Rapid Credit Growth in Central and Eastern Europe

Rapid Credit Growth in Central and Eastern Europe

Endless Boom or Early Warning?

Edited by
Charles Enoch
and
İnci Ötker-Robe

International Monetary Fund 2007

All rights reserved. No reproduction, copy or transmission of this publication may be made without written permission.

No paragraph of this publication may be reproduced, copied or transmitted save with written permission or in accordance with the provisions of the Copyright, Designs and Patents Act 1988, or under the terms of any licence permitting limited copying issued by the Copyright Licensing Agency, 90 Tottenham Court Road, London W1T 4LP.

Any person who does any unauthorised act in relation to this publication may be liable to criminal prosecution and civil claims for damages.

The authors have asserted their rights to be identified as the authors of this work in accordance with the Copyright, Designs and Patents Act 1988.

> Nothing contained in this book should be reported as representing the views of the IMF, its Executive Board, member governments, or any other entity mentioned herein. The views expressed in this book belong solely to the authors.

First published 2007 by
PALGRAVE MACMILLAN
Houndmills, Basingstoke, Hampshire RG21 6XS and
175 Fifth Avenue, New York, N.Y. 10010
Companies and representatives throughout the world

PALGRAVE MACMILLAN is the global academic imprint of the
Palgrave Macmillan division of St Martin's Press LLC and of
Palgrave Macmillan Ltd.
Macmillan® is a registered trademark in the United States, United Kingdom and other countries. Palgrave is a registered trademark in the European Union and other countries.

ISBN-13 978–0–2305–2151 3 hardback
ISBN-10 0–2305–2151 7 hardback

This book is printed on paper suitable for recycling and made from fully managed and sustained forest sources.

A catalogue record for this book is available from the British Library.

Library of Congress Cataloging-in-Publication Data
Rapid credit growth in Central and Eastern Europe : endless boom or early warning? / edited by Charles Enoch and İnci Ötker-Robe.
    p. cm.
 Includes bibliographical references and index.
 ISBN-13: 978–0–230–52151–3 (cloth)
 ISBN-10: 0–230–52151–7 (cloth)
    1. Credit control—Europe, Eastern. 2. Credit control—Europe, Central. 3. Credit control—Former Soviet republics. I. Enoch, Charles. II. Ötker, İnci.

HG3711.E85R37 2007
332.709443—dc22   2006051551

10 9 8 7 6 5 4 3 2 1
16 15 14 13 12 11 10 09 08 07

Printed and bound in Great Britain by
Antony Rowe Ltd, Chippenham, Wiltshire

Contents

List of Tables	vii
List of Figures	ix
List of Boxes	xiii
List of Abbreviations	xiv
Preface	xvii
Notes on Contributors	xviii

Part One. Assessing and Managing Rapid Credit Growth—General Framework

1. Introductory Remarks: Credit Growth in Central and Eastern Europe 3
   Charles Enoch
2. The Causes and Nature of the Rapid Growth of Bank Credit in the Central, Eastern, and South-eastern European Countries 13
   Calin Arcalean, Oscar Calvo-Gonzalez, Csaba Móré, Adrian van Rixtel, Adalbert Winkler, and Tina Zumer
3. Using Fundamentals to Identify Episodes of "Excessive" Credit Growth in Central and Eastern Europe 47
   Frédric Boissay, Oscar Calvo-Gonzalez, and Tomasz Koźluk
4. Fast Credit Expansion in Central and Eastern Europe: Catching-up, Sustainable Financial Deepening, or Bubble? 67
   Peter Backé, Balázs Égert, and Tina Zumer
5. Analysis of and Policy Responses to Rapid Credit Growth 84
   Paul Hilbers, İnci Ötker-Robe, and Ceyla Pazarbasioğlu
6. Rapid Credit Growth—The Role of Supervisors 137
   Mats Josefsson

Part Two. Assessing and Managing Rapid Credit Growth—Country Experiences

7. Credit Growth Slowdown: The Experience of Bulgaria 145
   Veselka Petkova and Stoyan Manolov
8. The Croatian Experience with Rapid Credit Growth 154
   Maroje Lang
9. Estonia's Experience with Rapid Credit Growth 172
   Raoul Lättemäe
10. Latvia's Experience with Rapid Credit Growth 181
    Uldis Rutkaste
11. Assessment of Credit Growth in Lithuania 190
    Tomas Ramanauskas

12. Poland's Experiences with Rapid Credit Growth—the 1996–97 Episode 203
    Piotr Szpunar
13. Fast Credit Growth and Policy Response: The Case of Romania 214
    Cristian Popa
14. Slovakia: Credit Growth in the Household Sector and Response to the Related Risks 229
    Marek Ličák
15. Too Much of a Good Thing? Credit Booms in Transition Economies: The Cases of Bulgaria, Romania, and Ukraine 236
    Christoph Duenwald, Nikolay Gueorguiev, and Andrea Schaechter

Part Three. Regional Dimensions of Rapid Credit Growth and Perspectives from Euro Convergence Countries

16. The Role of Housing Markets and Foreign-owned Banks in the Credit Expansion in Central and Eastern Europe 267
    Dubravko Mihaljek
17. Regional Dimensions of Dealing with Rapid Credit Growth: Perspectives from Greece, 1998–2005 284
    Nicos Kamberoglou and Nikolaos Stavrianou
18. Debt Growth: Factors, Institutional Issues and Implications— the Portuguese Case 296
    Nuno Ribeiro
19. The Growth of Private Sector Debt in Spain: Causes and Consequences 312
    Carmen Martinez-Carrascal

Part Four. Cross-Border Dimension: Supervisory Coordination Between Bank Supervisors

20. Cross-border Supervisory Cooperation 321
    Karin Zartl
21. The Role of Cross-border Supervisory Coordination when Dealing with Rapid Credit Growth in Emerging Countries—Home Country Perspective 331
    Linda van Goor
22. Home and Host Supervisors' Relations—a Host Supervisor's Perspective 339
    Piotr Bednarski and Dariusz Starnowski

Part Five. Concluding Remarks

23. Lessons from Country Experiences with Rapid Credit Growth in Europe, and Policy Implications 349
    Charles Enoch and İnci Ötker-Robe

Index 367

List of Tables

1.1	Rates of Growth of Credit in Central and Eastern Europe	4
1.2	Credit to GDP Ratio	4
1.3	Rate of Foreign Bank Ownership in Selected Countries of Central and Eastern Europe	7
3.1	Share of Loans in Total Lending to the Private Nonfinancial Sector in 2004	54
3.2	Estimates of Relation (1)—Total Lending	56
3.3	Average Quarterly Excessive Credit Growth over the Period 2001–04	57
3.4	Average Quarterly Excessive Credit Growth over the Period 2001–04	58
5.1	Components of the Analysis of Rapid Credit Growth	89
5.2	Growth of Private Sector Credit in Selected CEE Countries	90
5.3	Policy Responses to Rapid Credit Growth in Selected CEE Countries	98
5.4	Key Risks Associated with Credit Growth	103
5.5	Prudential and Supervisory Measures to Manage Key Risks of Rapid Credit Growth	104
8.1	Basic Features of the Banking System in Croatia	157
8.2	Domestic Credits by Sector—Croatia	157
8.3	Main Macroeconomic Indicators—Croatia	159
8.4	Total Nonfinancial Private Sector Debt by Creditor—Croatia	164
8.5	Calculation of the Impact of the MRR on the Required Return to Make Profit on Domestic Credit Financed by Borrowing Abroad—Croatia	166
8.6	Currency Structure of Domestic Credits—Croatia	168
11.1	Main Structural Banking Indicators in Lithuania and the Euro Area	191
12.1	Average Quarterly Reserve Requirements—Poland	206
12.2	Personal Deposits at the National Bank of Poland	206
14.1	Sectoral Structure of Loans—Slovakia	230
14.2	Selected Macroeconomic Indicators—Slovakia	232
15.1	Basic Economic Indicators, 2000–05 (Bulgaria, Romania, Ukraine)	237
15.2	Bulgaria, Romania, and Ukraine in Comparison: An Overview	238
15.3	Basic Credit Indicators, 2000–05 (Bulgaria, Romania, Ukraine)	241
15.4	Ownership of the Banking Sector, 2000–05 (Bulgaria, Romania, Ukraine)	243
15.5	Sectoral Composition of Credit, 2000–04 (Bulgaria, Romania, Ukraine)	248
15.6	Impact of Credit Growth on the Trade Balance	251
15.7	Credit to GDP Ratio in Banking-Crisis Countries	255
15.8	Prudential Indicators of the Banking Sector, 2000–05 (Bulgaria, Romania, Ukraine)	255

16.1	Composition of Commercial Bank Lending	270
16.2	Housing Loans and Private Sector Credit Growth, 2003–05	272
16.3	Structure of the Commercial Banking Sector, 2004	275
16.4	Prudential Indicators	277
18.1	Authorization of New Institutions in Portuguese Financial System	301
18.2	Selected Financial Indicators in the Portuguese Banking System	302
18.3	Market Shares in Banking Markets—Portugal	303
18.4	Concentration in the Portuguese Banking Sector	304
23.1	Nature of the Credit Growth (by Country)	351
23.2	Factors Stimulating Credit Growth (by Country)	353
23.3	Risks Associated with the Credit Growth (by Country)	355
23.4	Policy Responses to Credit Growth (by Country)	357

List of Figures

2.1	Change in Ratio of Bank Credit to the Private Sector to GDP, 2000–03	14
2.2	Financial Assets and Liabilities of Households	18
2.3	Financial Assets and Liabilities of Nonfinancial Corporations	19
2.4	Financial Assets and Liabilities of Nonresidents vis-à-vis Residents by Category	20
2.5	Equity and Bonds Outstanding versus Loans to Resident Clients, end-2003	21
2.6	Credit to the Private Sector to GDP Ratio and Per Capita GDP (2003)	22
2.7	EBRD Index of Banking Sector Reform	23
2.8	Share of Assets Held by Foreign Banks in Total Banking Assets	24
2.9	Interest Rate Spreads	24
2.10	Foreign Liabilities to Total Banking Sector Assets	25
2.11	Real GDP Growth	27
2.12	Currency Boards and Tightly Managed Floats Against the Euro: Real Exchange Rate Developments	31
2.13	Managed and Independent Floaters: Real Exchange Rate Developments	31
2.14	Private External Debt and Private Sector Credit to GDP: Correlation of Changes from 2000 to 2004	32
2.15	Share of Foreign Currency Loans in Total Loans	35
2.16	Change in Credit to the Private Sector, Domestic Deposits and Banks' Net Foreign Liabilities, 2001–04	36
2.17	Return on Equity of Banking Sectors	38
2.18	Capital Adequacy Ratios at end-2004	38
2.19	Ratio of Nonperforming Loans to Total Loans	39
3.1	Credit to the Private Sector to GDP and Per Capita GDP, 2003 (124 countries)	48
3.2	Observed versus Projected Growth Rates of Total Lending	57
3.3	Credit Growth and Foreign Ownership of the Banking System	60
3.4	Mortgage Loans and Real Estate Prices in Bulgaria and Estonia	62
3.5	Evolution of Credit Composition in Croatia and Latvia	63
4.1	Credit Growth to the Private Sector, 1999–2005	69
4.2	Private Sector Credit/GDP Ratios, 1999–2005	71
4.3	Share of Household Lending in Total Domestic Lending, 1999 and 2005	72
4.4	Selected Banking Sector Assets and Liabilities, 1999 and 2005	73
4.5	Share of Foreign Currency Loans in Total Loans to the Private Sector, 1999 and 2005	73

4.6	Deviations from Long-run Equilibrium Private Sector Credit-to-GDP, 1990 to 2004: Baltic Countries, Central Europe, South-eastern Europe	80
5.1	CEE Countries: Real Credit Growth over 2000–04 vs. Credit to GDP in 1999	91
5.2	Is the Rapid Credit Growth in the CEE Countries part of a Catching-up Process?	91
5.3	CEE Countries: Funding of the Credit Growth	95
5.4	Menu of Policy Options in Responding to Rapid Credit Growth	97
7.1	Credits and Banking Assets to GDP—Bulgaria	146
7.2	Annual Growth of Selected Balance Sheet Aggregates—Bulgaria	147
7.3	Growth in Lending and Deposits—Bulgaria	148
8.1	Evolution of Interest Rates in Croatia	160
8.2	Credit to Nonfinancial Private Sector—Croatia	161
9.1	Dynamics of the Estonian Banking Sector	173
9.2	Capital Inflow into the Banking Sector and Annual Increase in Domestic Credit to GDP—Estonia	174
9.3	"Effective" Reserve Requirement and Capital Adequacy Requirement in Estonia	175
9.4	Money Market Risk Premium and Estonian Sovereign Rating	177
9.5	Real Sector Interest Rates vs. EURIBOR Rates—Estonia	177
10.1	Credit Growth in Latvia	182
10.2	Domestic Loan Market Share and Banks' Liabilities to Foreign Credit Institutions—Latvia	182
10.3	Interest Rates and Income—Latvia	184
10.4	Privatization of Flats and Residential Construction—Latvia	185
10.5	Monetary Policy Measures Taken to Date—Latvia	187
11.1	Contributions of Loans by Type to Growth of Total Bank Loan Portfolio—Lithuania	191
11.2	Recent Dynamics of Nominal Interest Rates—Lithuania	193
11.3	M2 Dynamics—Lithuania	195
11.4	M2 Growth Factors—Lithuania	195
11.5	Dynamics of the Market Value and the Balance Sheet Value of Equity—Lithuania	196
11.6	Nonfinancial Corporate Sector's Financial Position—Lithuania	199
11.7	Bank Exposure to the Nontradable and Real Estate Sectors—Lithuania	199
12.1	Loans to Enterprises and Households—Poland	204
12.2	Interest Rates—Poland	209
12.3	Households' Deposits at the National Bank of Poland	210
12.4	Excess Liquidity—Poland	211
12.5	Corporate and Households Lending Growth—Poland	211
13.1	Analysis Ratios for the Banking System—Romania	216
13.2	Total Credit and Nongovernment Credit—Romania	218
13.3	Interest Rates Applied by Credit Institutions—Romania	219

13.4	Foreign Exchange-Denominated Credit as Share to Total Nongovernment Credit—Romania	222
13.5	Household Loans and Deposits—Romania	224
13.6	Total External Debt—Romania	226
14.1	Growth of Housing Loans and Share of Housing Loans in GDP in EU Countries in 2004	231
14.2	Debt Burden and Gross Disposable Income of Households—Slovakia	234
15.1	Selected EBRD Transition Indicators, 2004 (EU-8)	240
15.2	Credit Growth in Transition Economies, 2002–04	242
15.3	Credit and Bank Liabilities, 2000–04 (Bulgaria, Romania, Ukraine)	249
15.4	Bulgaria and Romania: Selected Economic Indicators, 2000–05	252
15.5	Credit Growth in Transition Economies and Banking-Crisis Countries	256
15.6	Transition Economies: Credit-to-GDP Ratio and Institutional Reform, 2005	256
16.1	Bank Credit to the Private Sector, 2002–05	269
16.2	Bank Credit as a Percent of GDP	269
16.3	Real Credit Growth, 2003–05	271
16.4	House Prices and Housing Loans, 1997–2005	274
16.5	Foreign-owned Banks and Credit Growth in CEE, 1997, 2000, and 2004	276
16.6	Commercial Bank Liabilities, 2002–05	278
17.1	Loans to the Private Sector—(annual growth rate, year-end Greece and Euro Area)	285
17.2	Loans to the Private Sector—(annual growth rate, year-end Greece)	286
17.3	Loans to the Private Sector—(as a percentage of GDP Greece and Euro Area)	287
17.4	Loans to Households—Greece and Euro Area	288
17.5	Retail Interest Rates—Greece	288
17.6	GDP Growth Rate—Greece	289
17.7	The Securities Portfolio of Greek Banks	290
17.8	BoG's Management of Credit Growth	291
18.1	Bank Loans to the Private Sector—Portugal	297
18.2	Household Indebtedness—Portugal	298
18.3	Interest Rates on Loans for House Purchase—Portugal	298
18.4	Regulatory Straitjacket in the 1980s—Portugal	300
18.5	New Banks in Portuguese Banking System	301
18.6	Share of the 20 to 34 Years Old Cohort of the Population—Portugal and EU Area	306
18.7	Indebtedness of Portuguese Households	309
18.8	Indebtedness of Nonfinancial Corporations in Portugal	309
19.1	Private Nonfinancial Sector Indebtedness Ratios—Spain, Euro Area, USA	313
19.2	Domestic Banks' Loans by Purpose—Spain	313
19.3	Structure of Spanish Household Debt	314

20.1	The Supervisory Review and Evaluation Process: An Illustration	325
21.1	Total Exposure of Dutch Banks: Market Share in CEE Area (per country in billion euro)	333
21.2	Total Exposure of Dutch Banks: Market Share in CEE Area (%)	333
21.3	Foreign Bank Exposure in CEE Countries	334
22.1	Predominant Presence of Foreign Investors in the Banking Sector Assets in the New Member States of the EU	339
22.2	Share of Foreign Financial Groups in the Banking Sectors in CEE Countries via their Subsidiaries	340
22.3	Share of Foreign Subsidiary in the Polish Banking Sector and Share in its Parent Bank	340
22.4	Share of Polish Banking Sector in Parent Institution Assets	341

List of Boxes

2.1	Financial Structure and Economic Growth	16
5.1	Analysis of the Nature of Credit Growth	87
12.1	Problems with the Monetary Transmission Mechanism (MTM)	207
12.2	NBP Collection of Deposits	210
13.1	Measures Taken by the NBR to Deal With the Rapid Credit Growth	221
15.1	Macroeconomic Background	239
15.2	Monetary Policy Frameworks	245
15.3	The Relationship Between Credit Growth and Trade Balance in Bulgaria and Romania	253
20.1	What is the Committee of European Banking Supervisors (CEBS)?	322

List of Abbreviations

ACB	Association of Commercial Banks
ARDL	Autoregressive Distributed Lag
BIS	Bank for International Settlements
BL	Bank of Lithuania
BNB	Bulgarian National Bank
BoE	Bank of Estonia
BoG	Bank of Greece
BoL	Bank of Latvia
BoP	Bank of Portugal
BoS	Bank of Spain
CAR	Capital Adequacy Ratio
CBA	Currency Board Arrangement
CCR	Central Credit Register
CEBS	Committee of European Banking Supervisors
CEE	Central, Eastern and South-eastern Europe
CEPI	European Council of Real Estate Professionals
CNB	Croatian National Bank
CPI	Consumer Price Index
CRD	Capital Requirements Directive
CZ	Czech Republic
DC	Domestic Currency
DEM	Deutsche mark
DIT	Direct Inflation Targeting
DNB	The Netherlands Bank (De Nederlandsche Bank)
EBRD	European Bank for Reconstruction and Development
EC	European Commission
ECB	European Central Bank
EE	Estonia
EEA	European Economic Area
EEK	Estonian kroon
EFTA	European Free Trade Association
EMS	European Monetary System
EMU	European Economic and Monetary Union
ERM	Exchange Rate Mechanism
ESCB	European System for Central Banks
EU	European Union
EUR	Euro
Euribor	Euro Interbank Offered Rate
FDI	Foreign Direct Investment

FSAP	Financial Sector Assessment Program
FSIs	Financial Soundness Indicators
FX	Foreign Exchange
FYR	Former Yugoslav Republic
GPS	Greece, Portugal, and Spain
GDP	Gross Domestic Product
HU	Hungary
IFRS	International Financial Reporting Standards
IMF	International Monetary Fund
IPOs	Initial Public Offerings
IT	Information Technology
KredEx	The Estonian Credit and Export Guarantee Fund
LI	Lithuania
LIBOR	London Interbank Offer Rate
LOLR	Lender of Last Resort
LTL	Lithuanian litas
LTV	Loan to Value
LV	Latvia
LVL	Latvian lat
M2	Broad Money
MCM	Monetary and Capital Markets Department
MFIs	Monetary Financial Institutions
MGE	Mean Group Estimator
MoUs	Memoranda of Understanding
MRR	Marginal Reserve Requirement
MTM	Monetary Transmission Mechanism
NBP	National Bank of Poland
NBR	National Bank of Romania
NBS	National Bank of Slovakia
NBU	National Bank of Ukraine
NPL	Nonperforming loan
OECD	Organization for Economic Cooperation and Development
OLS	Ordinary Least Square
PL	Poland
PPI	Producer Price Index
RAS	Risk Assessment System
ROA	Return on Assets
ROE	Return on Earnings
RON	Romanian leu (*pl.* lei)
RR	Reserve Requirements
SEE	South East Europe
SEOs	Seasoned Equity Offerings
SI	Slovenia
SK	Slovakia
SMEs	Small and Medium-size Enterprises

SoEs	State-owned Enterprises
SREP	Supervisory Review and Evaluation Process
TALSE	An index that reflects changes in the prices of shares listed in the Main and Investor lists of the Estonian Stock Exchange, and the Tallinn Stock Exchange
VAR	Value at Risk
VECM	Vector error correction model
VILSE	Lithuanian Broad Stock Market Index
WIBOR	Warsaw Interbank Offer Rate
ZL	Polish zloty

Preface

The chapters in this volume derive from the presentations made at a two-day conference jointly organized by the National Bank of Romania and the International Monetary Fund in Sinaia, Romania on October 7–8, 2005. We would first and foremost wish to thank the National Bank of Romania, in particular Governor Isarescu and Deputy Governor Popa, for hosting the conference. The conference brought together central banks and national supervisory and regulatory authorities of a number of Western, Central, Eastern and South-eastern European (CEE) countries. The conference and discussions were expertly organized, and certainly helped participants in their thinking and work on credit growth issues. We are also grateful to all the authors of the papers and other participants at the seminar for their many contributions and lively discussions.

The timing of the conference and the book is certainly not a coincidence. Rapid credit growth continues to be pervasive across almost the whole of the CEE region, and is recognized as a potentially serious problem. Assessing credit growth and developing an adequate policy response when such growth is viewed as excessive continue to occupy the minds of policymakers in the region. A regional conference on this topic provided an excellent opportunity to exchange information and experiences among the participants. We hope that this volume offers a useful contribution to the ongoing policy debate on these issues in the CEE region as well as in other regions experiencing a similar phenomenon.

We are grateful to many colleagues in the Monetary and Capital Markets Department (MCM) of the International Monetary Fund for working with us on the range of issues associated with the rapid credit growth phenomenon. Our papers are the result of collaboration with, and comments from, many colleagues, as well as several seminars and internal discussions within MCM and more widely within the IMF. The papers have also benefited from the able editorial work of Mr. Graham Colin-Jones. We also thank Maria Delia M. Araneta and Erik William Churchill for their excellent assistance in producing this volume, and Shannon Bui, Hortense N'Danou, and Roxana Nikdjou, for providing back-up support.

Finally, we would like to acknowledge the patience, advice, and general support received from Sean Culhane in the IMF's External Relations Department, who coordinated the arrangements for publication, and the guidance of the staff at Palgrave Macmillan.

Charles Enoch
İnci Ötker-Robe

Notes on Contributors

Calin Arcalean, Department of Economics, Indiana University, USA

Peter Backé, Head of Unit, Foreign Research Division, Oesterreichische National Bank, Austria

Piotr Bednarski, National Bank of Poland, Poland

Fréderic Boissay, European Central Bank, Germany

Oscar Calvo-Gonzalez, Principal Economist, EU Neighboring Regions Division, European Central Bank, Germany

Christoph Duenwald, Senior Economist, European Department, International Monetary Fund

Balázs Égert, Oesterreichische National Bank, Austria

Charles Enoch, Deputy Director, Monetary and Capital Markets Department, International Monetary Fund

Nikolay Gueorguiev, Senior Economist, European Department, International Monetary Fund

Paul Hilbers, Advisor, European Department, International Monetary Fund

Mats Josefsson, Senior Financial Sector Expert, Monetary and Capital Markets Department, International Monetary Fund

Nikos Kamberoglou, Senior Economist, Statistics Department, Bank of Greece, Greece

Tomasz Koźluk, European Central Bank, Germany

Maroje Lang, Head, Monetary Analysis Division, Research Department, Croatian National Bank, Croatia

Raoul Lättemäe, Head, Monetary Policy Unit, Economics Department, EEST 1 Pank (Bank of Estonia), Estonia

Marek Ličák, Banking Specialist, Banking Supervision, Risk Management, National Bank of Slovakia, Slovak Republic

Stoyan Manolov, Director, Off-Site Supervision & Analysis, Bank Supervision Department, Bulgarian National Bank, Bulgaria

Carmen Martinez-Carrascal, Economist, Monetary and Financial Studies Department, Research Department, Banco de España, Spain

Dubravko Mihaljek, Senior Economist, Bank for International Settlements, Switzerland

Csaba Móré, Senior Economist, Financial Stability, Magyar Nemzeti Bank, Hungary

İnci Ötker-Robe, Deputy Area Chief for TA Europe, Monetary and Capital Markets Department, International Monetary Fund

Ceyla Pazarbasioğlu, Division Chief, Emerging Markets Surveillance Division, Monetary and Capital Markets Department, International Monetary Fund

Veselka Petkova, National Bank of Bulgaria, Bulgaria

Cristian Popa, Deputy Governor, National Bank of Romania, Romania

Tomas Ramanauskas, Macroeconomics and Forecasting Division, Economics Department, Lietuvos Bankas (Bank of Lithuania), Lithuania

Nuno Ribeiro, Head of Financial Stability Division, Research Department, Bank of Portugal, Portugal

Uldis Rutkaste, Chief Economist, Monetary Policy Department, Macroeconomic Analysis Division, Bank of Latvia, Latvia

Andrea Schaechter, Senior Economist, European Department, International Monetary Fund

Dariusz Starnowski, National Bank of Poland, Poland

Nikolaos Stavrianou, Bank Examiner, Department for the Supervision of Credit and Financial Institutions, Bank of Greece, Greece

Piotr Szpunar, Deputy Director of Macroeconomic Analyses Department, National Bank of Poland, Republic of Poland

Linda van Goor, The Netherlands Bank, The Netherlands

Adrian van Rixtel, Principal Economist, Capital Markets and Financial Structure Division, European Central Bank, Germany

Adalbert Winkler, Deputy Head of Division, EU Neighboring Regions Division, European Central Bank, Germany

Karin Zartl, Member of the Secreteriat, Committee of European Banking Supervisors, Great Britain

Tina Zumer, Economist, EU Countries Division, European Central Bank, Germany

Part One

Assessing and Managing Rapid Credit Growth—General Framework

1
Credit Growth in Central and Eastern Europe

Charles Enoch[1]

Rapid credit growth is one of the most pervasive developments in recent years in the countries of Central, Eastern, and South-eastern Europe (CEE). The benefits of this growth are unquestioned; but so are the potential risks.

The following chapters derive largely from presentations prepared for a conference in Sinaia, Romania in October 2005, organized jointly by the National Bank of Romania (NBR) and the IMF.[2] Additional contributions are drawn from ongoing work on rapid credit growth in a number of the participating institutions. The objectives of the conference, and of this book, are to provide a channel to share experiences and counteractive measures, and to consider how best to take policy work forward.

I. The IMF and rapid credit growth in the region

The IMF has been focusing on rapid growth in CEE in a number of different fora. The chapters in this volume add to the ream of statistics showing that credit growth across the region has been running for several years at extremely rapid rates. Table 1.1 shows rates of credit growth for ten of the countries in the region. Ukraine showed the most rapid rate of growth of credit over the 2001–04 period, with an annual average of almost 37 percent per year, followed closely by Latvia with over 35 percent per year. Although the stock of credit relative to GDP started from a low base in all these countries, over this period there was a substantial increase, as shown in Table 1.2, with the credit to GDP ratio for Ukraine for instance rising from 11 percent of GDP in 2000 to almost 25 percent in 2004, and that in Latvia rising from 17 percent to over 45 percent of GDP over the same period. Recent evidence is that rapid growth rates continue in many of the countries in the region.

IMF involvement with this issue has a number of interrelated forms. First, as the central part of surveillance, the IMF Article IV consultations focus on monetary and

4 General Framework

Table 1.1 Rates of Growth of Credit in Central and Eastern Europe

	2000	2001	2002	2003	2004	Average (2000–04)
Growth of Credit						
Ukraine	32.9	25.5	48.8	55.7	21.6	36.9
Latvia	28.1	33.5	34.3	41.2	41.1	35.6
Albania	33.9	38.9	25.6	23.0	28.5	30.0
Bulgaria	6.0	23.0	34.6	45.4	40.5	29.9
Lithuania	-7.0	4.9	30.1	60.8	38.1	25.4
Russia	27.2	25.1	12.3	27.4	34.0	25.2
Belarus	6.8	8.3	16.2	43.8	36.1	22.2
Estonia	7.4	12.1	15.6	30.9	39.5	21.1
Moldova	6.1	26.2	31.0	29.8	7.9	20.2
Hungary	30.3	8.0	13.6	27.4	11.2	18.1

Source: Hilbers et al (2005).

Table 1.2 Credit to GDP Ratio

	2000	2001	2002	2003	2004	Average (2000–04)	Cumulative Change (1999–2004)
Credit to GDP Ratio							
Ukraine	11.1	12.9	17.5	24.3	24.9	18.1	16.4
Latvia	17.2	21.3	26.5	34.6	45.4	29.0	30.9
Albania	4.6	5.9	7.3	8.4	9.9	7.2	6.0
Bulgaria	12.6	14.9	19.6	27.4	36.7	22.2	24.6
Lithuania	11.4	11.4	14.0	20.4	25.6	16.6	12.8
Russia	13.3	16.5	17.7	21.0	24.5	18.6	11.5
Belarus	8.8	8.2	8.9	11.9	13.9	10.3	4.7
Estonia	23.9	25.2	26.9	33.1	43.3	30.5	19.0
Moldova	12.6	14.7	17.1	20.5	21.3	17.3	9.5
Hungary	32.4	33.7	35.8	43.0	46.0	38.2	19.9

Source: Hilbers et al (2005).

financial developments, in particular those that may indicate vulnerabilities for the country or more widely. With the IMF's ongoing medium-term strategy[3] containing a pledge to integrate more fully the macroeconomic and financial sector work, focus on areas such as rapid credit growth is likely to become more intense. Second, the IMF has conducted a number of studies on this topic to aid understanding, and give insights as to appropriate policy responses.[4] These studies also contain references to earlier IMF and other work in this area.[5] Third, a number of countries have approached the IMF, in particular its Monetary and Capital Markets Department, to discuss how to handle problems of rapid credit growth. The IMF has thus provided bilateral technical assistance on this subject for a number of countries. Fourth, beyond such assistance, there are a range of issues concerning rapid credit growth which are useful to discuss amongst the IMF and member countries, to reach a better understanding of rapid credit growth and how country authorities might design remedial action. Such discussions can often be most productive when handled on a regional basis, both because this can involve a relatively large group of people, and because sharing country experiences can serve to provide additional insights. It is with these last considerations in mind that the Sinaia conference was organized, and the papers prepared for wider dissemination.

II. Measuring credit growth

Rapid credit growth is a particularly difficult topic to address, for a number of reasons. First, it is hard to measure. Probably most observers would agree that the figures quoted are the lower bound of what is actually happening. These may be just flows through the banking system—which may well be the dominant flows, but are certainly not the whole story. In many countries nonbank financial institutions are now conducting a significant part of the overall intermediation. Also, close substitutes for lending are appearing—leasing is one example, and the IMF has in recent months received a number of requests from country authorities for assistance with assessing developments regarding leasing companies and designing regulations and supervisory practices to manage them. This may well be an example of what is known as Goodhart's law—as the authorities move to control one activity, there will be a shift away from institutions or mechanisms conducting the activity that is being controlled to those conducting activities that are not. Indeed, I will return to this phenomenon later.

III. Rapid credit growth may be very popular

Second, rapid credit growth is particularly hard to assess and determine how to handle because credit growth is inherently beneficial, and indeed is a basic underpinning for economic growth and development. In many countries of the CEE region there are recent memories of credit crunches, and then stagnation in credit while economic needs were clear and urgent. Banks seemed to be too restrictive in providing credits to the real sector and thus not contributing to economic growth. Revivals in credit growth may be seen as signs of a healthy banking system and returning confidence in the economy. There is likely to be irritation and disbelief then, just when it seems that things are turning out right, central bankers and regulators start issuing warnings of problems ahead, and urging that remedial action is needed. The message is bound to be a hard sell to a politician, for the politicians of course are dependent on a public that is, at least in the short term, the beneficiary of the credit growth. Credit is being used for home ownership or improvement, and purchases of cars and consumer durables, and anyone who suggests limiting such activity, or making it more expensive, is not likely to be very popular.

IV. Is it too much?

In this connection, it would be very helpful if there were a well-accepted threshold number beyond which credit growth would be consistently deemed as excessive. The third difficulty with handling rapid growth is that a definitive number beyond which credit growth can be deemed excessive is not known, and indeed if it exists would be unlikely to be constant across space or time. In those cases where credit growth starts from a lower base, one can broadly expect that a high growth rate may be sustainable for a longer period than in a situation where there are high levels of credit to begin with. Also, where the monetary and financial systems are well managed, a higher rate of growth can be sustained longer than where monetary and prudential management capacity is yet to be developed. And where the economy is simultaneously undertaking substantial structural reforms, as in many of the countries at the Sinaia conference, rapid credit growth may be seen as evidence of the success of the reform program. Indeed, this is not just an issue for transition or emerging market economies. Both the United Kingdom in the late 1980s and the United States in the late 1990s downplayed the risks of rapid credit growth in the exuberance of their ongoing structural reforms. In both cases the credit growth proved not to be sustainable, and the countries experienced a period of reversal. For many other countries the reversals after unsustainable credit growth were even more significant.

On the side of quantification, much has been achieved in recent years. One of the problems of rapid credit growth is that it may undermine financial system soundness. Until recently there have been no commonly-accepted measures of financial system soundness. The Asian financial crisis, however, showed the perils of leaving policymakers and regulators without a good quantitative basis for identifying weakening soundness in their financial systems. As a result, considerable efforts have been put into developing financial soundness indicators (FSIs). A core set, and an encouraged set, of FSIs were endorsed by the IMF Board, after extensive interaction with member countries, amongst which are indicators related to credit growth.[6] Many member countries have now put considerable efforts into compiling such indicators; some, including many from CEE, are participating in the coordinated exercise being run by the IMF's Statistics Department. Nevertheless, there is still some way to go. These indicators are compiled on a national basis, and there are ongoing struggles with harmonization. FSIs certainly do not provide a black box from which one can effortlessly determine if credit growth is too fast or if a system has become unsound.

Thus the demonstration that credit growth is excessive will generally need to be made through detailed analytical demonstration, and remedial action justified on the basis of demonstration of the desirability and efficacy of the proposed remedial action. The chapters presented in this volume provide additional insights to make these demonstrations.

V. The monetary/prudential interface

Fourth, credit growth is hard to handle because the concerns it raises are both monetary and prudential. Indeed, it was probably because the issues are at the interface between monetary and prudential management that it took so long to develop FSIs. The interface between monetary and prudential concerns and actions is an issue which all policymakers need to be fully aware of. It has both analytical and organizational implications. From an organizational point of view, the two sets of issues may involve very different sets of people, even from different institutions, perhaps with not much experience of communication with each other, and little experience of interfacing and understanding the concerns of the other. One of the purposes of the Sinaia conference was to bring these two sets of people together, and for all to be exposed to the range of issues. Hopefully one of the results will be a more comprehensive understanding of the issues, and so a better grasp of appropriate policy responses, even those outside one's own field of responsibility.

VI. The international dimension: the banks

Fifth, credit growth is hard to handle because of its international and institutional dimensions. Many of the causes of credit growth are nationally determined, and the case studies presented tell us much about these. But to an important extent the causes are externally driven. There is amongst many of the countries here the prospect of early accession into the European Union (EU), so EU policies and developments will have an important influence on credit growth across the region. Not unrelated, in many countries a large part of the credit growth derives from the activities of international banks, often from outside the region, that are likely to have a regional strategy on how they will grow their business in the countries of the region. Table 1.3 shows the share of foreign banks in total assets in a number of the countries in the region. In Estonia, Lithuania, and the Czech and Slovak Republics foreign-owned banks account for over 90 percent of total banking sector assets. In both Hungary and Poland more than two thirds of banking sector assets are held by foreign-owned banks.

Table 1.3 Rate of Foreign Bank Ownership in Selected Countries of Central and Eastern Europe

Country	Number of Banks	Number of Foreign-owned Banks (%)	Asset Share of Foreign-owned Banks (%)	Private Sector Credit Growth end-2004 (%)
Estonia	6	50.0	97.3	43.8
Slovak Republic	21	90.5	96.3	7.0
Czech Republic	35	77.1	96.0	13.3
Lithuania	13	76.9[b]	95.6	39.8
Hungary[a]	36	80.6	83.3	18.8
Poland[a]	60	76.7	67.8	3.6
Malta	16	62.5	67.6	–
Latvia	22	40.0	47.2	50.0
Slovenia	22	27.3	36.0	20.1
Cyprus[a]	14	42.0	12.3	6.7

Source: European Central Bank (2005).
[a] Excludes cooperative banks and international banking units, but includes the Cooperative Central Bank (in Czech Republic).
[b] Includes foreign bank branches.

In this connection, it should be noted that only a relatively small number of foreign banks account for the major share of this foreign penetration, and also that it tends to be the same banks that are active across the various countries in the region. Banking behavior in the region is thus not only subject to regulators in Bucharest, Sofia, and Zagreb, but also to those in Amsterdam, Brussels, and Vienna. It also means that regulatory action in one country in the region, or monetary action in a single country to curb excessive credit growth, may lead much of that growth to reappear elsewhere in the region. And while the actions of a particular bank may be of systemic importance to a country in this region, if that country accounts for only a small part of the overall activities of that bank, they may not register heavily with the regulators in the bank's parent country. This all adds to the case for discussing the subject on a regional basis, and to include participation also from outside the region.

VII. The international dimension: the currency

The sixth issue is a further aspect of the international dimension: the role of foreign currencies. In many countries a large part of the credit growth has been in foreign currencies. This carries additional risks, even if the authorities design and enforce appropriate limits on banks' net open positions. It seems to be the case in many countries that lending in foreign currency is made available to even those borrowers without an assured foreign currency income. The appearance of lower nominal interest rates on foreign currency borrowing has encouraged such borrowing, notwithstanding that the associated exchange rate risk may not be appropriately hedged, or indeed even recognized.

An additional wrinkle in this region is that a number of countries have aspirations to join the European Economic and Monetary Union (EMU) within a few years. At that time much of what is now foreign currency lending would become domestic currency lending. Before one gets there, however, vulnerabilities associated with rapid foreign currency borrowing may add to the strains on the convergence process.

VIII. What part of credit growth is the problem?

A seventh issue, looking particularly at the prudential side, why it is hard to handle the issue of credit growth, is because it is not clear whether one needs primarily to focus on aggregate growth, or some components of it.

To some extent, it is aggregate credit growth that is the problem, even as regards prudential concerns, and—notwithstanding the point above that rapid growth may be sustainable for longer when it begins from a low base—one can argue that rapid growth may even be a larger problem when it starts from a low base. When there is little history of granting commercial credit, or of enforcing regulations governing banks' prudential behavior, there is likely to be little capacity to manage it, whether in the commercial banks or amongst the regulators. Evidence of overall lack of capacity, particularly during the early stages of the economic transition in the region, was the repeated poaching that occurred of newly-trained regulators by the emerging commercial banks, thereby compelling regulators in many of the countries in the region to retrain their supervisory teams from scratch more than once. Rapid credit growth in such an environment might be considered particularly risky.

In the early days of the transition, observers were concerned primarily at continuing rapid growth of public sector credit, on the grounds that such credit might be politically driven and not subject to proper prudential oversight, and might be directed into sectors of the economy that were not likely to be sustainable on a commercial basis. Indeed, banks in many transition economies suffered serious difficulties from nonperformance of loans to government entities. More recently, the focus of concern has shifted to private sector credit growth, in part because that is now the dominant component of credit growth, and because its rates of growth have generally been the most spectacular. Such concern also results because of questions regarding governance of the corporate sector, and the relationships of the corporates with the banks. In environments where many local banks started essentially as treasury functions for corporate partners, rapid private sector credit growth leads to questions as to whether the banks are sufficiently separate from their customers to make—and enforce—sound judgments as to whether they should be lending to them.

While concern is frequently voiced at overall levels of credit growth to the private sector, specific concern also focuses on its components. At the present time, credit is in many countries expanding rapidly both to the corporate and to the household sectors. The issues affecting the respective sectors may be somewhat different. As regards corporate lending, again one has issues of corporate governance, including that the corporation should have a viable business plan that involves it making productive use of its borrowings, and that it should be sufficiently separate from its lender that the latter is able to decide whether or not to lend purely on prudential criteria. As regards consumer lending, on the other hand, a key issue may be that of consumer protection. Are lenders misleading their customers as they advertise their services? Do they make clear the borrowers' repayment obligations and how these might change, for instance if interest rates rise? Do borrowers understand the implications of pledging collateral? And, overall, have lenders an adequate system of risk analysis on which to base their lending decisions, or are they focusing purely on the current values of their collateral? Such issues are not only of relevance to transition economies. Consumer protection has come very much to the fore also in industrial countries in recent years, with several scandals that have undermined both the regulators and the authorities that drew up the regulations. And concerns over possible excessive consumer indebtedness have emerged also in advanced countries, including perhaps most significantly in the United States.

There are also issues of sectoral concentration that frequently raise concern. In many countries the most rapid source of credit growth is into property, and property prices have risen substantially in many countries. To some extent this is a healthy development. It is a widespread aspiration to own one's own house, and house purchase is likely to involve the single largest credit transactions that most of us ever undertake. Nevertheless, credit crises in many countries have in the past frequently been attributable to over-exuberance in the property sector. Borrowings are inherently frequently long term, which creates additional vulnerabilities both for the borrower and lender: risks of changes in the borrower's earning capacity, or of payment obligations in the case of floating rate loans. Also, banks may seek to sweeten such lending by low initial interest or principal payment requirements, without making clear that payment obligations are likely to rise subsequently. On the banks' side, while deposits continue to be very much short term, there is a serious risk of liquidity pressures if loans do not continue to perform. Moreover, lending may be on the basis of collateral, although the collateral may be difficult to seize, and its value will be closely linked to that of other properties, so that if economic conditions change and the banks have to seize a number of properties, their value could fall substantially, leaving the banks unprotected and vulnerable.

IX. Credit growth and inflation

Much of the above discussion has related to the financial stability aspects of rapid credit growth. Rapid credit growth also of course can have important monetary implications, which indeed are arguably more urgent. Unless counteracted, credit growth increases liquidity in the economy, raising the risk of a resurgence of inflation. For many transition economies, where the hyperinflations of the early transition periods are not-very-distant memories, this risk would be especially worrisome. As inflation has been brought down, it has in some cases taken many years for the public to regain confidence in the currency, and to behave with the expectation that monetary savings will retain their value rather than be rapidly eroded away. The substantial reduction in inflation over the past few years has no doubt made a significant contribution to the economic recovery in many economies of CEE. If rapid credit growth leads to a resurgence of inflation, these hard-won gains may be quickly jeopardized. And if liquidity also leads to problems on the external accounts and to exchange rate pressures, these macroeconomic policy difficulties will be compounded further.

In this connection the recent slight pickup in inflation in a number of countries may be a cause for concern. There are, as always, arguments that the pick up has little or nothing to do with credit growth, so that addressing credit growth would not address the problem of inflation. It would however be reckless, at a minimum, not to watch credit, liquidity and inflation developments very closely, and to be prepared to take prompt action. Many countries in this region have only limited powers to dampen liquidity expansions, whether because of institutional constraints such as those imposed in a currency board system, or because of lack of market development. The country presentations in Part Two of this volume give further details of both these types of constraints. In general, however, these constraints increase the case for the response to be firm and timely, since it is that much harder to take effective remedial action once the situation has seriously deteriorated.[7]

X. Targets and instruments

Much of the discussion of rapid credit growth concerns the choice of measures to address the problems of rapid credit growth. This introduction will not go far into this fascinating area, but I would like to raise two broad issues, that are among the major themes in the chapters that follow: assigning instruments to targets, and ensuring that remedial measures are, to the extent possible, market friendly.

There are two broad targets when one acts to contain rapid credit growth: achieving financial stability and achieving monetary stability. It is a well known maxim that instruments should be matched to the targets that they most directly affect. Thus, financial stability should in principle be achieved through prudential measures, while monetary objectives require the use of monetary instruments. There is a considerable variety of instruments of both types at least potentially available. Monetary instruments include, for instance, interest rate tightening, and sterilization measures, and correction of any exchange rate misalignment. Prudential measures include promulgation and enforcement of best practice prudential regulations, including on classification and provisioning, and liquidity, concentration and net open position limits.

In practice, however, targets and instruments have in some countries become mixed. First, the monetary and financial effects may be difficult to distinguish: developments that cause monetary distress are likely also to cause financial distress. Second, some types of measures may be regarded as politically difficult—it may be thought easier, for instance, to put extra regulations on to the banks than to raise interest rates. While a number of the chapters focus on dilemmas in this area, it would be worth observing here that regulators and policymakers should be very leery about easily accepting political difficulties as an excuse to move toward second or third best solutions—such acceptance could quickly lead to recommendations that are no solution at all.

In this connection, it is worth stressing the desirability of finding solutions that are market friendly. Sterilizing liquidity by issuing paper, for instance, can help to develop markets, while adding regulations—such as imposing high reserve requirements—might harm market development and financial intermediation. Although one might appear to be addressing the credit growth problem one may largely be diverting resources into other sectors or countries—an example of the Goodhart's law to which I referred at the outset. Given constraints on more market-friendly interventions, there may be cases where the less preferred forms of approach are the only ones available—perhaps especially where a country has a tight exchange rate peg, in its most extreme form a currency board arrangement. But in such cases, if one seeks directly to impose controls, their impact is in the present environment of multiple types of institutions and sources of financing, likely to be at best only partial and temporary, and—while having a helpful impact in the short term—could serve in the longer term to undermine and threaten the financial development that the countries in the region have achieved over the past few years.

XI. Conclusion

To summarize, the rapid credit growth that has been experienced for several years across much of the CEE region is in many ways welcome, and one should not forget the importance of nurturing credit growth. It is indeed with the objective of safeguarding credit growth, and ensuring its sustainability that one is looking at measures that may serve to contain it. A variety of measures may be brought into play, and these are examined in the contributions in this volume. While there have been periods of rapid credit growth in the past, the present experience of the region seems new in a number of regards. One important regard is the international dimension, with the dominant role of foreign banks and foreign currencies, and the international constraints on, and interrelationships between, national policy responses. It is this dimension that certainly will add to the value of the exchanges of information and analyses of policy options contained in the remaining papers.

Notes

1. International Monetary Fund (IMF).
2. I would like to thank the NBR, and in particular Governor Isarescu and Deputy Governor Popa, for providing the facilities for these discussions.
3. Please see the Managing Director's Report on the Fund's Medium-Term Strategy.
4. See Cottarelli, Dell'Aricca' and Vladkova-Hollar (2003); Hilbers, Ötker-Robe, Pazarbasioğlu, and Johnsen (2005); and Maechler and Swinburne (2005).
5. Please note that these papers are at this stage the responsibility only of the authors, and do not necessarily reflect an official IMF view.
6. See Sundararajan, Enoch, San José, Hilbers, Krueger, Moretti, and Slack (2002).
7. Also, while the pickup may be slight, it could well be significant in determining whether a Euro aspirant meets or breaches the Maastricht criteria.

Bibliography

Cottarelli, C., G. Dell'Aricca and I. Vladkova-Hollar, 2003, "Early Birds, Late Risers, and Sleeping Beauties: Bank Credit Growth to the Private Sector in Central and Eastern Europe and the Balkans," IMF Working Paper 03/213 (International Monetary Fund).

European Central Bank, 2005, "Assessing Financial Stability: Conceptual Boundaries and Challenges," *Financial Stability Review*, June, Frankfurt am Main.

Hilbers, P., İ. Ötker-Robe, C. Pazarbasioğlu, and G. Johnsen, 2005, "Assessing and Managing Rapid Credit Growth and the Role of Supervisory and Prudential Policies," IMF Working Paper 05/151 (International Monetary Fund).

Maechler, A. and M. Swinburne, 2005, "Rapid Credit Growth: A Framework for Policy Responses," unpublished paper.

Managing Director's Report on the Fund's Medium-Term Strategy, April 2005.

Sundararajan, V., C. Enoch, A. San José, P. Hilbers, R. Krueger, M. Moretti, and G. Slack, 2002, *Financial Soundness Indicators: Analytical Aspects and Country Practices*, IMF Occasional Paper 212 (International Monetary Fund).

2
The Causes and Nature of the Rapid Growth of Bank Credit in the Central, Eastern and South-eastern European Countries

Calin Arcalean, Oscar Calvo-Gonzalez, Csaba Móré, Adrian van Rixtel, Adalbert Winkler, and Tina Zumer[1]

Credit growth has taken center stage in the policy arena in Central, Eastern, and South-eastern Europe (CEE).[2] To some extent, this has not been a surprising development. Indeed, given the under-development of the financial sector at the beginning of the transition, and particularly with regard to lending to the private sector, financial deepening in the region was to be expected. In 1998, the EBRD Transition Report, with a special focus on the financial sector in transition, had already raised the question of whether financial sector development would be a stable process.[3] Six years later, stability issues related to strong credit growth have become a key policy challenge, with the 2004 Transition Report warning of financial and macroeconomic "risks over the medium term" posed by the "substantial increases in domestic bank lending" witnessed in many transition countries.[4]

Bank credit to the private sector has increased significantly in many, though not all, CEE countries. The average annual credit growth in real terms over the last five years has been above 20 percent in five of the countries under consideration (Latvia, Albania, Bulgaria, Lithuania, and Estonia) and three other countries have exhibited average annual real growth rates above 10 percent (Hungary, Croatia, and Romania).[5] By contrast, credit growth in real terms has been below 5 percent or even negative in Poland, the Czech Republic, and Slovakia.[6] Slovenia, Bosnia and Herzegovina, and the FYR Macedonia cover the middle ground, with real credit growth on average below 10 percent in 2000–04, but with several years showing rates above 10 percent or even 20 percent.

When compared with the growth of the economy, a similar picture evolves. The significance of the increase in the ratio of private sector bank loans to GDP in most countries of the region can be grasped best if compared with developments in other regions of the world, as shown in Figure 2.1.

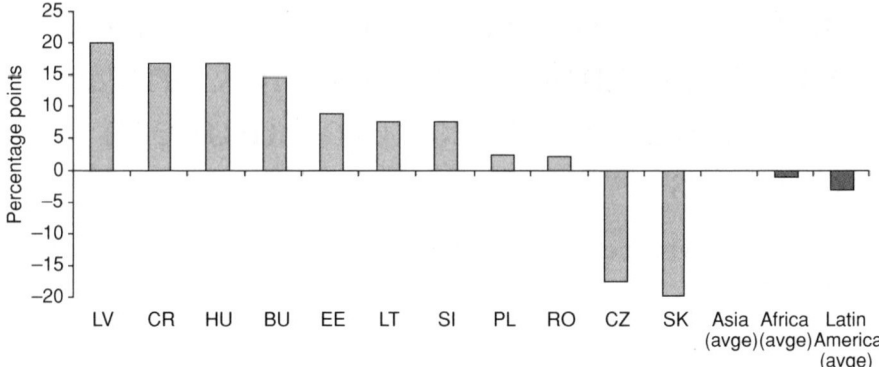

Figure 2.1 Change in Ratio of Bank Credit to the Private Sector to GDP, 2000–03

Source: IMF.

LV=Latvia; CR=Croatia; HU=Hungary; BU=Bulgaria; EE=Estonia; LT=Lithuania; SI=Slovenia; PL=Poland; RO=Romania; CZ=Czech Republic; SK=Slovak Republic.

It is well known that on the one hand, financial development and economic growth are typically seen mutually feeding each other and thus credit growth may support faster economic growth and vice versa. However, on the other hand, credit booms have been associated with financial and exchange rate crises as well as substantial output losses. Around three quarters of the episodes of credit booms in emerging markets from 1970 to 2002 were associated with banking crises, 85 percent with currency crises and, ultimately, real GDP usually fell by about 5 percent below trend after a credit boom (IMF, 2004). Thus, it is key to reflect on the causes and nature of credit growth in CEE countries, as this may help in assessing the benefits and risks of the respective developments in this region.[7]

Against this background, the chapter is organized as follows. Section I discusses the importance of bank credit as a source of finance in the new member states of the EU, presenting data from financial accounts recently compiled at the ECB (in cooperation with the national central banks concerned), which sheds light on how important credit is as a financing source for companies and households in those countries. The second section moves on to consider what the main causes of credit growth have been in the larger region, thus also including south-eastern European countries. Section III discusses the relationship between credit growth, financial development, and economic growth in this region. Section IV presents an overview of potential macroeconomic risks emanating from the rapid credit growth, and Section V investigates possible concerns for financial stability. Finally, Section VI concludes.

I. The importance of credit as a source of finance: a look at financial structures in the new EU member states

Since the early and mid-1990s, the countries in the CEE region have experienced substantial changes in the structure of their financial markets and financial institutions, in parallel with the transformation and further development of their economic structures and practices. This process of catching up with the existing EU countries has been important, since, for example, enhanced financing opportunities of the corporate sector may promote the further financial and economic development of these countries and their degree of convergence towards the euro area (for an overview of the related literature on financial structure and economic growth see Box 2.1).[8]

However, despite the progress that has been made regarding the development of both banking systems and capital markets in the countries in the CEE region, their overall degree of financial depth is still relatively subdued when compared with that in the euro area. This applies particularly to financial intermediation both by banks and households. For example, for most CEE countries, the provision of bank financing represents a much smaller share of GDP than in the euro area. At the same time, households may be restricted in their access to and choice of various types of loans, such as housing loans and consumer credit. Furthermore, capital markets remain relatively underdeveloped, implying that the issuance of quoted or listed equity and debt securities by nonfinancial corporations as sources of corporate financing is not that important yet (Köke et al, 2001; ECB, 2002a; Bonin and Wachtel, 2003). This does not automatically suggest that equity is not an important source of financing in most CEE countries: as a matter of fact, non-quoted equity—such as family capital—does play a major role in corporate financing in a significant number of countries. Thus, although relatively few companies are listed on stock exchanges and the amount of equity that is raised via publicly listed shares is very small, equity as such, including also non-quoted equity, is used as a corporate financing instrument.

Overall, there are significant differences between the countries in the region in terms of the degree of financial development. Thus, given these institutional characteristics, it may be expected that the importance and relevance of credit may differ substantially across countries, and thus also the impact of the rapid credit growth that has been observed for many of them. In general, in countries which have relatively well-developed financial markets in addition to bank financing, or have other potential sources for private sector financing, possible crises arising from "boom and bust" credit cycles may be absorbed relatively easily.[9] As already mentioned, however, it is fair to say that this level of development has not been reached yet in the region. Thus, the argument of "completeness" of financial systems may suggest that for most countries in the region, from a fundamental and theoretical perspective, financial stability concerns could arise more easily than in countries where both direct and indirect financing have reached more mature stages of development.

> **Box 2.1: Financial Structure and Economic Growth**
>
> Over the past decades, it has been increasingly recognized that the specific nature of an economy's financial structure is of crucial importance for the financing decisions of households and corporations. Differences in financial structures between countries exist due to a large number of factors such as historically determined characteristics, technological innovations, monetary and fiscal policies, and specific legal and accounting systems (Levine, 1997 and 2004; Rajan and Zingales, 2001). The regulatory framework may have a strong influence on the structure of financial institutions and markets as well, since it might result in different incentives for firms to provide information to financial markets and consequently stimulate the development of the financial structure towards a dominance of either direct or indirect finance. For example, a well-developed accounting system in combination with a relatively high degree of disclosure might promote the use of direct finance, as information regarding firms is more readily available to investors against relatively low costs. Thus, the overall use of indirect finance—i.e., the use of credit extended by financial intermediaries which are mainly banks—is embedded in this whole complex of institutional factors, which constitute a country's financial structure. In other words, the use of credit as a source of financing for enterprises and households may differ from country to country due to fundamental differences in their financial structures.
>
> Financial development has been the focus of theoretical as well as empirical research (Gertler, 1988; Hubbard, 1998; Allen and Gale, 2000). A large number of empirical studies find that the level of financial development, measured in terms of various financial variables which indicate the development of indirect and direct finance, is positively related to the rate and structure of economic growth. First, both financial intermediaries and financial markets matter for economic growth (Levine, 2003). Second, economic growth may benefit substantially from financial structures that allow for the development of specialized capital, such as private equity and venture capital by financial intermediaries (Stulz, 2000). Third, according to the so-called "financial services view," quality and availability of financial services are the key variables influencing a country's growth performance, whereas the indirect versus direct finance debate is only of second-order importance (Rajan and Zingales, 1998; Beck and Levine, 2004). However, Ergungor (2003) provides evidence that structure still matters, and that more market-oriented financial systems are beneficial to economic development. Lopez and Spiegel (2002) find that while financial development is beneficial over the long run, it may exacerbate short-term volatility. Fourth, empirical research has also shown that for nonfinancial firms that rely predominantly on external finance the legal framework, including the level of protection of outside investors and accounting standards, is of more importance than the extent of indirect or direct finance (so-called "legal view") (La Porta et al, various papers; Demirgüç-Kunt and Maksimovic, 2002; Levine et al, 2000; Modigliani and Perotti, 2000; Shleifer and Wolfenzon, 2002; Beck et al, 2003). For example, financial structures characterized by well-developed legal frameworks regarding bankruptcy proceedings could stimulate the growth of relatively risky sectors such as high-tech industries.
>
> Overall, more research is needed before conclusions can be drawn about the dominance of one financial structure over another and its benefits to corporate financing decisions and economic growth.

To assess the potential challenges and risks arising from the high credit growth that has been observed in numerous CEE countries, one needs to make an analysis of the fundamental characteristics of their financial structures. Preferably, this should be done on the basis of harmonized statistics, which would enable an objective assessment of comparative structures. This is particularly important for the CEE countries, as they have experienced relatively fast development in their banking systems and financial markets in recent years.

The ECB, in close cooperation with the countries involved, very recently has developed financial accounts statistics for the CEE new EU member states (i.e., CZ, EE, LV, LT, HU, PL, SI, and SK). Financial accounts provide a detailed and complete overview of the various financial relationships that exist between the different economic sectors of a country (see also: ECB, 2002b). The sectors that are identified are households, nonfinancial corporations, financial corporations, the general government, and nonresidents. Data are available on the structure of both their assets and liabilities, with the latter providing specific information on the structure of the particular sources of financing used. This allows for a relative and comparative analysis of the significance of credit in the financing of the various sectors in the economy. Unfortunately, harmonized financial accounts statistics are not available for the south-eastern European countries, which are covered in the other sections of this chapter. Thus, the following analysis only relates to financial structures in the new EU member states from CEE.

Figure 2.2 shows the assets and liabilities structure, in terms of amounts outstanding, of the households sector. With respect to their financial liabilities, households in the majority of the countries finance their activities predominantly in the form of loans,[10] in a degree rather similar to that in the euro area, indicating the importance of credit for households. The major exceptions are the Czech Republic and Slovakia and to a lesser extent Poland and Slovenia, where households finance a considerable part of their activities through "other accounts payable." This source of financing includes miscellaneous non-paid items, most importantly non-paid interest which is accrued over the course of the year.

Figure 2.3 shows the financial structure of the nonfinancial corporations sector, which has a much broader range of financing opportunities available than households since such corporations can issue bonds and shares. The country that is the closest to the euro area in terms of the use of loans by the nonfinancial corporate sector as defined in amounts outstanding is Hungary, where around one third of the financial liabilities of enterprises consist of credit. Interestingly, for all countries the share of loans in corporate financing is below the share seen in the euro area (37 percent). As a matter of fact, for the Czech Republic, Lithuania, Poland and Slovenia, this share is around 20 percent and for Slovakia even below 20 percent. It needs to be emphasized that an important part of corporate loans originates from foreign sources (see also financial assets of nonresidents below).

The main source of financing of nonfinancial corporations in the CEE new member states, similar to the euro area, is shares and other equity. The important use of this category as a source of corporate finance (in terms of amounts outstanding) for nonfinancial corporations is mainly due to the high contribution of non-quoted shares, in the form of for example foreign equity stakes.[11] This largely reflects the rather underdeveloped character of equity financing in these countries through financial markets in the form of quoted (or listed) shares, both as initial public offerings (IPOs) and seasoned equity offerings (SEOs). For the six new member

18 General Framework

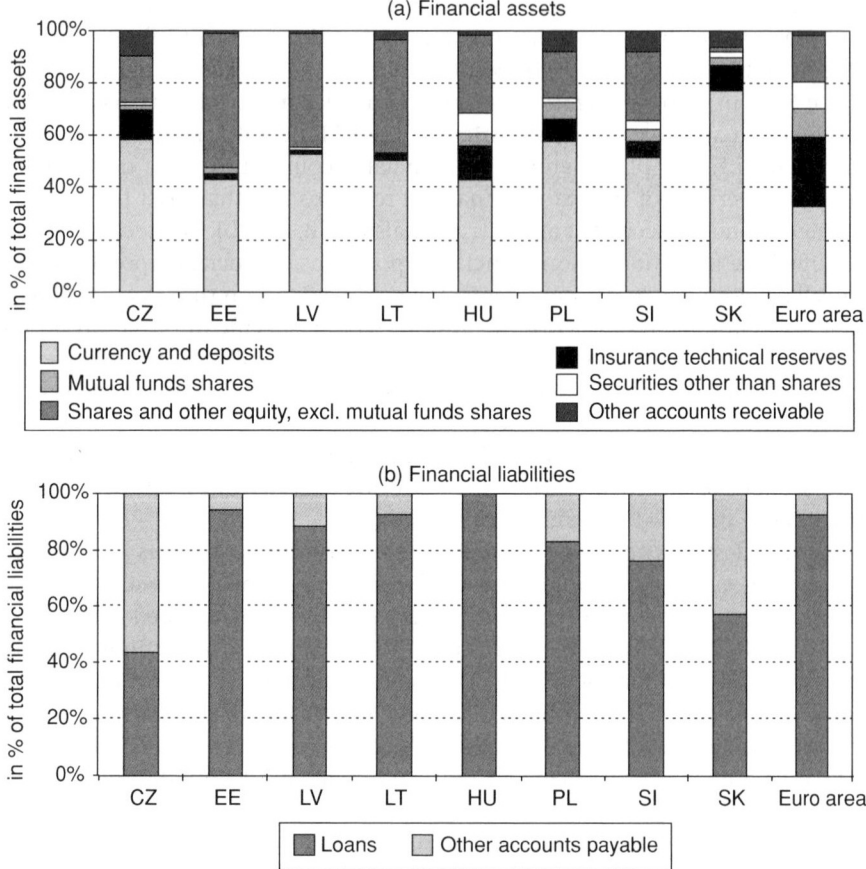

Figure 2.2 Financial Assets and Liabilities of Households (in percent of total financial assets/liabilities)

Source: ECB.

Note: Households include nonprofit institutions serving households. CZ, HU, LT, PL, SK, euro area as of 2003; EE, LV, SI as of 2002; non-consolidated data.

states for which data on non-quoted shares are available (CZ, EE, LT, HU, PL and SI), the percentage of total equity financing is 80 percent or more. To some extent, the significant percentage of non-quoted equity in corporate financing is due to the fact that often large nonfinancial corporations in these countries are owned by foreign multinationals, which finance these companies through foreign direct investments (which include equity stakes) and direct transfers (see also below).

Foreign sources of financing play an important role in the overall financial structure of most CEE new member states. In this respect, the financial assets of nonresidents should be analyzed (see Figure 2.4), because they are reflected in the financial liabilities of the various resident sectors. For the majority of countries,

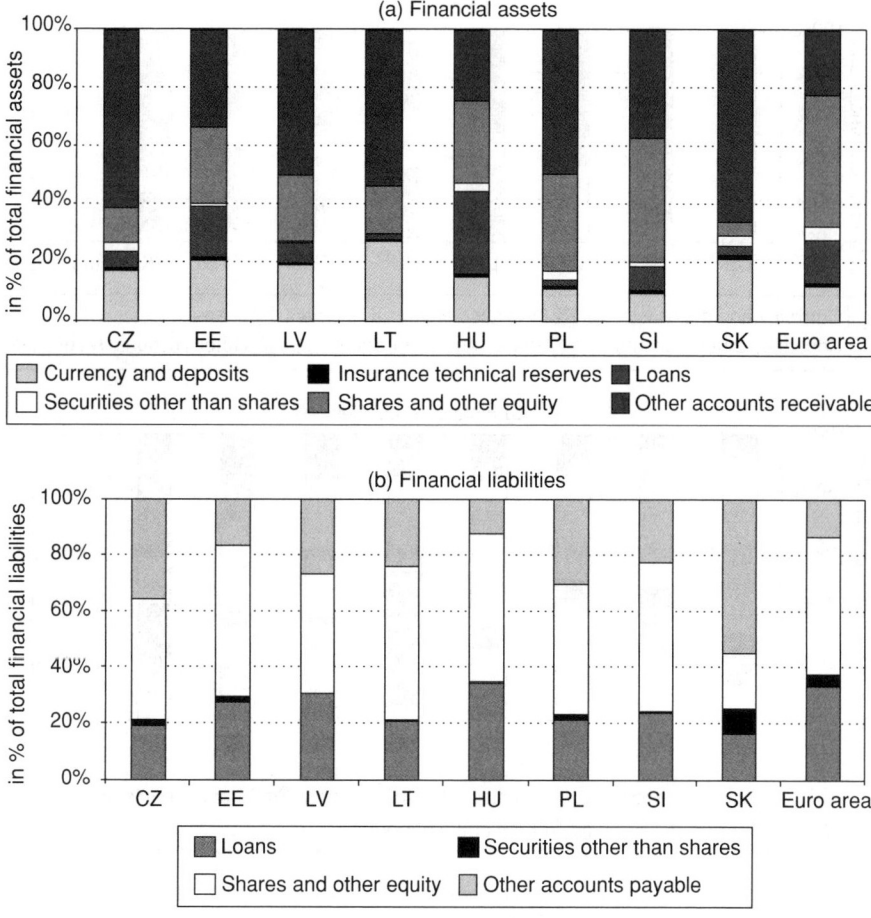

Figure 2.3 Financial Assets and Liabilities of Nonfinancial Corporations (in percent of total financial assets/liabilities)

Source: ECB.

Note: CA, HU, LT, PL, SK, euro area as of 2003; EE, LV, SI as of 2002; non-consolidated data.

equity is the single most important financial instrument representing the financial involvement of nonresidents. Notable exceptions are Latvia and Slovenia, whereas for Lithuania and Poland the importance of equity is relatively similar to the share of loans. The relatively important role of nonresident equity stakes can be explained by the rather significant degree of foreign ownership in both the real and financial sectors of the economies in most of the new member states in CEE (the picture for the banking sector is discussed in Section II). For most countries, the second most important financial asset of nonresidents is loans. These may take the form of intercompany loans from foreign owners to their domestic subsidiaries, including credit

20 *General Framework*

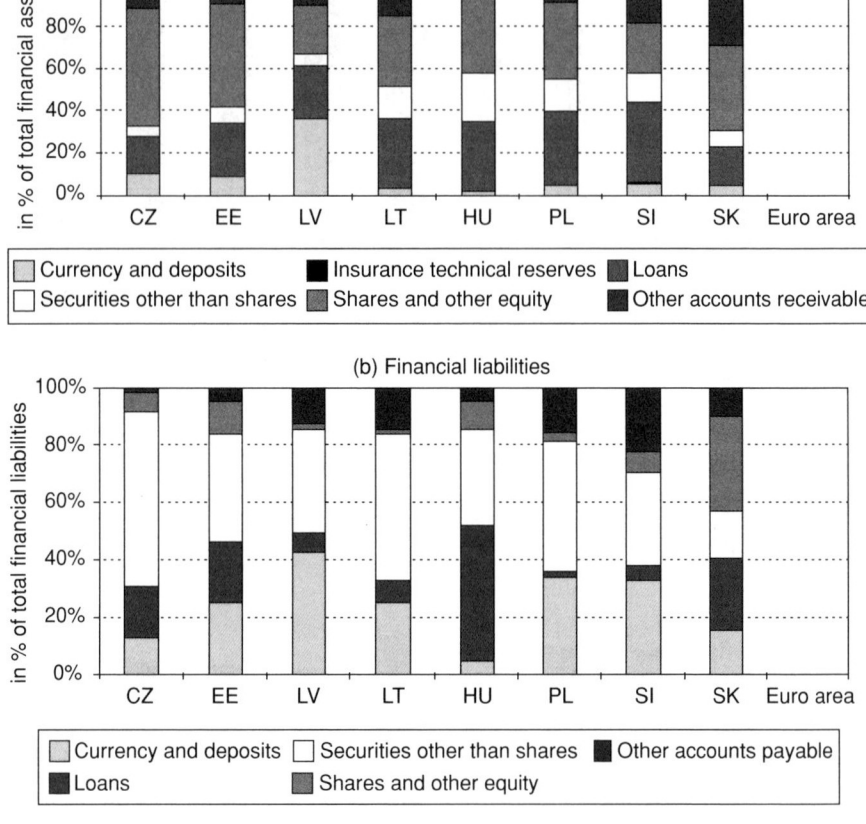

Figure 2.4 Financial Assets and Liabilities of Nonresidents vis-à-vis Residents by Category (in percent of total financial assets/liabilities)

Source: ECB.

Note: CZ, HU, LT, PL, SK, euro area as of 2003; EE, LV, SI as of 2002.

lines from foreign parent banks to domestic banks, and borrowing by domestic companies from foreign banks.

Finally, in order to assess the overall importance of loan financing in the countries discussed in this section, it may be useful to compare them as percentage of GDP with two important sources of external financing, i.e., debt securities and equity (Figure 2.5), with equity also including non-quoted equity. Figure 2.5 shows that in only two countries (Estonia and Latvia), the share of loans is higher than that of the two other financial instruments. This is mainly caused by the significance of non-quoted equity, as discussed above. Hence, from a static point of view (based on amounts outstanding), the macroeconomic role of credit for the majority of countries seems to be rather subdued at the moment. This changes when taking a

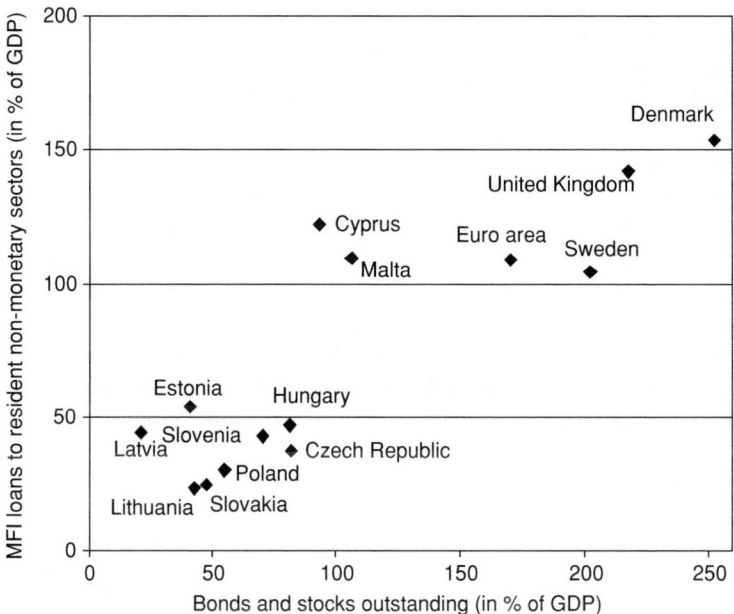

Figure 2.5 Equity and Bonds Outstanding versus Loans to Resident Clients, end-2003

Source: ECB; Eurostat; national central banks; national regulatory authorities and statistical offices; national stock exchanges.

Note: MFI loans are to resident nonfinancial and nonmonetary financial sectors; equity includes both quoted (or listed) and non-quoted equity.

dynamic point of view, i.e., when looking at credit growth, which will be the focus of the next section.

II. Causes of credit growth

The determinants of credit growth can be classified in several ways, for example in terms of structural versus cyclical factors, microeconomic versus macroeconomic factors, demand versus supply factors or market versus policy driven factors. These classifications are to some extent overlapping, but, because they each focus on different aspects of credit, they are also complementary. They help to highlight the multiple, and often interdependent, causes of credit growth.[12] In addition, the relevance of the specific factors underlying the expansion of bank credit has been changing over time, also because the countries in the region have been at different stages of the transition process over the last 15 years. Below, the factors behind the growth of credit that have been important in many, although not necessarily in all countries, are summarized in three main groups: transition-related, policy-related, and cyclical factors. This grouping of factors is purposefully eclectic, in recognition of the multifaceted and ever-changing causes of credit growth.

Transition-related factors

In its early stages, the credit expansion in these countries was facilitated by a number of "transition factors." The most obvious transition factor relates to the fact that due to the inherent nature of a planned economy, at the beginning of the 1990s the countries in the region were confronted with the task "... to create a functioning financial system where none had existed before" (EBRD, 1998, p.52). Thus, to a certain extent, the credit expansion in these countries may be attributed to a "pure" catch-up effect.

As shown in Figure 2.6, there is a positive relationship between the level of economic development (measured as GDP per capita) and financial sector depth (measured as credit to the private sector to GDP ratio). A simple regression analysis on the basis of worldwide cross-country data suggests that, among the countries in the region, only Bosnia and Herzegovina and Croatia have a credit-to-GDP ratio higher than what would be expected given their levels of economic development.

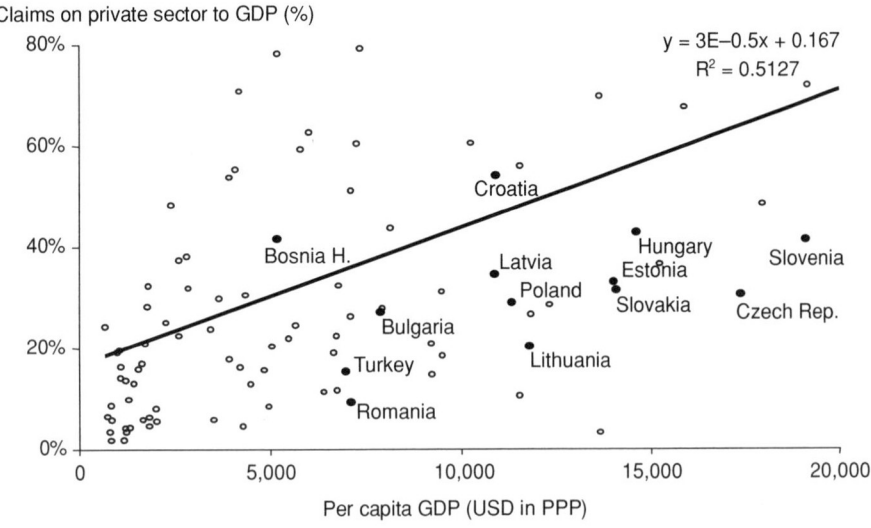

Figure 2.6 Credit to the Private Sector to GDP Ratio and Per Capita GDP (2003) (on the basis of 124 countries)

Source: IMF.

Transition involved deregulation, liberalization, and privatization across these economies (the only exception being Turkey). These transition elements affected both the demand for and the supply of credit. As new firms were set up in the countries in the region and these economies started to (re)capitalize, the demand for credit became particularly intense. In fact, lack of access to external sources of finance, including credit from banks, was seen as a key feature hampering enterprise development in the region, particularly among the south-eastern European countries.[13] In time, deregulation, liberalization, and privatization also brought an increase in the supply of credit. For example, improvements in the financial infrastructure were vital for establishing a well functioning credit market. Improvements in the legal systems enhanced contract enforcement and enabled the expanded use of collateral, which was needed for the development of mortgage markets. The adoption of new banking supervision and regulation mechanisms, often within the EU framework, was also essential for the development of banking intermediation. Therefore, as the institutional ground for financial sector development was set, a mix of supply and demand factors supported the expansion of domestic credit.

The EBRD index of banking sector reforms shows how countries in the region have advanced with the banking sector reforms (see Figure 2.7). The reforms, which have progressed in line with the overall transition process, were fastest in the new member states, followed by the candidate countries, while potential candidate countries still show a less advanced stage of reforms, despite evident progress since 2001. As banking sectors became more advanced, this process amplified the supply of bank credit available in the economies via several channels.

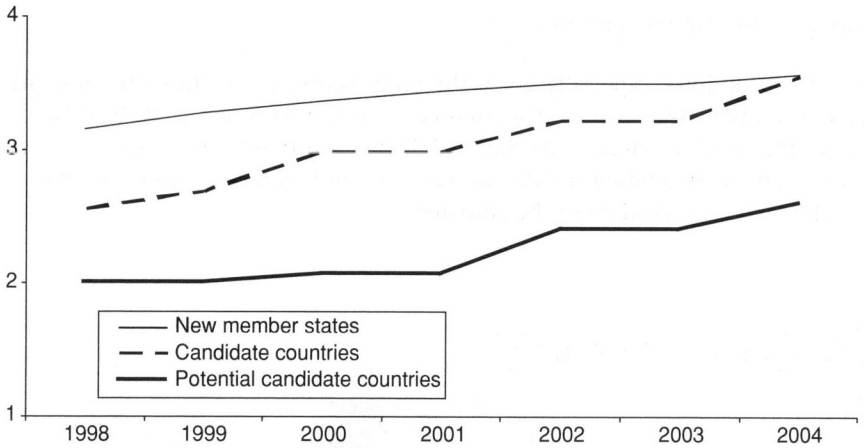

Figure 2.7 EBRD Index of Banking Sector Reform (higher values indicate more advanced stage of reforms; unweighted averages)

Source: EBRD.

First, foreign entry has played an important role in banking intermediation development. As Figure 2.8 shows, in most countries in the region the banking sector became predominantly foreign-owned by the turn of the century, mainly reflecting bank privatization which typically leads to efficiency gains, especially in the case of privatization to foreign strategic investors. Empirical research has indicated that a more efficient banking sector will increase financial intermediation (see Clarke et al, 2005).

Growing foreign investment in the respective banking sectors has been largely motivated by high returns on equity, which are typical for transition and lower income countries. Growth and profit seeking foreign-owned banks thus spurred

24 *General Framework*

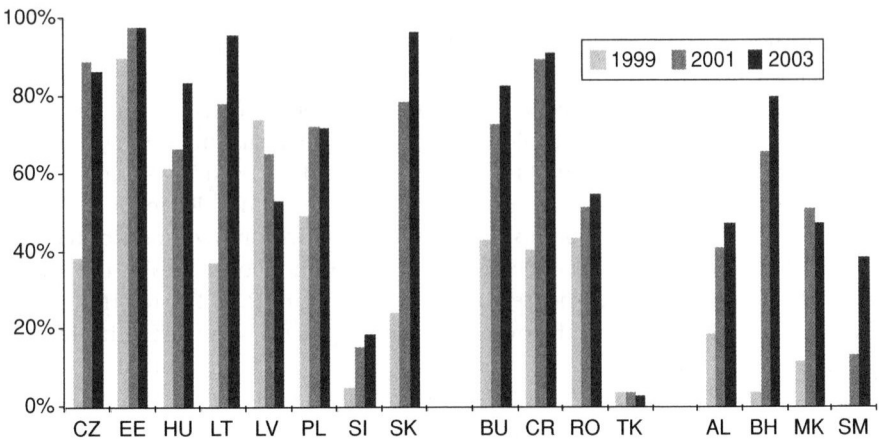

Figure 2.8 Share of Assets Held by Foreign Banks in Total Banking Assets

Source: EBRD, IMF, national central banks.

large capital inflows, especially given the profit squeezing in shrinking domestic markets, an issue that will be discussed below when considering cyclical factors behind the credit expansion. As Figure 2.9 shows, interest rate spreads (i.e., the difference between lending and deposit rates) in the region have been high, mostly well above those prevailing in the euro area.

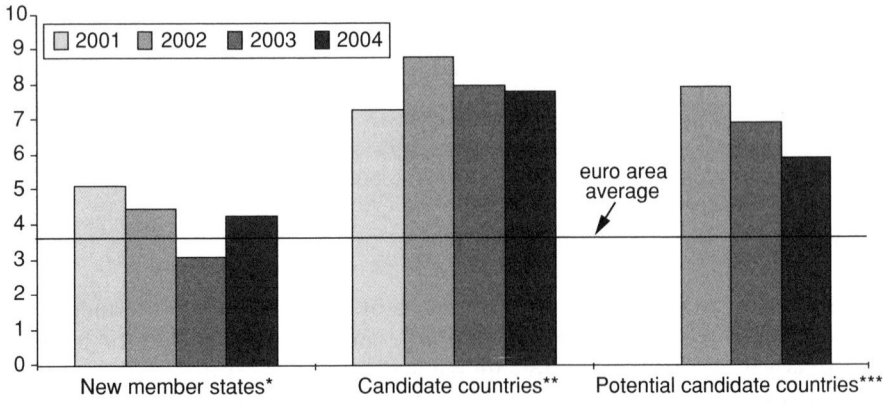

Figure 2.9 Interest Rate Spreads (lending minus deposit rates, percentage points)

Source: IMF.

Note: Unweighted averages; * refers to Czech Republic, Estonia, Hungary, Latvia, Lithuania, Poland, Slovakia, and Slovenia; ** refers to Bulgaria and Croatia; *** refers to Albania, Bosnia and Herzegovina, and FYR Macedonia.

Moreover, foreign-owned banks often prompted the development of "new" market segments, like mortgage lending, importing their experience and knowledge to the respective local banking sectors. At the same time, competition in the financial sector increased, which on one hand led to a greater variety of products offered by banks, and on the other hand made banks, which benefited from the ample liquidity conditions, more willing to extend loans. Favorable liquidity conditions in the financial sector resulted not only from strong capital inflows, but also from accumulating domestic bank deposits, which increased after confidence in the banking sector had been restored. In fact, during its early stages, credit expansion was usually predominantly financed by domestic sources, while foreign sources became increasingly important only later.[14] This is reflected in a large and, in several countries, growing share of foreign liabilities as of total assets of the banking sector, particularly in those countries which recorded rapid credit growth (Figure 2.10).[15]

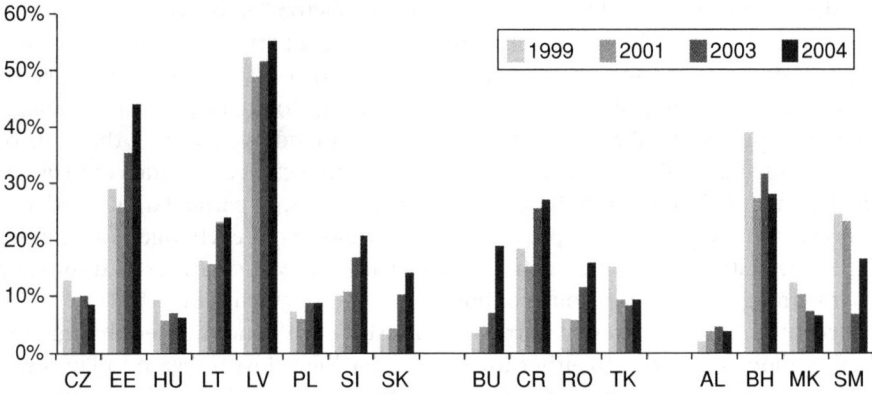

Figure 2.10 Foreign Liabilities to Total Banking Sector Assets

Source: IMF, national central banks.

Increased credit supply has been met by increased credit demand by households and nonfinancial corporations, in addition to increased demand stemming from improvements in the business cycle (e.g., cyclical factors discussed below). A common factor behind this development has been the stabilization of macroeconomic conditions, which raised confidence in domestic policies and contributed to favorable economic outcomes and prospects. Overall, higher economic growth increased the need for external financing of domestic investment and thus the demand for credit by the business sector, as in these countries other sources of external finance are typically scarce. Similarly, rising personal incomes boosted households' consumption and this in turn encouraged borrowing not only against current incomes, but also borrowing against future expected incomes.

Macroeconomic stability and nominal convergence have also significantly improved overall financing conditions. The outcome has been diminishing risk premia and gradually decreasing lending margins, allowing interest rates to decline further. As in several countries nominal interest rate convergence has occurred faster than convergence in inflation rates (due to, for example, structural factors and the Balassa–Samuelson effect), the decline in the real interest rate has often been even more pronounced, thus making borrowing more attractive.

A final transition-related cause behind the high growth of credit is the role that asset prices have played in shaping credit demand, in particular by households.[16] On the one hand, rapidly growing house prices in a number of countries in the region have stimulated buying real estate against the prospects of further price rises in the context of price convergence. In turn, demand for loans, particularly housing loans, has increased, as prices of and demand for real estate surged.[17] On the other hand, higher house prices have raised households' wealth and thus their potential against which they can borrow.

Policy-related factors

In addition to transitional factors, "policy-related factors" have also contributed to the dynamism of credit expansion. Besides the overall attitude of the authorities towards deregulation and liberalization, the policy-mix that the countries pursued may have sometimes played a role in contributing to credit growth. Although monetary policy can directly impact on credit demand by changing the costs of borrowing, it actually became less important in some cases as several countries in the region opted for more active exchange rate policies. In particular, the evidence suggests that countries that pursued fixed or quasi-fixed exchange rate regimes experienced stronger credit growth dynamics, particularly in countries with currency board arrangements, on account of borrowing in foreign currency.

Recently, foreign currency borrowing, mostly euro denominated, has gained further momentum due to either the advances achieved with regard to European integration or improved prospects for such integration. The link between exchange rate stability and credit expansion can be explained by the fact that better predictability of exchange rate movements has stimulated foreign currency borrowing, which has typically been at a lower cost than domestic currency borrowing.[18] In addition to monetary and exchange rate policies, also fiscal policies have been important. In one way, government financing per se impinged on credit supply, which could allow for some degree of crowding in.[19] In addition, specific schemes and guarantees, like mortgage loan subsidies or tax deductibility of mortgage repayments, gave an additional impetus to credit developments.

Cyclical factors

The third group of factors in broad terms can be classified as "cyclical factors." As shown in the literature, credit expansion may experience normal cyclical upturns because firms' investment and working capital needs fluctuate with the business cycle (IMF, 2004). The result is that credit expansion may prove to be pro-cyclical. The extreme example of this type of cyclicality can be seen in the recovery phase in financial intermediation in the aftermath of a macroeconomic and financial crisis, such as those experienced in Bulgaria in 1997 or in Turkey in 2000 and 2001. Whether stemming from extreme or other cyclical developments, the implication of this pro-cyclicality in credit is that the robust growth performance recently seen across the region may have contributed to faster credit growth. It is important to make a clear difference between the catch-up effect, discussed above, and this cyclical effect. While the catch-up effect would be driven by a higher growth trend, the cyclical aspect would stem from deviations around the trend. As Figure 2.11 shows, countries in the region have recently recorded very high GDP growth rates, well above not only the growth seen in the euro area but also above available estimates of potential output growth.[20]

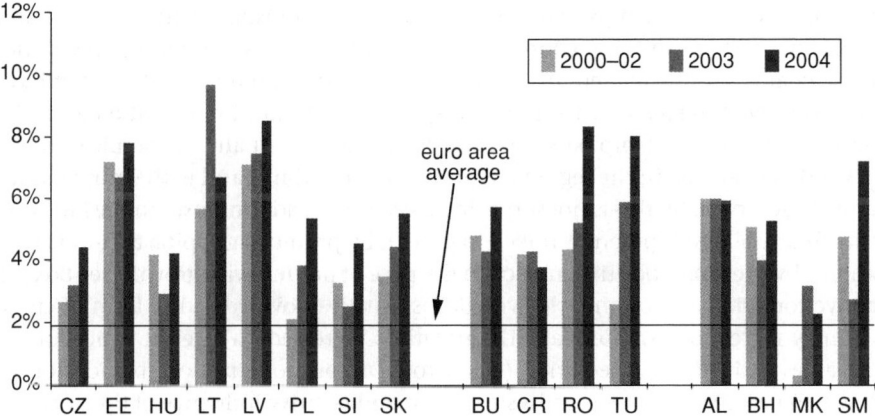

Figure 2.11 Real GDP Growth

Source: Eurostat.

All of the above cyclical factors refer to economic conditions in the countries of the region. However, the fact that the financial institutions operating in most countries of the region are predominantly foreign-owned also has implications for possible cyclical factors. The available evidence, both quantitative and qualitative, suggests that both the economic situation in the home country of the parent bank and the financial situation of the parent bank matter for the decisions made by the subsidiaries.[21] In general, local bank subsidiaries are found to increase lending in situations where economic conditions in the home country of the parent bank are subdued, as investment opportunities decrease, but are also particularly sensitive to the financial health of the parent bank, as exposures in these markets are likely to be among the first to be curtailed in situations of increased fragility of the parent institution.

Looking ahead, most of the above factors can be expected to continue to play a role in the countries in the region in the coming years. First, transition and catch-up are expected to continue, though their impact has become gradually less and less important given the advances achieved in the countries of the region. Next, these countries are expected to continue with economic and monetary integration, which should generate further fiscal consolidation and eventually lead to more exchange rate stability. And finally, the prospects for growth in the region are favorable, which should stimulate borrowing requirements. Nevertheless, as in some countries credit has been growing fast for a rather long period, saturation effects may become more important.

III. Credit, financial development, and economic growth

In order to understand properly the specific causes of the high credit growth observed in the countries in the region, it may be helpful to have a better insight into the fundamental relationships between the main characteristics of the financial and economic systems in these countries. This is particularly so because of the rather rapid changes in the related institutional frameworks in these countries that have been observed in recent years. In this respect, one of most important issues is the nature of the relationship between financial development and economic growth.

Credit expansion in the region has been going hand-in-hand with strong output growth. At first sight, this is not surprising given the broad consensus in the literature that financial development is linked to growth by promoting capital accumulation and/or by exerting a positive impact on the pace of productivity growth (see Box 2.1 above for details). Econometric evidence is usually provided in the form of cross-country regressions where real GDP growth is regressed on a set of conditioning variables and the intermediation (credit-to-GDP) or monetization (broad money-to-GDP) ratio. Most studies find a significant and positive influence of the financial variables on economic growth.

However, applying a standard empirical framework of the finance and growth nexus to the countries in the region does not suggest that finance has had a significant impact on the growth performance of countries in the region (Koivu, 2002; Fink et al, 2005; and Mehl et al, 2005). Indeed, financial variables may even be negatively counter-intuitive, signaling that an increase in financial depth has been associated with lower growth.

There are several possible explanations for this result. First, available time series may be still too short for applying this form of analysis to the region. Second, the specific nature of transition countries, i.e., economies with comparatively high per-capita incomes shifting from a planned to a market economy, may inhibit application of the standard growth regression framework. This view is supported by evidence showing that many of the control variables that are usually included in the regression, like the initial GDP per capita, to capture a convergence effect, and the initial secondary school enrolment rate, to proxy human capital investment, are also found to be not significant.

A third interpretation takes into account the quality of the financial sector environment, which is emphasized in both the "financial services" and "legal" views of the relationship between finance and growth (see Box 2.1). According to the literature, the financial sector is growth-supportive only if financial institutions are subject to proper governance structures. In particular, it is crucial that the behavior of banks is incentive-compatible with that of depositors and borrowers.[22] This relates most importantly to banking regulation and supervision (Dewatripont and Tirole,

1994) as well as the overall institutional and legal framework governing contractual relationships between economic agents (Levine et al, 2000).[23]

Since the beginning of transition, countries in CEE have engaged in efforts to reform their financial systems, reflecting the fact that under central planning financial sectors did not play a part in the allocation of resources. Thus, there was no need for banking supervision and regulation, or for an appropriate legal framework. However, the effectiveness and speed of financial sector reform efforts in the 1990s differed considerably among countries in the region (Bokros, 2002). Only recently has the region witnessed a convergence in terms of tightening regulations and supervision as well as the opening of domestic banking sectors to foreign investors.

Mehl et al (2005) explicitly include variables in the growth regressions that account for the quality of the financial sector environment, namely an index of creditor rights protection, the EBRD indicators for transition and banking sector reform and the share of foreign-owned banks in the total number of banks. Their results suggest that an improvement in the quality of finance is positively linked to growth. The creditor rights indicator is always found to be positively related with growth and in most cases highly significant. Indeed, it is the only variable, in addition to inflation, which captures the effect of macroeconomic stability on growth[24] and is always found to have the right sign and be highly significant.[25] Thus, there is evidence that the quality of financial development matters, lending support to both the "financial services" and "legal" views on the relationship between finance and economic growth (see Box 2.1). Moreover, this result may indicate that a further strengthening of the financial infrastructure and the legal framework, together with sound macroeconomic policies, can be an effective way to ensure that the current credit expansion will continue to be associated with economic growth.

IV. Credit growth and macroeconomic risks

While financial development has been found to be positively linked with growth, historical evidence and academic research also suggest that at times episodes of strong credit growth have been associated with substantial macroeconomic risks. In particular, these risks relate to an overheating economy and a worsening of the current account. Overheating pressures may reflect a surge in domestic demand, consumption, and investment, which are not accompanied by an equally large supply response, leading to inflation. Rising current account imbalances may be caused by stronger import demand and a loss of competitiveness due to an appreciating real exchange rate. Together with an increasing level of external debt this could make the economy vulnerable to sudden stop phenomena and balance of payments crises.[26]

An analysis of the key variables indicating the macroeconomic risks of the credit expansion in the region during the period 2000–04 gives mixed results. Inflation, in terms of consumer price inflation, has generally been contained in the new member states and has even been declining in the candidate and potential candidate countries, although it has picked up recently in the Baltic countries. At the same time, gross fixed capital formation, as a share of GDP, increased in most of the new member states and in all candidate and potential candidate countries, indicating an increase in domestic demand via investment.[27]

Current account imbalances have been significant. In general, countries show substantial current account deficits with an increasing trend over time, with the Czech Republic, Slovakia, Poland, and Slovenia being the exceptions. In line with this trend, external debt—expressed as a share of GDP—has increased substantially in Croatia, Latvia, and—to a lesser degree—in Estonia, Poland, and Slovenia. In other countries, however, the external debt–GDP ratio has been largely stable, reflecting that many countries have benefited from substantial inflows of (non-debt creating) foreign direct investment flows. Moreover, several countries with improving fiscal positions have seen declining external public debt to GDP ratios. By contrast, external private debt rose—both as a share of total external debt and as a share of GDP—in Bulgaria, Croatia, Estonia, Latvia, and—to a lesser degree—in Romania and Slovenia.

Given the short time period, it is difficult to link developments in these key macroeconomic variables with credit growth. However, a simple correlation analysis for the period 2000–04, covering 14 of the 16 countries under review (only Turkey as well as Serbia and Montenegro were excluded, the latter because of lack of comparable data) suggests that credit expansion in the region has indeed been associated with rising domestic demand, in particular with rising investment. Countries with stronger credit growth have also seen a stronger increase in the investment ratio, which is in line with the evidence from other credit boom episodes in emerging market economies. Moreover, countries with higher credit growth also have seen higher inflation, albeit this relationship was found to be somewhat weaker than in the case of investment. Correlation analysis also suggests a weak link between fiscal imbalances and credit growth, as at least some of the correlation exercises indicate that stronger credit growth seems to go hand in hand with an improvement in fiscal balances.

The effect of credit growth on the current account balance seems to be—recalling all the caveats of such a simple analysis—the most clear-cut one, suggesting that credit expansion has been associated with a worsening of current account imbalances in the region. However, the real exchange rate does not seem to be the channel through which this effect has been working. This may be explained by the fact that most countries that link their exchange rate to the euro, either in the form of a currency board or a tightly managed float, have been able to stabilize their real exchange rate, while countries with a managed or independent floating exchange rate regime saw much higher fluctuations in the real exchange rate and—as seen in the trend over the last two years—an appreciation (see Figures 2.12 and 2.13). At the same time, as indicated before, five of the seven countries with a fairly stable exchange rate against the euro have been among the countries experiencing strong credit expansion, while—with the exception of Hungary and Albania—countries with more flexible exchange rate regimes have seen a comparatively low rate of credit growth—on average—over the last five years.

Finally, it is revealing that absolute changes in the private external debt to GDP ratio are highly correlated with absolute changes in private sector credit to GDP ratio

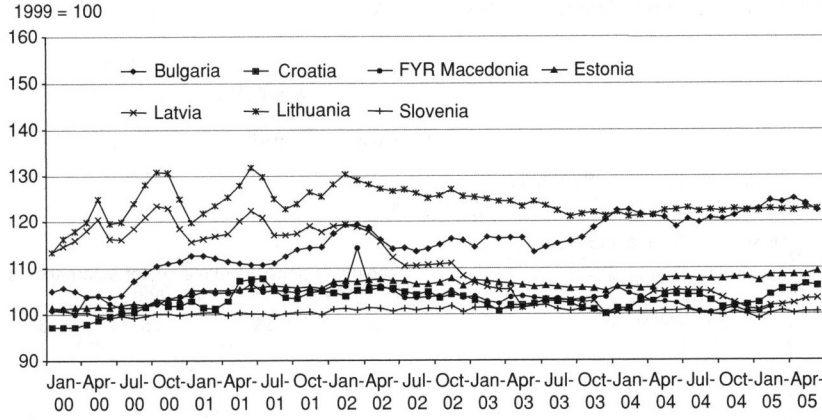

Figure 2.12 Currency Boards and Tightly Managed Floats Against the Euro: Real Exchange Rate Developments

Source: IMF, authors' calculations.

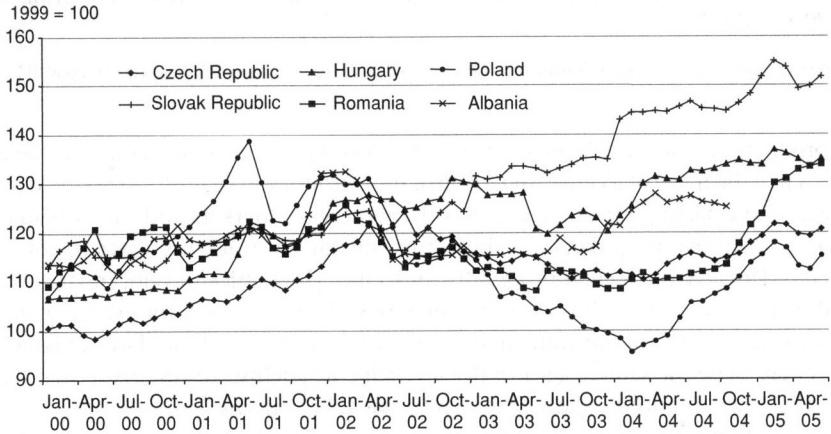

Figure 2.13 Managed and Independent Floaters: Real Exchange Rate Developments

Source: IMF, authors' calculations.

in the period 2000–04 (see Figure 2.14). Indeed, the correlation coefficient amounts to 0.62 when considering all countries, and increases to 0.90 when disregarding the outliers, i.e., the Czech Republic and Slovakia.

The analysis suggests that the macroeconomic risks in the region associated with strong credit growth seem to be more pronounced on the external side, as up to now signs of domestic overheating have been subdued on goods and labor markets. Inflation has been contained, reflecting the global low inflation environment and substantial slack in domestic labor markets at the beginning of the decade. High unemployment rates have been reduced only slowly as growth has been associated

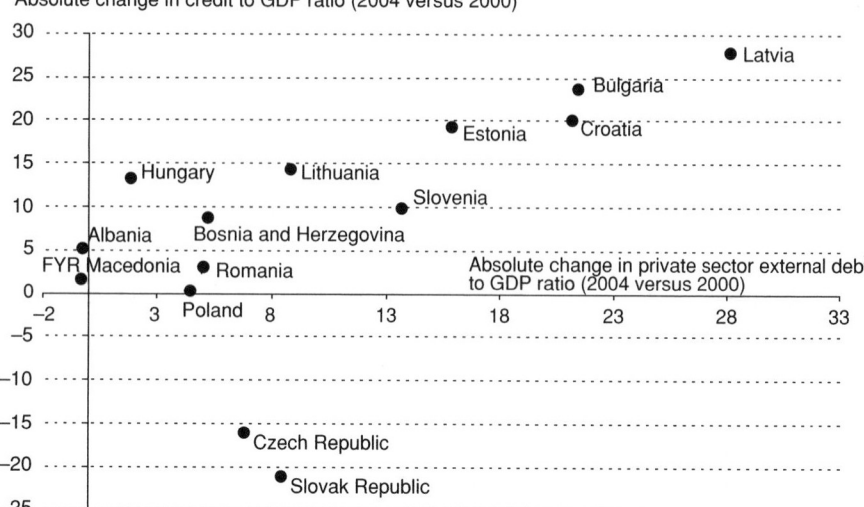

Figure 2.14 Private External Debt and Private Sector Credit to GDP: Correlation of changes from 2000 to 2004

Source: IMF, authors' calculations; Bosnia and Herzegovina: 2002–04 change; FYR Macedonia: 2000–03 change.

with productivity increases in many countries. Developments in asset and real estate markets may be more of a cause for concern. Indeed, stock markets have boomed in the region, outpacing price increases in other emerging markets and the available evidence on housing markets also indicates substantial price increases in some countries. However, it is even more difficult to link these price developments in a causal way to credit growth. While this may have been the case, for example, via the financial accelerator mechanism (see Section V below), credit and asset market booms may have the same origin in the favorable financing conditions in mature market economies and the global "search for yield" phenomenon.

On the external side, against the background of the available evidence on factors associated with "boom-bust" episodes of credit markets, substantial and increasing current account deficits in the region, linked with an increasing external indebtedness of the private sector, are a cause for concern. There are, however, also some mitigating factors, as current account deficits have been matched to a considerable amount by nondebt creating capital inflows, mainly in the form of foreign direct investment (for example, as evidenced by the high share of equity in nonresident portfolios; see also Section I) or—in some potential candidate countries—via capital transfers as one form of remittance and donor support (Zeuner, 2005).[28] Moreover, in the candidate and potential candidate countries, foreign exchange reserves held by the authorities have continued to increase strongly, both as a share of GDP and expressed in months of imports.

As credit growth has been most prominent in countries with a currency board or a tightly managed float, fiscal policies remain key in containing demand pressures and acting as a restraint for further increases in current account deficits. While several countries experiencing strong credit growth have seen an improvement in fiscal balances and a reduction of external public debt (expressed as a percentage of GDP), it is difficult to gauge the extent to which this trend is primarily a result of strong economic performance or due to active consolidation efforts. Modest deficits in years of extraordinarily high growth suggest that the fiscal stance has been less tight than the deficit reduction might indicate at face value. Against this background, a strengthening positive correlation between credit growth and fiscal balances would represent a considerable achievement in containing the macroeconomic risks associated with strong credit expansion.

V. Financial stability implications of rapid credit growth

Besides its impact on macroeconomic stability, rapid credit expansion can have important implications for financial stability. This relationship may be attributed to the procyclicality of bank lending behavior: risks may be underestimated during expansionary phases of the business cycle, thereby resulting in loosening credit standards and a lower average quality of borrowers,[29] and higher credit losses when the next economic downturn occurs. Another often cited theory related to the over-expansion of credit is the "financial accelerator" mechanism.[30] Over-optimism about future returns could boost asset valuations and thus firms' net worth, which then feeds back into higher investment and credit demand and a further increase in asset prices. Consequently, this self-reinforcing mechanism may lead to excesses in the growth of credit and asset prices. A negative change in expectations could then precipitate a reverse process with falling asset prices and a credit crunch, which may significantly increase repayment difficulties for borrowers and may ultimately lead to higher loan losses for banks.

Notwithstanding the role of credit booms in increasing the likelihood of banking crises, it is important to stress that rapid credit expansion may not necessarily be harmful for financial sector health. There is empirical evidence that many episodes of rapid credit growth have not been followed by banking crises.[31] This, coupled with the role of financial deepening in economic growth, may pose important dilemmas for policymakers (Kraft and Jankov, 2005). Given the difficulties in distinguishing between "good" and "bad" lending booms ex ante, however, rapid credit growth should remain a key concern for policymakers from a financial stability perspective. In particular, the speed of credit growth may put strain on banks' risk assessment and risk management capacities which, coupled with over-optimism about future prospects, may lead to a misallocation of credit (Hilbers et al, 2005). Given the lack of long enough credit histories for borrowers, this challenge may be all the more important for banks in CEE countries due to measurement difficulties in estimating default probabilities. This problem may be even more pronounced in the case of relatively new, previously under-serviced, market segments such as households and SMEs.

Risk factors associated with rapid credit growth

One of the main features of the fast credit growth in the CEE region is the substantial rise in household debt, albeit from a low initial level. Notwithstanding the rapid pace of lending growth to households, credit risk is contained by the fact that household indebtedness is still low by international standards. Only Croatia has indebtedness ratios comparable to the euro area average, with household debt amounting to 70 percent of disposable income in 2004. Among other countries, the household indebtedness ratio in Estonia (45 percent) is at a similar level to the euro area countries with the lowest household indebtedness, for instance, Italy. In other countries characterized by very strong growth in household loans, the indebtedness ratio stood just above 30 percent at the end of 2004 (Hungary and Latvia).[32] Credit risk is also mitigated by the favorable growth outlook, improving income prospects for households as well as a low interest rate environment.

As regards the repricing characteristics of household loans, mortgage loans granted at floating interest rates are the most common in the new member states (ECB, 2004a).[33] Given the current low level of interest rates, an abrupt upturn in short-term interest rates could expose borrowers to a considerable increase in their repayment burdens. Information on the interest payment burden is only available for a few countries. The ratio of debt servicing costs (interest payments) to disposable income varied between 1.3 percent and 3.8 percent across the new member states in 2003, compared to the euro area average of 4.5 percent (ECB, 2004b). Based on the comparatively modest proportion of interest payments to income, the negative impact of interest rate hikes on household debt servicing ability is expected to be subdued.

A common feature of rapid credit growth in the region is the high or increasing share of loans denominated in foreign currencies. At the end of 2004, the share of foreign currency loans in total loans exceeded 50 percent in seven countries, and it was between 30 and 50 percent in four countries (see Figure 2.15). Due to the high or increasing share of foreign currency lending, the vulnerability of borrowers to adverse exchange rate movements may be significant. Currency mismatches in nonfinancial sectors' balance sheets may translate into higher credit risk for banks. For the corporate sector, the importance of foreign currency loans is partly explained by the large presence of multinational companies[34] The subsidiaries of these foreign-based corporations predominantly operate in the tradable sectors, and typically have a natural hedge against adverse exchange rate movements. Conversely, the debt burden of households or small and medium-sized firms, operating in non-tradable sectors, may considerably increase in case of unexpectedly large adverse exchange rate movements and thus may lead to growing repayment difficulties.[35]

In a related empirical study, Glogowski and Zochowski (2003) investigated the potential impact of an exchange rate shock on foreign currency loan quality for Poland. They found that a large one-time depreciation could potentially lead to a significant deterioration in loan quality and to a considerable increase in loan losses. According to their model estimations, a one-time 15 percent depreciation of the zloty increased the expected value of loan losses by an amount which would have corresponded to more than one-third of average annual net profits, calculated for

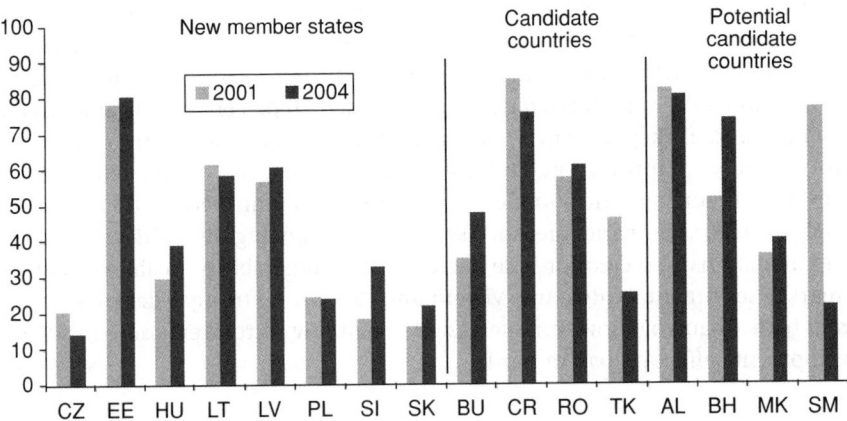

Figure 2.15 Share of Foreign Currency Loans in Total Loans (percent)

Source: National central banks.

Note: Foreign currency loans do not include indexed loans for Serbia and Montenegro and for Bosnia and Herzegovina in 2001.

the period between 2000 and 2004, or to a 0.5 percentage point reduction of the capital adequacy ratio within one year.

It is important to stress, however, that the above estimations cannot be generalized across countries. While the probability of adverse exchange rate movements may vary across different exchange rate regimes, the degree of vulnerability will largely depend on the credibility of economic policies which target a convergence to the euro area or a future accession to the EU.

As shown by the analysis in Section IV, rapid expansion of bank credit seems to be associated with high current account deficits and an increasing dependence on foreign funding in several countries.[36] This may suggest that the vulnerability of banking sectors to external shocks has increased recently. Risks associated with high external imbalances are alleviated by favorable deficit financing patterns, characterized by sizable FDI inflows in several countries.[37] In a few cases, however, significant portfolio inflows have also played a role, thereby increasing the risk of capital flow reversals. In particular, portfolio inflows have been supported by the low level of global interest rates and a lower risk aversion of investors. Thus, a potential change in this favorable external environment could precipitate a reverse process. This could then feed back into increasing repayment difficulties for borrowers with substantial foreign liabilities.

Another aspect of external vulnerability is the increasing reliance on foreign funding in financing credit growth (see also Section I). Since the growth of domestic deposits was outpaced by that of loans, banks increasingly tapped the interbank markets in search for alternative funding sources. Consequently, the growth of foreign liabilities accelerated simultaneously with the rapid expansion of credit (Figure 2.16). Looking at the maturity breakdown of banks' foreign debt in selected countries with fast credit growth, there are no clear signs of a shift towards shorter maturities.[38] Note, however, that in some countries the share of short-term bank debt is rather high. For the past three years, the share of short-term debt in banks' total foreign debt has exceeded 70 percent in Bulgaria, Latvia, Lithuania, and Turkey. However, given the high foreign ownership of banking sectors in most countries, foreign borrowing is likely to be dominated by intra-group bank financing. Thus, in view of the strong commitment of their strategic foreign owners, subsidiaries are not likely to face financing difficulties. Moreover, the extremely narrow creditor base decreases the vulnerability to abrupt changes in market sentiment (Kutos and Vogelmann, 2005). A stronger dependence on parent bank financing, however, increases the banking sectors' exposure to adverse developments affecting parent banks.

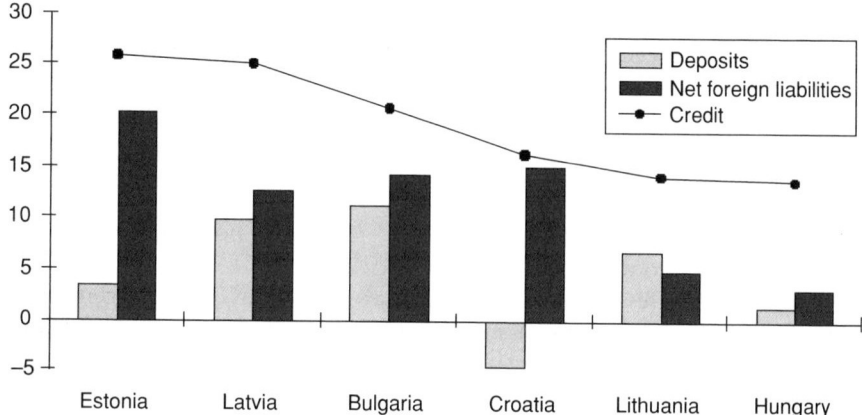

Figure 2.16 Change in Credit to the Private Sector, Domestic Deposits and Banks' Net Foreign Liabilities (2001–04, percent of GDP)

Source: National central banks, IMF, authors' calculations.

Another risk factor related to rapid credit growth concerns the impact of strengthening competition in banking markets, in particular in CEE countries. Intensifying competition among banks may erode their net interest margins and put pressure on profitability. To compensate for the adverse impact of narrowing margins, banks may be inclined to increase lending volumes. This might be enhanced by the strong incentives for parent banks to exploit the significant growth potential of CEE markets due to limited growth and squeezing profit margins in their home markets (see also Section II). This process may result in higher risk taking by banks, which could become a source of rising loan losses if macroeconomic conditions worsen. According to assessments by central banks in some new member states (Estonia, Hungary), there are signs of increased willingness by banks to take on more risks as a result of increased competition and lower margins.

The development of interest margins paints a mixed picture. (Net) interest margins for banks in the new member states as well as in candidate and potential candidate countries are generally higher than in the euro area. This may suggest that price competition in the banking market as a whole might still be less intense than in the euro area. The decomposition of margins indicates, at least for the new member states, however, that price competition may have strengthened significantly in certain market segments, in particular in the mortgage lending market. Lending margins on housing loans, defined by the difference between lending rates and money market rates, reached levels close to the euro area average by the end of 2004 (e.g., in Estonia and Lithuania). The degree of price competition in the market for consumer loans seems to be lagging behind that of the euro area (Eesti Pank, 2005b). Finally, margins on corporate loans are comparable with the euro area average in several new member states. Thus, higher overall net interest margins may be explained by higher deposit margins on time deposits and sight deposits, in addition to higher margins on consumer loans.

Credit standards also give a mixed picture. Quantitative information on the development of credit standards is very scarce even for CEE countries. The limited evidence, provided by bank lending surveys in Hungary and Poland, suggests that banks may have eased their credit standards for the past few years, especially in lending to households and SMEs.

Given the potential risk of asset price bubbles associated with rapid credit growth, it may also be important to examine the dynamics of housing prices. Limited data availability does not allow for drawing general conclusions on house price developments in the region. Recent evidence on real estate price dynamics indicates a relatively great diversity across countries. For instance, a sharp rise in house prices has been observed in recent years in the Baltic countries, in Bulgaria, Romania and Turkey (see Mihaljek in this volume). In other countries, such as the Czech Republic, Hungary, or Slovenia, the growth of housing prices had slowed down by 2004. In the longer term, an increasing trend of housing prices is expected across the region due to further convergence to price levels in "old" EU countries.

Shock-absorbing capacity of banking sectors

An essential component of financial stability is that a smooth and efficient allocation of resources from savers to investors is facilitated by the financial system. Another important aspect of financial stability is that the financial system is in such a condition that it can smoothly absorb financial or real shocks. Given the prevalence of bank-dominated financial structures in CEE countries, it follows that the impairment of the credit providing function of the banking system could have relatively severe consequences on the real economy in these countries.

After taking stock of potential vulnerabilities stemming from rapid credit growth, it is thus of key importance to assess banks' ability to withstand shocks. Some comfort can be taken from the fact that bank profitability has improved significantly in most new member states and candidate countries during the past few years (Figure 2.17). On the other hand, banking sectors in the potential candidate countries, with the exception of Albania, have continued to show weak performances indicating persistent fragilities in their banking systems.

38   *General Framework*

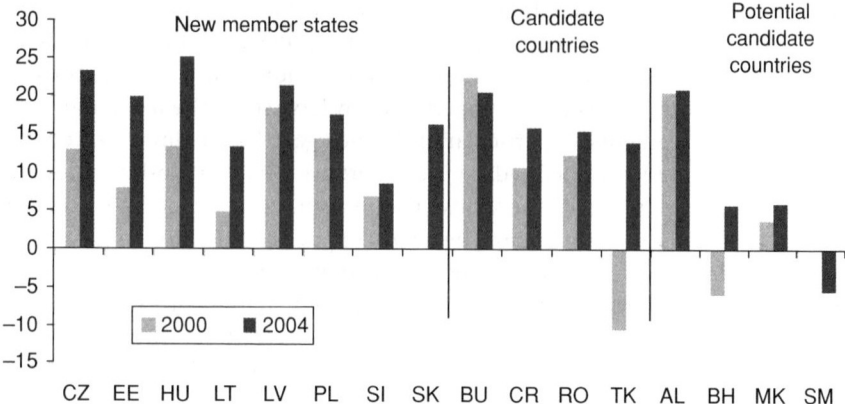

Figure 2.17   Return on Equity of Banking Sectors

Source: National central banks, IMF, Banking Regulation and Supervisory Agency (Turkey), authors' calculations. ROE is calculated with after-tax profit, except for Bosnia and Herzegovina where it is calculated with profit before tax.

Improved profitability in many countries helped banks maintain a solid capital base, thereby contributing to increased shock absorbing capacity of banks. While strong loan growth, through a dynamic increase in risk-weighted assets, contributed to the decrease in capital adequacy ratios in many countries, banking sectors maintained adequate solvency buffers, well in excess of minimum requirements, even in countries with a higher-than-8 percent required minimum ratio (Figure 2.18).

Judging from the change in nonperforming loan (NPL) ratios over the past few years, asset quality seems to have improved in most countries (see Figure 2.19). Improved loan quality may reflect mostly benign macroeconomic conditions as well

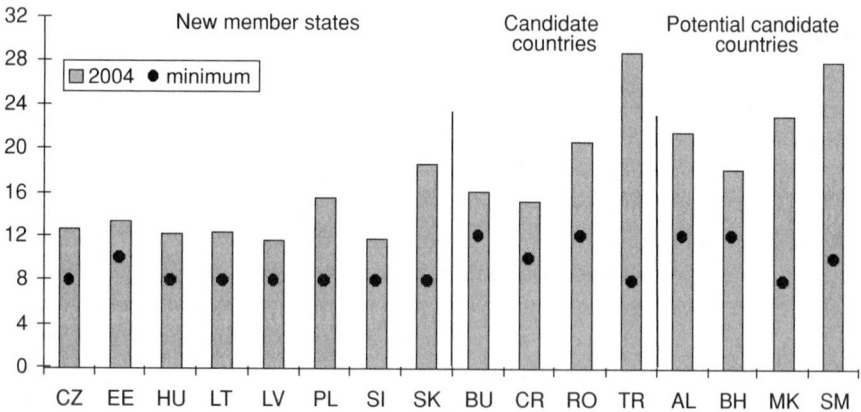

Figure 2.18   Capital Adequacy Ratios at end-2004 (percent)

Source: National central banks, IMF, Banking Regulation and Supervisory Agency (Turkey).

as improving risk management by banks. In some potential candidate countries (FYR Macedonia, Serbia and Montenegro), however, banking sectors are still burdened by high NPL ratios, highlighting the need for further efforts to strengthen risk management and prudential supervision of banks. As for countries with low NPL ratios, some caution is also warranted as these indicators of banks' asset quality are affected by "loan seasoning" (Berger and Udell, 2003). Since loan performance problems usually materialize only with a significant lag, the large volume of new loans associated with rapid credit expansion tends to depress NPL ratios. As in most countries banks' asset quality has been supported by relatively buoyant cyclical conditions in recent years, the resilience of loan portfolios to economic downturns remains untested up to now.

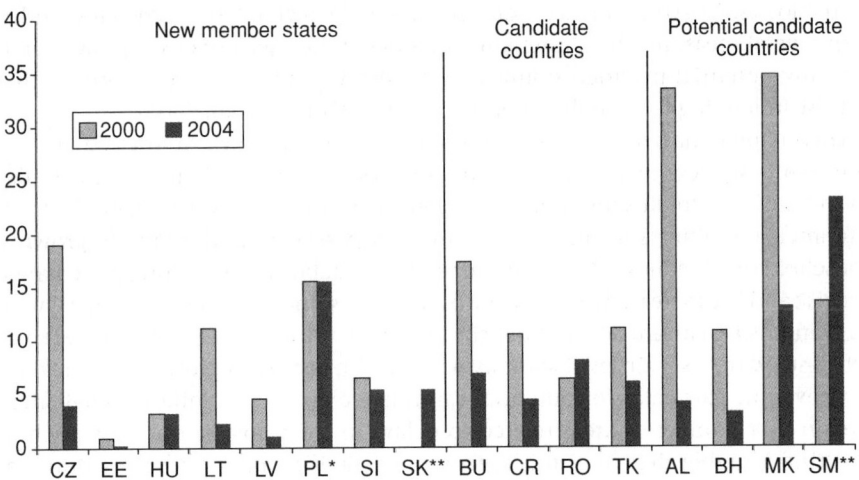

Figure 2.19 Ratio of Nonperforming Loans to Total Loans (percent)

Source: National central banks, IMF, Banking Regulation and Supervisory Agency (Turkey), authors' calculations.

* Data for Poland are not directly comparable to other countries due to different classification criteria.
** Data refer to August 2004 for Slovakia.

Besides the significant improvement in financial strength, a strong ownership background should provide banks with a second line of defense against potential shocks. Many banks in the region are owned by reputable, well-capitalized banks from EU-15 countries. Looking at different sub-groups, in 2003 foreign ownership was the highest for the new member states (77 percent), followed by the candidate (76 percent) and potential candidate (53 percent) countries. Financial support is likely to be provided by the strategic foreign owners in case of need, as already indicated by some recent examples. It should be noted, however, that there were a few cases where foreign owners did not provide financial support for their troubled subsidiaries and withdrew from the market. But overall, the knowledge transfer and improved risk management systems facilitated by foreign ownership should be beneficial for banking sector stability in CEE countries in the longer term.

VI. Conclusions

Since the beginning of the decade CEE countries have seen a period of strong credit growth, which in several cases has reached more than 20 percent per year in real terms. Up to now, the credit expansion has gone hand in hand with strong economic growth, demonstrating the beneficial side of an increase in financial intermediation for economic development. However, the experience of many emerging market countries, albeit by no means unambiguous, also suggests that fast credit growth may end in a "boom–bust" scenario, culminating in financial crisis and the associated output losses. As a consequence, policymakers in the region have already responded with several measures that either aim at reducing the speed of credit growth or at reducing potential macroeconomic and financial stability risks associated with a fast rise in lending to households and businesses (Hilbers et al, 2005).

This chapter analyzed the causes and nature of credit growth in the CEE region. The results suggest that there are several factors that have characterized similar episodes of fast credit growth in other countries and regions. For example, from a financial stability and macroeconomic risk perspective, the rapidly growing household indebtedness, the significant exposure of borrowers to foreign exchange rate risk and the increased external vulnerability of some countries—associated with high and rising current account deficits and an increasing level of private external debt—stand out as main risk factors associated with fast credit growth in the region. Moreover, in particular for potential candidate countries, significant challenges remain in a number of areas related to delays in the transition process, such as ensuring a higher degree of macroeconomic stability, developing institutional frameworks and strengthening the prudential supervision of banks.

However, some of the causes of credit growth have been unique to the region, in particular, those related to the transition process, namely the catching-up in financial development with market economies with similar per capita incomes and the predominance of foreign-owned banks in the region. Both factors affect the nature of credit growth in a way that can be seen as mitigating the risks, both from a macroeconomic and a financial stability perspective.

At the same time, the main policy recommendations for reducing risks stemming from strong credit growth also apply to the region (Papademos, 2005). First, banking supervision and regulation should be strengthened, ensuring that banks' risk management practices live up to the challenges linked to a rapid expansion of credit. Second, fiscal consolidation should be used as the main instrument to address the macroeconomic challenges, in particular in countries with an exchange rate peg or a tightly managed float.

With regard to the first element, considerable improvements in supervision and regulation in the region have been achieved. Moreover, the evidence presented also suggests that a higher quality of the financial sector environment may have contributed even more to output growth in the region than the increase in financial depth. Nevertheless, there are still significant variations across different country groups as regards their institutional framework and banking sector performance.

As far as fiscal policy is concerned, further consolidation may be needed in countries experiencing strong credit and output growth, even though the fiscal position has improved in several countries over the last few years, as this may reflect strong economic performance rather than active consolidation efforts.

Notes

1. European Central Bank (ECB). The contribution of Calin Arcalean (Indiana University) was made during his stay at the ECB in 2005. The authors would like to thank Georges Pineau and Cristina Vespro for helpful comments and André Geis for excellent research assistance.
2. This chapter analyzes the causes and nature of rapid credit expansion in most of the new EU member states and the EU candidate and potential candidate countries (Czech Republic, Estonia, Hungary, Latvia, Lithuania, Poland, Slovakia, and Slovenia, Bulgaria, Romania, Croatia, Turkey, Albania, Bosnia and Herzegovina, the former Yugoslav Republic of Macedonia, and Serbia and Montenegro). However, data availability limits the analysis of parts of the chapter to a narrower set of countries, in which case this is indicated in the text.
3. EBRD Transition Report 1998, p. vii.
4. EBRD Transition Report 2004, p. 27.
5. IFS data. For country by country data see Hilbers et al (2005) or the IMF's September 2005 Global Financial Stability Report, pp. 61–3.
6. For the Czech Republic and Slovakia, the interpretation of the data before 2002 is distorted due to the consolidation of the banking sector.
7. Thus, the chapter does not analyze the policy responses already taken by the authorities in the region. An overview is provided in Hilbers et al (2005).
8. Financial structures differ from country to country and also change over time in relation to the stages of economic development (Demirgüç-Kunt and Levine, 2001). In general, financial structures are classified in terms of the significance of indirect versus direct finance. In financial structures characterized by indirect or bank-based finance, surplus funds of savers are channeled to entities short of funds (e.g., households, companies, and governments) through financial intermediaries that are mostly monetary financial institutions (MFIs) such as private banks. By contrast, in direct or market-based finance, borrowers obtain funds directly from lenders by issuing debt securities or financial instruments in financial markets.
9. This argument of the so-called "completeness" of financial structures has been emphasized by various observers (Greenspan, 1999; Allen and Gale, 2000). In this regard, the prolonged banking and economic crisis that Japan experienced during the 1990s could be partly due to the lack of well-developed capital markets that could replace the credit providing function of the banking system when the latter was seriously impaired (van Rixtel, 2002).
10. Loans typically represent the largest proportion of bank credit.
11. Equity financing in the form of non-quoted shares, for example family capital invested in small companies, also contributes to the high share of equity financing used by euro area nonfinancial corporations. See ECB (2001).
12. For a literature overview, see for example Backé and Zumer (2005), and IMF (2004).
13. Results from the latest EBRD-World Bank Business Environment and Enterprise Performance Survey conducted in 2002 showed the still very high reliance on internal funds and retained earnings for the south-east Europe (SEE) countries; see EBRD (2004b).

14. For the new member states, foreign sources particularly gained importance since 2001/02 (Backé and Zumer, 2005).
15. As discussed in Section I, loans by nonresidents play an important role in the financing of the economies in the new member states.
16. One should bear in mind that the causality of the relationship between asset prices and credit demand is difficult to define due to the endogeneity problem.
17. As households move homes, they are likely to increase consumption of other goods, like furniture and household appliances; therefore overall demand for loans, not only for housing loans can increase.
18. Generally, the share of foreign currency loans is the highest in countries with the most dynamic credit expansion (for the new member states, see Backé and Zumer, 2005).
19. This may have been particularly relevant at the beginning of transition, when public sector deficits started to decline due to privatization and governments started to consolidate their budgets. In fact, Cottarelli et al (2005) suggest crowding in may have been a factor in the countries with rapid credit growth. However, looking at a more recent period (2001–04), there is no evidence for crowding in of private sector credit as a consequence of lower public borrowing in the new member states (Backé and Zumer, 2005).
20. For example, the actual economic growth rates among the four countries that exhibited the highest GDP growth in 2004 (Latvia, Romania, Turkey, and Estonia) were above the estimated potential output growth as presented by the governments of those countries to the EU in the context of their 2004 Convergence or Pre-Accession Economic Programmes (potential growth in 2004 was estimated to be 7.9 percent in Latvia, 6.4 percent in Romania, 7.2 percent in Turkey, and 6.2 percent in Estonia).
21. De Haas and Naaborg (2005) on the basis of focused interviews with managers of foreign parent banks and their subsidiaries in the region and de Haas and van Lelyveld (2005) on the basis of banks' balance sheet data reported to Bankscope.
22. Indeed, depositors have limited information on banks' activities, as banks extend loans on the basis of private information, and are unable to exert proper governance on banks' management and owners.
23. Several cross-country regressions for Latin America in the 1970s and 1980s (De Gregorio and Guidotti, 1992) as well as countries experiencing a financial crisis (Johnston and Pazarbasioğlu, 1995) have also found a negative and significant coefficient of the financial variable in the regression, suggesting that in a low quality financial sector environment "expansions of financial intermediation do not appear to improve growth and efficiency" (Johnston and Pazarbasioğlu, 1995, p.20).
24. Macroeconomic instability, as proxied by inflation higher than a 4 percent threshold, was found to have a significant and detrimental impact on growth (see also Cottarelli et al, 2005). Also in line with other studies on the finance–growth nexus (Khan et al, 2001), the impact of inflation on growth is non-linear as inflation lower than the threshold had no significant effects.
25. Somewhat weaker is the evidence of possible growth effects related to the EBRD indicators of transition and banking sector reform as well as the degree of foreign ownership in the banking sectors.
26. The risks, including the channels through which they come about, are analyzed in detail in the emerging "boom-bust" financial crisis literature (Bordo and Jeanne, 2002; Jaeger and Schuknecht; 2004, and Detken and Smets, 2004).
27. By contrast, evidence on gross private savings (as a share of GDP) is more diverse. Among the new member states, gross private savings have been on a declining trend in Estonia and Latvia, while it has slightly increased in Slovakia. For the remaining countries, including candidate and potential candidate countries, the data do not show a clear trend.
28. In some countries, like Estonia (Lutz, 2004), current account deficits may also reflect reinvestments of sizable profits earned by the large stock of inward foreign direct investment. These profits are recorded as an outward payment in the current account,

with reinvestments recorded as an offsetting inflow in the financial account, with no actual financial transactions taking place.
29. For an overview of theories on the cyclical variations in banks' credit standards, see Berger and Udell (2003) or Jiménez and Saurina (2005).
30. For models where credit market imperfections can lead to the amplification of initial shocks, see Bernanke and Gertler (1989), Bernanke et al (1998), and Kiyotaki and Moore (1997).
31. See Gourinchas et al (2001) or Tornell and Westermann (2002).
32. Sources: National central banks, ECB.
33. The Czech Republic and Hungary are exceptions to this, as housing loans with longer initial rate fixation periods have the highest share in total housing loan stock. Similar information is not available for SEE-countries.
34. In addition to foreign currency loans granted by local banks, loans by nonresidents also play an important role in the financing of the nonfinancial corporations in the new member states (Section I).
35. Note that the negative impact of a currency depreciation on debt repayments could be partly compensated for those borrowers who also hold foreign currency deposits. However, for borrowers whose income is mainly generated in local currency, the average amount of foreign currency deposits is likely to be much lower than the average amount of foreign currency denominated debt.
36. In 2004, the current account deficit as a percentage of GDP exceeded 6 percent in seven CEE countries: Bosnia and Herzegovina, Bulgaria, Estonia, Hungary, Latvia, Romania, and Serbia and Montenegro.
37. It is to be noted that the role of FDI inflows, albeit increasing, is still less significant in the potential candidate countries.
38. Except for Croatia, where the share of short-term debt in total foreign bank debt has significantly increased since the first quarter of 2004, albeit from a zero level.

Bibliography

Allen, F. and D. Gale, 2000, *Comparing Financial Systems*, Cambridge, MA and London: MIT Press.

Backé, P. and T. Zumer, 2005, "Developments in Credit to the Private Sector in Central and Eastern European EU Member States: Emerging from Financial Repression—A Comparative Overview," *Focus on European Economic Integration*, Oesterreichische Nationalbank, October.

Beck, T. and R. Levine, 2004, "Stock markets, Banks, and Growth: Panel Evidence," *Journal of Banking and Finance*, vol. 28(3), pp. 423–42.

Beck, T., A. Demirgüç-Kunt and R. Levine, 2003, "Law, Endowments, and Finance", *Journal of Financial Economics*, vol. 70(2), November, pp. 137–81.

Berger, A. and G. Udell, 2003, "The Institutional Memory Hypothesis and the Procyclicality of Bank Lending Behaviour," BIS Working Papers No. 125, Bank for International Settlements, January.

Bernanke, B. and M. Gertler, 1989, "Agency Costs, Net Worth and Business Fluctuations," *American Economic Review*, vol. 79(1), pp. 14–31.

Bernanke, B., M. Gertler and S. Gilchrist, 1998, "The Financial Accelerator in a Quantitative Business Cycle Framework," NBER Working Paper No. 6455, Cambridge, MA.

Bokros, L., 2002, "Financial Sector Development in Central and Eastern Europe," in A. Winkler (ed.), *Banking and Monetary Policy in Eastern Europe. The First Ten Years*. Houndmills and New York: Palgrave Macmillan, pp. 11–42.

Bonin, J. and P. Wachtel, 2003, "Financial Sector Development in Transition Economies: Lessons from the First Decade," *Financial Markets, Institutions and Instruments*, vol. 12(1), pp. 1–66.

Bordo, M.D. and O. Jeanne, 2002, "Monetary Policy and Asset Prices: Does 'Benign Neglect' Make Sense?" IMF Working Paper No. 114, Washington, D.C.
Borio, C. and P. Lowe, 2002, "Asset Prices, Financial and Monetary Stability: Exploring the Nexus," BIS Working Paper No. 114, Bank for International Settlements, July.
Clarke, G.R., R.C. Cull and M. Shirley, 2005, "Bank Privatization in Developing Countries: A Summary of Lessons and Findings," *Journal of Banking and Finance*, vol. 29, pp. 1905–30.
Cottarelli, C., G. Dell'Ariccia and I. Vladkova-Hollar, 2005, "Early Birds, Late Risers, and Sleeping Beauties: Bank Credit Growth to the Private Sector in Central and Eastern Europe and in the Balkans," *Journal of Banking and Finance*, vol. 29(1), pp. 83–104.
De Gregorio, J. and P.E. Guidotti, 1992, "Financial Development and Economic Growth," IMF Working Paper No. 92/101, Washington, D.C.
De Haas, R. and I. van Lelyveld, 2006, "Foreign Banks and Credit Stability in Central and Eastern Europe. A Panel Data Analysis," *Journal of Banking and Finance*, vol. 30(7), pp. 1927–52.
De Haas, R. and I. Naaborg, 2005, "Foreign Banks in Transition Economies: Small Business Lending and Internal Capital Markets," International Finance Working Paper No. 0504004, Economics Working Paper Archive at WUSTL.
Demirgüç-Kunt, A. and R. Levine, 2001, "Financial Structure and Economic Growth: Overview," in A. Demirgüç-Kunt and R. Levine (eds.), *Financial Structure and Economic Growth: A Cross-Country Comparison of Banks, Markets, and Development*, Cambridge, MA and London: MIT Press, pp. 3–14.
Demirgüç-Kunt, A. and V. Maksimovic, 2002, "Funding Growth in Bank-Based and Market-Based Financial Systems: Evidence from Firm Level Data," *Journal of Financial Economics*, vol. 65(3), September, pp. 337–63.
Detken, C. and F. Smets, 2004, "Asset Price Booms and Monetray Policy," ECB Working Paper No. 364, May, Frankfurt am Main.
Dewatripont, M. and J. Tirole, 1994, "The Prudential Regulation of Banks," Cambridge, MA and London: MIT Press.
EBRD, 1998, *Transition Report*, London.
——, 2004a, *Transition Report*, London.
——, 2004b, *Spotlight on South Eastern Europe*, London.
Eesti Pank, 2005a, *Financial Stability Review*, May 2005.
——, 2005b, *Monetary Developments and Policy Survey*, March 2005.
Eichengreen, B. and C. Arteta, 2000, "Banking Crises in Emerging Markets: Presumptions and Evidence," Centre for International and Development Economics, WP No. C00–115, University of California at Berkeley.
Ergungor, O.E., 2003, "Financial System Structure and Economic Development: Structure Matters," Working Paper Series No. 0305, Federal Reserve Bank of Cleveland.
European Central Bank, 2001, "Characteristics of corporate finance in the Euro area," *Monthly Bulletin*, February, Frankfurt am Main, pp. 37–50.
——, 2002a, *Financial Sectors in EU Accession Countries*, October, Frankfurt am Main.
——, 2002b, *Report on Financial Structures*, October, Frankfurt am Main.
——, 2004a, *Financial Stability Review*, December, Frankfurt am Main.
——, 2004b, *EU Banking Sector Stability*, November, Frankfurt am Main.
——, 2005, "Assessing Financial Stability: Conceptual Boundaries and Challenges," *Financial Stability Review*, June, Frankfurt am Main.
Fink G., P. Haiss and G. Vukšić, 2005, "Importance of Financial Sectors for Growth in Accession Countries," paper presented at the conference on European Economic Integration organized by the ECB, OeNB and CFS, Vienna, November 14–15.
Gertler, M., 1988, "Financial Structure and Aggregate Economic Activity: An Overview," *Journal of Money, Credit and Banking*, vol. 20(3), pp. 559–88.
Glogowski, A. and D. Zochowski, 2003, "Modeling the Impact of the Zloty Depreciation on the Quality of Foreign Currency Assets of Banks," *Financial Stability Report*, Narodowy Bank Polski, May.

Gourinchas, P., O. Landerretche, and R. Valdes, 2001, "Lending Booms, Latin America and the World," NBER Working Paper No. 8249.

Greenspan, A. 1999, speech at the "Financial Markets Conference" of the Federal Reserve Bank of Atlanta, 19 October.

Hilbers, P., İ. Ötker-Robe, C. Pazarbasioğlu, and G. Johnsen, 2005, "Assessing and Managing Rapid Credit Growth and the Role of Supervisory and Prudential Policies," IMF Working Paper No. 05/151.

Hubbard, R.G., 1998, "Capital-Market Imperfections and Investment," *Journal of Economic Literature*, vol. 36(1), pp. 193–225.

IMF, 2004, "Are Credit Booms in Emerging Markets a Concern?" *World Economic Outlook*, April, pp. 147–66, Washington, D.C.

———, 2005, *Global Financial Stability Report*, September, Washington, D.C.

Jaeger, A. and L. Schuknecht, 2004, "Boom-Bust Phases in Asset Prices and Fiscal Policy Behavior," IMF Working Paper No. 04/54.

Jiménez, G. and J. Saurina, 2005, "Credit Cycles, Credit Risk, and Prudential Regulation," paper presented at "Banking and Financial Stability: A Workshop on Applied Banking Research" held in Vienna on April 20–21, 2005.

Johnston, R.B. and C. Pazarbasioğlu, 1995, "Linkages Between Financial Variables, Financial Sector Reform and Economic Growth and Efficiency," IMF Working Paper No. 95/103, Washington, D.C.

Kaminsky, G. and C. Reinhart, 1999, "Twin Crises: The Causes of Banking and Balance-of-Payment Problems," *American Economic Review*, vol. 89(3), pp. 473–500.

Khan, M., A. Senhadji, and B. Smith, 2001, "Inflation and Financial Depth," IMF Working Paper No. 01/44, Washington D.C.

Kiyotaki, N. and J. Moore, 1997, "Credit Cycles," *Journal of Political Economy*, vol. 105(2), pp. 211–48.

Köke, J., T. Reininger and R. Schneider, 2001, "The Future Role of Capital Markets in Central and Eastern Europe for the Domestic Economy," in M. Schröder (ed.), *The New Capital Markets of Central and Eastern Europe*, Heidelberg, pp. 398–465.

Koivu, T., 2002, "Does Financial Development Affect Economic Growth in Transition Countries?" paper presented at the BOFIT seminar, Bank of Finland, May 20.

Kraft, E. and L. Jankov, 2005, "Does Speed Kill? Lending Booms and their Consequences in Croatia," *Journal of Banking and Finance*, vol. 29, pp. 105–21.

Kutos, P. and H. Vogelmann, 2005, "Estonia's External Deficit: A Sign of Success or a Problem?" *Country Focus*, vol. 2(13), July. European Commission, Brussels.

LaPorta, R., F. Lopez-de-Silanes, A. Shleifer, and R.W. Vishny, 1997, "Legal Determinants of External Finance," *Journal of Finance*, vol. 52(3), pp. 1131–50.

———, 1998, "Law and Finance," *Journal of Political Economy*, vol. 106(6), pp. 1113–55.

———, 2000, "Agency Problems and Dividend Policies around the World," *Journal of Finance*, vol. 55, pp. 1–33.

Levine, R., 1997, "Financial Development and Economic Growth: Views and Agenda," *Journal of Economic Literature*, vol. 35(2), pp. 688–726.

———, 2003, "More on Finance and Growth: More Finance, More Growth?" *Federal Reserve Bank of St. Louis Review*, vol. 85(4), pp. 31–46.

———, 2004, "Finance and Growth: Theory and Evidence", in P. Aghion and S. Durlauf (eds.), *Handbook of Economic Growth*, Elsevier Science, preliminary draft.

Levine, R., N. Loayza and T. Beck, 2000, "Financial Intermediation and Growth: Causality and Causes," *Journal of Monetary Economics*, vol. 46(1), August, pp. 31–77.

Lopez, J.A. and M.M. Spiegel, 2002, "Financial Structure and Macroeconomic Performance over the Short and Long Run," Pacific Basin Working Paper Series No. 02–05, Federal Reserve Bank of San Francisco.

Lutz, M., 2004, "Estonia's External Debt and Domestic Balance Sheet Developments, in: Republic of Estonia: Selected Issues," *IMF Country Report No. 04/357*, Washington, D.C.

Magyar Nemzeti Bank, 2005, *Report on Financial Stability*, April, Budapest.

Mehl, A., C. Vespro and A. Winkler, 2005, "The Finance-Growth Nexus and Financial Sector Environment: New Evidence from Southeast Europe," paper presented at the Joint Conference of the ECB-CFS Research Network on "Capital Markets and Financial Integration in Europe" and the Oesterreichische Nationalbank in Vienna on "European Economic Integration: Financial Development, Integration and Stability in Central, Eastern and South-Eastern Europe," Vienna, November 14–15.

Mihaljek, D., "The Role of Housing Markets and Foreign-owned Banks in the Credit Expansion in Central and South-Eastern Europe," paper presented at the Conference on Rapid Growth of Banking Sector Credit to the Private Sector, Sinaia, Romania, October 7–8, 2005.

Modigliani, F. and E. Perotti, 2000, "Security Markets versus Bank Finance: Legal Enforcement and Investor Protection," *International Review of Finance*, vol. 1(2), pp. 81–96.

Ottens, D., E. Lambregts and S. Poelhekke, 2005, "Credit Booms in Emerging Market Economies: A Recipe for Banking Crises?" DNB Working Paper No. 46, De Nederlandsche Bank, June, Amsterdam.

Papademos, L., 2005, "Financial Structures, Credit Growth and House Prices in the New EU Member States: Policy Challenges on the Road to the Euro", Speech at the Conference held by Latvijas Banka, Riga, 19 September; <www.ecb.int>.

Pistor, K., M. Raiser, and S. Gelfer, 2000, "Law and Finance in Transition Economies," *Economics of Transition Journal*, vol. 8(2), pp. 325–68.

Rajan, R. and L. Zingales, 1998, "Financial Dependence and Growth,"*American Economic Review*, vol. 88(3), June, pp. 559–86.

——, 2001, "Financial Systems, Industrial Structure, and Growth", *Oxford Review of Economic Policy*, vol. 17(4), Winter, pp. 467–82.

Shleifer, A. and D. Wolfenzon, 2002, "Investor Protection and Equity Markets," *Journal of Financial Economics*, vol. 66(1), October, pp. 3–27.

Stulz, R., 2000, "Financial Structure, Corporate Finance and Economic Growth," *International Review of Finance*, vol. 1(1), pp. 11–38.

Tornell, A. and F. Westermann, 2002, "Boom-Bust Cycles: Facts and Explanation," *IMF Staff Papers*, 49 (Special Issue), pp. 111–55.

Van Rixtel, A.A.R.J.M, 2002, *Informality and Monetary Policy in Japan. The Political Economy of Bank Performance*, Cambridge: Cambridge University Press.

Walko, Z. and T. Reininger, 2004, "Credit and Deposit Interest Rate Margins in Four New EU Member States," in *Financial Stability Report*, No. 8, Oesterreichische Nationalbank, December.

Zeuner, J., 2005, "International Experience with Credit Booms and Large Current Account Deficits, in: Bosnia and Herzegovina: Selected Economic Issues," *IMF Country Report No. 05/198*, Washington, D.C.

3
Using Fundamentals to Identify Episodes of "Excessive" Credit Growth in Central and Eastern Europe

Frédric Boissay, Oscar Calvo-Gonzalez, and Tomasz Koźluk[1]

Bank credit to the private sector has seen a significant increase among many Central, Eastern, and South-eastern European (CEE) countries.[2] To what extent can this credit expansion be explained by the rapid transition from a centrally-planned to a market-based economy in just over a decade? This question brings to the fore the importance of the developmental path that these countries have followed since the early 1990s. The early years of the transition usually exhibited a significant slump in GDP followed by a period of rapid economic growth. In some cases, during the turbulent years of the 1990s, rapid privatization of the banking sector and expansion of the undeveloped financial markets, which were basically set up from scratch, resulted in excessive lending booms followed by credit crunches and bank runs and crises that in some cases spilled over to the entire economy.

Perhaps the most illustrative example is that of Bulgaria, where problems in the banking sector were at the heart of the macroeconomic crisis that would see the annual inflation rate reach 2,000 percent in March 1997. The largely state-owned Bulgarian banking system had been financing for years the mounting losses from nonrestructured enterprises, leading to a gradual erosion of the balance sheets of banks. By the time the crisis broke out, nine out of the ten state-owned banks, which accounted for 80 percent of banking assets, had negative capital, and around half of the private banks were technically bankrupt. The Bulgarian National Bank increased liquidity to support the ailing banking sector, attempting to sterilize it through open market transactions. In the end, the crisis led to the closure of 17 banks, which accounted for around one-third of total banking assets (Yotzov, 2002). Across the region, the immature banking system was often flawed by inadequate regulation, corruption, and the simple lack of experience of the agents involved.

Financial liberalization during that first phase of transition may have in some cases undermined real sector development (Berglöf and Bolton, 2002). This turbulent recent history, together with the low levels of financial intermediation at the beginning of transition, helps to explain why the CEE countries still exhibit significantly lower levels of lending in terms of GDP compared not only to developed countries but also to countries in a similar state of economic development. As shown in Figure 3.1, all CEE countries with the exception of Croatia stood in 2003 below a simple regression line fitted for the correlation between private credit to GDP and per capita GDP across all countries in the world for which data were available.

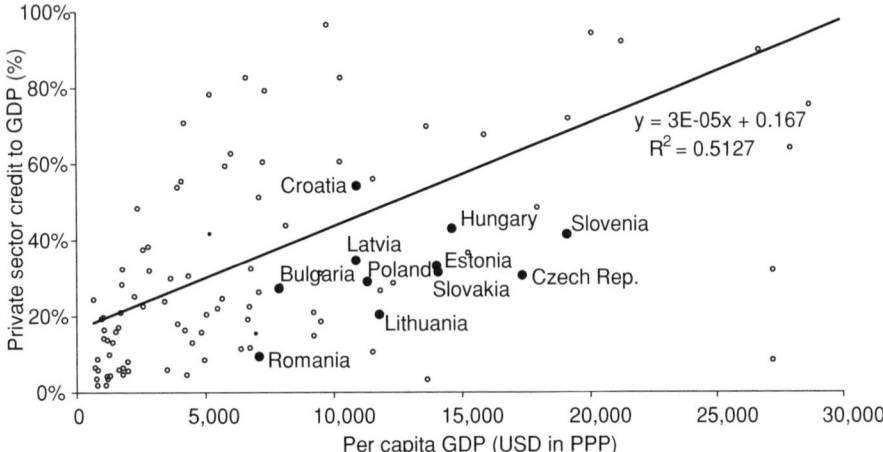

Figure 3.1 Credit to the Private Sector to GDP and Per Capita GDP, 2003 (124 countries)

Source: IMF (IFS and WEO).

Figure 3.1 suggests that there may indeed be sound reasons to expect credit growth in CEE countries to be faster than in both developed countries and other emerging regions of the world. While in the early and mid-1990s banks were often engaged in connected lending to a rather restricted number of corporate borrowers or lending into arrears to state-owned enterprises that faced soft budget constraints, progress in the transition process has done away with those practices (Bokros, 2002; Mehl et al, 2005).

Assuming that the catch-up in incomes will proceed and that it will be accompanied by financial deepening, as suggested by the simple correlation shown above, credit will necessarily have to grow faster than GDP in the CEE countries. There are numerous reasons that may help to explain the recent acceleration of credit growth in the region. A noncomprehensive list of such factors would include: foreign bank entry (which may have brought both improved risk management techniques as well as increased access to funding from parent banks); a more competitive environment in the banking sector (that may have contributed to declining interest rates); improvements in the institutional environment; improvements in the creditworthiness of borrowers on the back of improved economic prospects; as well as growing property prices (which may have led to higher financing needs). The reform of the banking sector is also a key development among these transition countries. Privatization may have led to faster financial deepening through foreign bank entry, but this is not the only channel through which banking sector reform may affect the pace of financial deepening. Banking sector reform brought about both new market segments and increased competition, thus increasing the range of products available to potential borrowers and reducing the costs. This led to faster financial deepening.

However, while credit growth can be seen as a natural adjustment due to recent banking system reforms, improved bank efficiency, and capital inflows from western European countries, some concerns have been raised as regards the speed of these adjustments. As Borio and Lowe (2002) put it, "one of the relatively few robust findings to emerge from the literature on leading indicators of banking crises is that rapid domestic credit growth increases the likelihood of a problem," and in some CEE countries the growth rate of the credit-to-GDP ratio is close to that observed in, for instance, Indonesia, Korea, or Sweden, prior to their financial crises in the 1990s.

The purpose of this chapter is to incorporate this key characteristic among CEE countries of catching up in both real incomes and in financial deepening into a statistical framework that provides a way to address the question of whether credit may be growing excessively fast. In doing so, the chapter builds upon a limited existing literature that is discussed briefly below. Following the discussion of the existing literature, two methods are proposed to address the question of what may be considered "excessive" credit growth given the catching-up process. The chapter then cross-checks the results obtained from these two methods, explores a number of themes highlighted by the results and finally provides some concluding comments.

I. Overview of the empirical literature on lending booms

The empirical literature on lending booms faces the enormous challenge of having to provide a working definition of what can be considered to be an "excessive" rate of credit growth. In theory, an episode of credit growth can be thought of as excessive if either (i) it endangers financial stability via financing undeserving projects that will eventually turn into bad loans; or, (ii) it leads to unsustainable macroeconomic developments, such as a deteriorating external position leading to an unsustainable buildup of external debt. Neither of these two effects can be easily measured or forecast. It is thus not surprising that the empirical literature on the measurement of "excessiveness" has been very limited.

Despite this intrinsic difficulty, policymakers and market participants alike are faced with the need to assess credit growth developments. From an operational point of view an episode of rapid credit growth is typically labeled excessive or as an unsustainable "credit boom" when the observed growth rates exceed a given threshold. This threshold is usually estimated on the basis of the country's trend credit growth, using a Hodrick-Prescott filter. For example, IMF (2004a) labels a credit expansion a credit boom if it exceeds 1.75 times the standard deviation of the country's average credit fluctuation around the trend. The threshold value in this case is selected because, assuming the observations of credit growth were drawn from a normal distribution, there would only be a 5 percent probability that they would lie more than 1.75 times outside the standard deviation. While the specific thresholds may differ, it is common in this literature to focus on deviations from an estimated trend (Gourinchas et al, 2001; Tornell and Westermann, 2002; Ottens et al, 2005). However, as has been often pointed out in the literature, in the context of transition this is particularly difficult, given both the short time series and the likely structural breaks in the series (Duenwald et al, 2005). This difficulty is particularly problematic given the acceleration in the pace of credit in the region in recent years.

There has been in fact a growing literature on lending booms in European transition economies. However, most of these papers describe credit developments and their implications for the rest of the economy (Cottarelli et al, 2005; Duenwald et al, 2005; Hilbers et al, 2005; Kraft and Jankov, 2005). While extremely valuable in themselves, none of these papers provide an econometric analysis of the growth of the credit-to-GDP ratio. In particular, Cottarelli et al (2005) explicitly refrain from exploring this question, focusing instead on deriving a static model of the expected credit-to-GDP ratio on the basis of economic fundamentals. Their conclusion that many countries in the region exhibited credit-to-GDP ratios below the level that would be warranted by their economic fundamentals only serves to underscore the importance of exploring what can be said about the different paths followed by these countries in their approach towards their credit-to-GDP equilibrium levels.

Schadler et al (2004) provide a useful approach to the question of measuring excessive credit growth, even though their paper deals mainly with the issue of whether rapid credit growth should affect plans for euro adoption in new member states. Acknowledging the challenges posed by the transition, their approach is to draw on the experience of existing members of the euro area to infer likely trends in the new member states since "historical data from the CEE countries would not be relevant to predicting future credit developments" (Schadler et al, 2004, p.4). The paper estimates a vector error correction model (VECM) on quarterly euro area data for 1991–2002. The VECM of the demand for credit includes three variables: (i) the credit-to-GDP ratio; (ii) a proxy for the cost of credit (long-run real interest rate on government bonds); and (iii) per capita income. A co-integrating relationship between these variables is then found, which can be used to draw some inferences about likely future developments in the CEE countries. For example, a 10 percent increase in per capita income raises the credit-to-GDP ratio by around 3 percentage points in the long run.

II. Detecting excessive credit growth

In the absence of a generally accepted way of determining what rate of credit growth may be deemed to be "excessive" we propose to focus on both macroeconomic fundamentals as the main macroeconomic determinants of credit growth (namely

GDP growth and interest rate), as well as on the gap between the actual credit-to-GDP ratio and its equilibrium level. The latter is important for the analysis since the countries in the region have been experiencing major structural changes related to the transition process. This allows us to estimate the elasticity of credit with regard to those variables and to derive estimates of expected credit growth in the countries of the region. The comparison between observed and expected credit growth provides us with a measure of excessive credit growth. We will consider that credit growth is excessive when it is higher than the level implied by its three main determinants given the estimated elasticities. Two key steps in this simple approach are the determination of the equilibrium credit-to-GDP ratio and the estimation of the credit elasticities.

Equilibrium credit-to-GDP ratios

For CEE countries, the equilibrium credit-to-GDP ratio is difficult to measure because it has to account for the effects of the transition from a centrally-planned to a market-based economy, which themselves are not straightforward to measure. Credit does not only depend on its traditional macroeconomic determinants, but also on the new circumstances arising from the financial liberalization during the transition process.

These new circumstances may affect the banking sector and credit supply in various ways. For example, free entry into the banking sector, the possibility for foreign banks to own local banks or create local branches, and the gradual expansion of these banks in the retail credit markets have certainly worked to increase credit supply and lower lending rates (De Haas and Naaborg, 2005). On the other hand, stricter supervisory requirements might have had opposite effects. The fact that the overall impact of financial liberalization on credit supply is probably gradual and perhaps ambiguous makes it difficult to measure and, a fortiori, to model. For simplicity, however, we will assume that the effects over time of financial liberalization on aggregate credit supply can be approximated by a deterministic non-linear time trend (see below).

Our formal definition of the equilibrium level of credit builds on the following credit demand/supply nexus:

$$\begin{cases} C^s = C^s\big((+)R^\ell - R, (+)Y, (?)Z\big) \\ C^d = C^d\big((-)R^\ell, (+)Y\big) \end{cases} \Rightarrow C^* = C\big((+)Y, (-)R, (?)Z\big)$$

where C^s, C^d, and C^* denote the aggregate real credit supply, demand, and equilibrium levels respectively, Y is real GDP, R is the real interbank rate, R^ℓ is the real retail lending rate, and Z captures the effects of financial liberalization on credit supply. While Y and R are the main standard determinants of aggregate credit, the Z factor is specific to transition economies. As is common practice in the literature, at this stage we will model the equilibrium credit-to-GDP ratio rather than credit itself. For transition economies the evolution of the credit-to-GDP ratio can be seen as depending not only on the real interest rate but also on the transition path to a market-based economy, which we will model as a gradual time trend:

$$\left| \frac{C_{it}}{Y_{it}} = \alpha_i + \beta_i R_{it} + \gamma_i Z_{it} = \left(\frac{C}{Y}\right)^*_{it} + \varepsilon_{it} \right. \quad (1)$$
$$Z_{it} = \gamma_{i1}.t + \gamma_{2i}.t^2$$

where t stands for time (quarters) and i for the country, $(C/Y)^*_{it}$ denotes the equilibrium credit-to-GDP ratio, and ε_{it} is the gap between the observed credit-to-GDP ratio and its equilibrium level. This equilibrium ratio represents the credit-to-GDP ratio that we would expect to observe in the absence of short-term shocks, given the interest rate, R_{it}, and the position of the economy on its way to a market-based economy, Z_{it}. To overcome the issue of the nonmeasurability of financial liberalization, and in line with the observation, we model the Z factor as a deterministic and non-linear time trend, so that the residual ε_{it} obtained in equation (1) is a mean stationary.

Estimates of credit elasticities

We estimate elasticities on the basis of the following short-run dynamic equation of credit growth:

$$\Delta \log C_{it} = \beta + \beta_c \Delta \log C_{it-k} + \beta_y \Delta \log Y_{it-l} + \beta_r \Delta R_{it-j}$$
$$+ \lambda \left[\log\left(\frac{C_{it-m}}{Y_{it-m}}\right) - \log\left(\left(\frac{C}{Y}\right)^*_{it-m}\right) \right] + \gamma_i.1_\Delta + \varepsilon_{it} \quad (2)$$

where 1_Δ is a dummy variable equal to one during period Δ and to zero otherwise, the coefficients (β, β_c, β_y, β_r, λ) are credit elasticities and ε_{it} is the residual. The dummy variable 1_Δ allows us to design a test for "excessive" credit growth since the coefficient on this dummy variable is, by construction, the difference between the observed credit growth and the credit growth implied by the macroeconomic variables (GDP and interest rates) and the gap between the observed credit-to-GDP ratio and its equilibrium level.

The limited availability of data poses, however, a challenge to estimate these elasticities for each of the countries in the region. To circumvent this issue, and to gain some comfort that the results are not driven exclusively by the choice of methodology, we will estimate two sets of elasticities:

First, we will estimate the credit elasticities for a number of benchmark countries where the credit-to-GDP ratio had been relatively stable over a long period of time. These countries are chosen for two main reasons: (i) the long time series available for these countries makes it possible to derive robust estimates of the elasticities for each of these countries; (ii) precisely because we use countries with stable credit-to-GDP ratios as benchmarks, we are likely to obtain lower elasticities than may be expected for catching-up countries. Since we use these elasticities to derive the expected credit growth in the CEE countries, and the measure of excessive credit growth is the difference between the actual and the expected credit growth, we are likely to bias the results toward making it more likely that we will detect excessive credit growth. This gives us an upper bound for our measure of excessive credit growth.

Second, we will estimate the credit elasticities using data for the countries in the region. Given the limited length of the time series of data available for each country, we will estimate relation (2) using a data panel but constraining the elasticities to be identical across all CEE countries. We thus estimate elasticities for the "average" country in our panel. In contrast to the benchmark countries, most of the countries in the panel experience rising credit-to-GDP ratios. Therefore, we are likely to obtain higher elasticities than with the benchmark countries and to bias our results towards making it less likely that we will detect excessive credit growth. This gives us a lower bound for our measure of excessive credit growth.

Test strategy

Our test for "excessive credit" growth during a period Δ focuses on parameter γ_i, which is the only country-specific parameter in relation (2). A strictly positive γ_i means that credit in country i grew faster during period Δ than its standard determinants would have implied. In this case, we conclude that credit growth was excessive by γ_i percent on average through the period Δ. Note that an appealing feature of our test strategy is the comparability of the coefficient γ_i across countries, which enables us to rank countries according to the excessiveness of their credit growth: the higher γ_i, the higher excessive credit growth during period Δ. To sum up, the steps to perform our test are the following:

- Estimate relation (1) and compute the implied equilibrium credit-to-GDP ratio $(C/Y)^*_{it}$ for each country;
- For the test using the elasticities of the benchmark countries:
  - Estimate the short-run elasticities (β, β_c, β_y, β_r, λ) for each benchmark country (relation (2));
  - Use these estimates and the data from CEE countries to compute the implied growth rates of credit for each CEE country;
  - Compute the average difference γ_i between observed and implied growth rates of credit for each CEE country;
  - Discuss whether $\gamma_i > 0$ or not and rank the countries according to their γ_i.
- For the test using the elasticities of the average CEE country:
  - Estimate the short-run elasticities (β, β_c, β_y, β_r, λ) common to all CEE countries as well as the country-specific coefficients γ_i (relation (2)); and
  - Test whether $\gamma_i > 0$ or not and rank the countries according to their γ_i.

The above test for excessive credit growth must be interpreted with caution since our working definition of excessiveness is necessarily conditional on the model that we use. In particular, macroeconomic variables other than those considered here (GDP and interest rates) could also influence credit growth. In addition, our test is also conditional on the equilibrium level of the credit-to-GDP ratio, which is estimated to fit the data. While the increase in the latter may reflect the nature of the transition process, it cannot be ruled out that it may lead to unsustainable developments and financial and/or macroeconomic instability.

Data

The CEE countries had credit-to-GDP levels significantly lower than the EU average throughout the sample period (1996–2004). By 1998 all eight of the countries considered in the study had total outstanding loans-to-yearly GDP ratios below 40 percent, the lowest being Bulgaria (which was still coping with the aftermath of the banking crisis), Latvia, Lithuania, and Romania. All four of these countries had a ratio below 20 percent. Croatia had the highest stock of loans at around 40 percent of GDP. By 1996–97, the vast majority of loans were denominated in domestic currencies (DC), apart from in Latvia and Romania. In Estonia, Hungary, Lithuania, Slovenia, and Croatia, the share of DC loans was around 70 to 80 percent. In 2004 however, the Baltic states and Romania all had a share of DC loans below 50 percent, while Croatia and Slovenia remained at around 70 to 80 percent. In 1996 only Estonia and Slovenia had a share of long-term loans (i.e. with a maturity of more than one year) higher than 50 percent, while in 2004 this share was above 50 percent in practically all the countries. Regarding the share of loans to households, only Hungary and Slovenia reported shares above 20 percent in 1997, while by 2004 this share was around 30 percent in Slovenia and Bulgaria, slightly higher in Latvia, and around 45 to 55 percent in Croatia, Estonia, Hungary, and Romania (see Table 3.1).

Table 3.1 Share of Loans in Total Lending to the Private Nonfinancial Sector in 2004 (in percent)

	Domestic Currency	Long-Term Loans	Credit to Households
Bulgaria	53.5	86.5	32.1
Croatia	88.0	–	54.5
Estonia	20.0	91.4	47.0
Hungary	56.0	62.3	44.6
Latvia	40.8	85.3	35.4
Lithuania	36.5	–	–
Romania[a]	39.1	49.9	46.2
Slovenia	69.3	69.1	28.9

Source: Authors' calculations.

[a] As the breakdown short-term/long-term and households/corporates is available only for domestic currency denominated loans, the figures are in percentage of domestic currency denominated loans.

Some of the more detailed credit developments in the sample countries have been the following:

- As a result of the banking crisis, in Bulgaria the total loans to GDP ratio dropped from levels reaching 70 percent to below 10 percent in 1996–97. Subsequent years brought a gradual recovery, with growth picking up especially after 2000 and total loans reaching levels that were more than half those prior to the crisis. Before the crash, the vast majority of loans were denominated in foreign currencies while this ratio is now more balanced. About half of the loans before the crisis were loans to private enterprises, while households had a share of about 20 percent, with most of the loans to these two sectors being short-term loans. However, this changed during the recovery, as most loans went to the private sector and now have a longer maturity.
- In recent years, Croatia has been characterized by a fairly steady growth of loans, mainly to households and denominated in domestic currency. While loans to corporations constituted the majority of loans in 1998, this fell to about 50 percent in 2004; in addition, there were previously far fewer loans in foreign currency than in domestic currency. Both of these categories (loans in domestic and foreign currencies) remained fairly constant in comparison to GDP.
- In the case of Hungary, total loans have doubled in the last nine years, reaching 45 percent of GDP. Most of this growth was attributable to long-term loans, foreign currency denominated loans, and loans to households, while domestic currency loans and short-term loans stayed fairly stable and loans to enterprises grew at a relatively slow pace.
- In Romania, total loans (as percentage of GDP) fell from 1998 to 2000, and picked up from 2000 onwards to double in the following four years and reach about 20 percent of GDP. While credit to corporations was not as severely affected by the fall, most of the recovery was due to a rise in credit to households. The currency composition was almost unaffected by these movements.
- Total loans in Slovenia doubled with respect to GDP from about 28 percent in 1996 to almost 50 percent in 2004. Foreign currency-denominated loans grew faster than those denominated in domestic currency, growing from 5 percent of GDP in 1996 to 33.1 percent in 2004.
- Overall, the fastest expansion of credit relative to GDP took place in the Baltic states. Starting from the lowest levels in our sample in 1996, Estonia and Latvia now have the highest credit-to-GDP ratios of our sample. In the case of Lithuania, the credit-to-GDP ratio has doubled over the last decade.

Test using benchmarks

We estimated relations (1) and (2) for 11 benchmark countries whose credit-to-GDP ratio had been stable over a long period of time (on average 19 years) since 1960. These countries are Australia (1960Q2–1984Q3), Belgium (1989Q4–2004Q4), Finland (1960Q2–1980Q4), France (1974Q1–1986Q4), Germany (1968Q1–1983Q4), Greece (1960Q2–1978Q4 and 1981Q2–1995Q4), Ireland (1979Q2–1995Q4), Norway (1960Q2–1983Q4), Spain (1973Q1–1996Q4), Sweden (1970Q1–1988Q1), and United

States (1981Q2–1995Q4). For comparison purposes and given the availability of data, we considered total lending to the private sector only.

We also estimated relation (1) for the eight CEE countries in order to compute their equilibrium credit-to-GDP ratio. As the interbank interest rate was not available for all these countries, and given that a large fraction of the CEE country banking system is owned by foreign (European) banks, we used the Euribor in the estimations. The estimates of relation (1) are reported in Table 3.2.

Table 3.2 Estimates of Relation (1)—Total Lending

Outstanding loans of MFI sector (excluding NCB) to non-MFIs end of quarter, as a ratio of yearly GDP

	Bulgaria	Croatia	Estonia	Hungary	Latvia	Lithuania	Romania	Slovenia
$time^2$	0.0006	0.0004	0.0005	0.0002	0.0005	0.0003	0.0002	−0.0000
	(14.58)*	(5.76)*	(11.79)*	(13.22)*	(16.24)*	(5.73)*	(2.45)**	(−0.97)
time	−0.0064	−0.0032	−0.0042	−0.0001	−0.0010	−0.0070	−0.0110	0.0074
	(−5.82)*	(−1.51)	(−3.42)*	(−0.23)	(−1.19)	(−3.95)*	(−4.24)*	(7.28)*
RIR	0.26	0.77	1.02	0.89	−0.21	−0.91	−1.62	−0.26
	(0.82)	(0.72)	(1.77)***	(3.61)*	(−0.9)	(−1.24)	(−1.74)***	(−0.9)
const	0.11	0.37	0.31	0.21	0.14	0.17	0.31	0.40
	(15.06)*	(11.16)*	(16.84)*	(27.45)*	(25.71)*	(7.78)*	(10.59)*	(42.49)*
obs.	24	28	28	28	28	28	28	28

Source: Authors' calculations.

Note: Numbers in brackets are t-statistic values. *, **, *** denote 1 percent, 5 percent, 10 percent significance respectively.

The quadratic time trend is significant in all countries but Slovenia and the comparison of the equilibrium with the realized credit-to-GDP ratios shows that the quadratic time trends capture a great deal of the evolution of credit in CEE countries over the past seven years. As this trend is assumed to control for the effects of transition-related processes such as banking sector reform, we therefore implicitly assume that the banking sector reform explains a large part of the acceleration of credit observed over the past seven years.

The growth rates of credit implied by the standard elasticities and its three main determinants are reported in Figure 3.2, and the average difference between these growth rates over the period 2001–04 for each CEE country are reported in Table 3.3. We find that Slovenia and Romania are the only two countries where aggregate credit grew in line with its main determinants. In contrast, the quarterly rate of credit growth in Bulgaria and Latvia was on average more than 7 percentage points higher than the evolution of GDP, interest rates, and financial liberalization would have implied. Although to a lower extent, we find that Lithuania, Estonia, Hungary, and Croatia have also experienced excessive credit growth since 2001.

Using Fundamentals to Identify "Excessive" Credit Growth 57

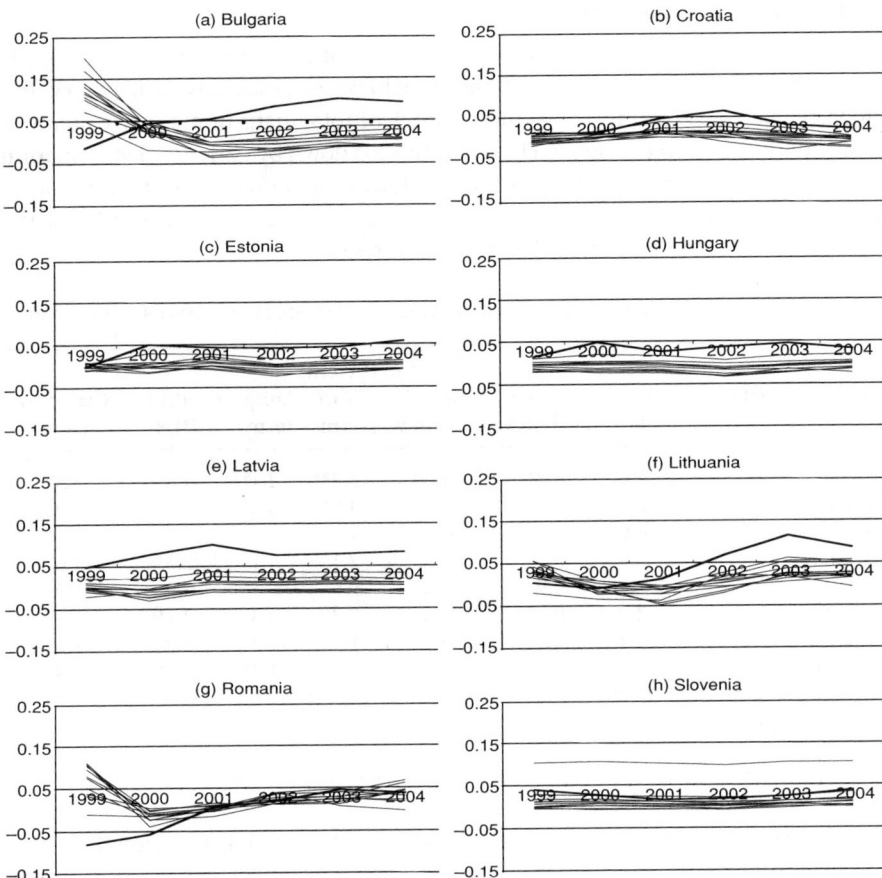

Figure 3.2 Observed (bold lines) versus Projected (thin lines) Growth Rates of Total Lending

Source: Authors' calculations.

Table 3.3 Average Quarterly Excessive Credit Growth over the Period 2001–04 (in percent)

Countries i (ranked)	Coefficients γ_i
Bulgaria	7.8
Latvia	7.4
Lithuania	5.5
Estonia	4.1
Hungary	3.9
Croatia	2.9
Slovenia	0.3
Romania	0.0

Source: Authors' calculations.

Test using CEE country data

We now turn to our second test and use our panel of quarterly observations for the countries in the region starting in 1998. We will consider various credit aggregates, in particular, total lending (outstanding stock of total loans of monetary financial institutions (MFIs) to the non-MFIs), loans broken down by currency denomination (domestic and foreign), maturity (short and long term) and by type (to households or corporations). Table 3.4 summarizes the results (the detailed results of the estimations are available from the authors on request).

Table 3.4 Average Quarterly Excessive Credit Growth over the Period 2001–04 (in percent)

Countries i (ranked)	Coefficients γ_i						
	Total loans	Foreign currency	Domestic currency	Short term	Long term	Credit to HHs	Credit to corp.
Bulgaria	5.6*	6.4*	5.6*	3.4**	2.1***	4.8*	5.5*
Latvia	5.4*	5.2*	5.1*	4.8*	0.5	4.5*	5.0*
Lithuania	4.0*	2.0	6.0*	–	–	–	4.9*
Estonia	2.9*	2.5**	3.8*	2.1	–3.1	2.5**	1.6
Croatia	2.2*	0.9	3.3*	–	–	0.9	1.0
Hungary	2.0*	0.1	0.6	0.3	0.4	3.1**	0.0
Slovenia	0.4	4.1*	0.4	1.1	–0.2	–1.8	1.7**
Romania	0.0	2.1	4.2*	1.4	1.2*	5.6***	0.5

Source: Authors' calculations.

Note: *,**,*** denote 1 percent, 5 percent, and 10 percent significance respectively.

The results of Table 3.4 broadly confirm those of Table 3.3. The growth of total lending in Slovenia and Romania has not been excessive since 2001, while for Bulgaria and Latvia it has exceeded the level implied by fundamentals by more than 5 percentage points. The two tests also give similar results regarding the ranking of the countries, as Bulgaria and the Baltic countries still appear to have the highest excessive growth rate of total lending. Moreover, for these countries, our results suggest that most credit sub-components have grown too fast, which is not the case for the other countries. Notably, excessive credit growth seems to originate from loans denominated in domestic currency (which still represent a low proportion of total credit) in Croatia,[3] and from credit to households in Hungary (where they represent 44.6 percent of total loans). That total lending has grown in line with its main determinants in Slovenia and Romania should not mask the fact that some sub-components of lending have recently developed rapidly in these countries. Our results indeed suggest that lending in foreign currency and in domestic currency have on average grown excessively by 4.1 percentage points and 4.2 percentage points per quarter in Slovenia and Romania respectively since 2001. These developments may, however, be interpreted as a catch-up effect to the extent that these two types of loans still represented a very low percentage of total lending in Slovenia and Romania in 2004.

III. Selected issues: exchange rate regimes and composition of credit

Exchange rate regimes

A key result from the disaggregated analysis is that credit growth in countries with relatively fixed exchange rate regimes is faster than what may be reasonably explained by the macroeconomic fundamentals considered and the gap to the equilibrium credit-to-GDP ratio. Bulgaria, Estonia, and Lithuania all feature currency boards whereby the exchange rate is fixed to the euro.[4] In addition to these countries with hard pegs, both Croatia and Slovenia have followed tightly managed exchange rate regimes, and hence fluctuations in the real exchange rate have been limited. In fact, despite pursuing a managed float, fluctuations in the real exchange rate of both Croatia and Slovenia have been particularly limited. In contrast, countries which have typically exhibited more limited credit expansions have also seen greater flexibility in their real exchange rate (see Arcalean et al, 2005).

This prompts the question of whether the exchange rate regime may have influenced credit developments. One possible mechanism through which the exchange rate regime may lead to higher credit growth is through encouraging lending in foreign currency. As borrowing in foreign currency is usually associated with lower interest rates, perhaps borrowers in those countries are taking increasing amounts of debt denominated in foreign currency in the belief that there is no foreign exchange rate risk associated with such borrowing. Perhaps lenders in those countries are content to lend in foreign currency to nonforeign currency earners, and thus transform the exchange rate risk into credit risk. This may be the case if lenders also share the view that countries with hard pegs such as the currency boards to the euro (Bulgaria, Estonia, and Lithuania) do not in fact pose a significant exchange rate risk. Moreover, the regulations in some of these countries allow lending in euro not to be considered as foreign currency exposure when calculating the net open foreign position of banks,[5] as in Estonia, where the share of loans in foreign currency is indeed very high (80 percent of total loans in 2003). Other countries like Croatia and, to a lesser extent, Latvia, Lithuania, Romania, and Bulgaria have also relatively high shares of foreign loans in total loans. Moreover, in some cases there is a very large discrepancy between the share of loans in foreign currency and the corresponding share for deposits, which is possibly explained by the lack of a need to match open positions in foreign currency. Based on this view, the presence of foreign banks would also play an important role, as they would be in principle more comfortable extending loans in their own currency.

Overall, this scenario of fast credit growth driven by a perception of no exchange rate risk in the context of hard pegs seems plausible. Under this scenario, however, lending in foreign currency should not only accelerate but also should do so at a faster pace than lending in domestic currency. In other words, one should observe an increase in the share of foreign currency lending. This is only the case in Bulgaria among the countries that have been detected as experiencing "excessive" credit growth. In other prominent cases such as Estonia, Latvia, or Lithuania no clear trend can be observed, and in the case of Croatia the share of foreign currency lending has actually decreased in recent years. This suggests that, while lending in foreign currency in some cases may be proceeding at too fast a pace, this is not a distinctive feature of foreign currency lending only. Moreover, while Bulgaria, Estonia, Lithuania, and, to a lesser extent, Croatia have been identified as cases where credit growth may be deemed to be excessive according to our tests, Slovenia stands out as a case of very limited exchange rate fluctuations with contained credit growth thus far.

Beyond the idea that foreign banks are more likely to lend in foreign currency than domestic banks, the presence of foreign banks also helps explain fast credit growth through various other channels. For example, foreign banks may have access to additional sources of finance as they can typically tap the parent bank. Moreover, foreign banks are widely seen as bringing know-how, and empirical studies have shown that bank privatization leads to efficiency gains especially in the case of privatization to foreign strategic investors.[6] A more efficient banking sector will increase financial intermediation. In fact, as shown in Figure 3.3b, there is some indication that foreign bank presence in these countries has been associated with higher credit growth.

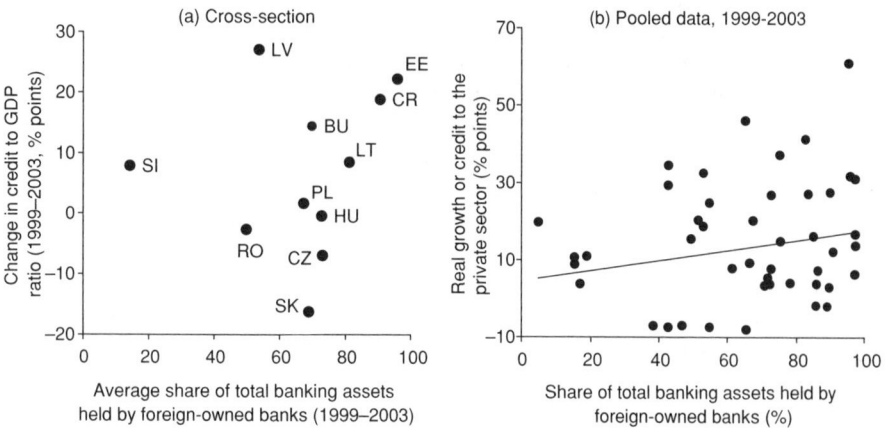

Figure 3.3 Credit Growth and Foreign Ownership of the Banking System*

Source: EBRD, Authors' calculations.

Note: * available years, time-span differs for some countries.

Figure 3.3a shows how, with the exception of Slovenia, the average share of banking assets owned by foreign banks' subsidiaries or branches has been above 50 percent for all countries in the region. It is also worth highlighting the relatively limited foreign bank penetration of the Slovenian banking system since, if it were confirmed that foreign bank entry is associated with a faster financial deepening, it would help explain why, among the CEE countries with relatively fixed exchange rate regimes, Slovenia stands out as having experienced the slowest growth of credit. At the other extreme, Croatia and Estonia stand out as having the highest penetration rate of foreign banks. Regarding Croatia, the other CEE country with a relatively fixed exchange rate that has not seen such fast credit growth, it is worth noting that the Croatian National Bank (CNB) took measures already in 2003 to curb credit growth.[7] Estonia is the country with the largest foreign bank presence and one of the largest increases in financial deepening. In this country, privatization and consolidation took place in the mid-1990s and by 1998 there were only five private banks in the country, down from 42 banks in 1992. As in other Baltic countries, one channel through which the presence of foreign banks appears to have contributed to the fast pace of financial deepening in Estonia is through access to foreign sources of finance to fund the domestic credit expansion.

Overall, it is precisely in those countries for which our proposed methodologies suggest credit growth has been above the level that can be explained by economic fundamentals (Estonia, Bulgaria, Latvia, Lithuania, and Croatia), that we see either sharp increases in (and/or high levels of) the ratio of foreign liabilities to total banking assets. In this regard, Slovenia, Slovakia, and Romania stand out from this analysis as possible cases where, while our methodologies did not detect abnormal developments yet, external funding may be currently fueling an acceleration in credit growth.

One possible explanation for these phenomena is that the perception of limited foreign exchange rate risk does not only affect borrowers but also the foreign bank subsidiaries, which would be induced to expand their loan portfolios in local currencies to take advantage of an interest rate differential that is perceived to come with no or little exchange rate risk. In addition, foreign bank entry and a limited perception of foreign exchange rate risk could lead to excessive credit growth of both foreign and domestic currency lending through competitive pressures in the marketplace. Increased lending in foreign currencies could potentially lead also to a greater supply of domestic currency loans by banks which, perhaps more reliant on deposits or other domestic sources of funding, still strive to keep market share.

Credit composition

A second key result from our disaggregated tests on credit growth is that, for countries exhibiting "excessive" credit growth at the aggregate level, the result also typically applies to both credit to households and credit to corporates. This is the case for both Bulgaria and Latvia, while data were not available for Lithuania. In Estonia, however, credit growth was only deemed to be excessive in the case of lending to households. The fact that credit growth to corporates appears to be excessive is somewhat surprising to analysts of developments in the region, who often refer to the appearance of new products such as mortgages and the launch of consumer credit as key factors in explaining credit growth. In fact, credit growth in certain retail segments has grown spectacularly high. Moreover, this rapid credit growth has been indeed accompanied by rising house prices (Papademos, 2005).

As shown in Figure 3.4a, in Bulgaria, there has been a recent acceleration in the mortgages segment, which may have repercussions for real estate prices in the near future. Figure 3.4b illustrates the close connection between house prices and the development of mortgage lending for Estonia. In Estonia, whereas we saw that credit growth appears to be excessive in the case of lending to households but not

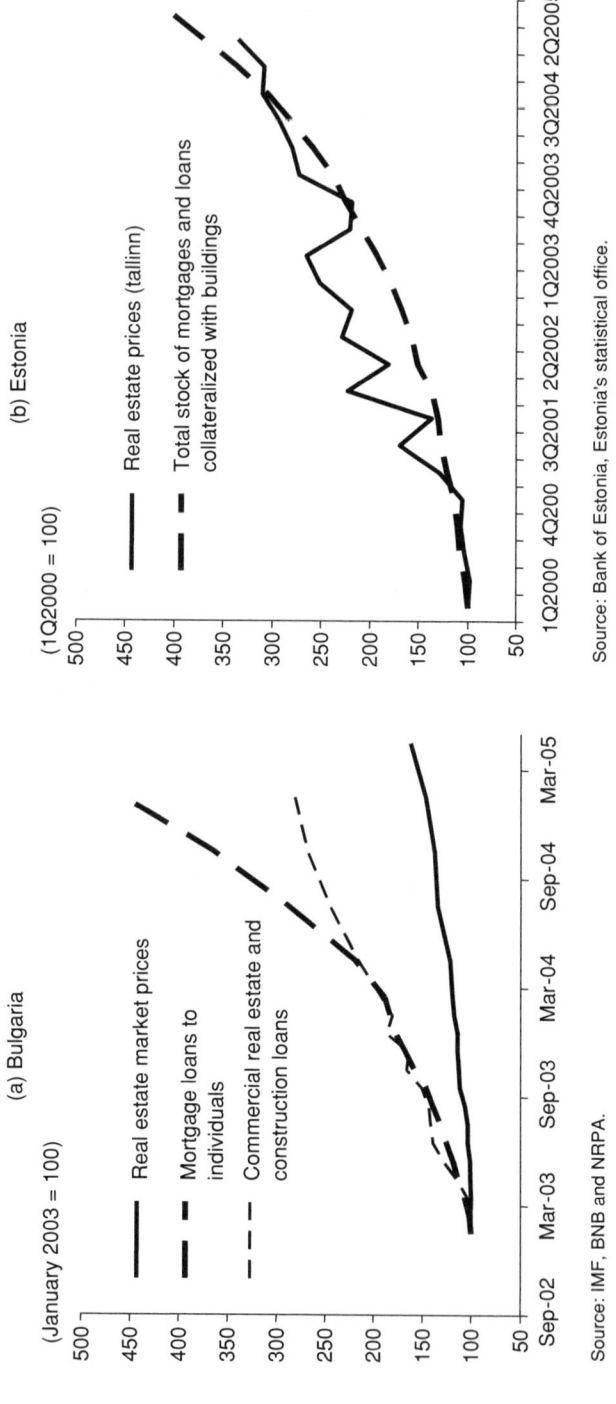

Figure 3.4 Mortgage Loans and Real Estate Prices in Bulgaria and Estonia

to corporates, a number of policy measures help to explain the prominent growth of home mortgage loans. In particular, through a state-owned credit guarantee foundation, KredEx, Estonian families and young adults can obtain a guarantee of up to 24 percent of the value of the collateral provided they have their own funds equivalent to 10 percent of the value of the property being purchased. Set up in 2000, the activity of KredEx as a provider of mortgage loan guarantees has increased significantly in recent years, also through the introduction in 2003 of a new KredEx service aimed at providing grants for revamping Soviet housing. In addition, tax deductibility of mortgage payments may have helped to increase demand for mortgage loans and housing, which has experienced an increase in prices since mid-2003 far above the growth of wages.

However, while the mortgage and consumer credit markets have been undoubtedly developing fast in the region, interpreting the rates of credit growth in these market segments needs to take account of the low starting levels.[8] As shown in Figure 3.5, the case of Croatia provides a clear example of the trend of shifting from loans to enterprises to loans to households. Data for Latvia show how, while also gaining ground at the expense of industrial credit, consumer credit is still limited.

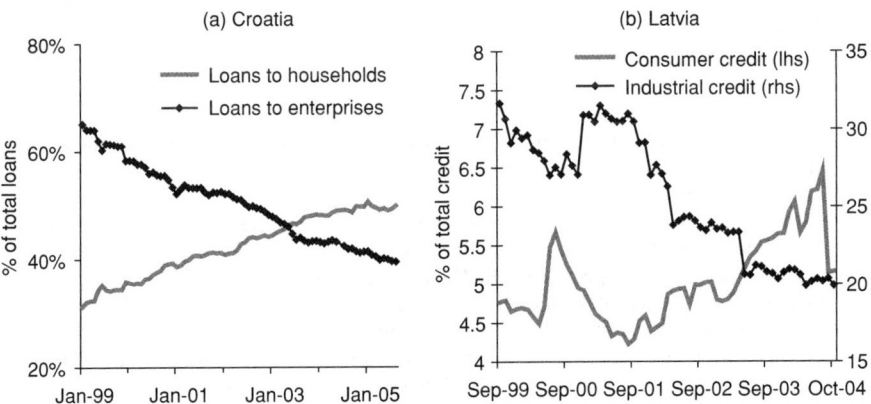

Figure 3.5 Evolution of Credit Composition in Croatia and Latvia

Source: Hrvatska Narodna Banka, Latvijas Banka.

V. Conclusions

The experience of many emerging market countries suggests that episodes of fast credit growth often, though by no means always, end in financial and currency crises. Given the high output costs of such crises, policymakers in CEE countries have been paying increasing attention to developments in the provision of credit to the private sector in the region. Increased attention has also been followed up by a number of policy measures aimed at slowing down the pace of credit growth. Curbing credit growth is not, however, without welfare costs as financial deepening is in principle associated with increased economic growth and efficiency. In this context, empirical work on the nature of the observed credit growth in the region can be a useful input for the policymaker. This chapter provides one such empirical study of credit growth in the region. Its main contribution is to suggest a methodology for assessing credit growth in the region while accounting for the catching up in incomes associated with the transition process that the region is undergoing.

A key result from this chapter is that, even accounting for a rising trend in the equilibrium credit-to-GDP ratio, a number of countries in the region have experienced "excessive" credit growth, in the sense that the observed credit growth has been higher than what we would have expected, given the evolution of macroeconomic variables. In particular, countries with fixed exchange rate regimes appear to have experienced credit growth well beyond what would have been expected according to our model. However, tests on disaggregated credit data by currency suggest that "excessive" credit growth is not limited to lending in foreign currency but is also a feature of lending in domestic currency. This somewhat puzzling result calls for further research on the mechanisms through which the exchange rate regime may impact credit developments in the region. While the results from this exercise necessarily depend on our narrow definition of "excessive" credit growth, they bring a new perspective that enhances our understanding of credit developments in the region.

Notes

1. European Central Bank (ECB). The authors would like to thank Georges Pineau and Cristina Vespro for helpful comments and André Geis for excellent research assistance.
2. See Arcalean et al (2005).
3. Data on which the estimations for the foreign/domestic currency are not corrected for indexed loans and therefore results are less informative.
4. The Lithuanian litas was pegged to the US dollar prior to 2002.
5. For example, in the case of Bulgaria the limits on open foreign exchange positions are such that each bank must maintain daily (i) a maximum ratio of up to 15 percent between its open position in any particular currency and the amount of its own funds, excluding the euro and (ii) a maximum ratio of up to 30 percent between its net open foreign currency position and the amount of its own funds, excluding the euro (IMF, 2004b, p. 164).
6. See, for example, Clarke et al (2005) overview paper in the special issue on bank privatization in developing countries (including emerging Europe).
7. In particular, banks were made to hold CNB paper bearing low interest rates if their growth of assets exceeded 4 percent in a given quarter. While these measures were repealed as from 2004, banks were then made to hold liquid foreign exchange assets equal to at least 35 percent of their total foreign exchange liabilities.
8. The difficulty in interpreting growth rates given low starting levels of credit to the private sector in general, has recently prompted some researchers to shift their focus of analysis to credit flows, rather than stocks. See, for example, Arpa et al (2005).

Bibliography

Arcalean, C., O. Calvo-Gonzalez, C. Móré, A. van Rixtel, A. Winkler, and T. Zumer, 2005, "The Causes and Nature of the Rapid Growth of Bank Credit in the Central, Eastern, and South-Eastern European Countries," paper presented at the Conference on Rapid Growth of Banking Sector Credit to the Private Sector, Sinaia, Romania, October 7–8, 2005.

Arpa, M., T. Reininger and Z. Walko, 2005, "Can Banking Intermediation in the Central and Eastern European Countries Ever Catch Up with the Euro Area?" Mimeo, Oesterreichische Nationalbank.

Backé, P. and T. Zumer, 2005, "Developments in Developments in Credit to the Private Sector in Central and Eastern European EU Member States: Emerging from Financial Repression—A Comparative Overview," *Focus on European Economic Integration*, 2/05, Oesterreichische Nationalbank, October.

Berglöf, E. and P. Bolton, 2002, "The Great Divide and Beyond: Financial Architecture in Transition," *Journal of Economic Perspectives*, vol. 16(1), Winter, pp. 77–100.

Bokros, L., 2002, "Financial Sector Development in Central and Eastern Europe," in A. Winkler (ed.), *Banking and Monetary Policy in Eastern Europe. The First Ten Years*. Houndmills and New York: Palgrave Macmillan, pp. 11–42.

Borio, C. and P. Lowe, 2002, "Asset Prices, Financial and Monetary Stability: Exploring the Nexus," BIS Working Paper No. 114, Bank for International Settlements, July.

Clarke, G.R., R.C. Cull and M. Shirley, 2005, "Bank Privatization in Developing Countries: A Summary of Lessons and Findings," *Journal of Banking and Finance*, 29, pp. 1905–30.

Cottarelli, C., G. Dell'Ariccia and I. Vladkova-Hollar, 2005, "Early Birds, Late Risers, and Sleeping Beauties: Bank Credit Growth to the Private Sector in Central and Eastern Europe and in the Balkans," *Journal of Banking and Finance*, vol. 29(1), pp. 83–104.

De Haas, R. and I. van Lelyveld, 2006, "Foreign Banks and Credit Stability in Central and Eastern Europe. A Panel Data Analysis," *Journal of Banking and Finance*, vol. 30(7), pp. 1927–52.

De Haas, R. and I. Naaborg, 2005, "Foreign Banks in Transition Economies: Small Business Lending and Internal Capital Markets," International Finance working paper 0504004, Economics Working Paper Archive at WUSTL.

Duenwald, C., N. Gueorguiev and A. Schaechter, 2005, "Too Much of a Good Thing? Credit Booms in Transition Economies: The Cases of Bulgaria, Romania and Ukraine," IMF Working Paper No. 05/128.

EBRD, 2004, *Transition Report*, London.

Gourinchas, P., O. Landerretche and R. Valdes, 2001, "Lending Booms, Latin America and the World," NBER Working Paper 8249.

Hilbers, P., İ. Ötker-Robe, C. Pazarbasioğlu, and G. Johnsen, 2005, "Assessing and Managing Rapid Credit Growth and the Role of Supervisory and Prudential Policies," IMF Working Paper No. 05/ 151.

International Monetary Fund, 2004a, *World Economic Outlook*, April.

——, 2004b, *Annual Report on Exchange Arrangements and Exchange Restrictions*, August.

——, 2005, *Global Financial Stability Report*, September.

Kraft, E. and L. Jankov, 2005, "Does Speed Kill? Lending Booms and Their Consequences in Croatia," *Journal of Banking and Finance*, 29, pp. 105–21.

Lepik, I. and J. Tõrs, 2002, "Structure and Performance of Estonia's Financial Sector," in C. Thimann (ed.), *Financial Sectors in EU Accession Countries*, European Central Bank, Frankfurt.

Mehl, Arnaud, Cristina Vespro and Adalbert Winkler, 2005, "The Finance-Growth Nexus and Financial Sector Environment: New Evidence form South-Eastern Europe," paper for the Conference on Financial Development, Integration and Stability in Central, Eastern and South-Eastern Europe, Oesterreichische Nationalbank, November 14–15.

Ottens, D., E. Lambregts and S. Poelhekke, 2005, "Credit Booms in Emerging Market Economies: A Recipe for Banking Crises?" DNB Working Paper No. 46, De Nederlandsche Bank, June.

Papademos, L., 2005, "Financial Structures, Credit Growth and House Prices in the New EU Member States: Policy Challenges on the Road to the Euro," speech at the Conference held by Latvijas Banka, Riga, September 19, 2005; <www.ecb.int>.

Schadler, S., Z. Murgasova and R. van Elkan, 2004, "Credit Booms, Demand Booms, and Euro Adoption," paper for the Conference on Challenges for Central Banks in an Enlarged EMU, Oesterreichische Nationalbank, February 20–21.

Tornell, A. and F. Westermann, 2002, "Boom-Bust Cycles: Facts and Explanation," *IMF Staff Papers*, 49 (Special Issue), pp. 111–55.

Yotzov, V., 2002, "The Financial Sector in Bulgaria: Structure, Functioning and Trends," in C. Thimann (ed.), *Financial Sectors in EU Accession Countries*, European Central Bank, Frankfurt.

4
Fast Credit Expansion in Central and Eastern Europe: Catching-up, Sustainable Financial Deepening, or Bubble?

Peter Backé, Balázs Égert, and Tina Zumer[1]

In recent years, most Central, Eastern, and South-eastern European (CEE) countries have recorded rapid rates of growth of banking system credit and, consequently, sizable increases in the ratio of credit to GDP. Not surprisingly, therefore, the assessment and the implications of credit expansion have become a key policy issue across the CEE region. In particular, the question arises whether or not the observed credit expansion can be viewed as excessive, that is, disconnected from economic fundamentals, or whether it reflects catching-up effects due to low initial credit-to-GDP ratios and sustainable financial deepening.

In this chapter,[2] we proceed in two steps to contribute to answering this question. First, we review briefly the main stylized features of bank credit expansion in 11 CEE countries, namely Bulgaria, Croatia, the Czech Republic, Estonia, Hungary, Latvia, Lithuania, Poland, Romania, Slovakia, and Slovenia (Section I). In doing so, the focus is on the most dynamic components of credit developments, that is, on credit to the private sector.[3] Second, we examine the equilibrium credit/GDP level for transition economies (Section II). In particular, we explore the extent to which recent lending booms in CEE countries have already lifted private sector credit/GDP ratios possibly even beyond equilibrium levels, and thus consider whether strong credit expansion was "excessive" with respect to the underlying economic fundamentals. We rely on econometric estimates obtained for small open OECD countries to derive the equilibrium level of private credit to GDP in transition economies.

Although our results show a substantial degree of uncertainty with regard to the equilibrium private credit-to-GDP ratios, they also indicate that none of the countries displayed clearly excessive levels by 2004. Nevertheless, the rapid move toward equilibrium in a number of cases (Croatia, Estonia, Latvia, Hungary, Slovenia, and Bulgaria) may suggest that the ongoing credit growth could potentially result in an overshooting in the coming years.

I. Stylized features of credit expansion in Central and Eastern Europe

The key facts about the developments in credit to the private sector in these 11 CEE countries (CEE-11) can be summarized in four main points:

- In most countries, one can observe dynamic growth in credit to the private sector well above the pace seen in the euro area. This is generally, but not necessarily, reflected in sizable increases in the private credit-to-GDP ratios.
- Strong credit growth is primarily attributable to the strong growth of loans to households.
- Foreign borrowing has become an increasingly important source of financing for the expansion of domestic credit in these countries.
- Foreign-currency-denominated or foreign-currency-indexed loans have taken a rising share in total private sector loans in most of the CEE-11.

Strong credit growth and the rise of credit-to-GDP ratios

Since 1999, nominal growth rates of credit to the private sector (Figure 4.1a) have been especially high in the Baltic countries, Bulgaria, Hungary, and Romania, and to a somewhat lesser extent also in Slovenia and, at times, in Croatia. Whereas Estonia, Hungary, and Slovenia displayed relatively steady annual average rates of credit expansion throughout the sample period, credit growth accelerated visibly in Latvia (until 2001 and again in 2005), Lithuania (until 2004), Bulgaria (in 2001–03) and Romania (until 2003); in 2005, it decelerated in Bulgaria and Romania while still being buoyant. The annual average growth rates of credit to the private sector differ substantially within these seven countries, ranging, in 2005, from around 17 percent in Hungary to about 54 percent in Latvia. It is noteworthy that the Baltic countries and Bulgaria recorded very high nominal credit growth rates in an environment of low or relatively low inflation, while in Hungary, Slovenia, and Romania credit dynamics have to be seen to some extent in the context of higher and only gradually falling inflation, implying less rapid growth rates of credit in real terms (Figure 4.1b).

In the Czech Republic and Slovakia, growth in credit to the private sector picked up more recently after a period of rather moderate or, at times, negative growth before 2004 (Czech Republic) and 2002 (Slovakia). In the two countries, the interpretation of credit data before 2002 is somewhat difficult due to the consolidation of the banking sector and the cleaning of the credit portfolios of selected banks at the time. In any case, banking sector "rehabilitation" facilitated the subsequent acceleration of bank lending activity in these countries since 2002.[4]

In Poland, lending to the private sector has decelerated from relatively high rates recorded in the period up to the end of 2000, to average annual growth rates of around 5 percent since 2002. This was related to the economic slowdown and,

Catching Up, Sustainable Financial Deepening, or Bubble? 69

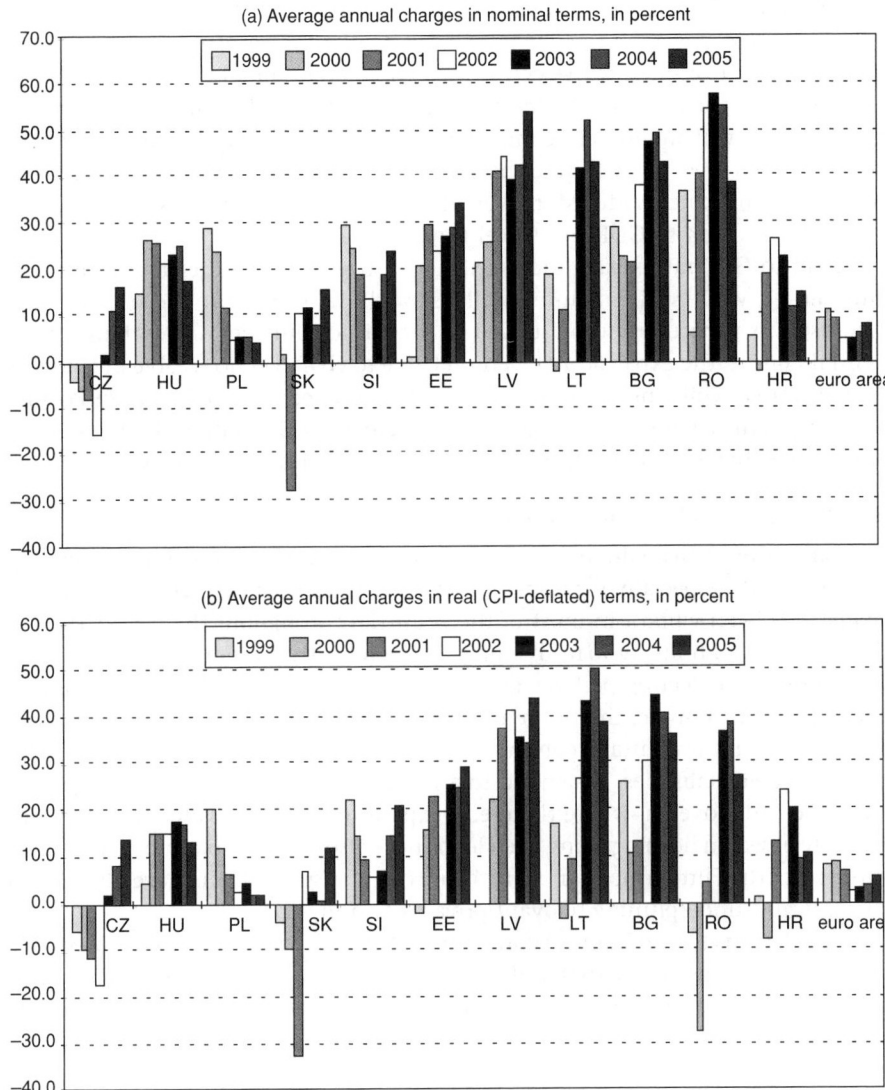

Figure 4.1 Credit Growth to the Private Sector, 1999–2005

Source: National central banks.

Note: The contraction in 2001 and 2002 in Slovakia is due to bank rehabilitation measures.

in particular, the severe contraction of gross fixed capital formation during the earlier years of this decade. In the more recent economic upswing since 2003, the ample profit situation of the enterprise sector has promoted internal financing of corporate sector activities and thus curbed overall credit demand in the economy. Household borrowing in contrast expanded dynamically.

High nominal credit growth does not necessarily imply correspondingly high growth rates in the credit-to-GDP ratio, in particular for countries with low credit-to-GDP ratios. Considering two countries with different initial credit-to-GDP levels and with similar credit-to-GDP flows, it becomes apparent that although the credit-to-GDP ratios will progress at a comparable pace, the "low-credit" country will have high nominal credit growth rates because of the low base effect, i.e., the initially low level of nominal credit. Moreover, differences in inflation rates also affect the dynamics of credit-to-GDP levels over time.

Credit-to-GDP ratios have increased (or are beginning to increase) in most of the CEE-11, while still remaining well below those of the euro area (Figure 4.2). The rise was particularly pronounced in the Baltic countries and in Bulgaria. In central Europe, the expansion of credit relative to GDP was noticeable in Hungary and Slovenia, while much more moderate in the Czech Republic and in Poland. Slovakia, in turn, has recorded broadly steady credit-to-GDP ratios, though starting from levels that were above those of the other countries under review.

Strong growth of loans to households

Although growth in credit to the private sector has varied across countries, lending to households, especially for home purchases (primarily mortgage-based housing loans), has been vibrant in most of the countries throughout the period 1999 to 2005. However, housing loan dynamics have recently started to decelerate in a few countries, reflecting perhaps the result of measures taken by the authorities, including, for example, the tightening of mortgage scheme subsidies (Hungary). In Slovakia, on the contrary, commercial banks adjusted their interest rate policies to offset lower subsidies, which led to a further strengthening of mortgage loan dynamics. In Slovenia, where the credit expansion to the private sector was not strongly based on housing loans, such loans have also begun to pick up considerably more recently. Furthermore, in some countries, consumer loans have also grown dynamically, underpinning buoyant private consumption.

Overall, loans to nonfinancial corporations have grown at a more measured pace than loans to households, so that the share of household lending in total domestic lending increased considerably in most countries during the period under review (Figure 4.3).

Foreign borrowing as an important source of funding credit growth

Credit expansion in most of the CEE-11 has been financed by both domestic and foreign sources (Figure 4.4). However, while deposits of domestic residents played the main role in funding credit growth until 2001/02 and are still the largest item on the liability side of banks, foreign borrowing has become an increasingly important source of financing for the expansion of domestic credit in these countries, particularly in those CEE-11 which have recorded rapid credit dynamics. The net foreign position of banks in most CEE-11 countries that have recorded high and rising credit growth has deteriorated noticeably more recently (as net foreign liabilities increased or net foreign assets turned into net foreign liabilities). Still, net foreign liability positions of CEE-11 banking sectors continue to be comparatively

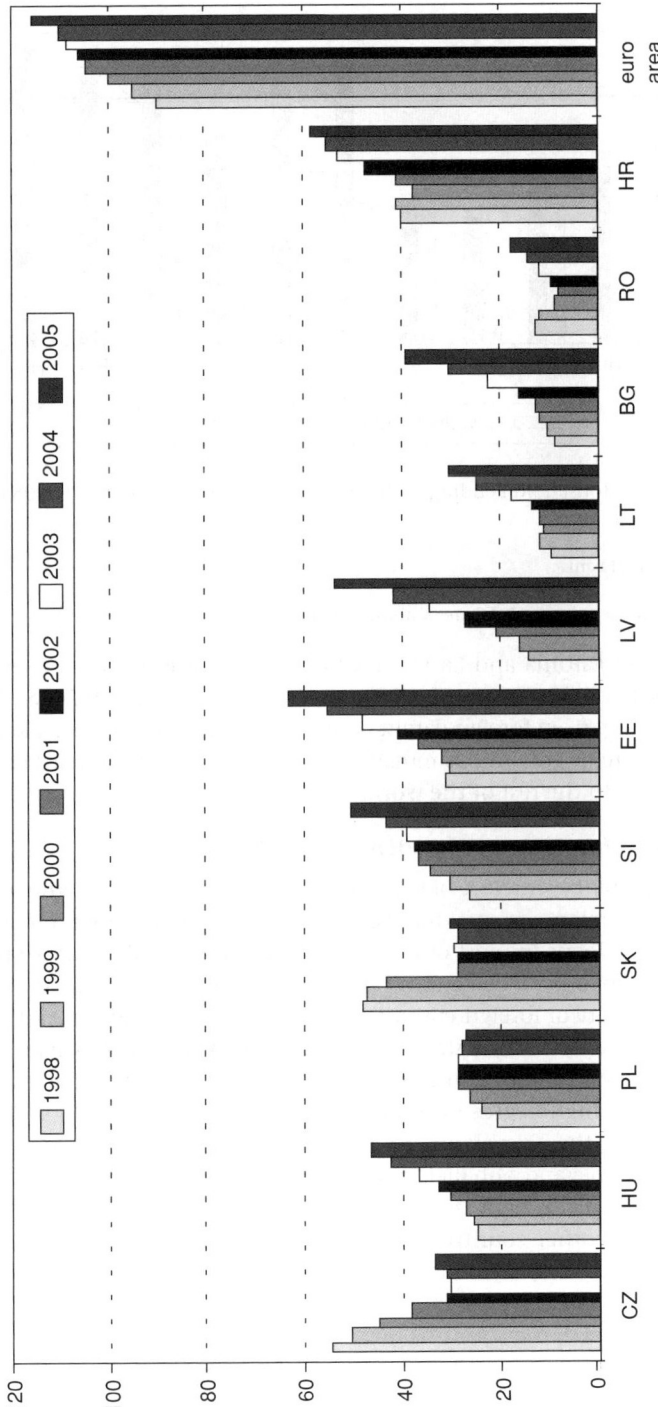

Figure 4.2 Private Sector Credit/GDP Ratios, 1999–2005 (in percent)

Source: National central banks.

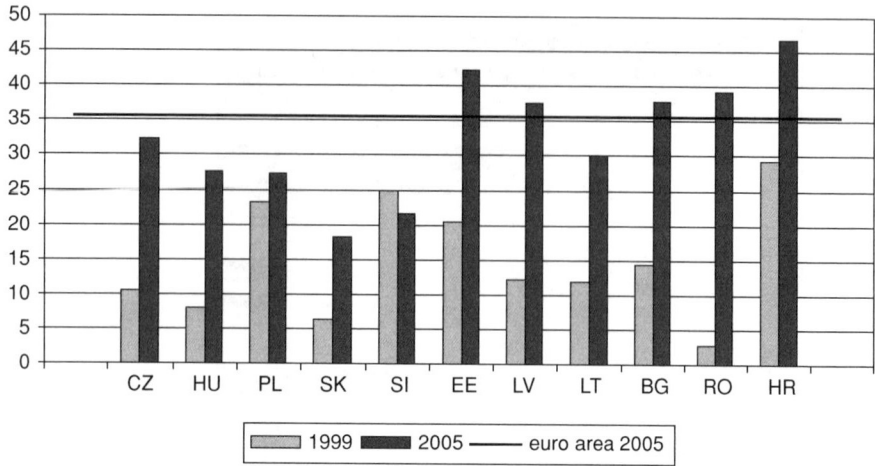

Figure 4.3 Share of Household Lending in Total Domestic Lending, 1999 and 2005 (in percent)

Source: National central banks.

Note: The horizontal line refers to the share of household loans in the euro area.

moderate; only in Estonia and Latvia have they reached more sizable levels (of about 22 percent and 30 percent of GDP, respectively, at the end of 2005), in part driven by borrowing from foreign parent banks. In Poland and the Czech Republic, where aggregate credit growth has remained moderate, banking systems continue to be net creditors to the rest of the world.

The rising role of foreign-currency-denominated loans

In terms of the currency structure of lending to the private sector, foreign-currency-denominated or foreign-currency-indexed loans have had an important share in total private sector loans in most of the CEE-11, ranging in 2005 from 10 percent in the Czech Republic to 80 percent in Estonia (Figure 4.5). In the Baltic countries and Croatia, the share of foreign-currency-denominated loans (around 60 percent or more) has remained relatively steady between 1999 and 2005, as such borrowing had already built up in these countries during the 1990s. Long-standing exchange rate stability and a high degree of foreign ownership in the banking sector may have played a role in these developments (also see Arcalean et al, 2005; Boissay et al, 2006 and this volume; and Mihaljek, this volume). The share of foreign-currency-denominated loans is also high and fairly steady in Bulgaria and Romania (around 50 percent). In the other countries, with the exception of the Czech Republic, the share of foreign-currency-denominated borrowing increased over the same period, most notably in Slovenia and Slovakia, where it tripled or almost doubled, respectively.

Foreign-currency-denominated loans in the CEE-11 are mainly granted to the nonfinancial corporate sector, and in some countries, in considerable magnitudes

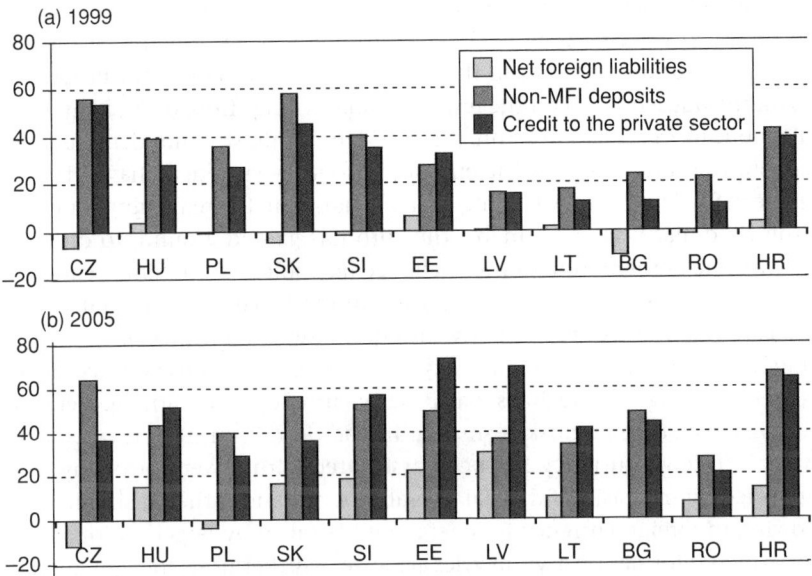

Figure 4.4 Selected Banking Sector Assets and Liabilities, 1999 and 2005 (in percent of GDP)

Source: National central banks.

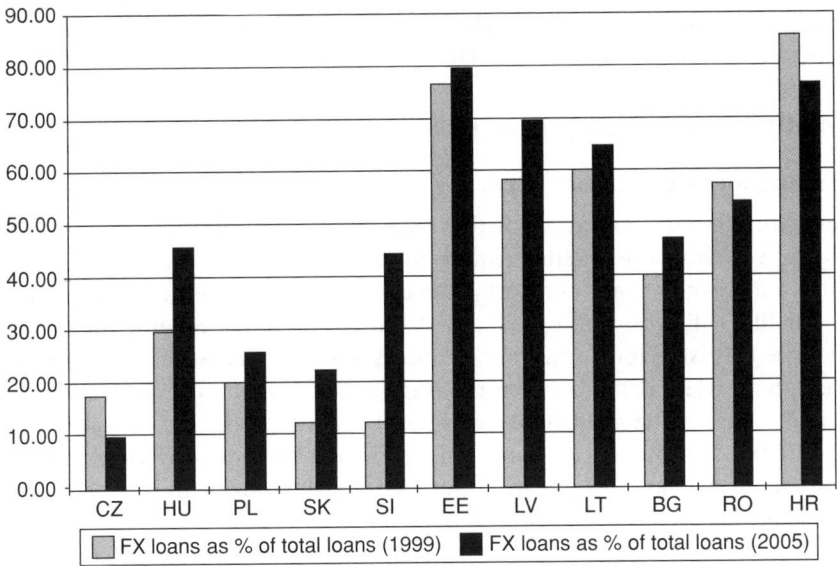

Figure 4.5 Share of Foreign Currency Loans in Total Loans to the Private Sector, 1999 and 2005 (in percent)

Source: National central banks.

Note: The figures on Croatia include domestic currency loans indexed to foreign currency (see ECB, IRC, TF ENL 2006 for more information on this aspect).

also to households. Such loans to nonfinancial corporations represent an important share in total loans outstanding to this sector in all CEE-11, ranging, at the end of 2005, from around 16 percent in the Czech Republic to 83 percent in Estonia, whereas for the household sector the respective shares range from 0.3 percent in the Czech Republic to 75 percent in Estonia. These loans are mostly euro-denominated. In most countries under review, the euro and its legacy currencies have played a leading role in foreign currency lending from the outset. In the remaining countries, where the US dollar was preeminent, the euro has gained ground, to different degrees, with the reorientation of the exchange rate policy to the single currency. However, in some countries, other currencies, in particular the Swiss franc, have begun to gain importance very recently, also in household borrowing.

Overall, borrowing in foreign currency has been more extensive in countries with pegged exchange rate regimes, particularly currency board arrangements, as the perceived exchange rate risk is smaller. In addition, in most of the countries borrowing in foreign currency has been associated with lower borrowing costs and supported by increasing financial liberalization. Besides that, a sizable share of borrowing in foreign currency is generally undertaken by larger multinational firms, for which information asymmetries are lower. Furthermore, foreign-currency borrowing by the corporate sector is frequently used for hedging purposes. Large multinational firms play a prominent role in this respect, as the greater part of their revenues is in foreign currency. The rationale for household borrowing in foreign currency is much less clear cut, even where sizable interest rate differentials to key currencies still prevail, as it substantially increases their exposure to exchange rate risk, especially for loans denominated in other foreign currencies than the euro.[5]

Estimating equilibrium private sector credit-to-GDP levels

Estimation method and data issues

We now turn to the question of whether credit growth in transition economies is excessive. Answering this question requires assessing the equilibrium level of private credit as a share of GDP and comparing the equilibrium level to the observed data.

Cottarelli, Dell'Ariccia, and Vladkova-Hollar (2005) were probably the first to investigate this issue for transition economies. The authors estimate a model of the long-term relationship between the private sector credit/GDP ratio and a set of variables (per capita GDP, public debt/GDP, inflation, financial liberalization, legal origin) for a panel of nontransition economies. Subsequently, they produce out-of-sample estimates for private sector credit/GDP ratios of 15 CEE countries. As actual private sector credit-to-GDP levels were considerably lower in 2002 than the authors' estimates of the expected long-term credit/GDP ratios, they conclude that private sector bank credit levels in that year were not inconsistent with the structural characteristics of the economies under examination. The key motivation of this section therefore is to revisit the issue by examining the period up to 2004 and by using estimation strategies that differ, to some degree, from those of Cottarelli, Dell'Ariccia, and Vladkova-Hollar (2005).

There are two other recent studies, to our knowledge, which also investigate the equilibrium level of private credit and the possible "excessiveness" of credit growth in transition economies.

First, Boissay, Calvo-Gonzalez, and Koźluk (2006) estimate time series models including GDP-per-capita and real interest rates for a number of established market economies[6] for periods with stable credit-to-GDP ratios.[7] They then compare the average of the credit growth rates for transition economies obtained using the error correction specifications estimated for the developed countries with the observed credit growth in the transition economies. The authors also estimate time series models for transition economies, which include the real interest rate, a quadratic trend, and a dummy aimed at capturing changes in credit growth after 2001. Their results indicate excessive credit growth in the three Baltic states and in Bulgaria and to a lesser extent also in Hungary and Croatia. At the same time, credit growth in Romania and Slovenia does not seem to be excessive. Looking at disaggregated credit series for transition economies (domestic vs. foreign-currency-denominated; short-term vs. long-term credit; and credit to households vs. credit to nonfinancial corporations) cannot identify any particular sector common for the countries under study that seems to drive the excessive credit growth observed in aggregate credit.

Two observations come to mind with regard to these findings. First, the quadratic trend may be capturing missing variables from the model (which indeed only contains real interest rates) and explosive trends due to credit boom or to adjustment from initial undershooting of credit levels.[8] It is in fact curious to see that a sizable number of countries have excessive credit growth, given that the quadratic trend has a very good fit thus leaving very little unexplained variation in the credit series. Second, the use of Euribor for the real interest rate variable may not be able to capture some foreign-currency-denominated loans that are linked to other currencies than the euro (e.g., as in Hungary), and also Euribor neglects the country risk and default risk at the micro level.

Second, Kiss, Nagy, and Vonnák (2006) estimate a dynamic panel (Pooled Mean Group Estimator) model including GDP-per-capita, real interest rate and inflation of 11 euro area countries (excluding Luxembourg) to generate out-of-sample estimates for private sector credit-to-GDP ratios of the three Baltic countries and of the CEE-5 (Czech Republic, Hungary, Poland, Slovakia, and Slovenia). They find that only Estonia and Latvia may have come close recently to equilibrium while the other countries have credit-to-GDP ratios below the estimated equilibrium levels.

Besides being above the estimated equilibrium credit level, Kiss, Nagy, and Vonnák (2006) define two other criteria which may indicate a credit boom: (a) if the observed credit growth exceeds the one implied by the long-run equilibrium relationship and (b) if the observed growth rate is higher than the speed of adjustment to equilibrium in the error-correction model. Overall, the authors find that the risk of a credit boom is high in both Estonia and Latvia according to these criteria, whereas Hungary, Lithuania, and Slovenia might be in the danger zone because the observed growth rates are higher than the one derived from the long-run equilibrium relationship. In addition, the authors argue that possible credit booms are mainly due to credit expansion to households and not to the nonfinancial corporate sector. It is important to note, however, that the observed growth rates may be in excess of the one derived from the long-run equilibrium relationship because of the adjustment from initial undershooting. Moreover, the speed of adjustment to equilibrium differs if the actual observations are below or above the estimated equilibrium.

We contribute to this literature by expanding the list of countries (11 transition, OECD, and emerging market economies) and explanatory variables, by constructing several possible benchmark country groups which share common characteristics with the transition economies (emerging markets, small emerging markets, small and open OECD countries) and by performing an extensive sensitivity analysis of the estimation results.

Three points need to be made at the outset: First, in such an econometric framework, equilibrium is defined as behavioral equilibrium, that is, the level of private credit, which can be explained by economic fundamentals with the unexplained part being considered as deviation from the equilibrium level. This notion of equilibrium is indeed very close to the one used for instance in the literature on (behavioral) equilibrium exchange rates and in other fields of the economic profession. Second, our definition of equilibrium is not suitable for analyzing the connection between credit growth and external sustainability, financial stability aspects of credit growth or the optimal currency (foreign currency vs. domestic currency) or sectoral (households vs. corporate sector) composition of the credit-to-GDP ratio. Third, in a setting where the credit-to-GDP ratio is regressed on both supply-side and demand-side variables, the implicit assumption is that the credit market is in continuous equilibrium.

Our baseline specification uses explanatory variables employed in previous studies (see Calza, Gartner, and Sousa, 2001, and Calza, Manrique, and Sousa, 2003, for industrial countries, Cottarelli, Dell'Ariccia and Vladkova-Hollar, 2005, and Brzoza-Brzezina, 2005), but also extends on them. The explanatory variables include per capita GDP, bank credit to the public sector as a percentage of GDP, long-term nominal lending rates, inflation rates measured by the producer price index and the spread between lending and deposit rates to capture the degree of liberalization of the banking sector.[9]

$$C^P = f(\overset{+}{CAPITA}, \overset{-}{C^G}, \overset{-}{i^{lending}}, \overset{-}{p^{PPI}}, \overset{-}{spread}) \quad (1)$$

where C^P is bank credit to the private sector expressed as a share of GDP. In order to check the robustness of the variables included in the baseline equation, we undertake various sensitivity checks. In particular, we estimate alternative specifications, employing alternative measures often used in the existing body of literature. Concretely, we subsequently replace in the baseline specification one-by-one GDP per capita by real GDP growth and by real industrial production, long-term lending rates by short-term lending rates, and the PPI by the CPI, which yields four additional equations that are being estimated. Moreover, we substitute (where available) a financial liberalization index for the spread variable. In addition, further alternative specifications include the (public and private) registry variable.

Equation (1) is estimated using quarterly data covering 43 countries, which are grouped into three main panels: (a) the CEE-11 economies, (b) developed OECD countries, and (c) emerging market economies from Asia and the Americas.[10] The CEE panel is further subdivided into three presumably more homogeneous groupings: (a) the Baltic countries (B-3): Estonia, Latvia, and Lithuania, (b) the CEE-5: the Czech Republic, Hungary, Poland, Slovakia, and Slovenia, and (c) southeastern Europe (SEE-3): Bulgaria, Croatia, and Romania. The OECD panel is also split into two subpanels: (a) small OECD countries (excluding transition economies that have joined the OECD),[11] and (b) large OECD countries.[12] In addition, we also analyze a panel including catching-up old EU countries: Greece, Portugal, and Spain and a panel composed of small emerging market economies: Chile, Israel, Peru, and South Africa. The beginning of the sample periods are 1975–80 for the OECD countries, 1980–93 for the emerging market economies, and 1990–96 for the transition economies; the sample ends in 2004.

We first check whether the series under consideration are stationary in levels, applying various panel unit root tests. The results of the panel unit root tests (not reported here) show that most of the series are I(1) processes. In some cases, the tests yield conflicting results for level data. However, since the tests do not indicate unambiguously in any case that the series are stationary in level, we conclude that they are I(1).

Subsequently, in order to make sure that the variables are cointegrated, the error correction terms issued from the estimated error correction form of an Autoregressive Distributed Lag (ARDL) model, the Mean Group Estimator (MGE) proposed by Pesaran, Shin, and Smith (1999) are used. The variables are cointegrated in the event that the error correction term is statistically significant and has a negative sign. As reported in Égert, Backé, and Zumer (2006), most of the error correction terms fulfill this double criterion. A notable exception is the panel composed of the three Baltic countries, as there seems to be only one cointegration relationship out of the eight tested equations.

Finally, the long-term coefficients from equation (1) are obtained from three alternative estimation techniques: (a) fixed-effect ordinary least squares, (b) panel dynamic OLS estimates, and (c) the MGE.

Estimation results

The estimation results, reported in more detail in Égert, Backé, and Zumer, 2006, are the following. First, GDP per capita is found to be positively connected with private credit for the OECD and the emerging market panels. This result is especially solid for small open OECD and emerging market economies. By contrast, GDP per capita is not always significant for the transition countries, in particular not for the CEE-5, while the size of the coefficient is much larger for the B-3 and the SEE-3 than for the OECD and emerging market economies.

As far as credit to the public sector is concerned, the estimations confirm that an increase in credit to the public sector causes a decline in private credit and vice-versa. This result is very robust for emerging market economies and for the CEE-5, thus supporting the crowding-out/-in hypothesis in these countries. Some empirical support for this hypothesis can be also established for the advanced OECD and for emerging market economies, but not for the B-3 countries (possibly due to their low public debt) and the SEE-3 sub-sample.

As regards long-run nominal interest rates, reasonably robust empirical support is found for nominal lending rates being negatively linked to private credit in the CEE-5 as well as in emerging markets and small open OECD countries. In contrast, the finding for the Baltic countries and the SEE-3 is that interest rates mostly have a positive sign if they turn out to be statistically significant.

For inflation, particularly strong negative relationships could be established between the rate of inflation and private credit for the group of emerging market economies. This negative relationship between inflation and credit is also supported to some extent for the CEE-5 and for small OECD economies. Nevertheless, inflation does not seem to have a role in the equations estimated for the Baltic and SEE countries.

For the spread variable, which is meant to capture the degree of financial liberalization, the expected positive relationship is detected in small OECD economies and in the CEE-5, and also in the other transition economies.[13]

Finally, it is noteworthy that our baseline specification is fairly robust to the use of the aforementioned alternative variables. Two exceptions merit mention here. First, the financial liberalization index proposed by Abiad and Mody (2005) does not perform very well. Also, the credit registry variable measuring the existence of private and/or public credit registries is usually not significant. Interestingly, the two narrower panels of catching-up old EU countries and small emerging market economies yield rather shaky estimation results.

Comparison of the estimated and observed credit-to-GDP ratios

The final stage of our analysis helps us answer the question of possible deviations from the equilibrium private credit-to-GDP ratio. This consists of the comparison of the fitted values derived from the panel estimations to the observed values for the CEE-11. We face the following problem here: it might be that at the beginning of the transition process the private credit-to-GDP ratio was lower (or higher) in transition economies than in other countries at a similar level of development and that this gap was closing gradually. This point was first put forward in the context of equilibrium exchange rates by Maeso-Fernandez, Osbat, and Schnatz (2005). If this were true, the use of panels that only include transition economies may lead to severely biased constant terms and coefficient estimates. The fact that the coefficients on the GDP per capita variable are considerably larger than unity for the B-3 and (to a lesser extent) for the SEE-3, might reflect such an upward bias. However, even if the coefficient estimates would not suffer from bias, we could not use the estimation results obtained for transition economies, because there is no single equation where most coefficients are statistically significant and correctly signed.[14]

Therefore, we have to rely on nonbiased and robust estimations, which could be obtained in principle from nontransition economies, such as emerging market economies and OECD economies. Once again, the lack of robustness of the coefficient estimates for emerging markets makes it impossible to use these estimations to derive equilibrium credit levels for transition economies. Hence, we can count only on the OECD panels. The baseline specification estimated by means of fixed effect OLS for small open OECD economies appears to be the single solution given that it is the only equation where all coefficients bear the right sign and all but one are statistically significant.

Consequently, we plug in the macroeconomic series of the transition economies into this selected equation obtained for the small open OECD panel to derive the equilibrium credit level for transition economies. The underlying assumption of such an exercise is that there is long-run parameter homogeneity between the small developed OECD panel and the transition countries. This supposes that in the long run, the behavior of private credit in transition economies will be similar to the present behavior of small open OECD economies.

A problem we face when deriving the fitted value for transition economies is the lack of country-specific constant terms for the transition economies. To be on the safe side, we use the largest and the smallest constant terms obtained on the basis of the small OECD panel, which gives us the whole spectrum of estimated values for private credit.

There is a considerable amount of uncertainty with regard to the equilibrium level of the private credit-to-GDP ratio, as suggested by the rather large derived ranges of deviations (Figure 4.6), especially given the range of constant terms we use. Consequently, if one considers whole ranges, Croatia is the country which has the largest share of the range above equilibrium, while Bulgaria, Estonia, Hungary, Latvia, and Slovenia might have already reached equilibrium as well, even though the mass of the estimated deviation was still located mostly on the undershooting side in 2004. Finally, it is interesting to see that Lithuania, Poland, and Romania are below equilibrium throughout the period.

IV. Concluding remarks

This chapter investigated credit growth in 11 CEE economies, which has by now become a key policy issue across the region. We summarized the stylized facts with regard to private sector credit growth in transition economies, namely that: since 1999, credit growth has been substantial in most economies; the rate of growth was usually higher in nominal terms than for the private credit-to-GDP ratio, primarily because of the initially low stock of private credit; credit expansion is mainly attributable to credit growth to households; there is increasing reliance by banks on foreign sources to fund their domestic lending; and there seems to be some shift toward more foreign-currency-denominated credit in total private credit.

In the second part of the chapter, we attempted to answer the question of whether the observed credit expansion is a bubble phenomenon or whether it only reflects changes in economic fundamentals and catching-up effects. For this purpose, we estimated the determinants of private credit on the basis of a number of dynamic panels containing quarterly data for transition economies, developed OECD economies, and emerging market economies. Our results showed a varying importance of our selected explanatory variables (GDP per capita, public credit, interest rates, inflation, and a spread variable) for the different groups of countries.

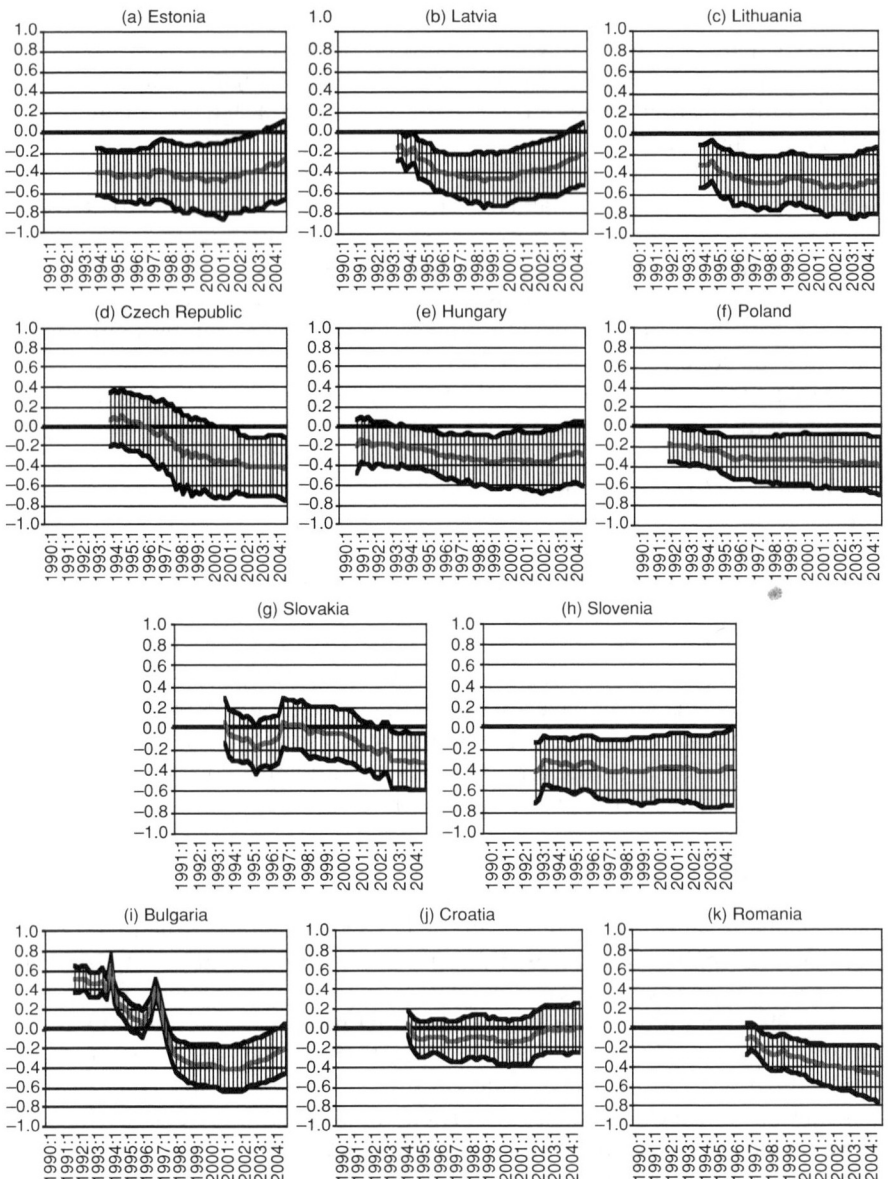

Figure 4.6 Deviations from Long-run Equilibrium Private Sector Credit-to-GDP, 1990 to 2004: Baltic Countries (a–c), Central Europe (d–h), South-eastern Europe (i–k)

Source: Égert, Backé, and Zumer (2006).

Note: negative values indicate that the observed private credit-to-GDP ratio is lower than what a particular country's GDP per capita would predict ("undershooting"). Conversely, positive figures show an "overshooting" of the private credit-to-GDP ratio. For Bulgaria, Romania, and the three Baltic states, private credit includes both public and private nonfinancial corporations, while the results reported in Égert, Backé, and Zumer (2006) disregard public nonfinancial corporations for these countries (available data—IFS data base—do not allow such a desegregation on a fully comparable basis for the remaining transition economies).

Generally, relying on in-sample panel estimates for transition economies appears to be problematic, because of a possible bias in the estimations due to the so-called initial undershooting or overshooting of credit levels, but also because the equations estimated for the transition economies are not sufficiently stable. Given similar difficulties encountered for emerging market economies, we employed estimations obtained for the small open OECD country sample to get around these problems and to obtain estimates of equilibrium levels of private credit for transition economies.

We obtained relatively wide ranges of equilibrium private-sector credit-to-GDP levels. Considering these ranges, we cannot state with confidence that fast credit growth has resulted in overshooting, that is, private credit-to-GDP ratios are consistently above the estimated equilibrium levels, in any of the transition economies. At the same time, for Croatia a substantial part of the estimated range is above equilibrium by 2004, while Bulgaria, Estonia, Hungary, Latvia, and Slovenia might have already reached equilibrium as well, even though the mass of the estimated deviation was still located mostly on the undershooting side in 2004. Finally, the initial undershooting remains relatively stable for Lithuania, Poland, and Romania throughout the period. Nevertheless, considering recent dynamics, the rapid adjustment that has been observed in some countries, notably in Croatia, Estonia, Latvia, and possibly Bulgaria, might lead to a surpassing of the equilibrium and thus to the emergence of overshooting instances in the near future, unless private sector credit growth slows.

However, we also emphasized that our notion of equilibrium cannot tackle issues related to financial stability aspects of credit growth, the optimal currency (foreign currency vs. domestic currency denomination) and sectoral composition (household vs. corporate sector) of private credit and the implications of credit growth on the trade balance and external sustainability. As a matter of fact, credit growth can pose risks, even if overall levels of private sector credit-to-GDP appear to be broadly in line with equilibrium ranges, especially if the adjustment from an undershooting situation to an equilibrium level takes place rapidly. In financial stability terms, a persistent rapid credit expansion does by itself pose the risk of a deterioration in the asset quality of banks. If a sizable share of lending takes place in foreign currencies and if borrowers are not sufficiently hedged against foreign exchange risk—a feature that is certainly pertinent in CEE countries—this creates risks for borrowers and lenders. On the macroeconomic front, a rapid adjustment process toward equilibrium levels may trigger aggregate demand booms and worsening savings-investment balances, thus causing current account deficits to move above levels that can be sustained over a longer period of time. Countries with persistent and high external imbalances may be particularly susceptible to discontinuities in the pricing of risk by global financial markets.

Notes

1. Backé and Égert: Oesterreichische Nationalbank (Austrian central bank); Zumer: European Central Bank (ECB).

2. This chapter summarizes the key findings of Backé and Zumer (2005, with selective updates) and Égert, Backé and Zumer (2006).
3. We define the private sector as the nonbank nongovernment sector, i.e., households, (public and private) enterprises, and nonbank financial institutions. Apart from the early years of transition when credit to state-owned enterprises was still sizable in CEE countries, the nonbank nongovernment sector comes in fact very close to the (nonbank) private sector. Thus, for reasons of simplicity, we denote the nonbank nongovernment sector as the private sector in this study. It should be noted that fully comparable disaggregated data for credit to enterprises according to their ownership structure is only available for some countries.
4. In addition, the fact that more dynamic credit expansion took place only recently can be attributed to the cautiousness of banks to finance longer-term capital projects in the business sector and, in the Czech Republic, also to relatively moderate real GDP growth prior to 2005. Moreover, FDI (which also includes credit transactions between affiliated enterprises) has been a particularly important source of financing in these two countries and has thus substituted for bank credit.
5. For a discussion of the factors driving private sector credit growth in CEE countries see Backé and Zumer (2005), as well as Hilbers, Ötker-Robe, and Pazarbasioğlu in this volume, and Arcalean et al (also in this volume).
6. Australia, Belgium, Finland, France, Germany, Greece, Ireland, Norway, Spain, Sweden, and the USA.
7. These periods mostly concern the 1960s, 1970s, and 1980s.
8. Initial undershooting could occur in transition economies because of their underdeveloped financial systems under the previous system of central planning. In such a case, credit-to-GDP ratios would be considerably lower than implied by economic fundamentals in countries with similar levels of development. The subsection "Estimation Results" in section II spells out the implications of an initial undershooting for the econometric estimations.
9. We recognize the limitations of the spread variable. Ideally, we would have liked to use a financial liberalization index for all estimations. However, this can be done only for a limited set of countries, as the indexes that are available only partially match our country and time coverage, and we do so in our sensitivity checks wherever possible (using the financial liberalization index constructed in Abiad and Mody (2005)).
10. Argentina, Brazil, Chile, India, Indonesia, Israel, Mexico, Peru, Philippines, South Africa, South Korea, Thailand. Although South Korea and Mexico are OECD countries, they can be viewed as catching-up emerging market economies for most of the period investigated in this chapter.
11. Austria, Australia, Belgium, Canada, Denmark, Finland, Greece, Ireland, the Netherlands, New Zealand, Norway, Portugal, Spain, and Sweden.
12. Germany, France, Italy, Japan, United Kingdom, and the United States.
13. The estimation results for the specifications including credit registries and house prices (not reported here) can be summarized as follows: While changes in credit registries produce the expected effect on private credit in OECD countries, the estimation results show the opposite happening in the transition economies. The estimation results for the specification including house prices are not particularly robust for the small and large OECD economies. For transition economies, even though the results are somewhat more encouraging, the estimated equations seem to be rather fragile too. The inclusion of house prices yields robust results only if large price increases have taken place on the property markets.
14. Note that the analogy with the literature on equilibrium exchange rates in transition economies ends here, given that it is possible to establish robust relationships between the real exchange rate and its most important fundamentals, such as productivity (see e.g., Égert, Halpern, and MacDonald, 2006).

Bibliography

Arcalean, C., O. Calvo-Gonzalez, C. Móré, A. van Rixtel, A. Winkler, and T. Zumer, 2005, "The Causes and Nature of the Rapid Growth of Bank Credit in the Central, Eastern, and South-Eastern European Countries," paper presented at the Conference on Rapid Growth of Banking Sector Credit to the Private Sector, Sinaia, Romania, October 7–8, 2005.

Abiad, A. and A. Mody, 2005, "Financial Reform: What Shakes It? What Shapes It?" *American Economic Review*, vol. 95(1), pp. 66–88.

Backé, P. and T. Zumer, 2005, "Developments in Credit to the Private Sector in Central and Eastern European EU Member States: Emerging from Financial Repression – A Comparative Overview," Oesterreichische Nationalbank, *Focus on European Economic Integration*, vol. 10(2), pp. 83–109.

Boissay, F., O. Calvo-Gonzalez and T. Koźluk, 2006, "Is Lending in Central and Eastern Europe Developing too Fast?" Paper presented at the conference "Finance and Consumption Workshop: Consumption and Credit in Countries with Developing Credit Markets", Florence, June 16–17.

Brzoza-Brzezina, M., 2005, "Lending Booms in Europe's Periphery: South-Western Lessons for Central-Eastern Members," ECB Working Paper No. 543.

Calza, A., C. Gartner and J. Sousa, 2001, "Modeling the Demand for Loans to the Private Sector in the Euro Area," ECB Working Paper No. 55.

Calza, A., M. Manrique and J. Sousa, 2003, "Aggregate Loans to the Euro Area Private Sector," ECB Working Paper No. 202.

Cottarelli, C., G. Dell'Ariccia and I. Vladkova-Hollar, 2005, "Early Birds, Late Risers and Sleeping Beauties: Bank Credit Growth to the Private Sector in Central and Eastern Europe and in the Balkans," *Journal of Banking and Finance*, 29, pp. 83–104.

Égert, B., P. Backé and T. Zumer, 2006, "Private Credit in Central and Eastern Europe: New (Over)Shooting Stars?" *Corporate Economic Studies*, forthcoming.

Égert, B., L. Halpern and R. MacDonald, 2006, "Equilibrium Exchange Rates in Transition Economies: Taking Stock of the Issues," *Journal of Economic Survey*, vol. 20(2), pp. 257–324.

European Central Bank, International Relations Committee, Task Force Enlargement, 2006, "Macroeconomic and Financial Stability Challenges for Accession and Candidate Countries," Occasional Paper No. 48.

Hilbers, P., İ. Ötker-Robe, C. Pazarbasioğlu, and G. Johnsen, 2005, "Assessing and Managing Rapid Credit Growth and the Role of Supervisory and Prudential Policies," IMF Working Paper 05/151 (International Monetary Fund).

Kiss, G., M. Nagy and B. Vonnák, 2006, "Credit Growth in Central and Eastern Europe: Trend, Cycle or Boom?" Paper presented at the conference "Finance and Consumption Workshop: Consumption and Credit in Countries with Developing Credit Markets," Florence, June 16–17.

Maeso-Fernandez, F., C. Osbat and B. Schnatz, 2005, "Pitfalls in Estimating Equilibrium Exchange Rates for Transition Economies," *Economic Systems*, vol. 29(2), pp. 130–43.

Pesaran, M.H., Y. Shin and R. Smith, 1999, "Pooled Mean Group Estimation of Dynamic Heterogeneous Panels," *Journal of the American Statistical Association*, 94, pp. 621–34.

5
Analysis of and Policy Responses to Rapid Credit Growth

Paul Hilbers, İnci Ötker-Robe, and Ceyla Pazarbasioğlu[1]

This chapter discusses the phenomenon of rapid growth in bank credit to the private sector, which in recent years has been particularly prominent in many Central, Eastern, and South-eastern European countries (CEE). In the past few years, real growth rates of credit to the private sector in these countries were often in the range of 30–50 percent per year, albeit beginning from a low base. This trend has generally been viewed as a normal and positive consequence of the growing degree of deepening and restructuring of the financial system. It fits in with the transition process from centrally planned to market-based economies and has often been supported by the prospect of European Union (EU) accession. At the same time, there are growing concerns about the implications for macroeconomic and financial stability, in particular where rapid credit growth has coincided with a weakening current account and vulnerabilities in the financial systems.

The chapter reviews the trends in bank lending to the private sector in CEE countries; discusses possible implications for macroeconomic and financial stability; provides a framework for analyzing rapid credit growth; and discusses the pros and cons of a number of instruments—both macroeconomic and prudential in nature—that could be used to counter and reduce these risks. The chapter concentrates, in particular, on the supervisory and prudential implications of rapid credit growth, their relationship to macroeconomic policy responses as part of an overall policy mix, and on how prudential and supervisory policies could be used in strengthening the resistance of the financial system to adverse consequences of rapid credit expansion.

I. Analysis of rapid credit growth

This section provides a brief overview of the factors underlying a rapid expansion of bank credit to the private sector and its possible implications for macroeconomic and financial stability. It establishes a framework to analyze a credit growth process by providing a menu of indicators of vulnerability that could be examined and monitored to assess the possible risks.

The literature generally identifies three main drivers of rapid credit growth:[2]

- During the development phase of an economy, credit grows more quickly than output (Favara, 2003; King and Levine, 1993; and Levine, 1997). This "financial deepening" argument is supported by empirical work suggesting that a more developed financial sector helps promote economic growth.
- Credit expands more rapidly than output at the beginning of a cyclical upturn due to firms' investment and working capital needs, according to the conventional accelerator models (see, e.g., Fuerst, 1995; and IMF, 2004a).
- Excessive credit expansions may result from inappropriate responses by financial market participants to changes in risks over time. According to the "financial accelerator models,"[3] over-optimism about future earnings boosts asset valuations, leads to a surge in capital inflows, increases collateral values (increases the relative price of nontradables), and allows firms and households to borrow and spend. If performance falls below these expectations, asset prices and collateral values decline. This reverses the financial accelerator, increasing the indebtedness of the borrowers, decreasing both their capacity to service their loans and their access to new loans. These factors play an important role in extending a boom and increasing the severity and length of a downturn.

In practice, it has proven difficult to distinguish among these three factors driving credit growth and to determine a "neutral" level or rate of growth for credit.[4] When assessing rapid credit growth, it is therefore necessary to carefully consider the potential implications for macroeconomic stability. A rapid expansion of bank credit to the private sector may affect macroeconomic stability by stimulating aggregate demand compared to potential output and creating overheating pressures, as bank lending fuels consumption and/or import demand, with subsequent effects on the external current account balance, inflation, and currency stability. A continued deterioration in the current account deficit may in turn trigger a cutback of external credit lines and foreign liquidity and thus lead to a deterioration in the condition of the banking system, potentially bringing about a full-fledged financial and economic crisis.

Rapid credit growth also has implications for financial stability. There is a large body of literature that links credit overexpansion and banking crises.[5] Kaminsky, Lizondo, and Reinhart (1997), in a survey of the literature, report that five out of seven studies find credit growth to be an important determinant of banking and/or currency crises. Goldstein (2001) provides evidence on the link between a credit boom and the likelihood of twin crises (banking and currency crises) as a result of capital flows. Similarly, IMF (2004a) concludes that credit booms pose significant risks for emerging market countries, as they are generally followed by sharp economic downturns and financial crises. In a broad sample of boom episodes over 40 years, lending booms are often found to be associated with a domestic investment boom, an increase in domestic interest rates, a worsening of the current account, a decline in international reserves, a real appreciation of the exchange rate, and a fall in growth of potential output. About three-fourths of credit booms are shown to be associated with a banking crisis and almost seven-eighths with a currency crisis.

The macroeconomic and microeconomic implications of rapid credit growth are interrelated. On the one hand, in a situation of continued macroeconomic deterioration (inflation and/or external imbalances), financial stability will likely also deteriorate. For example, macroeconomic imbalances impact the stability of the financial system as the repayment capacity of borrowers may worsen with the slowdown in economic activity and the movements in interest and exchange rates associated with the macroeconomic instability. On the other hand, concerns about financial sector health may lead to macroeconomic instability, as markets react to such concerns by adjusting investment portfolios, including holdings of currencies.

These risks are generally underestimated during booms due to measurement difficulties both in forecasting overall economic activity and its link with credit losses, and in assessing how correlations of credit losses across borrowers and lenders change over time. This under-estimation of risk may result in over optimism about the degree of structural change that may be fueling the credit growth and a socially suboptimal reaction to risk by market participants. Incentive structures that reward short-term performance further contribute to credit growth even if risk is measured properly. Certain accounting and regulatory frameworks may also encourage or lead to lending decisions that may contribute to financial system vulnerability. Moreover, rapid credit growth may result from certain micro- or bank-level factors that create incentives for banks to take on excessive risk, including moral hazard arising from implicit or explicit government guarantees or inappropriate governance structures.

The banks' ability and resources to monitor and manage risks are also stretched by the increased volume and speed of credit expansion. Substandard loan-granting procedures and unrealistic projections of future repayment capacity of borrowers may distort the growth and allocation of credit. Such exuberance would allow large exposures to develop, which could magnify real sector costs in the event of a shock. Governance issues related to insider or connected lending may be aggravated under these circumstances. Apart from developments in the amount of credit, the nominal increase in the number of loans is a relevant factor, also in terms of the ability of the banks and supervisors to assess credit quality. Banks need to have sufficiently trained credit assessors to determine which credit requests should be honored. However, even if the assessors are skilled, the sheer number of credit applications in an upswing may be so large that the existing staff cannot handle them. In that case, requests that should not be considered may be accepted. Credit bureaus may help to alleviate the problems but may not always be established or functioning properly.

The inter-relationship between macroeconomic and financial sector stability suggests that in determining the risk profile of and policy responses to rapid credit growth, a more detailed analysis of its characteristics is important. When it has been determined that bank credit to the private sector is growing at a rapid pace, there will be a need to collect and monitor more detailed information about this process. It is no less important to have a detailed breakdown of aggregated credit data according to the borrower and to have information on the purpose, use, and specific features of the loans. All these aspects are relevant to assess the risks and to determine the best policy response, since the magnitude of losses in the event of an adverse shock will depend on the degree of maturity mismatches, the sectoral composition and concentration of credit, the relative importance of collateral-based lending, the currency exposure of banks and borrowers, the availability of hedging instruments, and the extent to which banks and borrowers use these instruments to cover their exchange and interest rate risks. Box 5.1 further discusses the various ways to assess the nature of credit growth.

Box 5.1. Analysis of the Nature of Credit Growth

In determining the risk profile of, and policy response to, rapid credit growth, a more detailed analysis of its characteristics is important. Such analysis would include a detailed breakdown of aggregated credit data according to the borrower, the purpose and use of the loans, their sectoral composition and concentration, the currency denomination, and the maturity and other conditions of the loans.

In terms of the breakdown of credit data, a key element is the **type of borrower**, in particular, the distinction between households and the corporate sector. **Households** tend to borrow for purchases of durable consumer goods (e.g., cars) or for real and financial assets. Consumer loans are generally relatively small; there may be substantial risks involved on a case-by-case basis, but the overall risk is diversified due to the large number of the debtors. There have been few cases where rapid expansion of consumer loans has led to systemic problems. Household borrowing for purchases of assets has a very different risk profile. Mortgage lending and lending for equity purchases involve higher amounts—in the case of real estate lending, often a multiple of the household's income—but are generally supported by collateral. Key variables in assessing the risks are loan-to-value ratios, the effectiveness of collateral legislation, and the financial health of the borrowers. With regard to the latter, it is important to closely monitor the overall balance sheet of the household sector and in particular the degree of indebtedness in relation to disposable income. But these indicators may not be sufficient to detect asset price bubbles, and therefore a careful analysis of the relationship between asset prices and, in particular, rates of return on assets may be needed in cases where bubbles are suspected.

Within the **corporate sector**, it is useful to conduct a **sectoral breakdown of the borrower**. A distinction between various sectors (agriculture, manufacturing, construction, services, etc.) is useful to determine the likely character and purpose of the loan—e.g., whether the credit provided will be used for productive economic activities. A careful analysis of sectoral balance sheets and financial results plays a key role in assessing corporate sector credit risk. In addition, it may be relevant to include the ownership of the industry sector as a relevant factor, distinguishing between credit to state-owned enterprises, domestic private enterprises, and foreign-owned industries. Risks involved in corporate lending are often increased by weaknesses in transparency, accounting, contract enforcement, etc.

▶

> The **currency denomination** is another key factor in assessing rapid credit growth. Borrowing in foreign currency is generally driven by lower foreign interest rates compared to domestic rates. The main risk is related to the exchange rate. Banks are generally constrained by limits on open foreign exchange positions, which forces them to fund these credits in foreign currency as well, e.g., through foreign currency deposits, credit lines with the banks' foreign owner, or other borrowing from abroad. But their customers may not be hedged, hence it will be important to assess whether the borrower has foreign exchange income that can be used to repay the debt and/or whether hedging instruments are available and used. Even if the banks are fully covered against currency risk, the exchange rate risk for their clients may translate into sizable credit risk for the banking sector.
>
> Other relevant factors include **maturity, interest rate conditions, and collateral**. When maturities are short, repayment problems surface at an early stage, unless evergreening practices are widespread. In general, maturities in emerging markets will tend to be shorter than in fully developed markets, due to a lack of available long-term funding. For the same reason, interest rate fixation periods will tend to be shorter. If expectations of interest rate declines prevail, unexpected interest rate increases may result in debt servicing problems for debtors. Collateral—if it can readily be accessed and used to cover defaults—reduces the risk for financial institutions and creates an incentive for debtors to meet their obligations. It may, however, also exacerbate cycles in real estate lending.
>
> More generally, rapid credit growth and **asset market developments** are often closely related, which makes close monitoring of the latter essential in assessing credit growth. Booms and busts in asset prices (in particular for real estate) can contribute to unbalanced credit growth, resulting in financial sector distress and macroeconomic imbalances. There are various channels through which, for instance, real estate cycles and bubbles can develop. Optimistic investors may drive up prices since the supply reaction is slow due to lags in construction. Cycles can be exacerbated by the use of real estate as collateral for financing, and by financial institutions' capital gains on their own holdings of real estate, which increase their ability to lend. In addition, financial sector liberalization can extend the sector's ability to finance real estate transactions in an environment of potentially insufficient credit assessment skills. A lack of good quality and timely data on real estate developments, however, can complicate assessment of the risks associated with real estate market developments.*
>
> * On the specifics of real estate markets and related measurement issues, see Hilbers, Lei, and Zacho (2001), Sundararajan et al (2002), and BIS (2005).

More generally, assessing risks associated with rapid credit growth involves a comprehensive analysis of the stability of the macro economy and the financial system (Table 5.1). Such an assessment includes a variety of relevant macroeconomic and financial sector data (financial soundness indicators and structural financial sector data), as well as information from stress tests and scenario analyses to determine the sensitivity of the financial system to macroeconomic and market shocks (IMF, 2005a). Real estate developments require special attention. Market-based information complements the financial sector data by conveying market perceptions of the health and stability of the financial system. Information on the quality of the institutional and regulatory frameworks, mostly through assessments of compliance with international financial sector standards, helps in interpreting and assessing developments in prudential variables.

Table 5.1. Components of the Analysis of Rapid Credit Growth

Key data	Provide information on
Macroeconomic data (inflation, current account, etc.)	Pending macro risks or vulnerabilities
Financial Soundness Indicators (capital, asset quality, earnings, liquidity)	Soundness and resilience of the financial sector
Sectoral balance sheets (corporate sector, households)	Corporate sector debt and earnings Household sector indebtedness
Stress tests of the financial system (sensitivity of balance sheets to shocks)	Vulnerability to changes in key macro and market variables
Real estate market developments (price developments, rents, vacancy levels, etc.)	Unbalanced developments and potential bubbles in the market
Other market data (stock prices and yields, credit ratings)	The markets' expectations about future risks and returns
Structural financial sector information (size, ownership, concentration, legal framework)	Risks of contagion and owner's obligation and ability to control such risks
Qualitative information (compliance with financial sector standards)	Quality of data (transparency) and of supervision and regulation of markets and institutions

II. Recent developments in credit growth in the CEE countries

Given the framework suggested in Section I, this section assesses the challenges associated with the continuing rapid credit growth to the private sector in some of the CEE countries. It provides an overview of the recent developments regarding credit growth in these countries and assesses the risks associated with the ongoing credit booms.

Many of the CEE countries have been experiencing a rapid expansion of bank credit to the private sector in recent years. This process, which was already apparent at the beginning of this decade, has only become stronger since.[6] During 2000–04, credit increased by about 17 percent a year on average in real terms across the region (Table 5.2).[7] In 2004, credit to the private sector increased by about 30–45 percent in real terms in six of the countries in the region. As a result, the ratio of private sector credit to GDP has also been increasing significantly in these countries, albeit from a low base.[8]

This expansion in credit occurred at relatively low levels of financial intermediation, providing support for the "catching-up" hypothesis. With the exceptions of Estonia and Hungary, the countries with the fastest growth in private sector credit had credit-to-GDP ratios below the group average of 22 percent (compared to the average for the EU-15 countries of over 100 percent of GDP) (Figures 5.1 and 5.2). In contrast, in those countries where the real credit growth has been relatively low, the credit-to-GDP ratio has been generally above the group average (except in Macedonia and Romania).[9]

Table 5.2 Growth of Private Sector Credit in Selected CEE Countries

	2000	2001	2002	2003	2004	Average (2000–04)	Cumulative Change (1999–2004)[a]
Real Growth of Credit							
Countries with real credit growth higher than the sample average (16.8%)							
Ukraine	32.9	25.5	48.8	55.7	21.6	36.9	...
Latvia	28.1	33.5	34.3	41.2	41.1	35.6	...
Albania	33.9	38.9	25.6	23.0	28.5	30.0	...
Bulgaria	6.0	23.0	34.6	45.4	40.5	29.9	...
Lithuania	–7.0	4.9	30.1	60.8	38.1	25.4	...
Russia	27.2	25.1	12.3	27.4	34.0	25.2	–
Belarus	6.8	8.3	16.2	43.8	36.1	22.2	...
Estonia	7.4	12.1	15.6	30.9	39.5	21.1	...
Moldova	6.1	26.2	31.0	29.8	7.9	20.2	...
Hungary	30.3	8.0	13.6	27.4	11.2	18.1	...
Countries with real credit growth lower than the sample average (16.8%)							
Croatia	1.4	17.2	27.5	13.1	11.3	14.1	...
Romania	–10.2	16.5	14.2	23.7	18.9	12.6	...
Slovenia	7.6	9.6	5.2	9.3	16.0	9.5	...
Bosnia	0.7	–26.7	27.3	19.5	14.9	7.1	...
Macedonia	–9.0	–7.3	2.3	14.0	24.0	4.8	...
Poland	5.8	1.9	2.4	5.8	0.1	3.2	...
Czech Republic	–9.7	–15.0	–22.8	8.5	10.3	–5.8	...
Slovak Republic	–7.1	–26.2	10.9	–19.8	–0.4	–8.5	...
Sample Average	8.4	9.7	18.3	25.5	21.9	16.8	
Credit-to-GDP Ratio							
Countries with real credit growth higher than the sample average (16.8%)							
Ukraine	11.1	12.9	17.5	24.3	24.9	18.1	16.4
Latvia	17.2	21.3	26.5	34.6	45.4	29.0	30.9
Albania	4.6	5.9	7.3	8.4	9.9	7.2	6.0
Bulgaria	12.6	14.9	19.6	27.4	36.7	22.2	24.6
Lithuania	11.4	11.4	14.0	20.4	25.6	16.6	12.8
Russia	13.3	16.5	17.7	21.0	24.5	18.6	11.5
Belarus	8.8	8.2	8.9	11.9	13.9	10.3	4.7
Estonia	23.9	25.2	26.9	33.1	43.3	30.5	19.0
Moldova	12.6	14.7	17.1	20.5	21.3	17.3	9.5
Hungary	32.4	33.7	35.8	43.0	46.0	38.2	19.9
Countries with real credit growth lower than the sample average (16.8%)							
Croatia	37.2	42.2	50.7	54.2	57.5	48.4	20.3
Romania	7.2	7.7	8.3	9.5	10.0	8.5	2.0
Slovenia	36.4	38.4	38.9	41.5	46.3	40.3	12.4
Bosnia	43.3	30.1	36.3	41.4	45.2	39.2	–0.6
Macedonia	17.8	17.6	17.7	19.5	23.6	19.3	2.8
Poland	27.3	27.9	28.4	29.0	27.7	28.1	1.7
Czech Republic	47.9	39.6	29.8	30.7	32.2	36.0	–21.1
Slovak Republic	51.3	37.6	39.6	31.6	30.6	38.1	–23.9
Sample Average	23.1	22.5	24.5	27.9	31.4	25.9	8.3

Source: International Financial Statistics, World Economic Outlook, and IMF staff calculations.

[a] Percentage point difference between figures for 2004 and 1999.

Analysis of and Policy Responses to Rapid Credit Growth   91

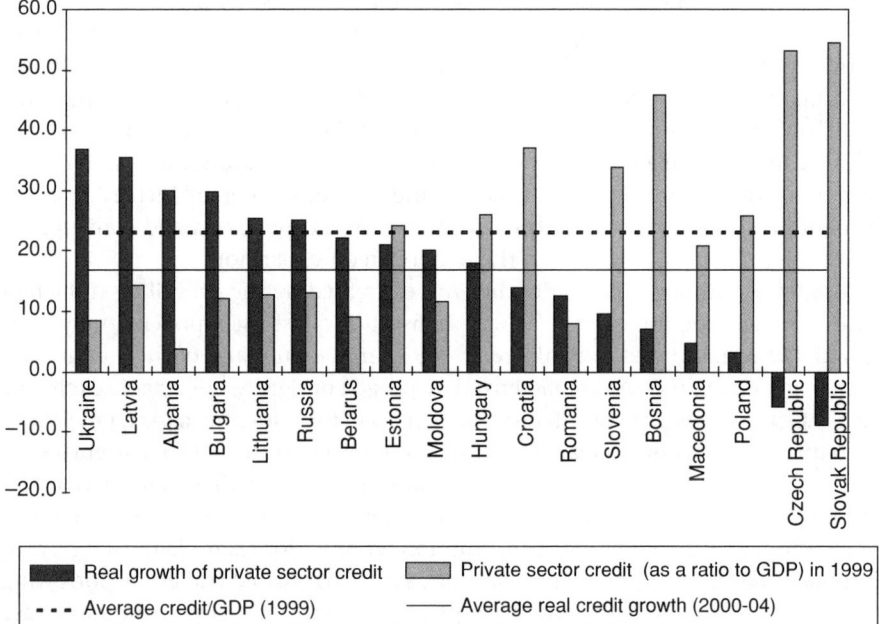

Figure 5.1 CEE Countries: Real Credit Growth over 2000–04 vs. Credit to GDP in 1999 (in percent)

Source: International Financial Statistics; World Economic Outlook; and authors' calculations.

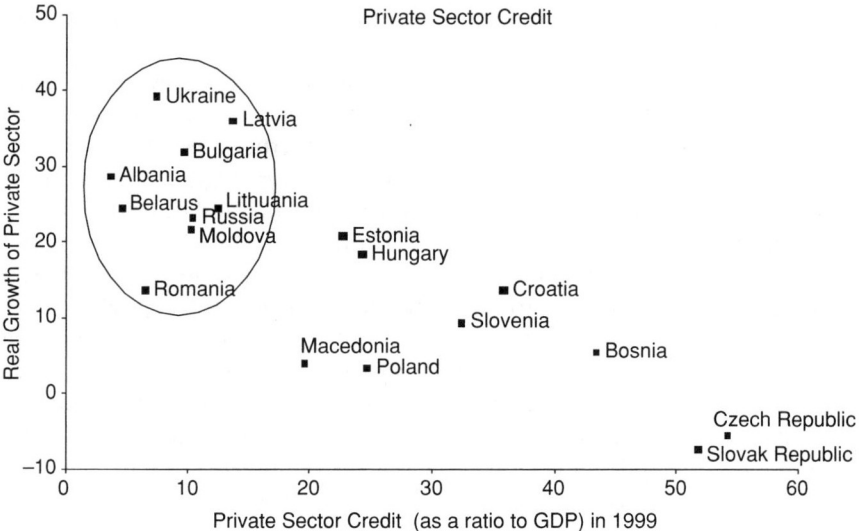

Figure 5.2 Is the Rapid Credit Growth in the CEE Countries part of a Catching-up Process? (Credit to GDP Ratio in 1999 vs. Average Real Credit Growth over 2000–2004)

Source: International Financial Statistics; World Economic Outlook; and authors' calculations.

Rapid credit growth in the region has been supported by a general easing of monetary conditions and improved economic prospects. Consistent with the "over-optimism" argument discussed in Section I, favorable economic conditions, combined with macroeconomic stability and progress in financial sector reforms, have led to an upward revision in income expectations of the private sector. Consequently, strong consumption and investment in a number of these economies has emerged (e.g., Bulgaria, Estonia, Latvia, Lithuania, and Romania), thereby increasing credit demand. For some of the countries in the region, EU prospects and convergence expectations also played a role in the pace of credit expansion.

Also, in a number of countries, incentives created by the prevailing monetary and exchange rate policy mix, as well as fiscal or quasi-fiscal policies, may have stimulated certain types of bank credit. For example, in many of these countries, exchange rate regimes are characterized by pegged or tightly predictable exchange rates.[10] Combined with wide interest rate margins in the domestic market, predictable exchange rates may have created incentives for borrowing in foreign currencies (by banks and/or borrowers) and led to capital inflows that helped stimulate credit expansion. On the fiscal side, open-ended government interest rate subsidies may have stimulated the growth of consumption lending, for example in Hungary; in Estonia, interest rate deductibility of mortgage loans created real estate borrowing incentives; and in Belarus, government guarantees to support bank loans rose sharply in 2004.

In most CEE countries, the banking sector is the most important channel of funds to support increased demand for credit, with capital and equity markets still small and relatively underdeveloped. The share of bank assets in total assets of the financial system (including also insurance companies, pension funds, securities firms, investment funds, and leasing companies) is in fact very high, generally exceeding 75 percent.

Privatization of the banking sector and increased participation by foreign banks has also contributed to rapid credit growth in a number of countries. Banks have now been largely privatized in most of the countries with the fastest growth of credit. The share of foreign ownership of banks has also been very high, with the share of assets ranging from around 60–70 percent (Latvia, Romania, and Hungary) to about 80–90 percent (Bulgaria, Croatia, Estonia, and Lithuania). The expectation of high profits has been an important motive for foreign investors to move into the CEE banking market. While exposure to these countries in foreign banks' overall portfolio remains quite small, the steady expansion of the foreign (mainly European) banking groups in the CEE region has had a positive impact on the profitability of the banks. In some of the CEE countries, foreign banks have engaged in aggressive lending to the private sector to raise their share in these profitable markets; this has resulted in downward pressure on lending rates and has helped stimulate credit demand.[11]

The lending boom episodes seem to be associated with a deterioration in external imbalances and high dependence on foreign funding, suggesting increased vulnerabilities in most of the CEE countries. In particular, the rapid expansion of bank credit seems to be coupled with high current account deficits in most of the CEE countries, where the deficits are partly caused by increasing import demand stimulated by credit growth. The low savings rates in most of the countries imply that they are highly dependent on the willingness of foreign investors to fund these deficits. An additional source of vulnerability is that the strength of the credit growth has been sustained by an increase in net foreign liabilities of the banks in many of the countries (Figure 5.3). In fact, for most of the countries in the sample, loans are also being financed increasingly with liabilities other than deposits (loans are almost 50 percent higher than deposits). Banks have been borrowing funds from abroad (including from parent banks) and/or have been drawing down their foreign assets.

It is not clear how well the comparatively new and untested credit risk systems of many banks in CEE markets are able to cope with a (potential) lending boom. In most CEE countries, the prudential indicators do not seem to indicate a sizable increase in financial vulnerabilities in the banking system: banks are highly capitalized and profitable, either with relatively low or declining nonperforming loans (see Appendix 5.1). However, nonperforming loans are usually a lagging indicator of banking system problems, and there have been some indications of a decline in capital adequacy and some increase in credit risks in many of the countries in the group. Potential risks from greater lending to the household/consumer sector are increasing, and in some cases, rapid credit growth started to put some strain on bank supervisors' and banks' capacity to assess risks. In many CEE countries, banks' potential exposure to indirect foreign exchange risks may have increased: foreign-currency-denominated lending represents a substantial proportion of total loans in many CEE countries, while information on customers' foreign currency positions and the extent of their hedging has remained limited. There are also indications of potential liquidity risks in some of the countries, as suggested by the maturity of loans.

A decline in margins may also create strains on the banking system. In the medium term, a lower country risk premium (due to convergence) and increased competition should lead to a convergence of margins towards the EU average (a decline in margins has already been observed in some countries for corporate lending but not for consumer and mortgage lending). Competition should increase as countries become EU member states, because entry barriers will decline under the European single passport regime under which any bank registered in an EU member state can establish branches in another EU country without a local banking license (Breyer, 2004). Potential EU accession has led to increased competition among banks (for example, in Bulgaria and Romania; Duenwald, Gueorguiev, and Schaechter, 2005), as these banks have a strong incentive to increase market shares ahead of full membership. The compression of margins in EU accession countries may come to a point where the margins may become too narrow to compensate for the risks in lending.

III. Policy responses to rapid credit growth in the CEE countries

The experiences of many countries that have undergone financial crises suggest that misperceptions of the evolution of risks over time and inadequate or inappropriate

94 *General Framework*

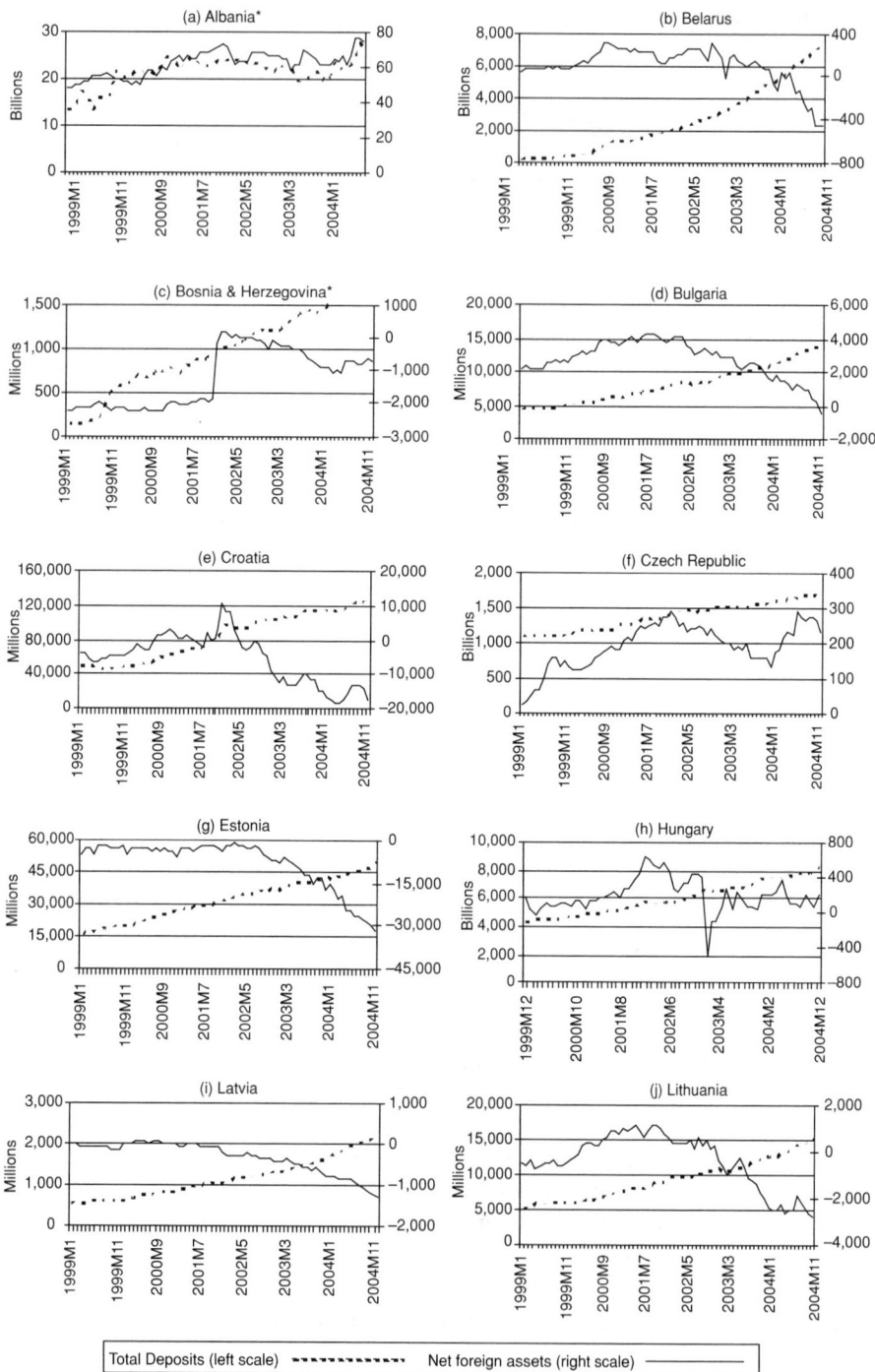

Analysis of and Policy Responses to Rapid Credit Growth 95

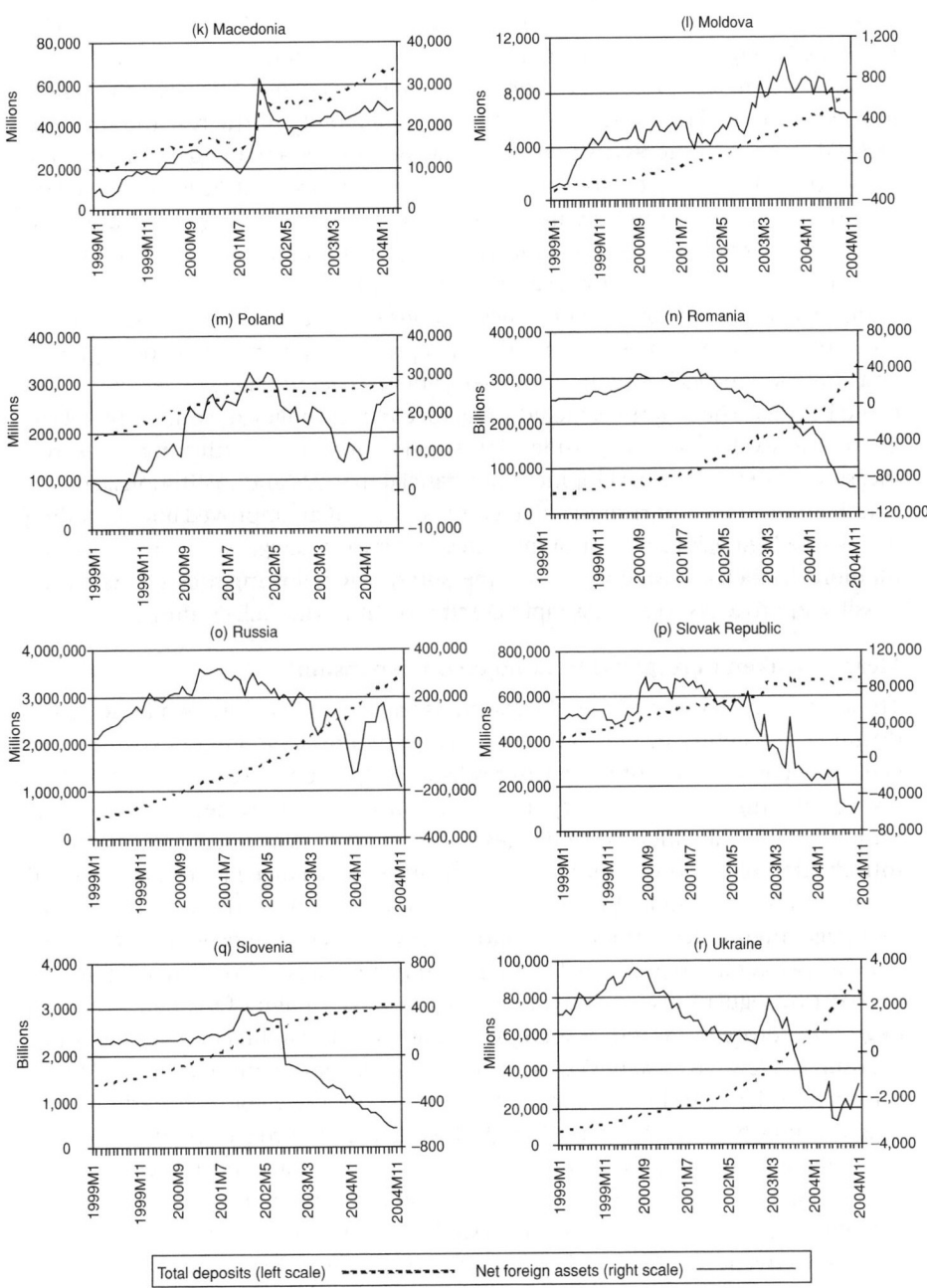

Figure 5.3 CEE Countries: Funding of the Credit Growth (in national currencies)

Source: International Financial Statistics.

* Only demand deposits

policy responses can have costly consequences. As Borio, Furfine, and Lowe (2001) note, there may be a case for a public policy response if it is likely that rapid credit growth is due to inappropriate responses by financial system participants to changes in risk over time. Policies designed to limit vulnerability of the real and financial sector may hence be necessary to prevent macroeconomic and financial instabilities. While there is a need to avoid "crying wolf" when observed developments may be a simple result of catching-up, it would be unduly optimistic to assume that rapid credit growth to a new, and much higher, "equilibrium" level of credit would automatically be without any risks or need for action.[12]

In considering the appropriate policy response, it would be useful to start from a menu of possible measures and consider their pros and cons, negative consequences and limitations in dealing with the problem, and the circumstances under which they could be used. These options include: macroeconomic policy measures (monetary, fiscal, and exchange rate); prudential, supervisory, and monitoring measures; measures fostering the development of financial markets and institutions; administrative/more direct measures; and measures aimed at an improved understanding of risk (see Figure 5.4 for a list of measures under each category and Appendix 5.2 for more detailed assessments of these measures). The following subsections discuss possible approaches to address rapid credit growth in the CEE countries.

Measures taken in response to rapid credit expansion

The authorities in many of the CEE countries have taken measures while facing the dilemma of whether or not to interfere with ongoing rapid credit expansion. In general, a combination of the measures listed in Figure 5.4 was used, rather than a single instrument.[13] Monetary measures that have been widely used took the form of interest rate increases, changes in the parameters of reserve requirements, introduction of liquidity requirements, and greater exchange rate flexibility. Fiscal policy has been tightened in some countries or fiscal incentives in the form of mortgage interest deductibility and mortgage subsidies have been reduced (Table 5.3). Many have taken prudential and supervisory measures in the form of tightening the existing regulations, or close monitoring and assessment of loan underwriting or granting procedures, and/or surveys of banks' direct or indirect foreign exchange exposures. A few have established a credit registry system, credit bureaus, and wider information bases to improve market discipline. In a few countries, administrative measures have been taken through direct credit controls or marginal reserve requirements on foreign borrowing. Moral suasion has also been used on a few occasions. The measures have been, in general, motivated by concerns about emerging signs of external problems as well as the stability of financial systems.

The effectiveness of these policy responses has varied.[14] In a few of the cases, the measures seem to have been effective in reducing credit growth or certain targeted types of lending (e.g., Bosnia, Croatia, and Poland). As discussed in Section II, in many of the countries concerned, credit growth remains strong, with few signs of abating, and in a few others, despite some indications of a slowdown, the rate of growth remains high. Persistent strength of foreign-currency-denominated lending

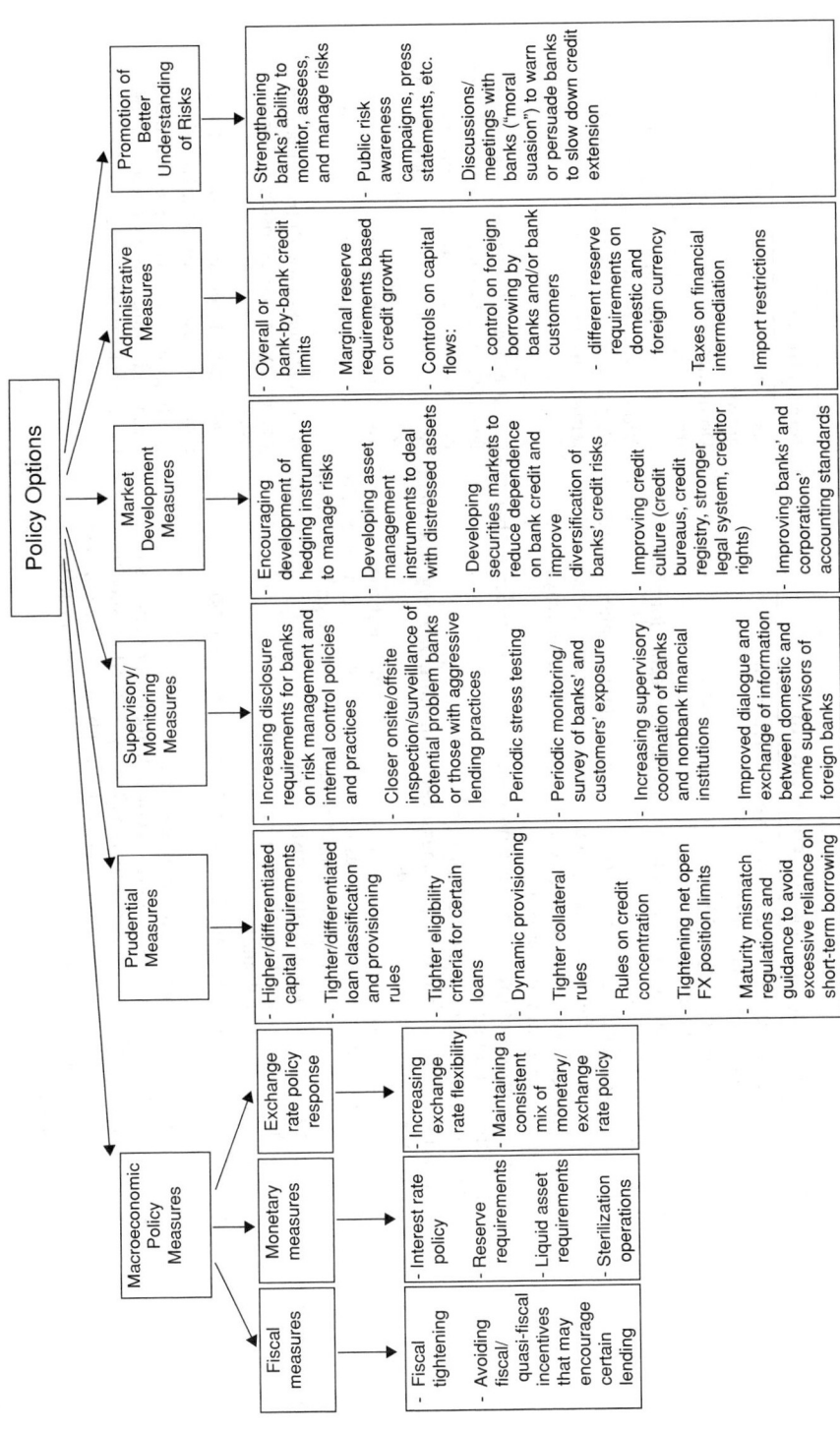

Figure 5.4 Menu of Policy Options in Responding to Rapid Credit Growth

Table 5.3 Policy Responses to Rapid Credit Growth in Selected CEE Countries

Country	Measures with potential impact on credit growth	Impact to date
Bosnia (2003)	• Monetary measures (tightening—reserve requirements) • Prudential measures (tightening)	Seems to be effective in easing the credit growth.
Bulgaria (mid-2003 to Feb 2005)	• Monetary measures (tightening—reserve requirements) • Fiscal measures (tightening) • Prudential and supervisory measures (tightening of regulations and supervision) • Market development measures (credit registry, wider information base) • Administrative/other measures (credit controls—marginal reserve requirement for banks exceeding a certain level of credit growth) • Other measures (moral suasion)	Domestic credit growth remains strong (though with some stabilization in the growth rate during January–February 2005). Banks remain vulnerable to indirect FX risk. Effect of the recent credit controls remains to be seen.
Croatia (2000–05)	• Monetary measures (moderate tightening—interest rates, foreign exchange liquidity requirements) • Fiscal measures (some consolidation) • Prudential, supervisory, reporting measures (tightening of many prudential regulations and supervision practices) • Administrative measures (direct credit controls—requirement to purchase CNB securities at below-market rates when loan portfolio exceeds a certain level of credit growth; marginal reserve requirement on foreign borrowing)	Credit growth slowed significantly since late 2003, but impact on aggregate demand limited: credit controls circumvented via switch to nonbank and foreign borrowing, with potential adverse impact on soundness of the financial system. Banks remain vulnerable to indirect FX risk.
Estonia (2004)	• Fiscal measures (reducing existing distortions) • Supervisory measures (close monitoring of developments) • Other measures (moral suasion)	Domestic credit growth has remained strong; continued exposure to potential FX risk.
Latvia (2004)	• Monetary measures (tightening—interest rates, reserve requirements)	Credit growth remained strong. Banks remain exposed to indirect FX risk.
Moldova (2004)	• Monetary measures (reserve requirement rules) • Prudential/supervisory measures (the central bank required banks to have separate risk management units to identify and reduce specific risk exposures; assessment of credit risk is made on a borrower-by-borrower basis, and banks share information on problem borrowers on an informal basis, in the absence of a credit registry)	Credit growth slowed somewhat but still remained strong. Banks remain vulnerable to indirect FX risk.

Country	Measures with potential impact on credit growth	Impact to date
Poland (2001)	• Monetary measures (narrowing domestic interest rate differentials, increasing flexibility of the exchange rate) • Prudential, supervisory, reporting measures (adjusting capital requirements for FX risk, periodic surveys/close monitoring of banks' FX exposure, risk management, and internal controls) • Other measures (moral suasion)	Rapid growth of FX-denominated loans slowed significantly and households became more careful about unhedged borrowing. Total credit growth subdued since 2000.
Romania (2003–05)	• Monetary and fiscal measures (tightening) • Prudential and supervisory measures (tightening—especially tightening of loan classification, eligibility criteria, reserve requirement on banks' FX denominated liabilities; provisioning/classification taking into account borrowers' FX risk) • Market development measures (credit bureau, widening information base) • Administrative measures (postponement of FX liberalization measures; limits on banks' FX credit exposure to unhedged borrowers)	Credit growth slowed somewhat from August 2003 to April 2004. Growth in leu credit nearly came to a halt, partially offset by a continuing expansion of FX-denominated credit.
Serbia (2004–05)	• Monetary measures (tightening—reserve requirements) • Prudential and supervisory measures (tightening): tightening conditions for consumer loans, broadening the reservable base to include banks' foreign borrowing, increase in capital adequacy ratio; plan to introduce a regulation on monitoring/ managing credit risk from borrowers' exposure to FX risk	Monetary measures did not have a tangible impact, under high euroization. Given the fairly recent implementation of the prudential measures, effectiveness viewed only on a preliminary basis. Consumer lending and credit to non-government slowed down after the tightening measures. Banks vulnerable to indirect FX risk.
Ukraine (2004)	• Monetary measures (limited tightening) • Prudential and supervisory measures (tightening—rules on capital adequacy, quality of bank capital, loan classification, provisioning for FX-denominated loans, related party lending, risk management etc.)	The rate of growth of bank credit slowed down significantly, though still at a relatively high rate. Banks remain vulnerable to indirect FX risk.

Source: See Appendix 5.3 for details on these measures, their timing, and the impact to date.

Note: FX = foreign exchange.

in several countries has continued to keep banks vulnerable to potential (direct or indirect) foreign exchange rate risk.

Efforts to slow down credit have in general been frustrated by a number of factors. The measures had little impact on banks' sources of funds for lending, given their ability to obtain funding through rapid deposit growth and borrowing from abroad (in particular through parent banks). The process was further supported by high profitability of domestic lending, often in the wake of EU accession. Some measures were rendered ineffective by the circumvention of regulations by borrowers (through the ability to borrow directly from abroad or from less supervised/regulated nonbank financial institutions) and by banks (e.g., through window-dressing activities). Integration of domestic markets in the euro environment brought a general easing of monetary conditions that likely stimulated credit demand. The high degree of euroization of the economies, a lack of effective instruments of monetary control, and weaknesses in the monetary transmission mechanism have limited the capacity to effectively use monetary measures.

Further policy options

The key question is what further options are left for the CEE countries in dealing with rapid credit growth. In contemplating the appropriate policy response, policymakers need to focus on the nature of the associated risks, in particular macroeconomic and financial risks. Given that these risks are interrelated, particularly when the growth of credit is very rapid, with one possibly leading to, or reinforcing, the other, the policymakers need to focus on both the macroeconomic and financial implications of the credit growth. This in turn calls for a package of measures that contains both macroeconomic and prudential tools. Adding to the need for a broader policy package is the fact that macroeconomic and prudential measures affect each other. Prudential measures to preserve credit quality may limit certain types of lending (e.g., FX-denominated lending) that have negative implications for macroeconomic and financial sector health. Similarly, an appropriate macroeconomic policy mix may limit incentives for excessive borrowing and FX lending, hence limiting the scope for deterioration in credit quality. An appropriate combination of macro and prudential measures could then be used to achieve a desired effect on the quality as well as quantity of bank loans.

The choice of particular measures will be affected by an assessment of the nature of risks implied by the nature of the credit growth. The starting point for such an assessment should be an analysis of the credit growth on the basis of detailed underlying data, including the speed of the growth, breakdown of aggregate credit in terms of the borrower (households, corporate sector, exporters, etc.), the sectoral concentration and allocation of the loan (mortgages, durable consumer goods, investments), the currency composition of loans (foreign exchange versus local currency), the maturity of the loans, availability of adequate collateral, and the funding sources of the credit.

The appropriate policy response will also be affected by the prevailing macroeconomic policy framework. In this context, managing rapid credit growth has been a significant challenge for some of the CEE countries, since the set of available measures is limited due to the specific characteristics of these countries:

- Tightening monetary conditions in response to credit growth may help dampen over-heating pressures by impacting aggregate demand, helping to reduce demand for bank loans, or reducing banks' liquidity base that helps finance the credit growth. However, in many of the CEE countries, the ability to use monetary policy has been constrained by the underlying monetary policy regime. Most have pegged or tightly managed exchange rate regimes that limit the use of market-based monetary tools in coping with credit growth. In several countries, effective monetary instruments are not fully developed, constraining the ability to manage liquidity in the system. The relatively high level of euroization (and other structural factors) weakens monetary transmission mechanisms, making it difficult to influence lending and retail rates through changes in policy rates. An open capital account limits the ability to use monetary policy effectively in a number of countries, especially those with pegged exchange rate regimes, because interest rate tightening may attract capital inflows that can further boost money and credit. Monetary policy can be used effectively if efforts are put into developing market-based monetary instruments and eliminating obstacles to monetary transmission.
- Where there is a significant increase in foreign-currency-denominated lending and a tendency to borrow from abroad, increasing the flexibility of the exchange rate and maintaining a consistent monetary-exchange rate policy mix would help limit direct and indirect foreign currency exposures by reducing perceptions of low exchange rate risk.[15] For example, increasing the flexibility of the exchange rate and allowing domestic interest rate differentials to narrow in combination with supervisory tools helped reduce foreign currency denominated bank lending in Poland during the early 2000s. However, where the monetary framework is characterized by formal peg commitments (e.g., in a currency board or under ERM II in a run-up to joining the euro area), room for such policy maneuvering is limited; the best policy in this case would be to keep domestic interest rates consistent with the exchange rate commitment to limit incentives for excessive lending and borrowing and to address any structural factors that may be contributing to high interest margins (e.g., high risk premium, high transaction or operational costs, tax distortions, etc.).
- Tightening fiscal policy further and maintaining a prudent stance would help counter the expansionary pressures that may be brought by credit expansion in some of the CEE countries. In a number of others, however, where the fiscal position is already tight, the authorities may find limited room to resort to fiscal measures. Where there are fiscal incentives that may be encouraging certain types of borrowing or lending (such as interest deductibility for mortgage loans, explicit subsidies or government guarantees for housing loans, interest rate subsidies, etc.), addressing these distortions would be an appropriate policy response.

The key question is whether prudential and supervisory measures could substitute for monetary and fiscal policies in coping with rapid credit growth when the latter policies are not a viable option. When rapid credit growth (e.g., with excessive concentration in certain types of loans such as mortgages or in foreign-currency-denominated lending to unhedged borrowers) is generated by inconsistencies or distortions in macroeconomic/structural policies, the first best policy response should be to eliminate those distortions or policy inconsistencies. The use of prudential and supervisory measures should be genuinely justified on prudential grounds (e.g., when there are financial stability risks and/or there is room to bring the country's prudential and supervisory framework in line with best practices). Otherwise, excessive tightening of the prudential and supervisory framework would inflict an undue burden on the supervisory authorities and banks, and result in efforts to circumvent such measures by switching to activities offshore or to institutions less subject to scrutiny. Supervisory measures would also lose credibility if they are used for purposes other than prudential concerns (see also Josefsson in this volume).

Given the inter-linkages between macroeconomic and financial concerns discussed above, however, prudential measures could be used to support macro policies to limit a deterioration in the quality of banks' assets, including when rapid credit growth is encouraged by incentives created by the macroeconomic policy mix.[16] Since prudential measures, also in these cases, are aimed at ensuring sound lending practices and maintaining the resilience of the financial system to adverse shocks, they should not automatically be relaxed when the threat to macroeconomic stability subsides.

The scope for tightening further prudential/supervisory policies varies across the CEE countries. In many of the countries, the frameworks have been strengthened significantly and there may be limited room for further tightening. In others, efforts have been ongoing to strengthen the prudential and supervisory systems, although there is still room for improvement, particularly where there are weaknesses in banks' and supervisors' ability to assess and monitor the risks. Strengthening the capability of banks and supervisors to better assess and manage indirect exposure to foreign exchange risks is an area that needs to be addressed, specifically considering the large proportion of lending in foreign currencies and limited information on the degree of hedging by borrowers in many of the CEE countries. The type of prudential/supervisory measures that could be tightened, or introduced, would in general be guided by the nature of the risks associated with the nature of the credit growth. Table 5.4 provides a mapping from various features of the credit growth to different types of risks and Table 5.5 lists prudential tools that could be used to deal with each type of risk.

Prudential policies should hence be considered as part of a comprehensive package of measures to deal with rapid credit growth. While supervisory and prudential measures alone may not lead to a significant reduction in credit growth, they contribute to both limiting its growth and preserving banks' asset quality, if implemented along with appropriate macro policies. In fact, there are limits to what prudential policies can do in the absence of prudent fiscal policies, or if monetary/fiscal regimes persistently create perverse incentives that encourage credit growth.

Table 5.4 Key Risks Associated with Credit Growth

Aspects of Credit Growth	Type of Risk Associated
Speed of credit growth	• Credit risk (from inappropriate loan assessments, strain on ability to monitor and assess risks) • Macro risks
Main providers of credit (e.g., foreign versus domestic banks)	• Credit risk (from aggressive lending strategies) • Macro risks
Main borrowers (e.g., households, corporate sector)	• Credit risk (sensitivity of repayment capacity of corporate loans to the economic situation, that of consumer loans to collateral values) • Macro risks (likely impact of loans on the current account) • Market risks (sensitivity to economic activity and price changes)
Sectoral loan concentration/composition of credit (e.g., mortgages, durable consumer goods, investments)	• Credit risk (e.g., stemming from concentration, collateral values for mortgages) • Macro risks (e.g., impact on the current account in the case of consumer/investment loans) • Market risks (e.g., sensitivity to real estate prices)
Currency composition of loans	• Direct (through banks' net open positions) and indirect (via borrowers') exposure to foreign exchange risk
Maturity of loans	• Maturity/liquidity risks (longer-term loans financed through shorter-term borrowing by banks)
Sources of credit	• Foreign exchange risk (loans funded by bank borrowing) • Maturity risks (when liabilities short-term, assets longer term) • Macro risks (from exposure to market sentiment)

However, when applied as part of a comprehensive package of measures, such policies can serve to address distortions in bank lending associated with, for example, risky sectoral loan concentrations, unhedged currency borrowing, imprudent funding behavior by banks, or real estate bubbles. Appropriate disclosure requirements for banks of their risk management and internal control policies and practices can also strengthen market discipline, limiting imprudent lending practices.

Effective implementation of the prudential/supervisory measures requires an adequate enforcement capacity, cross-border supervisory cooperation, and effective coordination between supervisors of nonbank financial institutions. Bank and nonbank supervisory coordination is essential to avoid loopholes (e.g., a shift away from bank lending toward direct foreign borrowing or borrowing from less well-regulated and less supervised nonbank financial institutions, which perform quasi-bank activities and fall outside the regulatory framework).[17] Similarly, creating an effective dialogue with home supervisors of foreign banks (e.g., through memoranda of understanding bilaterally or multilaterally or regular exchange of information among supervisors) will be critical in many of the CEE

Table 5.5 Prudential and Supervisory Measures to Manage Key Risks of Rapid Credit Growth

Type of risk	Specific Measures
Credit risk	• Higher and/or differentiated capital requirements or application of risk weights based on loan type, maturity, and currency composition of credit; • Raising general provisions, incorporating various elements of risks (e.g., in foreign currency loans, offshore, derivatives, or other off-balance sheet activities) in loan classification and provisioning requirements (e.g., for banks with rapidly growing portfolios); or dynamic provisioning; • Tightening eligibility requirements for certain types of loans including through limits on loan-to-value ratios for certain loans (e.g., for mortgages or FX loans); • Tighter (or appropriate) collateral requirements (e.g., specifying assets eligible for collateral, marked-to-market asset valuation); • Rules on credit concentration (limits against large exposures to a single borrower or a group of related borrowers and against connected lending; and limits against credit concentration in particular industries, sectors, or regions); • Use of periodic stress tests of banks' balance sheets against interest rate, exchange rate, and asset price changes (by banks themselves as well as supervisory authorities); • More intensive surveillance and onsite/offsite inspection of potential problem banks; • Improved reporting/disclosure rules for banks' and their borrowers' balance sheets and banks' risk management, and internal control policies and practices; and • Periodic and close monitoring of banks' foreign-currency-denominated (or indexed) loans to domestic customers, which do not have adequate sources of foreign exchange or are otherwise unable to hedge the risks involved, including through requirements to conduct periodic surveys of banks' and their borrowers' foreign exchange exposures.
Direct/ indirect foreign exchange risks	• Tightening of net open position limits for banks to limit direct foreign exchange risks; • Imposing differentiated capital requirements or risk weights based on the currency composition of credit to limit indirect exposure to foreign exchange risks; • Incorporating unhedged foreign exchange exposure in the criteria for loan classification and provisioning rules; • Tightening eligibility requirements for foreign exchange loans, including by limiting such loans to borrowers with foreign exchange income or adequate hedging, to limit indirect exposure to foreign exchange risks; • Periodic stress testing of banks' balance sheets with respect to exchange rate changes (by banks themselves as well as supervisory authorities); • More intensive surveillance and onsite/offsite inspection of banks with a large share of foreign exchange lending in their overall portfolios, including to ensure that banks have appropriate internal procedures for risk measurement, assessment, and management; and • Adequate monitoring of banks' direct and indirect exposure to foreign exchange risks through improved reporting/disclosure rules for banks and their borrowers' open positions in foreign currency or through a requirement to conduct periodic surveys of banks' and their borrowers' foreign exchange exposures (by banks themselves and/or by supervisory authorities).

Type of risk	Specific Measures

Liquidity/ maturity risks	• Imposing differentiated capital requirements or risk weights based on the maturity composition of credit;
	• Maturity mismatch regulations (active management of maturity mismatches between bank assets and liabilities, with limits established against such gaps and limits on various instrument exposures incurred by the bank);
	• Use of periodic stress tests of banks' balance sheets under alternative scenarios for interest rate changes (by banks themselves as well as supervisory authorities);
	• Enhanced monitoring and reporting requirements on:
	  – the maturity structure of interest-sensitive assets and liabilities, broken down into several daily, weekly, monthly, and quarterly maturity "buckets";
	  – the maturity structure for each currency in which the bank has a substantive position; and
	  – the types of interest-bearing securities and their maturity breakdown;
	  – banks' liquid assets, expected future cash flows and liquidity gaps for specified future periods, and details of liquidity management; and
	• Guidance to banks to avoid over reliance on short-term interbank borrowing and encouraging access to diversified funding bases in terms of sources of funds and the maturity breakdown of the liabilities, taking into account differences in volatility and reliability of domestic and external sources of liquidity.

Source: Johnston and Ötker-Robe (1999), Delgado et al (2000).

countries where rapid credit growth is dominated by a group of foreign branches regulated/supervised by the home authorities of parent banks (see also Bednarski and Starnowski, van Goor, and Zartl, in this volume). This is an issue of particular concern since incentives to expand market share are strong and the relatively small share of the domestic banking market in foreign banks' portfolios makes their endeavor seem to be a low-risk strategy.

Beside these policies, it is important to promote a good understanding of risks, to help limit excessive risk-taking and potential deterioration in asset quality. Press conferences, financial stability reports, seminars/workshops, public awareness campaigns, and consultative meetings with banks could be used to warn borrowers and banks against risks of over-borrowing/lending (some CEE countries have already been using these tools recently, e.g., Bulgaria and Romania). Improving the credit culture, including through credit bureaus and registries, would also help enhance market discipline, while providing a valuable information base to monitor bank loan quality. Together with a better understanding of risks, availability and use of hedging instruments would help protect banks and their customers against risks associated with rapid credit growth. This would also help deepen financial markets and enhance capacity to cope with credit growth. Developing securities markets could reduce dependence on bank credit and provide banks with alternative assets to diversify risks.[18]

Finally, the authorities could consider administrative measures, but only as a last resort, if there are significant macroeconomic and prudential risks that justify curbing the amount or growth of credit, and market participants fail to respond appropriately to changing risks over time and to other instruments.[19] The decision regarding the use and timing of such measures would likely depend on the policymakers' perceptions and judgments on the vulnerability threshold of the perceived imbalances and risks. Although the probability of an adverse shock that may cause these risks to materialize may be small, the expected loss given a possible shock could be large and may prompt policymakers to take preemptive measures (in some cases drastic ones) in order to reduce the vulnerability of the system as a whole.

Since administrative measures are distortionary and entail costs (e.g., Alexander, Baliño, and Enoch, 1995), including for the stability of the financial system that the measures are intended to protect, a careful cost-benefit analysis is needed before such measures are adopted. Such analysis should take the potential risks into consideration and periodically assess the risk of circumvention through balance sheet manipulation by banks and borrowers switching to less supervised and monitored nonbank financial institutions for funding (direct credit controls were used in Croatia, for example, where such effects have been observed, and were subsequently removed). Imposing administrative measures may also send a negative signal of a lack of commitment to market-based policies, and the authorities should have sufficient confidence that the costs of resorting to such measures would not exceed their expected benefits. Since these measures likely have unintended and undesirable side effects, they should be temporary and designed to include some market-based features, to the extent possible, to avoid introducing long-lasting distortions and inefficiencies.[20]

IV. Concluding remarks

Rapid credit growth in CEE countries reflects, at least in part, a process of catching up from low levels of financial intermediation to the market economy levels that prevail elsewhere in Europe. However, even when moving to a new equilibrium, the process of credit expansion may become unbalanced and, if not well managed, many involve significant risks. To reap the benefits of credit growth while countering these risks, authorities should have in place policies designed to limit the vulnerability of the real and financial sectors. A key element in assessing the vulnerabilities is to accelerate the building of comprehensive information systems that would enable regular monitoring and analysis of credit developments, including, in particular, a breakdown of aggregate credit data in terms of the borrowers, the purpose of the loans, their currency denomination, and other relevant conditions of the loans.

Such a breakdown is necessary for an assessment of the possible macroeconomic as well as financial stability risks involved in rapid credit growth. Without such a comprehensive assessment, it will generally not be possible to determine whether and when an observed rate of credit growth is a cause for concern, given the difficulties in assessing the appropriate rate of growth in countries experiencing substantial structural change. The assessment should also include macroeconomic, macroprudential, and structural factors, including the existence of economic imbalances, the soundness of the financial system, the effectiveness of supervision and regulation, the structure of the financial system, and the financial health of borrowers.

Once the need for a policy response has been established, the authorities may be able to draw on a variety of instruments at their disposal, including both macro and prudential measures. Authorities will need to continue strengthening the prudential and supervisory framework to ensure sound lending policies, and stability and resilience of their financial systems to adverse consequences of credit growth. Administrative measures should be considered only as a very last resort, if at all, and, given their unintended and undesirable side effects, should be imposed temporarily and designed carefully to avoid long-lasting distortions and inefficiencies. Both supervisory and administrative measures will only be effective when supported by a sound macroeconomic policy mix focused on maintaining macro stability, effective cross-border supervisory coordination, improved awareness of risk by the private sector, and efforts to further develop financial markets and instruments that improve monetary transmission mechanisms and facilitate hedging against various risks associated with credit growth.

Notes

1. International Monetary Fund (IMF). This chapter is a shortened and updated version Hilbers, Ötker-Robe, Pazarbasioğlu, and Johnsen (2005).
2. See, for example, IMF (2004a) and Gourinchas, Valdes, and Landerretche (2001).
3. See Bernanke, Gertler, and Gilchrist (1999), Borio, Furfine, and Lowe (2001), Kindleberger (1996), Kiyotaki and Moore (1997), and Minsky (1992).
4. Cottarelli, Dell'Ariccia, and Vladkova-Hollar (2003) estimate an equation for bank credit to the private sector as a function of public debt, per capita income, inflation, financial liberalization, and the legal system, and they use this equation to determine an equilibrium level with which actual levels can be compared in a selected group of CEE countries. They note, however, that the ongoing transition process in these countries complicates the determination of a "normal" growth rate, and that the focus on aggregate credit developments may lead to an underestimation of risks.
5. See Demirgüç-Kunt and Detragiache (1997), Drees and Pazarbasioğlu (1995), Goldfajn and Valdes (1997), Goldstein (2001), Gourinchas, Valdes, and Landerretche (2001), and Kaminsky, Lizondo, and Reinhart (1997).
6. In all the countries that had been identified as "early risers" in Cottarelli, Dell'Ariccia, and Vladkova-Hollar (2003), with the exception of Croatia and Poland, credit continues to rise at a rapid pace (Bulgaria, Estonia, Hungary, Latvia, and Slovenia). Some of the "sleeping beauties" (Albania and Romania, and lately the Czech and Slovak Republics) seem to have woken up, while in "late risers" (Bosnia and Herzegovina, Serbia and Montenegro, and Lithuania), real growth of credit has continued to rise. Data for 2005 indicate a continued sharp increase in credit to the private sector in CEE countries.
7. This chapter focuses on bank credit to the private sector, excluding bank credit extended to the public sector and credit extended by nonbank financial institutions for which data availability is limited. Breakdown of credit between foreign and domestic currency denominated components is also not available across all countries in the sample, and hence no attempt has been made to treat them separately in the analyses. Moreover, the credit growth figures used in the analyses were all obtained from International Financial Statistics for purposes of comparability and may differ from those of the national authorities.
8. See also Cottarelli, Dell'Ariccia, and Vladkova-Hollar (2003), Schadler et al (2004), and IMF (2004b).

108 General Framework

9. Note that the negative growth of credit in the Czech and Slovak Republics in the early 2000s reflects, in part, the efforts to clean up the bad loans in the system.
10. These regimes include: currency board arrangements in Bosnia, Bulgaria, Estonia, and Lithuania; horizontal exchange rate bands in Hungary and Slovenia; fixed exchange rates in Latvia, Macedonia, and Ukraine; crawling bands in Belarus and Romania; and tightly managed floats in Croatia, Moldova, Russia, and Serbia.
11. It is reported that about 70 percent of the CEE banking market is currently controlled by western European banking groups (Breyer, 2004).
12. Computing the "equilibrium" level of credit in these economies is not a trivial exercise, given the structural changes that affected these economies and the short time span of economic and financial sector data. Estimation of the equilibrium level for Central and Eastern Europe and Balkan countries in Cottarelli, Dell'Ariccia, and Vladkova-Hollar (2003) suggests that in most of these countries the current credit-to-GDP ratios are still relatively low compared to the estimated equilibrium levels. Also, Schadler et al (2004) include estimates of equilibrium credit-to-GDP levels and dynamic paths toward them.
13. A combination of instruments has also been used by a number of other European countries that entered the EU earlier and have experienced rapid credit growth during the period of their accession to the euro area (see Appendix 5.3 for details): Greece, for example, imposed direct credit controls, Portugal tightened the prudential and supervisory framework accompanied by a rise in interest rates, while Spain introduced dynamic provisioning. Outside the EU, Iceland has used a combination of moral suasion and monetary measures, including a liquid asset requirement.
14. Note, however, that many of the CEE countries are still in the midst of a period of rapid credit growth, and some of the measures taken may not yet have demonstrated their full impact. Any assessment of the effectiveness of measures is, therefore, necessarily preliminary. There is also the problem of the counterfactual, that is, the difficulty of determining what could have happened in the absence of these measures.
15. Highly predictable exchange rates, combined with large domestic interest differentials that are inconsistent with the exchange rate regime, may create perceptions of low exchange rate risks and encourage foreign borrowing. On-lending in domestic currency creates exposure to direct foreign exchange risks, while on-lending in foreign currency to unhedged borrowers or those with no foreign exchange income raises exposure to indirect foreign exchange risks.
16. Macro policies generally limit credit by raising the price—the interest rate—while prudential policies tend to make such lending decisions more expensive by raising the associated costs for the banks in the form of capital requirements, provisioning rules, and liquidity requirements, or limit the quantity through, for example, loan-to-value ratios.
17. IMF (2004c) points to greater challenges for financial sector regulators brought by growing integration across various types of financial institutions and by cross-border financial integration, and the need, in turn, for closer and more systematic monitoring of cross-border contagion risks and of opportunities for regulatory arbitrage.
18. A supportive borrowing strategy by the government would be essential to ensure that banks would have the incentive to invest in such instruments.
19. These measures are steps back in the process of financial liberalization that took place worldwide during the past decades; see Abiad and Mody (2003).
20. Reserve requirements on excessive credit growth or on banks' foreign borrowing (including from parent banks) may discourage lending by making it more costly for the bank rather than limiting credit outright.

Bibliography

Abiad, A. and A. Mody, 2003, "Financial Reform: What Shakes It? What Shapes It?" IMF Working Paper 03/70 (International Monetary Fund).

Alexander, W.E., T.J.T. Baliño and C. Enoch, 1995, *The Adoption of Indirect Instruments of Monetary Policy*, IMF Occasional Paper 126 (International Monetary Fund).

Ariyoshi, A., K. Habermeier, B. Laurens, İ. Ötker-Robe, J. Canales-Kriljenko, and A. Kirilenko, 2000, *Capital Controls: Country Experiences with their Use and Liberalization*, IMF Occasional Paper 190 (International Monetary Fund).

Bank for International Settlements, 2005, "Real Estate Indicators and Financial Stability," *BIS Papers* No. 21 (Basle: Bank for International Settlements).

Bednarski, P. and D. Starnowski, 2005, "Home and Host Supervisors' Relations—a Host Supervisor's Perspective," paper presented at the Conference on Rapid Growth of Banking Sector Credit to the Private Sector, Sinaia, Romania, October 7–8, 2005.

Bernanke, B., M. Gertler and S. Gilchrist, 1999, "The Financial Accelerator in Quantitative Business Cycle Framework," *Handbook of Macroeconomics*, vol. 1C, pp. 1341–93, Handbooks in Economics, Vol. 15 (New York: Elsevier Science, North-Holland).

Borio, C., C. Furfine and P. Lowe, 2001, "Procyclicality of Financial Systems and Financial Stability," *BIS Papers* No. 1 (Basle: Bank for International Settlements).

Breyer, P., 2004, "Central and Eastern Europe—the Growth Market for Austrian Banks," *Monetary Policy and the Economy*, Issue Q3/04 (Vienna: Austrian National Bank).

Cottarelli, C., G. Dell'Ariccia and I. Vladkova-Hollar, 2003, "Early Birds, Late Risers, and Sleeping Beauties: Bank Credit Growth to the Private Sector in Central and Eastern Europe and the Balkans," IMF Working Paper 03/213 (International Monetary Fund).

Delgado F., D. Kanda, G. Mitchell Casselle, and R. Morales, 2000, "Banks' Domestic Lending in Foreign Currency," *Operational Paper*, 00/4 (International Monetary Fund).

Demirgüç-Kunt, A. and E. Detragiache, 1997, "The Determinants of Banking Crises—Evidence from Developing and Developed Countries," IMF Working Paper 97/106 (International Monetary Fund).

Drees, B. and C. Pazarbasioğlu, 1995, "The Nordic Banking Crisis: Pitfalls in Financial Liberalization?" IMF Working Paper 95/61 (International Monetary Fund).

Duenwald, Christoph, N. Gueorguiev and A. Schaechter, 2005, "Too Much of a Good Thing? Credit Booms in Transition Economies: The Cases of Bulgaria, Romania, and Ukraine," IMF Working Paper 05/128 (International Monetary Fund).

Favara, G., 2003, "An Empirical Reassessment of the Relationship Between Finance and Growth," IMF Working Paper 03/123 (International Monetary Fund).

Fernandez de Lis, S., J.M. Pages and J. Saurina, 2000, "Credit Growth, Problem Loans, and Credit Risk Provisioning in Spain," paper prepared for the Bank for International Settlements Autumn Central Bank Economists' Meeting (Madrid: Banco de Espana).

Fuerst, T., 1995, "Monetary and Financial Interactions in the Business Cycle," *Journal of Money, Credit and Banking*, vol. 27 (November), pp. 1321–38.

Goldfajn, I. and R. Valdes, 1997, "Capital Flows and the Twin Crises: Role of Liquidity," IMF Working Paper 97/87 (International Monetary Fund).

Goldstein, M., 2001, "Global Financial Stability: Recent Achievements and Ongoing Challenges," Global Public Policies and Programs: Implications for Financing and Evaluation, Proceedings from a World Bank Workshop (World Bank), pp. 157–61.

Gourinchas, P., R. Valdes and O. Landerretche, 2001, "Lending Booms: Latin America and the World," *Economia*, vol. 1, pp. 47–99.

Hilbers, P., Q. Lei and L. Zacho, 2001, "Real Estate Market Development and Financial Sector Soundness," IMF Working Paper 01/129 (International Monetary Fund).

Hilbers, P., İ. Ötker-Robe, C. Pazarbasioğlu, and G. Johnsen, 2005, "Assessing and Managing Rapid Credit Growth and the Role of Supervisory and Prudential Policies," IMF Working Paper 05/151 (International Monetary Fund).

International Monetary Fund, 2004a, "Are Credit Booms in Emerging Markets a Concern?" *World Economic Outlook*, April 2004, Chapter IV.

———, 2004b, "Bulgaria's Credit Boom: Characteristics, Consequences and Policy Options," *Selected Issues and Statistical Appendix*, Country Report 04/177.

——, 2004c, *Financial Sector Regulation: Issues and Gaps* (August) (International Monetary Fund).

——, 2005a, *Financial Sector Assessment Program—Review, Lessons and Issues Going Forward* (International Monetary Fund).

——, 2005b, "Credit Boom in Ukraine: Risks for Banking Sector Stability," *Selected Issues and Statistical Appendix*, Country Report 05/20.

Johnston, B. and İ. Ötker-Robe, 1999, "A Modernized Approach to Managing the Risks in Cross-Border Capital Movements," IMF Policy Discussion Paper, 99/6 (International Monetary Fund).

Kaminsky, G., S. Lizondo and C. Reinhart, 1997, "Leading Indicators of Currency Crises," IMF Working Paper 97/79 (International Monetary Fund).

Kindleberger, C.P., 1996, "The Lender of Last Resort: Pushing the Doctrine Too Far?" *Monetary Economics in the 1990s: The Henry Thornton Lectures*, Numbers 9–17 (New York: St. Martin's Press), pp. 122–36.

King, R.G. and R. Levine, 1993, "Finance and Growth: Schumpeter May Be Right," *Quarterly Journal of Economics*, vol. 108(3), pp. 717–37.

Kiyotaki, N. and J. Moore, 1997, "Credit Cycles," *Journal of Political Economy*, vol. 105(2), pp. 211–48.

Kraft E. and L. Jankov, 2005, "Does Speed Kill? Lending Booms and Their Consequences in Croatia," *Journal of Banking and Finance*, 29, pp. 105–21.

Levine, R., 1997, "Financial Development and Economic Growth: Views and Agenda," *Journal of Economic Literature*, vol. 35(2), pp. 688–726.

Lukonga, I. and K. Nakamura, 2003, "Private Sector Credit Expansion in Selected Eastern European Countries: Developments, Risks, and Policy Issues," (International Monetary Fund), unpublished.

Mann, F. and I. Michael, 2002, "Dynamic Provisioning: Issues and Application," *Financial Stability Review*, Issue No. 13 (London: Bank of England).

Minsky, H.P., 1992, *Profit, Deficits and Instability* (London: Macmillan Academic and Professional), pp. 11–22.

Schadler, S., P. Drummond, L. Kuijs, Z. Murgasova, and R. van Elkan, 2004, *Adopting the Euro in Central Europe—Challenges of the Next Step in European Integration*, IMF Occasional Paper 234 (International Monetary Fund).

Sundararajan, V., C. Enoch, A. San Jose, P. Hilbers, R. Krueger, M. Moretti, and G. Slack, 2002, *Financial Soundness Indicators: Analytical Aspects and Country Practices*, IMF Occasional Paper 212 (International Monetary Fund).

Van Goor, L., 2005, "The Role of Cross Border Supervisory Coordination when Dealing with Rapid Credit Growth in Emerging Countries—the Case for Cooperating Supervisors," paper presented at the Conference on Rapid Growth of Banking Sector Credit to the Private Sector, Sinaia, Romania, October 7–8, 2005.

Watson, M., 2004, "Financial Stability in Converging Economies: Macro-prudential Challenges," unpublished.

Zartl, K., 2005, "Cross-Border Supervisory Cooperation," paper presented at the Conference on Rapid Growth of Banking Sector Credit to the Private Sector, Sinaia, Romania, October 7–8, 2005.

Appendix 5.1 The Nature of Credit Growth in the Group of Countries with Rapid Credit Expansion (as of March 2005)

	Speed of Credit Growth	Signs of Macroeconomic/ Financial Stress?	Main Providers of Credit	Sectoral Loan Composition	Loan Currency Composition	Maturity of Loans	Funding Sources of Credit
Belarus	Accelerating growth of credit, particularly fast since 2003 (>40% in real terms at low levels of financial deepening (9% in 2000–04).	Strong GDP growth with high but somewhat falling inflation and moderate current account deficit. Strong growth fueled by consumption boom driven in turn partly by strong credit growth; government guarantees to support bank loans rose sharply in 2004. Vulnerabilities in the banking sector (with exposure to various risks, low profitability, weaknesses in loan classification regulations/ practices, weak loan recovery and creditor rights' protection, difficult enforcement, limited ability to price risks given limits on lending rates).	Foreign participation is 21% of the assets of commercial banks as of mid-2004.	Many banks apparently have sectoral lending concentration (e.g., agriculture, industrial sector, etc.). Overall, largest share in loans belongs to industry (38%), and households (20%).	About half of bank loans to residents are denominated in foreign currency; indirect exposure to FX risk by unhedged borrowers. FX loans rose by 32% y/y in October 04. FX liabilities at about 40% of total liabilities.	On balance short-term (28% of assets and 8% of liabilities are long term), though with variations across banks; some state banks have interest rate and liquidity exposure. Liquid assets to short term liabilities at 58% in mid-2004, below prudential 70% minimum.	Financed mainly by a strong deposit base.
Bulgaria	Very strong growth since mid-2001 (32% in real terms in 2000–04) at a still relatively low level of financial deepening (20% over the same period—but second largest rise in loan to GDP since 1999).	No apparent sign of inflation, but a sharp deterioration in current account; strong import growth. Prudential indicators appear strong, though capital ratio has been falling, with some banks close to the minimum required; latest stress tests imply a rise in vulnerability of a large number of banks (maturity risks and indirect FX risk).	Banking sector dominates financial sector; credit growth mainly driven by foreign banks with asset market share of 80%. Foreign banks lending aggressively to raise market share.	Commercial loans (70% of total), consumer loans (20%), residential mortgage loans (5%), with fastest growth in the latter two (over 50% and 100%, respectively).	About 46% of total bank loans are FX denominated as of end-September 2004 (from 35% in 2000).	About 75% of total credit is extended at maturity>1 year with the share of banks' foreign 5 year loans rising in the last two years, suggesting rising liquidity risks.	Mainly the sharp rise in deposits (esp. FX deposits), and the share of banks' foreign liabilities (drawing down of foreign assets and borrowing from parent banks).

Appendix 5.1 continued

	Speed of Credit Growth	Signs of Macroeconomic/ Financial Stress?	Main Providers of Credit	Sectoral Loan Composition	Loan Currency Composition	Maturity of Loans	Funding Sources of Credit
Croatia	Following a sharp rise in credit from 2001–03, credit growth slowed down sharply; but has the third largest rise in loan/GDP since 1999.	No major sign of inflation, but sharp deterioration of the current account. Increase in net open positions since 2001 and exposure to indirect FX risks, with most borrowers unhedged; higher credit risk; fall in capital ratios since 2001 (but still high).	Asset market share of foreign banks at 90% at end-2003.	Household credit (49% of total and grew markedly); enterprise loans (40%) at end-2003; some rise in the former's share.	While the share has fallen since 2000, FX denominated lending still make up 75% of total loans.	n.a.	Growth of credit supported by a strong deposit base growth, foreign borrowing from abroad, and easier monetary policy.
Estonia	Bank credit has been rising persistently since 1999, over 30% in real terms since 2003, with a sharp rise in credit to GDP since 1999.	Strong GDP growth with low inflation, but a sharp deterioration in the current account deficit. Banks highly capitalized, profitable, low NPLs. But potential risks from rapid growth of household credit and indirect FX exposure.	About 90% of bank assets are foreign owned. These banks have been lending aggressively to gain market share, putting pressure on loan rates.	Household loans growing (28% of total in 2003); share of corporates falling (34% from over 50% in 1999); all sectors grew.	Share of FX denominated lending has been rising, close to 60% in 2003; extent of hedging unknown.	n.a.	Steady rise in bank deposits and a rapid rise in banks' net foreign liabilities (particularly since 2002).
Hungary	Rapid growth of credit during 2001–03, with some deceleration since 2004, but a rapid rise in credit-to-GDP ratio.	Steady economic growth with slowing inflation, but with a large current account deficit (8.9% of GDP). Banks highly capitalized, profitable, low NPLs. But potential risks from rapid growth of household credit and indirect FX exposure.	Banks mostly private (about 90%). About ²/₃ of bank assets are foreign owned.	Corporate sector loans have the largest share, but household credit (incl. mortgage loans) accounted for most of the credit expansion.	Share of FX credit remained around 30% of total credit; some reported reluctance by the corporate sector to hedge FX risks.	n.a.	Financed mainly by a steady deposit base, and some increase in net foreign liabilities of banks.

	Speed of Credit Growth	Signs of Macroeconomic/ Financial Stress?	Main Providers of Credit	Sectoral Loan Composition	Loan Currency Composition	Maturity of Loans	Funding Sources of Credit
Latvia	Persistent rise since 1999 (over 30% in real terms since 2001), also with the largest rise in credit-to-GDP (28 percentage points).	Strong economic growth with low inflation; current account deficit remains very high (9% in 2003), with short-term external debt rising. Banks highly capitalized, profitable, with low NPLs, small direct, potentially large indirect, FX exposure.	Financial sector dominated by banks (mostly private); foreign ownership at 70% of capital and asset share at 54%. Competition creates pressure on margins.	Credit to corporates (the largest share) rose sharply since 2000. Mortgage loans also rose from a low base, doubling its share.	More than 50% of the loans are FX denominated.	More than 80% of loans in long term, suggesting vulnerability to liquidity risks.	Steady rise in bank deposits (almost doubled to 27% of GDP) and rising net foreign liabilities (part. since mid-2001).
Lithuania	Persistently strong growth since 2001 (over 30% per annum from 2002, with some sign of easing during 2004); large rise in credit/GDP ratio.	Strong economic growth with very low inflation; current account deficit deteriorating (about 7% in 2003), with non-FDI component rising. Banking sector highly capitalized, profitable, falling NPLs, with small direct, but potentially significant indirect FX exposure.	Financial sector dominated by banks (fully private), with 89% of asset share at end-2003 and 90% of share capital.	Majority of loans to corporate sector (69% in 2001); but consumer loans (at 21% of loans) rose rapidly since 2001.	53% of loans FX-denominated but fell from 2000–01 levels; rising FX loans to corporate sector. Consumer loans mainly in domestic currency.	About 73% of loans in long term, suggesting vulnerability to liquidity risks.	Strong growth in bank deposits and increasing net foreign liabilities, with increasing credit lines from parent banks.
Moldova	Rose strongly from 2000; around 30% in real terms in 2002–03, also with some sign of deceleration in the rate during 2004.	Strong economic growth with relatively high inflation; current account deficit remains large (about 7% of GDP). Banking sector indicators broadly favorable, with some weaknesses in bank risk management capacities and potential for deterioration in the process of credit approval. A loan category introduced (loans under supervision), requiring 5% provision; loans in this category (35.3% of total loans) potentially signal future problems.	Foreign and state ownership low (3 and 1 out of 16 banks, respectively). Foreign banks make up about 38% of total assets in 2003.	Industrial/commercial loans (46%), real estate (6.6%), consumer loans (2.7%) (in 2003).	Stable around 42% of total loans in 2003. Banks' FX liabilities are 49% of total liabilities. Banks are not allowed to lend exporters, but can extend FX loans to importers without FX income.	Ratio of liquid to total assets low at 32%.	Banks use a large share of their foreign currency resources for lending, instead of holding foreign exchange deposits in correspondent accounts, being exposed to FX risks.

Appendix 5.1 continued

	Speed of Credit Growth	Signs of Macroeconomic/ Financial Stress?	Main Providers of Credit	Sectoral Loan Composition	Loan Currency Composition	Maturity of Loans	Funding Sources of Credit
Romania	Credit has been rising at a strong rate since 2001, at a rising but still low level of financial deepening (7.8% of GDP in 2000–04).	Strong economic growth with relatively high inflation. Current account deficit remains relatively high. Banking sector highly capitalized, profitable, some rise in NPLs. Direct FX exposure of banks limited, but potential indirect FX exposure, due to large FX denominated lending and unknown extent of hedging.	Financial sector dominated by banks. Asset market share of foreign banks 58%. Share of foreign ownership at 33% in mid-2003.	Consumer and mortgage loans rose rapidly; household loans at about 22% of total, and 70% of which is mortgage loans.	FX denominated loans at 75% in 2003; 30% of loans to households and 65% of loans to business sector are FX denominated.	About 50% of loans in long term—small liquidity mismatch.	Mainly by a steady growth in deposits, and some increase in net foreign currency liabilities.
Serbia	Private sector credit has been rising very rapidly since 2002, with 28% real growth in 2003 albeit from a low base (17% of GDP).	Moderate growth with relatively high inflation; deteriorating current account; rising imports believed to be fed by rapid credit growth. Signs that this is putting strain on bank risk management. Banks not FX-exposed directly, but likely exposed indirectly.	Most lending is by foreign banks that are well-capitalized, get long-term funding from headquarters but with Serbia making a small share of their portfolio.	Consumer loans rose by 93% in 2003 in real terms.	Almost all loans are denominated in or indexed to foreign currency.	n.a.	Rapid growth of foreign currency deposits, and a surge in foreign loans to banks in Serbia.
Slovenia	Credit has been rising at a moderate but steady pace since 2003, with a significant rise in financial deepening since 1999.	Moderate growth with some fall in inflation. No significant external problem. Banking sector relatively well-capitalized, profitable, stable NPLs. While banks argue that FX loans are mostly to exporters, degree of indirect FX exposure unknown.	The share of foreign ownership is low (about 35%) with ¾ of banks private.	Loans to both corporate and households sector grew rapidly, with about ⅔ of credit to the corporate sector.	About ⅘ of the expansion in credit to corporate sector was in foreign currency, financed by higher bank foreign borrowing.	About 61% of loans in long term, suggesting some vulnerability to liquidity risk.	Mainly by a steady growth in deposits, and some increase in net foreign currency liabilities.
Ukraine	Persistently strong growth (39% on average, with some recent deceleration); a sharp rise in credit-to-GDP to a still relatively low level—26%).	Strong growth with recently rising inflation; current account in surplus. Banking sector stronger in recent years but some vulnerabilities remain (high credit risk with high NPLs, direct/indirect FX exposure, some maturity risk, need to increase capital, connected lending).	Foreign ownership is quite low (about 13% of capital)	Majority of loans is to enterprises while consumer lending has also risen significantly in recent years.	Significant FX-denominated lending (about 38% in 2004), incl. to borrowers with no significant FX earnings and hedging.	Less-than-balanced lengthening of funding of FX loans compared with maturity of FX loans.	Mainly by steady growth of bank deposits (except recently); since late 2003 also by higher bank borrowing from abroad (with a sharp fall in banks' net foreign assets).

Appendix 5.2 Policy Options to Cope with Rapid Credit Growth

Measures	Impact	Limitations	Examples where they have been used	Appropriate situation to apply
I. Macroeconomic Measures				
• Fiscal measures: tightening fiscal policy; reducing distortions that may create incentives for borrowing or certain types of credit (e.g., interest rate deductibility of mortgage loans, explicit subsidies/guarantees for housing loans).	• Help reduce overheating pressures that may be associated with credit expansion. • Reduce structural distortions that bias economic incentives.	• Task of restructuring government spending or broadening tax bases may be difficult in the short run and may not be available as a quick measure to deal with emerging problems. • Limited room for maneuver if fiscal position is already fairly tight. • Potential political resistance given output costs that may be associated with significant tightening.	Bulgaria (further tightening of fiscal stance); Croatia, Romania; Estonia (limited mortgage interest deductibility); Netherlands (reduced tax relief on mortgage payments).	• When rapid credit expansion creates overheating pressures that may undermine macroeconomic/external stability; • Especially when ability to use monetary policy tools is limited or nonexistent.
• Monetary measures	Reduce liquidity in the banking system to contain/counter the expansionary impact of credit expansion.	• Face constraints depending on the type of the monetary regime (e.g., under currency board arrangements, currency unions, etc., there may be incentives to build unhedged foreign exchange positions which help finance credit growth, and monetary autonomy is limited at best).	See below	• To reduce overheating pressures that may undermine macroeconomic external stability; • When the underlying monetary regime does not limit/preclude use of monetary instruments.

Appendix 5.2 continued

Measures	Impact	Limitations	Examples where they have been used	Appropriate situation to apply
• Reserve requirements (RR) (changes in the level, eligible assets, and eligible liability base associated with the requirement).	• Help to induce demand for reserves and hence enhance predictability of reserve demand. • Increase in the requirement can be useful in one-off sterilization of excess liquidity or otherwise to accommodate structural changes in demand for reserves.	• High requirement is a tax on financial intermediation and a source of spread between lending and deposit rates, potentially reversing financial deepening. The adverse effect could be reduced, e.g., if the tax it imposes is neutralized through reserve remuneration at market rates, but at the expense of limited effectiveness on credit growth. • Could push financial intermediation offshore where there may be a more favorable regulatory environment. • Affect all types of credit (do not address distortions between different credit categories, unless different ratios imposed). • With an open capital account and ability to borrow from abroad, including by banks from their parent banks, they cannot be effective in reducing liquidity unless the base of the requirement is broadened to cover such liabilities. • Not convenient for short-term liquidity management as frequent changes can disrupt bank portfolio management. • There is a risk that the rise in the cost of capital through RR could encourage banks to focus their lending on high risk—high return projects rather than higher quality customers. • Discriminates against banks vis-à-vis nonbanks.	• Used in many countries but active variation for policy purposes declined in industrial countries. • Recently used in Bosnia, Bulgaria, Croatia, Latvia, Moldova, and Romania in dealing with rapid credit growth.	• Could be effective temporarily when reserve requirements are the most effective monetary instrument to affect liquidity and when designed appropriately in a way to minimize loopholes for circumvention.

Measures	Impact	Limitations	Examples where they have been used	Appropriate situation to apply
• Liquid asset requirements/ (LARs)/statutory liquidity ratios (introduction or tightening).	• Could provide "sand in the wheels" against rapid lending, provided they are carefully designed: by forcing banks to hold funds in liquid assets, help reduce total potential loans, if effective.	• Adverse impact on financial market development by creating a captive market for certain papers, distorting interest rate structure, hence affecting monetary transmission mechanism and stifling secondary trading. Hence inefficient and distortionary as a monetary policy tool and not a desirable instrument for liquidity control purposes. • Could reduce fiscal discipline, thereby losing effectiveness as means to control money. • Distort competition by constraining bank asset management. • By imposing a tax on financial intermediation, a high LAR may reverse the process of financial deepening, pushing financial intermediation offshore where there may be a more favorable regulatory environment. • Unlikely to be effective beyond the very short term as banks may attempt to circumvent them (at least to some extent) through creative accounting practices, by borrowing from abroad under an open capital account (including by banks directly from their parent banks abroad), unless such liabilities are included in the base of the requirement. • There is a risk that the rise in the cost of capital through LAR could encourage banks to focus their lending on high risk-high return projects rather than higher-quality customers, affecting asset quality and financial stability.	Croatia, Iceland, Singapore	• May be effective in controlling lending capacity of banks if designed properly, with appropriate choice of eligible securities, eligible maturities, and averaging methods. • May be helpful in short-term liquidity management when proceeds of security sales are sterilized (as in Singapore).

Appendix 5.2 continued

Measures	Impact	Limitations	Examples where they have been used	Appropriate situation to apply
• Tightening of monetary policy (e.g., rise in key policy rates).	• By transmitting the higher policy rates to bank lending rates, could help slow down demand for credit. • Could help reduce the impact of credit expansion on inflation and current account (i.e., the overheating pressures).	• May have the unintended effect of stimulating capital inflows that may further support credit growth, in particular under relatively open capital account. • Limited effectiveness if monetary transmission mechanism is not working properly (i.e., changes in key policy rates are not reflected to lending-deposit rates to affect lending). • Limited room to affect interest rates under certain monetary regimes, such as currency boards, unions, or rigid pegs, with limited room at most for monetary autonomy. • Negative impact on fiscal position by raising the cost of borrowing for the government.	Croatia, Iceland, Latvia, Romania	May be more effectively used under a relatively closed capital account, and where monetary transmission mechanism is working properly, as well as when there is supportive fiscal situation.
• Shifting of government deposits in commercial banks to the central bank.	• Would have a direct impact of reducing bank liquidity available for lending.	• Likely to have only a short-term and limited impact on its own as banks could find resources through other sources to support bank lending (foreign borrowing, private sector deposits, etc.).		Could perhaps be helpful as part of a package of other measures aimed at reducing banks' ability to lend.
• Increasing the flexibility of exchange rates.	• May help limit inflows of capital, attracted by the relative predictability of the exchange rate that may provide funding to finance banks' lending. • Could help counter inflationary effects of credit growth by putting downward pressure on prices via appreciation.	• May be associated with greater exchange rate volatility, particularly in thin, shallow markets that may have some undesirable effects on competitiveness or private sector balance sheets.	Poland, Romania	• It may be an appropriate measure when rapid credit growth is stimulated by perceptions of low exchange rate risk provided by highly predictable exchange rate path. • Could be useful to deal with both macroeconomic (by limiting overheating pressure on the economy) and prudential concerns (by reducing incentives to build unhedged FX positions).

Measures	Impact	Limitations	Examples where they have been used	Appropriate situation to apply
• Maintaining a consistent monetary-exchange rate policy mix (monetary policy set consistent with the exchange rate regime: e.g., if the exchange rate is pegged, interest rates set based on those in the anchor country).	• Limit incentives for excessive foreign currency borrowing stimulated by high domestic interest rate differentials and stable/predictable exchange rates.		Poland, Romania	• When rapid credit growth is financed by increased borrowing from abroad and banks and their customers are building unhedged FX positions under perceptions of little/no FX risk.
II. Prudential Regulation and Supervisory Measures	• Strengthening prudential regulation/supervision can limit macro-prudential risks and hence contribute to the resilience of banks to adverse shocks. Supervisory techniques can help address distortions in lending that are associated with real estate bubbles, sectoral loan concentrations, unhedged currency borrowing, or imprudent external funding behavior by banks. • Less distortionary and intrusive and more market-based compared with direct/administrative measures.	• Needs to be justified by financial sector stability concerns. • Ability for effective regulation and supervision may be limited unless there is significant cross-border supervisory cooperation (e.g., including with parent supervisors). • Supervisory and prudential measures alone may not lead to a reduction in credit growth but rather aim at maintaining asset quality. • There are limits to what prudential policy can deliver in the absence of a prudent and consistent fiscal, monetary, exchange rate policy mix. • The impact of prudential policy will also be limited by the scope for disintermediation and direct cross-border borrowing as a loophole, particularly for households and domestic borrowers such as large firms. • Concern about further tightening may create incentives for changing the structure of domestic banks, pushing business to less monitored and/or less supervised nonfinancial institutions.	See below	• In general, use of such measures may be warranted when there are serious systemic risks for the financial and real sectors of the economy, and/or when there is a need to preempt potential financial sector difficulties, including to ensure that macroeconomic policy inconsistencies do not end up causing a deterioration in soundness of banks' financial condition.

Appendix 5.2 continued

Measures	Impact	Limitations	Examples where they have been used	Appropriate situation to apply
II.A. Prudential Measures				
• Higher and/or differentiated capital requirements or risk weights based on loan type, maturity and currency composition of credit; incorporation of market and other risks in capital adequacy ratios.	• Help reduce total lending capacity. • Enhance resilience of banks' capital base against adverse shocks to the system.	• Raising capital ratios may not be effective in countries where such ratios are already at well above Basle requirements. • There is a risk that the regulations may get overly complicated and enforcement cumbersome, undermining the effectiveness of the system.	Bulgaria, Bosnia, Croatia, Norway (raised capital requirements on certain categories of loans in the late 1990s), Poland, Ukraine (to some extent)	• Would be effective in countries where the existing ratio is not already unbinding (that is, already well above Basle requirements). • Would be effective if certain risky categories of lending have been rising very rapidly and raising systemic risks.
• Tighter/differentiated loan classification and provisioning requirements (e.g., for banks with rapidly growing portfolios, or imposing differential provisioning requirements for different types of loans, raising general provisions, etc.).	• Help reduce total lending capacity by requiring greater resources to allocate to provisioning. • Enhance resilience of banks' capital base against adverse shocks to the system.	• May not be effective where such requirements are already tight compared with international standards. • Excessive application may reduce the profitability of the banks, risking disintermediation. • There is a risk that prudential regulations may get overly complicated and enforcement cumbersome, undermining the effectiveness of the system.	Bulgaria, Croatia, Romania, Ukraine	Would be effective where there is room to tighten the regulations (i.e., the existing system has weaknesses) and where there are macro-prudential risks associated with the particular patterns of lending.

Measures	Impact	Limitations	Examples where they have been used	Appropriate situation to apply
• Dynamic provisioning' (accounts for the phase of economic cycle in calculating loan-loss provisions and limits their procyclical behavior, with quarterly loan-loss provisions reflecting average losses over a business cycle).	• Additional provisions set aside in lending booms, rather than in downturns when loan quality worsens; seeks to moderate upswing of a credit cycle, ensure prudent reserves for downswings. • Provisioning that looks at borrowers over the cycle would reduce fluctuations in bank profits and lending, helping to reduce risk of financial instability. • Provides incentives for better pricing, risk management and appraisal and internal models.	• Not compatible with the international accounting standards (IAS 39) that the EU plans to implement in 2005. • Not as simple and transparent, since provisions are calculated based on averages over a cycle and as it may be difficult to estimate the amount of provisioning. • Requires confidence that future declines in provisioning will follow the same pace as past decreases and assumes losses in the next business cycle will be the same on average as in the last business cycle.	Spain	• Easier to implement in stable markets with long data series and stable provisioning levels, and where incompatibility with IAS39 is not an issue.
• Tightening eligibility requirements for certain types of loans including through limits on loan-to-value ratios (e.g., mortgages), limiting FX-denominated loans to those with FX income or adequate hedges.	Help avoid very high levels of mortgage leverage, to avoid risks in market behavior or asset prices.	May raise the risk of borrowers switching to alternative sources of funds from unregulated/weakly regulated nonbank financial institutions.	Hong Kong, Romania, Singapore	Could be a very effective tool to reduce bank lending, provided that reporting requirements are adequate and supervision of banks and nonbanks are well-coordinated to limit risk of circumvention.
• Tight/adequate collateral requirements (e.g., specifying assets eligible for collateral, marked-to-market asset valuation).	Protects banks' asset portfolios against a deterioration in loan quality and risk of asset price bubbles, thereby increasing the resilience of the banking system.	Does not in itself lead to a reduction in rapid credit growth, though helps a more prudent allocation of credit.	Ukraine	Effective instrument to increase the resilience of banking systems against bad shocks, where legal system works properly and efficiently.

Appendix 5.2 continued

Measures	Impact	Limitations	Examples where they have been used	Appropriate situation to apply
• Rules on credit concentration (limits on large borrowers, related lending, sectoral concentrations).	Help limit excessive expansion of credit to risky sectors and ensure diversification of sectoral/single borrower risks.	Limited effectiveness in slowing credit growth if banks could engage on window-dressing activities and where there are difficulties in identifying related parties.	Ukraine (efforts to strengthen rules against connected party lending)	Effective to increase resilience of banking systems where such concentration is an existing problem.
• Tightening of net open position limits and other prudential regulations against foreign currency denominated lending.	Help limit exposure to direct (through net open position limits) and indirect FX rate risks (i.e., credit risks associated with banks' exposure through borrowers' FX positions).	• Net open position limits by themselves would not help if banks are hedged in their FX positions; hence if not accompanied by regulations protecting against indirect FX risks. • The latter also would not help slow down credit growth or address its negative consequences, if FX denominated lending is not a significant part of banks' portfolios.	Bosnia (tightening FX exposure regulations, including off-balance sheet activities)	Where banks are borrowing significantly from abroad to finance rapid expansion of credit and where FX denominated lending is a significant part of banks' loan portfolios.
• Maturity mismatch regulations.	Help limit exposure to interest rate and liquidity risks, increasing the resilience of bank balance sheets vis-à-vis market risks.			Where there is significant mismatch between the maturity of banks and their borrowers' assets and liabilities.
II. B. Supervisory/ Monitoring Measures		May in general adversely affect financial intermediation if tightened excessively and may lead to disintermediation toward cross-border flows or nonbank financial sector activity which is not in general regulated/supervised. May lead to a move from foreign subsidiaries (which can be made subject to regulation/supervision) to foreign branches (supervision/ regulation of which will require cooperation with parent banks).		In general, appropriate where there are weaknesses in the supervisory system, systemic risks for financial and real sectors, and/or when there is a need to preempt potential financial sector difficulties, particularly if there is concern that the speed of credit growth puts additional strain on an otherwise strong system.

Measures	Impact	Limitations	Examples where they have been used	Appropriate situation to apply
• Use of periodic stress tests of banks balance sheets w.r.t. interest rate, exchange rate, and asset price changes (by banks themselves as well as supervisory authorities).	Provide a systematic tool to assess risks and continued monitoring and assessment of capital adequacy of the financial institutions. Market based, less intrusive supervisory tool.	Should be done by bank supervisors as well as banks themselves, not to have a limited impact due to potential limitations in the capability of banks to conduct such tests. As the sophistication of the banking system increases, such tools may not be adequate by themselves, but may need to be accompanied with other sophisticated methods (risk metrics to perform VAR analysis, credit scoring models, etc.).		Appropriate in any circumstances to systematically identify, assess, and manage risks in the financial system.
• More intensive surveillance and onsite/offsite inspection of potentially problem banks.	Provide a systematic tool to have close monitoring of bank balance sheets, risk assessment and management capabilities to identify risks on time.	Potential strain on supervisors' resources and capability to do adequate assessments especially in an environment with a large and rapid expansion of bank credit.	Bulgaria, Croatia, Estonia (close monitoring of credit developments)	Appropriate under any circumstances to systematically identify, assess, and manage risks in the financial system.
• Improved reporting/disclosure rules for banks and borrowers' balance sheets, risk management, internal control policy.	Improve market discipline on banks and transparency of the financial system, limiting room for aggressive lending practices.	Existence of legal limitations on disclosure such as bank secrecy laws, etc.	Croatia, Poland	Appropriate under any circumstances to systematically identify, assess, and manage risks, particularly where financial system is characterized by non-transparent lending practices.
• Guidance to banks to avoid over reliance on short-term borrowing.	Help limit maturity and liquidity risks associated with excessive accumulation of short-term borrowing.	Effectiveness depends on how forceful these guidelines are. May require repeated monitoring and assessment of banks' balance sheet positions through disclosure and reporting requirements and on site inspections.		Where there is significant mismatch between the maturity of banks and their borrowers' assets and liabilities.

Appendix 5.2 continued

Measures	Impact	Limitations	Examples where they have been used	Appropriate situation to apply
• Requirement to conduct periodic surveys of banks' and their borrowers' foreign exchange exposures (by banks themselves or by supervisory authorities).	• Help banks and supervisors better monitor and assess overall unhedged exposures of borrowers and hence banks' indirect FX exposure. • Also increases transparency, facilitates identifying risks.	None.	Israel, New Zealand, Poland	Where there is significant currency mismatches in banks' and/or their borrowers' assets and liabilities and banks' own risk assessment and management capabilities are weak and inadequate.
• Strengthening the coordination of bank and nonbank supervision.	Helps monitor the potential risk of prudential and supervisory measures on banks from being circumvented through greater lending activity by less regulated nonbank institutions.	None, except, strengthening capability of regulatory and supervisory institutions may take time.	Croatia (plans ongoing), Greece	Particularly relevant where there are many nonbank financial institutions that are performing quasi-bank activities (e.g., leasing companies, etc.) that are not well regulated and outside the regulatory framework.
• Increased dialogue with home supervisors of foreign banks.	May help limit foreign banks' exposures from creating systemic risks for local banks and domestic banking system as a whole.		Used/considered in Croatia, Greece	Particularly relevant when credit boom is dominated by foreign banks regulated and supervised by country authorities of parent banks; and where returns to aggressive lending may overshadow risks from a combined exposure of foreign banks to several regional banks.
IV. Financial Markets and Institutions Development Measures				
• Increasing the availability of hedging instruments to hedge exchange rate or interest rate risks, and asset management instruments to deal with distressed bank assets.	• Help raise resilience of balance sheets of banks and borrowers to changes in the exchange, interest rate and asset prices; deepen markets, and improve transmission mechanism; facilitate adopting flexible rates that help deal with credit growth.	• May take time to build, if at a very low starting point. • Requires private sector involvement.		When there are both macroeconomic and prudential concerns associated with rapid credit growth.

Measures	Impact	Limitations	Examples where they have been used	Appropriate situation to apply
• Government borrowing strategies, in particular, shifting from external to domestic borrowing by the government.	• Reduce liquidity. • Stimulate domestic market development, hence providing alternative assets for banks to invest and diversify their risks.	• Resistance from government (Treasury/MoF) given if borrowing terms from abroad more favorable as opposed to borrowing domestically. • Effectiveness depends on whether there is appetite for government securities by the banks, particularly when the yield on these securities are not attractive when there are more attractive returns to lending (e.g., with large lending-deposit spreads, high return-high risk projects, etc.).	Bulgaria (being considered)	• Helpful in the medium to long term as a measure to enhance the resilience and depth of the financial system and markets. • Could be effective as part of a comprehensive package and with market-determined yields on the government securities.
• Developing securities markets (including domestic government securities markets).	• Help reduce dependence on bank credit and provide alternative assets for banks to invest and diversify risks.	May take time to build deep, liquid securities markets, hence may not be helpful in addressing the rapid credit expansion in the short run.	Considered in Bulgaria	Appropriate under any circumstances.
• Improving banks' and corporations' accounting standards.	Helps limit window-dressing activities that may be used to circumvent prudential and supervisory regulations.	Insufficient on its own to cope with excessive credit growth problem, unless used as part of a comprehensive set of measures.	Many countries as part of the transition process	Helpful where accounting and disclosure systems are opaque and there are large incentives to evade existing regulations.
• Improvement in credit culture, including via establishment of credit bureaus, credit registry.	Improves market discipline, and provides important information, data to supervisors, and limits deterioration in loan quality.	None	Bulgaria, Romania	Appropriate under any circumstances.

Appendix 5.2 continued

Measures	Impact	Limitations	Examples where they have been used	Appropriate situation to apply
V. Administrative/Direct Measures				
• Controls on capital flows (e.g., on borrowing by banks and/or customers) to limit resources to extend credit, including; reserve requirements on bank borrowing from abroad (including borrowing by foreign branch from parents). differentiated reserve requirements on domestic and foreign currency deposits.	Limit the source of funding for banks that would be financing rapid credit growth for a limited time.	• Provide at most only temporary effect. • Induce incentives to circumvent the controls, leading to disintermediation from the domestic banking system. • Difficult to enforce unless the enforcement and implementation capacity of the authorities are very strong; particularly difficult to enforce when there are weaknesses in cross-border regulation/supervision. • Adverse impact on market confidence and credibility of the prevailing monetary regime (e.g., under a currency board that relies significantly on full currency convertibility). • May lead to a move from foreign subsidiaries (which can be made subject to regulation/supervision) to foreign branches (supervision/regulation of which require parent cooperation).	Croatia (imposed marginal reserve requirement on foreign borrowing), Romania (increase in reserve requirement on FX liabilities and postponement of capital account liberalization)	Should be used only as a last resort if everything else fails and there are significant macroeconomic and prudential risks.

Measures	Impact	Limitations	Examples where they have been used	Appropriate situation to apply
• Direct credit controls.	Can deliver effective control over bank credit if reserve money creation is otherwise controlled, if the enforcement capacity is adequate, and in less well-developed financial markets and closed capital account. Can reduce loss of monetary control during transition to indirect instruments if transmission is uncertain.	• Since not market-determined, progressively distort the allocation of bank resources and competition. • Can lead to disintermediation and ultimate loss of effectiveness (including by circumvention through borrowers' switching to less supervised nonbank financial institutions such as leasing/insurance companies or to direct borrowing from abroad, which increases private sector external indebtedness). • Encourage balance sheet manipulation by banks. • Difficult to implement under free capital inflows. • Not consistent with a move toward market based monetary and financial sector policies; strong negative signal of lack of commitment to market mechanisms.	In western Europe until late 1980s, some African and Asian countries during 1990s, and in transition economies; more recently in Greece (1999) when faced with capital inflows ahead of euro adoption and in Croatia (during 2003)	• Could be an instrument during transition to indirect instruments; when transmission mechanism is uncertain; if the enforcement capacity is adequate with small risk of circumvention, and in less well-developed financial markets with closed capital account. • Should be used only as a last resort if everything else fails and there are significant macro-economic and prudential risks; use relatively more market-based versions of such controls.
• Taxes on financial intermediation.	Makes financial intermediation costly, likely reducing lending activities.	• Distortionary for efficient allocation of resources. • May encourage window-dressing activities in banks' balance sheets to circumvent the taxes. • May lead to disintermediation if the tax level is prohibitive.	In several Latin American countries	

VI. Other (Measures to Promote Better Understanding of Risks)

Measures	Impact	Limitations	Examples where they have been used	Appropriate situation to apply
• Strengthening banks' ability to assess, monitor, and manage risks through workshops, training, etc.	Limits banks from taking excessive risks associated with liquidity, maturity, currency structure of their balance sheets and hence improve the quality of their asset portfolios.	None	Ukraine (ongoing efforts)	Appropriate under any circumstances.

Appendix 5.2 continued

Measures	Impact	Limitations	Examples where they have been used	Appropriate situation to apply
• Consultative meetings with banks (including moral suasion) to persuade/warn banks to slow down credit.	Effective measure if the financial system is relatively small and easy to monitor and if authorities have alternative instruments to back up in case concerns persist.	• May be perceived intrusive if it takes the extreme forms. • Difficult to monitor in a well-developed sophisticated financial system. • No systematic mechanisms to ensure banks comply with the warnings.	Bulgaria, Estonia, Iceland	Where the financial system is small and closely integrated, banking system dominates the financial system, and there are good, working relations between banks and supervisory authorities.
• Public risk awareness campaigns, press statements, etc.	May help limit excessive risk taking by banks and customers and resulting deterioration in banks' assets.	None	Poland	Appropriate under any circumstances.

* The fundamental principle underlying dynamic provisioning is that provisions are set aside against loans outstanding in each accounting time period in line with an estimate of the long run, expected loss (Mann and Michael, 2002). Additional provisions are set aside in lending booms rather than in downturns when asset quality deteriorates, thereby making the level of provisioning less subject to sharp swings stemming from the strength of economic activity.

Source: Hilbers, Ötker-Robe, Pazarbasioğlu, and Johnsen (2005).

Appendix 5.3 Measures Used to Deal with Credit Growth in Selected European Countries

Country	Measures with potential impact on credit growth	Impact to date
Bosnia	• Reform of reserve requirements in mid- and end-2003 (including foreign currency in the base, excluding vault cash from assets eligible to meet reserve requirements) to withdraw bank liquidity, and a reduction in the remuneration of excess reserves at the central bank (twice); • New tighter bank core capital requirements, tighter foreign exposure regulations (including off-balance sheet activities) and strengthened application of bank liquidity regulations.	• The credit boom that followed the surge in bank deposits since 2001 has eased somewhat (as of early 2004), in the wake of the mid-2003 monetary and regulatory tightening that has been stimulated by macroeconomic concerns. Banks seemed to comply with these measures and overall credit to private sector slowed down (from about 26 percent in 2002 to 21 percent in Nov. 2003 as a whole, although credit to enterprises accelerated). The regulatory reforms also raised banks' demand for excess central bank deposits, stemming the growth of credit.
Bulgaria	• As a first phase in their strategy to deal with credit growth, the authorities also used suasion through public statements and meetings with banks, especially those with aggressive lending behavior. More recently, the BNB embarked on a series of meetings with CEOs of commercial banks to discuss the ongoing credit expansion and possible measures to dampen credit. • Since mid-2003, the BNB has been implementing a set of sequential measures to strengthen bank supervision, including tightening of loan classification and provisioning requirements; increasing the frequency and focus of onsite inspections, and restricting conditions under which current profits can be included in regulatory capital. • On the fiscal side, the authorities tightened their fiscal stance, in response to the widening of the current account deficit. • On the monetary side, given the limited options under a currency board, the authorities try to reduce banking system liquidity by tightening reserve requirements (by reducing the share of vault cash in eligible assets and broadening the liability base subject to RR by including deposits and securities with longer term maturity and repos); considered also to introduce a liquid asset requirement as a further measure to reduce bank liquidity to limit banks' capacity to lend. • To reduce information asymmetries and their adverse impact, the authorities also aim to strengthen information on retail lending conditions (e.g., overall indebtedness of particular households). • Consistent with its overall strategy to raise the share of domestic debt in total debt, as well as to limit credit growth by reducing bank liquidity while stimulating domestic market development, the government plans to shift from external borrowing to domestic borrowing (which is envisaged to be mostly absorbed by banks). • Introduced marginal reserve requirements for banks exceeding certain rate of credit growth (Feb. 2005).	• Domestic credit growth has remained strong (as of late 2004). Financed by a sharp rise in deposits (in particular foreign exchange (FX) deposits) and in bank foreign liabilities, 12-month growth in claims to the non-government sector rose to 52.5 percent in July, after having fallen to 47.8 percent in June. Financing of the credit expansion relied more on the rapid increase in banks' foreign liabilities than drawing down their foreign assets which was the case before. The share of corporate credit continued to fall gradually, but still remained at about two-thirds of the total; corporate credit rose nearly 42 percent, while consumer credit by 76.3 percent, down from the January–July average of 80.7 percent. • The anticipated impact of the various credit and prudential measures has been reduced by rapid deposit growth (much of it from non-residents) and greater-than-expected bank foreign borrowing, with banks being able to obtain loans from abroad much easier than assumed (mostly from parent banks to their Bulgarian subsidiaries, given the continued high profits Bulgarian banks are generating, the investment grade rating recently given to Bulgarian sovereign debt, and rising confidence in timely EU accession).

129

Appendix 5.3 continued

Country	Measures with potential impact on credit growth	Impact to date
Croatia	• Macroeconomic policies (some fiscal consolidation) to contain the domestic demand surge financed by bank credit (during 2000–mid-2003); some moderate tightening of interest rates, though using monetary policy was in general constrained by the commitment to a stable exchange rate policy and a very open capital account. • Direct credit controls—banks whose lending grew by more than 4 percent per quarter would be obliged to buy CNB bills at penalty rates in an amount twice as high as excess credit (Jan. 2003, removed in end-2003). • Additional FX liquidity requirements—the required FX coverage of banks' FX liabilities was increased (24 percent of banks' foreign borrowing had to be held in foreign liquid assets) (Jan. 2003). The coverage was further raised to 35 percent in Feb. 2005, then lowered to 32 percent in Mar. 2005. • Strengthening of prudential regulation and supervision (by-laws implementing a new Banking Law that came into force in Jan. 2004 included charges for market risk into capital adequacy calculation and increased provisioning for banks with rapidly growing portfolios. The CNB's banking supervision department was reorganized to operate more on risk basis, and its staffing was strengthened. • CNB introduced regulations requiring rapidly growing banks to meet even higher capital adequacy standards or be subject to mandatory retention of a portion of profits (early 2004). • Attempts to introduce counterparty exposure reporting systems, but with limited success due to weak reliability of data from the corporate sector. • Introduction of marginal reserve requirement on foreign borrowing (Jul. 1, 2004) to reduce external vulnerability (from 11 percent of foreign borrowing to 35 percent of their new foreign borrowing). • The authorities saw introduction of (price-based) capital controls as last-resort policy option, in case of unexpected capital inflows that may threaten macroeconomic stability. • The authorities appointed a working group (Oct. 2004) to unify supervision of nonbank institutions to cover supervision gaps (due to the rapid expansion of unregulated and unsupervised leasing companies and significant risk transfer from banks to insurance companies with limited risk management capacity and supervisory capacity in the insurance sector). The group is actively planning to implement the reform. • Recent agreement with the Fund on the need to closely monitor customers' FX risk during onsite inspections (including asking banks to inquire and report on the largest customers' FX exposure).	• Macroeconomic policies did not manage to contain the surge in domestic demand, as fiscal consolidation was not sufficient to offset the growth in private consumption and investment; current account deficit rose sharply (above 8 percent of GDP). But credit boom unwound in 2002 and early 2003, likely reflecting debt carrying constraints as well as credit controls imposed by CNB, although lack of data precludes a full assessment of trends. • Direct credit controls were not successful in controlling aggregate demand or current account deficit: bank credit decelerated significantly since mid-2003), possibly affecting spending by households that do not have easy access to foreign borrowing, but corporates moved significantly out of borrowing from domestic to foreign banks (local banks typically directed most of their best corporate customers to their parent banks abroad) and used leasing and other forms of financing provided by unsupervised and unregulated leasing companies. Foreign debt rose strongly in 2003 with borrowing by banks and nonfinancial enterprises. • The limits hence also had a negative impact on the soundness of the financial sector. Anecdotal evidence suggests that insurance companies have taken on a substantial part of the credit risks associated with banks' retail portfolios, which is a concern given the limited risk management and supervisory capacity in the insurance sector. Also transparency of monetary and banking statistics deteriorated as banks engaged in some activities designed to circumvent the limits, such as collateralization, asset swaps, and accelerated NPLs write-offs. • Private sector borrowing in FX remains a concern. Banks are vulnerable to indirect FX risk (credit risk due to currency mismatch between assets and liabilities of some clients) (about 78 percent of bank loans are denominated in or linked to FX and a significant share of those loans (about 60 percent) is extended to borrowers with kuna denominated sources of income and often with limited access to hedging instruments).

Country	Measures with potential impact on credit growth	Impact to date
Estonia	• The authorities recently reduced borrowing incentives by limiting mortgage interest deductibility to address the rise in households' real estate related borrowing, with plans for further reduction. • Moral suasion: the central bank and the financial supervisory authority repeatedly discussed and stressed with banks the need for continuing conservative lending practices. • Close monitoring of developments in credit.	• Domestic credit growth has remained robust to date (Oct. 2004), financed increasingly by bank borrowing from abroad, mainly from foreign parent banks. Bank credit to household sector (mainly to acquire real estate) at 50 percent y/y in Q104 and credit to enterprises at 30 percent in H104. Around 65 percent of household loans and 78 percent of enterprise credits are in FX (95 percent in euros).
Greece	• In response to an acceleration of credit growth (in particular credit to households expanded by around 30 percent), stimulated by the favorable economic environment ahead of EU accession, Greece imposed credit controls in the form of non-remunerated deposits for an amount equivalent to the growth of credit above specified rates (mid-Apr. 1999); at end-July 1999, in the face of still rapid consumer lending, penalty for excess lending in this category was doubled. Non-remunerated deposits were extended through the end of Mar. 2000. Restrictions were lifted in April 2000. • Additional measures were taken to prevent a surge in liquidity when reserve requirements were reduced to the euro area's 2 percent, with freed-up reserves converted into blocked interest bearing deposits at the central bank, to be gradually released until end-2001. • Attention was then given more to greater monitoring of qualitative aspects of banks' activities, notably their credit management processes through stress testing and scenario analysis, to enhancing market discipline through greater public disclosure, improvement of coordination between supervisory agencies, and strengthening the independence of the supervisors.	• Credit growth has remained robust following the Apr. 1999 measures, which necessitated further tightening several times until April 2000. In general the extent of slowdown in bank credit was limited by the increasingly accommodative monetary conditions in the run-up to the monetary union with a general decline in interest rates, easing of reserve requirements, lifting of credit restrictions in April 2000 and integration into the interbank euro market.
Iceland	• In response to a rapid rise of credit growth by deposit money banks during 1998–99, which was being increasingly financed by foreign borrowing by banks (with high proportion being short-term), the central bank took a few measures: • Moral suasion: it issued cautionary remarks to parties capable of influencing this development (management of banks and government authorities as the main owners of some of the players); • Tightening of interest rates: the central bank raised its key policy rate three times during 1999; • It set liquidity requirement ratios for credit institutions (Feb. 1999) to counter the deteriorating liquidity position of credit institutions and their increasing use of short-term foreign capital.	• As a result of the liquidity requirements, the commercial and savings banks' liquidity positions improved significantly and the share of short-term foreign borrowing in liabilities were reduced. • The real growth of bank lending also slowed down somewhat (from 30 percent in 1998 to 15 percent until about early 2000), but it picked up again subsequently and remained at high levels during 2000. Whether the initial decline could be entirely attributed to the new liquidity rules was also uncertain, since the decline could also reflect the warnings and the impact of interest rate rises. • The liquidity rules, along with other factors, also led to some reduction in trading in bank and treasury bills.
Latvia	• Raised interest rates—refinancing rate (Mar. 2004), and increased reserve requirements (Jul. 2004) partially reversing an earlier decline to bring them in line with European Central Bank (ECB) requirements to stem private sector credit growth and inflation.	• So far the measures have had limited effect, since banks' funding is mainly derived from abroad (Eurobond floatation and credit from parent banks) and domestic loans are extended mainly in FX. • Higher interest rates likely attracted additional capital inflows.

Appendix 5.3 continued

Country	Measures with potential impact on credit growth	Impact to date
Moldova	• Responding to rapid bank credit growth over the past four years, the National Bank of Moldova (NBM) gradually implemented a system where required reserves for FX deposits are held in FX (since Jul. 04). • The NBM required banks to have separate risk management units to identify and reduce specific risk exposures. The assessment of credit risk is generally made on a borrower-by-borrower basis, and the banks share information on problem borrowers on an informal basis, in the absence of a credit registry.	• Credit growth decelerated somewhat in 2004 but still remained strong.
Poland	• In response to increased foreign currency lending by banks from mid-2000, the supervisory authorities adopted a new capital adequacy regulation (in line with EU standards) that expanded the existing FX regulation to cover other risks (market, interest rate, commodity price and equity or debt instruments price risks), and required banks to increase capital to incorporate the aforementioned risks (this is in addition to the regulatory capital for credit risk). The previous limits on FX open positions were hence replaced with capital charges, implying higher capital for higher FX risks. • Periodic surveys of banks' FX exposure by supervisors to obtain specific information on banks' foreign currency lending, including borrowers' appetite for foreign currency loans, percentage of customers hedging their exchange rate risks, the form of hedging offered to customers, foreign currency loans protected by guarantees, costs for hedging loans as ratio to the loan, loan classification and provisions made, foreign exchange positions, by currency, receipts/costs of foreign exchange transactions, extent of engagement in arbitrage transactions, surveys followed up by action on procedures and banks stress tests. • Close monitoring of banks' exposure to FX risk and quality of FX risk management, internal controls. The authorities developed a credit information database and formed a unit to monitor vulnerabilities from credit risk associated with FX denominated lending. • Some form of moral suasion: From 2001, supervisors' warning of banks and written guidance from head of supervision, and press coverage of risks to households.	• The rapid increase in FX denominated credit since mid-2000 reversed in late 2002 (at an average of around 26 percent of total loans during 2000–03). The depreciation of the zloty against the euro and the narrowing of the spreads between zloty and foreign interest rates were also believed to have reduced foreign currency borrowing. The rapid growth of FX-denominated housing loans slowed significantly in the last quarter of 2003 as zloty interest rates declined and households became more careful about unhedged borrowing. Nonetheless, about half of the outstanding stock of housing loans was still FX denominated or indexed.

Country	Measures with potential impact on credit growth	Impact to date
Portugal	• The authorities strengthened regulatory measures further by tightening rules governing general provisions, large exposures, connected lending, and capital adequacy. • However, in response to the rise in private sector bank borrowing, which led to a surge in domestic demand and a widening of the current account deficit financed by reduced holdings of government paper and increased borrowing from abroad, the authorities took further measures: (i) the authorities tightened further prudential and supervisory measures to safeguard continued soundness of the financial sector, tightening of capital requirements for housing loans with loans-to-value ratios exceeding 75 percent as well as tightening provisioning requirements for consumer loans in early 1999—with household credit growth rising strongly from mid-1996 and helping finance the ongoing boom in housing and durables consumption through imports; (ii) new reporting requirements for liquidity monitoring purposes were put in place, as well as guidance for controlling the reliance on short-term market borrowing; (iii) the authorities increased reporting and disclosure requirements for banks on their risk management and control policies and practices to enhance market discipline, undertook impact studies within the scope of amending capital and provisioning requirements, and strengthened coordination between different supervisory agencies of the financial sector, forming in 2000 the National Council of Supervisors comprising all financial sector supervisors. Promoting the coordination of the action, facilitating and coordinating the exchange of information, and formulating proposals for the regulation of matters undertaken by the financial system's supervisory authorities are among the responsibilities of the Council. Since its establishment, the Council has had regular meetings. Supervision of financial conglomerates, anti-money laundering rules, and structured deposits were some of the main issues discussed.	• During the second half of the 1990s, the marked fall in interest rates contributed to the strong growth in loans granted to the nonfinancial private sector. These developments resulted in large borrowing requirements, which translated into a large current and capital account deficit. • In 1999, following the ECB interest rate rise, a significant decline in credit growth was observed. The economic slowdown that culminated in the 2003 recession implied a further reduction in the pace of growth of credit to non-financial corporations and consumer credits. However, housing loans' growth slowly declined but persisted growing at a nominal rate in excess of or around 10 percent. • Initially, banks financed the rapid credit growth by disposing government debt holdings and resorting to money market borrowing. Later in the process, an increase in the maturity of bank debt stock has been observed, in particular by substituting interbank liabilities by longer-term debt securities issues. In addition, the possibilities opened by securitizations also expanded the banks' liquidity management options.

Appendix 5.3 continued

Country	Measures with potential impact on credit growth	Impact to date
Romania	• Fiscal and monetary tightening. • Strengthened bank supervision with stricter loan classification rules and introduction of prudential norms to tighten eligibility for consumer and mortgage loans (in particular, limiting the monthly-payment-to-net income ratio to 30 percent, imposition of mandatory 25 percent down payment or cosigner/insurance for consumer loans, and a cosigner, insurance, or collateral for personal loans, and reducing the monthly-payment-to-net-income ratio to 35 percent and introducing a maximum loan-to-value ratio (75 percent) for mortgage loans). • Introduction of a regulation that limits insurance companies' exposure to bank loans. • Establishment of a credit bureau to monitor consumer loans and business credit (expected to be operational in the last quarter of 2004). The authorities recently expressed commitment to measures for expanding the database of the NBR's credit bureau. • Postponement of the liberalization of permitting leu deposits by nonresidents in the local banks. • Increase in the mandatory reserve requirement on banks' foreign currency denominated liabilities from 25 percent to 30 percent (from Aug. 2004). Extension of the 30 percent reserve requirement to such liabilities with maturity over two years (since Feb. 2005). • Cutting of policy interest rates and increased flexibility of the exchange rate to limit capital inflows and discourage FX borrowing (2004–Nov. 2005). • Enforcement of additional prudential regulations aimed at tightening eligibility criteria for individuals (Aug. 2005). • Limits on banks' FX credit exposure to unhedged borrowers and refining the regulations on provisioning and loan classification taking into account the FX risk of borrowers (Sep. 2005).	• Private sector credit growth has slowed from Aug. 2003 to Apr. 2004, but picked up again afterwards. Growth in leu credit nearly came to a halt, reflecting high interest rates and the effects of the regulatory measures approved in late 2003. But, the FX-denominated credit has started to pick up again, driven by strong mortgage demand and a switch for some consumer durables from lei to foreign currency credit, though the end-August increase in RR on FX-denominated loans seems to have helped slow down its growth. About 75 percent of the growth is in FX credit, out of which 30 percent is to households, and 70 percent of this comprises mortgage loans. • The authorities remain alert to persistent strength of credit growth in FX-denominated credit; additional measures being contemplated to slow credit growth. • Cutting of policy interest rates through 2004 to Mar. 2005 has not had a major effect on leu denominated credit, owing to the large interest rate differential between leu and FX-denominated loans and the expectations for exchange rate appreciation.

Country	Measures with potential impact on credit growth	Impact to date
Serbia	• Tightening of monetary policy by raising the required reserve ratio on all dinar and enterprise FX deposits by 3 percentage points to 21 percent and stepping up open market operations (Aug. 2004) as a result of a strong growth in bank credit to nongovernment sector (25.8 percent real growth year on year in Jul. 2004). • The authorities issued a guideline tightening conditions for bank consumer loans and requested the banks to adopt the guideline in Dec. 2004. They have also increased the capital adequacy ratio to 10 percent (effective Mar. 2005) and broadened the reservable base to include commercial banks' foreign borrowing (effective Jan. 2005). Specifically, the reservable base now includes the stock of all foreign borrowing with a maturity of up to four years and all new foreign borrowing independent of the maturity. In addition, they are currently preparing a regulation on monitoring and managing credit risk resulting from borrowers' exposure to exchange rate risk. Moreover, they are exploring possibilities to start regulating and supervising leasing companies.	• The monetary tightening in mid-2004 did not have any tangible impact on credit growth, which accelerated further in the second half of the year, reaching 32.9 percent in real terms in November. This largely reflects the limited effectiveness of monetary policy under the conditions of high euroization, with 67 percent of total credit to nongovernment being extended in foreign currencies or indexed to foreign currencies, and limited instruments for indirect monetary control. • Consumer lending slowed down significantly in the three months after the tightening measures. Credit to nongovernment also slowed down, but in a less pronounced manner. Banks remain vulnerable to indirect FX risk.
Spain	• Dynamic provisioning: Concerned that banks' loan portfolios continued to expand and that loan provisions were not keeping pace with potential credit losses latent in new lending, the Bank of Spain introduced a new "statistical provisioning" method, effective Jul. 2000. The provision is dynamic as it is envisaged to increase when specific provisions (i.e., actual losses) for a year are lower than expected credit losses, and used to set against specific provisions in years when specific provisions are higher than expected credit losses. The statistical provisions are subject to an upper limit and are not tax deductible. • With continued growth of housing credit, the authorities closely monitored forward looking indicators of potential debt-servicing difficulties, placing emphasis on continued vigilance, accompanied with moral suasion, to ensure that credit institutions exercised adequate caution, with effective credit approval and monitoring processes in place.	• The statistical provisions grew significantly over 2000 to 2002. While growth of housing credit slowed down temporarily from 2000 to 2002, it resumed its pace of growth, from 14 percent in 2002 to about 21 percent in 2004. The share in total credit to the private sector from credit institutions rose from 28 percent in 1997 to around 34 percent in 2004. • Dynamic provisioning was eliminated in Dec. 2004.

Appendix 5.3 continued

Country	Measures with potential impact on credit growth	Impact to date
Ukraine	• In response to a very rapid growth of banking system credit to the private sector (from about 33 percent y/y in early 2002 to a peak of 64 percent in Nov. 2003) and with a view to reducing the credit risk in the economy and strengthening the banking sector a number of prudential and supervisory measures were taken: the minimum capital adequacy ratio was raised from 8 percent to 10 percent (Mar. 2004); resolutions were issued in early April to increase and improve the quality of bank capital; loan classification rules were somewhat strengthened; related-party lending regulations were tightened by requiring lending to related-parties at favorable terms to be fully matched by set-aside capital; methodological guidelines were introduced on the inspection of banks based on a "Risk Assessment System" in Mar. 2004. While they may not be specifically aimed at addressing rapid credit growth, a number of measures taken may contribute to strengthening creditor rights and integrity of the financial system (a law on mortgages was passed, new civil and commercial codes were adopted, amendments were made to anti-money laundering (AML) legislation, and a regulator for nonbank financial institutions established). • Limited monetary measures during 2004: an increase in the overnight refinancing rates, a change in reserve requirements to reduce the eligible amount of vault cash in reserve requirements, elimination of the long-term refinancing facility that could potentially distort the credit market, and a change in the requirements for banks' access to NBU resources.	• The rate of growth of bank credit slowed down significantly from early 2004, to about 45 percent as of Oct. 2004, though still at a relatively high rate.

Source: IMF Country Reports (Staff Reports and Selected Issues), Annual Reports of Central Banks, Kraft and Jankov (2005), and Fernandez de Lis, Pages, and Saurina (2000).

6
Rapid Credit Growth—The Role of Supervisors

Mats Josefsson[1]

Many countries in Central, Eastern, and South-eastern Europe (CEE) are currently facing a rapid increase in bank lending, which, if not properly addressed, could create asset bubbles, threatening bank solvency and undermining economic stability. It is a well-known fact that large increases in bank lending explain most of the banking problems many countries have experienced during the last two decades, particularly the Asian and Nordic countries. What are the lessons to be learned from those crises in relation to bank supervision? What can bank supervisors do to influence bank lending? Should supervisory instruments and measures be used to implement macroeconomic policies? These are the key questions that this chapter considers by focusing on banking supervision and the role of bank supervisors. The conclusion is that since the objective of banking supervision is to maintain a sound banking system, prudential regulations should not be used to correct imbalances in the economy or to substitute macroeconomic policies.

I. The role of supervisory policies

Many of the countries participating at the Sinaia conference are facing, if not a credit boom, at least a rapid increase in lending. I will try to highlight the major risks facing these countries and what actions supervisors should take to address those risks.

Why are banks being supervised and what is the objective of banking supervision? When Sweden experienced banking problems in the early 1990s we, bank supervisors, asked ourselves: what is the role of banking supervision and what are the objectives we are supposed to achieve? Undoubtedly, banks have many very important roles to fulfill, acting as intermediaries between depositors and borrowers, but did that mean that no bank should be allowed to fail, and what were the responsibilities of bank supervisors when banks were facing problems? No one could provide clear answers, and we also in vain checked for a legal definition of the objective of banking supervision. The only guidance we found was that bank supervisors should try to maintain a sound banking system, meaning that banks should be operating in a prudent manner and in full compliance with all prudential regulations.

Banking is mainly about trust and confidence. Banks are very special, trusted to invest people's money and acting as intermediaries between savers and borrowers. That is why trust and confidence are so important in banking. Without the trust of the public, no banking system will be able to fulfill its obligations. Moreover, no depositor, small or big, would put his/her money in a "weak bank."

Thus, bank supervisors have a responsibility to maintain a sound and efficient banking system. They should check that (i) banks are operating in a prudent manner under the control of fit and proper owners, managers, and board members; (ii) risks are being managed professionally; (iii) deviations from sound banking practices are promptly corrected; and, (iv) failing banks exit the market before their capital has been exhausted. It is important to note that it is always the owners and managers—those who make the commercial decisions and thus ultimately are responsible for how a bank is being managed—who are responsible when a bank fails, and not the bank supervisors.

Assuming the banking system is sound, supervisory instruments should not be used to influence bank lending. If the banking system is not sound and the supervisory framework has weaknesses, there is an urgent need to quickly bring supervisory practices up to international standards, irrespective of a credit boom. However, if the banking system and its supervisory framework are strong and sound, supervisory instruments and measures should not be revised or tightened to try to reduce or influence bank lending.

Macroeconomic policies can have a large impact on the financial condition of banks. Macro, fiscal, and monetary shocks can all substantially undermine the financial condition of banks, as can disasters such as earthquakes and hurricanes. The question is how bank managers and bank supervisors should prepare themselves for something unknown or for something they are not sure whether and/or when it will effect them.

Prudential regulations are the tool available to bank supervisors to ensure that banks are properly managed and risks are minimized. The regulations address most risks banks are facing in their operations, such as credit risks, market risks, and operational risks. If banks are in full compliance with all regulations, and acceptable accounting standards have been adopted, banks should be able to withstand most shocks.

Credit losses are the most common cause of bank failures. The Asian and Nordic bank crises as well as the Savings and Loans crisis in the USA were all caused by credit losses due to excessive lending. Thus, there are numerous examples around the world of bank failures caused by credit losses, but very few cases of banks failing because of other risks such as market risks.

This is also the explanation why most prudential regulations are related to lending activities. There are a number of prudential regulations that, if properly defined and implemented, will minimize risk taking by banks in providing credits. These prudential regulations include capital adequacy, large exposures, loan classification, maturity and interest mismatches, provisioning, and connected lending.

If regulations had been properly implemented, some bank failures would not have happened. The key lesson to be learned from countries which have experienced banking problems because of excessive lending is the importance of proper and consistent implementation of all prudential regulations. With such implementation, it seems likely that some bank failures or bank crises in the past could have been, if not prevented, at least less severe and the cost for bank restructuring substantially lower.

To ensure a sound banking system, banking supervision must be forward looking. This is the key issue in effective banking supervision—to be forward looking and to identify potential risks at an early stage. This is particularly important when new elements and/or new products are being introduced. In my view, this is what is now happening in many countries in CEE. People who earlier did not have access to bank credit can now borrow at historically low rates, and many of them realize that through credit they can buy their own dwellings, renovate their houses, or buy new cars. New products such as mortgage lending are also being introduced. In such an environment, it is particularly important that bank supervisors, at an early stage, have thought through what the risks might be and what the supervisory framework should look like. The "rules of the game" should be defined upfront. Given that most of the CEE countries are facing a rapid increase in bank lending, it is essential that the policymakers have thought through the supervisory framework and feel comfortable that the systems in place are adequate to prevent banks from taking excessive risk.

The agency in charge of banking supervision should be independent and free from political pressure. Undoubtedly, it is a tough job to be a bank supervisor and bank supervisors are often criticized—both in good and bad times. In the initial phase of a credit boom, the economy normally is performing well, the growth rate is high, and banks are profitable. Politicians want the banks to continue to support economic growth by extending credits, and do not see the risks banks are facing by being too lenient in providing credits. Normally, there is a lag of a few years from the time loans are granted until they turn nonperforming. Thus, bank supervisors must resist any interference from politicians or the government to relax prudential regulations so as to allow banks to relax loan approval procedures. A lesson to be learned from other countries is that it is too late to implement or tighten prudential regulations when problems have started to surface.

Prudential regulations should not be used to correct imbalances in the economy. As stated, the purpose of prudential regulations is to maintain a sound banking system. Thus, prudential regulations should be no substitute for macroeconomic measures. If there is a need to slow down/stimulate the economy, it should be done through fiscal or monetary measures. Most prudential regulations are defined according to best practice; to influence the economy by relaxing or tightening the regulations will dramatically undermine the credibility of banking supervision and open it up to political interference. Bank supervisors do not have the skills needed to conduct macroeconomic policies; conversely, the implementation of prudential regulations should be the responsibility of the supervisory agency and not of any ministry, such as the ministry of finance.

Off-site and on-site supervision must both be forward looking. Bank supervisors should on an ongoing basis make sure that a proper reporting system is in place, ensuring that supervisors always have the data needed to follow market developments in detail as well as individual banks' risk exposures. A decision about the eventual set up of a credit bureau must be made at an early stage, since it takes time to get such a bureau up and running. Well-established administrative routines should also be in place for the coordination of supervisory responsibilities with other supervisory agencies, domestically and internationally. Moreover, priorities should on an ongoing basis be reviewed for on-site examinations, where preferably the focus should be on weak banks.

When problems start to surface, there is a limited role for banking supervision. As stated above, for effective banking supervision, it is important to be forward looking and to take early action. If systems and procedures are not in place when problems start to surface, there is not much that supervision can do. Thus, when the supervisors are not comfortable with the supervisory framework when facing a credit boom, it is advisable that they promptly strengthen supervisory procedures and bring them up to international standards.

Bank supervisors should not conduct macroeconomic analysis. Bank supervisors normally do not have the skills to do macroeconomic analysis. Moreover, resources available to the supervisory agencies are in most countries scarce and should be focused on supervisory issues rather than macroeconomic analysis. While there is a need for the supervisory agency to follow what is happening in the economy, such analysis should be provided by the central bank or the government. Thus, it should not be up to the supervisory agency to determine whether growth in lending is too high and should be brought down. Against the background of the macroeconomic analysis provided by the government to the central bank, the responsibility of the bank supervisors should be to maintain a sound banking system and to monitor that all banks are in full compliance with prudential regulations and operating in a prudent manner.

It is important that supervisory frameworks are not adjusted in an ad hoc fashion. To plan their activities, it is important that banks know the "rules of the game" at an early stage and that they can trust that ratios and other prudential requirements, in line with best practices, will not be changed. Undoubtedly ad hoc changes in definitions of prudential regulations undermine the credibility of banking supervision, particularly if the rules are already in line with best practices. Besides, it is difficult and costly for banks to quickly adjust to a tightening of prudential regulations or to correct imbalances in their portfolios.

It may be useful to give a real life example of when bank supervisors need to be forward looking. In one of the countries of the CEE region, the authorities are planning to introduce a new mortgage law, which is likely to fundamentally change over time the way loans are provided by banks and other credit institutions. This could almost serve as a textbook case on how bank supervisors need to be forward looking, to thoroughly think through what the risks are, and to inform market participants at an early stage what the supervisory framework will look like. The country is already facing a rapid increase in lending, housing credits have more than doubled over the last nine months, there is a sharp increase in housing prices, and the demand for credit continues to grow. Undoubtedly the new mortgage law is a much needed reform, but, given the already high growth in lending, the issue is how the authorities can make sure there will not be an uncontrolled increase in lending that would create a bubble in the real estate market similar to what the Nordic and Asian countries experienced in the early and mid-1990s. The authorities, however, should be commended for taking the risks seriously, since it has been announced that the new law will be phased in over a period of at least two years. Initially only banks will be allowed to participate in securitization and the supervisory agency will at an early stage define the supervisory framework through a number of sub-regulations.

II. Concluding remarks

The following recommendations can be made on the role of bank supervisors in dealing with credit growth:

- The objective of banking supervision should be to ensure bank soundness;
- Banking supervision should be independent and free from political interference/pressure;
- The credibility of banking supervision can easily be undermined, if used for other purposes than to maintain bank soundness;
- With supervisory procedures and regulations in line with best practice, banks should be able to withstand most shocks, provided they are in full compliance with the regulations;
- If the supervisory framework is not in line with best practice, actions should urgently be taken to bring it up to international standards;
- It is too late to strengthen supervisory procedures when problems start to materialize—a lesson to be learned from other countries;
- Banking supervision should be forward looking and identify potential risks at an early stage; and
- Banking supervision should not be used to control credit growth, to correct imbalances in the economy or to implement macroeconomic policies.

It is essential that we learn from experiences in other countries that excessive lending can cause many bank failures and, in a worst case scenario, a systemic bank crisis. As we all know, many of the countries in central and eastern Europe are currently facing a rapid increase in bank lending, which could be quite risky given that the supervisory framework may not be fully in line with best practice. It is important not to be misled by a booming economy and by the fact that banks are profitable. That could quickly change if loans start to turn nonperforming, although we know from other countries' experiences that it takes about three to five years from the time loans are granted until this might start to happen. Thus, there might still be some time to strengthen prudential regulations and to make sure that supervisory practices are well in line with best practice.

Note

1. IMF, previously with the Bank of Sweden.

Part Two
Assessing and Managing Rapid Credit Growth—Country Experiences

7
Credit Growth Slowdown: The Experience of Bulgaria

Veselka Petkova and Stoyan Manolov[1]

The banking sector in Bulgaria currently consists of 28 domestic banks and six foreign branches. The number of banks may seem large, but in relative terms the sector is small—before the beginning of the credit boom in 2002, total assets and loans represented 45 percent and 19 percent of GDP, respectively (see Figure 7.1). Foreign-owned banks hold about 80 percent of total assets; most domestic banks are affiliated with corporations and state ownership is limited to one bank. The banking system has experienced a rapid expansion of credit, especially since 2001. This chapter reviews the experience of credit growth and discusses the policy response by the Bulgarian authorities.

I. Factors underlying the credit growth

A combination of factors have played a role in the steady growth of banking sector credit in Bulgaria in recent years. After the banking crisis in 1997–98, a currency board arrangement was introduced in Bulgaria, yet confidence in the banking sector was damaged for a number of years. The successful macroeconomic stabilization after the crisis combined with robust growth and sizable foreign direct investment are among the main factors contributing to the credit expansion after 2001. The successful privatization of the big state-owned banks by prominent European banks as well as the restoration of confidence in the financial sector also contributed. To a certain extent, the credit expansion is also due to a catch-up effect and is a part of the ongoing process of "financial deepening."

Recognizing that the Bulgarian banking sector was not (and still is not) mature, the owners of the newly privatized banks came to this market for several reasons: there were better opportunities for higher profits; the capital adequacy ratios (CARs) were generally well above both international CARs and the Basel requirements; there were very good corporate and retail margins; and banks' balance sheets

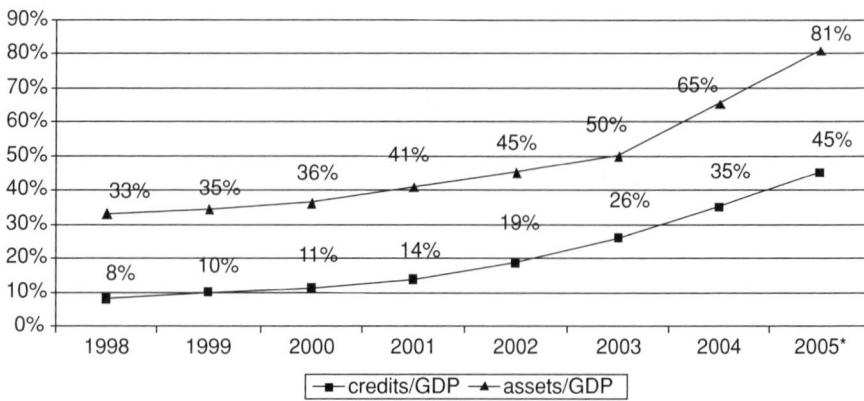

Figure 7.1 Credits and Banking Assets to GDP—Bulgaria

Source: BNB.

* Estimation for 2005.

were quite liquid with loans representing less than 40 percent of total assets. Both foreign and domestic banks shifted the composition of their assets toward loans so as to increase their profitability and gain bigger market shares. The influence of some external factors was also very important. These included: low interest rates (especially in the euro area), relatively stable exchange rates (the Bulgarian lev is pegged to the euro as required by the currency board arrangement), and high liquidity in international markets.

At the same time, there was increased demand from companies and households alike. From a business perspective, the high demand was due to positive trends in macroeconomic stability, employment, and investment—both FDI and domestic; and, in the absence of a developed capital market, the only source of finance has been bank loans. The rising wage incomes and the growing demand for durables, and to some extent for real estate, are some of the main reasons behind the household demand. After the arrival of strong foreign banks, competition in the sector has become more intense and bank customers have enjoyed more attractive new products and pricing.

Over the period 2002–04, the Bulgarian banking system experienced a continued and rapid increase in lending. Loans grew 49.6 percent in 2002–03 and 48.0 percent in 2003–04, while total assets of the banking system grew by only 18.4 percent and 43.6 percent, respectively (Figure 7.2). At the same time, deposits increased by 20.6 percent during the period 2002–03, and by 43.6 percent in the following year. Although the restored trust in the banking system, as well as improved wealth levels and high corporate liquidity, supported the increase in the deposits of nonfinancial institutions, the main source of funding was not the domestic market. Most of the foreign-owned banks attracted cheaper financing from abroad through short-term and/or long-term borrowing (mainly from their parent organizations), to lend in local markets at higher interest rates. But small and medium-sized banks financed their lending from more expensive sources—either by domestic deposit accumulation (high pricing strategies for longer-term saving accounts) or more expensive borrowings (e.g., a few banks issued domestic and euro bonds to raise funds).

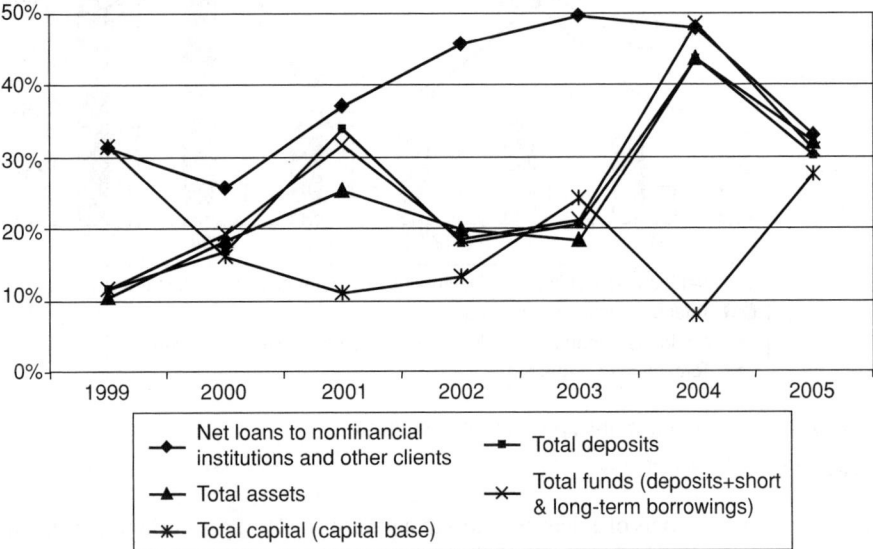

Figure 7.2 Annual Growth of Selected Balance Sheet Aggregates—Bulgaria

Source: BNB.

This process increased the pressure on banks' profitability as well as on capitalization and the balance between risks and rewards. Although a large portion of the borrowings and financing is conducted in euros (42 percent and 38 percent, respectively, as of December 2004), the foreign exchange risk for both the lender and the borrower is reduced by the euro-based currency board arrangement.[2] Capital growth fell from 24.2 percent in the first period of observation (2002–03) to 7.8 percent in the second year (2003–04). Although the capitalization of the banking sector remained adequate, it progressively declined from the previous high levels. Gradually, the share of loans in total assets went up from 41.2 percent at year-end 2002 to 52 percent at year-end 2003 and to 53.6 percent at year-end 2004. As the credit growth outpaced that of deposits, the ratio of loans to deposits from nonfinancial institutions of the banking sector rapidly increased from 60 percent at year-end 2002 to 82.5 percent at year-end 2004 (Figure 7.3).

The expanding credit has been a driver of widening macroeconomic imbalances in Bulgaria. Current account deficits ballooned as a percentage of GDP in 2002–04, largely driven by the robust growth in consumer goods imports, which was in turn facilitated by households' easier access to loans.

The very dynamics of the rapid credit growth also increased the risk of financial sector instability. In late 2004 and early 2005, the credit risk became higher due to explosive loan growth. Although the asset-quality indicators remained tolerable,

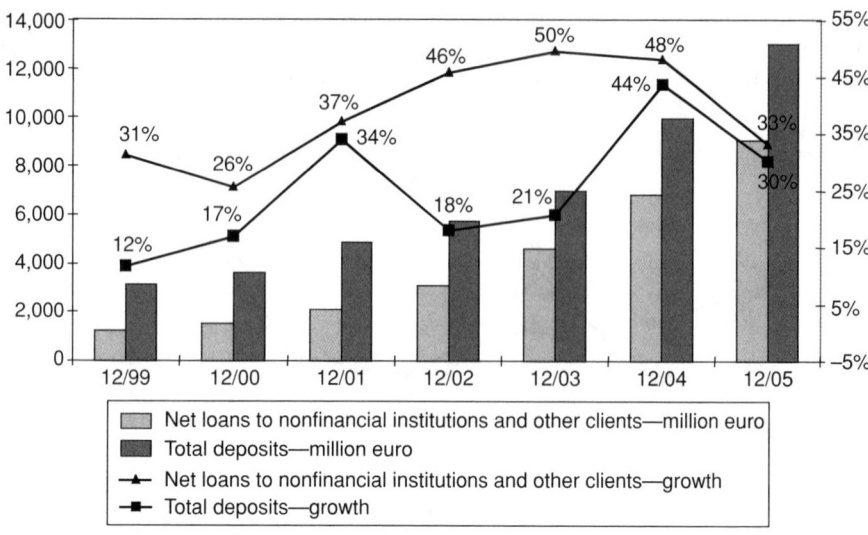

Figure 7.3 Growth in Lending and Deposits—Bulgaria

Source: BNB.

there were some signals of a deterioration in a part of the loan portfolio (especially in consumer lending) and the rates of loan impairment started to accelerate. The fierce competition between banks led to the hasty introduction of new credit products, while diminishing the requirements set out in the banks' procedures, rules, and internal control systems. The main concerns of the Bulgarian National Bank (BNB) are related to the growing indebtedness, the underdeveloped credit culture, the untested performance of companies in different phases of the economic cycle (especially in the recession phase), and the unsatisfactory enforcement of creditor rights. The BNB's numerous warnings about the necessity of greater discretion in the lending process were neglected.

II. Measures taken by the BNB to slow the credit growth

Having understood the risks associated with the rapid credit growth, the key policy challenge for the BNB was to take measures to slow down the pace of this process. The available policy options in Bulgaria were limited because the BNB was operating under a currency board arrangement. The practical measures that the BNB adopted in order to moderate credit growth to the private sector can be categorized into three groups: (i) information enhancing (reducing asymmetric information), (ii) prudential and regulatory, and (iii) administrative (quantitative limits).

Information enhancing

In 1998, the BNB established the Central Credit Register (CCR), which collects information from commercial banks for loans granted above lev 10,000 (Regulation 22 of the BNB on the Central Credit Register of Banks). Banks were required to supply this information on a monthly basis. The BNB collected a fee of lev 40 (EUR 20.5) for any inquiry that commercial banks submitted to the CCR. In 2003, the growth rate of credit to the private sector started to accelerate in line with the sharply rising growth rate of consumer credit. Since consumer credits were in small amounts (usually lev 3,000–5,000), they were not reported in the CCR, creating opportunities for some borrowers to accumulate consumer credits from several commercial banks, exploiting information asymmetries. On February 5, 2004, the Governing Council of the BNB changed Regulation 22 and abolished the lev 10,000 threshold for reporting loans to the CCR, thereby requiring that all consumer credits be incorporated into the CCR. In addition, reporting to the CCR was reduced to five days after the origination of the loan. Banks could make on-line, virtual, real-time checks on the indebtedness of the potential borrower, and in order to encourage the submission of inquiries to the CCR, the fee was reduced to lev 0.5 (EUR 0.26).

Increasing competition among banks led to the distortion of information that they provide to their customers (households) on effective interest rates on consumer and mortgage loans. At the BNB's request, in December 2005, banks signed an agreement through the Association of Commercial Banks (ACB) to disclose effective interest rates on their consumer loans. Such disclosure will be extended to all household loans following the adoption of the new consumer protection law, scheduled for June 30, 2006.

The BNB, like many other central banks in countries experiencing rapid credit growth, tried to convince the banks' management of the far-reaching effects of credit growth. However, moral suasion does not seem to have been a very effective tool in constraining credit growth.

The objective of the second set of measures introduced in 2004–05 (prudential and regulatory, and administrative) was to bring credit growth down to 25–30 percent per year.

Prudential and regulatory

The coverage for reserve requirements has been broadened; on May 20 and November 18, 2004, the Governing Council of the BNB changed Regulation 21: Minimum Required Reserves Maintained with the Bulgarian National Bank by Banks. From July 1, 2004, the deposit base included some liabilities for which banks had previously been exempted from the obligation to maintain reserves (long-term deposits with a maturity of over two years and the repos of end-clients). These liabilities are now counted in determining the amount of the minimum required reserves with a reduced rate of 4 percent against 8 percent for the remaining deposits. Since December 2004, the 8 percent minimum reserve requirement has become applicable to all bank deposits, meaning that the special 4 percent rate is no longer applicable to repo transactions and deposits over two years. In addition, the proportion of cash in vault that can be used to fulfill reserve requirements has been lowered. From October 1, 2004, only 50 percent of cash stocks in the vaults counted as deposited reserves, instead of 100 percent. Since December 2004, all of the cash holdings of banks have been excluded for calculating minimum reserves. The BNB's observations showed that the tightening of reserve requirements did not succeed in solving the credit boom problem, but it was at least a warning to market participants that the Central Bank would no longer tolerate the ongoing credit growth.

Capital adequacy requirements have been changed. On December 17, 2004, the Governing Council amended Regulation 8 on the Capital Adequacy of Banks. Mortgage credits are now treated with 50 percent risk weight and the amount of credit should not exceed 70 percent of the value of collateral (70 percent LTV ratio). In addition, on April 21, 2005, the Governing Council amended the Regulation, excluding current profit from the capital base of commercial banks to stop the so-called profit accelerator. Before this revision, commercial banks could in the middle of the year include in their capital base audited profit from the current year, thus increasing their capital base to support a further increase in their credit portfolio. The BNB also introduced a monthly requirement for reporting of capital adequacy (previously on a quarterly basis). Since July 1, 2005 new capital requirements for market risk have been introduced in the Regulation, requiring banks to maintain a higher level of capital. Finally, on February 24, 2006, the Governing Council amended the Regulation to increase the risk weighting used for calculating the CAR for mortgage loans by lowering the maximum LTV ratio from 70 percent to 50 percent from April 1, 2006.

Loan classification and provisioning requirements have also been changed. On January 23, 2004, the Governing Council amended Regulation 9 on the Evaluation and Classification of Risk Exposures of Banks and the Allocation of Provisions to Cover Impairment Loss. From April 1, 2004 classification groups were reduced from five (Standard, Watch, Substandard, Doubtful, and Loss) to four (Standard, Watch, Substandard, and Nonperforming). The "doubtful" and "loss" categories were amalgamated into the "nonperforming" loan category. Under the old classification rules, a loan was classified as "loss" after 120 days in arrears. Under the new classification rules, a loan is classified as "nonperforming" after 90 days in arrears. The provisioning requirements for impaired loans overdue by 60–90 days have been raised from 30 percent to 50 percent.

Loan classification and provisioning requirements have been adjusted further. On April 21, 2005, Regulation 9 introduced a provision which allows reclassification of a provisioned loan in a less risky group at least six months after the grounds for the original classification have been rectified. On November 10, 2005, the provisioning requirements for impaired household credits have been raised for loans overdue by 30–60 days from 10 percent to 20 percent and for loans overdue by 60–90 days from 50 percent to 75 percent, and provisions made for such credits may not be released until six months after the credits have begun to be fully serviced again.

Finally, some changes were made in eligibility requirements. In February 2006, the BNB issued a recommendation to the banks not to extend credit to households which do not have disposable income of at least lev 100 per household member per month after taxes, and all debt service (including that for the requested loan) have been deducted from the officially declared income. Where regular supervisory examinations reveal that this recommendation has not been followed, inspectors will reflect this in their reports and suggest appropriate supervisory measures.

Quantitative limits

Limits on excessive credit growth have been introduced. On February 22, 2005, the Governing Council amended Regulation 21, introducing additional required reserves from April 1, 2005. Banks whose credit portfolio expands by more than 6 percent per quarter are subject to an unremunerated deposit requirement of twice the excess credit expansion, unless the ratio of their credit minus capital deposit is below 60 percent. The measure, which had been announced well in advance, led, unintendedly, to a 22 percent month-on-month expansion of credit by banks in March 2005, as banks attempted to create a large base from which to calculate growth rates. On April 21, 2005, Regulation 21 was revised again, with the BNB deciding to use end-February instead of end-March as a base for the most aggressive lenders. Thus, for banks whose credit portfolio had increased by more than 4 percent in March compared to February 2005, the BNB used as a base February 2005 plus a 4 percent increase. In addition, the BNB changed computation of the credit growth rates from the end of the quarter to a quarterly average.

There were initial signs that the measures were effective, although the regulations had to be adjusted as the BNB observed some signs of circumvention. After the amendments to the Regulation on the minimum reserve requirements for the period March–July 2005, credit growth was negative, compared to 19 percent in December 2004 (for the first seven months of 2004 it had been 26.7 percent). The target for annual credit growth is within the range of 30–35 percent. After the first quarterly period of observation (April–June 2005) only four banks (there are 28 banks in the system) and one foreign bank branch (six branches) failed to achieve the limits prescribed in the Regulation. However, on November 10, 2005, the Governing Council amended Regulation 21. The quarterly limit on the penalty-free growth of credit, due to be phased out on March 31, 2006, was extended until the end of 2006. In addition, the penalty deposit rate for banks exceeding the limit by 1–2 percent was raised from 200 to 300 percent, and to 400 percent for excesses of more than 2 percent. On February 24, 2006, the Governing Council amended Regulation 21 further. In order to prevent circumvention of quantitative limits for credit growth, the BNB included in the definition of credit according to Regulation 21, bonds and other debt instruments acquired by banks after December 31, 2005.[3]

III. Effectiveness of the measures and implications

Overall, the measures taken by the BNB to curb credit proved to be effective. The most important conclusion after one year of intensive measures is that the BNB succeeded in achieving the two main targets: (i) to slow down credit growth and bring it to a similar level to the growth in assets and deposits, mainly through capital growth; and (ii) to keep the drop in the capital adequacy ratios at a comfortable level, which is appropriate for each bank's risk profile. While for the period December 2003–December 2004, the capital adequacy of the banking system shrunk by almost 600 basis points, for the period December 2004–December 2005, the drop was less than 100 basis points. At the end of 2004, capital growth was 5 percent while loans grew by 47 percent. As a result of the credit limits, at the end of 2005, the growth of capital and credit came within range for comparison—31 percent for the former and 33 percent for the latter. For the first quarter of 2006, the observed credit growth is less than 1 percent, while the annual credit growth for the period February 2005–February 2006 is below 30 percent (28.2 percent),[4] compared with 47.4 percent for the period February 2004–February 2005.

The measures also had other significant effects. First, the risk appetite of the main market players abated. The imposed measures helped improve risk management systems and facilitated knowledge transfer, something that was difficult during the period of fierce competition for clients. Second, speculative capital outflows are going mainly into the parent companies.

The measures, however, also forced banks to be more creative in their attempts to circumvent them. One of the most popular channels for banks to avoid the limitations was to establish their own leasing companies. Of the 50 leasing companies in Bulgaria, ten of them were established by banks. As of end-2005, the total amount of the claims of financial and operating leasing is lev 1.197 billion (about EUR 612 million). The development of leasing activities in the last two years resulted in a significant increase in its share of GDP, which by the end of 2005 reached almost 3 percent in comparison with 43 percent for credits as a percentage of GDP.

Another medium used by some banks to circumvent the BNB's measures was to fund some domestic customers through bonds and other debt instruments. At end-2005, the amount of these types of investment was about lev 340 million (EUR 174 million). The risk with this type of lending is much higher compared to the standard credit and this was one of the main reasons for the BNB to include in the definition of credit in Regulation 21, bonds and other debt instruments acquired by banks after December 31, 2005.

Looking back, the adopted measures as a whole proved to be effective. Although some could argue that prudential regulations should not be used to control credit growth, in the case of Bulgaria they have been an important part of the overall policy to offset and moderate rapid credit growth. Since policy options are constrained by the currency board arrangement, prudential regulations have become a crucial part of the BNB's policy to curb credit. The measures so far did not have undesirable side effects for the financial system as a whole. In addition, circumvention through lending by the nonbank financial sector shows that in the short run, the credit risk is still much higher in the banks' balance sheets than in that of some other financial institutions. To date, the current situation is not associated with a great shift from a closely monitored financial sector to a less supervised nonbank financial sector, although the authorities have also intensified their efforts recently to closely monitor the activity and supervision of nonbank financial institutions such as insurance and leasing companies.

Notes

1. The Bulgarian National Bank (BNB).
2. The limited exchange rate risk for Bulgarian banks and borrowers is the reason why the experience of the country is different from that of some other countries in the region where credit risk was also associated with an exchange rate risk.

3. With the exception of bonds issued by governments, central banks, and debt instruments with credit ratio higher than "Baa3" by Moody's or "BBB-" by Standard & Poor's or FITCH.
4. As the banks used different schemes to manipulate the initial base for calculation in March 2005, here the annual credit growth rate is calculated for the period February 2005–February 2006.

8
The Croatian Experience with Rapid Credit Growth

Maroje Lang[1]

In recent years, dealing with rapid credit growth has been one of the main issues for central banks in the countries of Central, Eastern, and South-eastern Europe (CEE). In many ways, these episodes resemble the credit booms that took place in other countries and generally resulted in banking crises. Recognizing that the main challenge now is how to design policies to deal with such credit booms, central banks in the region are adopting a range of different measures depending on their specific circumstances.

A variety of factors has contributed to the rapid growth of credit in the CEE countries. The transition, and particularly the liberalization of the banking sector, has played a profound role in the process. Demand for credit that was restricted in the past is finally being matched with an increasing supply of credit. In particular, many of these countries are experiencing a household credit boom following a long period prior to the transition in which it was not possible to do consumption-smoothing through borrowing because such loans were not available.

External factors have also played an important role. The most important of these are the historically low international interest rates and the process of EU accession. Low international interest rates helped increase the supply of credit, as international investors looked for higher than meager returns achievable in industrial countries. At the same time, the attainment of greater economic stability contributed to a willingness to take risks. This has been particularly the case in the CEE countries, which have been perceived as increasingly attractive destinations for foreign investment in the process of their joining the EU. Demand for credit also increased with the expectation of rising incomes and living standards brought by EU accession.

With a tradition as a local financial center, Croatia inherited a relatively well-developed financial sector[2] that responded to the above factors at a relatively earlier stage compared to the other countries in the region. Thus, Croatia experienced a rapid credit expansion relatively early, and was one of the first countries in the region to have implemented measures dealing with strong credit growth. As such, the Croatian experience can provide useful lessons for those countries that are currently experiencing credit booms and are devising policies to deal with it.

There is abundant literature on rapid credit expansion in Croatia. Kraft and Jankov (2004) give a good overview of the causes of lending booms in Croatia and the policies adopted for dealing with it up to 2004. Šonje and Vujšić (1999) describe banking sector developments in the late 1990s. Kraft (1999) and Jankov (2000) describe the banking crises in Croatia. Kraft (2004) describes the entry and impact of foreign banks in Croatia. Biannual banking surveys conducted by the Croatian National Bank (CNB) from 1997 identify the issue of fast credit growth as a potential cause for prospective macroeconomic imbalances.

In addition to presenting a case study of the Croatian experience with rapid credit growth, this chapter extends the existing literature by incorporating recent developments. It also puts a stronger emphasis on how the banks have responded, and often circumvented, the measures taken by the central bank. In the following two sections, the two distinct episodes of credit boom in Croatia are discussed, with particular emphasis on their causes, macroeconomic effects, and the policies undertaken to contain the rapid credit growth. Section III concludes.

I. The first credit boom (1995-98)

Post-war restoration and excessive liberalization of the banking industry

The first lending boom in Croatia started with the end of hostilities in 1995 and lasted until the banking crisis in 1998. During the four-year period, bank credits increased one and a half times (average annual rate of growth of 25 percent). Measured as a percentage of GDP, the share of credits increased from 26.3 percent at end-1994 to 36.6 percent at end-1998.

The major factors underlying the first credit boom developed in the years preceding the end of hostilities, with the latter acting more as a trigger for the overall economic revival. As a result of the war following the breakup of the former Yugoslavia, the drop in output in the early years of transition was more pronounced than in other CEE countries. The war also negatively affected the demand for and supply of credit. Some of the existing loans were written off as the result of bank rehabilitation in 1991, while subsequent write-offs occurred as the result of the war.

The liberalization of the banking system contributed to the rapid credit growth and eventually a banking crisis ensued. The banking system was dominated by the two largest banks with a presence throughout Croatia, while a number of regional banks enjoyed regional dominance. In order to support the development of the banking sector, bank entry was liberalized by introducing low initial capital requirements and relatively loose licensing criteria with the Law on Banks and Savings Banks in 1993 (Kraft and Jankov, 2005). As a result, many new private banks and savings banks were formed; the number of banks increased from 43 in 1993 to 60 in 1997, and 33 savings banks were formed (Table 8.1).

Some of the new private banks adopted a very aggressive growth strategy. With the liberalization of interest rates early on, they offered very high deposit rates in order to attract savings; those banks were offering annual rates on deposit in excess of 20 percent despite low inflation since late 1993. This aggressive strategy increased competition for deposits and led to an overall increase in deposit rates. However, high rates on deposits had also a major influence on the repatriation of deposits held by Croats abroad;[3] from 1995 to 1997 domestic deposits increased by 17.4 percent of GDP.

High deposit rates led to high lending rates, thereby attracting mostly riskier lending. Risk assessment was poor, and some of the fastest growing banks were engaged in significant connected lending. Both factors contributed to the failure of those banks in 1998 and 1999.

Households were interested in borrowing despite the high cost. Under socialism, banks had collected household deposits and extended credit primarily to companies; it had been difficult for individuals to obtain credit (at the end of 1994, almost 80 percent of domestic credit to the non-banking private sector was extended to companies—see Table 8.2). In addition, existing loans were in domestic currency and fell in real terms, since interest rates often did not keep up with inflation. Thus, the collective wisdom had been to take a loan if it was offered and to worry about repayment later. Most of the new credit offered by banks in the 1990s, however, was indexed to the exchange rate; hence the debt burden did not diminish.[4]

The first credit boom ended with the banking crisis in 1998 and 1999. The crisis started in March 1998 when one of the fastest growing regional banks failed, and gradually gathered momentum during 1998, peaking in February and March 1999. Overall, 16 banks representing 16.2 percent of total banking assets failed (Kraft and Jankov, 2005).

Current account deficit and monetary policy responses

Strong credit growth contributed to increased domestic demand, which was already strong as a result of the post-war economic expansion. Indeed, Croatia experienced its fastest economic growth immediately after the end of hostilities. Due to the openness of the economy and a stable exchange rate used as the main anchor for price expectations, strong domestic demand did not have an immediate effect on inflation.[5] Instead, higher demand was mostly met through merchandise imports.

Bank lending contributed particularly to the growth of car imports, the largest item among merchandise imports. With the restoration of stability and growth following the end of the war, households started upgrading their cars. Banks started offering loans for car purchases, since such loans were for relatively small amounts (compared to housing loans), and it was easier to collateralize them.[6] The gradual removal of car import duty exemptions enjoyed by war veterans also encouraged additional purchases of cars. The value of imported cars doubled during the credit boom peak in 1997.

There was consequently a significant deterioration in the current account to 12.3 percent of GDP during the height of the credit boom in 1997. During this period,

Table 8.1 Basic Features of the Banking System in Croatia

	1993	1994	1995	1996	1997	1998	1999	2000	2001	2002	2003	2004	2005
Number of banks	43	50	54	58	60	60	53	43	43	45	41	37	34
Total banking assets (% of GDP)	–	57.5	70.3	68.4	71.8	70.3	66.1	73.3	89.6	96.2	103.1	107.7	113.8
Number of foreign banks	0	1	1	5	7	10	13	20	24	23	16	15	14
Share of foreign banks in total assets, %	0.0	0.0	0.0	1.0	4.0	6.7	39.9	84.1	89.3	90.2	91.0	91.3	91.3
Capital-adequacy, %	–	–	19.6	17.7	16.4	12.7	20.6	21.3	18.5	16.6	15.7	15.3	13.4
Non-perf. loans, %	–	–	8.3	7.3	5.2	9.3	10.3	9.2	7.3	5.8	5.1	–	–
ROA, %	–	–	0.3	0.6	1.2	-2.8	0.7	1.4	0.9	1.6	1.4	1.7	1.7

Source: CNB.

Table 8.2 Main Macroeconomic Indicators—Croatia

	1994	1995	1996	1997	1998	1999	2000	2001	2002	2003	2004	2005
As a % of GDP												
Enterprises	21.2	22.9	21.4	25.3	26.6	22.1	20.7	23.1	25.9	24.9	25.1	27.1
Households	4.0	4.8	6.1	10.3	12.9	13.6	15.3	18.2	23.8	27.7	30.7	34.3
o/w: Housing loans	0.0	0.0	0.0	0.0	0.0	5.3	5.4	5.7	6.8	8.5	10.1	12.0
Total domestic credits*	26.3	28.7	27.9	36.6	41.0	43.2	44.2	49.7	60.6	65.9	60.5	67.6
Annual growth (in %)												
Enterprises	26.1	21.2	2.6	35.6	17.1	-14.5	0.9	21.3	22.6	5.1	8.0	16.3
Households	84.2	35.4	39.5	93.4	38.4	8.6	21.0	29.3	43.0	27.7	18.7	20.3
o/w: Housing loans							10.6	14.4	30.8	36.7	26.6	28.8
Total domestic credits*	30.9	22.8	6.7	50.4	24.5	-4.8	10.1	23.2	33.6	16.8	13.1	20.3

Sources: CBS, MoF, and CNB.

* All bank credits included, including credits to local and central government, and credits to financial sector.

Croatia also received an investment grade, and the government started borrowing abroad and accumulating foreign debt.

Monetary policy in the mid-1990s was primarily directed toward maintaining price stability achieved during the Stabilization Program in 1993 after the hyperinflation of the 1980s and the early 1990s. Monetary policy focused on a stable exchange rate as the main anchor for price expectations, as well as to contain import prices. This policy was very successful and Croatia for almost a decade enjoyed one of the lowest inflation levels in the region (Table 8.3).

Measures to tackle the lending boom came relatively late. In late 1996, the CNB increased the reserve requirement ratio. Further monetary tightening was attempted in mid-1997 by reducing money creation through reduced purchases of foreign exchange from banks.[7] Both measures, however, failed to reduce the credit expansion (Kraft and Jankov, 2005). Chilean-style capital controls were introduced in April 1998 (a non-remunerated 30 percent deposit requirement on all financial credits from abroad with a maturity of less than one year, and 5 percent on those up to three years). As the credit boom ended with the banking crisis in 1998, there was not enough time for the measures to have an effect.

II. The second lending boom, 2000–present

Key factor underlying the boom: foreign ownership of the banking sector

As a result of the banking crisis of 1998 and the continuation of economic reforms, the Croatian banking sector has changed significantly since 1999. It was privatized and taken over by foreign banks, primarily those in neighboring countries with an interest in extending their presence in the region—in particular, Italy and Austria. These changes helped the restructuring and modernization of the banking system, but also established the circumstances for the second lending boom, which has been ongoing since 2000 with a temporary slowdown in 2004.

The foreign banks took over the Croatian banking sector in just two years (see Table 8.1 above). The asset share of foreign-owned banks in the Croatian banking sector increased from 6.7 percent at end-1998 to 84.1 percent at end-2000, and continued to increase further; the foreign share as measured by shares in assets now amount to more than 90 percent of the banking industry. During the same two-year period, the number of banks with majority foreign ownership doubled from 10 (out of a total of 60) at end-1998 to 20 (out of a total of 43) in 2000. All major banks are currently majority owned by foreigners, with the exception of the state-owned Croatian Postal Bank; only smaller banks remain domestically owned.

The foreigners acquired the Croatian banking market in two ways: through purchases of existing banks and setting up new banks. Major entrants chose outright purchases in order to position themselves as important players early on, and thus to get ahead of possible international competitors interested in investing in the CEE. The largest share of the banking market was acquired through the privatization of (previously rehabilitated) state-owned banks. The banks that were privatized earlier (including the largest domestic banks) were acquired from private owners. Some foreign investors chose to set up new banks and opted for organic growth, with one

Table 8.3 Main Macroeconomic Indicators–Croatia

	1996	1997	1998	1999	2000	2001	2002	2003	2004	2005
GDP per capita (in EUR)	3,531	3,891	4,284	4,102	4,560	4,998	5,507	5,906	6,397	6,972
GDP growth (annual growth in %)	5.9	6.8	2.5	-0.9	2.9	4.4	5.6	5.3	3.8	4.3
Inflation (in %)	3.5	3.6	5.7	4.0	4.6	3.8	1.7	1.8	2.1	3.3
Current account balance (as of % GDP)	-4.8	-12.3	-6.8	-7.0	-2.4	-3.7	-8.6	-7.1	-4.9	-6.3
External debt (as of % GDP)	27.0	38.0	47.6	54.1	60.6	60.7	61.5	75.5	80.2	82.5
Average exchange rate (HRK : 1 EUR)	6.80	6.96	7.14	7.58	7.63	7.47	7.41	7.56	7.50	7.40
Consolidated central government deficit (as % of GDP)	–	–	–	-6.5	-7.1	-6.7	-4.5	-4.6	-4.6	-3.4
Unemployment rate (ILO, persons above 15 years of age)	10.0	9.9	11.4	13.6	16.1	15.8	14.8	14.3	13.8	12.7
Employment rate (ILO, persons above 15 years of age)	50.6	49.3	47.0	44.8	42.6	41.8	43.3	43.1	43.5	43.3

Sources: CBS, MoF and CNB.

bank being particularly successful in pursuing this policy. As the first foreign bank to enter the Croatian banking sector before its privatization, it managed to profit from foreign ownership; with many people considering it safer than domestically owned banks, especially during the banking crisis of 1998, it gained many new clients and deposits.

The acquisition of banks by foreigners had a profound effect. New owners brought new technology, improved the efficiency of Croatian banks, although this was to some extent achieved by cutting the number of staff, and also brought new products. While the former socialist banks predominantly lent to enterprises, the new owners focused primarily on the retail sector (lending to households). Squeezed by historically low interest rates and low margins in their domestic markets, the foreign owners sought to invest further in the Croatian market (and other transition economies), and hence were willing to extend funds to their banks in Croatia to meet credit demand. Some owners, especially those interested in a long-term presence in Croatia, aimed at increasing their share in the Croatian banking market. The increased competition among banks led to a continued decline in active interest rates and easier conditions for access to credit (Figure 8.1).

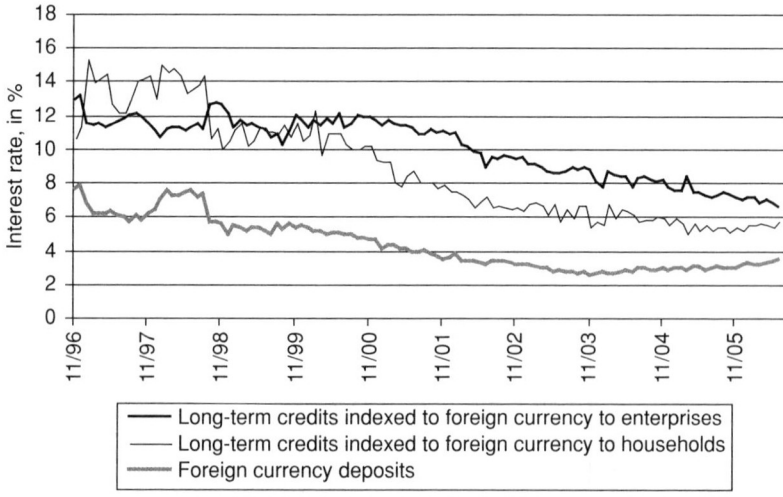

Figure 8.1 Evolution of Interest Rates in Croatia

Source: CNB.

The entry of foreign banks also had a major macroeconomic effect, in particular on the monetary policy transmission mechanism. Although the largest Croatian banks had received credit from abroad from the mid-1990s, foreign ownership significantly increased the availability of foreign funds. Indeed, most capital inflows to Croatia since 2002 came through banks, which used foreign funds to finance the rapid growth in domestic credit. The availability of foreign funds reduced further the effectiveness of monetary policy (see, e.g., Lang and Krznar, 2004, which shows that foreign ownership weakened the credit channel of monetary policy in Croatia). As discussed below, this has limited the use of monetary policy and induced the CNB to use more direct methods to deal with rapid credit growth.

Restoration of credit growth

Although the small, privately-owned banks suffered the most during the banking crisis of 1998 and 1999, bigger banks also slowed down their lending activity as the share of bad loans increased. The rise in bad loans was primarily due to the weaker lending policies of the previous few years, but the recession, and to some extent the drop in real estate prices, also contributed.

While all credits slowed in 1998 and 1999, lending to enterprises was the most affected. As noted above, credits to enterprises dominated old banks' portfolios, and banks started gradually shifting to households from the mid-1990s. Thus, while lending to enterprises actually declined, banks continued to lend to households, albeit at lower rates. Strong growth of credit to households resumed in 2000, while credit to enterprises started growing only in 2001 (Figure 8.2). In fact, the payment of government arrears accumulated in the late 1990s improved enterprise liquidity and their balance sheets, which may have reduced their demand for loans. As a whole, domestic credit to the nonfinancial private sector declined by 7.0 percent in 1999 due to the write-offs, and grew by a moderate 8.5 percent in 2000; domestic credit to households increased by 8.6 percent in 1999 and 21.0 percent in 2000, while that to enterprises fell by 14.5 percent in 1999 and stagnated in 2000.

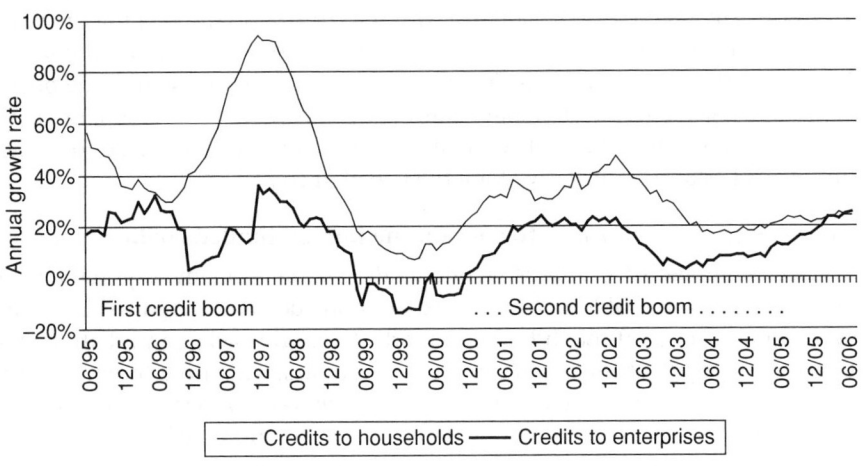

Figure 8.2 Credit to Nonfinancial Private Sector—Croatia

Source: CNB.

The entry of foreign banks in 1999 and 2000 and the subsequent changes in the banking sector contributed to such moderate credit growth, as the new owners were primarily interested in consolidating new acquisitions and increasing their efficiency rather than their growth. The Asian and Russian crisis experiences were also still recent, and the new owners of the major banks did not want to push ahead with credit expansion.

Overall credit growth resumed in 2001 when lending to the nonfinancial private sector increased by 24.7 percent (29.3 percent for households and 21.3 percent for enterprises). The growth of credit was further supported by the euro changeover, in a somewhat peculiar way. Traditionally, Croatians saved in foreign currencies[8] (mostly in deutsche mark), with the bulk of savings being held in foreign currency cash, particularly the legacy currencies. A strong campaign orchestrated by the CNB convinced the public that the best way of exchanging the old legacy currency banknotes was to deposit them in domestic banks.[9] As a result, domestic banks experienced a massive inflow of foreign currency deposits (53.2 percent rise in 2001) and an overall asset growth of 27.7 percent.[10] The huge increases in bank assets were initially placed abroad, but banks subsequently increased lending to the private sector as they started to look for better investment opportunities. In a few months, banks managed to lend all the deposits acquired during the euro changeover. As the demand for loans has remained strong, banks turned abroad for additional sources of financing (primarily to their foreign owners). Historically low international interest rates and a good initial experience with investment in Croatia motivated the owners to continue financing banking operations in Croatia, and they have maintained the ample supply of credit ever since.

The increased supply of banking loans was met by increased demand, as they were offered at lower interest rates and conditions that were more favorable to borrowers. Demand increased gradually, with the growing strength of the Croatian economy and better prospects for long-term growth associated with an improved political situation that helped accelerate the process of EU accession.[11] The prices of real estate also recovered after falling during the recession of 1999, supported by stronger housing demand from Croatians, as well as by increased foreign demand for prime real estate, particularly along the Croatian coast.

Rising foreign debt: measures to contain the foreign funded credit expansion

The macroeconomic effects of the second lending boom in many ways resembled those of the first one (Table 8.3). Increased domestic demand supported by credit growth was again met through higher imports; the slight pickup in inflation was primarily the result of increased administered prices. This time, however, the increase in the current account deficit was less pronounced, owing to strong tourism revenues. However, largely foreign-owned banks relied more on foreign funding for their credit expansion, which led to significant capital inflows, appreciation pressures on the exchange rate, and a buildup of foreign debt (over 15 percentage points of GDP in 2003 alone). The high level of foreign debt that exceeded 80 percent of GDP by end-2004 put pressure on the CNB to adopt measures to contain the credit expansion financed from abroad.

In devising the measures, the CNB had to take into account the new structure of the banking sector. As indicated above, foreign ownership of the banking sector weakened the credit channel of monetary policy in the sense that the commercial banks depended less on the CNB for liquidity. The CNB believed that, in addition to being ineffective for containing the credit growth, a decision to increase the short-term interest rates would be very expensive and could in fact encourage additional portfolio inflows. The capital inflows created appreciation pressures on the currency, leading to increased foreign exchange interventions so as to prevent further appreciation and a further worsening of the current account. In order to have the desired effect, the increase in interest rates would need to be substantial; the latter, however, would have negative implications for public finances, both directly and indirectly, as the CNB was trying to mop up the excess liquidity by issuing short-term CNB bills.

One of the main policy decisions was to stop the planned reduction of the reserve requirement that was much higher than in the euro zone, as well as in most of the countries in the region. The reserve requirement was levied on the entire liabilities of the commercial banks excluding capital and the rate amounted at that time to 22 percent. Since 2000, the same rate has applied to all liabilities; however, liabilities in domestic and foreign currency have been treated differently, in the sense that the reserve requirement on liabilities in foreign currency is maintained partly in domestic and partly in foreign currency, and a part of it can be maintained abroad in the form of liquid assets (mostly deposits with foreign banks).

Instead of relying on indirect monetary policy instruments, the CNB directly targeted rapid credit growth. Those banks for which the growth of risk assets exceeded 4 percent in a given quarter were required to buy low-yielding CNB paper (at an interest rate of 0.5 percent). The obligatory CNB bills measure (often called the "16 percent rule": 4 quarters × 4 percent growth = 16 percent annual growth) was meant to be temporary and was kept in place only during 2003.

To discourage banks from borrowing abroad, the CNB modified an older regulation that required the banks to meet their short-term liabilities in foreign currencies with liquid foreign assets, so as to include all liabilities in foreign currency. The motivation for this change was that foreign bank owners avoided the previous rule by extending longer-term financing to domestic banks. The regulation was further tightened in order to force banks to redirect a part of their domestic assets abroad, thereby further reducing the funds available to finance domestic credit growth. This measure was called the "35 percent rule" since banks were required to maintain the liquidity provision of 35 percent of their liabilities in foreign currency in the form of liquid foreign currency denominated assets. The list of assets which were considered liquid was very restrictive and did not include any domestic placements except those with the CNB. Both measures were aimed at slowing credit growth, not at preventing asset quality problems per se.

The measures undertaken at the beginning of 2003 produced mixed results. Headline credit growth fell from 30.2 percent in 2002 to 14.6 percent in 2003, and 13.0 percent in 2004. However, those numbers do not fully reflect the slowdown of lending activity in Croatia. In fact, banks shifted their assets within categories (Kraft and Jankov, 2005): they decreased available but unused lines of credit, increased write-offs, and sold some of their credit portfolio; there was also a rapid growth in leasing activity, and greater direct foreign borrowing by enterprises (Table 8.4). The

Table 8.4 Total Nonfinancial Private Sector Debt by Creditor—Croatia

	1999	2000	2001	2002	2003	2004	2005	2000	2001	2002	2003	2004	2005
	share in GDP (in %)							annual growth (in %)					
Household debt	14.2	15.9	19.0	24.7	28.9	32.1	35.9	21.1	29.7	42.5	27.9	19.2	20.3
banks	13.6	15.3	18.2	23.8	27.7	30.7	34.3	21.0	29.3	43.0	27.7	18.7	20.3
housing savings banks	0.0	0.0	0.0	0.1	0.1	0.2	0.3		1,933	686.7	105.8	98.6	54.2
foreign debt	0.1	0.2	0.2	0.3	0.3	0.3	0.3	38.5	45.9	36.9	15.2	21.0	9.4
savings and loans associations	0.4	0.4	0.5	0.5	0.6	0.6	0.6	14.8	29.0	15.7	24.4	9.8	11.5
leasing	0.0	0.0	0.0	0.1	0.1	0.3	0.3	91.5	48.4	122.6	119.0	91.1	22.7
insurance companies	0.0	0.0	0.0	0.0	0.1	0.1	0.1	94.1	164.8	-1.4	37.9	52.5	30.6
Nonfinancial enterprises debt	44.4	43.0	42.9	45.0	45.3	47.9	52.5	4.1	8.5	14.6	10.4	13.3	18.0
banks	24.9	23.5	25.9	28.5	27.1	27.6	29.3	1.8	19.5	20.6	4.0	9.0	14.3
foreign debt	18.0	18.1	15.7	14.7	15.9	17.5	19.5	8.3	-6.0	2.8	18.4	17.7	20.2
leasing	0.1	0.2	0.3	0.7	1.4	1.8	2.8	91.5	48.4	122.6	119.0	39.6	70.5
other (funds and insurance companies)	1.4	1.1	1.0	1.0	0.9	1.1	1.0	-16.9	2.0	9.6	-1.1	25.4	-5.8
Nonfinancial private sector debt	58.6	58.9	61.9	69.7	74.2	80.0	88.4	8.2	14.2	23.2	16.6	15.6	18.9
banks	38.5	38.8	44.1	52.3	54.8	58.2	63.6	8.6	23.3	29.9	14.8	13.9	17.5
housing savings banks	0.0	0.0	0.0	0.1	0.1	0.2	0.3		1,933	686.7	105.8	98.6	54.2
foreign debt	18.1	18.2	15.9	15.0	16.2	17.8	19.8	8.5	-5.5	3.2	18.4	17.8	20.0
savings and loans associations	0.4	0.4	0.5	0.5	0.6	0.6	0.6	14.8	29.0	15.7	24.4	9.8	11.5
leasing	0.2	0.3	0.4	0.8	1.5	2.0	3.1	91.5	48.4	122.6	119.0	44.6	64.3
other (funds and insurance companies)	1.4	1.1	1.1	1.1	1.0	1.2	1.1	-16.0	5.0	9.1	0.5	27.0	-3.3

Note: Estimate based on data of the CNB, CBS, FINA, DINADOS, HAGENA, CROSEC, and MoF.

growth of bank loans, leasing and enterprise foreign borrowing by the nonfinancial private sector was 23.3 percent in 2002, and 16.6 percent in 2003, and so it is evident that the decline in overall credit growth was much smaller than the fall in bank loans alone. This was also reflected in the sectoral distribution of credits. The annual growth of credits to enterprises fell from 22.6 percent in 2002 to 5.1 percent in 2003 and 8.0 percent in 2004, as enterprises were able to use other sources of financing more easily compared with households. Indeed, credits to households decreased less, from 43.0 percent in 2002 to 27.7 percent in 2003, and 18.7 percent in 2004.

Contrary to what was intended, the measures actually encouraged foreign borrowing, as banks responded to the 35 percent liquidity coverage by borrowing more instead of less. Since the banks received financing from their foreign owners, they actually withdrew more funds than they required and placed part of it with their owners to fulfill the liquidity requirement. As a result, both foreign assets and liabilities increased in 2003 and banks' foreign liabilities grew from 19 percent of GDP in 2002 to 25 percent in 2003. Banks continued to borrow abroad in 2004, with their foreign liabilities rising to 29 percent of GDP. The overall Croatian foreign debt increased from 62 percent of GDP in 2002 to 77 percent of GDP in 2003.

As the temporary penalty for fast growing banks expired, the CNB introduced new measures. Instead of directly targeting the credit growth, the new regulation focused more on the source of financing since the credit growth in excess of domestic sources (i.e., growth of domestic deposits) was considered excessive. Such an approach was taken as the CNB was particularly concerned about containing the growth of foreign debt that could in the medium term threaten overall macroeconomic stability.

The decision was therefore to start penalizing bank foreign borrowing directly. Despite the observed growth of foreign borrowing by enterprises, the CNB refrained from widening the scope of its measures and using broad capital account restrictions, and instead targeted banks exclusively, for which it could devise finer measures. The new Marginal Reserve Requirement (MRR) was imposed on new foreign borrowing by commercial banks (July 2004). The intention was to immobilize a part of the funds borrowed from abroad, reducing the room for profiting on the differential between active interest rates on credits and the cost of foreign funds. The existing reserve requirement was also modified and commercial banks were required to deposit the entire reserve requirement levied on foreign liabilities with the CNB, instead of keeping a part of it abroad in liquid assets.

The Marginal Reserve Requirement, however, was updated a couple of times by increasing its rate and scope as banks have continued to attempt to circumvent existing measures:

- The MRR was initially set at 20 percent, which meant that commercial banks, in addition to the regular reserve requirement, had to deposit 20 percent of the increase in their foreign liabilities after June 2004 with the CNB. Banks continued to borrow abroad, since this percentage was not enough to cover the marginal profit the banks were making on the spread between domestic and, historically low, international interest rates at which they were borrowing. The initial calculation was that the marginal rate would need to be in excess of 55 percent (in addition to the existing reserve requirement which at that time amounted to 19 percent and was levied on all liabilities) to fully eliminate the earning potential of such activity.

- As banks continued to borrow abroad in 2004 and 2005, the CNB increased the MRR on three occasions: to 30 percent in February 2004 and 40 percent in May 2005, levied on the same basis, calculated as the increase in foreign liabilities since June 2004. The latest increase took place in November 2005 when an additional 15 percent rate was levied, bringing the total MRR to 55 percent.
- As banks attempted to avoid the measure by trying to present the new foreign borrowing as domestic, the CNB broadened the base on a few occasions. Since its introduction, the basis for calculating the MRR included all deposits placed by the companies owned by the same foreign owner (including domestic ones). As banks devised new vehicles for channeling foreign borrowing, the CNB extended the MRR coverage. One bank was providing guarantees to Croatian companies who then received credits directly from its owner. Another issued domestic bonds that were initially purchased by domestic companies who were planning to sell the bonds on the secondary market to the bank's foreign owner (in monetary statistics these counted as domestic liabilities/bonds). The CNB responded to these circumvention attempts by including guarantees in the calculation of the MRR in November 2005 and domestically issued bonds in February 2006 (Special Reserve Requirement).

As can be seen in Table 8.5, subsequent tightening of the MRR increased the return that banks needed to make foreign funded lending activity profitable. Competition among banks and plenty of domestic sources, however, prevented the lending rates from rising. Interestingly, with the increase in the cost of funding as international interest rates increase, the required return will increase even more.

Table 8.5 Calculation of the Impact of the MRR on the Required Return to Make Profit on Domestic Credit Financed by Borrowing Abroad—Croatia

Source of Funding	Cost of funding	Reserve requirement	Marginal reserve requirement	Minimum required FX liquidity	Funds available for granting credits	Required return
Foreign liabilities (EUR)—MRR 55%	3.5%	17	55	0	28	12.2%
—MRR 40%	3.5%	17	40	0	43	7.8%
—MRR 35%	3.5%	17	35	0	48	7.0%
—MRR 25%	3.5%	17	25	0	58	5.8%
Foreign liabilities (CHF)—MRR 55%	1.5%	17	22	0	61	5.0%
Household deposits (HRK)	5.0%	17	0	0	83	4.8%
Household deposits (indexed in FX)	4.8%	17	0	0	83	4.6%
Household deposits (EUR)	4.3%	13.6	0	26.9	59.5	3.9%

Source: Author's calculation.

Note: Assumes no additional cost on receiving funding and granting credits; current reserve requirement rate at 17 percent and foreign currency liquidity coverage at 32 percent.

In addition to taxing foreign borrowing, the CNB tried to contain the growth of foreign debt by gradually reducing other reserve and liquidity requirements, effectively freeing bank assets previously unavailable for financing credit expansion. The required reserve ratio was lowered from 19 percent to 18 percent in November 2004, and to 17 percent in January 2006. In addition, the minimum required amount of foreign currency claims was lowered in March 2005 from 35 percent to 32 percent, and additionally modified in March 2006 to include a particular bridge loan to the government.

In most cases, the CNB reduced the existing requirements together with other monetary or fiscal operations. In particular, funds were freed when the government refinanced its foreign debt on the domestic market. Commercial banks, however, were not obliged to invest the freed assets in government paper. Only in one case—provisional modification in March 2006—was the freeing of funds explicitly tied to government financing. In addition to the immediate effect of freeing funds, these measures also increased the credit multiplier which could reduce the need for foreign funding in the future.

The CNB indicated to the banks that a further reduction of reserve requirements would take place if banks limited their growth of foreign liabilities, while the MRR would be increased if foreign borrowing continued. The approach was asymmetrical in the sense that the largest banks would benefit the most through compliance. On the other hand, banks which increased their foreign liabilities would be taxed with further increases in the MRR. This type of moral suasion, however, was not effective, since individual banks followed different business strategies. For some banks, an increasing share of the banking market was the target, which depended on borrowing abroad.

The CNB also used prudential measures for containing the credit expansion: the minimum capital adequacy requirement was raised to 10 percent (since the 1999 Law on Banks). From 2004, banks that grew faster than 20 percent were required to form special reserves (0.10 percent of risk assets) which acted as a temporary increase in capital requirements for the fast growing banks. Banks were exempt from this requirement if they met higher capital standards (15 percent for growth between 20 percent and 30 percent, 20 percent for growth between 30 percent and 40 percent, etc). Exceptions also existed for new banks (for the first three years).

Since 2006, more emphasis has been put on foreign exchange induced credit risk—a risk that a bank faces in providing credits in foreign currency (or indexed to foreign currency) to a client without income in that currency. The weight for calculating risky assets was increased by an additional 25 basis points. This measure is particularly important since more than three quarters of domestic credits are in, or indexed to, foreign currency (Table 8.6). The commercial banks extend their loans in foreign currency (or index it, since households are not allowed to borrow in foreign currency) to limit their currency mismatches, as most of their liabilities (deposits) are in foreign currency.[12] Loans are mainly indexed to the euro (also the case for deposits); however, banks recently started offering loans in Swiss francs, which became very popular due to the lower interest rate. Such loans carry larger exchange rate risk, as the CNB focuses on the stability of the exchange rate vis-à-vis the euro. Lending in Swiss francs hence has potential implications for financial stability; in particular, the expectation that the future adoption of the euro would remove the exchange rate risk from borrowers' balance sheets is put in question by the increased lending in Swiss francs.

Table 8.6 Currency Structure of Domestic Credits—Croatia

	1999	2000	2001	2002	2003	2004	2005
Total domestic credits							
Credits in domestic currency	14.5	14.6	15.3	20.2	25.8	24.3	22.6
Credits indexed to foreign currency	71.2	72.5	72.5	67.0	63.4	64.1	63.7
Credits in foreign currency	14.3	13.0	12.2	12.8	10.8	11.6	13.7
Currency structure of credits in foreign currency or indexed to foreign currency							
EUR	81.2	91.0	93.8	93.6	94.2	91.3	83.1
CHF	2.0	1.2	0.7	0.9	1.1	4.0	12.4
USD	7.4	7.6	5.4	5.1	4.5	4.5	4.3
other currencies	9.4	0.1	0.1	0.5	0.2	0.2	0.2
Enterprises							
Credits in domestic currency	14.6	14.4	19.5	25.4	28.6	25.9	24.9
Credits indexed to foreign currency	63.6	65.5	61.7	52.5	51.8	54.3	54.2
Credits in foreign currency	21.8	20.1	18.8	22.1	19.6	19.8	20.9
Households							
Credits in domestic currency	10.9	10.6	10.2	11.7	18.7	20.6	20.1
Credits indexed to foreign currency	88.9	89.2	89.6	88.1	81.0	79.0	79.5
Credits in foreign currency	0.2	0.2	0.2	0.2	0.3	0.4	0.4

Source: CNB.

Conclusions

Given its relatively well-developed banking sector, Croatia experienced rapid credit growth before the other countries in the region. Indeed, in just a decade and a half, Croatia has experienced two credit booms and one banking crisis. The causes of the credit booms were somewhat different between the two episodes, but in both cases were on the supply side. The first credit boom was to a large extent caused by bank liberalization, while the second was marked by the entry of foreign banks that provided ample funding for continued credit expansion.

The demand for credit has also remained strong throughout the period. External factors, including the historically low international interest rates, contributed to the strong demand for credit, suggesting that tightening of interest rates by major central banks might raise interest rates in emerging markets as well, and slow down the credit expansion. Monetary policy that focused largely on exchange rate stability might also have contributed to the demand for loans, particularly those denominated in or indexed to foreign currency, which are cheaper than loans in domestic currency; borrowers are willing to take such loans when they expect stable exchange rates to continue.

The macroeconomic effects of the two credit booms were similar. Credit activity stimulated domestic demand that led to increased imports and a worsening current account deficit. In both cases, the bulk of financing came from abroad, thereby leading to rising foreign debt; in less than a decade Croatia became a highly indebted country. Interestingly, inflation was unaffected by the credit growth owing to a stable exchange rate.

In dealing with the credit growth, the CNB did not rely on monetary tightening through higher interest rates. It was presumed that such a move would only trigger additional portfolio inflows and would be counterproductive. It appears that monetary policy in small countries, especially those experiencing strong capital inflows during the European integration process, have limited ability to control credit growth. These countries are facing very similar circumstances to the members of the euro zone, which are also experiencing rapid credit growth and are unable to effectively control it with the use of monetary policy instruments.

Prudential measures also appear to have had only a limited effect as they were primarily oriented to individual loans and banks, and were not tightened enough to have significant macroeconomic implications. As mostly foreign-owned banks were competing for market share, it was difficult to use moral suasion and convince banks to engage in a collaborative action of slowing down credit activity and borrowing from abroad.

The CNB therefore focused more on direct measures for containing the credit growth and the foreign borrowing that was financing it. Initial experience with such measures has been mixed. On one hand, the headline credit numbers look as though the direct measures for containing the credit expansion worked. However, a more in-depth analysis shows that banks by-passed the credit restrictions by reducing credit lines, writing off loans, selling their loan portfolio, and directing some of the lending activity to leasing companies and abroad.

Given the outcome, the CNB proceeded by differentiating the funding sources. It started penalizing the foreign borrowing by banks and the MRR in effect reduced the possibility of profiting from interest rate spreads between Croatia and abroad. However, this measure would not work unless the rate became very high, since banks managed to extract profit from such activity under the lower rate. Although further tightening of this requirement should at some point stop foreign borrowing by the banks, the level that would be necessary to do so remains to be seen. With a view to ensuring the success of future measures to stop banks from borrowing abroad to finance domestic lending, the central bank needs to consider simultaneously appropriate action to prevent the banks from circumventing such measures.

Notes

1. The Croatian National Bank (CNB).
2. Croatia has the largest share of domestic credits in GDP among CEE countries.
3. In addition to the deposits of Croats living abroad (approximately one quarter of Croats live abroad, mainly in western Europe, Americas, and Australia), a number of Croatian residents had transferred and kept their savings abroad (mostly Austria and Italy) due to instability caused by the war. In addition, after the breakup of Former Yugoslavia, foreign

exchange deposits had been temporarily frozen which reduced the confidence in the domestic banking sector.
4. Real exchange rate appreciation of course reduces the debt burden in the process of convergence to the EU.
5. However, the prices of the real estate increased as a result of the stability and higher demand for housing.
6. Croatian banks in general over-collateralized their loans. Banks usually combined a number of instruments to insure the loan repayment: permission to directly take a part of the borrower's salary, 2–3 guarantors and possibly a co-borrower who also signed a similar permission against their salaries (very important due to a relatively tight society and the importance of social connections), physical collateral (usually the same items purchased by the same credit, such as homes and cars), insurance of the collateral, life insurance of a debtor, and a bank deposit in the value of 10–20 percent of the loan. If the borrower did not honor a repayment or two, and it was not possible to directly charge his salary, the banks usually went directly to the guarantors' salaries without initiating other insurance instruments. As a result, there were very few nonperforming loans.
7. The CNB conducts unsterilized foreign exchange interventions for money creation.
8. Foreign currency deposits were permitted in 1967 in order to encourage growing ex-Yugoslav Diaspora to bring in their savings from abroad. In addition, episodes of hyperinflation in the 1980s and the early 1990s diminished the value of domestic currency deposits, and households learned from this. Also, the temporary freeze of foreign currency deposits in 1991 and the banking crisis in 1998 further encouraged households to hold their savings abroad or in cash.
9. During the last few days of 2001, people were forming queues in banks to pay-in their legacy currencies.
10. Some outflow from the banking sector took place in March and April 2002 after the news of a major loss caused by a rogue trader in one of the largest banks temporarily reduced the confidence in the banking system. The overall effect of deposit increase was nevertheless huge.
11. The left-center coalition, which won the 2000 election, enjoyed better reputation with the western countries, than the former government that led Croatia during the 1990s. This helped to accelerate the process of EU accession, and in 2001 the Stabilization and Association Agreement was signed.
12. During the last few years, banks started encouraging depositors to switch their savings from foreign currency into kuna deposits indexed to foreign currency in order to avoid fulfilling the minimum foreign currency coverage requirement. As a result, those deposits are rising significantly, while foreign exchange deposits are growing at lower rates than before. The CNB has not yet responded to such behavior.

Bibliography

Croatian National Bank. Annual Reports.
Croatian National Bank. Bulletins.
Croatian National Bank. Banks Bulletins.
Galac, T., 2003, Results of the Third CNB Bank Survey: Croatian Banking in the Consolidation and Market Positioning Stage, 2000, to date. CNB Survey Series 14, Croatian National Bank, Zagreb.
Galac, T. and L. Dukić, 2005, Results of the Fourth CNB Bank Survey, CNB Survey Series 20, Croatian National Bank, Zagreb.
Jankov, L., 1999, "Banking System in 1998," CNB Survey Series 1, Croatian National Bank, Zagreb.
——, 2000, "Banking Sector Problems: Causes, Ways of Resolving Them, and Consequences" (in Croatian), CNB Survey Series 2, Croatian National Bank, Zagreb.

Kraft, E., 1999, "Croatia's Second Banking Crisis," in *Enterprises in Transition*, Faculty of Economics, Split, Croatia.

——, 2004, "Foreign Banks in Croatia: Reasons for Entry, Performance and Impacts," *Journal of Emerging Market Finance*, vol. 3(2), pp. 153–74.

Kraft, E. and L. Jankov, 2005, "Does Speed Kill? Lending Booms and their Consequences in Croatia," *Journal of Banking and Finance*, vol. 29, pp. 105–21.

Lang, M. and I. Krznar, 2004, "Transmission Mechanism of Monetary Policy in Croatia," Paper presented on The Tenth Dubrovnik Economic Conference 2004, Croatian National Bank, Zagreb.

Šonje, V. and B. Vujčić, 1999, "Croatia in the Second Stage of Transition 1994–1999," CNB Working Paper Series 2. Croatian National Bank, Zagreb.

9
Estonia's Experience with Rapid Credit Growth

Raoul Lättemäe[1]

Estonia has experienced two rapid credit growth cycles: one in the mid-1990s and the second from 2001 onward. This has raised several questions about the sustainability of these developments and about possible policy reactions that the authorities can and should take.

The structure of the Estonian financial sector and the monetary policy framework based on a currency board arrangement (CBA) make coping with rapid credit growth a particularly challenging task for policymakers. The CBA itself is a certain form of a rigid, fixed-exchange rate regime, where there is practically no room for discretionary domestic monetary policy. The central bank's interventions in the foreign exchange market are basically automatic through the currency board-base money creation mechanism (base money is issued only against the respective change in foreign reserves), and there is legislation to inhibit any attempts to exit the regime (exiting a currency board usually requires a change in law). Hence, the set of tools that policymakers have at their disposal is certainly limited.

Further limitations stem from the structure of the financial sector. Estonian financial intermediation is based on the universal banking model, where the banking sector has a dominant role and the share of the securities market is relatively low. The Estonian banking system is concentrated, mainly foreign-owned, and fully privatized. Both credit expansion cycles have therefore been driven by market forces and have been run mostly on foreign capital inflows.

The rest of the chapter, which describes Estonia's policy experience during those cycles, is divided into two parts: (i) the first credit growth cycle (1996–98), and (ii) the second (current) credit growth cycle (from 2002 onwards).

I. The first credit growth cycle

The banking sector landscape was rather diverse in the early 1990s, with the number of banks peaking at 34 in 1992 (Figure 9.1). These banks, which were operating largely on the resources obtained from domestic deposits, were small and their risks were, on some occasions, not properly managed. This picture meant that rather harsh restructuring and consolidation of the banking sector was necessary by 1994, when the capital account in Estonia was opened up. The level of financial deepening was relatively low in the early 1990s, as the banks' assets made up less than 20 percent of GDP. Estonia experienced several banking crises, and periods of mergers and acquisitions, as a result of which the number of banks halved by the mid-1990s.

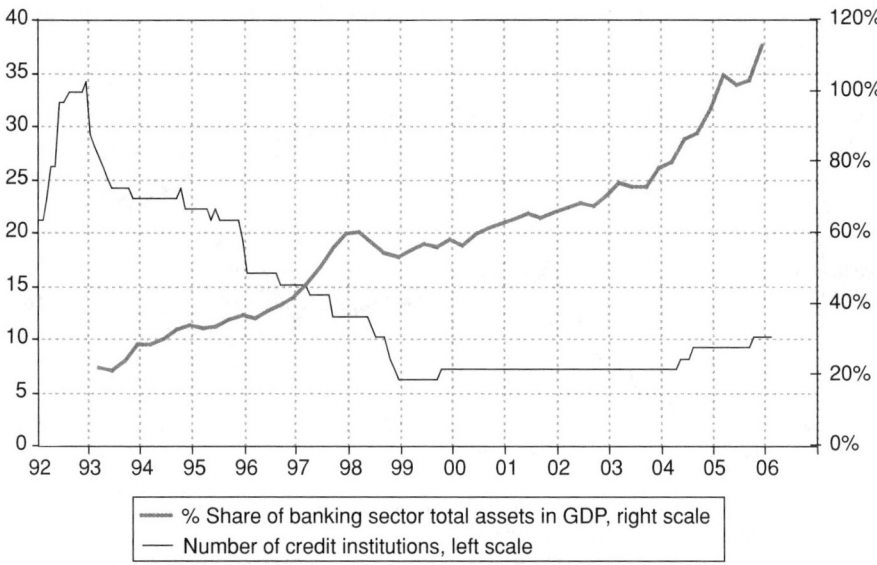

Figure 9.1 Dynamics of the Estonian Banking Sector

Source: BoE.

The strength of the financial sector became a crucial issue almost immediately after the capital account liberalization, given the limited lender of last resort (LOLR) capability of the central bank under the CBA. In addition, given that financial sector strength is one of the cornerstones of the CBA, the real sector was faced with a tough budget constraint from the beginning of the reforms.

Foreign capital inflow did not follow immediately after the liberalization of the capital account in 1994. However, from 1996 onward, foreign investors started to explore Estonian markets more actively. This period was marked by the increasing creditworthiness of Estonian enterprises and the growing presence of Estonian banks in European financial markets, both in terms of investment and borrowing. The latter also marked an early integration into European markets and a trend toward internationalization of Estonian financial markets.

Rapid pickup in foreign capital inflow through the financial sector, which started in 1996–97, led to extensive credit growth to the domestic real sector (Figure 9.2).

During the first stage, the banks' foreign borrowing supported the acceleration in banks' assets. In the later stages, the rapid credit growth was followed by rapid deposit growth as well. The strong monetary developments were reflected both in the skyrocketing equity market—with the increase in the stock exchange index (TALSE) peaking in 1997 at more than 200 percent in less than one year—as well as in strong domestic demand. The GDP growth rate in turn exceeded 10 percent and the current account deficit widened to 11.4 percent. At the same time, inflationary pressures were not a particular concern, as inflation rates were still on a downward trend from the very high levels of the early 1990s. Somewhat ironically, the Estonian inflation rate reached the single digit level in 1997 in an otherwise overheating environment.

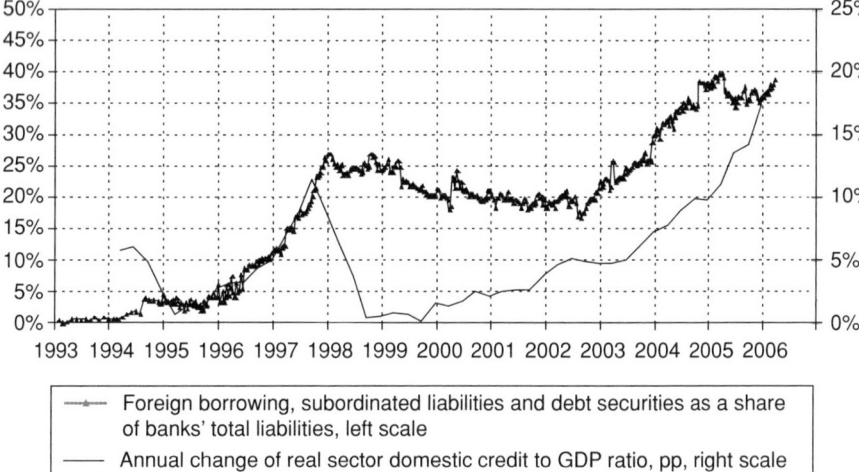

Figure 9.2 Capital Inflow into the Banking Sector and Annual Increase in Domestic Credit to GDP—Estonia

Source: BoE.

The authorities reacted to these developments with increased fiscal surplus, increased capital adequacy ratio, and several amendments to the compulsory reserve requirement framework. The changes were introduced due to concern that the monetary developments were excessive. More concretely, the increasing capital inflows, as well as financial sector over-borrowing from foreign markets during 1996–97, fostered domestic demand, which developed into a rapidly deteriorating current account deficit. As the currency board set clear limits on using monetary tools for implementing restrictive policies, the "stabilization package" contained not only the strengthening of compulsory reserves but also an increase in the prudential capital adequacy requirement from 8 to 10 percent (Figure 9.3) and the formation of Stabilization Reserves from the fiscal surplus. In the monetary framework, the steps meant a widening of the reserve base and an increase in banks' reserve balances with the Bank of Estonia (BoE), from 10 to 13 percent through the introduction of the additional liquidity requirement.

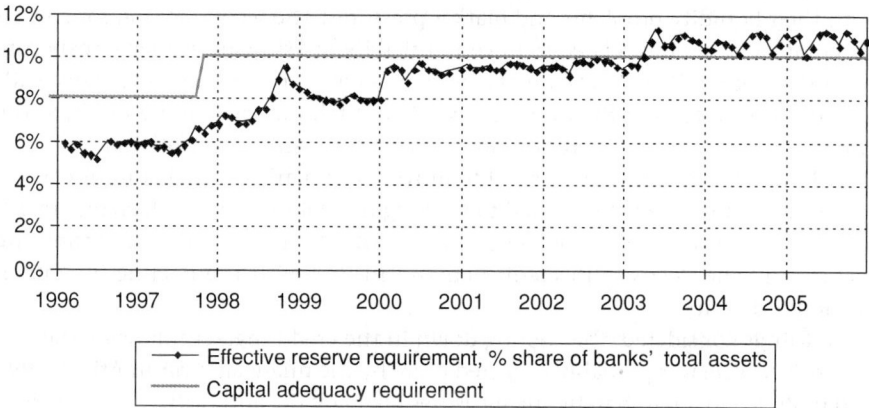

Figure 9.3 "Effective" Reserve Requirement and Capital Adequacy Requirement in Estonia

Source: BoE.

As noted above, the government surplus of 1997 was used to form a Stabilization Reserve. More importantly, those funds were shifted out from the commercial banks to locations abroad,[2] in an attempt to reduce the spare liquidity in the financial sector.

However, it is not clear whether the steps taken by authorities or the financial crisis in Asia in 1997 were more important in cooling down the credit market. In August 1997, the effect of the Asian crisis hit the emerging markets across the globe, and resulted in speculative contagion in Estonian financial markets as well. Like the Hong Kong CBA, Estonia also faced strong speculative pressure in the money and foreign exchange markets, with the halt of foreign capital inflows. This was particularly painful for some financial institutions, as in some cases short-term liquidity management was built up on a presumption of continuous foreign capital inflows. Credit growth therefore slowed down considerably in the last quarter of 1997.

The Asian crisis related pressures in financial markets seemed to ameliorate in early 1998, when money market rates decreased rapidly to the pre-pressures level. In spring 1998, it seemed even that the strong credit growth era was returning, as lending activities started to pick up again.

The Russian financial crisis in 1998, however, brought back strong pressures into the Estonian financial markets. Although the pressures in the interbank lending market were less visible than during the Asian crisis, the pressures in the foreign exchange market were evidently stronger. The main reason for the latter was probably the fact that foreign investors did not believe the fact that Estonia's banking sector exposure in Russia was relatively small, albeit concentrated on some particularly small banks that eventually indeed went into bankruptcy.

All banks faced serious liquidity constraints during the Russian crisis, and some banks had serious problems in fulfilling the compulsory reserve requirement. At the same time, banks practically stopped their real sector lending activities to struggle with their liquidity problems and market pressures. The second reason for halting corporate lending was related to uncertainties about Estonian real sector exposure toward Russia. In 1996–97, Estonian companies had started to expand rapidly, with a focus on Russia. After the Russian crisis, banks felt uneasy lending funds, as the size of the exposure in different industries and companies was not clear.

Although it is empirically difficult to prove, most market participants discussing the slowdown referred also to credit rationing in 1998–99. All in all, credit growth stopped in 1998 and 1999, apparently due to both the above credit supply limiting factors and the decrease in credit demand in line with the decline in general economic activity.

All things considered, the cooling down in the credit market following the first expansion cycle was probably triggered more by the financial crisis in Asia in 1997 and in Russia in 1998 than by the measures taken by the authorities. Nevertheless, the restrictive monetary environment (13 percent reserve requirement and 10 percent capital adequacy requirement) was maintained throughout the crisis years, as the authorities felt uneasy about relaxing banking sector liquidity buffers in this shaky environment. Estonia managed to circumvent a larger crisis in the aftermath of the Asian and Russian crises also due to the active involvement of Scandinavian investors in Estonia's banking sector in late 1998.

II. The second credit growth cycle

Scandinavian strategic investors bought into the Estonian banking sector at probably the most difficult time for the financial sector, i.e., soon after the Russian crisis in late 1998. This financial sector FDI brought Estonian financial intermediation into a new era. 1999–2000 were the years of restructuring by new owners: the loan portfolios of banks were cleared up, and the corporate governance and risk management schemes were effectively improved to bring them into line with those of their Swedish owners.

In 2000, domestic financing for the private sector started to pick up again. During the first stage, household mortgage loans started to pick up, and the recovery in corporate borrowing took place two years later, in 2002. In the background, the Estonian sovereign rating improved to investment grade (A-) level in late 2001, as the EU accession date became clarified. Competition in the financial sector intensified significantly due to the prospective EU accession and, as a result, whereas the real sector risk premium over the money market rates was around 3–4 percentage points in the early 2000s, it has now decreased to only 0.3–1 percentage point (depending on the sector and particular loan product, see Figures 9.4 and 9.5).

It is important to note that foreign currency borrowing has always been important in Estonia—its share in total borrowing has stayed around 80 percent since the mid-1990s. Since the currency board's base currency—EUR or DEM—has always made up a major part of foreign currency borrowing, the "euroization" of the borrowing

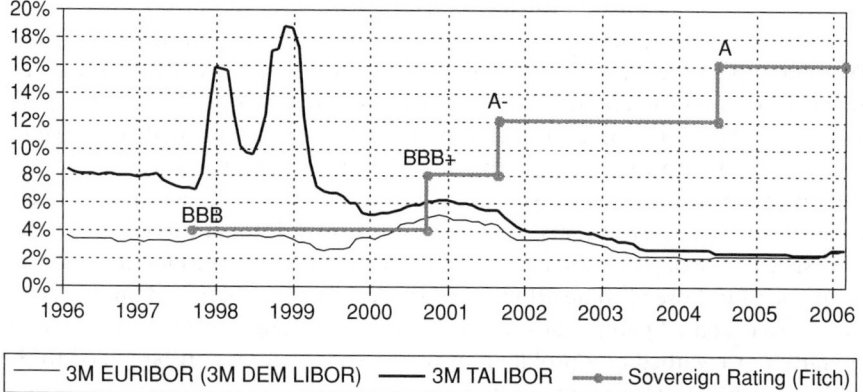

Figure 9.4 Money Market Risk Premium and Estonian Sovereign Rating

Source: BoE.

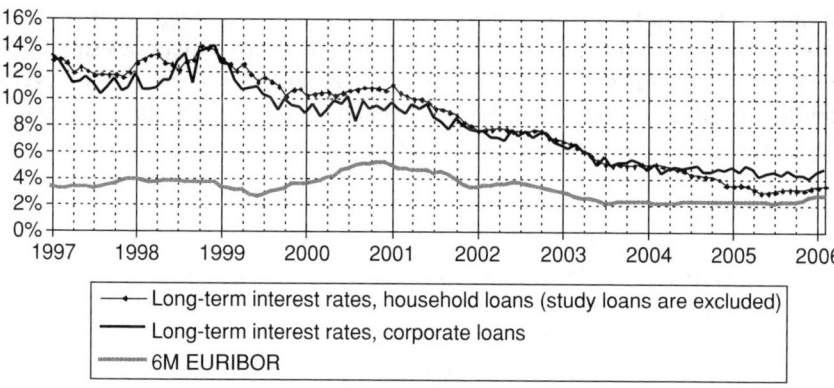

Figure 9.5 Real Sector Interest Rates vs. EURIBOR Rates—Estonia

Source: BoE.

has never been a particular problem in Estonia. Today it is more a reflection of habit than an indicator of some cost-based argument, as there is no interest rate discrimination between EEK and EUR based borrowing.

Risks associated with the current credit growth cycle

The reacceleration of household loan growth to 50 percent in 2001 started to attract the attention of the authorities. Since then, the authorities have been increasingly concerned about the sustainability of the strong credit growth, especially in the housing loan sector. This has resulted in the introduction of several measures, and on several occasions the BoE has pointed out the risk of the credit market overheating.

Nevertheless, it has been difficult to distinguish between convergence-related growth, the local impacts of the global credit expansion, and nonsustainable developments in the credit market. On the one hand, Estonia started from a very low level of domestic credit (about 8 percent of GDP at the end of 1993), and therefore some of the rapid growth can be attributed to a normal convergence process in line with income growth. On top of this, housing credit growth has been on an upward cycle across the globe, as interest rates have been at historically low levels for a number of years. On the other hand, in Estonia this expansion has been especially strong and some financial deepening indicators today are no longer lagging behind those of some other EU countries (e.g., the share of domestic credit in GDP exceeded 77 percent at the end of 2005). Although credit growth itself is generally not regarded as a problem, most current concerns can be linked to the rapid expansion of housing credit in particular.

Similar to the mid-1990s, the bulk of credit growth has been financed by foreign capital inflows, as domestic savings have not covered the domestic credit demand. This boosted growth in external debt, and the current account deficit deteriorated to 12 percent of GDP in 2004 in the strong growth environment. However, the main difference from the earlier period is that a large part of foreign financing has not been obtained from the markets but from parent banks, where ties should be stronger in tougher times. Another difference is that under the current credit cycle, the lending standards and risk management practices have been in line with those in Scandinavia (branches are supervised by the Scandinavian authorities).

Policy responses

Under the currency board regime, the authorities face serious constraints on implementing restrictive policies to cope with possibly unsustainable developments. There is no domestic interest rate policy in Estonia, and the euro area effectively determines the interest rate environment. There are also no capital controls or direct ceilings in Estonia, as Estonian economic policies have always been aimed toward a liberal and market economy-based approach. Nor would such controls be in line with EU directives.

Moreover, the financial sector structure poses additional limitations on the implementation of restrictive policies. Estonian banks today form financial conglomerates that consist of a bank, a leasing company, and several investment funds and insurance companies. In many cases, therefore, loan products have been directed into the market through leasing finance rather than through banks. These companies are not under the direct control of the central bank, as reserve requirements and other possible monetary measures do not apply to nonbank enterprises, so any direct credit ceilings (like those used in some southern-European countries recently) would be rather easy to circumvent by the Estonian financial sector. Moreover, foreign-owned banks already act as *de facto* branches, thus the step toward *de jure* branches (i.e., financial institutions that are not controlled by local Supervisory Authority) may not be so far away.

In spite of this, the authorities have tried to take several "measures" to point out the risks of excessive credit growth, especially in the household mortgage loan market. The reserve requirement framework has not been relaxed (with the ratio currently at 13 percent against the 2 percent in the euro area[3]) and its technical convergence towards the euro area system has been used to make the framework even more restrictive, including through the abolition of vault-cash deductibility and the inclusion of foreign liabilities into the framework on a gross basis from its initial net position (see Figure 9.3 above). The 10 percent capital adequacy requirement has been retained and the risk weightings of mortgage loans have been increased from 50 percent to 100 percent from March 2006 onward.

Also the "communication tool" and "moral suasion tool" have been used, and the BoE has recommended that the government abolish certain tax relief and guarantee schemes in the mortgage market. The "moral suasion" letters have been sent to the banks, to their Scandinavian owners, as well as to the respective Supervisory Authorities in the region, but the expansion has continued. The government has been relatively reluctant to make unpopular decisions to abolish relevant tax relief and state guarantee schemes in the housing loan market, especially in the context of the election cycle, with local elections taking place in 2005 and parliamentary elections to be held in 2007.

In summary, the rapid credit growth in the current cycle has continued and the annual growth in real sector credit peaked at more than 50 percent at the end of 2005. The measures that the authorities have taken throughout the last four years have not had any visible impact on these developments (although it is not evident whether the growth would have been even faster without those measures). Efforts to achieve a slowdown in real sector credit growth in Estonia have not yet proved to be successful, and it is not clear what direction credit growth will take in the near future.

III. Conclusions and lessons from the policies undertaken

The structure of the financial sector and the currency board based monetary policy make coping with rapid credit growth a particularly challenging task for policymakers. Firstly, although there is a full set of different kinds of financial sector companies, they are very bank-dominated and the financial sector is effectively owned by Scandinavian banks that act in the whole Baltic market. Secondly, the CBA sets clear limits on the use of monetary policy in general.

The policy responses in the two rapid credit growth cycles resemble each other to some extent. During the first credit growth cycle the reserve requirement was effectively increased, whereas during the second cycle the reserve requirement framework has not been relaxed and its operational convergence toward the euro area framework has been used to make the framework more restrictive in recent years. The authorities increased the capital adequacy requirement from the "standard" 8 percent to 10 percent in 1997 and this level has been retained in the current cycle. Moreover, in the current cycle the risk weightings of housing loans have been modified from March 2006 onward.

Moral suasion has been used more in the current cycle (probably also because the current cycle has lasted longer), but it also had its place in the mid-1990s. However, its impact has been limited, as credit growth instructions from parent banks seem to be more important for banks' local managers than credit growth curbing requests from the authorities. The existence of strong competition has hampered this effect also, as an uncoordinated slowdown in some banks would possibly lead to a loss of market share for these institutions. On the government side, the discussion today is aimed more at state distortions in the housing market, whereas in 1997 government funds were moved out of domestic commercial banks in order to curb monetary conditions. Today, such a measure would no longer be effective, as banks' access to foreign capital through their owners is much more fluid compared to the mid-1990s. The amount of government deposits in the domestic banking system was temporarily reduced in early 2003, without any serious impact on banks' behavior; conversely the need for a budget surplus has repeatedly been emphasized.

Estonia's current economic policies and political culture exclude capital controls or direct loan ceilings as policy instruments, in addition to the fact that such measures would not be in line with EU directives. Moreover, such measures would be easy to circumvent by the financial sector, either by changes in the legal structure of the group (e.g., by becoming a branch) or through the use of leasing companies; each bank in Estonia owns its own leasing company and has connected investment funds and insurance companies. It is, therefore, relatively easy for the financial sector to circumvent any entirely bank-based measure for slowing down credit growth.

As the majority (98 percent) of the financial sector is foreign owned, there is scope for extending the cooperation between home and host-country supervisors beyond a memorandum of understanding. In some cases, it may make sense to have a widespread regional cooperation agreement with shared tasks and resources in crisis management, as well as coordinated actions to curb unsustainable developments. In conclusion, it appears that there are questions regarding the pace and path of the current credit growth cycle in Estonia that remain unresolved.

Notes

1. The Bank of Estonia (BoE).
2. In Estonia, government deposits are held in commercial banks but not in the central bank.
3. In Estonia banks can fulfill up to 50 percent of the reserve requirement with the holdings of certain foreign securities. Hence the effective requirement held in the central bank is about half of the formal total requirement.

10
Latvia's Experience with Rapid Credit Growth

Uldis Rutkaste[1]

Until 2000, lending activities by the banking sector were rather subdued in Latvia. At the beginning of this decade, the resident loans-to-GDP ratio was just below 20 percent (Figure 10.1). However, the situation soon changed rapidly. From 2000 onwards, credit growth picked up substantially, and in terms of credit-to-GDP ratio, Latvia experienced fast convergence with the front-runners in the region of Central, Eastern, and South-eastern Europe (CEE). Initially, credit growth was largely driven by corporate borrowing, but recently, lending to households has also contributed substantially to credit growth, largely due to a significant increase in housing loans. In general, the fast credit growth in Latvia, similar to the situation in other CEE countries, largely represents a catch-up from a low base.

I. Factors underlying the lending growth

A combination of factors on both the supply side and the demand side is behind the swift credit growth in Latvia.

Supply factors

On the supply side, strong resident deposit growth and the increasing availability of funds abroad (particularly in the last few years) have substantially contributed to domestic credit developments. Resident deposits have grown at above 30 percent per year on average since 2000, and a similar growth rate was evident in mid-2005. Relatively high foreign ownership in the banking sector, especially in the group of banks that are engaged in domestic lending activities, facilitates access to foreign capital, mainly in terms of borrowing from parent banks abroad. These developments have been especially marked in the last few years as proxied by the considerable increase in the share of banks' liabilities to foreign credit institutions in total liabilities (Figure 10.2). It appears that accession to the EU and entry into

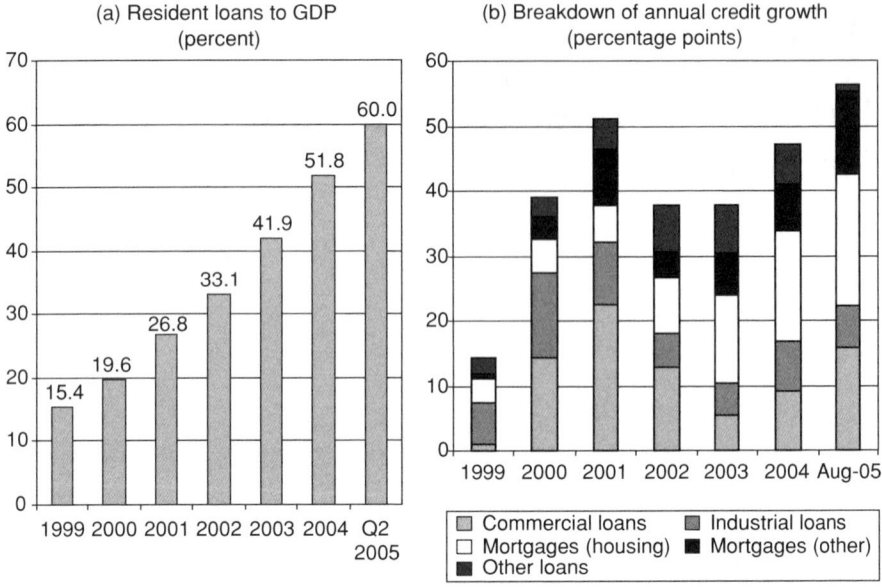

Figure 10.1 Credit Growth in Latvia

Source: BoL.

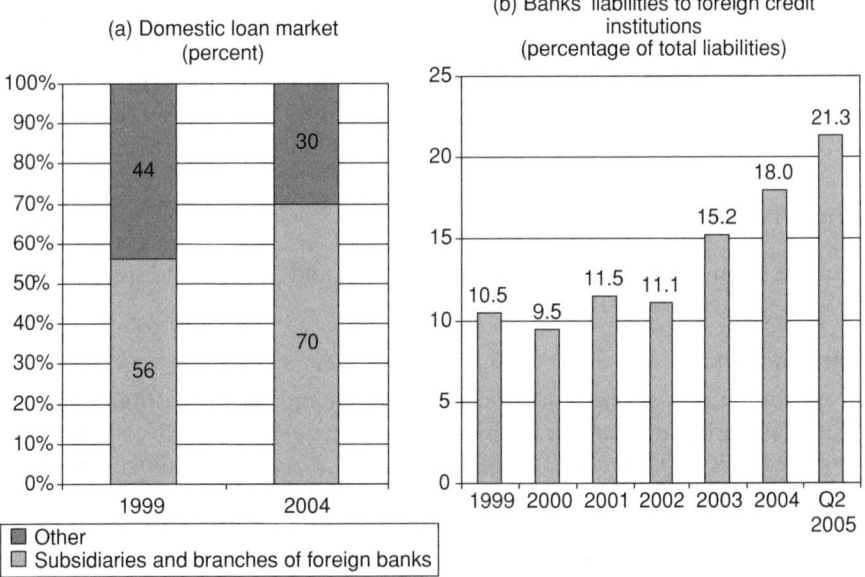

Figure 10.2 Domestic Loan Market Share and Banks' Liabilities to Foreign Credit Institutions—Latvia

Source: BoL.

the ERM2 have contributed to an increase in investors' confidence in the Latvian economy, and that, in turn, has reinforced inflows of foreign capital.

Stiff competition in the banking sector is another factor contributing significantly to credit supply incentives. Development of the domestic credit market and increasing profitability in the banking sector, as well as the entry of new market participants, encouraged banks to intensify the fight for market share. Interest rate margins on new loans decreased substantially, and presently, overall margins on new loans hover at about 2.5 percent.

Further widening of potential credit markets, the improvement in credit risk management techniques, the introduction of new financial products in the local market, and some institutional changes account for another group of factors that facilitated credit supply. From 2000, banks started to engage more actively in the development of new market segments by increasingly extending loans to SMEs and individuals (for individuals mainly in terms of housing loans), since credit markets for large enterprises gradually became saturated. Transfers of know-how from parent institutions abroad contributed to an improvement in risk management practices, and development of a register of collateral (created in 1998, and started to operate efficiently in mid-1999), and a register of bad debtors (created in 2003) provided a sound institutional background for the development of new market segments. The supply of some financial products was intensified in the local market as well, for example, mortgage loans for purchase of residential housing.

Demand factors

On the demand side, there are some common factors and others that are corporate and individuals specific, which are driving the demand for loans. Common factors include growing income, decreasing interest rates and, to some extent, rising property prices and the increase in collateral value. Robust economic development resulted in a strong increase in corporate profits and improvement in cash flows, which, when combined with a favorable economic outlook and huge investment needs for restructuring and technological innovations, reinforced corporate demand for bank loans. It must be noted that capital markets in Latvia are still tiny, and the role of the banking sector is dominant in corporate financing. Individuals' income has also increased considerably, and in conjunction with a relatively sharp decline in interest rates, it facilitated an increase in household borrowing. In addition, regional disparities in income levels and growth could also have played a role. Notwithstanding the comparatively low per capita income in Latvia as a whole, the income level in Riga has increased at a faster pace and is substantially higher than in the rest of the country on average (Figure 10.3a), thus adding considerably to the demand for loans.

Despite the strength of the economy, interest rates have decreased noticeably in recent years, contributing to a substantial reduction in borrowing costs, especially on the longer end of maturities. The decline in interest rates has been underpinned by an improvement in fundamentals, consistent economic policies, as well as increasing competition in the banking sector and greater loan availability. Proximity of the EU accession has also played a role in this regard. At the beginning of 2000, interest rates on loans granted in either lats or foreign currencies were mostly above 10 percent, but progressively declined in subsequent years, recently reaching 4–5 percent (Figure 10.3b).

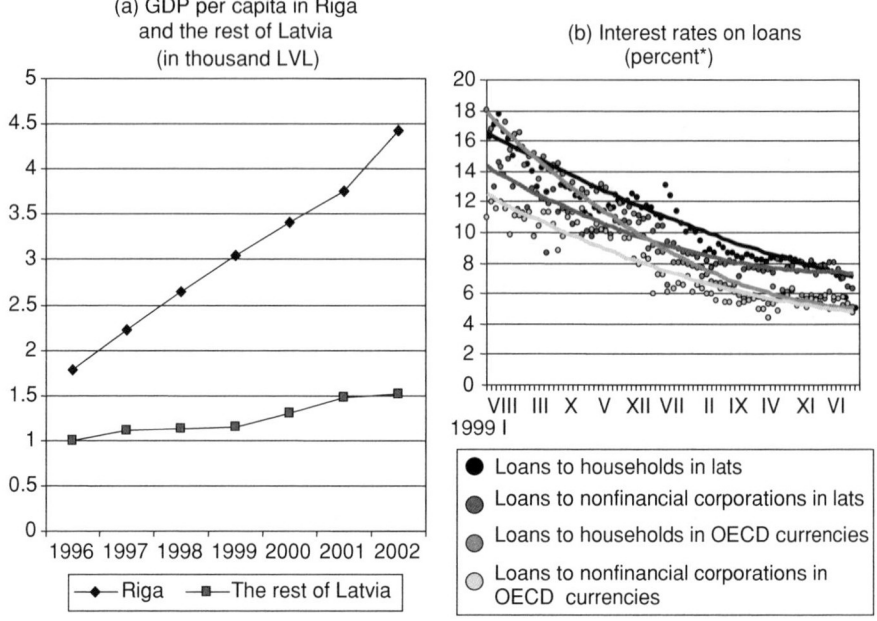

* Starting for January 2004 new methodology for interest rate statistics was applied.

Figure 10.3 Interest Rates and Income—Latvia

Source: BoL and Central Statistical Bureau of Latvia.

A number of corporate and individuals specific factors have also been driving the demand for loans. Among other factors that added to the demand for corporate loans were the need for investment related to the streamlining of production activities in line with EU requirements and the availability of EU funds. This has contributed to an increase in industrial loan growth since 2004. On the individuals' side, with virtually no new residential construction having taken place for a long period of time, older housing and the privatization of residential buildings constituted another group of factors determining demand for mortgage loans.

The acquisition of property rights and, lately, also the increasing supply of newly built dwellings have fostered activity in the real estate market, thereby having an impact on the demand for mortgage loans. Privatization of state-owned residential houses gained pace only in 1999, when, during the year, slightly more than 35 percent of all flats approved for privatization were privatized, whereas in 1998 the stock of privatized flats had constituted only 21 percent of all flats approved for privatization (Figure 10.4). Residential construction started to develop only in 2004, when real estate prices in the secondary market came close to replacement values. During the 1980s, the ratio of newly built dwellings stood at between 0.4 and 0.5 square meters per capita, before dropping to below 0.1 in the 1990s to increase again in 2004 to 0.2.

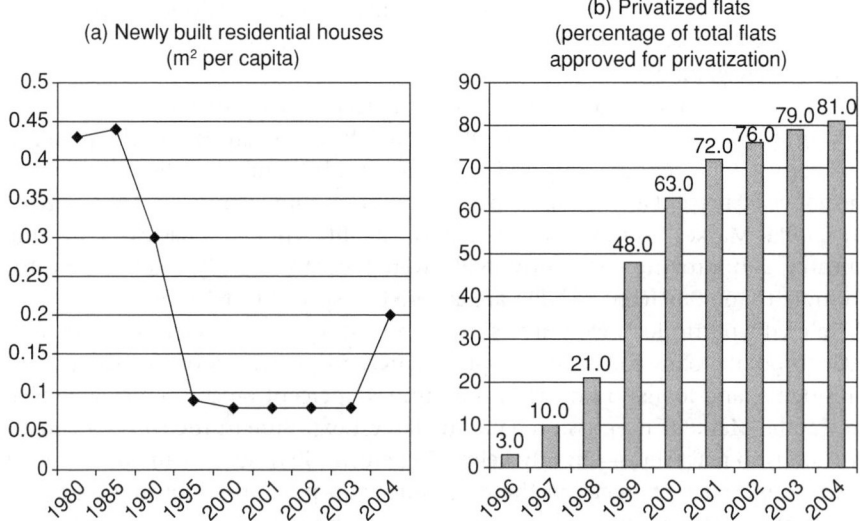

Figure 10.4   Privatization of Flats and Residential Construction—Latvia

Source: Central Statistical Bureau of Latvia.

Another factor driving demand for loans is the low level of household indebtedness. In 2004, household debt stood at below 20 percent of GDP, and according to survey data only around 10 percent of households held a mortgage loan by mid-2005, and they are obviously households with a high income. It seems that a shift in attitudes has also played a role in the increasing demand for loans. Partly as a result of intense marketing campaigns by commercial banks, households started to treat the possibility of taking out a loan as clearly beneficial to improve their living standards, largely in terms of the acquisition of housing most appropriate to their level of income.

II. The main risks of the credit growth: risks on the macro side

Even though credit development in Latvia could be largely explained by catching up and convergence to new levels of indebtedness, rapid growth in lending creates risks for the macroeconomic environment. External imbalances are relatively high in Latvia and have even increased in recent years (current account deficit exceeded 10 percent of GDP in 2004). The persistently high current account deficit in Latvia is largely explained by structural factors, namely, substantial investment needs that are partly financed by foreign savings; however, it seems that rapid credit growth also has added to the high level of the underlying current account deficit. In addition, recently we have seen strong domestic demand that is reinforced by credit development starting to have an impact on inflation in Latvia. The rise in inflation in 2004 to slightly above 6 percent from 2.5–3.0 percent in previous years can be well explained by supply-side pressures; however, there is some indication that domestic demand is starting to impose some inertia on disinflation processes, creating possible risks for the future and requiring the authorities to remain vigilant to further developments.

The financial system is sound and risks to financial stability are rather limited. The banking sector is profitable (presently ROE stays above 25 percent), well capitalized (CAR above 10 percent as compared to 8 percent minimum), and liquid (liquidity ratio above 50 percent as compared to 30 percent minimum defined by the Financial and Capital Market Commission). The credit quality, though a backward looking indicator, is improving constantly (NPLs were recently slightly below 1 percent) and more than 90 percent of NPLs are covered by special provisions.

The credit portfolio is well diversified across sectors of the economy. By mid-2005, corporate loans constituted approximately 51 percent of outstanding credit to residents, and loans to households around 37 percent. According to Financial and Capital Market Commission data, the largest exposure in the corporate loans portfolio is to real estate—slightly below 20 percent. Exposure to any other sector does not exceed 10 percent of the corporate loan portfolio. Housing loans are dominant in loans granted to households, and they take around 26 percent of outstanding credit to residents. However, according to statistics compiled for supervisory purposes by the Financial and Capital Market Commission, the loan-to-value ratio for housing loans is rather conservative, and it is below 70 percent for 75 percent of housing loans. In addition, monthly payments do not exceed 30 percent of income for around 80 percent of households holding a loan.

A substantial share of foreign exchange borrowing is a long lasting feature of the Latvian economy, and it has been underpinned by a credible fixed exchange rate arrangement as well as intense usage of foreign currencies in transactions. Presently, only around a third of credit to residents is granted in the national currency (the lat). The vast majority of foreign exchange loans are granted in euros, and the US dollar loan share has diminished progressively after the lat's repeg to the euro. On the one hand, taking into account that the national currency is pegged to the euro and Latvia is an ERM2 participating country, foreign exchange risks associated with day-to-day exchange rate volatility are only marginal. The high share of euro borrowing among other factors could be also explained by the fact that in the foreseeable future the euro is set to become the national currency, and thus, taking into account that mostly long-term loans are euro denominated, high foreign exchange borrowing may be attributed to agents' willingness to borrow in the currency of the expected future income.

On the other hand, while there are definite risks linked to foreign exchange borrowing, these risks are diminished by several factors. First, Latvia has managed to sustain a fixed exchange rate regime without any major tensions since 1994, and it appears that the current exchange rate framework is fairly credible. Second, there is some evidence that nonbank sector open foreign exchange positions are at least partly hedged by the substantial foreign exchange share in domestic deposits. In addition, the substantial share of foreign exchange deposits against a background of the high openness of the Latvian economy implies also that a certain share of agents' income is foreign exchange denominated.

All in all, even though there are a lot of risk-mitigating factors, credit risk is the most important risk to the financial system, and thus close monitoring and vigilance regarding future developments are of great importance.

III. Policy response to limit credit growth—a challenging task

Several measures have been taken to date to tackle issues related to the rapid credit growth, including tightening of monetary policy, improvements in prudential supervision, and so-called moral suasion measures.

Monetary policy measures

Regarding monetary policy measures, the Council of the Bank of Latvia (BoL), considering the risks posed by internal and external imbalances, has raised its main refinancing rate by a total of 100 basis points to 4 percent in March and November 2004 (Figure 10.5). Reserve requirements were raised from 3 percent to 4 percent in July 2004 and from 4 percent to 6 percent in June 2005. In addition, in November 2004 the minimum reserve base for commercial banks was extended to include bank liabilities to foreign banks and foreign central banks with an agreed maturity or redeemable at notice of up to two years. However, these measures were not sufficient to exert substantial downward pressure on lending growth, and credit

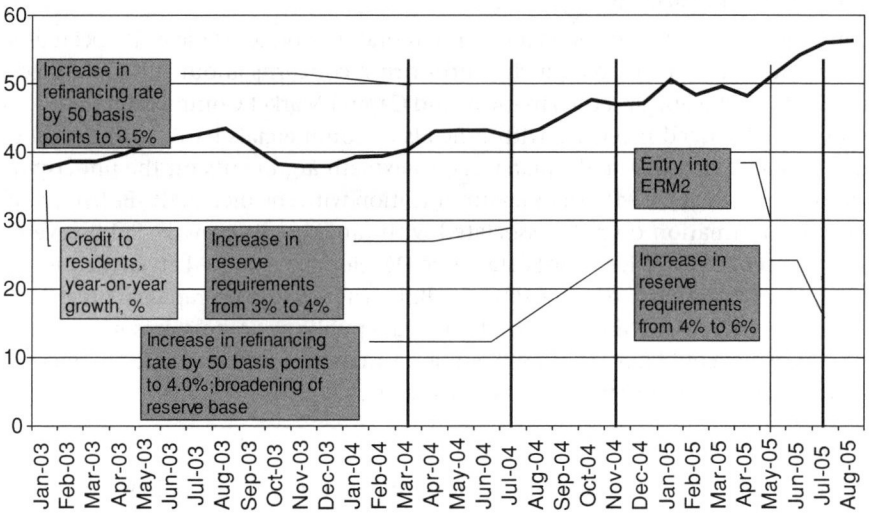

Figure 10.5 Monetary Policy Measures Taken to Date—Latvia

growth to residents continued to accelerate over time. However, the extension of the minimum reserve requirement base improved the term structure of banks' borrowing abroad, and currently the current account deficit is fully covered by long-term financial inflows.

The limited effectiveness of monetary policy measures is explained by several factors. First, the fixed exchange rate framework limits the use of any interest rate policy, and the wide usage of foreign exchange in the domestic economy decreases its effectiveness. In addition, high foreign ownership in the banking sector, almost unlimited availability of resources abroad compared with the small size of the local market, tight competition and high profitability in the banking sector, and the low level of household indebtedness provide a favorable base for further deepening of the credit market.

Supervisory and prudential measures

As regards supervisory and prudential measures, the policy of the Financial and Capital Market Commission—the supervisory authority in Latvia—has been to ensure a sound supervisory system, and presently it fully complies with the EU requirements and best international practices. Some recent measures that increased the supervisory reporting requirements imposed on banks' loan portfolios were implemented in 2004. These include the tightening of onsite/offsite inspections; the introduction of a rating system for banks; the carrying out of periodic stress testing activities; and the increasing supervision of banking groups on a consolidated basis. In addition, there are periodic consultations with the Association of Commercial Banks and with individual banks. Finally, dialogue and exchange of information between host and home supervisors is continually improving.

Moral suasion measures

Alongside the above-mentioned measures, moral suasion tools have also been used to communicate to the market the authorities' concerns about the rapid credit growth. Both the BoL and the Financial and Capital Market Commission have sent letters and arranged meetings with officials of commercials bank, at the level of both management and credit managers, to explain arguments on the underlying risks of rapid credit growth. In its communication with the media, the BoL provides relevant information on risks associated with rapid credit growth. Public events like the recent conference "The Sustainable Development of the Latvian Economy: Issues, Risks, Solutions" organized by the BoL, where issues on rapid credit growth were heavily discussed, are also used to increase public awareness. In some respect, these measures could have increased public awareness of risks associated with credit growth; however, their effects are hard to assess.

Future policy options

It is a challenging task to design an appropriate and effective policy package to bring down credit growth to a more appropriate level and/or to limit risks related to rapid credit growth. Clearly, one option is to pursue fiscal tightening at least to partly counterbalance the implications for the macroeconomic environment stemming from credit expansion. It should be mentioned that fiscal developments were rather favorable since 2000, and the government managed to progressively reduce the budget deficit to a relatively low level—0.9 percent of GDP in 2004. However, on the backdrop of the current cyclical position of the Latvian economy and government's announced budget deficit targets for following years, we consider fiscal policy as being insufficiently ambitious.

Administrative and tax related measures could be quite effective in restricting lending growth. However, at the same time, they could cause substantial market distortion and could be politically extremely costly, especially in post-Soviet countries, where markets were liberalized not so long ago, and thus such measures could be considered by the public as a backward step. In our view, such measures could be used only as a last resort if risks are aggravated further and there are no other policy options; however, the design of these measures would be of great importance. The effectiveness of administrative restrictions could vary depending on whether supply of or demand for loans is restricted. If the credit growth is substantially driven by expansion in a particular type of loan, like housing loans, demand-side restrictions could be the more appropriate choice.

Note

1. Bank of Latvia (BoL).

11
Assessment of Credit Growth in Lithuania

Tomas Ramanauskas[1]

The dynamic developments in the Lithuanian credit market have attracted observers' attention. The rate of banking intermediation growth, unthinkable for mature economies, is to a large extent justified on the grounds of financial convergence, improving economic outlook, changes in the interest rate environment, and so on. In this chapter we review the factors driving credit growth in the early 2000s and more recently. We also assess the current situation in the banking sector, and discuss briefly the main sources of risk. Finally, we touch upon policy dilemmas faced by policymakers, and briefly discuss the main policy measures taken by the Bank of Lithuania (BL) in dealing with rapid credit growth.

I. The Lithuanian banking sector: the ongoing catch-up processes

In Lithuania, bank lending to the private sector has been growing very rapidly since about 2002. Much of the strong dynamics are due to the fact that Lithuania was a "late riser" (in Cottarelli et al., 2003 terminology), catching up with levels of financial intermediation observed in advanced economies. A quick look at the main structural features reveals that back in 2002, there indeed was a huge gap, and even now there still is a long way to go to get anywhere near the average level of banking intermediation in the euro area; as all main structural banking indicators in fact remain well below those of the euro area (Table 11.1). More specifically, even though banks clearly dominate Lithuania's financial system, as of end-2001 bank assets and the total bank loan portfolio to the private sector amounted, respectively, only to 32 percent and 13 percent of GDP. By mid-2005, total bank assets rose to 51 percent of GDP, and loans to the private sector reached 30 percent of GDP.

Table 11.1 Main Structural Banking Indicators in Lithuania and the Euro Area, as Percent of GDP (as of end-2004)

	Total bank assets	Total loans to non-MFIs	Deposits from non-MFIs	Loans to non-financial corporations	Housing loans	Consumer credit
Lithuania	47	27	29	20	6	1
Euro area	266	117	97	41	34	7

Source: ECB, BL.

In terms of growth rates, over the period from 2002 to mid-2005 annual growth in total loans to customers averaged 37 percent, loans to enterprises on average grew by 32 percent per year, and loans to households—growing from minuscule levels—increased by an impressive 80 percent per year on average. At the initial stages, loans to enterprises contributed most to the growth of the total bank loan portfolio, but very recently the growth of loans to households has accounted for roughly one half of growth in total loans, despite the considerably smaller weights of loans to households in the overall structure of the loan portfolio (Figure 11.1); in mid-2005, 66 percent of bank loans to customers were extended to the nonfinancial corporate sector, 30 percent went to households (of which 80 percent were housing loans).

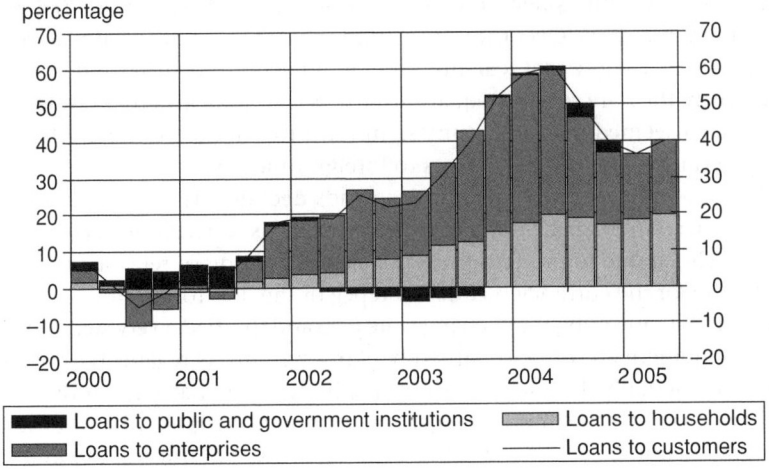

Figure 11.1 Contributions of Loans by Type to Growth of Total Bank Loan Portfolio—Lithuania

Source: Statistics Lithuania, BL calculations.

Apart from all other background information, the convergence processes in the credit market indicate relatively little about the financial instability risks involved: the size of the gap with activity in euro area countries should not provide an excuse to ignore those risks if they are present. It is often tempting to make judgments about risks to financial stability, assigning inadequately high weights to credit growth rates (or to the differential between the current level and some long-term level of credit penetration).

II. Drivers behind the lifting of the private sector's credit constraints in early 2000s

One should expect to see dramatic developments in the credit market once a full set of the preconditions necessary for efficient market functioning are put in place and, together with this, other strong exogenous factors stimulating credit growth come into play. That is what actually happened in Lithuania in the early 2000s. The whole sequence of drivers and shocks (both external and domestic, and supply and demand side), which were often quite coincidental, shook the stagnant banking sector in the early 2000s. As a result, the severe credit constraints faced by most economic agents due to high interest rates and the relatively low willingness by the banks to finance the private sector in the aftermath of the Lithuanian banking crisis (1995–96) and the Russian crisis (1998) were effectively lifted.

First, there were significant positive interest rate developments in major international money markets, and the decline in reference rates also had a profound effect on the domestic interest rates on loans.[2] As shown in Figure 11.2, average nominal interest rates on litas-denominated loans fell from 14 percent in 2000 to below 6 percent in mid-2005. Over the same period, real interest rates declined even more. It is interesting to note that real interest rates on deposits were even negative at times (currently they are roughly equal to zero), which indicates that domestic inflation has so far seemed not to play any significant role in determining interest rates, mainly because of banks' easy access to foreign funding.

Figure 11.2 also indicates that credit risk spreads declined as well. One could discern declines in country-specific and borrower-specific risks. The level of country-specific risks declined due to prudent fiscal policies and easing of tensions related to the functioning of the currency board. The repeg of the litas to the euro in 2002 contributed further to lowering the exchange rate risk, and this had a very significant impact on developments in the Lithuanian banking system. As regards borrower-specific risks, they actually declined because of the improving financial standing of individual borrowers and the improving general economic outlook, which turned from rather gray to quite positive following a couple of years of uncertainty in the aftermath of the Russian crisis. Finally, continuous development and improvements in the legal infrastructure and banking supervision also must have had some positive effect on both country-specific and borrower-specific risks.

Declining yields in major international financial markets and the cyclical downturn in the euro area in the early 2000s encouraged European banks to seek new business opportunities in the CEE countries, thereby contributing to the development of more efficient financial intermediation systems in those countries. Active involvement of foreign banks in the Lithuanian banking sector also was a crucial factor that drove the development of the domestic banking system to a

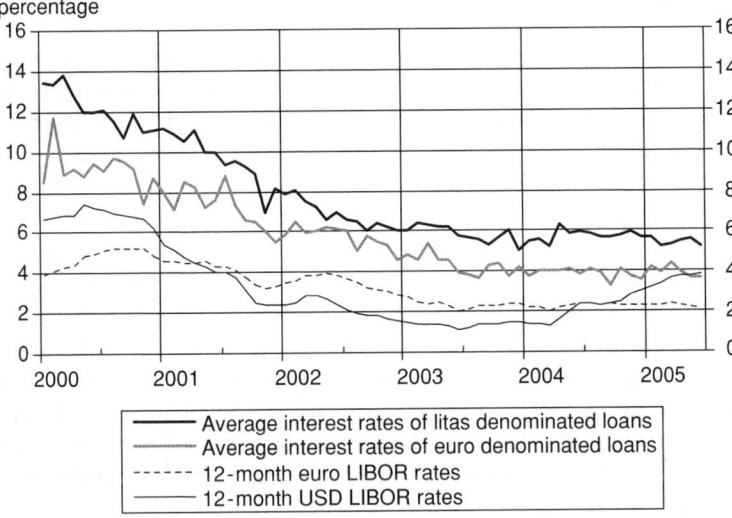

Figure 11.2 Recent Dynamics of Nominal Interest Rates—Lithuania

Source: Bloomberg, BL.

qualitatively-new level. In 2001 and 2002 foreign banks successfully participated in the concluding phase of the privatization of state-owned banks. At the same time, some foreign banks with a vested interest in expanding their activities in Lithuania established their subsidiaries or branches. As a result, at the end of 2002, the Lithuanian banking sector was fully privatized, and foreign banks constituted 88 percent of total capital. Not only did foreign banks bring new know-how, new risk management and operational practices, and take important steps to increase the transparency of the system (e.g., by cleaning up the balance sheets of privatized banks), but they also exploited access to ample financial resources from abroad. And, as was mentioned above, the credible peg to the euro was a very convenient circumstance for the efficient funneling of financial resources to the dynamic and promising market.

On the demand side, corporate and personal income tax reforms also provided a strong stimulus for developments in the credit market. In 2002, a (distortionary) corporate income tax exemption, which provided for zero percent tariff on reinvested profits, was abolished, thereby making investment financed with borrowed funds more attractive than it was before. In 2003, a personal income tax deductibility scheme, which is still in effect, was introduced. This effectively lowered by up to one third the interest rate burden borne by households taking housing loans. Demand for bank credit also increased due to the general economic recovery that led to the improving profitability of enterprises, rising household incomes, and, hence, an expanding pool of potential borrowers and decreasing riskiness of their loans.

III. The current phase of credit expansion

Prior to the recent developments in the credit market, restrictively high interest rates and banks' general reluctance to extend credit to the private sector actually put significant restrictions on economic agents' choices of their desired level of leverage. The factors mentioned above, however, contributed to an effective reduction in the private sector's credit constraints. Now that borrowing decisions depend more on economic considerations, such as the willingness to smooth consumption in expectation of higher future income, or the desire to bring forward consumption of housing, durables (the well-known theoretical principle of consumer impatience), some important new drivers behind rapid credit growth have emerged.

Some "crowding" effect could be observed, as economic agents driven by similar economic forces in the dynamically changing environment naturally tended to take similar actions. Historically low interest rates, low overall indebtedness, and rising income levels opened opportunities for a large number of households to increase their welfare by borrowing. In general, changes in a traditionally apprehensive attitude toward borrowing might be noted, as can be inferred from the dynamic growth of both housing and consumer loans.

The strong effect of the interest rate decline on real economic activity and the well-known feedback effects leading to some endogeneity of credit growth must also be recognized. Lower interest rates and associated credit growth have contributed to ample liquidity, strong aggregate demand, and asset price increases. All of this, and especially increases in the fundamental value of assets (housing, equity, investment projects, etc.), have provided incentives to invest (and borrow) and reduced the asymmetric information problems in the credit market; the latter, in turn, have facilitated credit growth. These are examples of the well-known *Tobin's q* and the financial accelerator effect.

To appreciate the relevance of this analysis in Lithuania's case, we must first consider the money creation processes. They have been quite dynamic recently (Figure 11.3). High growth rates of M2 resumed quite soon after the Russian crisis, more precisely in 2000, and the share of currency in circulation in M2 declined significantly, indicating the increasing role of the money multiplier effect in driving monetary dynamics. Over the period of accelerated credit growth (i.e., from 2002 onwards), the average annual growth of broad money exceeded 20 percent, and currently is close to 30 percent. M2 growth is currently mostly driven by time and savings deposits (a contribution of 16 percentage points), whereas demand deposits and currency in circulation contribute, respectively, 10 and 4 percentage points (Figure 11.4).

A natural way to gauge investor confidence and incentives to invest in physical capital is to examine developments in the stock market. VILSE, the broad stock market index, has tripled over the period 2003–04 and rose by another 78 percent over the first three quarters of 2005. Of course, these developments should be interpreted with a grain of salt because of a possible undervaluation of equities in the recent past, and the fact that the shallowness of the market and the small share of free-float equities make stock indices very sensitive to certain demand factors.

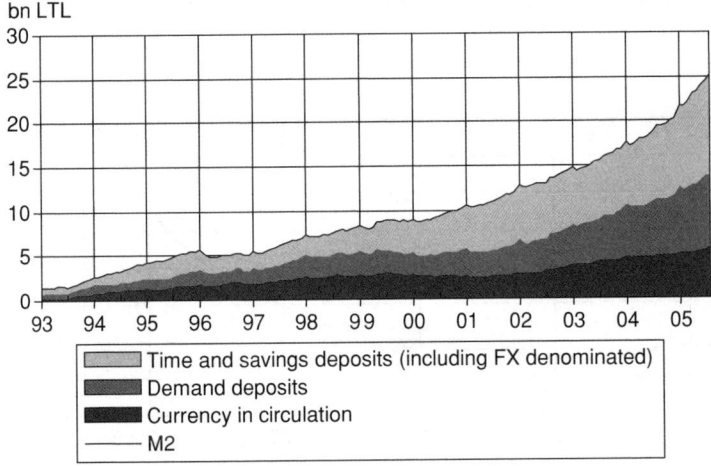

Figure 11.3 M2 Dynamics—Lithuania

Source: BL.

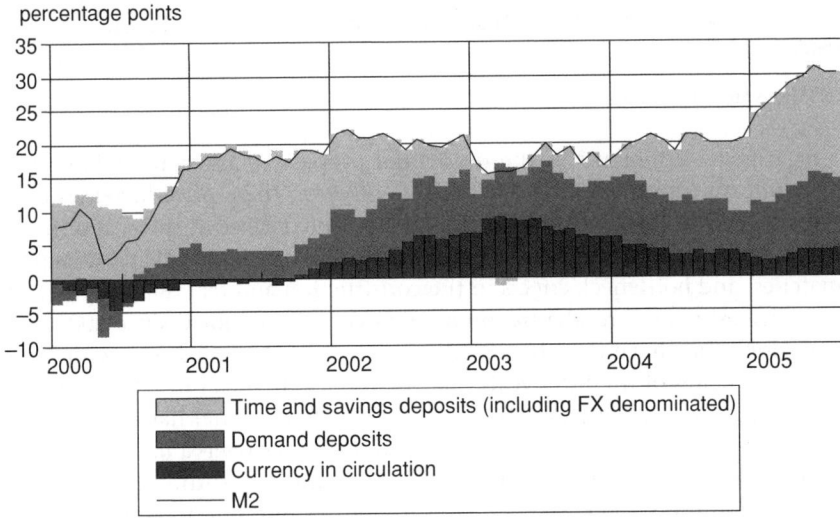

Figure 11.4 M2 Growth Factors—Lithuania

Source: BL.

Those factors are likely to have included (a) the increasing activity of institutional investors against the backdrop of the integration of stock markets in the Nordic-Baltic region, and (b) the emergence of private pension funds. Bearing in mind these caveats, stock market developments still carry some information (with non-eliminated noise) about investment incentives. Figure 11.5 depicts positive and strong dynamics of a proxy for *Tobin's q*, that is, the gap between the market value and the replacement value of capital.

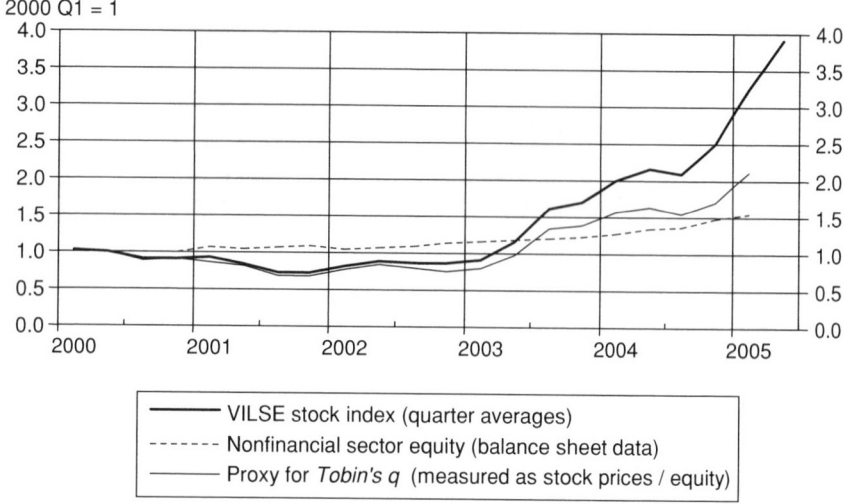

Figure 11.5 Dynamics of the Market Value and the Balance Sheet Value of Equity—Lithuania

Source: Vilnius Stock Exchange, Statistics Lithuania.

As regards developments in the residential property market, there have also been significant price rises in the last couple of years; these price increases have been fueled by the availability of credit and a drastic decline in the cost of funds (due to historically low interest rates plus tax incentives), strong demand–supply mismatches, and bottleneck effects in the construction and real estate sectors. By conservative estimates,[3] residential property prices have doubled since 2002, and in 2005 alone they have risen by 25–40 percent. A quick comparison with other new member states of the EU reveals that the real estate prices in Lithuania were still relatively low at the end of 2004 (CEPI, 2005). On the other hand, high price-to-income or price-to-rent ratios point to the risk of some overvaluation.

With the change in the financial and economic environment, therefore, households and firms had clear incentives to borrow and were in an increasingly better position to do so with their improving financial standing. In a nutshell, corporate earnings, though volatile, have been quite impressive, as those of the nonfinancial sector have doubled in the 2004–05 period.[4] Over the period of the accelerated credit growth, salaries on average grew by more than 9 percent per year, and at the same time unemployment fell from 13.8 percent in 2002 to 8.5 percent in the second quarter of 2005. Since the beginning of strong credit growth in 2002, the average annual real growth in gross capital formation was above 12 percent, and real consumption and real GDP grew on average by more than 7 percent per year, with little evidence of immediate risk of overheating. In fact, consumer price inflation remained quite low.[5] Government expenditure was quite expansionary and procyclical but budget deficits were not excessively high. The current account deficit at first grew somewhat and then moderated—in the second quarter of 2005, the four-quarter rolling sum of the deficit stood at 6.5 percent of GDP.

Bank loan pricing policies have adapted to these pronounced changes in the economic environment. The average interest rate margins declined from 5.2 percent in 2000 to 2.6 percent in the second quarter of 2005. In addition to the inherently positive effect of the economic upturn on the level of perceived risks, this marked decline in margins can be associated with a number of other factors:

- Economies of scale and recent cost restructuring measures allowed banks to increase their efficiency and extend credit at a lower cost.
- The structure of banks' loan portfolios has changed with a significantly larger share of loans recently being extended for housing acquisition (generally lower interest rates than for businesses).
- Banks tend to apply very active price and nonprice competition policies in order to win a higher market share and establish long-term bonds with customers. The difference from mature markets in this respect is that, in a young and dynamically evolving market, there is a relatively large number of potential first-time entrants into the credit market and they are the banks' main strategic target.
- Incentives for competition are further strengthened by the ongoing economic upturn and housing boom, as in this environment—which will inevitably become less favorable some time in the future—households (and firms) are more likely to make long-term credit commitments. In the context of banks' relatively easy access to financing, banks benefit from the ongoing housing boom because the average size of individual loans increases, which seemingly leaves room for interest rate (price) reductions and still allows banks to achieve profitability targets.

The ongoing processes in the credit market should also be seen against the background of economic integration. The need to co-finance projects supported from EU structural funds provides additional stimulus for credit growth. The effect of this factor, already recorded, should intensify in the medium term.

IV. Assessing risks to the banking sector

From the supervisory perspective, general banking risk indicators are quite good and all banks comply with regulatory requirements.

- Each bank and the banking system as a whole are sufficiently capitalized: as of July 1, 2005, the overall solvency indicator was above 11 percent (the minimum requirement was 8 percent), though this indicator has exhibited a decreasing trend as banks have been actively extending loans.

- The liquidity ratio for the banking system stood at about 40 percent, well in excess of the required 30 percent.
- The share of substandard loans increased somewhat to 2.8 percent of total loans in the second quarter of 2005, but this was mostly due to the broadened base of the substandard loan category, and the figure still remained well below the historical average.
- Owing to rapid credit expansion, growth in total interest income has had a tendency to outpace growth in operating expenses, which has resulted in improving cost-to-income ratios and a rise in profitability figures. All banks made profits in the first half of 2005, and altogether banks earned record profits. This allowed banks to accumulate protective buffers—as a consequence, general provisions have been rising recently.
- Banks' relatively strong financial position, and their strong ties with their parent institutions, should help them withstand moderate adverse shocks, as supported by some stress-testing exercises.

However, as well known, the above indicators are not very suitable for predicting periods of financial distress, because most of them are backward looking, and they can only show, to some extent, banks' resilience to adverse shocks without giving an indication as to the risks to which banks are most exposed.

Credit risks are by far the most important source of risk to the Lithuanian banking sector, but due to the lack of historical experience of business cycles and episodes of accelerated credit growth it is extremely difficult to judge how material these risks are. On the one hand, the financial position of the nonfinancial corporate sector, which absorbs the bulk of bank credit to the private sector, is relatively solid, as indicated by historically high profitability, low overall financial leverage and low debt-to-GDP ratios, and only moderate increases in these two indebtedness indicators (Figure 11.6). On the other hand, risks of potential over-investment exist. As widely discussed in the literature, in periods of accelerated credit growth, bank exposure to the nontradable sector, and construction and real estate sectors in particular, requires close surveillance. In fact, bank exposure to the nontradable sector has been increasing moderately in recent years (Figure 11.7), but has broadly remained in line with the structural developments in the real economy. However, direct bank exposure to the real estate and construction sectors has been much swifter; since these sectors have been among the most profitable in the economy, they have attracted greater financial resources, and the share of bank loans attributed to these sectors increased quite sharply, from 9 percent of total loans at end-2001 to 20 percent in the second quarter of 2005. While this might be seen as a somewhat worrisome process, it does not stand out from global tendencies (see, e.g., BIS 2005, pp.129–31).

As regards the riskiness of bank exposure to the household sector, the overall indebtedness of the latter remains very low (bank credit to households stood at 9 percent of GDP in the second quarter of 2005). Nevertheless, due to the lack of appropriate micro-level statistics, little can be said about the actual position of households taking housing loans. Risks are aggravated by several factors, including the softening of credit standards (as banks have done in Lithuania). Also, market risks

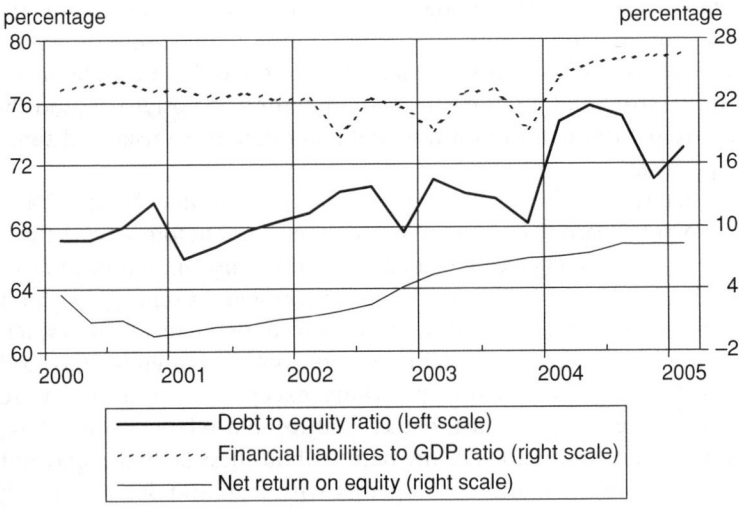

Figure 11.6 Nonfinancial Corporate Sector's Financial Position—Lithuania

Source: Statistics Lithuania, BL calculations.

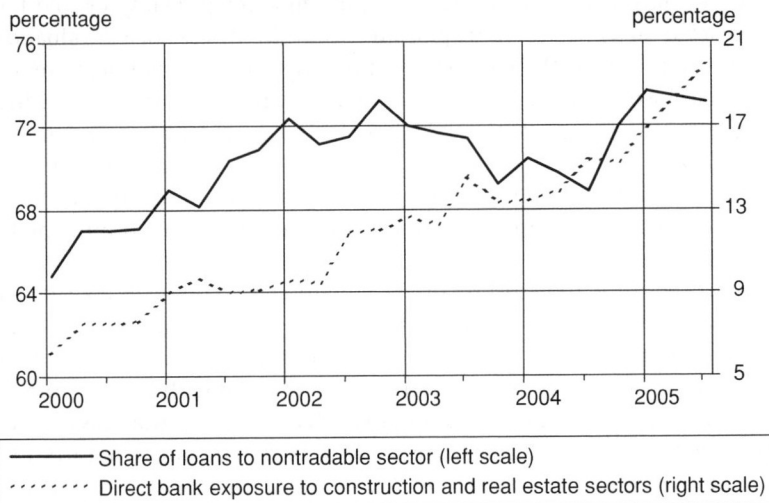

Figure 11.7 Bank Exposure to the Nontradable and Real Estate Sectors—Lithuania

Source: BL.

are usually passed on to households as most housing loans are variable rate loans and, in addition, households take up real estate price risks, which are considerable. All of these risks may turn into credit risks, of course, but any attempt to estimate them would be of a rather speculative nature.

In other words, the financial sector's position will depend, to a great extent, on households' and firms' ability to adapt to possible changes in the economic and interest rate environment. Observing quite broadly based economic growth, neither domestic nor foreign institutions currently forecast any abrupt economic slowdown. The downside risks are also alleviated by projected significant financial inflows from the EU structural funds in the medium term. The upside risks mostly relate to the above-mentioned interest rate and real estate price risks and some possible over-optimism.

Foreign exchange risks to the banking system are quite limited. In mid-2005, about 60 percent of total loans to customers were denominated in foreign currencies (mostly euros), whereas only 33 percent of all deposits from customers were foreign-currency denominated. However, the maximum open foreign exchange position requirements limit individual open positions to 15 percent of the regulatory capital (although maximum open euro position limits were abolished at end-2004), and at the sector level all foreign exchange positions, except euro positions, were almost completely hedged. In contrast, banks tend to hold relatively large long euro positions. Factors such as habits or the nature of business activities may not fully account for this situation, and this, together with loan and deposit pricing policies, must also reflect banks' attitude toward the currency peg. The long euro position and the relatively large spread between litas- and euro-denominated loans, compared with the spread on the deposit side, imply that banks perceive upside adjustment of the litas against the central rate of the euro as highly improbable, but they put themselves in a position to reap positive gains in the case of a devaluation of the litas against the euro. The latter event is very unlikely too, but pressures on the currency board would rise if control on inflation were to be lost, resulting in a severe loss of competitiveness. In any case, litas exchange rate adjustments might be perceived as catastrophic events—from the probabilistic perspective; therefore, banks' open euro positions should probably be interpreted as some sort of hedging against macroeconomic crises rather than low confidence in the functioning of the currency board.

Finally, some other structural features of the banking sector should be considered. The fact that both absolute volumes and growth rates of total bank loans exceed those of deposits might indicate overly dynamic credit growth processes, but again, it is barely surprising bearing in mind the strong financial ties with affluent foreign banks. Together with rapid credit expansion, maturity transformation has become more pronounced. To illustrate, the share of long-term loans increased from 67 percent of total loans at end-2001 to 86 percent in mid-2005, and at the same time the share of sight deposits rose from 54 percent to 61 percent of total deposits.

V. Main policy dilemmas and measures taken to date by the Bank of Lithuania

The preceding discussion suggests that it is by no means a trivial question to determine whether rapid credit growth should be characterized as excessive and a call for action from policymakers. There is no consensus among Lithuanian economists regarding this issue, but the BL does not neglect current developments in the credit market and keeps a close eye on them, recognizing that the increasing indebtedness of firms and households—all other factors left unchanged—inherently implies their increasing vulnerability to adverse shocks.

It is clear, however, that it is macroeconomic and financial stability risks that should be identified and reduced rather than targeting credit growth rates per se. Therefore, the mechanical application of policy measures aimed at slowing credit growth is of dubious value. Another reason the BL refrains from hasty actions is that—while there are certain macroeconomic risks related to asset price booms (such as, exogenous oil price shocks, very low cost of funds, and possible over-optimism), general banking risk indicators are relatively good, implying that first-best policies should include tackling economic imbalances and reducing "wrong" incentives rather than putting restrictions on bank activities. Also, the benefits for economic growth and society's well-being of the credit market's deepening must be acknowledged, suggesting that policymakers dealing with rapid credit growth always face politically tough dilemmas, being forced to weigh between outstanding (partly credit-fueled) economic growth figures, falling unemployment, sizable corporate, personal and budgetary incomes on the one hand, and risks to financial stability and medium-term economic growth on the other.

Finally, in Lithuania's case it is quite likely that credit growth rates will naturally fall significantly once residential real estate prices reach the "affordability ceiling" and expectations regarding future price rises settle down. Against the background of expected interest rate rises, this is most probably going to happen in the very near term, the only question being whether this will stabilize prices (soft landing of credit growth) or set the market in the opposite direction (more abrupt landing of the credit boom). This mainly depends on the share of speculative investors in the residential real estate market.

The first actions that should probably be considered relate to reducing imbalances in the real estate market. This could include introduction of an effective property tax, abolition of household income tax deductibility schemes, and the reduction of administrative distortions in the land market and the "shadow" cost of housing. Possible over-optimism should also be cooled down by disentangling and quantifying effects of credit expansion on economic growth, so that economic agents make sure that they prudently assess risks in this "hothouse" environment.

The BL's ability to effectively control the pace of credit growth and associated risks is rather limited because the main policy tool—interest rate measures—is, of course, eliminated under the currency board regime. The scope is also limited because of banks' easy access to borrowing from abroad, and the ability to avoid restrictions by shifting to other forms of credit (e.g., via subsidiary leasing companies). Banks' high profitability implies that there would be relatively little impact from policy measures aimed at increasing lending costs.

Nevertheless, the BL has maintained a clear commitment to keep the exchange rate policy stance unchanged and consider a number of measures to deal with the problem. The planned reduction of reserve requirements to the euro area level has been postponed, and the requirement has remained at 6 percent. Required solvency ratios are kept higher for one bank specializing in housing loans (at 10 percent) and for credit unions (at 13 percent). As regards supervisory and monetary measures, they include continued bank monitoring measures (and relatively frequent bank inspections) and increasing cooperation with home supervisors of foreign-owned banks. The market development measures that have been taken include broader bank disclosure requirements, and collection of more comprehensive information in the credit registry for risk assessment and management purposes. The BL has also applied policies aimed at better understanding of risks: for instance, moral suasion letters to banks, a new initiative on financial stability monitoring and reporting, public statements on risks related to the housing boom, and consultations with banks regarding preparation for implementation of the Basel II and internal ratings based risk assessment measures.

VI. Conclusions

Financial deepening has so far contributed very strongly to real economic convergence processes. However, there are some concerns over rapid credit growth, such as those associated with uncertainties in asset markets, possible over-optimism, and an inherent impossibility to assess credit risks with sufficiently high confidence. At the current juncture, the BL refrains from applying mechanically policy measures affecting banks' activities and aimed at slowing credit growth, but recognizes the need to remain vigilant and place stronger emphasis on careful examination of the ongoing processes in the banking sector. Arguably, risks should ideally be mitigated by minimizing the economic incentives for banks to take on excessive risks rather than by restrictive policy measures.

Notes

1. Bank of Lithuania (BL).
2. The Lithuanian litas (LTL) was pegged to the US dollar from 1994, and in early 2002 was repegged to the euro.
3. Assessment of price developments in the real estate market is aggravated by the fact that no official real estate price indices are constructed.
4. It should be noted that the excellent performance of the Mazeikiai oil refinery has contributed significantly to the overall figure.
5. While empirical evidence on credit growth episodes in other open economies indicates that this is quite common; nevertheless, inflation figures in the other two Baltic states are considerably higher.

Bibliography

Bank for International Settlements, 2005, *Annual Report 2004*.
Bank of Lithuania, *Annual Reports 2000–2004*, <www.lb.lt>.
——, Quarterly reviews of activity of credit institutions, 2000–2005Q2, <www.lb.lt>.
C. Cottarelli, G. Dell'Ariccia and I. Vladkova-Hollar, 2003, "Early Birds, Late Risers, and Sleeping Beauties: Bank Credit Growth to the Private Sector in Central and Eastern Europe and the Balkans," IMF Working Paper 03/213.
European Council of Real Estate Professions (CEPI), 2005, *Annual Report 2004*, <www.cepi.be/>.

12
Poland's Experiences with Rapid Credit Growth—The 1996–97 Episode

Piotr Szpunar[1]

Periods of fast credit expansion are common phenomena in post-transition emerging economies. Typically, consolidation of the banking sector and a rise in expectations follow the improvement in fundamentals, which results from initially implemented reforms. Anticipating higher income in the future, households increase their current consumption and finance it with bank loans (according to the consumption smoothing hypothesis). In many cases, an accompanying investment boom arises and creates additional demand for bank loans.

A strong credit expansion may, however, have severe adverse consequences either for macroeconomic stability or for the stability of the financial system (or both). Rapid credit growth may place excessive pressure on inflation and/or the current account. In turn, higher inflation and/or deterioration in external imbalances may exert pressure on exchange rate adjustment and in extreme cases may increase the risk of speculative attacks against the national currency. At the same time, excessive lending may lead to problems connected with the accumulation of bad loans. In addition, asset price bubbles may arise. The bursting of such bubbles may result in a drop in the value of bank collateral and a deterioration in the quality of bank assets. All these factors can pose serious threats to the stability of the banking sector. Both currency and banking crises, as potential consequences of a fast credit expansion, might be very costly in terms of economic growth.

For these reasons, measures may need to be taken in order to moderate, or limit the adverse implications of, the pace of credit expansion. This chapter reviews the Polish experience with rapid credit growth during 1996–97.

I. Credit growth in the period 1996–97

In Poland, three main waves of fast credit growth can be identified: the first in 1996–97, the second in 1999–2000, and the third since 2003 lasting until now

(Figure 12.1). This chapter will focus solely on the first episode of rapid lending acceleration.[2] The episode occurred during a period of strong economic growth and reflected the post-transition improvement in fundamentals. The positive results of the economic reforms undertaken at the beginning of the 1990s began to spread over the household sector. Conditions in the labor market and, consequently, the financial standing of households improved significantly. Low levels of ownership of consumer durables and the obsolescence of equipment created strong incentives to purchase consumer goods. For this reason, the demand for consumer credit grew rapidly, fueled by individuals' increasing confidence and the prospects of rising incomes. Households started to increase their long-postponed consumption. During this period, the fast growth in household loans was accompanied by an even larger increase (in terms of volume) in corporate borrowing. The enterprises financed their rapidly growing investments on the wave of overly optimistic expectations. As a result, the overall credit growth rate reached 42.4 percent in 1996.

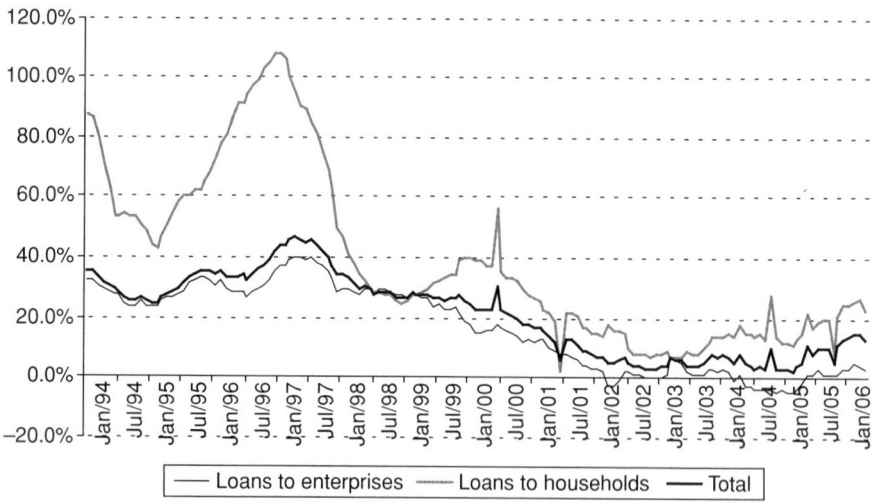

Figure 12.1 Loans to Enterprises and Households—Poland (year-on-year percentage change)

Source: NBP; author's calculations.

Note: In December 1996 and March 2002 the NBP changed the methodology of computing money and banking statistics. Therefore, for comparability reasons, the data for periods before the changes were re-estimated backwards, and do not necessarily comply with time series published on the NBP website.

II. Growing economic imbalances

It can be argued that banks were not sufficiently prepared for the first wave of rapid lending growth, despite significant consolidation prior to 1996: there was still no credit information bureau, bank customers' credit histories were relatively short, and credit risk assessment systems remained imperfect. Thus, the scope for proper credit risk assessment was limited. Despite that, there was no significant deterioration in loan quality, which at least in the initial period of lending acceleration did not seem to create problems. Banks were well capitalized and all important performance indicators seemed to remain in secure zones.

Serious problems, however, emerged as regards the macroeconomic situation. Domestic demand grew at a much faster rate than potential output, and the economy started to exhibit signs of overheating. Accelerated borrowing had become an important source for financing strongly rising consumption and investment. Moreover, fiscal policy was expansionary adding to the excessive domestic demand. The disinflation process slowed down, and the current account deficit started to widen rapidly.

Monetary policy operated under a kind of "eclectic" strategy: the crawling band exchange rate regime was combined with official monetary targeting. The policy of the National Bank of Poland (NBP) was aimed at gradual disinflation. The rate of crawl (devaluation of the central parity) was cut in successive steps as a compromise between disinflation and the speed of real appreciation of the domestic currency. The active interest rate policy was also subordinated to the final goal of gradual inflation reduction. Such a strategy had its limitations, as in periods of strong capital flows it was impossible to meet all the targets simultaneously. In such a case, the NBP tended to desist relatively easily from seeking to control the monetary aggregates. The exchange rate policy, however, was adjusted only when absolutely necessary, while the commitment to meet the final target of disinflation was very strong. Growing imbalances in the economy created the risk of capital outflows, especially after the Asian crisis in 1997 when financial markets became very sensitive to growing current account deficits. In view of the increasing risks regarding the sustainability of the disinflation process, monetary policy had to be tightened to stabilize domestic demand, and the NBP reacted promptly.

III. Measures taken

The fast credit growth was treated as part of a broader problem of excessive demand. As there were no signs of any serious threats to the stability of the banking sector, the NBP decided not to tighten its supervisory policy. Prudential measures were not considered to be a proper response to macroeconomic disturbances. Moreover, the room for further tightening of supervisory policy was limited as the regulations were already very strict. Since the beginning of the 1990s banking supervision had adopted a very restrictive approach in light of the experience with the bad loan problems of 1991–92.[3]

In 1997 the NBP focused on its monetary policy instruments. Acting in line with its "eclectic" strategy, the NBP maintained the crawling band mechanism, but refrained from further reductions in the rate of central parity devaluation. Despite falling inflation, the rate of crawl was maintained at 1 percent per month for a period of two years (January 1996–February 1998). The width of the band also remained unchanged (± 7 percent around the central parity). The whole exchange rate mechanism was practically frozen for two years, with the intention of reducing imports and supporting exports.

In order to maintain the crawling band system, the NBP purchased massive amounts of foreign exchange (FX) in the market via direct FX interventions and fixing transactions. The FX purchases were sterilized, and high excess liquidity was accumulated. This resulted in significant sterilization costs. The central bank treated it, however, as a price worth paying for its stabilization policy.

The cost of sterilization rose further after the NBP raised its interest rates. Starting from December 1996 it increased its open market operation rates several times. In August 1997, a hike in official rates followed (Lombard rate was raised by 2 percentage points).[4] As a result, the market rate represented by one month WIBOR rose by 5.4 percent (from 19.8 percent to 25.2 percent) between November 1996 and October 1997. In addition, the NBP significantly raised the rates of reserve requirements (see Table 12.1).

Table 12.1 Average Quarterly Reserve Requirements—Poland (in percent)

	1996				1997			
	Q1	Q2	Q3	Q4	Q1	Q2	Q3	Q4
Zloty deposits								
Demand	20.0	19.0	17.0	17.0	19.0	20.0	20.0	20.0
Time	9.0	9.0	9.0	9.0	9.0	11.0	11.0	11.0
Foreign currency deposits								
Demand	1.7	2.0	2.0	2.0	3.3	5.0	5.0	5.0
Time	1.7	2.0	2.0	2.0	3.3	5.0	5.0	5.0

Source: NBP.

Since the reaction of commercial banks to those measures proved to be insufficient in prompting a rise in banks' lending and deposit rates, additional actions had to be considered. The NBP decided to start collecting deposits directly from households. This was a supportive monetary policy tool aimed at creating direct competition to the commercial banks in the deposit market. The deposits collected at the NBP's branches were offered at fixed interest rates higher than those at commercial banks. During the three-month period (mid-September to mid-December 1997), the NBP collected ZL 3.6 billion in deposits (Table 12.2). The measure was intended to create a strong signaling effect and to increase competition in the deposit market, both aimed at promoting savings.

Table 12.2 Personal Deposits at National Bank of Poland (in ZL million)

1997	Level	Change
September	842.4	842.4
October	1984.6	1142.1
November	2731.8	747.2
December	3599.8	868.0

Source: NBP.

IV. Assessment of adopted measures

It is difficult to assess the efficiency of each of the measures separately. The specific effect of the exchange rate policy is particularly hard to judge. On the one hand, the lower value of the zloty must have led to a decrease in the purchasing power of households and companies for imported goods. In that way, it could have potentially weakened domestic demand. On the other hand, however, the weaker zloty contributed to higher exports and GDP growth and fueled higher incomes, which in turn boosted expectations and encouraged higher expenditures. There is no decisive hard evidence in evaluating the relative power of these two counteracting effects. Moreover, as this measure was aimed at the reduction of the current account deficit *via* relative prices of exports and imports, it is also difficult to assess its direct impact on the credit expansion.

The effectiveness of the interest rate policy was, at least initially, lower than expected. Whereas the NBP managed to maintain interbank market interest rates at the required level (the first stage of the monetary transmission mechanism (MTM)), serious problems emerged at the second and further stages of the MTM (Box 12.1). First, the impact of movements in official rates (and, following them, interbank interest rates) on commercial banks' lending and deposit rates proved to be limited. Second, the cost elasticity of the demand for credit proved to be low.

Box 12.1. Problems with the Monetary Transmission Mechanism (MTM)

The MTM starts with changes in the interbank interest rates, which reflect moves in the central bank's policy rates (usually carried out in open market operations). The interbank rates, in turn, affect the price setting behavior of commercial banks.

MTM First Stages

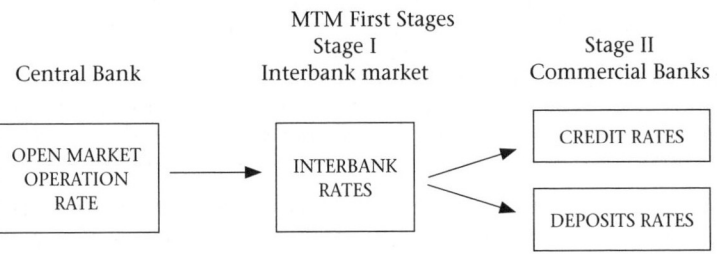

A change in the central bank's rates causes an immediate adjustment in the interbank rates, which move to a new level. This occurs both in a situation of liquidity shortage, as well as in the case of excess liquidity in the banking sector. Let us take the latter as an illustration that corresponds to the Polish experience. In a situation of excess liquidity, the central bank owes money to commercial banks. The money can come, for example, from the central bank's FX interventions against domestic currency appreciation. When a central bank intends to steer nominal interest rates at any level above 0 percent it must sterilize the surplus of liquidity. Sterilization means that the central bank sells interest bearing assets to commercial banks, e.g., the NBP bills in the Polish case. The

▶

> banking sector as a whole (but not necessarily one particular bank) no longer has to keep excess money on a no-interest bearing account with the central bank (as has been the case in, for instance, Japan). Excess money is invested in NBP bills and the surplus is in this way absorbed.
>
> The yield on NBP bills sets the market interest rate as it reflects the marginal adjustment to the reserve money demand and supply mismatch (it absorbs the excess on the supply side and in this way "balances the books"). From this point of view, there is no problem with sterilization, since commercial banks always buy an appropriate amount of central bank bills. There is no other possibility for the whole banking sector to invest the excess money. One commercial bank can invest the money (e.g., deposit it in the interbank market with another bank or buy T-bills or any other kind of instrument) but after the settlement of this transaction the account of another commercial bank with the central bank (e.g., selling the T-bill) will be credited. So, the excess in the banking sector still remains unchanged. When the banks buy too many bills, then they have a problem with meeting required reserves and risk paying a penalty. The interbank interest rates go up. When the banks buy too few bills, then they lose money by keeping it on no-interest bearing accounts with the central bank. The interbank interest rates go down.
>
> The central bank is thus in a position to control market interest rates. In order to do so it must, however, forecast the liquidity position of the banking sector. In practice the central bank must forecast its own balance sheet and adjust the scale of open market operations to the liquidity excess. By doing so, it is always able to steer the market interest rates as long as it is ready to accept the cost of sterilization.
>
> A problem with the transmission of the central bank's interest rate to the overall economy might, however, emerge at the second stage of the MTM. Commercial banks may not react properly in response to changes in the interbank market rates. This problem was apparent in Poland in 1997. Increases in market rates (following higher yields on bills offered by the NBP) did not induce adequate adjustments in commercial banks' credit and deposit rates. This was caused by segmentation and poor competition in the banking sector.
>
> Higher responsiveness of banks to the NBP's interest rate policy could have been achieved if there had been an improvement in the structure of the banking sector. This in turn could have been delivered by faster privatization of banks, faster abolition of government guarantees covering deposits in three state-owned large banks, and including those banks in the already-functioning universal deposit insurance scheme. These measures were, however, time-consuming and dependent on political decisions outside the central bank. In this situation the NBP chose to use a short-term measure and increase competition in the market by collecting deposits directly from the public.

The rates offered by banks did not respond properly to hikes in interbank market rates. Despite the increase in the market rates by more than 5 percentage points, commercial banks' prime lending rate rose only by 1.5 percentage points (Figure 12.2). This sluggish response of banks' interest rates to changes in market rates can be explained by their eagerness to expand lending activity in the environment of the segmented and not very competitive banking sector. The banking sector was dominated by a few strong, state-owned savings banks, equipped with government deposits guarantees. The state ownership, the guarantees, large size, wide net of branches, and fine reputation assured that group of banks a strong market-leader position. This enabled an oligopolistic-like price setting policy. Despite rising market rates, those banks managed not to raise their lending rates (or to raise them just slightly) to expand lending. The credit acceleration was easily financed by cheap deposits, as deposit rates were practically frozen at low levels. To avoid losing market share, other commercial banks had to shadow this kind of price-setting behavior, even at the cost of lower profitability.

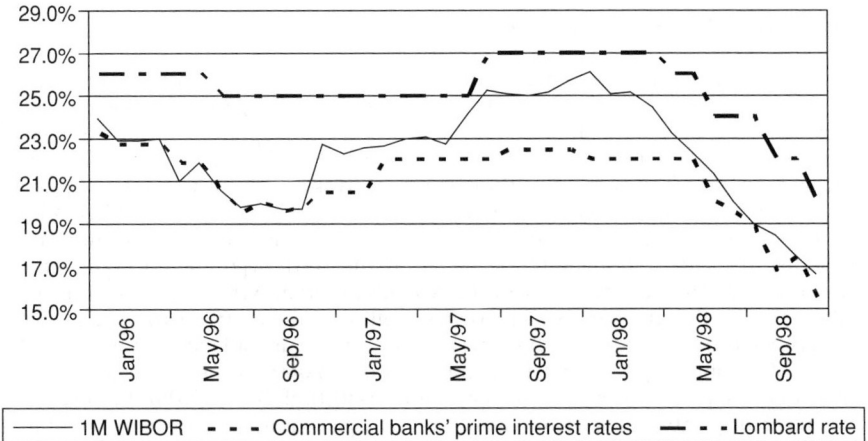

Figure 12.2 Interest Rates—Poland

Source: NBP.

Low price elasticity of the demand for credit was observed both in the household sector and in the corporate sector. In the case of households, this can be traced back to the rapid growth in real wages, optimistic expectations, and huge potential for consumption which had been deferred since the initial years of transformation. Additionally, the initial level of borrowers was very low. In the case of corporations, low sensitivity to the rising cost of borrowing can also be explained by overly positive expectations that led to very high investment activity.

The need to apply some additional measures hence became a matter of urgency and the NBP decided to accept deposits directly from households. Although this action was temporary, it substantially strengthened competition in the deposit market. During the period, nearly every second zloty of new deposits was paid in to the NBP (Figure 12.3). This limited the source of cheap funding and forced commercial banks to change their price-setting policies, despite the fact that the role of deposits in overall liquidity absorption was marginal (Figure 12.4). Interest rates offered to individuals went up, and new attractive saving products appeared. In the period of the NBP's deposit collection, deposit rates at the largest banks were increased. The signaling effect for both banks and households was also very important. As a controversial measure, it induced many public debates and criticisms of the NBP, which nevertheless provided it with the opportunity to explain the reasons for its action, thereby improving public awareness of the situation and, consequently, increasing the public's propensity to save. For the commercial banks, the acceptance of households' deposits at the NBP was a clear sign that the central bank would make determined efforts to rebalance the economic situation. All in all, the deposits proved to be an effective measure in support of monetary tightening (Box 12.2).

> **Box 12.2. NBP Collection of Deposits**
>
> Given the limited impact of changes in official base rates on the banks' lending and deposit rates, in mid-September 1997 the NBP began accepting personal deposits. These were offered at fixed rates of interest, with 6-month deposits earning 21.5 percent per year, and 9-month deposits earning 22.5 percent per year. These rates were at the time higher than those being offered by the commercial banks. During a 3-month campaign to attract personal depositors, the central bank took in funds totaling ZL 3.6 billion, with over two thirds of this sum placed in 9-month deposits. The NBP Management Board expected the banks to respond to this by raising their own deposit and lending rates, with higher real interest rates inducing households to curtail current consumption. The NBP estimates that the increases in base rates, allied to the central bank's acceptance of personal deposits, helped push up deposit rates at the largest banks by between 0.9 points (12-month deposits) and 1.6 points (1- and 3-month deposits). Prime lending rates rose 1.1 points. According to the Central Statistical Office (GUS), the ratio of savings to disposable incomes increased from 10.4 percent in 1996 to 10.9 percent in 1997, while growth in personal consumption slowed from 8.7 percent to 7 percent.
>
> Source: Annual Report 1997, Chapter on Monetary Policy, Exceptional Instruments, <www.nbp.pl>.

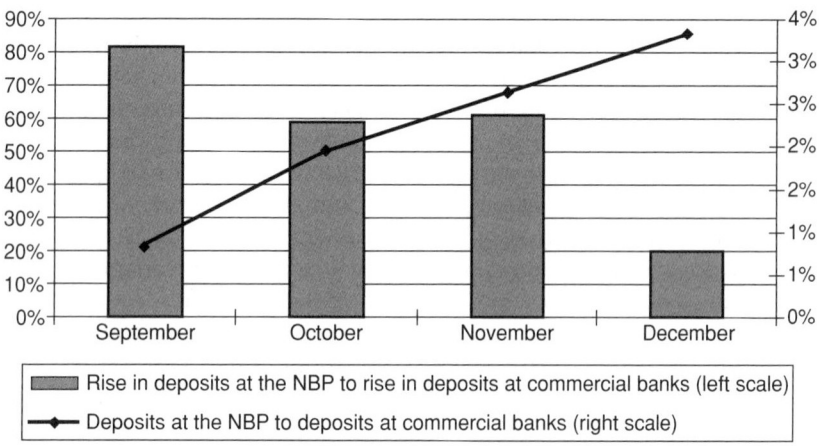

Figure 12.3 Households' Deposits at the National Bank of Poland

Source: NBP.

By contrast, the impact of changes in required reserve ratios can be assessed as very poor. Required reserves were not remunerated. In an environment of weak competition in the deposit market, it was easy for commercial banks to pass on the costs of required reserves to depositors. As the higher reserve ratios contributed to lower deposit rates, they could even have been assessed as counterproductive.

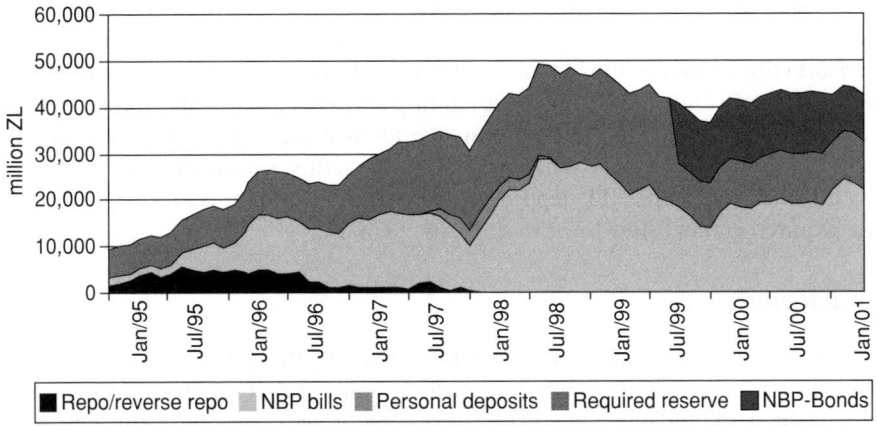

Figure 12.4 Excess Liquidity—Poland

Source: NBP.

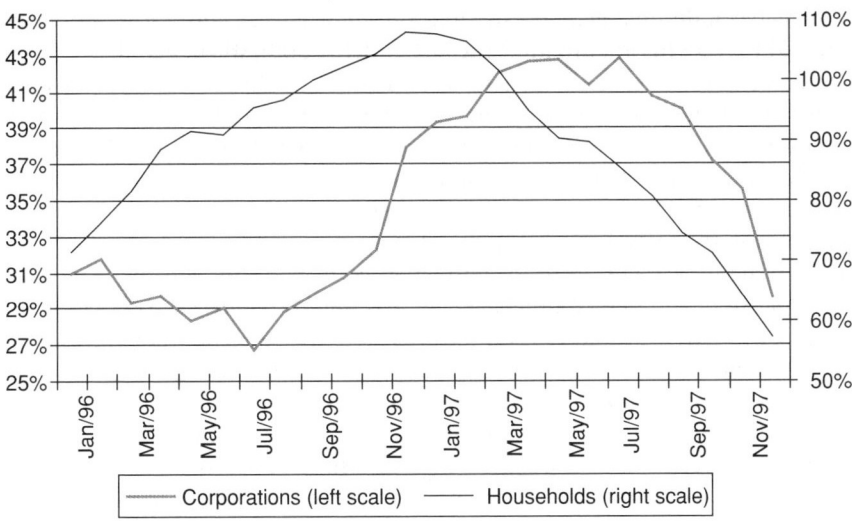

Figure 12.5 Corporate and Households Lending Growth (Year-on-year)—Poland

Source: The NBP Annual Report 1997.

Despite higher reserve requirements, banks did not face any liquidity constraints, as, in principle, newly granted loans create new deposits in the system. On the other hand, high reserve ratios helped the central bank to share sterilization costs with commercial banks. In this way, the higher costs of sterilization were not entirely passed on to the tax payer via lower NBP profits. This created more room for policy tightening without inducing tensions that could have emerged if the NBP had been generating losses.

To recapitulate, it is difficult to assess the effect of the individual instruments that were used to reduce the pace of credit expansion. However, the package of measures introduced seemed to prove effective. Banks started to pay more attention to deposit collection. The growth of lending slowed significantly from above 40 percent to less than 30 percent per year. Corporate credits responded more rapidly to the interest rate impulse, whereas household credits reacted stronger only after the introduction of the NBP deposit measure (Figure 12.5). This process supported the required gradual slowdown in domestic demand.

Conclusions

The Polish experience with rapid credit growth in the period 1996–97 can be considered as an example of a typical post-transition catch-up process. The initial improvement in fundamentals and high economic growth triggered overly optimistic expectations and led to high demand for borrowing. The supply of credits was also growing fast as domestic banks consolidated and restructured their activities. Such a process could have created problems for the stability of the banking sector and/or (as in the Polish case) macroeconomic stability of the country. The expansionary fiscal policy created additional demand and tensions. In these circumstances, monetary policy had to react in order to limit the fast growing domestic demand.

The adopted measures can be divided into three groups: (i) the conventional tools such as required reserve ratios and interest rate hikes were used; (ii) an unconventional measure of deposit collection was introduced, which supported the interest rate policy and increased its efficiency, as the low sensitivity of banks and economic agents to interest rate changes was finally overcome; (iii) the unchanged pace of exchange rate devaluation was maintained.

Overall, the package of measures implemented by the NBP effectively reduced credit expansion, and helped to rebalance the economy. During the period of fast credit expansion in 1996 and 1997 the drawbacks of the "eclectic" monetary policy strategy became apparent: the unchanged pace of crawl slowed down the disinflation process; the costs of sterilized intervention increased significantly; high interest rates attracted capital inflows, so that control over the exchange rate became difficult. Moreover, rapidly developing financial markets limited the scope for effective FX interventions. It became apparent that, in the long term, a switch from the "eclectic" approach to direct inflation targeting (DIT) would be inevitable. The successful implementation of measures aimed to slow down the credit growth paved the way for a gradual and orderly regime changeover. The gradual approach to the monetary policy regime changeover in turn gave economic agents enough time to prepare themselves for larger exchange rate fluctuations. While the application of unconventional instruments was temporarily helpful, in the longer run, the introduction of DIT as a pure corner solution was unavoidable, and ultimately improved the effectiveness of monetary policy.

Notes

1. National Bank of Poland (NBP). The author is grateful to İnci Ötker-Robe and Michał Brzoza-Brzezina for valuable comments and to Joanna Niedźwiedzińska for excellent research assistance.
2. Policy responses to a later episode from early 2000s associated with an expansion in bank lending in foreign exchange can be found in P. Hilbers, İ. Ötker-Robe, C. Pazarbasioğlu, and G. Johnsen, 2005, "Assessing and Managing Rapid Crdit Growth and the Role of Supervisory and Prudential Policies," IMF Working Paper 05/151 (International Monetary Fund).
3. The general prudential framework was not changed until the 2000s. In 2002, some major changes to the supervisory regulations were introduced, mainly in accordance with the EU harmonization process. The changes concerned capital requirements, loan classification criteria, FX exposures, and supervisory procedures.
4. Until February 1998 the yields offered on NBP bills were not treated as officially announced interest rates of the NBP.

13
Fast Credit Growth and Policy Response: The Case of Romania

Cristian Popa[1]

The evolution of credit growth in Romania, together with the macroeconomic consequences, has followed, albeit with a lag, similar developments in other economies in Central, Eastern, and South-eastern Europe (CEE), as well as in certain non-European emerging markets. However, the timing of the regulatory and supervisory overhaul and subsequent continued improvement of financial sector oversight, as well as the banking sector cleanup, have left their imprint on the Romanian economy. Financial market depth has been relatively low in comparison with that in other countries in the region. Only comparatively recent improvements in risk perception have made it possible for corporate entities and households to begin to make use of alternative nondomestic sources of financing. Both the similarities with other CEE countries and the particular features of the Romanian economy influenced macroeconomic policymaking and implementation, especially for the National Bank of Romania (NBR). This chapter presents these features and the attendant policy rationale in relation to Romania's experience.

I. The initial experience of credit expansion

Prior to 1997, credit expansion took place in Romania in an only partially reformed environment still dominated by state-owned enterprises. In this environment, the lack of widespread structural adjustment and the persistence of soft budget constraints resulted in distortions of behavior that affected not only large, loss-making publicly owned entities, but also segments of the private sector, including through the distortion of learning curves and their effect on corporate governance.

The expansion was mainly led by corporate borrowing, through a strong lending channel, where large, predominantly state-owned firms benefited from broader access to financial intermediation at the expense of smaller, mostly privately-owned companies. The state-owned firms were significantly less responsive to changes in the cost of credit (to the point that their demand for credit exhibited positive elasticity to interest rate increases) and displayed a greater ability to diversify into inter-company arrears when credit supply was adversely affected. Moreover, at that time, private sector companies, although more profitable, were usually more poorly capitalized than their public sector counterparts and also lacked supportive credit histories.[2] This resulted in adverse selection and moral hazard, visible in the significantly stronger impact of interest spread widening (as a proxy for deteriorating corporate net worth) on borrowing by private sector entities compared to larger, state-owned ones (Popa, 1998).

The important consequences of this credit channel were twofold. First, the banking sector, which was dominated by state ownership, was captive to important debtors even after directed and subsidized lending was discontinued, due to its significant exposure to them. Such exposure made the prospect of foreclosure unappealing from the creditors' point of view, given the low liquidity of eligible assets in the absence of specific markets, as well as their obsolescence, not to mention a significant worsening of prudential indicators for the lender, to the extent that it could compromise the lender's continued functioning. Second, given the presence of adverse selection and the need for tightening monetary policy in delivering sustainable disinflation, structural reforms became a necessity, in regard to both a comprehensive banking sector cleanup as well as improvements in financial discipline in the real sector. Thus, prudential and macroeconomic considerations were broadly overlapping and complementary, even in the early stages of Romania's systemic transformation.

II. The current credit expansion: underlying fundamentals, characteristics, and implications

Underlying fundamentals

The present credit expansion, which started in 2001–02, is based on a very different set of fundamentals. First, the banking sector cleanup effort, at an estimated cost of 10 percent of GDP, has resulted in a relatively small but clean and stable financial sector, where lending takes place on a sustainable basis. Importantly, banks are no longer captive to real sector debtors, and the persistently low and declining ratio of nonperforming loans[3] to own capital (even in the presence of pro-cyclicality), as well as the post-cleanup absence of arrears to banks, are significant indicators of this improvement in corporate governance.[4]

Second, the ownership pattern within the banking sector has shifted in favor of private capital, with a decisive role for foreign ownership. While private capital had a 54.7 percent share of banking sector assets in 2000 (and 55.1 percent and 67.9 percent of total deposits and credit, respectively), this grew to 94.1 percent (93.6 percent and 96.6 percent, respectively) in 2005. At end-2005, only two banks were majority state-owned, the larger of which (CEC, the former savings bank) is awaiting privatization in the near future.[5] Including the recently privatized BCR, in January 2006 foreign ownership amounted to 88.1 percent of assets, 86.6 percent of total deposits, and 89.3 percent of credit in the Romanian banking sector. The present ownership pattern, and especially the role played by experienced foreign credit institutions, is expected to yield further improvements in efficiency and competitiveness, in particular through the diversification of available products and services, knowledge transfer, and improvements in corporate governance (with special emphasis on risk management). The predominantly foreign ownership will also contribute to the resilience of the Romanian banking sector under potentially adverse economic conditions in the future. In contrast to experiences in some non-European emerging markets, the foreign bank presence in EU accession countries is regarded as a positive long-term development, and increased capitalization (above the minimum legal requirements) may be seen as evidence of this view.

Third, despite the significant rate of credit expansion over a number of years, the Romanian banking sector has maintained good solvency. Compared to the minimum 12 percent requirement, actual rates for the entire sector have stayed around 20–21 percent since August 2003, reaching 20.3 percent in December 2005. Recent capital increases undertaken in response to higher reserve requirements on foreign exchange liabilities and more stringent prudential measures also point to continued robust solvency in the future (Figure 13.1).

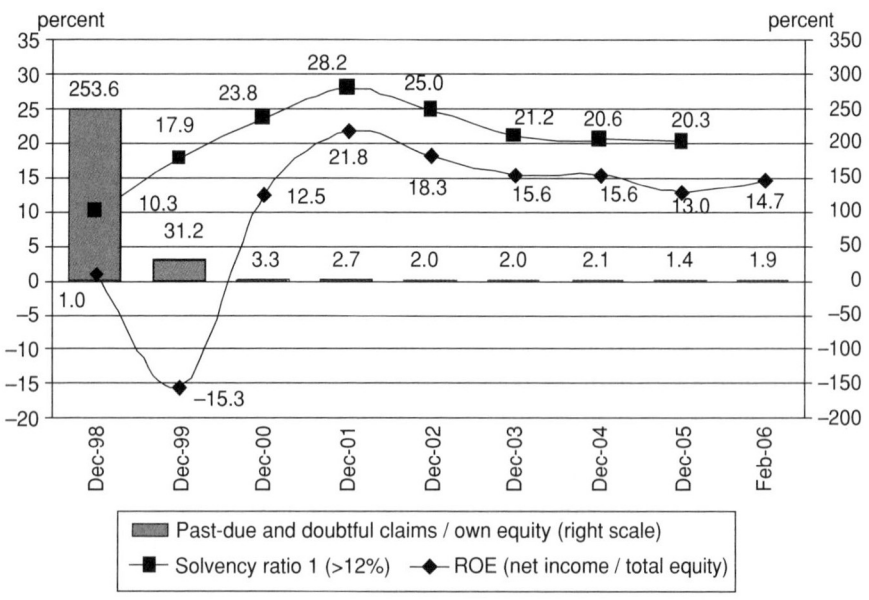

Figure 13.1 Analysis Ratios for the Banking System—Romania

Souce: NBR.

Fourth, the quality of regulation and supervision has improved dramatically. This concerns the legal underpinnings of financial sector oversight, the secondary legislation, the methodology and improved risk-based pro-active thinking of the central bank in this regard, and the cooperative efforts of regulators and supervisors responsible for different segments of the financial sector. In addition, benefits have arisen also from the common unifying approach of EU acquis transposition, which has not only allowed catching up in certain activities, but has also avoided considerable costs with regard to model search and has led to more consistency of regulation and supervision across the whole financial sector.

Fifth, the banking sector's resilience to shocks is significantly stronger. The first FSAP evaluation conducted by the IMF and the World Bank in 2003 showed the Romanian banking system to be performing well under rigorous stress testing (IMF, 2003). Repeated and more comprehensive evaluations conducted periodically by NBR staff have shown that this resilience is being maintained, even though credit flows have registered continued significant increases. Progress in securing improved banking sector quality has also been mentioned by the three EU peer review missions focusing on financial sector issues.

Finally, the current wave of credit expansion, besides being an expression of the catching-up process vis-à-vis the EU, is driven by improved country and debtor risk perception. The latter reflects, in turn, continued brisk economic growth, macroeconomic stabilization, and considerably lower systemic risk resulting from banking sector restructuring and consolidation, alongside the regulatory and supervisory improvements mentioned above.

Characteristics

As a first feature, credit expansion is taking place almost exclusively within the private sector. Indeed, the volume of credit extended to majority state-owned firms has remained roughly constant in nominal terms since end-1999 (and even declined after 2002), despite inflation having reached single digit levels for the first time only in 2004 (Figure 13.2).

Moreover, the most dynamic segment of credit has shifted over time from corporate to household lending, particularly through the introduction of new banking products and services. Whereas total nongovernment credit grew by an average of 32 percent per year in real terms in 2002–05, the analogous rate for household credit was 202.5 percent.

The above difference in growth rates is certainly also due to the presence of base effects, as can be seen in Figure 13.2. However, due to persistently high annual lending growth, these effects are starting to play a lesser role, as the share of household credit in total nongovernment credit has increased fivefold, from under 7 percent in 2001 to over 35 percent in 2005.

The start of sustained banking sector interest in household lending dates back to 2003, when lending rates fell significantly for the first time, while disposable incomes had been growing on the back of sustained GDP growth since 2000. It is important to note that, while most household borrowing is related to consumer finance, long-term borrowing is growing in importance in this market segment, in parallel with the growing demand for housing and the resultant takeoff in real estate prices, also fueled by nonresident capital flows.

The "new frontier" of lending to households appears to have led to increased competition within the domestic banking sector, with larger credit volumes going hand-in-hand with lower interest rate spreads (Figure 13.3). Indeed, while there was

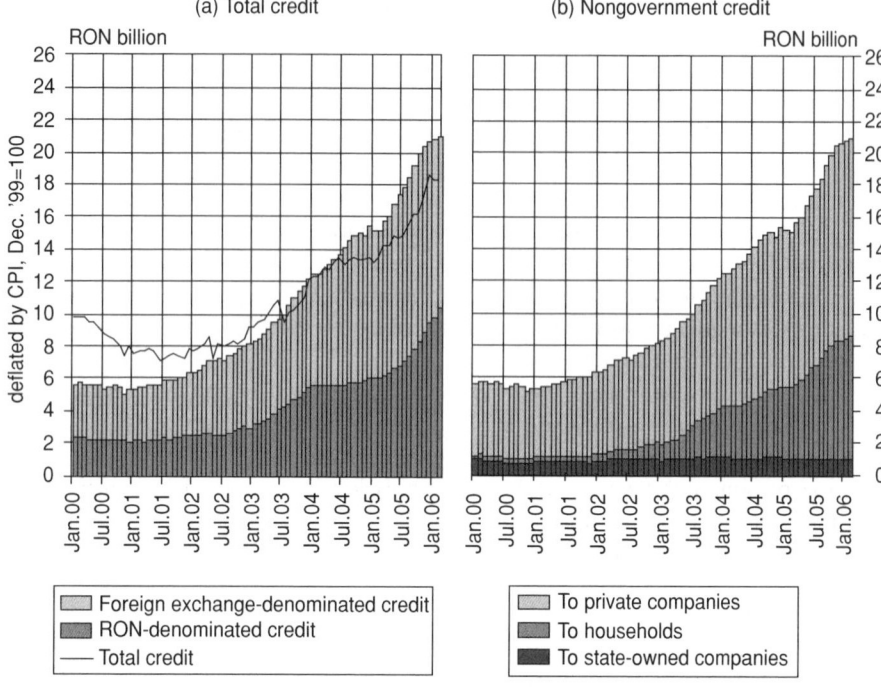

Figure 13.2 Total Credit and Nongovernment Credit—Romania (in real terms)

Source: NBR, National Institute of Statistics (NIS).

a contraction of spreads between lending and deposit rates for nongovernment, nonbank clients (with a decline from 10.8 percentage points to 7.5 percentage points from February 2005 to February 2006), it has been even more striking for household banking activity, where spreads dropped from 14.4 percentage points to 8.6 percentage points during the same period. The positive aspect is that existing efficiency reserves are beginning to be tapped into, with spreads starting to converge toward levels evident in more advanced markets. On the other hand, the sizable short-term compression also indicates that competition is concentrating more on generating higher volumes of activity through substantially lower credit rates (especially in domestic currency), with the result that the reaction to monetary policy signals is less immediate.

This ongoing spread compression has taken an inevitable toll on the profitability of credit institutions. The profitability has nevertheless remained high (with ROE of 13 percent in December 2005, down from 15.6 percent in the previous two years), prompting continued foreign interest in the sector and pointing to increased concentration as a probable future trend, analogous to similar developments taking place in the EU.

Another characteristic of the recent episode of credit expansion is represented by the fact that net banking sector claims on nongovernment, nonbank corporates

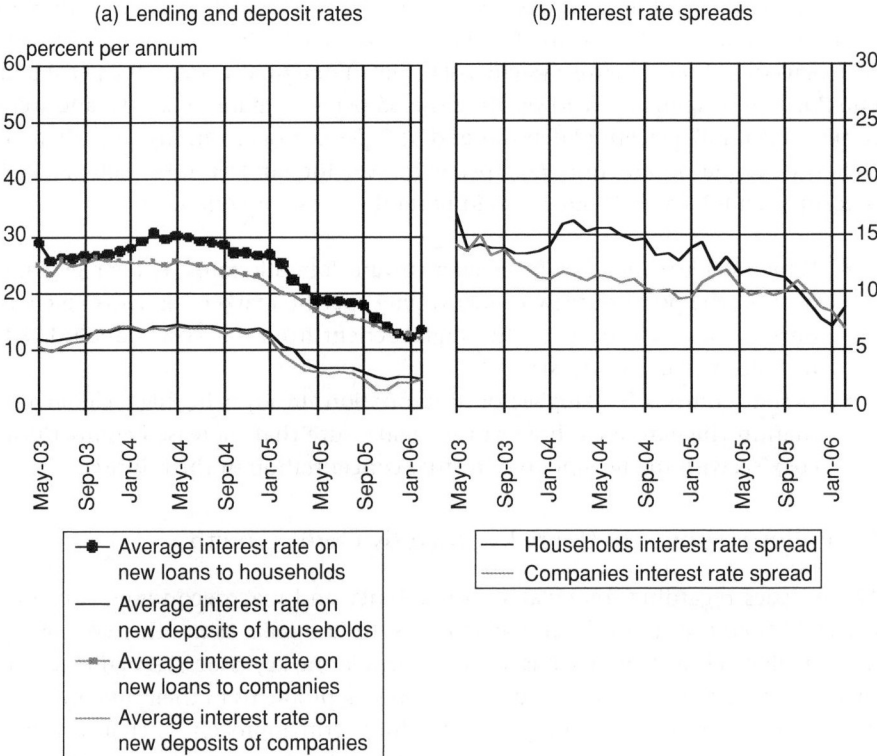

Figure 13.3 Interest Rates Applied by Credit Institutions—Romania

Source: NBR.

and households remain negative, despite having substantially dropped in absolute value over time. This not only provides part of the explanation as to why lending rates are falling more at present than deposit rates,[6] but also presents a positive view of the resilience of the credit institutions sector. Importantly, it reflects low, although increasing, financial depth in the Romanian economy, as well as the larger reliance of banks on household and nonbank firm deposits as financing sources, alongside lines of credit from abroad, given that interbank market activity (net of NBR liquidity sterilization) is still shallow.

External liabilities of the banking sector grew significantly, however, reflecting a substantial drawing of financial resources from abroad, in response to decelerating saving rates and a domestic borrowing appetite at higher spreads than in home markets. External liabilities as a share of total banking sector liabilities rose from 5.9 percent in 2001 to 20.9 percent in 2005. Also, net foreign assets of the banking sector as a share of total assets, which had been 8.5 percent in 2001, turned negative and became larger in absolute value at end-2005, reaching −17.4 percent.

Banking sector concentration is relatively high at present, with the declines in spreads perceived as related to a stepping up of competition, primarily over market share in consumer lending. In December 2005, out of a total of 39 banks (including six foreign bank branches), the five largest commercial banks in Romania held 58.8 percent of total banking system assets (down marginally from 59.2 percent at end-2004, and significantly lower than the 65 percent figure for 2001), and were responsible for 57 percent of deposits and 61.2 percent of credit. Also, the share of their own capital shrank from 60.5 percent of the total in December 2004 to 55.1 percent at end-2005. This poses two important supervisory questions:

- Which stable niches exist for smaller, private domestic banks, either regionally or from the point of view of identifying specific market segments (such as lower-income consumers who might benefit from low-cost, standardized, no-frills banking services)?
- Despite domestic banking sector concentration already being higher at present than in the euro area, how can we make sure that increased competition coexists with the likelihood of further concentration in the future?

III. Policy response to the risks posed by credit growth

Three issues regarding financial sector stability and macroeconomic concerns currently hold the attention of policymakers. In Romania, as in other economies in the region, a broad approach is taken in considering key issues, recognizing that there is a need to pro-actively address burgeoning problems in their infancy, with benign neglect representing only a costly, short-term approach. Therefore, a case can be made for enlightened activism, where financial stability and macroeconomic issues are approached in complementarity, and where awareness of the need for depth and diversity in financial intermediation goes together with the recognition of the paramount need to ensure the sustainability of credit dynamics by moderating the pace of its growth. This would prevent both a deterioration in the main macroeconomic equilibria and any complication of prudential considerations; the eventual resolution of such complication would potentially be more costly and difficult than the moderate constraints imposed for the purpose of prevention. Box 13.1 lists the measures taken by the NBR as of November 2005.

Currency mismatches

The first issue concerns the risks posed by the amplification of banking system asset–liability mismatch not just in terms of maturities, but, significantly, in terms of currency denomination.

The existence of a certain degree of euroization in Romania represents the legacy of persistently high inflation in the past, as well as of banking sector confidence problems prior to the cleanup. However, the increase in 2003–04 of the interest rate differential vis-à-vis international markets, driven by increases in the monetary policy rate,[7] resulted in a slight slowdown in domestic currency lending (accompanied by a pickup in domestic currency savings) that was offset by faster growth in lending in foreign exchange.

Box 13.1. Measures Taken by the NBR to Deal With the Rapid Credit Growth

Monetary policy measures to slow down credit growth

June, August 2003
- Halt of the declining trend of policy rate (June) given the unexpected acceleration in household consumption growth starting with Q2, and
- Gradual increase in policy rate (by 3 percentage points in three steps to 21.25 percent) (since August)

August 2004
- Keeping the nominal policy rate unchanged in H1, despite steady decline in annual inflation rate
- Rise in reserve ratio on foreign exchange (FX) deposits to 30 percent from 25 percent while keeping reserve ratio on RON-denominated deposits at 18 percent (August)

2005 (Switch to inflation targeting framework)
- Extending the reserve base for required reserves on FX deposits and lowering reserve ratio on RON-denominated deposits to 16 percent

Prudential measures to slow down credit growth

February 2004
- Enforcement of prudential regulations aimed at slowing down:
  consumer credit growth
  – installments (principal + interest) shall not exceed 30 percent of net incomes of the borrower and his/her family
  – down payment of at least 25 percent or cosigner commitment for purchases of goods
  – collateral and/or cosigner commitment for other types of consumer credit
  mortgage credit growth
  – credit value shall not exceed 75 percent of the building's value
  – collateral shall cover 133 percent of credit value
  – installments (principal + interest) shall not exceed 35 percent of net incomes of the borrower and his/her family

September 2004
- Inclusion of household credits over EUR 5,000 equivalent in Banking Risk Central; Credit Bureau starts operation

August 2005
- Enforcement of additional prudential regulations aimed at tightening eligibility criteria for individuals:
  – overall installments (principal + interest) associated with credit contracts (consumer and real estate), as well as with other similar liabilities resulting from other credit contracts, leasing contracts, installment purchases contracts, irrespective of the creditor, shall not exceed 40 percent of net incomes of the borrower and his/her family
  – installments (principal + interest) associated with consumer credit, and with other contracts similar to consumer credit, irrespective of the creditor, shall not exceed 30 percent of net incomes of the borrower and his/her family
  – installments (principal + interest) associated with real estate credit, and with other contracts similar to real estate credit, irrespective of the creditor, shall not exceed 35 percent of net incomes of the borrower and his/her family

September 2005
- Enforcement of new prudential regulations aimed at limiting FX credit exposure:
  – FX credit exposure of a credit institution arising from loans granted to unhedged individuals and legal persons (other than credit institutions) shall not exceed 300 percent of own funds
  – when determining the above-mentioned exposure, hedged borrowers (i.e. individuals and legal persons who generate net positive cash flows in FX) shall not be taken into consideration
- Refining the regulations on provisioning and loan classification taking into account the FX risk of the borrower

February 2006
- Enforcement of new legislation on regulating and supervising quasi-credit nonbank financial intermediaries (leasing, financial credit, etc.).

More recently, against the background of almost complete liberalization of capital movements, the preference for foreign exchange borrowing has been reinforced by the perceived appreciation trend of the domestic currency. The latter has raised wealth and balance sheet effects to a position of prominence for domestic economic agents, whose assets (as eligible collateral) and domestic currency income streams have increased in value in foreign exchange equivalent, thereby raising creditworthiness and making foreign exchange loans cheaper in relative terms.

The share of foreign exchange credit in total credit to nongovernment looked set to accelerate (Figure 13.4) from an already high level of 60 percent in early 2005. The increase reflected faster growth in borrowing in foreign exchange (with an increase of 55.8 percent in 2005 over 2004) than in lei (nominal growth of 38.4 percent in 2005 compared to 2004); the share of foreign currency deposits in total banking system deposits is only 40 percent, and was dropping at the time. Thus, the NBR decided (see Box 13.1) that it was necessary to take remedial action to discourage the most dynamic component of credit growth, thereby helping to correct the asset–liability mismatch and to contain the increase of aggregate demand fueled by borrowing in foreign exchange.

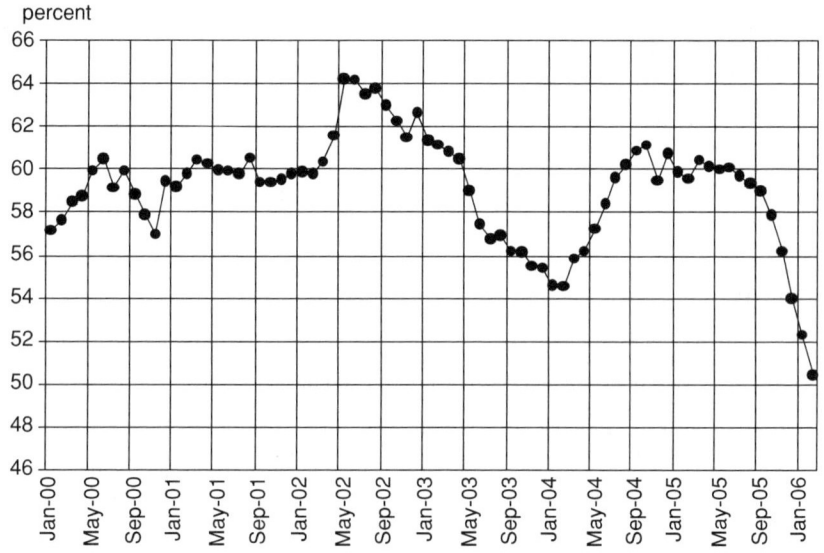

Figure 13.4 Foreign Exchange-Denominated Credit as Share to Total Nongovernment Credit—Romania

Source: NBR.

An additional consideration prompting action was that the increasing share of credit denominated in domestic currency would enhance monetary policy effectiveness. This is because, in the presence of euroization, interest rate changes tend to be transmitted only through one segment of the shallow credit market, and therefore fail to affect the entire economy in a direct manner. The latter is reinforced by the asymmetry between the size of the banking sector and that of capital markets and the insurance sector, similar to the situation in other European emerging markets. Also, the central bank has a limited set of instruments at its disposal to counter an increase in foreign exchange borrowing; these consist mainly of administrative or prudential tools, since sterilization and open-market operations are naturally centered on domestic currency.

Sustainability of credit dynamics

The second issue concerning financial stability has been the need to ensure sustainability in credit dynamics, especially with regard to household borrowing as its fastest growing component. While the need for further growth in intermediation is unquestionable, the speed at which this takes place matters both for the economy's capacity to absorb additional available financial resources in a noninflationary manner, as well as in relation to households' limited experience with indebtedness and capacity to manage such an important and growing constraint on income flows. Moreover, market share-oriented competition between banks, and the resulting strong contraction of spreads (mainly due to significantly lower borrowing rates) tend to reinforce household demand for credit, against the background of intertemporal consumption smoothing driven by the perception of higher future incomes associated with EU accession. As such, the limits on household indebtedness introduced in 2004 on both consumer borrowing and mortgage credit were further tightened in August 2005: the limits, at 30 percent and 35 percent, respectively, of an individual borrower's net monthly family income were further tightened by the introduction of a 40 percent overall limit, including exposures to nonbank financial institutions such as credit and leasing companies.

Indeed, mortgage and housing borrowing has been increasing rapidly, growing as a share of total nongovernment credit from 1.5 percent at end-2000 to 8.4 percent in January 2006. This reflects interest in a relatively new banking product, as well as the buoyancy of real estate prices, driven by domestic and nonresident purchases alike. However, housing finance is an especially complex issue. A sustained pickup in asset prices is important for the monetary authority: viewed from a regional perspective, similar developments are taking place in the new member states, and rising prices are underpinning the high demand for housing, which should be indirectly supportive of future productivity growth. It is important to note the increasing asset–liability mismatch that was taking place in Romania in the short run, as well as the pro-cyclical real estate price sensitivity of collateralization, which may directly affect its liquidity. Thus, the argument that mortgage-related foreign exchange borrowing may be less risky in relative terms, due to both its long-term maturity being longer than the planned date of euro adoption as well as the inherent existence of collateral, fails to provide complete reassurance.

The recent growth in mortgage borrowing and the more general shift into longer-term banking sector exposure to households also derive from the existence of limits on credit growth in foreign exchange and on household indebtedness. These limits are rapidly shifting banking business into long-term domestic currency loans (Figure 13.5), with longer maturities, making it possible for households to obtain access to credit within the existing loan-to-service ratios. There is also a transition from floating to fixed interest rates (which should increase interest rate sensitivity) taking place at the same time that interest rates are registering significant downward adjustment. Thus, the declining share of short-term credit in total nongovernment lending requires careful interpretation in the context of assessing risk developments.

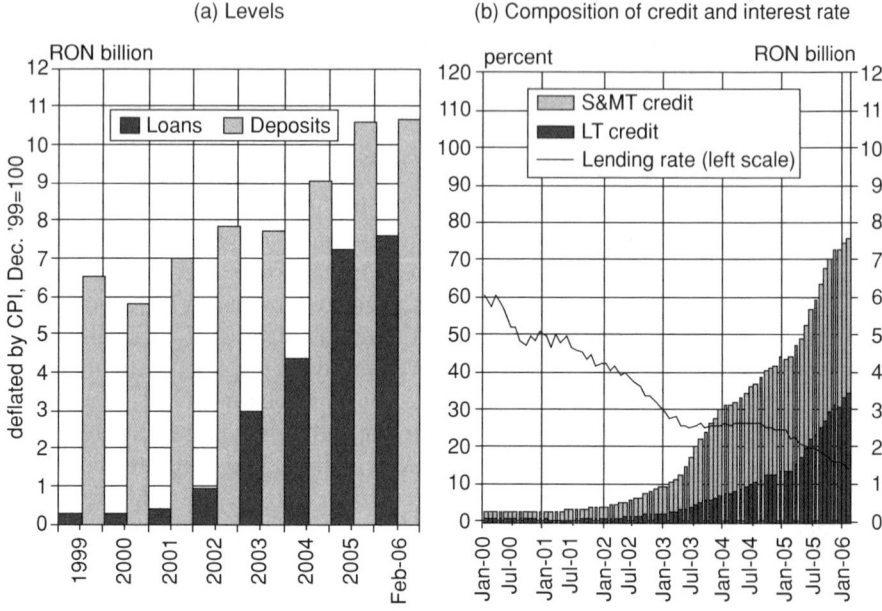

Figure 13.5 Household Loans and Deposits (in real terms)—Romania

Source: NBR, NIS.

An important element relating to the NBR's efforts to limit the expansion of foreign exchange credit is the overly optimistic perception of exchange rate risk exhibited by many borrowers as well as certain lenders. The experience of other emerging markets shows that the existence of a longer-term real appreciation trend may be undeniable, but shorter-run appreciation (especially in nominal terms) is less certain and prone to relatively high volatility; evidence for this is indeed provided by the significant depreciation episodes exhibited in the past five to eight years by most CEE new EU member states.

Lending in foreign currency to unhedged borrowers raises the significant problem of credit risk being magnified by exchange rate risk in a period of depreciation, especially if this were to coincide with an economic downturn. Accordingly, the authorities introduced further measures to deal with the growth of credit in foreign exchange: (i) the large increase in minimum reserve requirements on foreign exchange liabilities (from 30 percent in December 2005 to 40 percent in March 2006, aimed at reducing credit increase[8]), was accompanied, toward the end of 2005, by the introduction of a prudential limit of 300 percent of own funds in lending to unhedged borrowers;[9] and (ii) foreign exchange market intervention (up to October 2005) also sought to provide an element of two-way risk for both domestic and nonresident agents.

Monetary policy instruments

The final issue relates to the NBR Board's view on the complementarity between traditional and nontraditional monetary policy instruments in attaining the central bank's objectives, and to the constraints that both these categories face.

The traditional monetary policy instrument of interest rates, viewed in isolation, is faced with considerable constraints arising from the central bank's net debtor status, the presence of euroization and almost complete capital mobility. In a closed economy, the presence of excess demand requires interest rate increases through hikes in the policy rate. In a small open economy, such as Romania, sole reliance on the policy rate may bring about exchange rate appreciation that may prove unsustainable if not matched over time by productivity increases. The resultant unraveling of external positions at some point in the future would pose risks to the attainment of the proposed disinflation targets, especially given the asymmetric pass-through of import prices into domestic inflation (stronger at present for depreciation than for appreciation). Moreover, unsustainable appreciation also has prudential implications, since expectations of further appreciation will have stimulated foreign exchange borrowing by residents alongside nonresident inflows, including rapidly expanding lines of credit from foreign parent banks, in addition to the potentially volatile flows. However, resorting to frequent intervention may prove equally costly, especially under an inflation targeting regime, since it interferes with transparent policy signaling that is crucial for central bank credibility and the anchoring of inflation expectations.

Prudential and administrative measures, although not the first choice option, are therefore useful in addressing both macroeconomic concerns (including the consumption-driven component responsible for the widening of the current account deficit) and prudential considerations, and in complementing the traditional instruments of interest and exchange rates. However, their effectiveness tends to diminish over time, as credit institutions adapt their activity to existing restrictions,[10] including via the spillover of lending into the nonbank financial sector and by the direct recourse of firms to foreign borrowing.

The NBR's response has been to accept a broadening of its regulatory and supervisory responsibility by including nonbank financial institutions in its financial sector oversight. Legislation to this effect has recently been adopted, and the Romanian central bank is active in fulfilling its commitment to accelerate the implementation of its responsibilities in this area.

The trend in terms of direct foreign borrowing is evident in the rapid growth of private foreign debt, especially with regard to its short-term component (Figure 13.6). At end-2005, short-term foreign private debt was roughly equally split between banks and nonbank corporates, with nongovernment, nonbank corporates exhibiting a higher share of borrowing, as expected, while currency and deposits are still dominant for credit institutions.

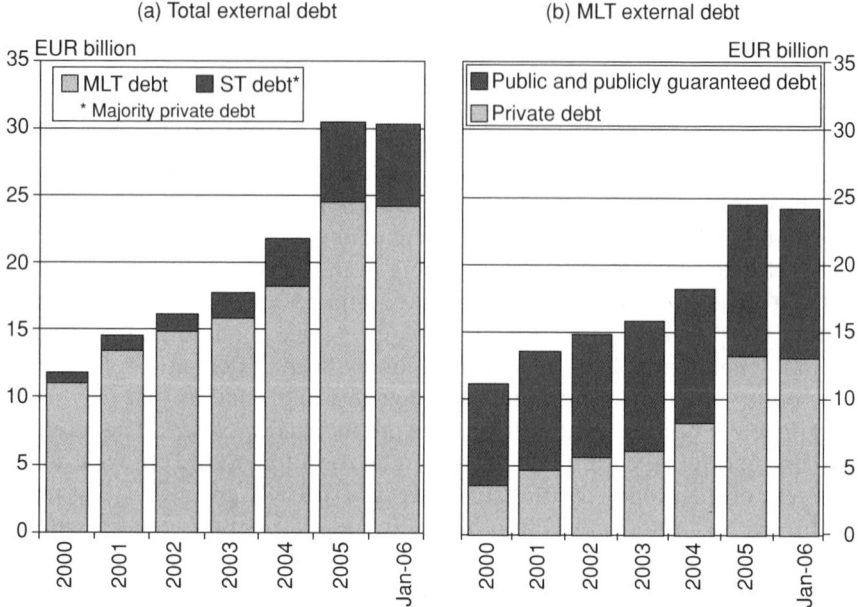

Figure 13.6 Total External Debt[a]—Romania

Source: NBR, Ministry of Public Finance.

[a] Public debt was 20.2 percent of GDP in 2005 (domestic debt 5.7 percent of GDP; external debt: 14.5 percent of GDP).

The increase in short-term private external debt accumulation is to be expected, given that it represents a response to improved corporate access to direct foreign borrowing, as indicated by the contraction in sovereign spread, and hence an indication of better risk perception and EU convergence.[11] However, the speed at which this is taking place is a matter of some concern. This concern is magnified by the negative external asset position of the banking sector, although the fact that official gross foreign exchange reserves represented a hefty 21.2 percent of GDP at end-2005 is a mitigating factor from the liquidity perspective of the foreign exchange market in the event of a large shock. For this reason, monetary policy austerity has tended to be delivered through a variety of instruments affecting monetary conditions, rather than just interest rates. Furthermore, the switch into domestic currency borrowing currently taking place (despite challenges to aggregate demand management) should help to a certain extent in providing alternatives to direct foreign borrowing for the more creditworthy domestic corporate segment and for high net worth individuals.

Conclusion

Romania provides an interesting case of rapid credit growth, where the fundamental catching-up drive present in many emerging market economies is influenced by the country's EU accession process. The economy's shallow financial depth, as well as initially high interest spreads over international rates and the perception of ongoing domestic currency appreciation, made foreign exchange-denominated credit the initial driver of fast intermediation and shaped the policy response to be more reliant on unorthodox measures, especially those of an administrative or prudential nature (higher minimum reserve requirements on foreign exchange liabilities, loan-to-income ceilings for household borrowing, limits on bank exposure to unhedged borrowers).

Such measures have been effective in slowing down credit in foreign exchange, but domestic currency credit dynamics have since picked up, while some foreign-owned banks have externalized part of their portfolios and corporate borrowing abroad has increased. The new economic context has in turn engendered a fresh policy approach, based on policy rate hikes, increases in reserve requirements on domestic currency liabilities, together with non-intervention for more than a year in the domestic foreign currency market. Unorthodox measures are seen as useful especially in the short run, and, via their effect on private consumption, they are also aimed at moderating the deeper current account deficits that Romania appears to be facing without adding to the burden of monetary policy. However, given the inherent limits to the effectiveness of such measures, further policy moves will likely increasingly favor using the interest rate.

Notes

1. National Bank of Romania (NBR).
2. Interestingly, it was not recent creditworthiness indicated by such credit histories, but rather the length of the credit histories, that mattered most. Ailing state-owned firms with long-standing credit relationships benefited from easier access to bank credit, largely due to creditors' familiarity with their financial performance in the past, even though this was under a different set of economic circumstances and incentives.
3. These are defined as loans classified in the lowest two (doubtful and loss) categories of the five employed in credit classification.
4. This has also been substantially influenced by stricter provisioning regulations: since early 2004, loans that are more than 90 days overdue must be fully provisioned and are moved off balance sheet; eventual repayment or collateral recovery is reflected in an improvement in the bank's profit and loss position. However, the improved condition of the banks is still observed even discounting for tougher prudential regulations.
5. The remaining entity, Eximbank, not only has a very low market share (1.6 percent of total banking sector assets in Jan. 2006) but is intended to increasingly acquire the characteristics pertaining to an export promotion-oriented government agency.
6. Another more prosaic explanation points to the fact that deposit rates have already fallen considerably, in light of commercial bank attempts to delay the effects of the contraction in spreads on profitability. However, deposit rates have stabilized and recently shown some increase.
7. Increases in the monetary policy rate were necessary in order to deliver tighter monetary conditions consistent with the achievement of the projected disinflation path.

8. Reserve requirements on foreign exchange were broadened in February 2005 to include all liabilities irrespective of their maturity (previously, liabilities carrying maturities of over two years were exempt).
9. The 300 percent limit was slightly wider than the overall banking system exposure to unhedged borrowers, but was meant to constrain the actions of a number of more risk-preferring credit institutions. Unsurprisingly, most of these have preferred to raise their capital endowment rather than restructure and reduce their credit portfolios.
10. For example, reserve requirement-driven increases in bank capitalization and portfolio externalization, together with increasing credit maturities in order to comply with household loan-to-service ratios are both testimony to this adaptive capacity.
11. Romanian long-term foreign bonds have for some time been trading around 50 basis points above bonds of similar maturity.

Bibliography

International Monetary Fund, 2003, "Romania: Financial Sector Stability Assessment," Country Report no. 03/389, Washington DC, December.

Popa, Cristian, 1998, "Nominal-Real Tradeoffs and the Effects of Monetary Policy: The Romanian Experience," Working Paper no. 244, William Davidson Institute, University of Michigan School of Business Administration, Ann Arbor, MI, December.

14
Slovakia: Credit Growth in the Household Sector and Response to the Related Risks

Marek Ličák[1]

Strong growth of credit in recent years has been one of the main factors that has caused changes in the asset structure of banks in Slovakia. The centrally planned economy of the past and the relatively late privatization and stabilization of the banking sector resulted in a rather marginal weight of bank credit in the economy. Growth of credit to enterprises in the early 1990s without sufficient know-how and risk management capacity in state-owned banks had led to high nonperforming loans (NPLs). Privatization of the banking sector, economic reforms accompanied by macroeconomic stabilization, and strong economic growth at the beginning of the new century created suitable conditions for banking sector credit growth to pick up, especially to the household sector.

I. Nature of the credit growth

More significant credit growth started in 2003 after the cleanup and stabilization of portfolios in major banks. Between end-2003 and end-2005, bank loans increased by 41 percent.[2] Loans denominated in foreign currencies grew in the same period by 70 percent, whereas loans in domestic currency increased by 34 percent.

The sectoral distribution of loans has been affected by the strong growth of household loans (Table 14.1), which increased by around 95 percent between 2003 and 2005, whereas loans to corporates grew only by 10 percent in the same period. In recent years, the export orientation of the corporate sector, strong economic growth, the inflow of foreign investments, and long-term investment purchases have contributed to increased financing of corporates in foreign currencies. Banks also increased financing of small and medium-size enterprises (SMEs), and some banks increased indirect financing of households through consumer credit companies.

Table 14.1 Sectoral Structure of Loans—Slovakia (in million SKK, end of year)

	2000	2001	2002	2003	2004	2005
Total loans	407,691	337,912	341,472	394,179	441,679	556,584
Loans to corporate sector	331,162	243,596	234,909	247,904	225,925	272,370
Loans to households	43,948	51,800	61,235	85,282	116,861	166,387
Of which in domestic currency						
Total loans	351,844	279,684	281,467	312,459	340,983	417,374
Loans to corporate sector	282,574	194,438	185,310	184,915	151,330	173,194
Loans to households	43,842	51,684	61,139	84,927	116,549	164,776
Of which in foreign currencies						
Total loans	55,847	58,228	60,005	81,720	100,680	139,210
Loans to corporate sector	48,588	49,157	49,599	62,989	74,595	99,175
Loans to households	106	117	96	355	312	1,610

Source: NBS.

The majority of loans have a maturity of over five years, with the increase in maturities in the last few years being driven by loans to households, mainly housing loans. Corporate loans denominated in domestic currency have mostly short maturities, while foreign currency denominated loans have mainly maturities of over five years, reflecting the investment nature of these loans.

Most of the new loans have the interest rate fixed for less than one year. Indirect interest rate risk is very evident in the corporate sector, where around 93 percent of new loans have their interest rate fixed for less than one year. The exposure of the household sector to changes in interest rates is lower, but still significant (80 percent of new loans have their interest rate fixed for less than one year).

The share of household loans that are denominated in foreign exchange is rather low (around 1 percent of total loans to households in 2005). On the other hand, foreign exchange loans are important in the corporate sector, with a share of 36 percent of all loans to the corporate sector in 2005. The latter is mainly driven by the strong export orientation of the corporate sector. Most corporates thus have a natural hedging, as their income is denominated in foreign currencies.

Although the credit market is highly concentrated, concentration ratios have decreased in the last few years because of growing competition between banks. The most significant reduction in concentration can be seen in lending to the corporate sector, where the share of the three largest banks was 39 percent in December 2005, whereas for the household sector it was around 65 percent.

Credit growth has been financed mainly by deposits, with the ratio of deposits to loans standing at 143 percent in December 2005. In the majority of banks, use of interbank and foreign funds to finance credit growth is somewhat limited, although foreign funds are partially used for financing loans denominated in foreign currencies. In addition, banks providing mortgage loans have to cover 90 percent of such loans through mortgage bonds.

It is also important to note that the initial level of credit was rather low in Slovakia. Despite the high credit growth to households, the share of household loans to GDP was around 11 percent in December 2005, whereas in EU-15 it was around 55 percent.

II. Determinants of the credit growth

When analyzing credit growth and questioning whether the growth is excessive or not, it is crucial to understand the determinants behind the growth. Understanding the reasons, and further monitoring the different indicators related to credit growth, can help in choosing appropriate measures and thus in avoiding negative effects on macroeconomic development and financial stability. Given that strong credit growth in Slovakia was mainly driven by loans provided to households, the following discussion will focus mainly on household loans when analyzing the determinants of credit growth.

The high rate of credit growth in the context of a low share of household loans in GDP and total banking assets can be considered as the so-called "catch up" effect, common in many Central, Eastern, and South-eastern European countries (CEE countries) with a relatively underdeveloped household credit market, in particular the housing credit market (Figure 14.1). The catch-up effect can be explained by positive macroeconomic developments that allow households to choose a path of consumption to maximize the use of credit over their lifetime. Households thus finance their current consumption by borrowing.

In addition to the low initial level of household indebtedness, a number of other factors also contributed to the rapid growth of household loans. On the supply side, financial liberalization, economic reforms (e.g., tax reform, law enforcement), privatization of banks, and high foreign ownership created a suitable environment for credit growth. This was accompanied by competition between banks to achieve a

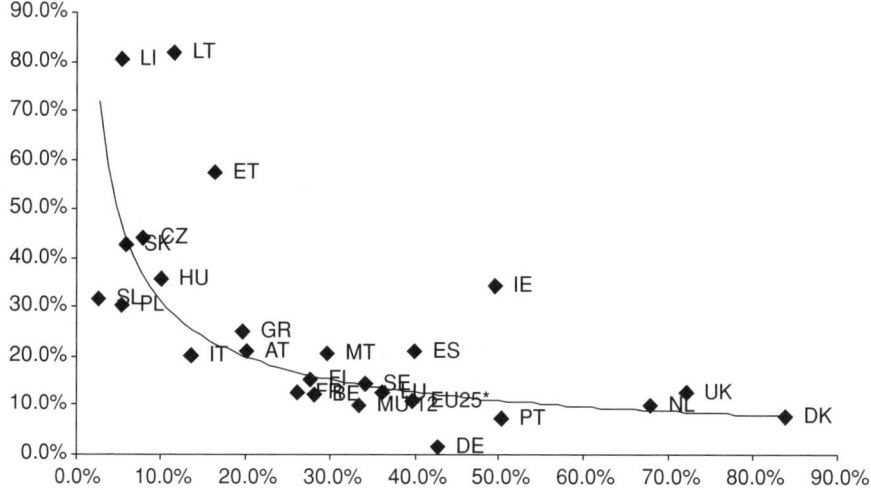

Figure 14.1 Growth of Housing Loans (in percent) and Share of Housing Loans in GDP in EU Countries in 2004

Source: ECB.

Note: Vertical axis indicates the growth of housing loans in percent (year-to-year changes). Horizontal axis indicates the share of housing loans in GDP.

larger share in the retail market, which is one of the most profitable sectors for banks. Unlike in other economic sectors, interest rate spreads in the household sector have not decreased in recent years. Despite growing competition, concentration has remained very high. Foreign owners also brought new products, risk management practices, and experience in the household sector from their home countries.

Notwithstanding the important role of the supply factors in boosting credit growth, demand factors that positively affected the income of households and asset prices have been the most important determinant of credit growth to households. Strong economic growth has been positively reflected in macroeconomic indicators, with the convergence of domestic interest rates to the low EMU levels, a significant fall in the unemployment and inflation rates, and growth in household income being the main drivers of the strong demand for loans (Table 14.2). The positive developments in the macro and microeconomic indicators were accompanied by optimistic expectations of households about their future financial position and economic growth.

Table 14.2 Selected Macroeconomic Indicators—Slovakia

	2000	2001	2002	2003	2004	2005
Gross disposable income (percent)[a]	9.8	7.1	8.2	6.4	10.2	8.8
Unemployment rate (percent)[b]	18.6	19.2	18.5	17.5	18.1	15.3
Economic sentiment indicator	104.0	101.3	102.6	107.1	106.0	113.4
GDP growth at constant prices (percent)	2.0	3.8	4.6	4.5	5.5	6.0

Source: Statistical office of Slovak Republic.

[a] Gross disposable income—year to year change.
[b] Unemployment rate—according the Labor force sample survey.

Fiscal incentives (in particular, interest rate subsidies) played an important role at the beginning of the cycle when interest rates were high. After a significant decrease in interest rates, the government abolished interest rate subsidies on mortgage loans[3] in 2004. The growth in housing loans has been accelerated also through rising real estate prices.

The concentration of household borrowing in regions with the most significant improvements in macroeconomic indicators supports the links between the positive macroeconomic developments and credit growth to households. For instance, around 65 percent of loans provided to households were concentrated in the Bratislava region.

III. Main risks stemming from the credit growth

Experience from different countries shows close links between rapid credit growth on the one hand and banking crises and macroeconomic deterioration on the other. So far there have been no significant macroeconomic imbalances in Slovakia caused by household credit growth. This can be explained by the low share of household debt in GDP. However, if the rate of growth experienced in recent years is maintained, this will require close monitoring. With a growing share of household loans in total assets of the banking sector (11 percent in December 2005), the significance of the household sector for the stability of the banking sector has increased. Therefore, the ability of the household sector to repay their loans has now assumed greater importance for the banks.

The stability of the banking sector can be affected through various channels. Direct credit risk, stemming from the inability and/or unwillingness of households to repay loans, has been relatively low. Measured by a backward looking indicator (the ratio of NPLs to total loans), the quality of household loans has been fairly good. The ratio has been stable in recent years, and in December 2005 reached 3.9 percent. However, the positive picture about the NPL ratio is driven by the high number of new loans. An upward trend in the number of NPLs can be partially caused by the easing of credit standards for clients (mostly reflected in the efforts of banks to simplify the process of providing loans), due to the growing competition between banks and their efforts to achieve a larger share in the retail market. Some banks thus have increased the share of loans provided to lower-income categories that are more sensitive to various shocks.

Despite the relaxing of credit standards and increased competition among banks, the picture of the overall distribution of loans by different income categories is fairly positive from a risk management point of view. Based on the household survey conducted in 2003, household loans are concentrated mainly in the highest income category, which normally has sufficient ability to overcome shocks. These households also hold the highest amount of financial assets.

The repayment burden on households, measured by the share of interest and principal payments on disposable income, has shown an upward trend, reaching 3.8 percent in the fourth quarter of 2005, from 2 percent in the first quarter of 2003 (see Figure 14.2). Based on the macroeconomic data, the household sector has sufficient financial assets (36 percent of financial liabilities were covered by the financial assets of households in 2005) to serve as a cushion if household income were to be hit by negative shocks.

Given the dominance of loans with a floating interest rate or interest rate fixed for less than one year, households' ability to repay can be negatively influenced by increases in interest rates. This risky behavior of households can be explained by the gradual decrease in interest rates in recent years, and households' presumption that they could fall further (in particular the loan rates with an interest rate fixed for less than one year).

IV. Measures taken by the banking supervisory authority

Measures taken against strong credit growth should be based on an understanding of the nature of the credit growth, its determinants, and its links to different areas in the economy. Despite the difficulty of this task, given the lack of data and lack of experience with the household sector, the National Bank of Slovakia (NBS) monitors all relevant risk categories and tries to identify potential vulnerabilities in

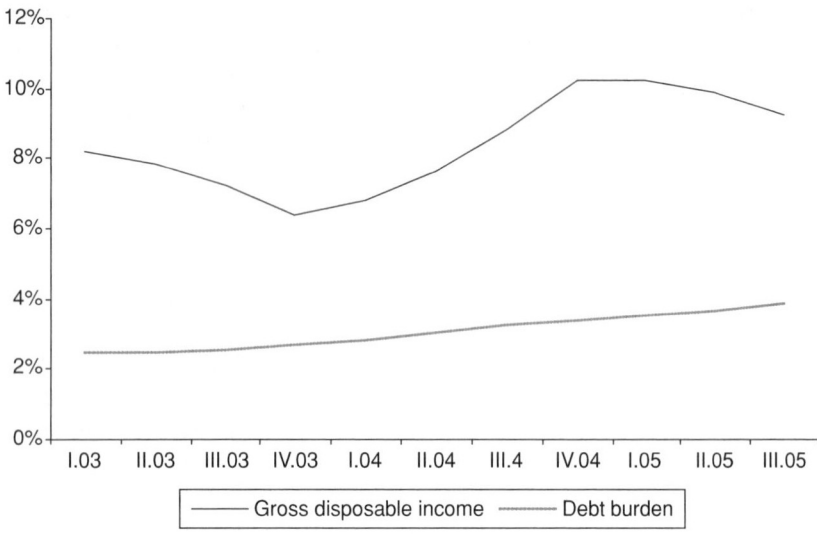

Figure 14.2 Debt Burden and Gross Disposable Income of Households—Slovakia

Source: Statistical office of Slovak Republic, own calculations.

Note: Debt burden defined as share of interest and principal payments on gross disposable income. Gross disposable income (year-to-year changes).

advance. In order to get relevant data, the NBS has introduced new reporting forms for banks and a bank lending survey, and increased the frequency of its meetings with commercial banks.

The current rate of credit growth derives mainly from the positive developments in macroeconomic indicators. Assessment of the impact of negative developments in the economy and in the quality of banks' portfolios is undertaken through stress testing. The latter is thus one of the major tools used by the NBS for forward-looking monitoring of credit growth. Results of stress testing scenarios related to the household sector do not show any significant impact on the banking sector. Nevertheless, given the growing indebtedness of the household sector and the potential impact of lending to households on the development of the financial markets and the economy in general, public awareness about risks is crucial. The NBS, in its regular publications, informs the public about the risks to which the household sector is exposed.

There are only two direct administrative measures that are related to the household credit market: an obligation for banks to finance mortgage loans through mortgage bonds; and a limit on the loan-to-value (LTV) ratio for mortgage loans. The first measure is related to banks' liquidity, and its objective is to limit banks' excessive funding of long-term mortgage loans through short-term domestic or foreign funds. Banks are therefore forced to cover 90 percent of mortgage loans through mortgage bonds. The objective of the latter measure is to limit the risk taken by banks in respect of the value of received collateral when providing mortgage loans. The limit is set at 70 percent LTV for mortgage loans.[4]

These measures were introduced together with interest rate subsidies on mortgage interest rates and positively influenced the liquidity gap of banks and the level of the LTV ratio in the banking sector. It should be stressed, however, that the regulations covering these two measures relate to only part of banks' housing loans, i.e., mortgage loans. Banks also provide other loans without a specified purpose that are mostly used for housing purposes. Hence, the final impact of the above-mentioned measures is limited.

V. Conclusion

Despite rapid credit growth to households, a growing exposure to this sector has not significantly influenced the stability of the banking system. Overall indebtedness of households is low in comparison with other countries, and, based on the macro data, the ability of households to repay loans is adequate. However, if the same rate of growth as in previous years is maintained, the impact of the credit growth on banks' stability could increase significantly. The main risks for the coming years are as follows:

- Credit growth will likely continue at a similar pace in coming years simply because of the catch up effect. The main question from the stability point of view is the behavior of banks. In particular, changes in credit standards are closely related to the quality of banks portfolio. Banks tend to ease credit standards in response to competition between banks.
- The financial position of households is closely related to the macroeconomic situation. Adverse macroeconomic developments could result in lower GDP growth and higher unemployment and thus an increase in the ratio of impaired loans. Despite the high interest rate sensitivity of households, however, a rise in interest rates is not expected to have a significant impact on the ability of households to repay their loans, given the rather low ratio of loan installments to disposable income.

Notes

1. The National Bank of Slovakia (NBS).
2. Several papers identify a negative credit growth rate in Slovakia between 2000 and 2004. It is worth mentioning the difference in data used for analyses. The NBS focuses on loans to clients (corporates, households, financial corporations other than banks, public sector, and non-residents) whereas most authors use data for the whole private sector including net claims on the government. Assets of Slovak banks were for a long time dominated by government securities, whereas the share of loans to corporates and particularly households was low. The decrease in net claims on the government in recent years was the main reason for the negligible or negative growth of loans to the private sector. Growth was also influenced by the stabilization of banks' portfolios in 2001 and 2002.
3. At present, the government's involvement in the banks' credit market is reduced to the state premiums on deposits in building societies.
4. Only 10 percent of mortgage loans can exceed this level, but they must not carry more than a 100 percent LTV ratio.

15
Too Much of a Good Thing? Credit Booms in Transition Economies: The Cases of Bulgaria, Romania, and Ukraine

Christoph Duenwald, Nikolay Gueorguiev, and Andrea Schaechter[1]

Rapid private sector credit growth has been among the most notable economic phenomena across many transition economies—particularly in the Central, Eastern, and South-eastern European (CEE) countries—over the past few years.[2] Such lending booms have presented both opportunities and challenges to economic policymakers. On the one hand, the surge in financial intermediation reflects a welcome catch-up from low levels, and financial deepening is generally associated with increased growth and efficiency. On the other hand, rapid credit growth has been associated with macroeconomic and financial crises, emanating from macroeconomic imbalances and banking sector distress. Policymakers therefore face the dilemma of how to minimize the risks of financial crisis while still allowing bank lending to contribute to higher growth and efficiency.

The recent experiences of three transition economies—Bulgaria, Romania, and Ukraine—provide useful case studies of credit booms in different macroeconomic and institutional settings. Recent papers on credit booms have focused on large cross-country data sets. In contrast, this chapter seeks to zero in on the experiences of a small set of countries with similar developmental characteristics. In Bulgaria and Romania, credit booms over the past two to three years have contributed importantly to widening macroeconomic imbalances and heightened external vulnerability. With limited monetary tools at their disposal, policymakers in these countries have tightened fiscal policy to offset the sharp increase in private sector consumption and investment. Nevertheless, sharply larger external current account deficits—albeit financed to a large extent by foreign direct investment (FDI) inflows—have generated concerns about external vulnerability, and the need to persevere with tight fiscal policies remains. In contrast, the credit boom in Ukraine was accompanied by strong output growth and large external current account surpluses, although inflation has picked up. Risks in terms of loan quality and the impact on banking sector stability are thus the predominant concerns rather than macroeconomic imbalances.

This chapter aims to address the following questions:

- What has caused credit to expand rapidly in all three countries despite the different institutional settings and macroeconomic conditions?
- What are the challenges and opportunities created by the credit booms?
- What have been the policy responses, and have they been effective?

The chapter is structured as follows. The next section discusses the causes and characteristics of the credit booms, emphasizing the similarities and differences between the three countries. The subsequent section outlines both the opportunities and the risks arising from the rapid credit expansions, followed in Section III by a discussion of the possible and actual policy responses. Section IV concludes.

I. Causes and characteristics of the credit booms

Background

Credit has expanded rapidly in all three countries in an environment of strong GDP growth and generally falling inflation (Tables 15.1 and 15.2, and Box 15.1). Driven by strong external and domestic demand, growth has averaged between 5 and 8 percent in the past five years. A generally countercyclical fiscal stance, as evidenced by the improving fiscal balances, and prudent monetary frameworks have led to single-digit or near-single-digit inflation. However, the external current

Table 15.1 Basic Economic Indicators, 2000–05 (annual percent change, unless otherwise indicated)

	2000	2001	2002	2003	2004	2005	Average
Bulgaria							
GDP growth	5.4	4.1	4.9	4.5	5.7	5.5	4.9
Inflation (end of period)	11.4	4.8	3.8	5.6	4.0	6.5	5.9
Current account balance (percent of GDP)	−5.6	−5.6	−2.4	−5.5	−5.8	−11.8	−5.0
Budget balance (percent of GDP)	−1.0	−0.9	−0.8	−0.4	1.8	2.3	−0.3
Romania							
GDP growth	2.1	5.7	5.1	5.2	8.4	4.1	5.3
Inflation (end of period)	40.7	30.3	17.8	14.1	9.3	8.6	22.4
Current account balance (percent of GDP)	−3.7	−5.5	−3.3	−5.8	−8.5	−8.7	−5.4
Budget balance (percent of GDP)	−4.0	−3.2	−2.6	−2.2	−1.1	−1.0	−2.6
Ukraine							
GDP growth	5.9	9.2	5.2	9.4	12.0	2.6	8.3
Inflation (end of period)	25.8	6.1	−0.6	8.2	12.2	10.4	10.4
Current account balance (percent of GDP)	4.7	3.7	7.5	5.8	10.6	3.1	6.5
Budget balance (percent of GDP)	−1.3	−1.6	0.5	−0.9	−4.4	−2.4	−1.5

Source: National authorities; and IMF staff estimates.

Table 15.2 Bulgaria, Romania, and Ukraine in Comparison: An Overview

	Similarities	Differences
Credit growth		
Speed	In the top ten of transition countries; average credit flows in percent of GDP above 5 percent on average since 2002.	*Romania:* Credit growth picked up later than in Bulgaria and Ukraine.
Level of credit	Level of credit, measured as credit-to-GDP ratio, is still relatively low (below 36 percent).	*Romania:* Credit-to-GDP ratio is about half of Bulgaria's and two-thirds of Ukraine's.
Causes	Macroeconomic stabilization; robust growth and strong economic outlook; regained confidence and bank restructuring; remonetization; parents of foreign-owned banks seek high yields.	*Ukraine:* Foreign banks have played only a subordinate role.
Characteristics	Funding mostly through deposit growth and capital inflows (in particular in Bulgaria and Romania); large share of foreign-currency-denominated lending; household loans have expanded most rapidly but remain below business loans in absolute terms; maturities of loans have lengthened; few other investment opportunities.	
Macroeconomic conditions	Inflation in mid-single to low-double digits; strong economic growth; relatively strong fiscal positions; large current account deficits in Bulgaria and Romania.	*Ukraine:* Large current account surpluses; substantial deterioration in fiscal position since mid-2004 and pickup in inflation.
Monetary policy regime	Exchange rate as nominal anchor (until November 2004 for Romania).	*Bulgaria:* Currency board arrangement (peg to euro). *Romania:* Managed float since November 2004; previously, managed crawl against euro within an unannounced band. *Ukraine:* De facto peg to U.S. dollar.
Capital account controls		*Bulgaria:* Open. *Romania:* Some controls, to be removed in part in 2005. *Ukraine:* Significant controls left.
Institutional environment	Improvements in the legal environment and financial supervision but still much need for further improvement to achieve EU standards.	Weakest institutions in Ukraine. According to EBRD index for financial sector reform (2004): *Ukraine:* 2.3; *Bulgaria:* 3.7; and *Romania:* 3.0.
Business environment/FDI	Bulgaria and Romania have benefited from their status as EU accession countries; large levels of FDI.	*Ukraine:* Weak business environment; lack of transparency; low level of FDI.
Banking system		
Ownership	Only small role for state-owned banks; mostly foreign owned in Bulgaria and Romania.	*Ukraine:* Mostly domestically owned.
Prudential indicators	Relatively strong in Bulgaria and Romania in terms of capital adequacy, provisioning, profitability, and nonperforming loans (NPLs).	*Ukraine:* Structural weaknesses, such as large share of related-party lending; inadequacy of provisions; high level of reported NPLs; low profitability.

account deficits have expanded considerably in Bulgaria and Romania, driven by strong domestic demand. In contrast, Ukraine has maintained large current account surpluses, largely driven by favorable terms of trade shocks and an undervalued exchange rate.

The three countries are at different stages of the transition process. Bulgaria and Romania are on the verge of European Union (EU) membership and have largely

---

Box 15.1. Macroeconomic Background

Bulgaria has enjoyed macroeconomic stability and sound growth since 1997. The establishment of the currency board set in train rapid disinflation to single digits and has helped restore confidence in the financial system. Tight fiscal policy and debt-management operations have cut public debt in half relative to GDP and sustained a manageable external current account deficit. Growth has been based on both external and domestic demand, with the latter assuming the leading role lately. Rapid credit growth has led to a construction and real estate boom, while privatization and good marketing have made tourism a leading sector as well. However, the sizable current account deficit has become a vulnerability, despite its being financed mostly by FDI.

Since mid-2001, Romania has enjoyed a period of strong real GDP growth and has generated steady disinflation. The country's gradual trade integration into the EU sustained double-digit export growth and gradually accelerating GDP growth. Budget and wage restraint and energy price adjustments moderated domestic demand initially. This allowed the National Bank of Romania (NBR) to successfully pursue disinflation by guiding exchange rate depreciation on a downward path. External competitiveness has been sustained through sizable productivity increases, moderate wage growth until 2003, and cuts in social security contribution rates. Beginning in 2002, improved macroeconomic conditions, the prospects for EU accession, and the wide yield differential between leu and foreign-currency-denominated assets resulted in sustained capital inflows, mostly in the form of bank borrowing and FDI, and substantial reserves accumulation. However, domestic demand accelerated in 2003–04, led by rapid credit expansion and fast real wage growth. As a result, the current account deficit surged to over 7.5 percent of GDP in 2004, almost double its level two years previously. The strength of domestic demand is forcing the NBR to allow substantial exchange rate appreciation in support of continuing disinflation.

Six years after the 1998 crisis, Ukraine has continued to recover strongly. Over 2000–04, GDP growth averaged 8.5 percent. External demand has been the main engine of growth, with buoyant metal prices and strong demand from Russia triggering a sharp and sustained export boom and resulting in consistent and large current account surpluses. The surge in credit to the private sector and rising disposable incomes have supported sizable consumption expansion. Fiscal policy remained prudent and inflation moderate through mid-2004. In the second half of 2004, however, the fiscal deficit surged to 4.5 percent of GDP against the backdrop of an election-motivated increase in transfers, thereby adding to inflationary pressures. Inflation picked up from an average of 6 percent in 2001–03 to 12 percent by end-2004. During the tumultuous presidential elections in late 2004, the National Bank of Ukraine (NBU) lost about one-fourth of its international reserves, and liquidity pressures emerged for the banking system when households withdrew 17 percent of their total deposits. Since the resolution of the political crisis, the financial market pressures have subsided, with sovereign spreads falling below pre-crisis levels, bank deposit flows reversing, and the NBU recouping more than its reserves losses by end-April 2005. In the context of an undervalued currency, rising capital inflows, and large increases in public wages and social spending under the 2005 budget, regaining control over inflation is the most important immediate challenge.

caught up with the central European transition economies in terms of structural reform indicators (Figure 15.1), although progress in corporate governance still lags behind. Structural reforms in Ukraine, on the other hand, have been much slower, and particularly accounting and reporting standards for corporates as well as corporate governance need to be strengthened for FDI to pick up.

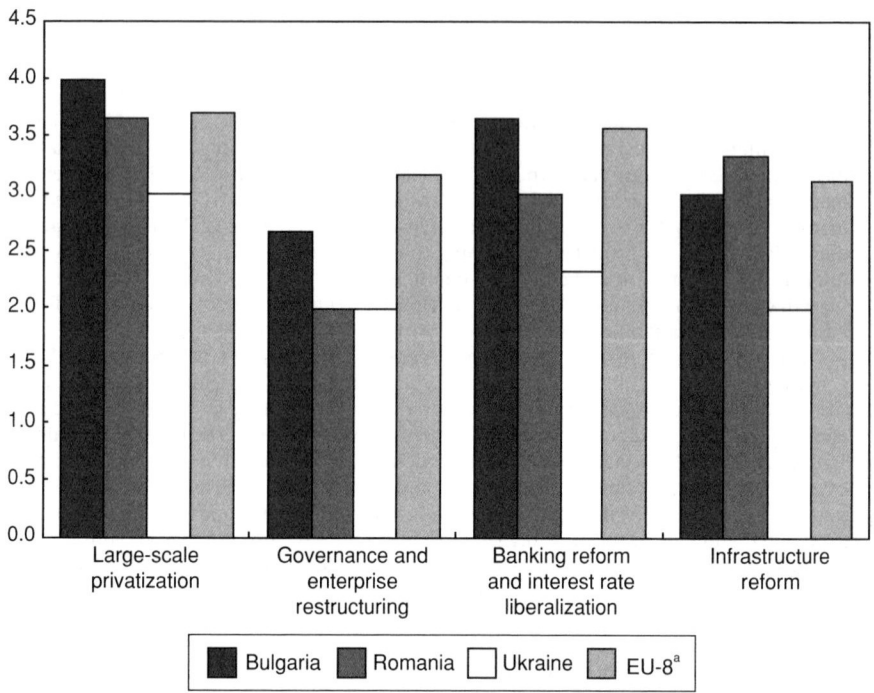

Figure 15.1 Selected EBRD Transition Indicators, 2004

Source: EBRD Transition Report, 2004.

[a] The EU-8 comprises the Czech Republic, Estonia, Hungary, Latvia, Lithuania, Poland, the Slovak Republic, and Slovenia.

Developments in credit dynamics in all three countries have followed a bust-boom pattern. After a sharp drop in financial intermediation during a deep macroeconomic/banking crisis, credit growth was initially subdued, reflecting low credit demand and banks' risk aversion. The subsequent stabilization and return of sound growth, together with banks' restructuring and balance sheet rehabilitation, has encouraged a rebirth of credit demand and banks to reassess positively their borrowers' creditworthiness, find new lending opportunities, and eventually even to engage in a race for market share, pushing up credit sharply.

As elsewhere in the region, credit has grown rapidly in the three countries in the acceleration phase, albeit from a small base. While credit-to-GDP ratios were in the teens when credit began to accelerate, real growth rates have been in the

30–50 percent range (Table 15.3). Annual flows, perhaps a better measure of the macroeconomic impact of credit, have ranged from 3 to 12 percent of GDP. Such credit dynamics are part of a regionwide trend. As Figure 15.2 illustrates, credit has been growing quickly in most CEE countries in the past three years as well.

Table 15.3 Basic Credit Indicators, 2000–05

	2000	2001	2002	2003	2004	2005
Bulgaria						
Real credit growth (in percent, year-on-year, deflated by CPI)	4.5	26.3	37.2	39.5	40.4	34.0
In local currency	11.9	26.6	23.7	37.7	27.9	35.5
In foreign currency	–6.6	25.9	61.8	42.1	57.3	32.4
Credit flows in percent of GDP	1.7	3.6	5.7	8.4	11.5	10.9
By currency: local	1.6	2.3	2.5	4.7	4.8	6.0
By currency: foreign currencies	0.2	1.2	3.2	3.7	6.7	4.9
By borrower: households	0.4	1.1	1.4	3.2	4.9	6.1
By borrower: companies	1.4	2.5	4.3	5.2	6.6	4.8
Credit stock in percent of GDP (year-end)	12.2	14.5	19.0	26.3	35.4	43.0
By currency: local	7.9	9.4	11.1	15.1	18.5	22.7
By currency: foreign currencies	4.3	5.2	8.0	11.2	16.9	20.2
By borrower: households	2.3	3.1	4.3	7.2	11.5	16.5
By borrower: private companies	9.3	10.8	14.1	18.4	23.2	26.0
Share of foreign currency deposits as percent of total	59.2	58.2	54.3	52.1	48.0	47.2
Share of household loans in total loans	18.9	21.6	22.5	27.6	32.5	38.4
Share of foreign currency loans as percent of total	35.5	35.4	41.8	42.5	47.6	47.1
Romania						
Real credit growth (in percent, year-on-year, deflated by CPI), composite	7.9	28.0	32.4	56.8	40.5	44.4
In local currency	–5.4	20.0	19.1	77.4	11.2	56.8
In foreign currency (in €)	15.8	33.2	40.4	38.1	60.5	34.3
Credit flows in percent of GDP	0.6	2.9	3.3	6.2	5.3	6.8
By currency: local	0.8	1.5	1.3	3.6	1.2	4.0
By currency: foreign currencies	–0.2	1.5	2.1	2.6	4.1	2.9
By borrower: households	0.1	0.3	0.8	2.9	1.9	3.3
By borrower: companies	0.4	2.6	2.5	3.4	3.4	3.5
Credit stock in percent of GDP (year-end)	9.3	10.1	11.8	15.3	17.0	21.1
By currency: local	3.8	4.1	4.4	6.8	6.7	9.7
By currency: foreign currencies	5.5	6.1	7.4	8.5	10.3	11.4
By borrower: households	0.5	0.7	1.4	3.8	4.8	7.4
By borrower: private companies	7.5	8.0	8.9	10.1	10.9	12.6
Share of foreign currency deposits as percent of total	47.0	49.3	44.7	42.5	41.2	34.7
Share of household loans in total loans	5.7	6.8	11.7	24.8	28.4	35.2
Share of foreign currency loans as percent of total	59.5	59.8	62.7	55.4	60.8	54.0
Ukraine[a]	2000	2001	2002	2003	2004	2005
Real credit growth (in percent, year-on-year)	28.6	32.7	48.4	51.2	16.9	46.4
In local currency	37.4	32.7	52.9	53.4	15.7	43.0
In foreign currency (in $)	17.9	32.8	41.9	47.8	64.0	36.7

Table 15.3 continued

	2000	2001	2002	2003	2004	2005
Credit flows in percent of GDP	4.7	4.2	6.2	10.5	6.4	13.8
By currency: local	3.1	2.5	4.0	6.6	3.8	7.9
By currency: foreign currencies	1.5	1.8	2.2	3.9	6.7	6.7
By borrower: households	0.2	0.2	0.8	2.1	1.7	4.5
By borrower: companies	4.5	4.0	5.4	8.4	4.8	9.2
Credit stock in percent of GDP (year-end)	12.3	14.4	19.3	27.0	27.0	36.1
By currency: local	7.3	8.5	11.7	16.6	16.5	21.5
By currency: foreign currencies	5.1	5.9	7.6	10.4	14.6	18.2
By borrower: households	0.6	0.7	1.5	3.3	4.2	8.0
By borrower: private companies	10.6	12.3	16.2	21.5	21.0	26.4
Share of foreign currency deposits as percent of total	38.5	32.9	32.6	32.2	36.5	34.2
Share of household loans in total loans	4.7	4.8	7.6	12.4	15.6	22.2
Share of foreign currency loans as percent of total	41.4	41.3	39.5	38.5	39.1	40.5

Source: Bulgarian National Bank; National Bank of Romania; National Bank of Ukraine; and IMF staff estimates.

[a] Ukraine: During the tumultuous presidential elections in late 2004, the banking sector lost substantial amounts of deposits and had to temporarily reduce lending.

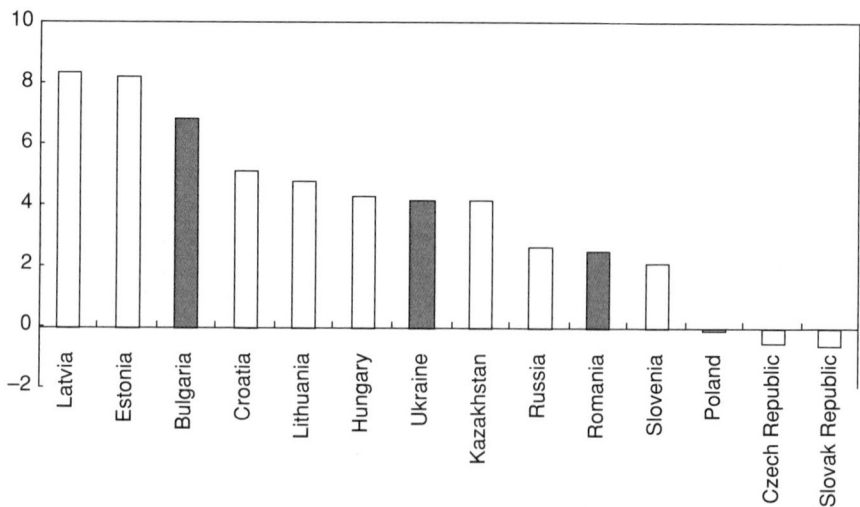

Figure 15.2 Credit Growth in Transition Economies, 2002–04[a] (average annual change in the credit-to-GDP ratio)

Source: IMF; International Financial Statistics; World Economic Outlook; and IMF staff estimates.

[a] Bank credit to the private sector. During the tumultuous presidential elections in Ukraine in late 2004, the banking sector lost substantial amounts of deposits and had to temporarily reduce lending.

The banking sector is still relatively small in all three countries despite the large number of banks and rapid asset growth over the past four years (Table 15.4). Relative to GDP, Bulgaria's banking system—consisting of 29 banks and six branches of foreign banks—is the largest, with total assets of 46 percent of GDP. The assets of Ukraine's 158 banks amount to 37 percent of GDP. However, many of the banks are small, and most are affiliated with corporates. Romania has 32 banks and seven branches, with assets of 35 percent of GDP.

Most banks are private now in these countries, and foreign ownership dominates in Bulgaria and Romania. State ownership is limited to two or three banks in each country, including the state savings banks in Romania and Ukraine, which have state guarantees for their deposits. In both countries, these institutions are being restructured, and Romania is aiming to privatize its bank by mid-2006. Through the privatization process, large European banks acquired most of the banking system assets in Bulgaria and Romania; however, the share of foreign-owned banks is much smaller in Ukraine, reflecting the difficult business environment.

Table 15.4 Ownership of the Banking Sector, 2000–05

	2000	2001	2002	2003	2004	2005
Bulgaria						
Number of banks and bank branches	35	35	34	35	35	35
Private	31	31	31	33	33	33
Domestic	10	11	12	12	12	12
Foreign[a]	21	20	19	21	21	21
o/w: foreign bank branches	8	7	6	6	6	6
State-owned[b]	4	4	3	2	2	2
Share of assets of largest 10 banks in total assets	76	75	74	73	73	74
Romania						
Number of banks and bank branches	41	41	39	38	39	39
Private	37	38	36	35	36	36
Domestic	8	6	4	7	6	6
Foreign[a]	29	32	32	29	30	30
o/w: foreign bank branches	8	8	8	8	7	6
State-owned[b]	4	3	3	3	3	3
Share of assets of largest 10 banks in total assets	–	–	–	80	80	80
Ukraine						
Number of banks and bank branches	153	152	157	158	160	165
Private	151	150	155	156	158	163
Domestic	120	122	135	137	139	140
Foreign[a]	31	28	20	19	19	23
o/w: foreign bank branches	0	0	0	0	0	0
State-owned[b]	2	2	2	2	2	2
Share of assets of largest 10 banks in total assets	55	53	54	54	53	–

Source: Bulgarian National Bank; National Bank of Romania; National Bank of Ukraine; and IMF staff estimates.

[a] Banks where foreign parties hold more than 50 percent of the total outstanding share value.
[b] Banks where state institutions yield effective control.

The institutional framework of the financial sector is generally adequate in Bulgaria and Romania, but still exhibits weaknesses in Ukraine, despite recent progress. Financial Sector Assessment Programs (FSAPs) conducted in the three countries in 2002–03 gave generally good marks to the authorities' regulatory framework and supervisory activity in Bulgaria and Romania but pointed out various shortcomings in Ukraine. Recommendations for Bulgaria and Romania included strengthening supervision on a consolidated basis and training bank supervisors in international accounting standards. For Ukraine, the advice focused on the need to achieve international standards, in particular in terms of related-party lending, identification of bank owners, banks' risk management practices as well as the need to raise capital requirements and tighten the definition of capital. While progress on the last two suggestions was made, including by raising the minimum capital adequacy ratio from 8 percent to 10 percent, the first three issues have not yet been appropriately tackled. These remaining institutional weaknesses, as well as the prominence of domestic bank ownership, make Ukraine's banking sector weaker than Bulgaria's and Romania's.

Episodes of economic instability in the past have caused dollarization, which has proved difficult to reverse. Even though confidence in local currencies has been partly restored following successful inflation stabilization, and real local currency deposit interest rates have been high in Romania and Ukraine, the share of foreign-currency-denominated deposits remains large in all three countries. At the same time, borrowers, mindful of the lower effective cost of foreign-currency-denominated loans, have maintained about 40–60 percent of their loans in foreign currency, thereby exposing the banking sector to indirect foreign exchange risk (see Table 15.3 above). By aiming, explicitly or implicitly, at some measure of exchange rate stability throughout most of the period analyzed (Box 15.2), monetary policy frameworks have inadvertently encouraged demand for foreign-currency-denominated loans.

Causes of credit booms

The common factors behind the sharp credit acceleration in all three countries are successful post-crisis macroeconomic stabilization and robust growth, restoration of confidence in the banking sector, and sizable foreign exchange inflows. All three countries went through deep macroeconomic and financial crises in the second half of the 1990s, which all but halted financial intermediation for a while. Prudent macroeconomic policies, leading to fast disinflation, quickly rebounding GDP, and rapidly rising profits and incomes, whetted the appetite for borrowing and improved banks' perception of borrowers' creditworthiness. The entry of reputable international banks and strengthening of the regulatory and supervisory frameworks of the central banks restored the populations' confidence in the banking sector, leading to a quick rise in deposits and pressure to find profitable asset placements. At the same time, sharply declining budget deficits and ample external budgetary financing limited government paper issuance. Finally, a fall in the country risk premium and improved business conditions gave and still give rise to large capital inflows, coming mainly through the mostly foreign-owned banking sector, and adding to supply-side pressures to lend.

Box 15.2. Monetary Policy Frameworks

The Bulgarian National Bank (BNB) operates a currency board arrangement. It has three key features: (i) a fixed exchange rate peg to the euro; (ii) automatic convertibility, a commitment on the part of the BNB to buy and sell foreign currency at the fixed rate; and (iii) a prohibition on domestic credit creation by the BNB. The last implies that the BNB cannot affect the money supply through open market operations or the extension of domestic credit. The only remaining monetary policy instrument is reserve requirements on commercial bank liabilities. Although this has generally not been used as a discretionary policy instrument, the credit boom recently prompted some adjustments to reserve requirements in an effort to reduce commercial bank liquidity. The BNB has also imposed quarterly ceilings on bank credit growth, with punitive marginal reserve requirements if those ceilings are exceeded.

The NBR is in transition from an effectively exchange-rate-based framework to inflation targeting. Until November 2004, the central bank relied on the exchange rate as an implicit nominal anchor, guiding it broadly in line with the annual disinflation target and moderate real effective appreciation. The existing restrictions on capital flows afforded the NBR a degree of autonomy in setting its policy interest rate, which it used mainly to support the targeted exchange rate dynamics and reserves accumulation. In view of its transition to inflation targeting in 2005, the NBR recently stopped announcing real appreciation targets and limited its interventions in the foreign currency market. The monetary policy stance is signaled through the main policy interest rate, which serves as a ceiling for the NBR's sterilization and liquidity-managing tools of deposit auctions and certificates of deposits. Changes in reserve requirements on leu and foreign currency deposits are a secondary, rarely used instrument. The forthcoming liberalization of nonresident deposits with local banks, a component of Romania's accession to the EU, will challenge monetary policy implementation, owing to the still wide yield differential between assets in leu and foreign currencies.

Although the de facto peg of the hryvnia to the U.S. dollar has been the main feature of the NBU's policy framework, a move to a new regime is contemplated. The exchange rate appreciated only marginally against the U.S. dollar between 2000 and March 2005, and monetary policy was largely accommodative. The strong accumulation of international reserves during that period was only partly sterilized, mainly by the relatively tight fiscal stance, rather than by active monetary policy operations. However, rapid base money and broad money growth was mirrored by strong money demand, thus keeping inflationary pressures in check before 2004. The surge of inflation to 15 percent since then has made it apparent that the de facto peg is unlikely to deliver low and stable inflation against the backdrop of an undervalued currency and prospects of rising capital inflows. In April 2005, the NBU therefore allowed the exchange rate to appreciate by 4.6 percent but has left it unchanged since, even though it contemplates a move to more exchange rate flexibility and inflation targeting in the medium term.

The foundation for the current credit boom in these countries was laid in the years following the crises. Banks initially maintained high cash balances, built up net foreign assets (Bulgaria), and invested mostly in government securities (Romania).[3] This risk-averse behavior in part reflected a lack of information (including too short a credit history) about prospective borrowers, doubts about contract enforcement, and the loss of a large client base, as the state-owned enterprises (SoEs) were now not deemed creditworthy without state guarantees. Aided by economic recovery, a return of confidence, strengthening of bank balance sheets, and privatization of state banks, this risk-averse behavior gradually gave way to increased lending. At the same time, the legal, supervisory, and accounting framework under which banks were operating was strengthened, laying the foundation for increased bank lending. The framework was strengthened by (i) expanding the regulatory powers of the central banks; (ii) strengthening prudential regulations and supervision, including raising minimum capital adequacy requirements; (iii) strengthening creditors' rights; and (iv) introducing international accounting standards.

The ongoing credit boom reflects a mix of supply- and demand-side factors. In broad terms, the credit boom reflects a catching-up from depressed levels of post-crisis bank lending and is thus part of a process of financial deepening. The following factors are especially important:

- The newly privatized banks have been keen to boost profitability and market share. With high capital adequacy ratios, banks managed to increase profitability by shifting the composition of their assets toward loans. In Bulgaria and Romania, this more aggressive stance has been actively encouraged by the banks' foreign parents. Many of the banks' foreign owners are domiciled in less profitable mature markets, so parents have encouraged their subsidiaries and branches to pursue aggressive loan portfolio expansion to gain market share and improve consolidated results, thereby contributing to the acceleration of credit. In Ukraine, where foreign banks are less prominent, the lack of other investment opportunities has forced banks to expand their loan portfolios in pursuit of higher profits.
- Banks' ability to fund loan expansion has been boosted by strong capital inflows, mostly through the banking system, amid high global liquidity, low interest rates, and increased confidence associated with Bulgaria's and Romania's prospective EU accession and Ukraine's large current account surpluses.
- The greater supply of credit has been matched by increased demand from both businesses and households. For the former, a newfound confidence in the future—prompted by rising profits and, for Bulgaria and Romania, strong EU accession prospects—has boosted investment intentions and demand for credit. For the latter, consumer and mortgage credit has taken off partly because household demand for durables and real estate has increased from previously depressed levels as households have felt more confident in their ability to service debt, and partly because the banks have offered new products with more flexible terms.
- Finally, an additional factor explaining the credit boom may be crowding in: bank credit to the public sector has declined substantially, reflecting small general government fiscal deficits or even surpluses and the availability of ample external financing and privatization revenue.

Characteristics of credit booms

A fast expansion of credit to households and a relative decline in loans to SoEs are common in all three countries (Table 15.3). Households have converted their confidence in a permanently rising disposable income into a sharp rise in consumer and mortgage loans. In Bulgaria and Romania, the share of household loans has surged to one-third of total loans while it is still much lower in Ukraine (16 percent) despite a rapid acceleration over the past years. The increase in credits to households has been matched by a declining share of SoEs in nongovernment credit, partly reflecting major progress in privatization. In all three countries, business credit remains the largest component of total credit.

Widespread lending in foreign currencies is another common feature (Table 15.3). Despite different monetary frameworks (Box 15.2), the expected cost of foreign currency credit is perceived to be lower than local currency loans in all three countries (a belief validated ex post for the time being as well). In Bulgaria, the currency board has assured borrowers of exchange rate stability, while banks still charge higher rates for loans in domestic currency.[4] In Romania, the sharp drop in the risk premium after EU accession became almost certain has led to strong and persistent inflows, which has significantly lowered the effective cost of foreign currency credit. In Ukraine, the de facto exchange rate peg has also provided an incentive for a rise in foreign currency credit, closely associated with the boom in loans to households; however, local currency loans in Ukraine have expanded even faster, in contrast to the other two countries. In all three countries, most enterprises that borrow in foreign currency do not appear to be hedged, except for the natural hedge enjoyed by exporters.

Services and industry still get the lion's share of credit in all three countries (Table 15.5). Trade and construction have been steadily gaining share everywhere, while industry has been increasing its relative borrowing (from a low level) only in Bulgaria. The share of loans going to the service sector has declined in Bulgaria—albeit from a high level—and was stable or increased in Romania and Ukraine.

There has been a marked shift from short- to medium- and long-term credit. Between end-2000 and end-2004, short-term credit (maturity less than one year) in Romania and Ukraine declined from 72 percent to 42 percent of the total, and from 82 to 46 percent, respectively. In Bulgaria, over the same period, short-term credit's share (including overdrafts) fell from 34 percent to about 24 percent. The preponderance of longer-term lending is a reflection of the increased confidence of both creditors and debtors.

In all three countries, banks have extended loans at very high, though falling, real interest rates and intermediation spreads in local currency. A dearth of alternative sources of corporate financing (e.g., corporate bonds and stock market initial public offerings) has led the banks to compete on terms like the range and fees for services rather than on deposit and loan rates. In Romania, the high reserve requirements have also contributed to the spread. Ukraine is an exception, as lower operating and provisioning costs have enabled banks to cut lending rates, causing an 18 percentage point fall in the deposit loan interest rate spread since end-2000.

Banks have funded the expansion of credit mostly through mobilization of deposits (Figure 15.3). Deposit growth has been relatively quick, owing to improved confidence, remittances from abroad, and, in Romania, high real leu deposit rates. In addition, a reduction of placements abroad, reflecting low global interest rates and a rapid accumulation of foreign liabilities, has resulted in a sharp drop in banks' net

Table 15.5 Sectoral Composition of Credit, 2000–04[a] (percent by total)

	2000	2001	2002	2003	2004
Bulgaria[b]					
Industry	–	–	26	30	31
Agriculture	–	–	2	3	4
Services	–	–	69	64	61
Trade	–	–	25	30	36
Transportation	–	–	5	3	3
Construction	–	–	1	2	4
Public administration and other	–	–	1	1	0
Romania					
Industry	53	52	48	44	41
Agriculture	4	3	3	3	3
Services	36	38	41	40	39
Construction	5	4	4	4	5
Public administration and other	2	3	3	8	12
Ukraine					
Industry	40	40	38	35	33
Agriculture	4	7	7	8	8
Services	40	39	44	46	47
Trade	37	36	40	42	42
Transportation	3	3	4	5	4
Construction	2	2	2	3	3
Public administration and other	13	12	8	9	9

Source: Bulgarian National Bank; National Bank of Romania; National Bank of Ukraine; and IMF staff estimates.

[a] Excluding credit to individuals. Data in this presentation deviate somewhat from the balance sheet numbers due to different data sources.
[b] Prior to July 1, 2004, only loans exceeding 10,000 leva were reported; since then, all loans have been reported.

foreign assets. To a lesser extent, additional capital—either from the parent bank or through issuance of subordinated debt—has also been a source, but only for banks with capital adequacy ratios near the regulatory minimum.

Opportunities and risks

Opportunities

An increase in the level of financial intermediation is associated with an increase in the long-run growth rate of the economy. The theoretical and empirical literature generally supports the view that financial sector development increases economic growth.[5] There are various channels through which financial development can contribute to economic growth, including by collecting information and thereby improving the allocation of capital; sharing risk; and pooling savings and raising the efficiency of financial intermediation. Indeed, by easing financing constraints, increased bank lending can contribute to higher investment and consumption, and, ultimately, a higher standard of living.

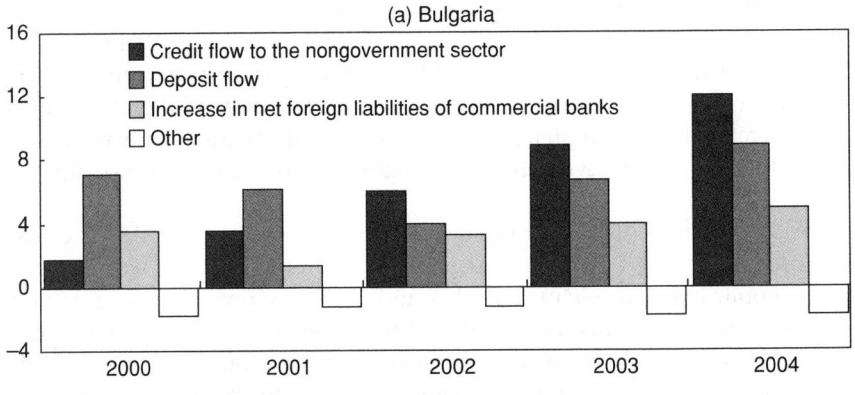

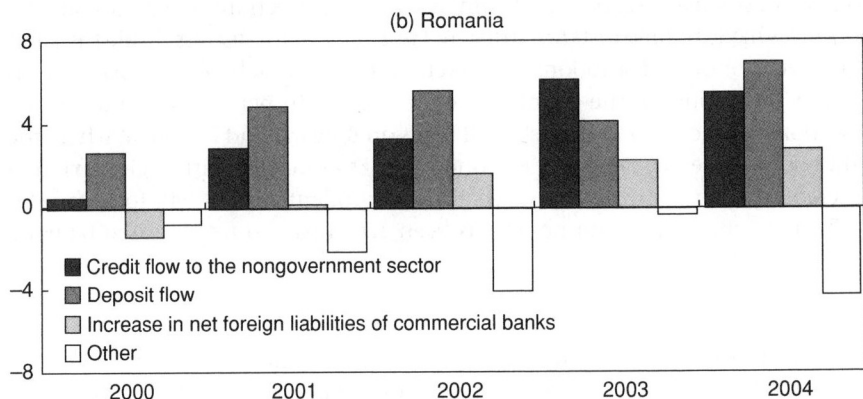

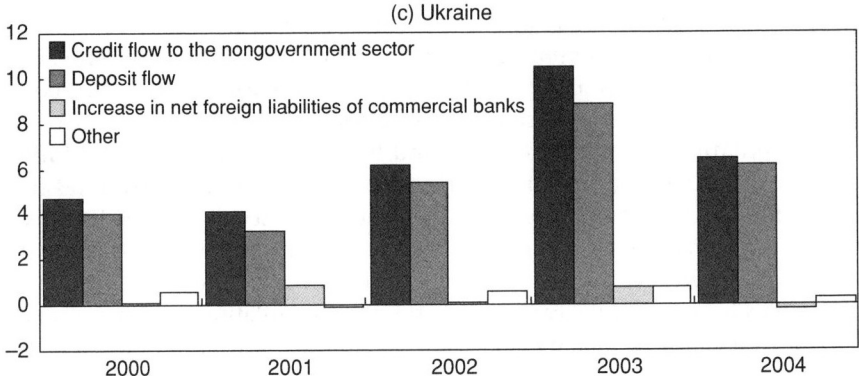

Figure 15.3 Credit and Bank Liabilities, 2000–04 (in percent of GDP)

Source: Central banks; and IMF staff estimates.

From a structural perspective, the increase in financial intermediation in the three countries can therefore be considered beneficial. Per capita GDP in Bulgaria, Romania, and Ukraine is still well below the average of EU countries and CEEs. To the extent that financial deepening raises the country's potential growth rate—through increases in the marginal productivity of capital and higher private savings and investment—recent developments in these countries should in principle be welcomed.

At the same time, episodes of rapid bank lending also entail risks. The risks can be broadly grouped into two categories: (i) the emergence or worsening of macroeconomic imbalances ("macro risk"); and (ii) risks to financial sector stability owing to deteriorating bank asset quality ("credit risk"). When they materialize, these two risks are typically mutually reinforcing, creating boom-bust cycles in credit and asset markets and large swings in macroeconomic fundamentals. Moreover, the two types of risk may also be causally linked: abrupt corrections of macroeconomic imbalances have in some instances triggered financial sector distress, while the latter has caused economic disruptions. This section discusses each of these risks in turn and how they apply to the countries being studied. In particular, the following subsection on macroeconomic risks will focus on Bulgaria and Romania, where the credit booms have increased macroeconomic risks associated with higher external vulnerabilities. In contrast, the subsection on prudential risks will focus mostly on Ukraine, where the credit boom has been accompanied by increased banking sector vulnerabilities.

Macroeconomic risks

Rapid credit growth poses potential risks for macroeconomic stability. Increased credit availability eases liquidity constraints on households and firms, leading to higher consumption and investment. Given short-run supply constraints, this upward shift in credit-financed domestic demand would tend to exert upward pressure on prices in asset, goods, and labor markets. Concurrently, demand for foreign goods—both consumption and investment—will rise, causing a deterioration in the trade balance. Thus, if left unchecked, a rapid increase in credit can boost domestic prices and wages—which at an unchanged nominal exchange rate could reduce international competitiveness—and heighten external vulnerabilities. Indeed, in characterizing emerging market credit booms, IMF (2004) notes that there is almost a 70 percent probability that a credit boom coincides with either a consumption or investment boom, and that credit booms are often associated with banking and currency crises. The same paper also concludes that emerging market credit booms have not, on average, resulted in higher inflation—partly reflecting the high degree of trade openness in these economies—but rather have led to a deterioration of the current account and nominal exchange rate appreciation.

The experience of Bulgaria and Romania accords well with these priors (Figure 15.4). Both countries have seen domestic demand contributions to real GDP growth rise sharply, while net export contributions have turned negative. These shifts have coincided with the rapid increase in bank lending documented in Section I above. Consumer price inflation has remained relatively tame in both countries, partly reflecting lower food prices due, in turn, to strong agricultural output, and nominal effective exchange rate appreciation in Bulgaria has offset the impact of higher oil prices. Thus, overheating has so far largely been manifested in widening trade deficits, owing to rapid growth in imports.[6]

In contrast, Ukraine's macroeconomic imbalances are of a different nature and have been driven by different shocks than in Bulgaria and Romania. Ukraine has registered large current account surpluses in recent years on the back of strong export commodity prices and an undervalued currency. With most of the terms of trade gains going to high-savings groups (a reflection of the ownership structure of Ukraine's economy, including the export sector) the impact on domestic demand and inflationary pressures remained subdued through mid-2004 against large idle capacities, a tight fiscal stance, and rapid remonetization. The subsequent pickup of inflationary pressures can be attributed mainly to expansionary fiscal policy, emerging capacity bottlenecks, rapidly rising wages and pensions, and an accommodative monetary policy stance.

Econometric analysis suggests that rapid credit expansion in Bulgaria and Romania has been a significant factor in explaining the deteriorating trade balance, although tighter fiscal policy has helped moderate the impact (Table 15.6; for an overview of the methodology, see Box 15.3). The estimation results suggest that each percentage point of GDP of additional credit leads to a deterioration in the balance of goods and nonfactor services (with a one-quarter lag) of about 0.4 percentage point of GDP for Bulgaria and 0.7 percentage point of GDP for Romania. The change in the fiscal stance is also an important determinant of changes in the trade balance: a 1 percentage point increase in the fiscal balance improves the trade balance by 0.2 percentage point (with a one-quarter lag). The same-size response in both countries probably reflects the broad similarity in the use of the exchange rate as a nominal anchor during the analyzed period, despite the different monetary policy frameworks (see Box 15.2 above). The results also suggest that private savings provide

Table 15.6 Impact of Credit Growth on the Trade Balance (dependent variable: trade balance-to-GDP ratio)

	Coefficient	Std. Error	t-Stat	Prob.
Constant	−0.031	0.010	−3.043	0.004
Fixed effects: Bulgaria	−0.008			
Romania	0.008			
Lagged trade balance	0.197	0.156	1.262	0.214
Lagged fiscal balance	0.190	0.097	1.952	0.058
Lagged credit flow				
Bulgaria	−0.442	0.151	−2.930	0.006
Romania	−0.706	0.189	−3.735	0.001
Change in GDP	−0.050	0.051	−0.982	0.332
Memo items:				
Sample: 1999Q2–2004Q4		Durbin Watson stat		1.975
Total pool (balanced) observations	46	F-stat		13.312
Adjusted R-squared	0.621	Prob(F-stat)		0.000

Source: IMF staff estimates based on data from national authorities.

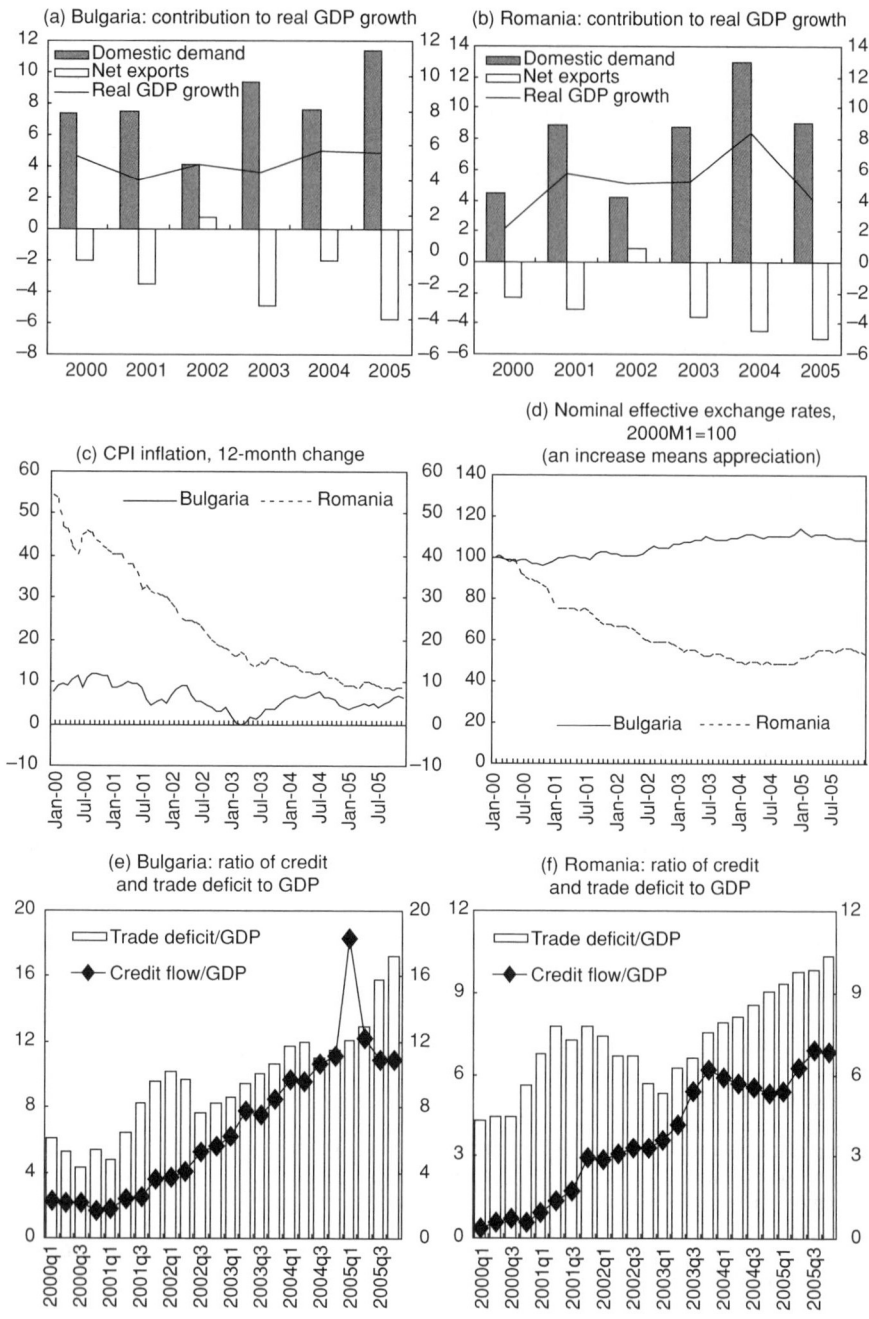

Figure 15.4 Bulgaria and Romania: Selected Economic Indicators, 2000–05 (in percent, unless otherwise indicated)

Source: National authorities; IMF, International Financial Statistics; and IMF staff estimates.

Box 15.3. The Relationship Between Credit Growth and Trade Balance in Bulgaria and Romania

There are different ways of analyzing the impact of credit growth on the external balance. One option, described in Duenwald and Joshi (2004), is to use a financial programming model in which an increase in credit to the nongovernment sector, for a given level of the change in broad money, the fiscal balance, and the change in net foreign assets of the nonbank sector, translates into a worsening of the current account balance. This effect can be numerically derived. A second approach, adopted in this chapter, is to specify a behavioral relationship between the two variables and fit this model to the data.

Our chosen model is loosely based on Bussière et al. (2004). Their paper uses a modified intertemporal current account model to analyze current account dynamics in a mix of advanced and transition economies. The standard model is augmented to explain two stylized facts: (i) the persistence of current account positions; and (ii) the observed impact of the fiscal balance on the current account. The authors explain the former by habit formation and the latter by the presence of liquidity-constrained agents whose current income (and thus spending) is influenced by fiscal policy. The following dynamic model is tested:

$$CA_{it} = \alpha + \beta CA_{it-1} + \phi X_{it} + \varepsilon_{it},$$

where i and t represent the cross-sectional and time dimensions, respectively, CA stands for the current account-to-GDP ratio, and X represents other explanatory variables: the change in net output (GDP less investment and government spending), the fiscal surplus, relative income, the relative investment ratio, and the relative public expenditure ratio (relative to the sample average, to capture the catch-up effect of higher growth and investment in lower-income countries). Using dynamic panel estimation, this model is fitted to data from 21 industrial countries and the EU-acceding countries, plus Bulgaria and Romania. The results suggest that the lagged current account and the fiscal balance have a significant impact on the current account for the panel of countries studied.

This chapter modifies the above model in three ways. First, we use the goods and nonfactor services trade balance instead of the current account balance, in part because movements in the current account partly reflect large inward transfers, which are not germane to the links we are trying to identify. Second, we replace the investment ratio, net output, and relative income variables with the credit-to-GDP ratio and the change in GDP. In Bussière et al (2004), these variables reflect two catch-up effects on the current account: consumption smoothing in anticipation of higher future permanent income and higher investment driven by the higher return on capital in poorer countries. We capture these effects from the financing side, as both consumption and investment are financed either out of current income (GDP) or by borrowing. Third, we lag by one period the fiscal balance and the credit variable to reflect the lags with which they likely affect the trade balance; however, we do not lag the change in current income (GDP), which is spent upon realization. Our tested model therefore takes the following form:

$$TB_{it} = \alpha + \beta TB_{it-1} + \gamma \Delta Y_t + \phi X_{it-1} + \varepsilon_{it},$$

where i represents Bulgaria and Romania, TB the trade balance (goods and services), X contains the flow in credit and the change in the fiscal balance, and Y is the change in GDP. All variables are quarterly, scaled by GDP, and seasonally adjusted. The data period is too short to conduct stationarity tests, but the flow specification of the variables and scaling by GDP suggest likely stationarity. Using the cross-section generalized least squares estimator, and allowing country-specific effects for several variables, the model was fitted to the data. The results (Table 15.6) suggest that, over this sample period, changes in the flow of credit and the fiscal balance (one-period lag in each case) had significant (and, of course, opposite) effects on the trade balances in the two countries.

a significant but incomplete Ricardian offset to changes in public savings, albeit somewhat above what is typical for a developing country (Chinn and Prasad, 2003). Finally, it seems that, in terms of the efficiency of policy instruments, moderating credit growth in these two countries is more powerful than attempts to offset it by tightening the fiscal stance (see Section III below).

Risks for banking sector stability

Rapid credit growth can trigger banking sector distress through two channels: macroeconomic imbalances and deterioration of loan quality. If the rapid expansion of bank loans leads to large current account deficits and is accompanied by fiscal deficits and inflationary pressures, as described in the previous subsection, an economy becomes increasingly vulnerable to macroeconomic shocks. A sudden reversal in capital flows or other external shocks, as well as the need for swift and drastic policy responses, could bring about a hard landing for the economy, as evidenced by higher interest rates, a slowdown in growth, a drop in asset prices, and pressures on the exchange rate. Whether this hard landing causes any distress for the banking sector will depend on the sector's exposure to those risks in relation to its financial buffers.

Loan quality is not only susceptible to macroeconomic shocks but also to banks' excessive risk taking. Risk assessments may suffer due to the vast amount of new loans extended. Loan officers may be overburdened and agree to riskier loans that are not appropriately priced. Moreover, lending booms can facilitate "evergreening" when new loans are used to service existing debt. At the same time, banks may neglect to further diversify their loan portfolios in an environment in which they can service existing clients. And finally, the perceived risk of loans may be underestimated during lending booms because the risk assessments are based on the current strong economy and rising values of underlying collateral.[7]

Thus, rapid credit growth has been one of the most robust leading indicators for banking distress even though the majority of lending booms has not resulted in banking crises.[8] Numerous studies have found that periods of significant and accelerating credit growth have often preceded banking crises.[9] The likelihood of a banking crisis following a lending boom is estimated to be as high as 20 percent, depending on the data set and methodology used. Prominent examples include the Scandinavian banking crises in the early 1990s, Mexico's banking crisis in 1994, and the Asian financial crisis in 1997–98. As depicted in Table 15.7, the ratio of credit to GDP increased rapidly in those countries, with the increase averaging 5.2 percentage points per year in the five years leading up to the crisis and dropping precipitously afterward.[10]

Prudential indicators point to the strength of banks in Bulgaria and Romania, while Ukraine's banking system seems plagued by structural weaknesses (Table 15.8). Despite the ongoing credit acceleration, banks in Bulgaria and Romania are well capitalized and liquid. Healthy profitability and low nonperforming loan (NPL) ratios foretell continuing credit expansion for years to come.[11] In contrast, Ukrainian banks suffer from large shares of related-party lending and NPLs, while profitability has remained low.

Table 15.7 Credit to GDP Ratio in Banking-Crisis Countries (in percent)

	t–6	t–5	t–4	t–3	t–2	t–1	t	t+1	t+2	t+3
Finland (t=1991)	60.1	63.9	69.2	78.3	81.2	86.0	93.7	89.8	81.0	69.0
Indonesia (t=1997)	45.8	45.5	48.9	51.9	53.5	55.4	60.8	53.2	20.5	21.1
Korea (t=1997)	52.6	52.2	52.2	53.8	53.2	57.6	64.8	71.7	79.5	87.6
Mexico (t=1994)	8.5	13.8	16.3	20.4	27.8	28.9	34.9	25.2	15.6	17.7
Norway (t=1987)	31.3	32.1	33.2	37.3	44.1	55.0	61.7	63.1	64.3	63.5
Philippines (t=1997)	17.8	20.4	26.4	29.1	37.5	49.0	56.5	48.0	42.0	39.2
Sweden (t=1990)	40.7	39.3	42.1	44.3	52.2	57.2	56.1	52.5	52.8	40.9
Thailand (t=1997)	67.7	72.2	80.1	91.0	97.7	101.7	121.1	114.6	108.1	85.7

Source: IMF, *International Financial Statistics*; and IMF staff estimates.

Note: *t* is the year of the crisis.

Table 15.8 Prudential Indicators of the Banking Sector, 2000–05 (in percent)

	2000	2001	2002	2003	2004	2005
Bulgaria						
Capital adequacy ratios	35.6	31.3	25.2	22.0	16.1	15.2
Nonperforming loans/total loans	17.3	13.1	8.6	7.3	6.9	7.7
Return on assets	3.1	2.9	2.1	2.4	2.1	2.1
Return on equity	22.5	22.0	16.4	22.8	20.6	22.1
Liquid assets/total assets	26.0	25.5	29.3	25.5	31.6	31.3
Romania						
Capital adequacy ratios	23.8	28.8	24.6	20.0	18.8	20.2
Nonperforming loans/total loans	6.4	3.9	2.8	8.3	8.1	8.3
Return on assets	1.5	3.1	2.7	2.4	2.5	1.9
Return on equity	12.5	21.8	18.8	18.2	19.3	15.4
Liquid assets/total assets[a]	–	–	78.6	62.7	63.6	61.8
Ukraine						
Capital adequacy ratios	15.5	20.7	18.0	15.2	16.8	15.0
Nonperforming loans/total loans[b]	29.6	25.1	21.9	28.3	30.0	19.6
Return on assets	–0.1	1.2	1.2	1.0	1.1	1.3
Return on equity	–0.5	7.5	8.0	7.6	8.4	10.4
Liquid assets/total assets	20.8	15.3	13.5	15.3	16.7	16.4

Source: Bulgarian National Bank; National Bank of Romania; National Bank of Ukraine; and IMF staff estimates.

[a] Liquid assets are assets with residual maturity of up to three months.
[b] The NBU estimates that about 94 percent of loans classified as substandard are being timely serviced.

While macroeconomic imbalances are largest in Bulgaria and Romania, the risks from financial sector distress are highest in Ukraine. The level of credit in all three countries is still much below that of many prominent crisis countries, but the speed of credit expansion in Bulgaria and Ukraine has reached levels comparable to them (Figure 15.5). However, institutional and structural factors put the banking systems in Bulgaria and Romania on a much stronger footing than Ukraine's. In the EBRD's index on banking sector reform, both surpass Ukraine (Figure 15.6), and Bulgaria is

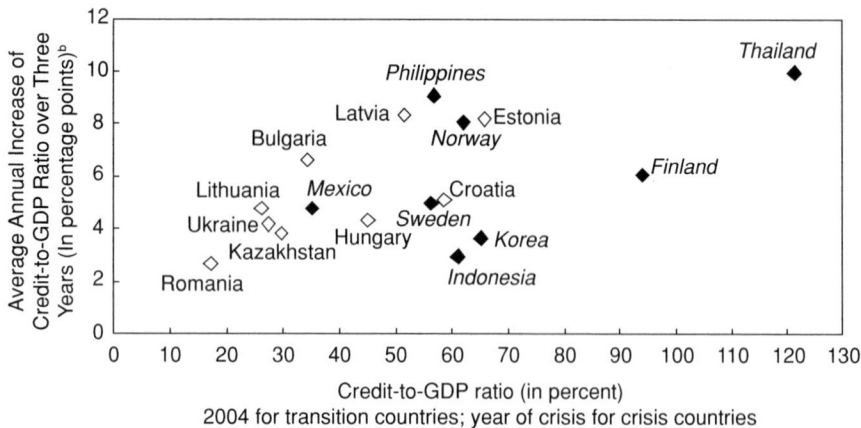

Figure 15.5 Credit Growth in Transition Economies and Banking-Crisis Countries[a]

Source: IMF, International Financial Statistics; and IMF staff estimates.

[a] Private sector credit. Crisis countries are depicted in italics.
[b] 2003–05 for transition countries. Biggest average annual three-year increase before crisis for crisis countries.

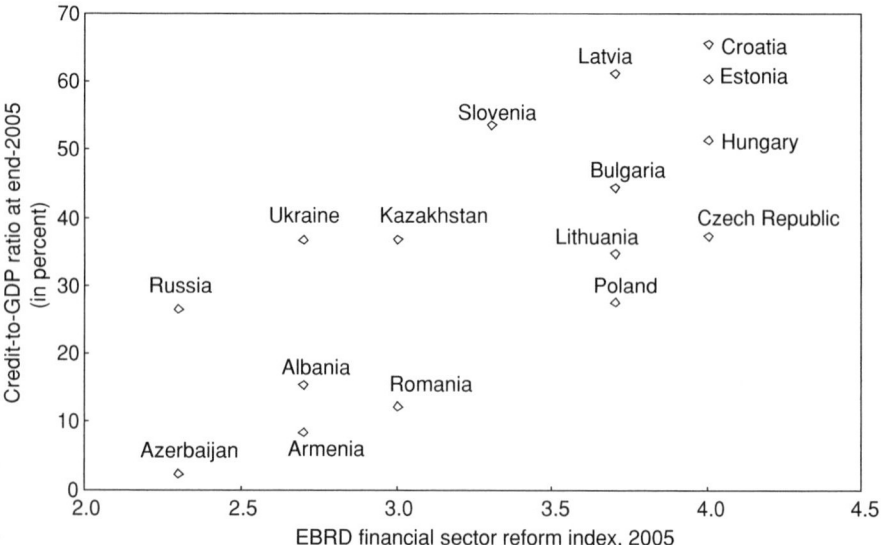

Figure 15.6 Transition Economies: Credit-to-GDP Ratio and Institutional Reform, 2005[a]

Source: IMF, International Financial Statistics; EBRD Transition Report 2005; and IMF staff estimates.

[a] Private sector credit.

now on par with countries that have already acceded to the EU. The large share of foreign ownership and relatively strong prudential indicators also indicate that the banking systems in Bulgaria and Romania are relatively well shielded from shocks. Nevertheless, credit risk through exchange rate exposure is a concern in all three countries, given the large shares of often unhedged foreign currency loans.

The financial condition of banks in Ukraine remains opaque. In light of widespread related-party lending practices, the only recently strengthened definitions of bank capital,[12] and weaknesses in banks' risk management and loan practices, the true resilience of banks to withstand a deterioration in credit quality is unclear. In particular, the buildup of cushions, in the form of capital and provisions, has not kept pace with the rapid credit expansion in Ukraine, and banks' profitability has remained much below that in most other transition economies. Poor asset diversification—due to the lack of other investment opportunities, about two-thirds of banks' total assets in Ukraine are loans, higher than in Bulgaria (56 percent of total assets), Romania (47 percent of total assets), or other transition economies—is another concern (see Schaechter (2005) for a more detailed analysis).

III. Policy options and authorities' responses

Policymakers face a number of difficult questions in deciding how to respond to a credit boom:

- On what basis should the judgment be made as to whether credit is expanding too quickly? Are there speed limits?
- Assuming it is decided that credit is growing too quickly, how should the policy response be apportioned between (i) offsetting the effects of the credit boom with other policy instruments and (ii) moderating the credit boom itself?
- Is it advisable to use prudential measures for macroeconomic objectives?

Deciding whether a credit expansion is excessive or not is difficult both in general and for the three countries. During the convergence process, a certain degree of reintermediation, higher consumption and investment growth, and wider external current account deficits is to be expected. Unfortunately, the academic literature provides few reliable guideposts in answering the question of "how fast is too fast." In principle, an equilibrium level of credit could be calculated, based on a country's economic and institutional fundamentals.[13] This can then be compared with the current level of credit. However, while such a calculation might provide a "target," it does not provide any guidance on how rapidly a country should move to that equilibrium level. In the case of Bulgaria, the gap between the estimated equilibrium ratio and the actual has been narrowing very rapidly: in 2001, before the credit boom got into full swing, the credit-to-GDP ratio was 15 percent, and by end-2004 it had reached about 34.5 percent. Thus, the credit-to-GDP ratio rose by about 6.5 percentage points on average per year, a pace that has been associated with banking crises in other countries. In Romania and Ukraine, the credit-to-GDP ratio has risen more slowly, at 2.5 and 4.25 percentage points, respectively, on average during the same period.

The test of whether credit is growing too rapidly should be based on the extent to which the risks identified earlier—macroeconomic and prudential—appear to be materializing. On the domestic side, is inflation (in goods, assets, and labor markets) rising, and if so, is this linked to the credit boom? On the external side, are trade/current account balances deteriorating beyond what could be deemed sustainable? In assessing the current account position, two questions are critical: (i) to what extent is rapid credit growth responsible for the deterioration in the current account balance? and (ii) what is the level of the current account balance that stabilizes the external debt-to-GDP ratio over the medium term?[14] Answering the latter question depends crucially on assumptions regarding the future size of nondebt-creating inflows.[15] Finally, an assessment of prudential risks would involve closely monitoring indicators of banking system health, such as NPL ratios, capital adequacy ratios, loan concentration ratios, and balance sheet mismatches (especially maturity and currency). Assessing such risks is a complicated task for supervisors, as it is difficult to disentangle boom excesses from equilibrium trends. In addition, certain indicators—for instance, NPL ratios—are lagging indicators of emerging risks, and reliable early warning indicators for banking fragility remain largely elusive.

These risks have emerged to varying degrees and in varying forms in Bulgaria, Romania, and Ukraine. As noted above, in Bulgaria and Romania external balances have tended to weaken beyond what would be considered prudent or sustainable levels, but no significant price pressures stemming from the credit boom have emerged. In Ukraine, the situation is reversed: the current account has been in a very large surplus and inflation has recently been trending up, driven mainly by large increases in social expenditure. On the prudential side, as previously discussed, the banking systems in Bulgaria and Romania appear to be healthy, while vulnerabilities are greater in Ukraine. Overall, these considerations point to a need to rein in these countries' credit expansions, a policy that has been pursued by all three in the past two years (see below).

The menu of available policy options depends on the country's policy framework and institutional setting.[16] The tools include macroeconomic policies (fiscal, monetary, and exchange rate policies), regulatory and supervisory policies, administrative measures (such as controls on capital inflows), and market development measures. Many credit boom countries have used a combination of the above policies. Constraints on policy options relate to the type of monetary/exchange rate policy framework and to the institutional setting: with a fixed exchange rate regime, traditional monetary policy tools (e.g., changes in interest rates, open market operations) are ineffective, particularly in cases with open capital accounts. In such a setting, efforts to drain liquidity from the domestic banking system to reduce funding sources will be frustrated: as long as returns on lending remain high, nonbank/cross-border flows will quickly replenish funding sources. Regulatory and supervisory policies aim to ensure banking sector health; their effectiveness in moderating credit growth has not yet been established, and there is a general consensus that such measures cannot substitute for monetary policy.[17] Thus, if supervisors try to reduce credit growth, they may in fact divert it to less supervised channels (e.g., leasing companies). However, in combination with monetary policy, changes in the prudential regime can help avoid excessive credit growth. Administrative measures—for instance, general or bank-by-bank credit ceilings, or capital inflow controls—are generally viewed as a last resort, owing to their bluntness and distortionary effects. Finally, market development measures—including establishment of credit registries to improve the credit culture and development of securities markets to reduce dependence on bank credit—may help, but the impact is likely to be marginal and of a more medium-term nature.

The authorities in the three countries understand the risks associated with the credit booms and have responded in varying ways and degrees to both offset and moderate rapid credit growth:

- In **Bulgaria**, policy options are constrained by the currency board arrangement. The main response has been a tightening of fiscal policy, both through higher revenue—reflecting mostly cyclical factors and improved compliance in the face of lower taxes—and expenditure restraint. A host of monetary measures—notably moral suasion, a tightening of reserve requirements and prudential supervision, and, most recently, quantitative restrictions on credit (enforced with the help of marginal reserve requirements for banks exceeding the limits)—have been implemented. The tightening of reserve requirements in 2004 does not appear to have reduced credit growth, although such growth may have been even higher otherwise. It is too early to assess the impact of the quantitative limits on credit expansion that took effect on April 1, 2005, but a significant diversion to other forms of financing (nonbank/cross-border) is likely. Going forward, it is possible that further fiscal tightening would be necessary should the monetary measures prove ineffective in preventing a further widening of external imbalances.
- In **Romania**, a combination of fiscal policy, monetary policy, and prudential measures has been used to both moderate and offset credit growth. Fiscal policy has been consistently tightened, with the general government deficit narrowing from 3.2 percent of GDP in 2001 to 1.1 percent in 2004. The NBR tried interest rate hikes in 2003 but had to reverse course in 2004, as falling inflation and large capital inflows made high real interest rates both unjustifiable and untenable. Moreover, these hikes merely changed the composition of credit in favor of foreign currency loans without reducing the overall credit flow. As the boom occurred mostly in loans to households, the NBR tightened households' eligibility for credit by lowering the ceiling on the maximum monthly payment-to-net income ratios, standardizing the downpayment for mortgage loans at 25 percent, and strengthening the required guarantees/collateral. Finally, the reserve requirement on foreign-currency-denominated bank liabilities was increased and extended to liabilities with residual maturity longer than two years. These measures did reduce credit growth somewhat, but a further fiscal tightening is likely to be necessary in the period ahead to support efforts on the monetary side.
- In **Ukraine**, the focus was on bank regulatory and supervisory measures. The NBU raised the minimum capital adequacy ratio, strengthened the definition

of capital, tightened loan classification rules, raised provisioning requirements for foreign- currency-denominated loans, tightened related-party lending regulations, and put in place a new risk assessment methodology for its supervisors. These measures were aimed at strengthening banks' resilience to shocks. Credit growth decelerated during 2004 (even when the sharp drop during the political crisis is excluded), but it is unclear to what extent this can be attributed to the NBU's responses. Going forward, further progress in strengthening bank regulation and supervision, as well as the institutional environment, is needed, with particular focus on related-party lending.

IV. Concluding remarks

Like other CEE countries, Bulgaria, Romania, and Ukraine have experienced rapid increases in bank credit to the private sector. In part, this reflects economic convergence and a reversal of years of financial repression, and is likely to give a much needed boost to per capita incomes. However, the credit expansion has been excessive: in Bulgaria and Romania, from the point of view of macroeconomic stability; and in Ukraine, from the point of view of financial sector stability.

The booms reflect broadly similar causes. On the demand side, macroeconomic stabilization and robust growth have lifted households' confidence that rises in income will be permanent and boosted businesses' willingness to invest. As for credit supply, bank privatization, improved creditor rights, large capital inflows triggered by low credit demand abroad, and diminishing opportunities for alternative asset placements have increased banks' propensity to lend.

The impact of the credit booms has varied in the three countries. In Bulgaria and Romania, rapid credit growth has contributed to wider trade and current account deficits. This hypothesis was tested and confirmed with the use of a pooled regression, which also suggested a significant role for fiscal policy in offsetting the impact of rapid credit expansion. In Ukraine, in contrast, concerns about the credit boom have largely reflected financial sector vulnerabilities.

Policy responses in the three countries have been tailored to address the identified risks, but further action is probably necessary. In Bulgaria and Romania, such action will probably continue to emphasize tighter macroeconomic policies, although supervisors will need to remain vigilant to ensure continued financial sector health, particularly as credit may be diverted to less supervised channels. In Ukraine, stronger prudential and supervisory policies will remain at the heart of efforts to reduce financial vulnerabilities. In all three countries, these efforts to maintain macroeconomic and financial sector stability will be part of a broader framework of prudent fiscal and incomes policies and structural reform.

Notes

1. International Monetary Fund (IMF).
2. IMF (2004) makes a distinction between rapid credit growth and a credit boom. The former can occur as part of financial deepening (trend) and normal cyclical upturns, while the latter represents an excessive and therefore unsustainable cyclical movement.

While such a distinction may be sensible for advanced economies, the short time series and likelihood of a structural break in the series make such a distinction less meaningful for economies in transition. We therefore use the terms "rapid credit growth" and "credit boom" interchangeably in this chapter.

3. Due to the financial crisis in Ukraine during which the government had to restructure its debt, banks in Ukraine initially shied away from government securities.
4. This partly reflects market segmentation, with households and businesses that do not have access to foreign currency loans having to borrow in domestic currency.
5. IMF (2004) summarizes the state of play in the literature; a more extensive discussion of both the theory and empirics regarding finance and growth can be found in Levine (2003).
6. Developments in bank credit are probably more closely mirrored in the trade rather than the current account. In Bulgaria, for example, the current account deficit narrowed in 2004 despite an acceleration in credit growth as the invisibles strengthened substantially; the trade deficit, meanwhile, remained at a very high level (14 percent of GDP) despite favorable movements in the terms of trade. Competitiveness does not appear to have been a significant factor in the deterioration of trade balances in Bulgaria and Romania.
7. As a result, in most countries lending is strongly procyclical: in upswings, lending is extended much faster than real GDP, and in recessions it contracts stronger than output.
8. The risks for financial sector stability are predominantly linked to the speed of credit growth rather than the stock of credit or money. Nevertheless, the level of financial intermediation may affect the costs for the economy of financial sector distress. See Hoelscher and Quintyn (2003) for an attempt to estimate the costs of financial crises.
9. Eichengreen and Arteta (2000) find robustness in these results by testing the findings of earlier studies by Gavin and Hausmann (1996), Kaminsky and Reinhart (1999), and Gourinchas, Valdes, and Landerretche (2001). Other papers that support the importance of lending booms for banking crises are, for example, IMF (2004), Drees and Pazarbasioğlu (1998), Hardy and Pazarbasioğlu (1998), and Demirgüç-Kunt and Detragiache (1997).
10. Cottarelli, Dell'Ariccia, and Vladkova-Hollar (2005) report that, in the years preceding banking crisis, countries' credit-to-GDP ratios grew by between 5 and 10 percentage points of GDP annually.
11. The NPL ratio includes loans classified as substandard, doubtful, and loss.
12. A major revision to the definition of capital was to exclude accrued income and tie the inclusion of revaluation gains of fixed assets to strict auditing procedures.
13. Given the ongoing structural changes in such transition economies, however, these estimates of equilibrium credit must be taken with a grain of salt. A recent attempt at such estimates is Cottarelli, Dell'Ariccia, and Vladkova-Hollar (2005), who calculate equilibrium credit-to-GDP ratios for a number of CEE countries. For Bulgaria and Romania, the estimated ratios are 52.6 percent and 58 percent, compared with ratios of 34.4 percent and 17.9 percent, respectively, at end-2004. These estimates are based on 2002 data and are now somewhat dated.
14. Aside from medium-term considerations, prudence suggests keeping the current account at manageable levels to reduce vulnerability to sudden reversals in capital. A recent survey of early warning system models by Berg, Borensztein, and Pattillo (2004) reports widespread use of the current account as one of the predictive variables. For instance, Goldstein, Kaminsky, and Reinhart (2000) find the current account deficit to be among the best predictors of currency crises.
15. In this context, imports related to FDI are often thought to be self-financing as they generate future exports; however, to the extent investment is made in nontraded sectors, this argument cannot be made.
16. For a fuller discussion of policy options, see Hilbers et al (2005).
17. Dynamic provisioning is one technique that has been used to address risks arising from the procyclicality of credit. The main rationale for its use is to address a systematic

underpricing of risk during cyclical upswings. Dynamic provisioning links the provisioning rates to the average probability of default for different types of assets over the business cycle (see e.g. Bank for International Settlements, 2001). However, the technique has generated objections from the accounting and tax professions on the grounds that these provisions do not relate to identified risks. Options for provisioning loans in partially dollarized economies are discussed in Del Mar Cacha and Morales (2003).

Bibliography

Bank for International Settlements, 2001, *Marrying the Macro- and Microprudential Dimensions of Financial Stability* (Basel).

Berg, Andrew, Eduardo Borensztein and Catherine Pattillo, 2004, "Assessing Early Warnings Systems: How Have They Worked in Practice?" IMF Working Paper 04/52 (Washington: International Monetary Fund).

Bussière, Matthieu, Marcel Fratzscher and Gernot J. Müller, 2004, "Current Account Dynamics in OECD and EU Acceding Countries—An Intertemporal Approach," European Central Bank Working Paper No. 311, February.

Chinn, Menzie D. and Eswar S. Prasad, 2003, "Medium-Term Determinants of Current Accounts in Industrial and Developing Countries: A Empirical Exploration," *Journal of International Economics*, 59, pp. 47–76.

Cottarelli, Carlo, Giovanni Dell'Ariccia and Ivanna Vladkova-Hollar, 2005, "Early Birds, Late Risers, and Sleeping Beauties: Bank Credit Growth to the Private Sector in Central and Eastern Europe and in the Balkans," *Journal of Banking and Finance*, Vol. 29, pp. 83–104.

Del Mar Cacha, Maria and R. Armando Morales, 2003, "The Role of Supervisory Tools in Addressing Bank Borrowers' Currency Mismatches," IMF Working Paper 03/219 (Washington: International Monetary Fund).

Demirgüç-Kunt, Asli and Enrica Detragiache, 1997, "The Determinants of Banking Crises: Evidence from Developing and Developed Countries," IMF Working Paper 97/106 (Washington: International Monetary Fund).

Drees, Burkhard and Ceyla Pazarbasioğlu, 1998, *The Nordic Banking Crises: Pitfalls in Financial Liberalization?* IMF Occasional Paper No. 161 (Washington: International Monetary Fund).

Duenwald, Christoph and Bikas Joshi, 2004, "Bulgaria's Credit Boom: Characteristics, Consequences, and Policy Options," in *Bulgaria: Selected Issues and Statistical Appendix*, Country Report No. 04/177 (Washington: International Monetary Fund), pp. 6–25.

Eichengreen, Barry and Carlos Arteta, 2000, "Banking Crises in Emerging Markets: Presumptions and Evidence", CIDER Working Paper No. C00–115, (Berkeley, California: University of California Center for International and Development Economics Research).

Gavin, Michael and Ricardo Hausmann, 1996, "The Roots of Banking Crises: The Macroeconomic Context," in *Banking Crises in Latin America*, ed. Ricardo Hausmann and Liliana Rojas-Suarez (Baltimore: Johns Hopkins University Press), pp. 27–63.

Goldstein, Morris, Graciela Kaminsky and Carmen Reinhart, 2000, *Assessing Financial Vulnerability: An Early Warning System for Emerging Markets* (Washington: Institute for International Economics).

Gourinchas, Pierre-Olivier, Rodrigo Valdes and Oscar Landerretche, 2001, "Lending Booms: Latin America and the World", NBER Working Paper No. 8249 (Cambridge, Massachusetts: National Bureau of Economic Research).

Hardy, Daniel C. and Ceyla Pazarbasioğlu, 1998, "Leading Indicators of Banking Crises—Was Asia Different?" IMF Working Paper 98/91 (Washington: International Monetary Fund).

Hilbers, Paul, İnci Ötker-Robe, Ceyla Pazarbasioğlu, and Gudrun Johnsen, 2005, "Assessing and Managing Rapid Credit Growth and the Role of Supervisory and Prudential Policies," IMF Working Paper 05/151 (Washington: International Monetary Fund).

Hoelscher, David S. and Marc Quintyn, 2003, "Managing Systemic Banking Crises," IMF Occasional Paper 224 (Washington: International Monetary Fund).

International Monetary Fund, 2004, *World Economic Outlook: Advancing Structural Reforms*, World Economic and Financial Surveys (Washington).

Kaminsky, Graciela and Carmen Reinhart, 1999, "The Twin Crises: The Causes of Banking and Balance of Payments Problems," *American Economic Review*, vol. 89 (June), pp. 473–500.

Levine, Ross, 2003, "Finance and Growth: Theory, Evidence, and Mechanisms" (unpublished; Washington: World Bank).

Schaechter, Andrea, 2005, "Credit Boom in Ukraine: Risks for Banking Sector Stability," in *Ukraine: Selected Issues*, Country Report No. 05/20 (Washington: International Monetary Fund), pp. 14–35.

Part Three

Regional Dimensions of Rapid Credit Growth and Perspectives from Euro Convergence Countries

16
The Role of Housing Markets and Foreign-owned Banks in the Credit Expansion in Central and Eastern Europe

Dubravko Mihaljek[1]

The past few years have seen a significant change in the bank lending landscape in Central, Eastern, and South-eastern Europe (CEE). In contrast to the late 1990s, when bank credit to the private sector was weak in most countries or even falling in those that had experienced a banking crisis, the ratio of private sector credit to GDP increased by 6 percent on average from 2000–04 in the 16 countries studied in this chapter.[2] Total bank credit (excluding credit to public enterprises and financial intermediaries) increased on average in the new EU member states from central Europe from under 40 percent of GDP in 1999, to over 50 percent in 2004; and in the countries of south-eastern Europe from 35 percent to 39 percent of GDP.

Several recent papers discuss whether credit expansion on this scale has been excessive; if so, what can be done to bring it under control; and if not, how far can the expansion proceed safely.[3] This chapter focuses on two particular aspects of the same phenomenon: first, the role of housing markets in credit growth development in CEE; and second, whether foreign-owned banks have somehow amplified the expansion of private sector credit in this region and made it more difficult for the authorities to control.

The main hypothesis is that the recent credit expansion largely reflects the rapid development of local housing markets. Housing loans have made the largest contribution to the growth of private sector credit in the majority of countries in the region over the past two to three years. Since the boom in mortgage lending has not yet been accompanied by an excessive increase in housing prices, the associated credit expansion seems to have been for the most part healthy. And as the development of housing markets still has a long way to go, property lending and overall private sector credit are not likely to slow significantly in the near term.

The main hypothesis on the foreign banks' role in credit expansion is that credit growth has not been solely the result of the activities of foreign banks; private domestic banks have also contributed to this development. The chapter further argues that foreign banks have played a leading role in improving the composition of lending and raising the efficiency level in the banking industry in CEE. However, some effects of foreign banks' activities have been less benign. As lending in CEE has been highly profitable for parent institutions from western Europe, foreign-owned banks have started to compete fiercely to increase their market share in the region. After years of pent-up demand, households were attracted by the opportunity to expand their consumption. This combination of supply and demand factors has led to buoyant growth of consumer loans, which has in turn contributed to the widening of current account deficits and the growth of external debt in some countries, as bank subsidiaries have borrowed from their headquarters in western Europe in order to expand lending in host countries. An additional concern is the growth of foreign currency lending, which might heighten longstanding external vulnerabilities in some countries.

The chapter is structured as follows. Section I sets the stage with a brief overview of trends in credit growth in the region. Section II discusses the role of housing markets in credit expansion in CEE. Section III looks at the role of foreign banks in credit expansion. Section IV concludes with some policy implications arising from the roles of housing markets and foreign-owned banks in the rapid credit growth.

I. Common trends in the credit expansion in the region

A revival in private sector credit growth has recently become a widespread phenomenon. Besides CEE, other emerging market economies as well as industrial countries have also experienced fast credit growth. For instance, domestic credit to the private sector in Latin America accelerated to about 15 percent year-on-year in 2004 and to 20 percent in 2005, while in Asian emerging economies credit has expanded by about 15 percent since 2003. In the euro area, banks expanded credit to households by more than 20 percent over the course of 2002–04, despite stagnant GDP growth.

Within CEE, there has been considerable diversity in the dynamics of bank credit. As shown in Figure 16.1, cumulative growth of private sector credit during 2002–05 exceeded 300 percent in nominal terms in half of the countries studied in this chapter, reflecting mainly the low base effect. In Bosnia and Herzegovina, Croatia, Hungary, Macedonia, and Slovenia, cumulative growth of credit over this four-year period was also high, ranging from 170 to 230 percent. But in the Czech Republic, Poland, and Slovakia, the expansion was considerably slower. In real terms, credit growth exceeded 30 percent per year in seven out of 16 countries; and in a further six countries it ranged from 10 to 20 percent (Figure 16.1). But in Slovakia, private sector credit expanded at a modest 3 percent annual real rate.

There is also considerable diversity in the composition of bank lending. It may come as a surprise that in 2004 claims on the government accounted for more than 20 percent of total bank loans in the Czech Republic, Poland, and Slovenia, not to mention Albania, Slovakia, and Turkey (Figure 16.2). Moreover, as discussed in

The Role of Housing Markets and Foreign-owned Banks 269

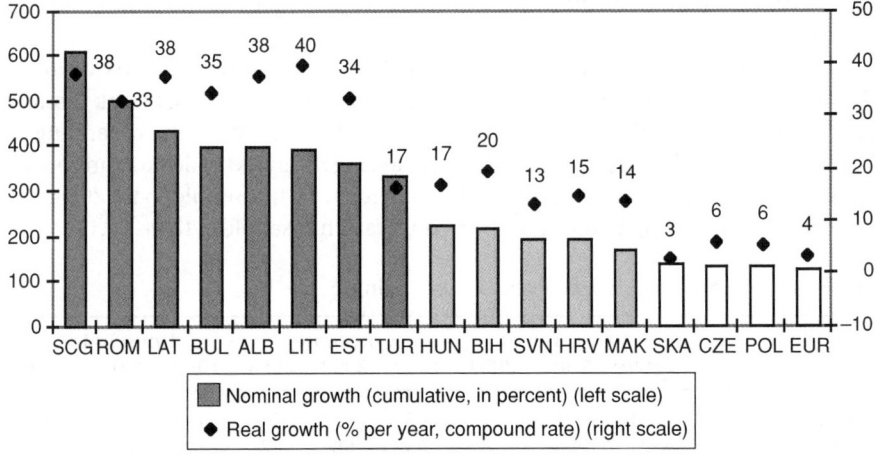

Figure 16.1 Bank Credit to the Private Sector, 2002–05

Source: IMF, International Financial Statistics; national data; author's estimates.

Note: ALB=Albania, BIH=Bosnia-Herzegovina, BUL=Bulgaria, CZE=Czech Republic; EST=Estonia, EUR=Euro area, HRV=Croatia, HUN=Hungary, LAT=Latvia, LIT=Lithuania, MAK=Macedonia, POL=Poland, ROM=Romania, SCG=Serbia-Montenegro, SVK=Slovakia, SVN=Slovenia, TUR=Turkey.

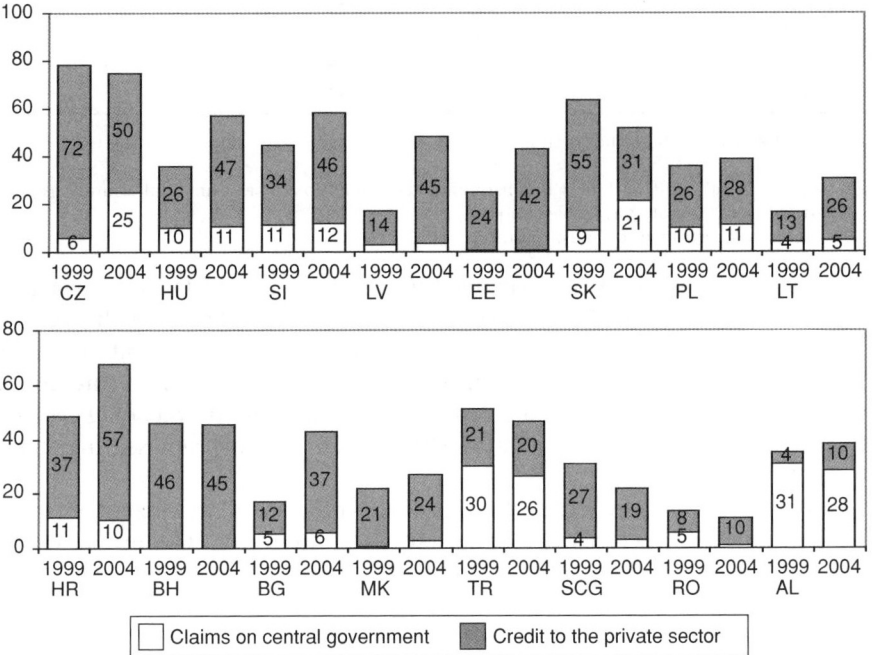

Figure 16.2 Bank Credit as a Percent of GDP

Source: IMF; national data; author's estimates.

Section III, the share of credit to the government has increased in some countries in recent years.

What are, then, some common characteristics of the growth of bank credit in CEE? One common feature is that the composition of commercial bank lending has changed very rapidly. Starting from a highly distorted structure of lending in the late 1990s—when 66 percent of loans on average were extended to enterprises, 20 percent to the government, and only 15 percent to households—by 2004, the composition of lending had clearly shifted toward households (Table 16.1).

Table 16.1 Composition of Commercial Bank Lending[a]

	Government[b]			Corporate			Household		
	1999	2003	2004	1999	2003	2004	1999	2003	2004
Bulgaria	21	8	−3	65	67	70	14	25	33
Croatia	21	8	8	65	68	42	14	25	50
Czech Republic	6	31	25	83	45	45	12	25	30
Estonia	3	6	4	71	52	50	26	43	45
Hungary	43	13	9	49	57	57	8	30	32
Latvia	11	10	9	76	63	59	13	28	32
Lithuania	29	20	4	62	63	70	8	17	26
Poland	5	6	7	62	53	46	33	31	46
Romania	35	9	5	62	68	68	3	23	27
Slovakia	29	49	49	64	37	34	7	14	17
Slovenia	22	22	22	52	57	55	26	21	23
Turkey	3	4	4	86	76	71	11	20	25
Average	*19*	*16*	*12*	*66*	*59*	*56*	*15*	*25*	*32*
Euro area	–	11	11	–	41	41	–	48	49

Source: Central banks; IMF; author's estimates.

[a] In percent of total credit, excluding interbank credit and credit to nonbank financial institutions. End of period or for 2004, latest available period.
[b] Net claims on government for most countries.

Lending to households has expanded nearly four times as fast on average as corporate lending during 2003–05 (Figure 16.3). There has been a high negative correlation (R = −0.60) between the growth of these two types of credit: the faster the growth of credit to households, the slower the growth of credit to enterprises. Yet only in Croatia, Estonia, and Poland has the composition of lending evolved closer to that found in the euro area, with household loans representing about one-half of total loans.

As will be discussed in Section III, this shift reflects, to a large extent, changes in the ownership structure of banking systems in the region. During the 1990s, households were largely ignored by the banking sector. However, this changed after the main banks had been sold to foreign institutions and started to compete for market share, introducing many new products and pushing down interest rates in the process. The increased supply of credit was matched by rising demand, as real household incomes have grown rapidly in recent years.

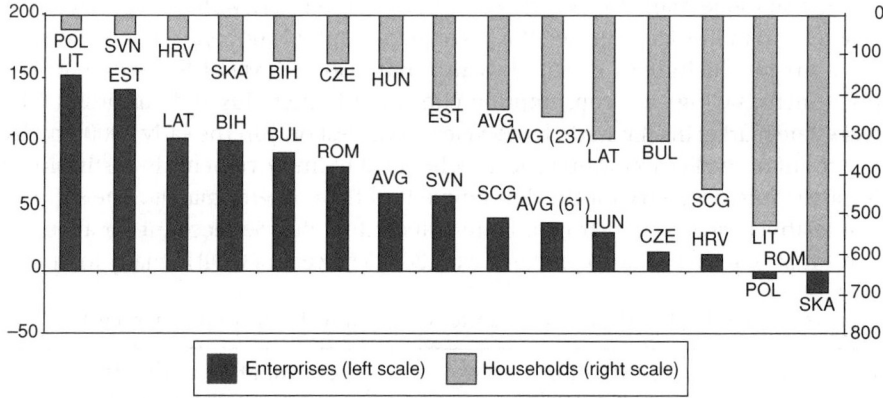

Figure 16.3 Real Credit Growth, 2003–05 (cumulative growth rate, in percent)

Source: National data; author's estimates.

Arcalean et al (2005) discuss other factors that contributed to the credit expansion in the region. These include the transition and catch-up effects related to financial deepening; policy-related factors including the nature of exchange rate regimes—countries with fixed or quasi-fixed exchange rate regimes have generally experienced faster credit growth dynamics than countries with more flexible regimes; as well as cyclical factors beyond those mentioned above, in particular strong economic growth in recent years. While certainly relevant, many of these factors have also been at play in episodes of rapid credit growth in other regions. What is specific to CEE, however, is the relationship between the development of housing markets and private sector credit growth.

II. Housing markets in CEE countries

One common feature of credit growth in the region is the large contribution of housing loans. As shown in Table 16.2, housing loans expanded on average by over 50 percent per year and contributed on average over 55 percent to the growth of total private sector credit during 2003–05. During this period, corporate lending was the dominant driver of credit growth only in Lithuania and Slovenia. Elsewhere, the contribution of household loans—and housing loans in particular—was larger than (or about equal to) that of corporate loans. Consumer loans made a larger contribution than housing loans only in Bulgaria and Croatia.

The recent expansion of private sector credit in CEE thus appears to be primarily related to the growth of housing loans. This in turn raises several questions about the nature of the property markets in CEE. Why is the housing market developing so fast so late in the transition process? Is the development of the housing market—and, hence, the associated credit growth—sustainable at the current pace? And how far might it continue without causing problems at the macroeconomic level and giving rise to challenges for financial stability?

The real estate market is usually one of the most closely watched sectors of the economy in industrial countries. It plays an important role not only because housing accounts for the bulk of personal wealth, but also because of linkages with key investment, saving, and consumption choices of households and businesses. The real estate market in CEE started to develop in earnest only in the early 2000s, partly as a result of the EU accession process, which led to improvements in institutional infrastructure necessary for the development of the property market. The sector is still relatively small—construction and real estate industries account for about 15 percent of GDP on average, compared with 20–25 percent of GDP in many industrial

Table 16.2 Housing Loans and Private Sector Credit Growth, 2003–05 (in percent)

Countries	Growth of private sector credit[a]				Contribution to growth of private sector credit[b]			
			Household				Household	
	Corporate	Total	Housing	Consumer	Corporate	Total	Housing	Consumer
Bulgaria	28.7	63.3	114.8	51.5	50.5	49.5	17.3	32.1
Croatia	8.4	16.7	23.3	13.7	22.4	62.7	24.9	37.9
Czech Republic	11.1	32.3	39.6	23.3	10.7	89.3	69.9	19.4
Estonia	30.5	48.1	56.1	29.9	48.8	51.2	42.2	9.0
Hungary	12.3	20.5	26.1	44.2	40.8	59.2	43.9	15.8
Latvia	16.4	53.2	60.0	42.4	43.0	57.0	35.5	6.4
Lithuania	27.6	67.1	68.9	3.3	59.0	41.0	40.7	0.3
Romania	30.8	64.8	67.8	42.9	50.7	49.3	46.1	3.2
Serbia	25.2	61.4	–	–	48.4	51.6	–	–
Slovakia	3.7	35.4	34.9	15.6	27.0	73.0	51.7	15.2
Slovenia	40.0	105.0	–	–	78.0	22.0	–	–
Average	21.3	52.3	54.6	29.6	43.6	55.1	41.4	15.5

Source: Central banks; author's estimates.

[a] Annual growth rate of private sector credit (excluding credit to financial intermediaries). Data for 2005 are for the latest month available.
[b] Percentage contribution to the annual growth rate of private sector credit; average for 2003–05 (for Slovakia, 2004–05). Based on monthly data.

countries. Research on the economics of the property market is not developed, and statistical data on the sector are very patchy.[4]

The key obstacle to the development of housing markets in CEE in the 1990s was the inadequate institutional and regulatory framework for the property market. Privatization of housing from the socialist period was mostly completed during the 1990s, but missing or unclear land and property titles, the difficulty of enforcing foreclosure of residential properties, and the lack of credit registries limited the supply of housing and of housing finance. In addition, the supply of new homes was constrained during the 1990s by the exit of the public sector from housing construction; slow growth of private property developers; and inadequate spatial plans.[5] In the secondary market, supply was constrained because of the poor quality of many existing homes and their uneven regional distribution (shortage of housing in large cities and surplus in small towns). These factors at the same time put pressure on housing demand, which was strong despite high owner-occupancy rates.[6]

The EU accession and the adoption of acquis communautaire accelerated the removal of legal impediments to property transactions and housing finance. Once the institutional preconditions for the real estate market fell into place, the supply of housing and of mortgage products started to improve relatively quickly. Private construction firms significantly expanded development of new housing, while many existing properties started to appear on the market after their owners had obtained clean property titles. On the financing side, once reforms in legislation and the judiciary made it easier for creditors to seize real estate collateral, many banks started to provide longer-term housing loans; the loan-to-value ratios increased; and mortgage rates started to decline.

A final impetus to the development of housing markets came from the demand side and included demographic factors, rapid growth of household incomes and—somewhat unusually for the property market—strong external demand. Most countries in CEE experienced small baby booms in the 1970s and the early 1980s, often following episodes of political repression under the communist regime. As the 1970s and the 1980s generations are gradually nearing their prime earning age, they are entering the housing market and providing a strong boost to demand, especially for quality housing.

Another factor adding to demand pressures in recent years is increased demand for second homes by residents of EU-15 countries. This phenomenon partly also reflects demographic factors, and partly the low interest rate environment of recent years. As the baby boomers (of the late 1940s and 1950s) from northern Europe near their retirement age, they are increasingly looking for second homes in southern Europe, where they could spend part of the year during retirement. Second homes in countries such as France, Italy, and Spain have become fairly expensive in recent years, so many households have turned their attention to properties in Bulgaria, Croatia, Romania, and Turkey. In addition, investment in commercial real estate by large international property developers is rising fast.[7]

Against this background, it is not surprising that housing loans have expanded at annual rates of 40–100 percent in several countries in the region since 2003. But despite the rapid growth of housing loans and strong demand for housing, house prices have not risen excessively so far. In nominal terms, house prices in Croatia, the Czech Republic, Hungary, and Poland—countries for which limited data on house prices are available—have increased on average by about 10 percent per year since 2000.

Moreover, as indicated in Figure 16.4, residential property prices have not been rising continuously over the past six years, but have occasionally also decreased, by up to 10 percent per year. One reason for the relatively slow growth of property prices is that access to housing finance remains difficult for an average family. Mortgage rates are still relatively high in most countries in CEE and loans provided with a fixed interest rate are still rare. With some exceptions, housing loans are typically denominated in foreign currencies or indexed to a particular exchange rate (usually the euro, but increasingly also the Swiss franc), so that households bear the currency risk, a factor which is constraining demand for housing loans by lower-income households.

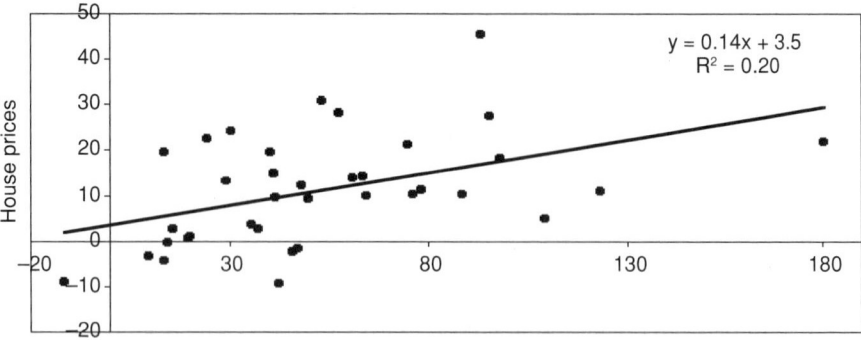

Figure 16.4 House Prices and Housing Loans, 1997–2005[a] (annual percentage changes)

Source: National data; author's estimates.

[a] Annual percentage changes; data for Croatia, the Czech Republic, Estonia, Hungary, Lithuania, and Portugal.

The fastest increases in house prices have been observed in large cities such as Budapest, Bucharest, Prague, Warsaw, and Zagreb, as well as in coastal areas of Bulgaria, Croatia, Romania, and Turkey. The growth of property prices has accelerated where foreign demand has strengthened and the regime for property sales to nonresidents has been liberalized. Constrained supply of quality housing and signs that the construction industry in several countries may have started to hit capacity constraints suggest that underlying price pressures are strong and could manifest themselves openly if the development of the real estate market becomes disorderly.[8]

Given the importance of the housing market for investment, saving, and consumption choices of households and the rapidly growing size of the mortgage portfolios of financial institutions, it seems appropriate for central banks to closely monitor developments in real estate markets. As shown in Figure 16.4, mortgage lending and residential property price increases are highly correlated. The direction of causality is not clear: rising house prices may have made it necessary for households to take on larger mortgages, but they may also have induced some individuals to invest in property, thus fueling speculative demand. At the same time, the greater availability of housing loans may have been the spur to the growth of house prices, especially in areas where housing supply is lagging behind demand. As in many industrial countries, a major part of the effort to monitor developments in the housing market will have to be focused on developing reliable statistics on the property market.

III. The role of foreign-owned banks in credit expansion

That foreign-owned banks should play a major role in credit expansion in CEE would seem to be more or less obvious, given these banks' dominant position in banking systems in the region. As shown in Table 16.3, foreign-owned banks accounted on average for 69 percent of total banking sector assets in 16 countries studied in this chapter, their share rising to 80 percent or more in Albania, Bulgaria, Croatia, the Czech Republic, Estonia, Hungary, Lithuania, and Slovakia in 2004.

Table 16.3 Structure of the Commercial Banking Sector, 2004

Countries[a]	Number of banks	Market share[b]				Ratio to GDP[c]		
		Foreign-owned banks	Private domestic banks	State-owned banks	Top five banks	Total assets	Private sector credit	Household deposits
Croatia	37	91	6	3	74	109	62	60
Latvia	23	47	50	3	63	96	51	16
Slovenia	19	36	40	24	64	89	48	51
Bosnia-Herzegovina	33	66	22	12	61	73	45	41
Hungary	35	83	16	3	53	79	45	40
Estonia	9	99	1	–	99	94	42	20
Bulgaria	35	83	15	2	55	66	37	39
Czech Rep.	35	96	1	3	63	107	32	64
Poland	54	68	8	24	50	65	31	39
Lithuania	14	96	4	–	82	39	29	14
Slovakia	21	96	–	4	67	83	24	54
Macedonia	21	47	51	2	76	57	23	30
Turkey	35	3	57	40	60	76	20	48
Romania	39	62	31	7	60	38	18	24
Serbia	43	37	28	35	47	39	17	20
Albania	16	89	5	6	77	54	9	47
Total/Average	469	69	22	12	66	73	33	38
Euro area	2,287	24	74	2	54	206	100	73

Source: ECB; Bank Austria Creditanstalt; national data; author's estimates.

[a] Ordered according to the private sector credit/GDP ratio.
[b] As a percentage of total assets.
[c] In percent.

It is only in Turkey that foreign-owned banks have not been prominent, although they have yet to make major inroads in Latvia, Macedonia, Serbia, and Slovenia. It is interesting in this respect that Latvia and Serbia have recently been at the top in terms of the rate of credit expansion (see Figure 16.1 above). A comparison of foreign banks' shares in total banking sector assets with the shares of private sector credit in GDP indicates that these two variables are basically uncorrelated (Figure 16.5). While other measures might reveal a stronger relationship between foreign banks' presence and private sector credit growth, one should recognize that private domestic banks and state-owned banks—where they still exist—have also participated in the recent credit expansion.[9] For instance, over the past five years private domestic banks were leading the credit expansion in Hungary, and state-owned banks in Turkey.

It seems therefore that the foreign-owned banks have contributed to the credit growth through more indirect channels. First, they have been instrumental in

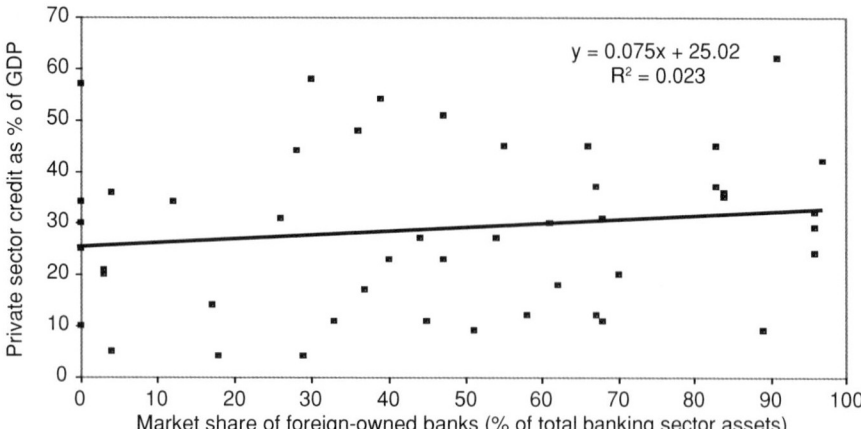

Figure 16.5 Foreign-owned Banks and Credit Growth in CEE, 1997, 2000, and 2004

Source: Bank Austria—Creditanstalt; author's estimates.

shifting the composition of loan portfolios from the highly biased structure inherited from the socialist period, to a structure closer to that found in the euro area. As with credit growth, it is not only foreign banks that have been instrumental in bringing about this shift. For instance, the share of credit to the government in total bank lending increased in central European countries that joined the EU in 2004 (by 4.5 percent of GDP on average between 1999 and 2004, to 11 percent of GDP), while in south-eastern Europe, the share of credit to the government in total bank lending declined on average by 1.5 percent of GDP since 1999, to 11 percent of GDP in 2004, even though foreign banks in the former set of countries accounted for a larger share of intermediation than those in the latter countries (77 percent versus 60 percent of total assets, respectively).[10]

Second, foreign-owned banks have been actively involved in the development of new banking products in the region. When they were established as part of the privatization process—typically through purchases of local state-owned banks—foreign-owned banks inherited a large portfolio of loans to the government and the corporate sector. Like private domestic banks, many foreign banks initially focused on the corporate sector. But as large firms strengthened their financial position and over time started to diversify their sources of finance by issuing bonds, equities and borrowing directly from banks abroad at lower interest rates, foreign-owned banks in CEE were more or less forced to turn to the household sector in search of business. More recently, as competition in consumer loan and mortgage markets has intensified, foreign-owned banks have turned to the next underserved segment of the market: small and medium-sized enterprises (SMEs).[11]

Third, in addition to stimulating competition and helping to develop new products, foreign-owned banks have made a major contribution to the improvement of efficiency in the banking industry in the region. Reflecting restructuring and better risk management, the share of nonperforming loans (NPLs) was reduced by more than 50 percent between 1999 and 2004; a high capital adequacy ratio was maintained (16.5 percent on average in 2004); provisioning against loan losses increased; and profitability improved to a level comparable with that of banks in countries such as Austria (Table 16.4).

Table 16.4 Prudential Indicators (in percent)

Countries[a]	Nonperforming loans[b]		Capital adequacy[c]		Loan-loss provisions[d]		Return on equity		Return on assets	
	1999	2004	1999	2004	2000	2004	1999	2004	1999	2004
Estonia	1.7	0.3	16.1	13.4	...	...	9.2	13.8	1.4	1.6
Czech Rep.	22.0	4.1	13.6	12.6	46.8	69.4	−4.3	23.4	−0.3	1.3
Lithuania	12.5	2.3	17.4	12.3	34.6	21.6	1.1	13.4	0.5	1.3
Slovakia	23.7	5.4	29.5	19.0	75.1	89.1	−36.5	11.9	−2.3	1.0
Croatia	11.8	4.5	20.6	14.1	79.9	60.3	4.8	16.6	0.7	1.4
Bulgaria	29.0	7.1	43.0	16.6	65.9	49.0	20.9	20.0	2.5	2.1
Hungary	3.6	2.7	14.9	11.2	57.0	51.1	7.1	25.2	0.6	2.0
Poland	13.2	15.5	13.2	15.6	40.5	58.0	12.9	17.6	0.9	1.4
Bosnia and Herzegovina[e]	9.9	3.5	26.3	18.0	64.2	96.1	−5.8	5.6	−1.3	0.6
Romania	35.4	8.1	17.9	18.8	–	34.3	−15.3	19.3	−1.5	2.5
Latvia	6.0	1.1	16.0	11.7	74.1	99.1	11.2	21.4	1.0	1.7
Macedonia	41.3	13.2	28.7	23.0	–	76.2	3.5	6.2	0.8	1.1
Serbia and Montenegro[f]	21.6	22.8	25.6	27.9	–	–	−60.6	−5.3	−8.4	−1.2
Slovenia	5.2	5.7	14.0	11.0	45.3	34.0	7.8	14.2	0.8	1.1
Turkey	10.5	6.0	8.2	28.8	59.8	88.1	33.1	17.4	3.3	2.5
Average	16.5	6.8	20.3	16.9	58.5	63.6	−0.7	14.7	−0.1	1.4
Memo: Austria	1.7	1.5	13.9	14.7	–	–	6.9	9.3	0.3	1.5

Source: Central banks; IMF; author's estimates.

[a] Ordered according to the share of foreign-owned banks in total banking sector assets shown in Table 16.3 (from 80–99 percent in Estonia, the Czech Republic, Lithuania, Slovakia, Croatia, Bulgaria, and Hungary; below 70 percent in other countries).
[b] As percent of total loans.
[c] Risk-weighted capital-asset ratios.
[d] Ratio of bank provisions for loan losses to nonperforming loans.
[e] End-2000 instead of 1999.
[f] End-2002 instead of 1999.

It should be noted that some of the improvements in prudential indicators probably reflect cyclical factors. For instance, many loans extended during the recent period of rapid credit growth have yet to mature, so the NPL ratios recorded at the end of 2004 may not fully reflect the quality of banks' loan portfolios. Part of the improvement in NPL ratios also reflects the fact that many banks—especially the former state-owned banks that were sold to foreign strategic investors—unloaded a significant portion of their NPL portfolios to asset management companies and other vehicles for resolution of bank distress.

One should recognize, however, that the increasing presence of foreign-owned banks in CEE has also been associated with some less benign effects. First, despite improvements in prudential indicators, it is doubtful that foreign-owned banks can continue to expand their balance sheets in CEE by 20 percent per year or more without running into funding difficulties. In many countries, deposits of residents expanded at annual rates of 20–40 percent from 2000 through mid-2002, making it possible to finance credit expansion from domestic sources. However, after the effects of the euro changeover in 2002 have dissipated, the growth of time, savings, and foreign currency deposits has decelerated in most countries. At the same time, foreign liabilities jumped sharply, implying that commercial banks have financed the continuing expansion of domestic credit to a great extent from foreign sources. The situation depicted in Figure 16.6—significantly faster growth of foreign liabilities than residents' deposits, implying rising external debt of the private sector—is not sustainable over a long period. It is therefore not surprising that several central banks (including those in Bulgaria, Croatia, and Romania) have taken precautionary measures to restrict the growth of consumer and mortgage loans over the past two years.

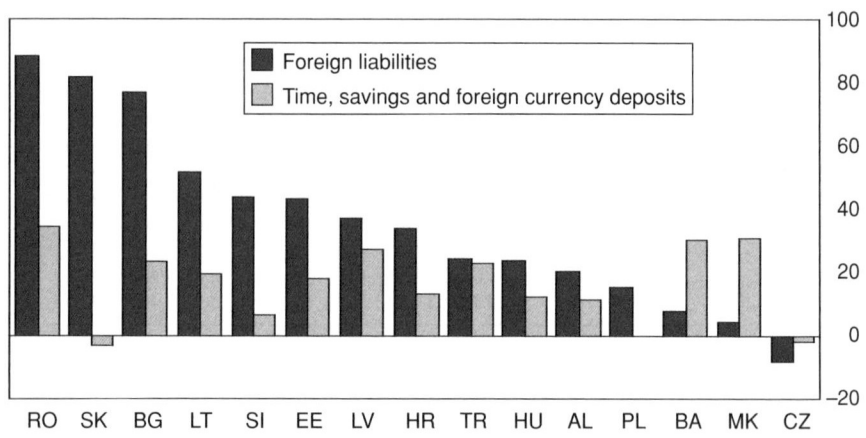

Figure 16.6 Commercial Bank Liabilities, 2002–05 (Annual changes in percent, quarterly average)

Source: IMF; author's estimates.

Note: AL=Albania; BA=Bosnia and Herzegovina; BG=Bulgaria; CZ=the Czech Republic; EE=Estonia; HR=Croatia; HU=Hungary; LT=Lithuania; LV=Latvia; MK=Macedonia; PL=Poland; RO=Romania; SI=Slovenia; SK=Slovakia; TR=Turkey.

A second concern is the rapid growth of foreign currency loans to domestic residents, including to households, for the purchase of housing.[12] Foreign currency borrowing is often rational from an individual borrower's perspective, because interest rates on foreign currency loans are lower than those on local currency loans and most currencies in the region are expected to strengthen against the euro in the medium term. But as most households and corporate borrowers taking foreign currency loans do not earn foreign currency income, a large currency mismatch might arise on the aggregate private sector balance sheet. In particular, commercial banks, whose open foreign currency positions are limited by prudential regulations, are nevertheless exposed to foreign exchange risk via the credit risk, i.e., the risk stemming from the deterioration in bank customers' ability to service foreign exchange debt in the event of adverse exchange rate movements.

Reflecting these concerns, central banks in Croatia, Hungary, and Poland recently launched media campaigns to increase public awareness of exchange rate risks involved in foreign currency borrowing. In Poland, the central bank also asked commercial banks to strengthen their foreign currency and property lending standards; while in Croatia and Romania central banks raised liquidity requirements for foreign currency loans.

Third, aggressive marketing of consumer loans may have contributed to the widening of external current account deficits and rising household indebtedness.[13] Initially, consumer loans—in particular car loans—have indeed expanded very rapidly and contributed to large current account deficits in many countries. However, judging from the experience of countries such as Croatia and Poland, which went through several consumer lending cycles over the past ten years, this type of credit growth tends to be self-correcting. As the stock of consumer durables is renewed and household indebtedness rises, households reduce their aggregate borrowing and adjust consumption, facilitating smooth reversal of current account deficits (see Mihaljek, 2004).

Whether the same tendency applies to any current account deficits and household indebtedness arising from the growth of mortgage loans remains to be seen. In most countries in CEE total household debt remains well below the levels that are common in western Europe. For instance, the ratio of household debt to GDP ranged in 2004 from 5–6 percent in Romania and Turkey, to 25–30 percent in Croatia and Estonia, compared with 50 percent in the euro area.[14] While many households in the region lack experience in managing their debt and payment discipline is low in several countries, the past 15 years of transition have also demonstrated that households in CEE have considerable capacity to adjust consumption and saving behavior under adverse economic circumstances.

IV. Policy implications

This chapter has argued that the recent credit expansion has largely reflected the rapid development of housing markets in the region, and that foreign-owned banks have been a major force behind the rapid credit growth. It also argued, however, that the latter occurred perhaps more by changing the composition of lending, introducing new products, and improving the efficiency of financial intermediation, than by increasing the quantity of loans, as other domestic banks have also been actively involved in the credit expansion per se. What are the main implications of these findings for financial stability and the supervisory regime?[15]

The impact on financial stability is difficult to assess at the moment given that the credit cycle has not yet run its full course, especially with respect to mortgage loans and the housing market. Key issues ahead will be: (i) how the banking system and the corporate and household sectors adjust to the normalization of global interest rates that is currently under way, and (ii) whether exchange rates in CEE remain on a broadly appreciating trend vis-à-vis the euro. Regular stress tests conducted by central banks indicate that commercial banks in the Czech Republic, Hungary, and Poland appear fairly resistant to large exchange rate depreciations or sharp interest rate increases.[16] As most banks have built up reserves and most of them are foreign-owned, the risks to the banking sector appear limited at the moment.

Regarding the impact on the supervisory regime, the presence of foreign banks has generally led the domestic supervisory authorities to upgrade the quality and increase the size of their staff in order to supervise the more sophisticated activities and new products that are being introduced by foreign banks. In addition, supervisory authorities in the region are cooperating closely with home-country supervisory authorities.

One should keep in mind, however, that foreign bank affiliates are often of marginal importance from the perspective of parent institutions and home-country supervisory authorities, but might well be systemically important for the host country. One issue that arises in this context is what would happen if a foreign-owned subsidiary that was systemically important locally ran into problems. There have been cases where a parent company helped its subsidiary immediately, without asking host country authorities for any assistance. But there have also been some cases of a parent abandoning its subsidiary (e.g., the case of Riječka Banka in Croatia). The response seems to depend mainly on the financial health of the parent. If the parent is in weak shape, it might care less about reputation costs and decide to abandon its subsidiary.

A related issue in this context is the possible conversion of systemically important subsidiaries of foreign-owned banks into branches. This development is facilitated in the EU by the adoption of the single EU banking passport. But the issue is more general, as the centralization of the decision making process in global financial institutions has led to a system in which subsidiaries operate more or less like branches (see Domanski, 2005). Again, the issue is whether such systemically important branches (or quasi-branches) might be abandoned in a period of distress, and how the supervisory authorities in the host country might prepare for such an eventuality.

Developments in the global banking industry are important for market discipline and supervision in emerging market host countries for yet another reason: mergers between parent institutions in industrial countries might result in a significant increase in concentration in host countries. For instance, the merger between Unicredito and HVB has implications for competition in Croatian and Polish banking markets, where these two parents own some of the largest domestic commercial banks. This raises questions about the best approach that the supervisory authorities could take in such circumstances.

The delisting of foreign-owned subsidiaries from local stock exchanges raises a different set of concerns. The delisting has occurred, for instance, in Croatia, the Czech Republic, and Poland. In Croatia, it involved the largest commercial bank in the country; in the Czech Republic, it involved one institution with a 12 percent share in market capitalization; and in Poland, three institutions with a combined share in stock market capitalization of 5 percent. Delistings on this scale can lead to a considerable loss of market prices and scrutiny by independent analysts. In addition, the disclosure of timely and meaningful information about developments in institutions might be impaired, making it necessary to significantly improve information flows from parent banks to markets, and from home supervisors to host authorities.

These considerations suggest that the rapid credit growth will continue to draw the attention of policymakers, economists, and industry analysts in the future. To date, the expansion of private sector credit in CEE has been mostly a benign phenomenon. But given the speed of financial deepening in the region, the time when credit growth becomes a normal cyclical phenomenon and raises the usual concerns about macroeconomic and financial stability might not be too far away.

Notes

1. Bank for International Settlements (BIS). Helpful comments from David Archer, İnci Ötker-Robe, and the Sinaia conference participants are gratefully acknowledged.
2. The countries studied in the chapter are eight new EU member states from central Europe (the Czech Republic, Estonia, Hungary, Latvia, Lithuania, Poland, Slovakia, and Slovenia) and eight EU candidate and potential candidate countries from south-eastern Europe (Albania, Bosnia and Herzegovina, Bulgaria, Croatia, Macedonia, Serbia and Montenegro, Romania, and Turkey).
3. See Arcalean et al (2005); Arpa et al (2005), Backé and Zumer (2006), Backé et al (2005), Boissay et al (2005), Coricelli et al (2005), Cottarelli et al (2005); Duenwald et al (2005), and Hilbers et al (2005).
4. This section draws on Mihaljek (2005) and references therein.
5. In the late 1990s, the number of newly completed dwellings per 1,000 inhabitants ranged from 1 to 3 units per year in CEE, compared with 7–13 units in western Europe (OECD, 2002).
6. In Bulgaria, Estonia, Hungary, Slovenia and Romania, the ratio of owner-occupied housing exceeds 90 percent, while in Croatia it exceeds 80 percent. For comparison, the share of owner-occupied housing in western Europe ranges from 38 percent in Germany to 80 percent in Ireland (OECD, 2002).
7. For instance, CB Richard Ellis (2005, p. 1) notes that the property investment markets in CEE continue to perform "exceptionally well," with the company's own investment of EUR 3.9 billion in 2004 growing by 64 percent year-on-year; and that investors looking at CEE who would only consider offices three years ago were now "so anxious to buy that they were open to the industrial, hotel, and residential sectors."
8. Hours worked and in particular wages in the construction sector in the Baltic states, Bulgaria, Slovakia, and Romania were growing at an annual rate of 10–20 percent during 2004 and the first half of 2005.
9. In a broader emerging market context, for every 10 percentage-point increase in the credit to GDP ratio, credit by private domestic banks has expanded on average by 8 percent of GDP over the past ten years; credit by foreign-owned banks by about 1.5 percent of GDP; and credit by state-owned banks by about 0.5 percent of GDP (Mihaljek, 2006).
10. Foreign banks in the Czech Republic and Slovakia in particular increased their lending to the government relative to the private sector (see Figure 16.2).
11. In terms of the growth rate, loans to SMEs have rivaled mortgage loans in the Czech Republic, Hungary, and Poland in the past two years; see Czech National Bank (2005a, 2005b); National Bank of Hungary (2005a, 2005b); and National Bank of Poland (2005).

12. See Backé and Zumer (2005) and Bokor and Pellény (2005) for a description of developments in foreign currency lending.
13. This concern is particularly strong in some media and among interest groups opposing foreign-owned banks. They typically argue that, by extending credit to the households and corporations, owners of foreign banks are serving primarily the interests of industry in their home countries, given that much of the bank credit is used for imports of consumer durables and other manufactured goods from western Europe.
14. See Coricelli et al (2005). The ratio of debt to disposable income in CEE was 18 percent on average in 2004 (rising to 80 percent in the case of Croatia), compared with 75 percent in the euro area.
15. This section draws on Mihaljek (2006).
16. See Czech National Bank (2005a, 2005b); National Bank of Hungary (2005b); and National Bank of Poland (2005).

Bibliography

Arcalean, Calin, Oscar Calvo-Gonzalez, Csaba Móré, Adrian van Rixtel, Adalbert Winkler, and Tina Zumer, 2005, "The Causes and Nature of the Rapid Growth of Bank Credit, with Particular Emphasis on Central, Eastern and South-eastern European Countries," paper presented at the IMF and National Bank of Romania Conference on the Rapid Growth of Bank Credit to the Private Sector, Sinaia, Romania, October 7–8.

Arpa, Marcus, Thomas Reininger and Zoltan Walko, 2005, "Can Banking Intermediation in CEE Ever Catch up with the Euro Area?" *Focus on European Economic Integration*, no. 2/05, pp. 110–33. <www.oenb.at>.

Backé, Peter and Tina Zumer, 2005, "Developments in Credit to the Private Sector Growth in CEE : Emerging from Financial Repression—A Comparative Overview," *Focus on European Economic Integration*, no. 2/05, pp. 83–109. <www.oenb.at>.

Backé, Peter, Balázs Égert and Tina Zumer, 2005, "Credit Growth in Central and South-eastern Europe: Emerging from Financial Repression to New (Over)Shooting Stars?" Unpublished manuscript, Austrian National Bank, December.

Bank Austria Creditanstalt, 2004, "Banking in Central and South-eastern Europe," April, <www.ba-ca.com>.

—— 2005, "Banking in South-Eastern Europe: On the Move," September, <www.ba-ca.com>.

Barisitz, Stephan, 2005, "Banking in CEE since the Turn of the Millennium—An Overview of Structural Modernization in Ten Countries," *Focus on European Economic Integration*, no. 2/05, pp. 58–82. <www.oenb.at>.

Boissay, Frederic, Oscar Calvo-Gonzalez and Thomas Koźluk, 2005, "Using Fundamentals to Identify Episodes of 'Excessive' Credit Growth in Central and Eastern Europe," paper presented at the IMF and National Bank of Romania Conference on the Rapid Growth of Private Sector Credit in Central and South-eastern Europe, Sinaia, Romania, October 7–8.

Bokor, László and Gábor Pellény, 2005, "Foreign Currency Denominated Borrowing in Central Europe: Trends, Factors and Consequences," *ICEG EC Opinion*, no. 5, February. <www.icegec.hu>.

CB Richard Ellis, 2005, "CEE Investment: Market View," First Quarter. <www.cbre.com/cee>.

Coricelli, Fabrizio, Fabio Muci and Debora Revoltella, 2005, "The New Europe Household Lending Market," paper presented at the Austrian National Bank Conference on European Economic Integration, November 14–15.

Cottarelli, Carlo, Giovanni Dell'Ariccia and Ivanna Vladkova-Hollar, 2005, "Early Birds, Late Risers, and Sleeping Beauties: Bank Credit Growth to the Private Sector in Central and South-eastern Europe and in the Balkans," *Journal of Banking and Finance*, vol. 29(1), pp. 83–104.

Czech National Bank, 2005a, "Banking Supervision 2004." <www.cnb.cz>.

——, 2005b, "Financial Stability Report 2004." <www.cnb.cz>.
Demirgüç-Kunt, Asli and Enrica Detragiache, 1997, "The Determinants of Banking Crises: Evidence from Developing and Developed Countries," IMF Working Paper No. 97/106. <www.imf.org>.
Domanski, Dietrich, 2005, "Foreign Banks in Emerging Market Economies: Changing Players, Changing Issues," *BIS Quarterly Review*, December. <www.bis.org>.
Duenwald, Christoph, Nikolay Gueorguiev and Andrea Schaechter, 2005: "Too Much of a Good Thing?, Credit Booms in Transition Economies: The Cases of Bulgaria, Romania, and Ukraine," IMF Working Paper No. 05/128, June. <www.imf.org>.
European Central Bank, 2005, "Banking Structures in the New EU Member States", January. <www.ecb.int>.
Hilbers, Paul, İnci Ötker-Robe, Ceyla Pazarbasioğlu and Gudrun Johnsen, 2005, "Assessing and Managing Rapid Credit Growth and the Role of Supervisory and Prudential Policies," IMF Working Paper No. 05/151, July. <www.imf.org>.
Mihaljek, Dubravko, 2004, "Challenges to Macroeconomic Stability: A Speed Limit on Croatia's Accession to the European Union?" *Financial Theory and Practice*, vol. 28(1), March, pp. 93–119. <www.ijf.hr>.
——, 2005, "Free Movement of Capital, the Real Estate Market and Tourism: A Blessing or a Curse for Croatia on its Way to the European Union?" in Katarina Ott (ed.), *Croatian Accession to the European Union*, vol. 3, Zagreb, Institute of Public Finance and Friedrich Ebert Stiftung, April. <www.ijf.hr>.
——, 2006, "Privatisation, Consolidation and the Increased Role of Foreign Banks," in *The Banking System in Emerging Economies: How Much Progress Has Been Made?* BIS Papers No. 28, August, pp. 41–66. <www.bis.org>.
National Bank of Hungary, 2005a, "Senior Loan Officer Survey on Bank Lending Practices," August. <www.mnb.hu>.
——, 2005b, "Report on Financial Stability," April. <http://english.mnb.hu>.
National Bank of Poland, 2005, "Summary Evaluation of the Financial Situation of Polish Banks 2004", July. <www.nbp.pl>.
OECD, 2002, "Housing Finance in Transition Economies." Paris: OECD. <www.oecd.org>.

17
Regional Dimensions of Dealing with Rapid Credit Growth: Perspectives from Greece (1998–2005)

Nicos Kamberoglou and Nikolaos Stavrianou[1]

Greece has recently entered a period of rapid increase of bank loans to the private sector, an episode that leads to a significant transformation of financial institutions' asset structure and an increase in the indebtedness of enterprises and, in particular, households. Rapid credit expansion is of particular interest to the central bank because of the implications this may have, both for price stability, and for the overall credit risk assumed by banks.

The chapter aims at a short examination of these developments and is organized as follows. Section I provides a description of the evolution of credit aggregates during the period 1998–2005; Section II discusses some factors underlying the rapid credit expansion to the private sector; Section III describes a series of measures the Bank of Greece (BoG) took as a response to credit developments, gives a brief overview of the prudential supervision framework, and provides an overview of recent developments in the Greek banking industry; Section IV offers some concluding remarks.

I. The evolution of loans to the private sector

A key feature of the Greek financial system throughout the period 1998–2005 is the rapid expansion of banking loans to the private sector. The annual growth rate[2] of these loans is quite close to 20 percent (see Figure 17.1) and reached a peak value of 27.5 percent in March 2001. Although credit growth has decelerated since then, it remains at high levels compared with the euro area average, with a differential close to ten percentage points per year.

Credit growth was relatively weak in the last quarter of 1999 and until June 2000, but picked up considerably in late 2000 and remained at very high levels until February 2002. The evolution of credit can be related to Greece's entry into

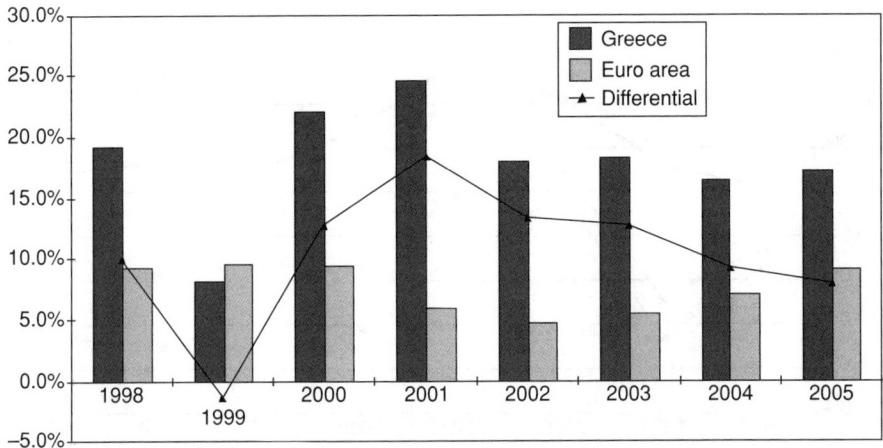

Figure 17.1 Loans to the Private Sector (annual growth rate, year-end)

Source: BoG, and European Central Bank (ECB).

the euro area on January 1, 2001 and to specific measures taken by the BoG in the run-up to euro area membership. The BoG, which had been monitoring credit developments very closely on a continuous basis, saw credit developments at the beginning of 1999 as a major threat to price stability and the fulfillment of the convergence criteria that would allow participation in the euro area in 2001. It decided to impose severe quantitative restrictions on the rate of increase of bank loans to the private sector. The measures were quite effective, as indicated by the very low growth of credit in December 1999 (even lower than the euro area average). The restrictions were lifted in March 2000, since they were only seen as a temporary ad hoc measure and not compatible with the way monetary policy is carried out in the euro area. The lifting of the restrictions clearly led to an immediate jump in credit growth in late 2000.

Specific policy measures are thus behind the abrupt ups and downs of credit growth during the period 1998–2000. However, abstracting from these short-term dynamics, one is left with the general picture of a rapid credit expansion to the private sector. A closer look at the sectoral distribution of banking loans indicates that it is mainly loans to households rather than businesses that are behind the credit growth (Figure 17.2). More specifically, the average annual rate of increase of loans to households during the period 2000–05 has exceeded 30 percent. Although some deceleration has been observed in 2004, it is mainly due to technical reasons, in particular, the removal of significant amounts of housing and consumer loans from banks' balance sheets, as banks have started carrying out securitization operations from mid-2003. By the end of 2005, the outstanding amount of these securitized loans was EUR 3.2 billion—4.9 percent of the outstanding amount of loans to households, which led to a reduction of 4 percentage points in the December 2005 growth rate of these loans.

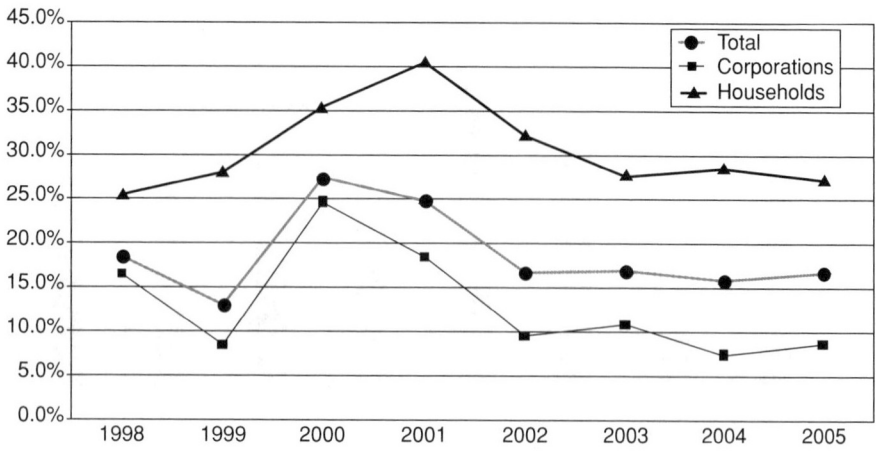

Figure 17.2 Loans to the Private Sector—Greece (annual growth rate, year-end)

Source: BoG.

Corporate loans have increased at much more moderate rates, which, at least in recent years, did not exceed 10 percent. However, even in this case there are some technical reasons behind the deceleration observed. More specifically, a number of corporations substituted their bank loans with securities which were purchased by banks. The switch from loans to securities was driven largely by fiscal reasons as it allowed corporations to avoid a 0.6 percent fee that is added to the interest cost of loans and which banks collect on behalf of the government. By the end of 2005, banks had accumulated EUR 9.8 billion of domestic corporate debt securities in their portfolios, amounting to 13.6 percent of the outstanding amount of domestic business loans, compared with just 1.5 percent in 2002.

In sum, one can conclude that bank loans to the private sector have increased at relatively high rates and, despite some recent signs of deceleration, the phenomenon of rapid credit expansion is by no means over. Loans to households have increased much faster than corporate loans and it was primarily the developments in household credit that are behind the rapid credit growth. However, there is no evidence of a crowding-out of firms by households and by no means should one conclude that banks are turning their backs on their business customers.

II. The causes of rapid credit growth

Rapid credit growth can be attributed to both demand and supply factors. Indeed, it was because of the simultaneous increase in demand and supply that the increase in bank loans was accompanied by significant reductions in prices, that is, interest rates.

On the demand side, the first reason behind the increase in bank loans is the catching-up effect. The indebtedness of the private sector in Greece was relatively low, and thus convergence to the euro area figures led to and actually necessitated a long period of high credit growth. In 1998, bank loans to the private sector as a percent of GDP were only 38.9 percent in Greece compared with 86.6 percent in the euro area (Figure 17.3). Even though by the end of 2005 the debt to GDP ratio has nearly doubled in Greece, it still remains substantially below the euro area average.

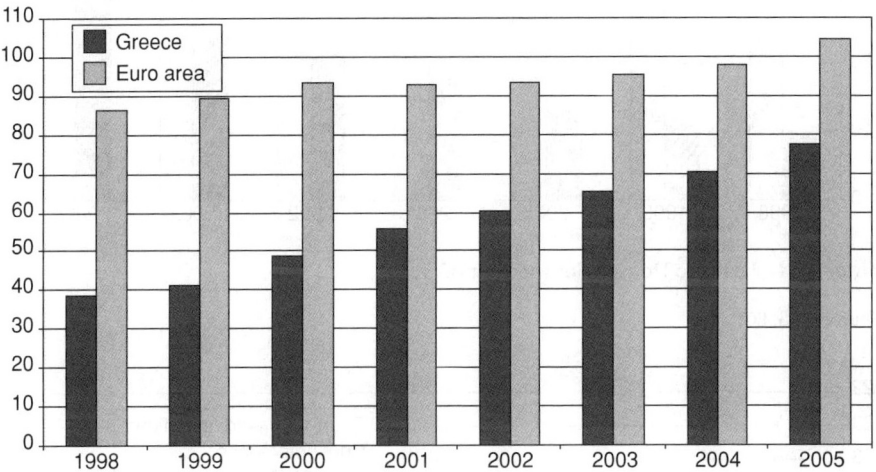

Figure 17.3 Loans to the Private Sector (as a percent of GDP)

Source: BoG, ECB.

Differences between Greece and the other euro area countries are much larger in the case of loans to households (Figure 17.4). In 1998, household debt in Greece was below 10 percent of GDP, compared with over 40 percent in the euro area. The limited amount of loans that banks extended to households was due inter alia to administrative restrictions that prevented (or discouraged) consumers and house buyers from seeking bank finance. Thus, loans to households were not simply at low levels, but at artificially low levels. Some administrative restrictions on consumer loans were actually in force until mid-2003. Once these restrictions were lifted, households entered a path of rapid convergence to the debt profile of households elsewhere in the euro area. By the end of 2005, the ratio of household loans to GDP had risen to 38 percent[3] in Greece compared with 53 percent in the euro area. As a matter of fact, consumer credit in Greece has been relatively larger than the euro area average since 2003[4] and it is only housing loans that are still relatively small.

The second factor that accounted for the increase in the demand for loans was developments in interest rates. Bank lending rates have declined sharply from the beginning of 1998 till mid-2001 (Figure 17.5), related to the convergence of Greek interest rates to the euro area ones.[5] At the beginning of 1998 the short-term lending rate for business loans was 19.5 percent in Greece compared with an average rate of 7.2 percent in the countries that were to form the euro area in January 1999.

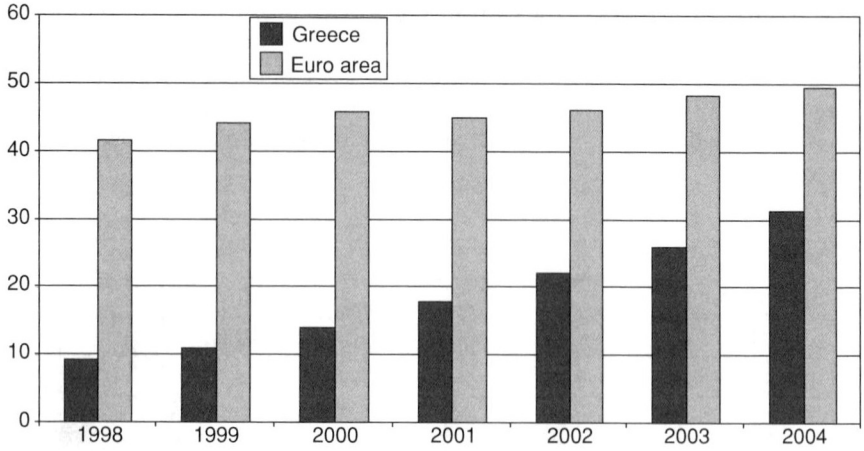

Figure 17.4 Loans to Households (percent of GDP)

Source: BoG, ECB.

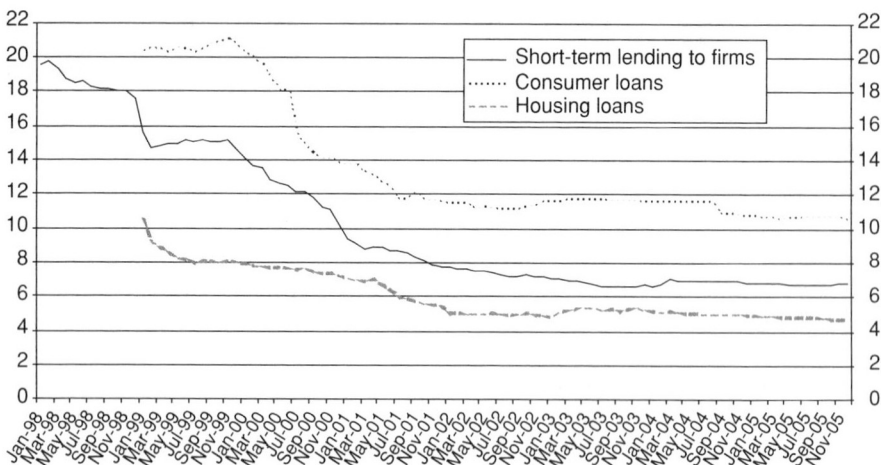

Figure 17.5 Retail Interest Rates—Greece (percent per year)

Source: BoG.

In June 2001, six months after Greece joined the euro area, the above rate had declined to 8.6 percent compared to 7.0 percent in the euro area. The sharp decline in nominal rates in Greece was broadly similar to the decline in real rates, since the inflation rate was broadly stable (4.4 percent in January 1998 and 3.9 percent in June 2001).[6]

One must again also note the differences between sectoral lending rates: the fall in the rates on consumption loans was much larger than that on business loans.[7] The rates on housing loans, on the other hand, did not decline significantly over this period, mainly because they were already much closer to euro area rates than the remaining interest rates in Greece.[8] While all lenders thus gained from a reduction in bank lending rates, consumers gained relatively more than businesses and house buyers.

In addition to the reduction in lending rates, macroeconomic conditions in Greece were quite satisfactory and boosted consumer and business confidence. Since 1997, GDP has been increasing at rates well over 3 percent (Figure 17.6), and it was thus natural for economic agents to be willing to assume more debt. The prospect of rising future income suggested that the servicing of loans would be problem-free. This has indeed been the case, and bad loans (as a ratio of the outstanding amount of total loans) have declined from 10 percent in 2000 to 7 percent in 2004. Moreover, debt service in Greece is still low, albeit rising. In 2004, for example, households' interest expenses amounted to 2.8 percent of their disposable income compared with 4.7 percent in the euro area. And as far as corporations are concerned, the debt to equity ratio has declined from an average of 1.3 during the period of 1997–2001 to 0.98 in 2003 and 2004.

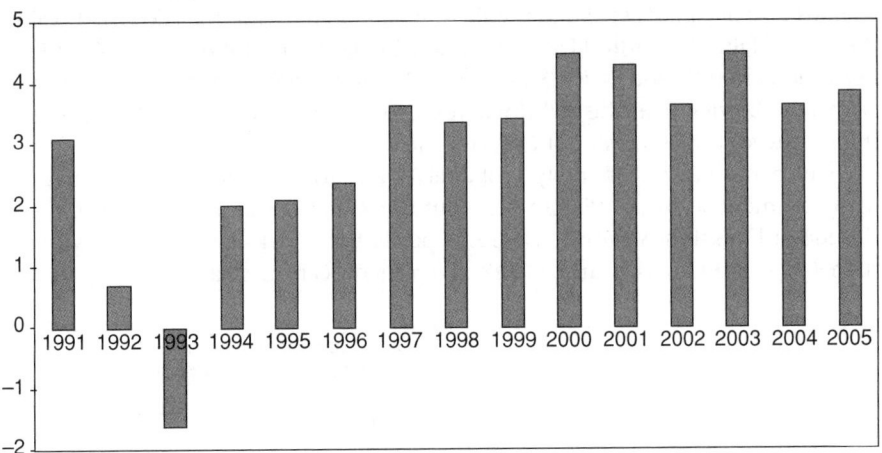

Figure 17.6 GDP Growth Rate—Greece (annual percentage change)

Source: National Statistical Service of Greece.

Turning to the supply side, there are two factors behind banks' willingness to increase the amount of loans they extend to the private sector, both related to Greece joining the euro area. The first factor is the sharp reduction in reserve requirements that boosted banks' overall liquidity. The second factor is the sharp reduction in the yields of Greek government bonds, which used to be a risk-free source of high and stable income for banks. The BoG used to impose a high reserve ratio on credit institutions in order to restrain liquidity and combat inflation pressures. The ratio was 12 percent compared with just 2 percent in the euro area until mid-2000. The subsequent reduction in reserve requirements had two effects. First, there was a one-off reduction in the stock of accumulated reserves, which amounted to EUR 13.5 billion. This amount was not immediately released to credit institutions but in tranches spread over three years. In 2000, EUR 0.25 billion was released, in 2001 EUR 8.08 billion, and in 2002 EUR 5.16 billion.

The funds released to banks were 16 percent of the outstanding amount of loans to the private sector in mid-2002. Credit institutions have an ongoing gain in their liquidity since their new deposits are only subject to the 2 percent reserve requirement rather than the 12 percent. In 2005 this gain is estimated at EUR 2.0 billion, and amounts to 10 percent of the increase in loans to the private sector during this year.

In addition to compulsory reserve requirements, the BoG offered a very high interest rate to collect voluntary interbank deposits. At the beginning of 1999, the rate was 11.5 percent, compared with 2 percent in the euro area. Even by June 2000, the BoG had a deposit rate of 7.25 percent, i.e., 4 percentage points above the ECB rate, since it was mainly in the last two months of 2000 that convergence to ECB rates took place. The sharp reduction in the official deposit facility rate in conjunction with the reduction in compulsory reserves is clearly reflected in the composition of banks' assets and the sharp reduction in claims (i.e., deposits) against the BoG. Claims fell from EUR 19.0 billion in December 1998 to EUR 7.1 billion in December 2001, and EUR 4.3 billion in December 2005. The reduction in these claims can be viewed as the additional resources banks had available for lending to the private sector, as a result of Greece's entry into the euro area.

Greek banks had traditionally kept a relatively large part of their assets invested in government securities (Figure 17.7) but this situation has changed recently. At the end of 1998 these securities were 22.1 percent of total assets compared with less than 9 percent in the euro area. Greek government securities had high coupon rates

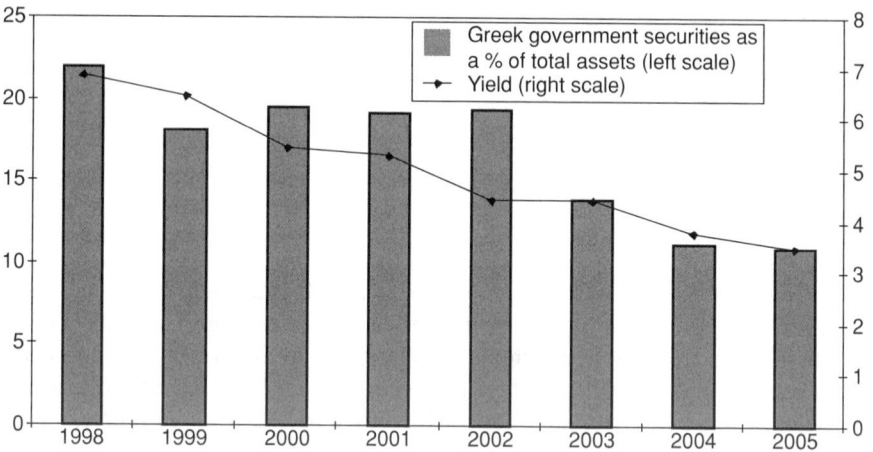

Figure 17.7 The Securities Portfolio of Greek Banks (in percent)

Source: BoG.

and, in the run-up to euro area membership, this offered the near certainty of large capital gains in addition to a perfectly safe income flow. However, as the coupon rates of these securities were reduced in 1999 and 2000, the opportunities for capital gains were quickly exhausted. Moreover, as their yield declined from 11.15 percent in January 1998 to 5.37 percent in January 2001 and 3.51 percent in December 2005, banks had to search for alternative profit sources. Thus, credit institutions shifted their attention from the government to the private sector, and especially to the household sector, where interest rates and profit margins are relatively high. This shift did not necessarily imply a significant increase in the amount of risk that Greek banks were willing to take, since the private sector, and households in particular, had low indebtedness.

III. Policy responses

In general, the BoG has been managing rapid credit growth with a diversity of prudential and supervisory measures (proactive or structural) (Figure 17.8).

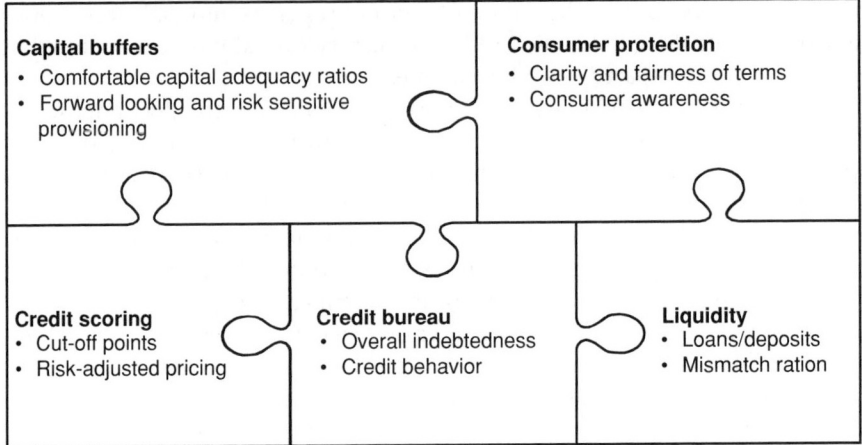

Figure 17.8 BoG's Management of Credit Growth

The prudential measures

The BoG linked the liberalization of household credit with the development of a stricter monitoring framework for credit institutions, especially regarding provisioning, capital adequacy, transparency, and credit bureau services and usage. More specifically, the BoG imposed in 1999 a supervisory provisions matrix with differentiated provisioning coefficients by loan type (business, mortgages, consumer) and time past due. To this end, provisions were calculated also for performing loans, while any shortfall of accounting provisions over supervisory provisions would be subtracted from regulatory capital toward the calculation of capital adequacy ratios. Coefficients for mortgage loans depended on the level of the loan-to-value (LTV) ratio (initially 70 percent of taxable value and later 75 percent of market value, favoring low LTVs). The BoG adjusted dynamically the provisioning coefficients responding to market developments (e.g., credit growth rate, competition, banks' credit policy):

- In January 2003, there was an increase in the provisioning coefficients for all loans overdue by more than 12 months or classified as doubtful, as well as for all consumer loans. On the other hand, there was a reduction for mortgage loans with low LTV ratios.
- In January 2005, there was a further increase in coefficients for consumer loans overdue by more than 12 months or classified as doubtful, to encourage prompt write-offs.
- In October 2005, there was a similar increase in coefficients for mortgages overdue by more than 12 months or classified as doubtful.

Furthermore, the BoG imposed higher minimum capital adequacy ratios for vulnerable banks, such as cooperatives and small credit institutions, and pushed for capital increases and higher provisioning when deemed necessary. Nonetheless, for the banking system as a whole the solvency ratios were comfortable throughout the period, while the good quality of the regulatory capital has been reflected in high Tier-I ratios compared with the euro area.

In the context of transparency and consumer protection, the BoG imposed in 2002 detailed minimum information requirements by product type (e.g., deposits, loans, cards) and distribution channel (e.g., branch, internet), as well as clear terms and conditions (e.g., fee structure, effective interest rates) and fairness (e.g., changes in variable rates linked with macroeconomic conditions and financial market developments). In parallel, the BoG demanded the establishment and operation by all credit institutions of customer complaints departments, and now continuously monitored compliance. Recently, the BoG, taking into account both risk management and consumer protection considerations, has issued a guideline that the total monthly installment payments should not exceed 40 percent of the gross disposable income of the obligor. The measure is intended to protect both households and credit institutions from the impact of potential adverse market developments.

The upgrading and sophistication of credit bureau services also supported the effort to mitigate credit risk. The well developed black list with extensive coverage (around 1.9 million citizens and legal entities are monitored) and widespread use by credit institutions (around 39,000 requests per day) was complemented by the development in July 2003 of a white list. The white list already covers new consumer loans and credit cards (around 100,000 new entries per month; 700,000 and 900,000 consumer loans and credit cards registered, respectively), while the inclusion of overdrafts and, more importantly, mortgages is planned in the course of 2006. The BoG cooperates closely with the credit bureau, gaining access to primary data for prudential supervision purposes and balancing efforts to ensure the quality of the database and the need for disclosure with the requirements for consumer protection of the Hellenic Data Protection Authority.

Supervisory framework

Prudential supervision plays a key role in monitoring the efficiency and health of the banking system and safeguarding financial stability, especially in a period of prolonged rapid household credit growth, when market conditions and risks evolve fast and often in unexpected ways. On-site inspections and continuous monitoring of risks to financial stability complement off-site supervision. The close collaboration with European and international institutions facilitates the transfer of know-how, the sharing of experiences, and the convergence of supervisory practices.

The Department for the Supervision of Credit and Other Financial Institutions (the supervisory department of the BoG) has dedicated sections for each group of credit and financial institutions, as well as dedicated bank examiners for major banks. Furthermore, there is a special department for the centralized processing and analysis of prudential returns and financial statements with the support of the information technology (IT) unit. Monitoring covers the full spectrum of reported data: capital adequacy, provisions and liquidity; large exposures, country exposures, and exposures above EUR 1 million; internal control systems; IFRS income statements; and FX positions, as well as authorizations of: mergers and acquisitions (as far as supervisory issues are concerned); branch network expansion; increase of participation in the financial sector; and expansion abroad (mainly south-east Europe).

Complementing off-site supervision, the BoG performs on-site inspections of all institutions on a regular basis, as well as ad hoc inspections. The main objectives include: validation of reported financial statements and prudential returns; control of adherence to required standards and procedures, as well as of efficiency of credit institutions' various departments; and monitoring and validation of banks' systems (e.g., IT) and methodologies (e.g., credit scoring).

Bank examiners coordinate with off-site supervision to validate findings or initiate unplanned inspections. On-site inspections are the major tool to ensure compliance of credit institutions, especially at times of rapid expansion and intensifying competition, which might induce them to loosen their standards and controls.

The Supervision Department has special sections monitoring credit and market risk applying modern techniques; extensively stress testing the banking system (credit risk, market risk, expansion in south-east Europe, macro stress testing); authorizing and validating banks' risk management systems, procedures, and employed techniques (e.g., VAR models); and monitoring new developments (e.g., credit derivatives, hedge funds). Last but not least, it has initiated consultations on the imminent implementation of Basel II, and encouraged the banks to make appropriate and timely preparations.

Risks are being monitored and assessed on a continuous basis. A recent example of a prudential supervisory measure in response to changing market conditions (i.e., intensified competition and increased risk taking) is the following: the reduced weighting by 50 percent (which corresponds to a capital adequacy ratio (CAR) of 4 percent) for the calculation of capital requirements against mortgage credit risk from December 31, 2005, only to those outstanding claims which are covered at least 75 percent by the market value of the mortgaged residential property; while for those with less coverage, a weighting of 100 percent applies (CAR of 8 percent).

The BoG is integrated in the System of European Central Banks and the BoG representatives participate in all relevant committees and working groups and exchange information with the ECB on a regular basis. This allows for ongoing knowledge transfer, and provides a framework for cooperation with other EU central banks, whenever this is deemed necessary. Furthermore, the BoG maintains a close relationship with the Fund, participates in the regular consultations in the context of Article IV, and has recently successfully completed the FSAP exercise for Greece. In parallel, the BoG maintains an ongoing relationship with other international institutions (e.g., BIS, Groupe De Contact, etc.). Finally, the BoG has signed Memoranda of Understanding with most countries where Greek banks are present.

Recent developments

The rapid credit growth to households has contributed to the increased sophistication of the Greek banking industry. We can identify three major recent trends:

- Maturing of the retail market in terms of product differentiation (i.e., innovative and client specific products), margin and fees compression, development of alternative distribution channels (e.g., PoS, internet, real estate agents), and the evolution of the industry structure (i.e., entry of specialist players such as consumer finance companies).
- Differentiation of funding, both in terms of maturities and of sources, with the exploitation of new products such as Euro Commercial Paper, Euro Medium Term Notes and securitization. Greek banks show an increasing interest in securitization to exploit both favorable market conditions and fund further credit growth. So far they have issued mainly Mortgage Backed Securities and there has also been recently an issuance of credit card receivables.
- Differentiation of capital structure with the issuance of subordinated debt instruments and hybrid capital, to improve their capital adequacy ratios and the return on shareholder capital. The BoG has developed a detailed framework for their regulatory treatment.

IV. Summary

The BoG has always been concerned with the adverse implications of credit growth. In 1999, it took ad hoc measures to restrain credit to businesses and consumers. This was indeed the last time such measures were taken, since at present the only measures that can be taken are of a "prudential supervision" nature.

In particular, the BoG monitors household debt very closely. It commissioned a survey on the subject in 2002, and a follow-up is currently under way. The 2002 survey did not, in general, reveal a problem of over-indebtedness. However, taking into account that the majority of loans are at a floating rate, an increase in ECB rates might lead to debt servicing problems, especially if coupled with adverse domestic macroeconomic conditions.

Since the adoption of the single currency, the BoG can no longer pursue an independent monetary policy, and refinancing rates are set by the ECB for the whole euro area. Nonetheless, domestic credit developments are closely monitored, since they might have a considerable impact on banks' risk exposure and hence the stability of the financial system, with a monitoring system that is accompanied by a diversity of prudential and supervisory tools to manage the financial sector risks.

Notes

1. Both the Bank of Greece (BoG).
2. Calculated on the basis of financial transactions. It thus excludes reclassifications, revaluations, exchange rate variations, and any other changes which do not arise from transactions.
3. Including securitized loans.
4. The ratio of consumer credit to GDP was 12 percent in Greece and 7 percent in the euro area in 2005.
5. It should be pointed out that the BoG had a very strict policy of high interest rates to combat inflation pressures. It had thus decided to keep its official rates at high levels for as long as possible and it was mainly in the second half of 2000 that it gradually reduced its rates to the ECB level.
6. In January 1999, there is a break in the series because of a change in the reporting system. Prior to 1999, short-term lending rates reported by banks to the BoG were actually an average of business and consumer loans. Because of the relatively small amount of consumer loans, this rate mainly reflected developments in business loans, but is clearly an overestimate of *the level* of business lending rates.
7. The spread of unsecured consumer loans over short-term business loans declined from 6.2 percentage points at the beginning of 2000 to 3.8 percentage points in June 2001.
8. The spread between Greece and the euro area in mid-1999 was 3.2 percentage points in the case of housing loans, compared with 9.7 points for short-term business loans.

18
Debt Growth: Factors, Institutional Issues and Implications—The Portuguese Case

Nuno Ribeiro[1]

In this chapter, I discuss some of the features underlying the private sector debt evolution in Portugal throughout the 1990s. Rapid private sector credit growth, both in the household and nonfinancial corporate sectors, together with a continuous edging up of debt-to-income ratios, has been observed since the mid-1990s. These developments occurred against the background of institutional change in several dimensions dating back from the mid-1980s, including: the liberalization of an almost fully nationalized and deeply regulated financial market; widespread privatization and consolidation of the banking sector; disintermediation; an evolving international environment towards more competition; easier entry into the banking business; capital mobility; and the adoption of post-Basel I supervisory requirements and tools.

A number of demand and supply factors played an important role in the expansion of lending, against the background of the gradual dismantling of the regulatory straitjacket prevailing until the late 1980s that opened up the doors to an increasing role for market forces. Demand factors played a major role in explaining debt growth, inter alia the much lower nominal (and real) interest rates applied to loans associated with nominal convergence. In the household sector, demographic issues, alongside a shortage of housing, also played a role, while in the nonfinancial corporate sector, the financing of significant foreign direct investments abroad and the building of road infrastructures in "public–private" partnerships explained part of the credit boom in the late 1990s. Supply-side factors were also important, with the banks' financial conditions and ability to adapt to the new competitive environment allowing for the swift intermediation of funds from abroad to finance high private sector borrowing requirements.

The rapid rise in aggregate debt levels has called for an increase in monitoring efforts, in particular of the potential liquidity pressures on banks and the concentration of borrowers facing common risk factors. Available evidence points to an increase in credit availability due to lower liquidity constraints as the major driving factor for higher aggregate household indebtedness, rather than more stretched financial positions for individual households.

Against the background of rapid credit growth and weak customer deposit developments, the banking system turned from a comfortable net liquidity surplus to a position in which market funding, most of it obtained abroad, became much more significant. Monitoring tools to analyze banks' liquidity positions were reinforced and a new emphasis was placed on supervisory guidance for banks' internal control, risk management, and contingency procedures. On the credit risk front, changes in general and specific provisioning and solvency requirements were fine-tuned to ensure adequate buffers under EU-type overall supervisory infrastructure. These measures were motivated by prudential goals and not designed to curb or target aggregate credit growth per se.

I. Stylized facts on private credit growth and indebtedness

The evolution of bank loans to the private sector in real terms was stagnant on average in the 1980s, a period in which the financial system remained strongly regulated and strict quantitative quotas prevailed at the bank level (Figure 18.1). A short-lived period of some credit acceleration was witnessed after the abolition of the system of credit ceilings in 1991, and strong aggregate credit growth resumed in 1995 and more particularly in 1997 by the nonfinancial corporate sector only.

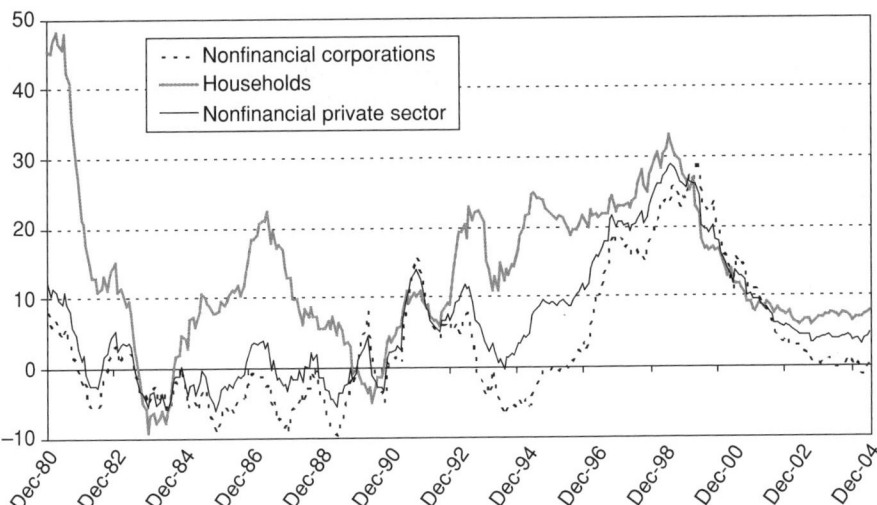

Figure 18.1 Bank Loans to the Private Sector—Portugal (year-on-year real rate of growth)

Source: Bank of Portugal (BoP).

As regards total debt levels scaled by income aggregates, the most striking observation is the high rate of change for the household sector; indebtedness remained very low until late 1992, but multiplied more than fivefold in the decade that followed (Figure 18.2). This development took place in the context of

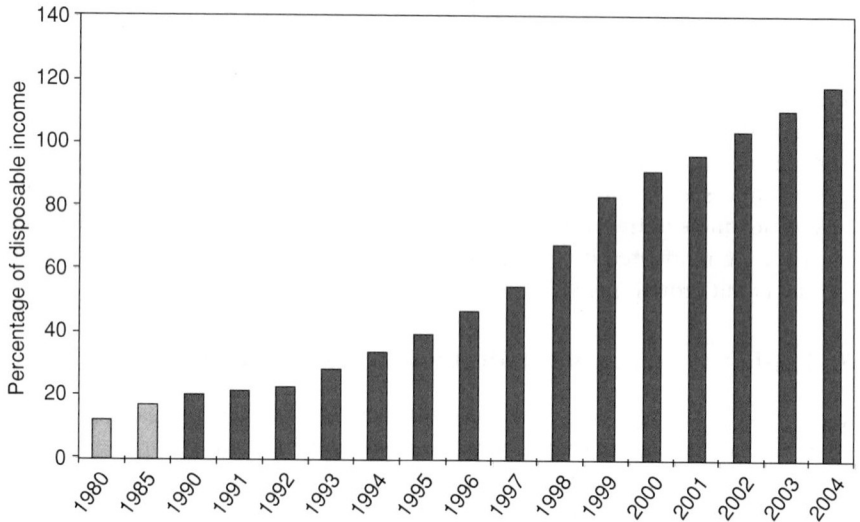

Figure 18.2 Household Indebtedness—Portugal

Source: BoP.

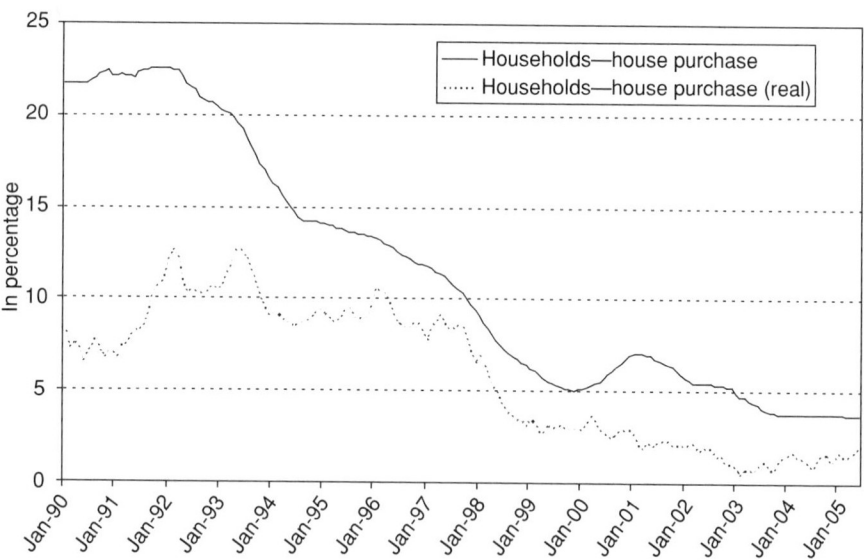

Figure 18.3 Interest Rates on Loans for House Purchase—Portugal

Source: BoP.

a continuous decline in nominal interest rates from 1992 (Figure 18.3). It is worth mentioning that the ECB interest rate rises between April 1999 and October 2000, and the related increases in short-term money market rates, mirrored the reversal in the credit growth peak in mid-1999, as shown in Figure 18.1.

As regards the nonfinancial corporate sector, the growth in indebtedness was not as marked as for the household sector. In 1995, the indebtedness of this sector stood at about 60 percent of GDP, rising to about 100 percent of GDP in 2003, and has remained virtually stable since then.[2]

II. An overview of banking liberalization

This section provides an overview of Portugal's financial liberalization and highlights some specificities of the Portuguese case as background information for the acceleration of credit since the mid-1990s.

State-owned banking sector: 1975–83

Banking liberalization began in 1980, when the first private investment companies were allowed to operate in a narrow segment usually classified as investment banking. Some of these companies were transformed into investment banks when the banking authorities opened up the banking sector to private operators at the end of 1983. Prior to that date, the banking sector primarily consisted of state-owned commercial banks whose operations were subjected to frequent government interference. The monetary authorities administratively set interest rates for both deposit and lending operations, established credit ceilings for each bank, and, therefore, controlled a sizable share of the sector's credit operations. In fact, the regulatory straitjacket on banks remained virtually unchanged following nationalization in 1975, when most of the sector fell under government control.

During this period, financial intermediation remained almost exclusively under the control of the nationalized banks, since no other financial intermediaries existed and capital markets had only a residual role. The absence of alternatives for financial investment, together with the persistence of high saving rates, provided the banking system with a significant flow of deposits, even though some volatility in the deposit base surfaced in periods of increased exchange rate uncertainty. On the other hand, the banking sector was burdened by the government's continuous deficit financing at below market rates. Public sector deficits were financed through monetization via the central bank, which used the credit ceilings to sterilize money creation stemming from the state financing. In this way, the implicit tax arising from monetary financing of the public sector was passed on to the banking system by the prevalence of credit ceilings coupled with retail interest rate control. In such a setting, banks accumulated involuntary excess liquidity which was invested with the central bank at below market rates.

In addition, political interference on bank management affected bank solvency, since it led to both the increase in nonperforming loans and to an insufficient capitalization of banks (Figure 18.4).

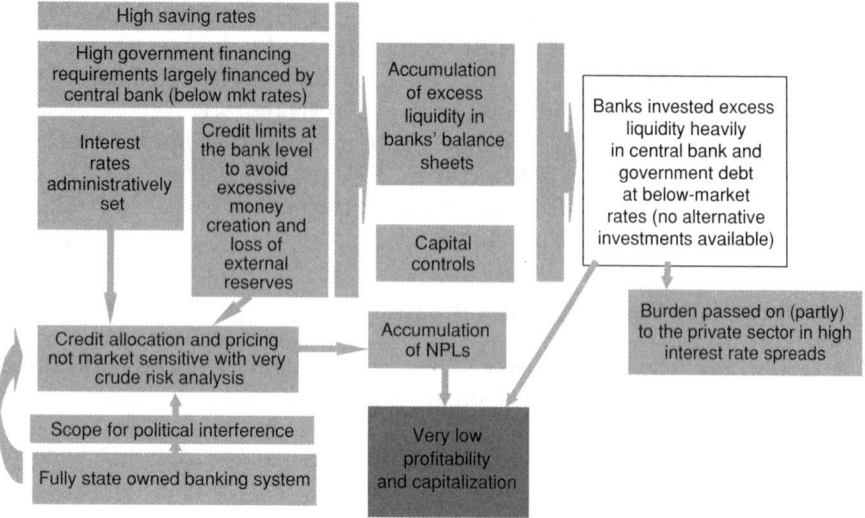

Figure 18.4 Regulatory Straitjacket in the 1980s—Portugal

The period 1984–90

Portugal's accession to the EC prompted a series of policy measures towards greater liberalization of the economy, reflecting a renewed political commitment to the establishment of an economic system free from all remaining controls and integrated into a much wider economic space. Contrary to previous liberalization episodes (see Macedo and Sebastião, 1989 and Barros and Leite, 1994), this time the liberalization process was supposed to affect both the real and financial spheres of the economy, encompassing simultaneously the mandatory adoption of EC-wide rules and the gradual opening up of the Portuguese economy. Accordingly, for most of the second half of the 1980s, Portugal's banking sector underwent a process of gradual liberalization which affected both the degree of competition and bank conduct.[3] The move towards both liberalization and financial integration resulted from the joint forces of several factors affecting most banking sectors in the EU: international financial deregulation; increased liberalization of capital movements; and changes in the structure and organization of the financial industry.

The first steps towards financial sector liberalization consisted of the authorization of new private financial institutions (Table 18.1). In the early 1980s, private insurance companies and banks were therefore allowed to operate in the Portuguese market, alongside a series of nonbank financial institutions, such as investment companies, leasing and factoring companies, venture capital companies and money market brokers.[4]

Even though the changes throughout this period marked the beginning of the banking sector liberalization, some restrictions on banks were kept in place for most of the period. For example, administratively set limits on interest rates on credit operations remained in effect until 1988–89, and credit ceilings stayed in place until 1991, when market-oriented monetary management was introduced. On the other

Table 18.1 Authorization of New Institutions in Portuguese Financial System

Type of Financial Institution	Year of Authorization
Leasing companies	1979
Investment companies	1980
Private banks	1983
Private insurance companies	1983
Factoring companies	1985
Investment funds	
Securities	1985
Real estate	1985
Money market brokers	1986
Pension funds	1986
Venture capital companies	1986
Stock market brokers and dealers	1988

hand, although possible since 1983, entry (especially de novo entry) by private players (both national and foreign) was subject to administrative discretion until the adoption of the EU Second Banking Directive in January 1993.[5] Notwithstanding, the number of banks increased every year, especially in 1985 (Figure 18.5).

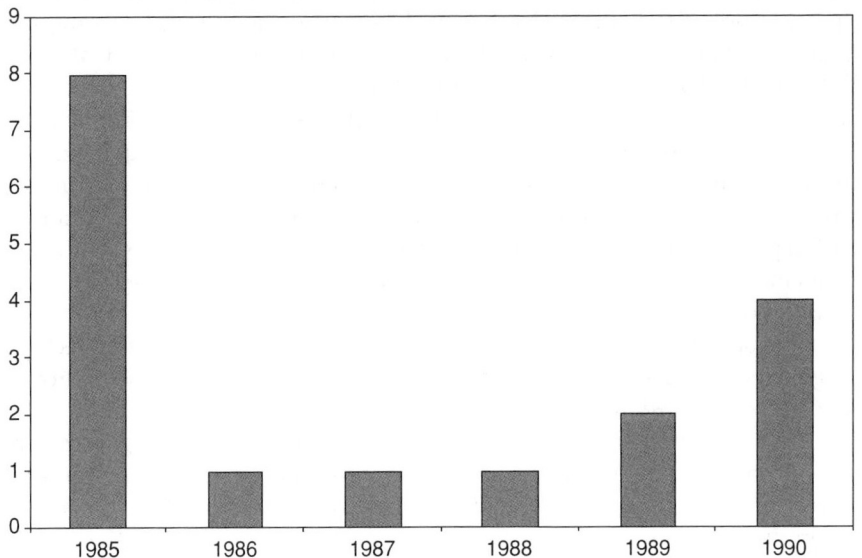

Figure 18.5 New Banks in Portuguese Banking System

Source: BoP.

These barriers to entry resulted in the prolonged protection of state-owned banks, which had been highly undercapitalized after a decade of mismanagement (especially in the credit market).[6] During this period these banks were given the opportunity to improve their prudential ratios by enjoying oligopoly rents resulting from operating in a protected environment (Table 18.2).

Table 18.2 Selected Financial Indicators in the Portuguese Banking System

	1984	1987	1989
Profitability (gross income[a]/assets) (percent)			
Banking sector	0.97	2.02	2.69
State-owned banks	0.92	1.96	2.62
Private domestic banks	–	2.43	2.97
Foreign banks	4.84	2.77	3.32
Solvency (own funds/credit) (percent)			
Banking sector	3.70	6.40	8.90
State-owned banks	3.60	5.80	7.90
Private domestic banks	–	11.50	13.10
Foreign banks	12.50	12.80	17.60

Source: BoP.

[a] Profits before depreciation, provisions and income taxes.

The persistence of low levels of competition in the banking sector also facilitated the privatization of state-owned banks, which became possible from 1989 onwards. This also seemed to correct for the high levels of implicit taxation to which the banking sector had been subjected throughout most of the 1980s. Given the inflationary dangers of monetary deficit financing and the rise in public debt, government financing had been achieved through the use of a non-explicit tax on financial intermediation by banks.[7] This was made possible by the control of money creation through the imposition of credit ceilings, which, as already mentioned, stayed in place until 1991. Since deposits grew faster than credit, banks were led to leave an increasing proportion of their assets idle, which were then used to finance successive government deficits at (relatively) very low cost.

It should be noted that this financing of public deficits was made both directly—through direct purchase of government debt securities by the banks—and indirectly, since banks channeled most excess liquidity to the BoP, which was then the major buyer of government debt. These funds were ultimately used to finance government fiscal imbalances at below market rates. This form of deficit financing caused a serious deterioration in the balance sheet of banks, thus hampering their competitive position. It was also widely recognized as a further reason to control the pace of liberalization.

Banks gradually learned how to circumvent the regulatory constraints that restricted their lending activity, in tandem with the initial steps to liberalize capital movements. By 1991, when credit ceilings were abandoned, the system was already showing strong signs of ineffectiveness. Banks resorted to their nondomestic branches to grant credit and, as a result, foreign credit grew as a proportion of total credit. Further, banks took advantage of the fact that credit ceilings were controlled only on an end-of-month basis. In addition, the aforementioned below-market rates earned on the banks' liquidity started to approach market levels as direct issuance of government debt in the market substituted the deficit financing with the BoP and the banking system.

Nevertheless, the entry of a number of banks to operate in Portugal during this period contributed to increased competition; by the end of 1989, 13 new private banks had entered the market since 1984, of which five were domestic. Nevertheless, the market share of privately-owned banks as a result of de novo entry remained small until 1989 (Table 18.3). After that date, the gradual privatization of state-held banks caused the market share of these banks to follow a declining trend. In any event, the growth in new entrants led to changes in the way banks approached the market: nonprice competition increased together with the rapid growth of bank branches. New entrants' market share, albeit small, grew consistently. In the credit market, they accounted for 11.1 percent of the market at the end of 1989, compared with 6.2 percent of all loans at the end of 1987.

Table 18.3 Market Shares in Banking Markets (in percent)—Portugal

	1984	1987	1989
Credit			
State-owned banks	95.9	89.8	83.9
Private domestic banks	3.1	6.2	11.3
Foreign banks	1.0	4.0	4.8
Deposits			
State-owned banks	96.2	93.6	88.7
Private domestic banks	2.5	4.3	8.6
Foreign banks	1.3	2.1	2.7

Source: BoP.

Concentration in the banking sector, though declining, remained high during this period (Table 18.4). Concentration in the loans market followed a decreasing trend, although the market share of the four largest banks accounted for nearly 50 percent of the market in 1990. Concentration in the deposits market remained at slightly higher levels, with the share of the four largest banks declining 8 percentage points from 1987 to 1990, when it reached 54 percent. It should be stressed that changes in market shares and concentration in the credit market were to a large extent the result of the changes in the credit ceilings imposed upon banks. That is, by setting credit ceilings at the bank level, the authorities pre-determined the changes in concentration in the loans market. This, in turn, affected competition in the deposits market, since banks could not guarantee that gains in market share in this market would be translated for certain into profitable investments, due to the restrictions in the credit market. However, as mentioned above, this situation changed somewhat in the late 1980s with the decreasing effectiveness of credit ceilings.

In spite of this gradual change toward lower concentration, entry restrictions allowed banks to enjoy oligopolistic rents. The interest rate spread between credit operations and deposits remained high and fairly stable from 1984 to 1990,

Table 18.4 Concentration in the Portuguese Banking Sector

	Major 4 market share		Herfindhal index	
	Deposits	Credit	Deposits	Credit
1987	61	56	1362	1338
1988	57	51	1195	1219
1989	52	54	1292	1137
1990	54	49	1219	1092

Source: BoP.

Note: Herfindhal index is the sum of squares of each individual bank market share.

falling only slightly from more than 10 percentage points in 1984–85 to around 9 percentage points in 1989–90.[8] The quantitative restrictions in the loan market may have contributed to this continuing high spread. Maximum limits for loan rates were eliminated toward the end of this period which, in a setting of persistent credit ceilings on individual banks and increased credit demand due to the acceleration of economic activity, created pressures for increases in loan rates. This partially compensated for the growing price competition in the loan markets, which worked in the opposite direction, pressuring loan rates downward.

From 1991 onward: the specificities of the Portuguese case

The pace of liberalization clearly increased in the early 1990s. After some preliminary steps, which included the lifting of upper limits on interest rates on credit operations and the liberalization of deposit rates, credit ceilings were abolished in 1991, leading to complete price liberalization.[9] Although entry remained somewhat restricted, the adoption of the Second Banking Directive at the end of 1992 led to full entry liberalization. Further, only after late 1991 did it become possible for banks at large to operate in the mortgage market, since prior to that date only three banks had been allowed to grant housing loans.

The adoption of the EU Second Banking Directive, establishing freedom of entry and service provision in the Portuguese banking market practically coincided with the lifting of barriers to all capital movements between Portugal and the other EU member states and the end of branching regulations. Most liberalization on the domestic front had taken place before full external liberalization, while the later stages in both external and domestic liberalization coincided with international upgrades in supervisory rules and instruments following the 1988 Basel Accord. As explained above, a distinctive aspect of the Portuguese liberalization was the time the banking system was given to adapt to market forces before privatization, which took place after a period of controlled co-existence of state-owned and lean and innovative de novo private banks.

In addition, the crisis in the Exchange Rate Mechanism (ERM) of the European Monetary System (EMS), which roughly overlapped with the later steps in liberalization, was an early live-test of the risks that could occur. The risks associated with possible disruptions in an exchange rate arrangement perceived as credible and stable in normal times, in conjunction with the 1993 recession, required considerable discipline on the part of the nonfinancial private sector, whose financing in foreign currency was never significant in the run-up to the European Monetary Union (EMU). This situation also provided banks with incentives to move away from hard price competition in the early years of the fully market-driven environment. Rather, nonprice competition seemed to be much more important, involving nonlegal barriers to entry into the retail market; this was subsequently reflected in the fairly low market share of nondomestic banks. Depositors have remained to a large extent faithful to recognizable brand names, and the expansion of branch networks by incumbents in the early 1990s has proven to be an effective means of capturing sizable resources.[10]

The abovementioned factors help to explain why credit growth remained relatively subdued until very late in the liberalization process, and still moderate in the few years after the lifting of all administrative entry, price, and quantitative restrictions in the banking business.

III. Debt growth in the run-up to EMU

In this section, private sector debt growth in Portugal is analyzed with a particular focus on the post-1995 period.

Demand-side factors

As mentioned above, nominal interest rates posted a continuous decline after late 1992, easing very significantly the liquidity constraints of households. The available estimates point to a relatively high share of liquidity-constrained households (representing around 60 percent of disposable income), in line with what could be inferred at that time in other southern European countries, such as Greece, Italy, or Spain (Luz, 1992). Not surprisingly, aggregate household debt grew quickly, as access to the mortgage market was widened as a result of the nominal interest rate reduction, the effect of which was further amplified by the existence of direct subsidies to new mortgages. Further, the housing shortage in the early 1990s represented potential demand for the mortgage market, which could materialize over time as more and more households were able to afford the typical installment plan at the prevailing interest rate. In addition to that, demographic factors added to the increase in housing demand. The mild baby boom observed in Portugal in the early 1970s implied an increase in the number of individuals reaching the age for forming a new household in the early 1990s. This increase in the proportion of potential first-time buyers in Portugal throughout most of the 1990s was contrary to experience in most other European countries and in the euro area as a whole (Figure 18.6).

At the same time, the supply side of the housing market was able to accommodate demand pressures. The housing stock increased by around 1 million dwellings in the ten years up to 2001, a 25 percent increase vis-à-vis the 1991 level. Simultaneously, although prices rose quickly for some time in the late 1990s, no continuous and persistent rise in aggregate house prices was observed for several years in a row.

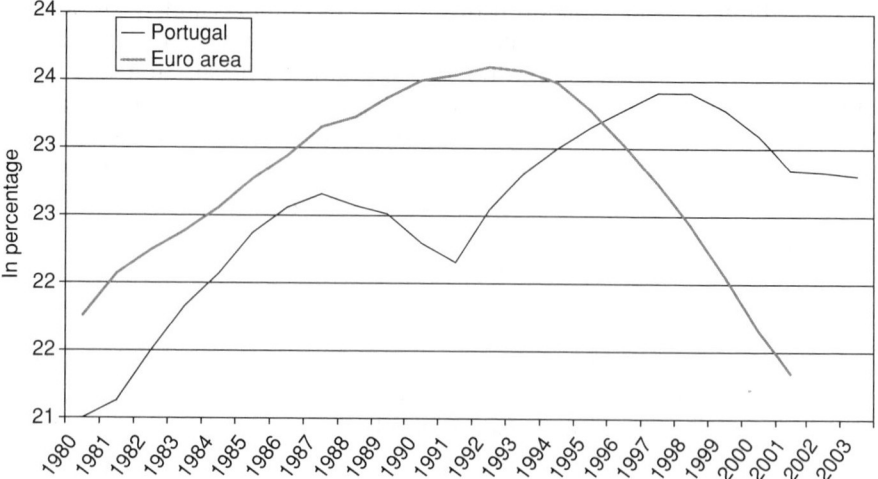

Figure 18.6 Share of the 20 to 34 Years Old Cohort of the Population

Source: BoP.

A third demand factor that played a role in the increase in household loans was a decline in the implicit cost of consumer loans. An almost prohibitive tax on consumer loans prevailed for most of the 1980s, and was lifted only in 1995.

As regards nonfinancial corporations, there is also evidence of significant liquidity constraints by the mid-1990s, implying that nominal rates were affecting firms' investment decisions (Farinha, 1995). Even though nominal interest rates started to decline already in 1992–93, real interest rates remained high until very late in the 1990s (notwithstanding the downward trend from the mid-1990s). In the late-1990s, two additional factors explained the high credit demand by nonfinancial corporations.

- First, Portuguese nonfinancial groups undertook large foreign direct investment operations abroad, which were facilitated by the momentum in the stock markets (high valuations of the acquirer firm eased the funding of operations in the capital markets) and the cheap funding in debt markets in domestic currency (the euro).
- Second, a change in the strategy used by the state to finance the building of roads also induced higher demand for funds by the private sector. These roads were built under project financing arrangements that utilize a shadow toll, that is, they are free of charge for the user but paid for by the State, and financed upfront by private consortia.

Supply-side factors

To understand the private sector credit dynamics in Portugal from 1995, it is important to take into consideration the ability that banks demonstrated to accommodate increasing private sector borrowing requirements. In fact, an ample liquidity pool of government debt, inherited from the 1980s, and the gradual amortization of central bank certificates, could be used to finance increasingly strong credit demand. Those central bank certificates resulted from a large liquidity absorption operation by the BoP in November 1994, when reserve requirements were reduced from 17 to 2 percent (the 17 percent rate had been in place since 1987). The amortization plan included tranches of similar size maturing annually from 1996 to 2004, with roughly one third of the amount being nonremunerated and the remainder at close to market rates. After EMU accession, banks started to have access to a large unified money market, without foreign exchange risk and with historically low interest rates. As expected, banks indeed resorted to the euro money market massively to finance the growing gap between credit and customer deposit growth. In parallel, the emergence of a pan-European private bond market allowed them to diversify their funding sources away from the short-term maturities typical of interbank markets and to diversify investor targets by geography and investment horizon.

As mentioned above, the mortgage market was only liberalized in late 1991, when the few banks allowed to operate lost their shelter from competition. The cyclical downturn that led to the 1993 recession shifted banks from the most risky segments (e.g., loans to nonfinancial corporations) toward the housing loan market. Households were much less indebted than nonfinancial corporations, and nominal interest rate declines were driving credit demand faster in this sector.

From 1997 onward, and more prominently since 2000, loan securitization showed a huge expansion, allowing banks to better manage their medium-term liquidity position and, in some circumstances, to pass on the credit risk to third parties. Securitization became an additional instrument to finance credit and also fostered changes in the design of contracts in order to facilitate arranging pools of homogeneous loans.

More recently, diversification of mortgage contracts tailored to meet the specific needs of different classes of customers emerged. Such diversification included, in particular, allowing more extended maturities and deferred redemption, such as requiring only interest payments in the first years and/or larger redemption at maturity.

Consolidation throughout the 1990s led the market share of the five major banking groups to rise to more than 80 percent. That was not detrimental to competition in the loan market, as spreads declined significantly, mostly as regards loans for house purchase. However, spreads in the housing loan segment, even though at historical lows recently, remain at an intermediate position among euro area countries.

The final factor on the supply side was the change in banks' loan approval and risk management systems. These have evolved in line with both the demands of the new competitive environment and the change of supervision from the 1980s administrative system to one that is market based and includes among its tools the fostering of internal controls and stress tests to analyze the banks' financial position.

IV. Monitoring issues related to the buildup of risks

The persistently high rates of growth of bank loans imply funding pressures on banks' liquidity, in particular in a small, open economy like Portugal. The change in the liquidity profile of Portuguese banks in the run-up to EMU from net external creditors to net debtors fostered increased liquidity monitoring, inter alia motivating the establishment of reporting requirements, including a liquidity map with each relevant asset and liability class broken down by residual maturity. Stronger analytical efforts to analyze banks' liquidity developments and profiles have been put in place both from the prudential and broad financial stability perspectives. Recognizing that a bank's liquidity is a multidimensional issue, the approach that was followed incorporated many qualitative features, rather than defining a quantitative requirement, and moral suasion through interactive dialogue with banks has been extensively used.

In the run-up to EMU, fine-tuning measures were introduced to ensure adequate buffers as the credit cycle matured, such as changes in (i) the general provisioning requirements to differentiate more consumer credit from other segments, (ii) the specific provisioning requirements to differentiate them more according to the existence of collateral and personal guarantees, and (iii) the solvency (and specific provisions) requirements for loans with loan-to-value ratio higher than 75 percent.

Looking forward, two main issues were identified regarding the concentration of risk: (i) the relatively low number of corporate debtors accounting for a significant share of total corporate loans (0.5 percent of individual debtors represent almost half the loan amount to corporations), and (ii) a concentration of borrowers facing common risks, such as real-estate related lending, mostly retail housing mortgages (representing 43 percent of bank loans to the resident private nonfinancial sector), but also construction (9 percent of this aggregate) and real-estate related services (roughly 8.3 percent of the same portfolio).

Concerning the first case, the fact that the larger companies are active essentially in the services sector, not exposed to international competition and enjoying a good financial position, is a mitigating factor, while the non-existence of a house price bubble in the Portuguese economy reduces the likelihood of sharp downward price corrections with related macroeconomic and default risk consequences. In both the household and nonfinancial corporate sector, the debt interest burden remains at a fairly low level, as are delinquency rates in the loan portfolio (Figures 18.7 and 18.8). At the same time, rapid credit growth induced relationships with customers with no previous credit history, and micro data show that the easing of liquidity constraints allowed less educated and younger people access to credit over the 1995 to 2000 period (Farinha, 2003). Nonetheless, personal (usually parental) guarantees are the norm in Portugal for those segments of the population at the margin of affordability. Further evidence based on micro data points also to a non-increasing household debt burden in the same period, after controlling for socio-economic characteristics of each household (Farinha, 2004).

From a macroeconomic point of view, higher debt levels are assessed as a constraint to household spending, as debt service takes an increasing proportion of disposable income. The estimates of the aggregate debt service burden of the household sector point to some stabilization over the last three to four years, after having risen continuously in the 1990s. The Portuguese banking system did not experience

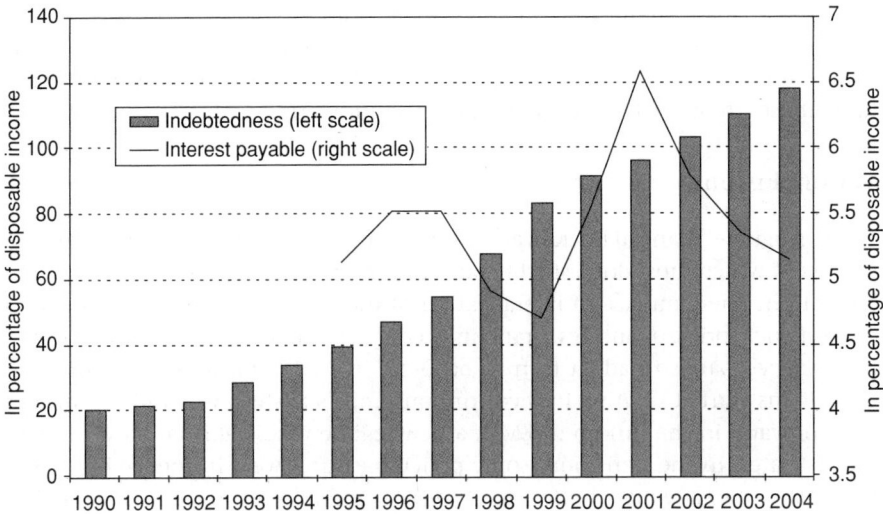

Figure 18.7 Indebtedness of Portuguese Households

Source: BoP.

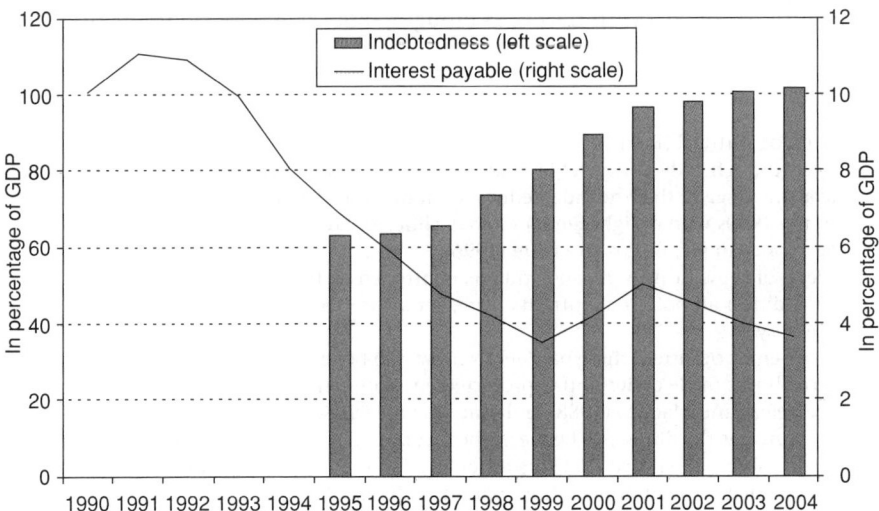

Figure 18.8 Indebtedness of Nonfinancial Corporations in Portugal

Source: BoP.

significant rises in loan losses, despite having operated in a market in which economic activity was stagnant and unemployment has been rising over the last few years. In the event short-term interest rates continue to rise, as was the case in late 2005, in particular if associated with a lag between Portuguese and euro area economic activity, credit risk materialization may increase from its current historically low level.

However, no material threats to financial stability are envisaged, given the evidence that households have not become significantly more burdened by debt obligations at the individual level and the fact that financial markets expect only gradual and limited rises in the ECB policy rates in the medium term.

V. Conclusions

The Portuguese financial liberalization started in the early 1980s and was a gradual process in which most domestic liberalization measures preceded full external liberalization. The sequence of liberalization of the instruments relevant for banks' performance (price, quantities, branching, entry, external activities) allowed former nationalized banks to adapt to market forces in a still controlled environment. Bank loans started to grow in a continuous and persistent way only from mid-1995 onward, in the run-up to EMU, a new regime with stable and low nominal interest rates. In the transition, some policy measures were introduced to ensure the existence of adequate buffers to absorb potential losses in the credit portfolio and the robustness of banks' risk management. Credit growth was not an issue of itself, and those measures were not designed to directly curb it per se or as a final objective. Key issues during this process were to establish an adequate supervisory infrastructure, and furnish the banking system with the appropriate skills to face competition and deal with new risks brought about by financial innovation.

Notes

1. Bank of Portugal (BoP).
2. Even though fully comparable figures are not available prior to 1995, the partial data available suggest that the indebtedness of nonfinancial corporations fluctuated cyclically in the 1980s with a slight tendency to decline, as a result of the credit ceilings system.
3. See, for example, Barros and Leite (1996).
4. Many of these firms were, and still are, controlled by banks.
5. In addition all potential entrants were, for a short period, required to pay fees to the Treasury.
6. Once entry occurred, these barriers to entry also benefited the new entrants, since their growth was made easier in this protected environment.
7. See Beleza and Macedo (1988) and Macedo and Sebastião (1989).
8. Measured as the difference between the (average) lending rate and the (average) deposit rate. It should be noted that this difference between average lending and deposit rates overestimates the intermediation margins of banks. Total credit was roughly 73 percent of deposits in 1985 and only 55 percent at the end of 1989.
9. The system of administratively-set interest rates prevailed in modified forms until May 1992, when the last administrative limits to deposit rates were abolished (the minimum rate on 180-day to one year time deposits, the maximum rate on demand deposits, which was indexed to the former, and also the minimum rate on deposits under the housing savings system). Total liberalization of lending rates had taken place by September 1988.
10. Empirical studies of branching decisions by banks in the Portuguese market (e.g., Cabral and Majure, 1993; Barros and Leite, 1994; or Barros, 1995) show that the sharp increase in the number of branches in both urban and rural municipalities was, to a large extent, a pre-emptive move by incumbents regarding possible entry by de novo entrants, both

national and foreign, in retail segments. Barros (1999) shows that in the deposits market, observed market power depends on product differentiation induced by the geographical location of branches and not on collusion at the industry level.

Bibliography

Barros, P., 1995, "Post-entry Expansion in Banking: The Case of Portugal," *International Journal of Industrial Organization*, 13.
——, 1999, "Multimarket Competition in Banking," *International Journal of Industrial Organization*, vol. 17(3), p. 335–52.
Barros, P. and A.N. Leite, 1994, "Conduct and Competition in Portuguese Commercial Banking," Working Paper 216, Faculdade de Economia, Universidade Nova de Lisboa.
——, 1996, "Competition in Portuguese Banking", *Economia*, vol. 20(1).
Beleza, M. and J.B. Macedo, 1988, "Implicit Taxes and Credit Ceilings: The Treasury and the Banks in Portugal," Working Paper N. 106, Universidade Nova de Lisboa.
Cabral, L. and R. Majure, 1993, "A Model of Branching with an Application to Portuguese Banking," WP 3–92, BoP.
Farinha, 1995, "Investment, Liquidity Constraints and Firm Size: The Portuguese Case," Economic Bulletin, BoP, December.
——, 2003, "The Effect of Demographic and Socioeconomic Factors on Households' Indebtedness," Economic Bulletin, BoP, June.
——, 2004, "Households' Debt Burden: An Analysis Based on Microeconomic Data," Economic Bulletin, BoP, September.
Luz, S., 1992, "The Effects of Liquidity Constraints on Consumption Behaviour: The Portuguese Experience," WP 3–92, BoP, February.
Macedo, J.B. and M. Sebastião, 1989, "Public Debt and Implicit Taxes: The Portuguese Experience," *European Economic Review*, vol. 33, pp. 573–9.

19
The Growth of Private Sector Debt in Spain: Causes and Consequences

Carmen Martinez-Carrascal[1]

The indebtedness of the Spanish nonfinancial private sector has increased significantly in recent years. For both households and nonfinancial corporations, the average annual growth rate of financing between 1995 and 2004 stood at around 15 percent and, as a result, the indebtedness ratios for both sectors have reached and subsequently exceeded the related figures for the euro area (Figure 19.1).

In the case of nonfinancial corporations, the sizable increase in indebtedness during the second half of the 1990s was associated with the internationalization of business by large Spanish corporate groups, which led them to increase their leverage considerably to meet their financing requirements. From the beginning of the current decade, the construction and property development sectors had the highest debt increases, against a background of sharp increases in house prices, with an average growth rate for domestic bank loans of around 25 percent (see Figure 19.2 for the breakdown of domestic bank loans growth). On the other hand, unfavorable developments in certain Latin American countries, together with the low return on some investments, led the large Spanish corporate groups to set about restructuring their balance sheets; the restructuring process, which now seems to be over, resulted in a negative growth rate of their debt between 2002 and 2004. In the case of households, loans for house purchases have been the most dynamic component (see Figure 19.3).

This significant increase in indebtedness can be mainly attributed to the structural changes observed in the Spanish economy in the recent period. The following section explains these changes, while Section II highlights the attendant macroeconomic and financial stability consequences. Finally, Section II draws conclusions.

I. Explanatory factors behind the increase in debt

The large increase in private-sector debt mainly reflects structural changes in the Spanish economy. Both demand and supply forces have played a role. This section summarizes the most important ones.

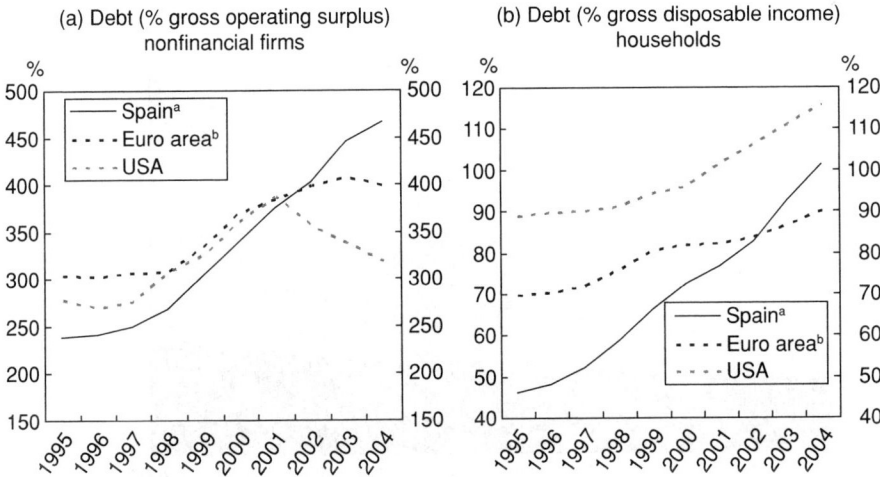

Figure 19.1 Private Nonfinancial Sector Indebtedness Ratios

Source: European Commission, Federal Reserve, and Bank of Spain (BoS).

[a] National Accounts base year 1995.
[b] Excludes Greece, Ireland, and Luxemburg. 2004 is an estimation.

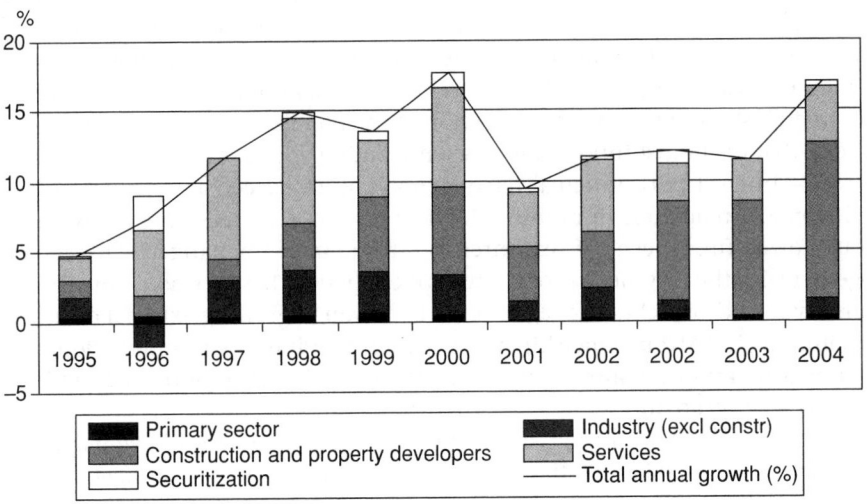

Figure 19.2 Domestic Banks' Loans by Purpose—Spain

Source: BoS.

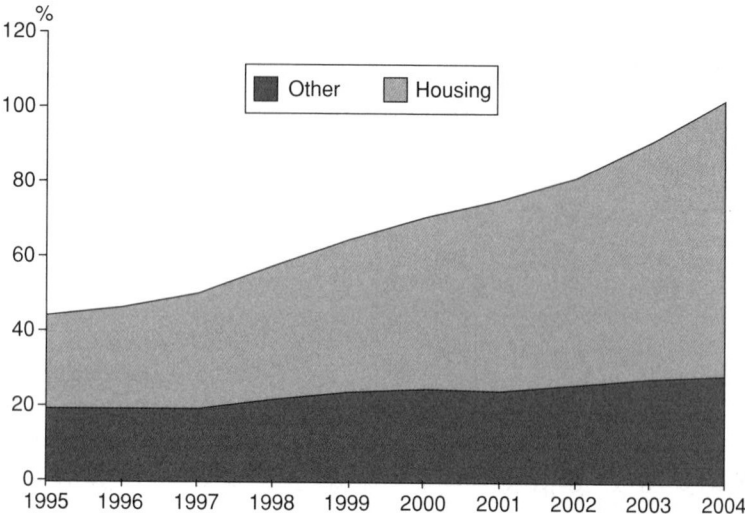

Figure 19.3 Structure of Spanish Household Debt (percent of disposable income)

Source: BoS.

The first factor was entry into the European Monetary Union (EMU), which resulted in improved income expectations (associated with an increase in the economy's potential growth), greater macroeconomic stability (and, therefore, lower uncertainty), and lower financing costs. These three factors have been conducive to a reduction in savings for precautionary reasons, an increase in desired spending levels, and, as a result, an increase in the volume of debt that households want to obtain. In addition, the reduction in financing costs, in nominal terms, has eased the credit restrictions for a certain fraction of the population: since one of the key criteria that credit institutions apply when granting a loan is that the initial debt burden—interest plus principal repayment—cannot exceed a given percentage of income, a reduction in nominal interest rates can increase the accessibility to borrowed funds, even if real interest rates remain unchanged. This factor, together with the lengthening of the repayment period, has increased households' capacity to take on debt. Also, against the backdrop of growing external openness culminating in EMU membership, there has been an increase in internationalization of corporations, contributing to the increased resort to borrowed funds by nonfinancial corporations.

Together with EMU entry, two additional structural changes have played an important role in explaining the observed increase in private sector indebtedness. First, the labor market reforms during the 1990s contributed to intensive job creation, labor market stability, and increased confidence. Through its impact on income expectations, this development has had a significant effect on spending decisions and, as a result, on indebtedness. Second, significant changes took place in the financial system, which played a pivotal role in the efficient use of savings. The deregulation and liberalization of the financial industry over the course of the

1980s resulted in more efficient and more competitive mortgage markets, leading in turn to lower interest rates and longer mortgage terms, and, therefore, better financing conditions for firms and households.

Finally, housing market developments are another key factor in explaining rapid household credit growth in Spain in recent years. Since the late 1990s, house prices have risen sharply, with an average annual growth rate of 16 percent from the beginning of this decade. Associated with this large increase are wealth effects and collateral effects, implying an increase in the quantity of funds that households want and can obtain. Loans for house purchases, in the case of households, and loans to construction and property developers, in the case of nonfinancial corporations, have shown the most salient rates of growth of debt in recent years.

II. Risks associated with the growth of private sector debt

Macroeconomic consequences

These changes in the Spanish financial system and those in the institutional environment noted in the previous section have contributed to relaxing some of the restrictions that limited the ability of households and nonfinancial firms to spread their spending decisions over time. In this sense, the increase in debt, as a counterpart of agents' desired spending decisions, has contributed to strong economic growth in recent years. Moreover, the relaxation in these restrictions has probably made consumption and investment less dependent on current income and more sensitive to their respective opportunity costs, and, therefore, to changes in interest rates (see Malo de Molina and Restoy, 2003, for a discussion on the macroeconomic implications of recent trends in households' and firms' balance sheets).

In addition, the rise in indebtedness means that the household sector is now more exposed than in the past to adverse shocks in income, interest rates, and house prices. This is especially so bearing in mind the high and increasing share of loans at variable rates and the large proportion of mortgage debt in total debt (see Figure 19.3 above). Also, the higher indebtedness of nonfinancial companies means that their exposure to variables that affect their debt repayment capacity is now greater than in the past. Moreover, price stability signifies that debt and debt service as a proportion of income will decline more slowly than in a high-inflation environment. Therefore, the low-inflation context implies that households and firms in a more vulnerable situation will remain so for a longer period of time.

While in other countries the adverse impact of a fall in house prices on household spending may be heightened by a turnaround in housing equity withdrawal, this channel is not expected to be so considerable for the Spanish economy, where there is no evidence of the significant use of mortgages to finance consumption.

In any case, to draw precise conclusions regarding the consequences of these changes in terms of the potential risks to macroeconomic and financial stability, the aggregate information needs to be supplemented by a distributional analysis, since aggregate indicators may conceal potential vulnerabilities in certain population groups. In this regard, empirical studies conducted in the BoS indicate that the impact of financial position on real decisions may be especially relevant up to a certain threshold. For example, in Hernando and Martinez-Carrascal (2003), it is found that financial pressure above a certain threshold negatively affects firms' investment and employment decisions, while under that threshold the impact is nonsignificant.

Therefore, it is worth analyzing financial ratios at a micro level taking a number of relevant characteristics (e.g., income, wealth levels, the age, and the employment status of the household head or the number of employed persons in the house). In this respect, the BoS analyzes the disaggregated information available for both Spanish households and nonfinancial firms. For households, the data from the Spanish Survey of Household Finances indicate that the financial position of the sector as a whole is sound, although for certain population groups concentrated in low-income segments, the financial pressure is considerably higher, and these groups may be particularly vulnerable to adverse shocks in employment, interest rates, and house prices.[2] As for nonfinancial corporations, information from the Central Balance Sheet Data Office (which contains data on a sample of Spanish nonfinancial corporations that report voluntarily to the BoS) indicates that the distribution of the indebtedness ratio with respect to gross operating profit plus financial revenue has moved upwards from the late 1990s, but it has remained quite stable when measured with respect to total assets.

Overall, all these aspects suggest that financial decisions will become more relevant for macroeconomic analysis and that micro studies will be useful tools in assessing the implications of credit growth. In addition, the changes in the balance sheets of households and firms and, in particular, their increased indebtedness may also have contributed to strengthening the transmission of monetary policy impulses to private expenditure. Given the absence of autonomous monetary policy, other instruments, such as fiscal policy, can contribute to the possible containment of macro-financial imbalances, while fiscal laxity can fuel them and increase the risk that correcting the imbalances entails, with subsequent adverse real effects.

In keeping with the increasing relevance of financial issues in the assessment of economic prospects, the BoS closely monitors financial developments and uses projections of financial indicators, such as indebtedness or debt burden, conditional upon the expected macroeconomic scenario, to identify to what extent the level of financial pressure borne may result in potential situations of stress. Along these same lines, stress test exercises are performed in order to evaluate the potential impact of (unlikely) negative shocks on the Spanish economy.

Consequences for financial stability

Given the predominant weight of credit in the liabilities of the nonfinancial private sector, financial stress situations that affect households or nonfinancial companies can have implications for banks' solvency. And, as pointed out above, the increase in indebtedness means that the financial position of the private sector is now more exposed to changes in interest rates and asset prices, as too, consequently, are financial institutions' balance sheets. In addition, price stability means that debt as a proportion of income declines slowly and, therefore, it is expected that individuals at risk will remain in that situation for a longer period.

As mentioned earlier, according to the disaggregated information available, the financial position of the private nonfinancial sector as a whole is sound, although for some groups of population the capacity to manage shocks may be limited and situations of financial distress may arise. From a financial stability perspective, it is also reassuring that, in the case of households, almost half of the debt is concentrated in the upper income quartile (15 percent of all households), while the self-employed (7 percent of household units), who have the highest levels of net wealth, account for almost 25 percent.

Moreover, although the banking sector may now be more exposed to changes in variables that affect the borrowers' repayment capacity, the comfortable levels at which the solvency ratio stands, together with the favorable evolution of financing institutions' profits in recent years, imply that banks, savings banks, and cooperatives have a wide safety margin to absorb the possible impact of existing risks. The soundness of the financial position that the sector enjoys has, moreover, been reinforced by the dynamic provisioning system introduced by the BoS, which became applicable in 2000 and has enabled a significant buffer to be built up.

The statistical or dynamic provision was a prudential tool designed to reduce the strong cyclical behavior that the loan loss provision ratio showed in Spain. As in many other countries, the ratio was closely linked to the volume of contemporaneous problem assets. Consistent with sound risk management practices, this prudential tool is aimed at a proper accounting recognition of *ex ante* credit risk, correcting the cyclical bias previously observed in the loan loss provisioning system. More specifically, the amount of the statistical provision is the difference between the measure of latent risk (expected losses) and the specific provision (that covering impaired assets).

It is important to note that the dynamic provisioning tool did not intend to restrict credit growth but to better synchronize risk-taking and provisioning.[3] In fact, although this instrument made credit growth significantly more costly (it absorbed close to 20 percent of banking institutions' pre-tax profits during 2002–04), it has not prevented credit to the private sector from continuing to grow at very high rates in recent years. Arguably, using prudential measures to limit credit growth is likely to require, in most cases, going further than what sound prudential principles would warrant.

On the other hand, the significant growth of the assets of the banking sector had some implications for banks' balance sheets. In particular, the large increase in debt to the nonfinancial private sector, together with the slower growth of banks' traditional liabilities vis-à-vis the nonfinancing sector, has resulted in a change in financing institutions' balance sheets. More specifically, the wider gap between bank credits and deposits has resulted in an increase of the funds raised from abroad through the issuance of assets other than equities, implying that the sector is now more dependent on this source of financing than in the past. The financial sector has also resorted much more actively to asset securitization. However, although on a growing trend, securitization is not yet very significant and, therefore, the risks of default on the repayment of loans are mainly concentrated in banking institutions.

III. Conclusions

In Spain, the indebtedness of the nonfinancial private sector has increased significantly in the past decade. This increase in leverage is mainly explained by the structural changes observed in the Spanish economy: EMU entry, labor market reforms and the deregulation and liberalization of the financial system. Also, housing market developments have been linked with the large growth rate of debt in recent years.

This higher leverage has important macroeconomic and financial stability consequences. It means that the financial position and spending decisions of the private sector will be more sensitive to changes in the macroeconomic environment, strengthening the transmission of monetary policy impulses to private sector expenditure. Moreover, the low-inflation context means that debt and debt burden as a proportion of income will decrease more slowly. Therefore, households or firms in a more vulnerable situation will remain so for a longer period of time.

Overall, increased indebtedness suggests that financial issues will play a more important role in the assessment of economic prospects and will become more relevant to macroeconomic analysis. Projections of financial indicators, such as debt ratios or debt burden, conditional upon the expected macroeconomic scenario, can prove worthwhile in identifying to what extent the level of financial pressure being borne can result in potential situations of stress. Also, micro data analysis complementing aggregate indicators will be very useful tools, since aggregate data indicators may conceal vulnerabilities in certain population groups that only a micro analysis can reveal.

Notes

1. Bank of Spain (BoS).
2. More specifically, the percentage of households with debt ratios over 3 or a debt burden over 40 percent (these are two of the figures most commonly used as benchmarks) is less than 10 percent of indebted households and slightly more than 3 percent of total households. For further details, see Banco de España, Economic Bulletin, January 2005.
3. The BoS Governor, in his occasional speeches, also warned about the risks associated with rapid credit growth.

Bibliography

Hernando, I. and C. Martinez-Carrascal, 2003, "The Impact of Financial Variables on Firms' Real Decisions: Evidence from Spanish Firm-Level Data," Banco de España, Working Paper No. 0319.

Malo de Molina, J.L. and F. Restoy, 2003, "Recent Trends in Corporate and Household Balance Sheets in Spain: Macroeconomic Implications," Banco de España, Occasional Paper No. 0402.

———, 2005, "The Spanish Survey of Household Finances (EFF): Description, Methods and Preliminary Results," Banco de España, Economic Bulletin, January.

Part Four

Cross-border Dimension: Supervisory Coordination Between Bank Supervisors

20
Cross-Border Supervisory Cooperation
Karin Zartl[1]

This chapter discusses the role played by the Committee of European Banking Supervisors (CEBS) in promoting the convergence of banking supervisory practices and supervisory cooperation in Europe (see Box 20.1 for a brief description of the CEBS). As an example of its work in this area, the CEBS has recently drafted "Guidelines for Cooperation Between Consolidating Supervisors and Host Supervisors," which sets out the key principles and practices that will enhance cross-border supervisory cooperation.

After describing briefly the structure of the Guidelines, I take a more practical approach by focusing on specific elements involved in a case study, the Supervisory Review and Evaluation Process (SREP) under Pillar 2. Within the framework of a generic risk assessment system, three issues are considered:

- an assessment of significance and systemic relevance;
- the exchange of information between home and host supervisors;
- the allocation of tasks and delegation of responsibilities.

Although specific suggestions are made in the discussion of each issue, it must be borne in mind that, most importantly, the Guidelines are aimed at enhancing the effectiveness of cross-border supervision.

I. Guidelines for cooperation between supervisors

Background

The working title of the "Guidelines for Cooperation Between Consolidating Supervisors and Host Supervisors" is the "Home-Host paper" or the "Home-Host guidelines."[2] They were launched as a Consultation Paper No. 9 in July 2005 and were open for comments for a four month period. The comments received will be thoroughly analyzed and assessed with a view to making further improvements to the paper.

Box 20.1. What is the Committee of European Banking Supervisors (CEBS)?

CEBS brings together supervisory authorities and central banks of the EU and the European Economic Area (EEA). CEBS is a "Level 3 Committee" in the new Lamfalussy framework, which has been created to speed up the legislative processes and to promote consistent implementation in the field of financial services supervision.

CEBS Members are high level representatives from 46 member organizations (supervisory authorities and central banks) from 25 countries and the European Central Bank. Observers come from the European Free Trade Association (EFTA) states (Iceland, Liechtenstein, and Norway), the EU accession countries (Bulgaria and Romania), the European Commission and the Banking Supervision Committee of the ESCB (European System for Central Banks).

CEBS has a Consultative Panel which consists of 20 members who have relevant experience of banking through either working in the industry or from representing the customers. The Consultative Panel assists in the performance of CEBS' functions and ensures that the consultation process functions effectively. The Panel acts also as a "sounding board" for CEBS on strategic issues.

One of CEBS' main tasks is to advise the European Commission on banking policy issues, in particular in the preparation of draft measures for the implementation of European legislation. CEBS also advises on technical details of banking regulation. An example in this field would be our advice on various aspects of deposit guarantee schemes.[1]

Secondly, CEBS fosters common, day to day implementation and application of Community legislation by issuing guidelines, recommendations, and standards. One of the main objectives of its work is to achieve convergence of supervisory practices within the new capital rules, i.e., the Capital Requirements Directive.[2] CEBS is drafting sets of standards and guidelines for supervisory practice that should be applied consistently by all national authorities. In this way, CEBS can ensure that banks face a more "level playing field," and that all institutions are subject to a cost-efficient supervisory system. An example of this is the Guidelines on Cross-border Cooperation.[3]

CEBS is part of the legal framework of supervision and it is the only committee that is formally charged with promoting convergence of banking supervisory practices and supervisory cooperation in Europe. This task has been assigned to CEBS by a Commission Decision, on the basis of an agreement among European finance ministers.[4] But it is not only the European Commission that will check whether CEBS is meeting this objective. CEBS is accountable to the Council and European Parliament; and its work will be closely monitored by the Inter-Institutional Monitoring Group, by the industry and by other market participants. CEBS also provides for the exchange of supervisory information and acts as an operational network for this.

CEBS is chaired by José María Roldán from the Banco d'España. Madame Danièle Nouy from the French Commission Bancaire is the Vice Chair. Mr. Andrea Enria is the Secretary General. He is seconded from the Banca d'Italia.

The London based Secretariat consists of eight full-time, long-term national experts and supports, coordinates, and assists the Committee in all its functions.

[1] For the publication of CEBS advice see <www.c-ebs.org/Advice/advice.htm>.
[2] The Capital Requirements Directive ("CRD"), which recasts Directives 2000/12/EEC and 93/6/EEC (see ECOFIN 299, Doc No. 12890/05).
[3] For the publication of CEBS standards and guidelines see <www.c-ebs.org/standards.htm>.
[4] European Commission Decision of November 5, 2003 establishing the Committee of European Banking Supervisors (2004/5/EC).

CEBS guidelines do not constitute enforceable rules and are not legal instruments, but they sit within the legal framework created by the Directives. By common consent of CEBS Members they carry a good deal of weight. These Guidelines have been adopted on a consensus basis and CEBS Members have committed to respect and be bound by them. The Home-Host guidelines were not created as something completely new, they are based on a long-established process of cooperation. Indeed, they are merely the accumulation of "best practices" as they have spontaneously developed between European supervisors.

The starting point for these Guidelines is the legal text, particularly Articles 129, 131, and 132 of the Capital Requirements Directive (CRD), which set out the statutory framework for a much enhanced collaborative approach to the supervision of cross-border banking groups. In line with the requirements of the Directive, this approach will be based on information sharing including, where necessary, consultation on supervisory action (Article 132 of the CRD), on joint model validation under the leadership of the consolidating supervisor (Article 129 of the CRD) and more generally on written arrangements for coordination and cooperation between home and host supervisors (Article 131 of the CRD).

The next challenge after finalizing the Guidelines will be to bring them to life. In the process of their application generally and in the course of agreements for individual groups, we will check carefully to determine if and where there are shortcomings in the guidelines and amend them accordingly. An important task will be to extend cooperation outside the EU. A common approach toward third countries based on these Guidelines should be devised. This concerns not only the relationship between EU Members and the USA, but also the relationship between EU Members and Central, Eastern, and South-eastern (CEE) countries.

The structure of the guidelines

There are three parts to the Guidelines: (i) the "Introductory statements" which prepare the ground for the individual guidelines that follow, (ii) an explanation of the framework within which these rules are elaborated, and (iii) practical examples of models of cooperation.

The introductory part

The overarching belief, expressed throughout the Guidelines, is that by working together supervisors will achieve more effective and efficient supervision. Avoidance of duplication of tasks and a streamlined information flow will lead to optimized use of supervisory resources and a reduction in the supervisory burden.

However, it is absolutely essential to bear in mind that—regardless of any cooperation agreements—supervisors will remain responsible at all times for any entity they have authorized.

The legal setting for these Guidelines is defined not only by the CRD, at present still the Banking Directive[3] and regulations connected to this, but also by other legislation. Obvious and influential examples of this are company law and tax law. Especially in the field of company law, the newly established European Company

Statute may impact on the group structures that supervisors will have to cope with and hence on the way groups are supervised.

The Home-Host Guidelines contain supervisory considerations with regard to this setting and these changes.

The basic principles of the framework

The framework is based on three basic principles.

- It differentiates between the host supervisors of branches and the host supervisors of subsidiaries. This is the reason for the "two scenarios" approach adopted in the practical framework set out in the Guidelines.
- It takes into account the fact that the CRD identifies features and functions which are likely to be centralized within a group, with the result that the consolidating supervisor and the host subsidiary supervisors are interested in many of the same group functions.
- It focuses on the need to coordinate supervisory approaches, to the extent possible, in order to streamline the overall supervision of the group. The CRD sets out several provisions that require cooperation, and the EU framework should conform to those provisions.

The EU framework is characterized by the concepts of significance and systemic relevance. The extent of cooperation and information sharing will be influenced by the significance or systemic relevance of the entities, both within the group and in their local market(s). The consolidating supervisor and the host supervisors may have different views on the degree of significance or systemic relevance of the various entities and on the risks stemming from these entities for the group. In such a case they should strive to reach agreement. Written agreements will specify their respective roles in their supervisory cooperation.

In determining cooperation arrangements, it should not be forgotten that supervisory responsibilities, as they are defined by the CRD, require the performance of the SREP on each authorized entity.

The models of cooperation

After explaining the general approach, the Guidelines then get down to more specific points. They are intended to be used as a checklist for supervisors and as such they were fleshed out for supervisors' practical application. After the overarching guidelines which sit on top, a chapter on information exchange and three examples of a practical framework follow. These three examples cover the practical framework for cooperation in the supervision of group and subsidiary, group and branch and model validation.

II. Case study: The "supervisory review and evaluation process"

In this section I will provide more details on one of the case studies. In doing so, I will concentrate on three main ideas and concepts contained in the Guidelines, and will not follow exactly the structure of the Guidelines. The example I have chosen is the "Supervisory Review and Evaluation Process in the Setting of Pillar 2." This process covers—on a very generic basis—the following elements (see Figure 20.1, which is intended to illustrate how every supervisory step taken by one authority is connected to the supervisory actions of the supervisors of an affiliated entity):

- Initiation of process
- Risk identification and assessment
- Planning supervisory action
- Performing supervisory tasks
- Evaluation
- Ongoing supervision

The notion of significance and systemic relevance

The first step in the SREP is the "Initiation of process." It consists mainly of three elements, starting with a preliminary assessment of cross-border issues within the group. The consolidating supervisor will then establish a communication strategy between all the supervisors, proportionate to the involvement of the different

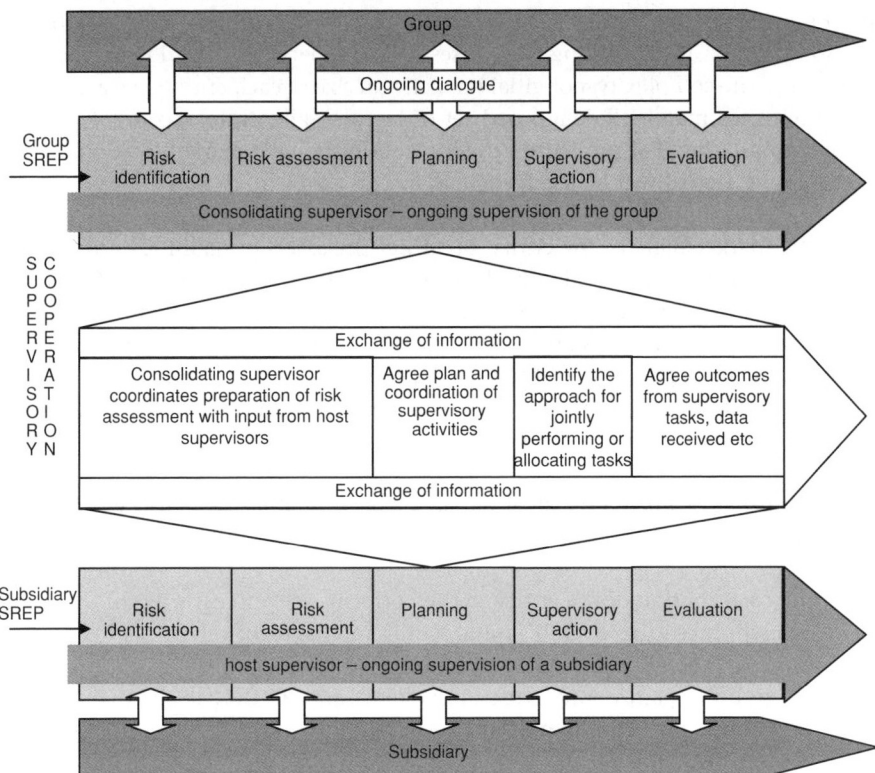

Figure 20.1 The Supervisory Review and Evaluation Process: An Illustration

supervisory authorities. For this, it is essential to agree on the significant subsidiaries in the group for the purpose of group and subsidiary supervision and on systemically important branches for the purpose of group and branch supervision.

The consolidating supervisor will undertake a preliminary risk assessment of the group, while the host supervisors will undertake a preliminary assessment of the group's entities within their jurisdictions.

Through dialogue with the host supervisors involved in the group's supervision, the consolidating supervisor will design a communication strategy proportionate to the involvement of the other competent authorities in the group's supervision.

To reach an agreement on the communication strategy, it is necessary to carry out an assessment of significance or systemic relevance, depending on whether the cross-border establishment is a subsidiary or a branch. This is necessary because the extent of cooperation and information sharing will be influenced by the significance or systemic relevance of the entities, both within the group and in their local market(s). The consolidating supervisor and the host supervisors may have different views on the degree of significance or systemic relevance of the various entities and on the risks stemming from these entities for the group. Significance and systemic relevance remain relative concepts, to be assessed by the consolidating and host supervisors on a case-by-case basis, and determined by the consolidating supervisor for the purposes of the group's supervision on a consolidated basis. In making their assessment, supervisors should consider, at a minimum, the complexity, potential impact, and size of each entity. The assessment of significance may include a broad set of factors, taken into account separately or in combination. For measuring the impact on the host market, predominantly quantitative factors will be used, such as:

- the market share of the entity, on either the assets or liabilities side (e.g., in relation to (mortgage) loans, deposits, or savings products);
- the role of the entity in specific markets (e.g., principal market-maker);
- whether the entity is an integral part of the infrastructure of the financial system (e.g., payment systems, exchanges, and clearing houses); and
- the extent to which the entity provides liquidity to the market (either generally or to individual key markets).

For measuring the impact on the group as a whole, qualitative factors will be more important:

- the contribution of the entity to the performance and earnings of the group as a whole (e.g., to overall capital requirements, turnover, or pre-tax profit);
- the risk of activities undertaken in the entity;
- the group's organizational structure, systems, and controls; its risk management functions; and senior management oversight to monitor and control risks in the entities;
- the extent to which the entities are autonomous; and
- the correlation of risks across entities.

Within the legal framework laid down in the CRD, which assigns to the authority having authorized the credit institution full responsibility for its branches, similar cooperation agreements can be established between the consolidating supervisor and host supervisor(s) with regard to systemically relevant branch(es), taking into account each supervisor's particular responsibilities, e.g., for local financial stability and liquidity. Such agreements will provide primarily for information exchanges and state clearly that, whenever an authority agrees to perform any work on behalf of another with respect to a branch, it does so within the framework of both the requesting and accepting authorities' competence and legal responsibilities.[4]

Please note that in the following subsections I do not distinguish between host subsidiary supervisors and host branch supervisors because the basic concepts are the same. It is necessary, however, to keep in mind the legal rights and obligations of each supervisory authority concerned.

Information exchange

The next and second step in the SREP and in the generic risk assessment system (the "RAS") outlined in this case study is the identification and assessment of risks. The consolidating supervisor and host supervisor need to understand fully the risks of the group and its subsidiaries. If more information is needed for the assessment, this constitutes an information gap which needs to be plugged by information exchange. The legal basis for information exchange is the new Article 132 of the CRD.

A free flow of information is an important building block in supervisory cooperation. The exchange of information is the starting point for developing sound relationships between supervisors, and building trust and confidence in their respective risk assessment processes. Moreover, it is a core element in the planning of supervisory tasks and in the coordination of the activities of supervisors under the umbrella of the consolidating supervisor. Any information exchange should start by communicating the status quo on the issues and sharing each party's own knowledge.

A communication strategy should be developed under the auspices of the consolidating supervisor in full consultation with the other supervisors concerned. The strategy should coordinate at a minimum the gathering and the dissemination of information. It should include defining by whom and to whom information should be disseminated, be it between host supervisors and a (sub)consolidating supervisor or, mutually, between host supervisors. In particular, supervisors should ensure that the consolidating supervisor has unfettered access to all relevant information and that essential information and, if deemed useful, relevant information is provided to all supervisors at an appropriate level. No undue limitations should be imposed on spontaneous communication between supervisors. The process may naturally lead to an asymmetric flow of information from consolidating supervisor to host supervisor or the other way round.

Article 132 of the CRD distinguishes between two types of information.

- *Essential information* is information which supervisors shall communicate on their own initiative. According to the CRD, information shall be regarded as

essential if it could materially influence another Member State's assessment of the financial soundness of a credit institution.
- *Relevant information* is information which supervisors shall communicate on request. Although the CRD does not define "relevant information," this is understood to mean information that is relevant to the performance of another supervisor's obligations. Supervisors should agree on the scope of relevant information to be communicated, and may consider specifying the content, format and manner in which information will be exchanged (e.g., ad hoc contacts, regular conference calls, regular meetings, written reports etc.). Supervisors requesting information should state clearly the purpose for which the information is requested. This will help to assess relevance.

The CRD states that the supervisors responsible for the consolidated supervision of EU parent credit institutions shall provide host subsidiary supervisors with all relevant information. In determining the extent of relevant information, the importance of the subsidiaries within the financial system of the Member States where they are licensed should be taken into account. That is where the notion of significance plays a role again.

The communication of information between supervisors should be a two-way process, but should be balanced to reflect the needs of the supervisors involved. For certain matters, such as those related to local market characteristics, the host subsidiary supervisor will be best placed to collect and assess information that could be of interest to the consolidating supervisor. Likewise, there are matters for which the host supervisor may find it necessary to obtain information which is best made available by the consolidating supervisor. The communication of information should be proportionate and risk-focused, to avoid unnecessary information flows and it should be as spontaneous as possible, allowing any supervisor to take the initiative, and should provide information on a timely basis.

Allocation of tasks and legal responsibilities

This third and final issue is of special importance and of great interest to the industry.

Supervisors will plan their supervisory actions like on-site inspections and other procedures in response to the risks and objectives identified in the risk assessment process. When supervisory tasks are planned, this should be done with the aim of eliminating duplication of tasks. If no common tasks are planned or identified, other tasks may then be allocated to one supervisor to achieve more effective supervision. This should lead to a decision on the most appropriate collaborative model for the planning of individual supervisory tasks.

During this step, in order to meet the objective of avoidance of duplication of tasks, it will be essential to decide which supervisor should do what. For every decision, the starting point naturally will be the legal allocation of responsibilities laid down in the Directive. For reasons of effectiveness it may then, however, be sensible to take advantage of the proximity of supervisors to the supervised entity. Within the framework of the CRD, certain tasks may be undertaken by one supervisor acting on behalf of another, thus making optimal use of resources and expertise. Supervisors may consider the resource implications, including the cost impact of such cooperation.

It therefore may be sensible to accept fully the supervisory actions of the consolidating supervisor with regard to functions centralized within the group headquarters. Host supervisors may, on the other hand, have advantages when conducting on-site inspections because of, but certainly not limited to, language.

It should be kept in mind that the practical arrangements set out in the Home-Host guidelines are intended only to improve efficiency and effectiveness in the performance of supervisory tasks. They can never lead to any alteration in the responsibilities and powers of supervisors as laid down in the legal text. It should be emphasized that the recast Banking Directive and the CRD provide the possibility for a host supervisor to delegate full responsibility for the supervision of a subsidiary to the consolidating supervisor. Although this possibility has already existed for many years, it has never yet been put into practice. Any such delegation should be based on a formal agreement that stipulates responsibilities and defines practical arrangements for the way supervisory tasks are organized. If, on the other hand, there is a decision to allocate tasks from the consolidating supervisor to a host supervisor, this can never lead to a change in legal responsibilities.

For the sake of completeness, the titles of the remaining steps in the generic SREP are: Step 4—Performing supervisory tasks; Step 5—Evaluation; and Step 6—Ongoing supervision.

III. Summary

The following is a summary of the key points of this chapter on cross-border supervisory cooperation.

CEBS brings together supervisory authorities and central banks of the EU and EEA. As such, it provides for an operational network, which is essential for effective supervision in normal times and even more so in a crisis situation.

CEBS has set out in its Consultation Paper No. 9 "Guidelines for Cooperation Between Consolidating Supervisors and Host Supervisors" how it envisages cross-border supervisory cooperation to take place. These Guidelines are based on long established "best practices" of cooperation, which are now reshaped in the light of the forthcoming CRD.

I touched briefly on the background and the structure of these Guidelines and then concentrated on one case study which is the Supervisory Review and Evaluation Process under Pillar 2. Within the framework of a generic risk assessment system I dug deeper into three issues.

Firstly, the extent of cooperation and information exchange should be based on the notion of significance of subsidiaries and systemic relevance of branches. This needs to be determined on a case-by-case basis and should be done by agreement between the supervisors involved.

Secondly, the key to effective supervision is a proportionate and spontaneous information exchange. For this, advantage should be taken of the proximity and oversight of every supervisor in the supervisory process.

The third and final issue I covered was the possibility of allocating and delegating tasks in the course of planning supervisory actions which should lead to more effective supervision. Such shifting of tasks will always need to be accompanied by written agreements.

The objective above all is "improved" cross-border supervision.

Notes

1. The Austrian Financial Market Authority and the CEBS Secretariat.
2. For the full text see <www.c-ebs.org/pdfs/CP09.pdf> (the "Guidelines" or the "Home-Host guidelines").
3. Recast 2000/12/EC Directive.
4. See Section II, Heading C "Allocation of tasks and legal responsibilities."

21
The Role of Cross-border Supervisory Coordination when Dealing with Rapid Credit Growth in Emerging Countries— Home Country Perspective

Linda van Goor[1]

The high growth figures of western European banks penetrating the Central, Eastern, and South-eastern European (CEE) markets are impressive. By October 2005, about 77 percent of banks in CEE countries were in foreign hands, and the number continues to increase.[2] The pace of internationalization gives opportunities, including for economic growth and for entrepreneurial initiatives,[3] but supervisors still need to maintain a grip on the solidity of the credit institutions.

Fragmented supervision of a group weakens the grip on its soundness as a whole, and an isolated view of a solo entity fails to consider its links with other entities in the group. Thus, the need for coordinated supervision, and the added value of consolidated supervision, should be evident. This chapter focuses on the rationale behind the supervision of a group as a group, instead of as the sum of solo entities.

As a home supervisor of three international groups, De Nederlandsche Bank (DNB) needs the support of its hosts to maintain an adequate grip on the groups. Since host supervisors request information from the home supervisors to make a balanced assessment of the solo entity's soundness, DNB views this relationship between home and host supervisors as an interdependent one. The supervisors on the Committee of European Banking Supervisors (CEBS) intend to coordinate their cooperation for internationally active European banks with immediate effect.[4] The new European approach is to supervise groups as groups, not fragmented, but coordinated among all the European supervisors involved in a group. This new approach might be crucial for Europe's stability. As new as it is for the western European financial system, it is even more so for the new member states, and the states that would like to become members. In addition to the new players entering their markets, the states also face the new supervisory framework, Basel II, that applies to those banks. Supervisors of international players will be facing major challenges in the coming years.

The initiators of the CEBS home-host cooperation framework are very much aware that important issues are still to be resolved before cross-border cooperation is possible on the broader supervisory spectrum. Those issues include depositor protection schemes, liquidity supervision, failure and crisis management, lender of last resort roles, and, perhaps the most difficult, integrity supervision. Some hosts might need more information sharing in those areas before they can enter into cooperation frameworks. Banking supervision is an area that is very much dependent on trust. In an area that is built on confidential relationships, cooperation evolves in three phases:

- Common language: giving the same issues the same name fosters common understanding.
- Information exchange: informing each other about the banks' activities using the common language, as well as getting to know how other supervisors tackle important issues, fosters trust among supervisors, and, as a result, they become convinced that other supervisors are indeed also competent.
- Division of tasks: cooperation through dividing tasks among the supervisors of a group, as a final phase, implies sharing the operational workload while aiming for a full picture.

I. Sector dynamics underlying DNB's thinking of home-host cooperation

The number of EU banking groups that earn more than 25 percent of their profits cross border is actually small, about 15 groups, all well-known: Deutsche Bank, BNP, HypoVereins, ABNAMRO, Fortis, Nordea, West LB, KBC, Santander Abbey, Dexia, HSBC, ING Group, Erste Bank, and Commerzbank, and also Citibank and Goldman Sachs. These groups, although small in number, are not expected to stop expanding, and more groups will likely follow them. The banking industry has always insisted on consistency and parallelism between supervisory frameworks. It claims that cross-border groups could be of benefit to European economies—for example, in facilitating corporate finance locally and cross border.

While some groups are supervised on a consolidated level, others are not. Since the Dutch groups are quite internationally oriented (see Figures 21.1–21.3 for Dutch banks' exposure in the CEE countries), the incentive for DNB to perform consolidated supervision has existed for some time, but for other supervisors the urgency has been less evident. There are several Memoranda of Understanding (MoUs) in place, which, in essence, serve the purpose of cross-border cooperation. Good decisions have been taken at the highest European level, such as the Lisbon agenda and the EU enlargement. But still, the European groups financing European entrepreneurs that should be driving the economic engine are facing a fragmented European supervisory system.

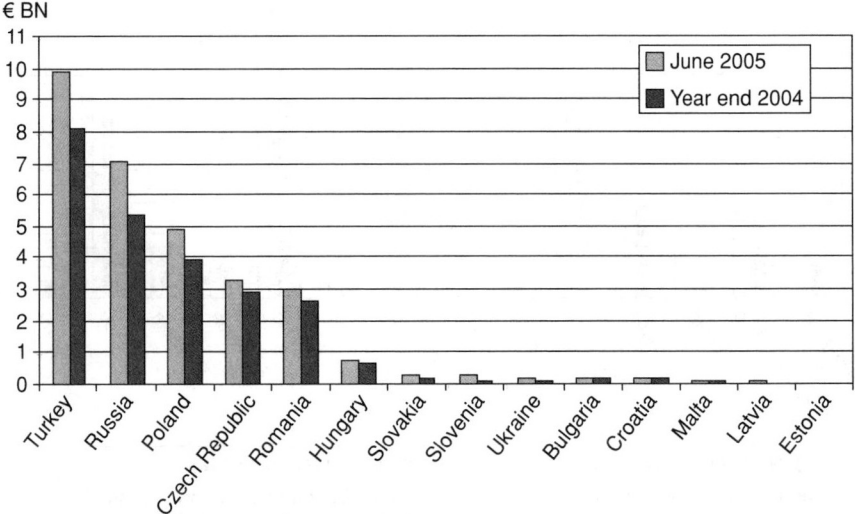

Figure 21.1 Total Exposure of Dutch Banks: Market Share in CEE Area[a] (per country in billion euro)

Source: DNB.

[a] Subsidiaries of ABNAMRO, ING and Rabobank are in the Czech Republic, Hungary, Poland, Romania, Russia and Turkey, some of which have specific market shares over 10 percent. Dutch branches are in the Czech Republic, Hungary, Slovakia, Bulgaria, Romania and Turkey.

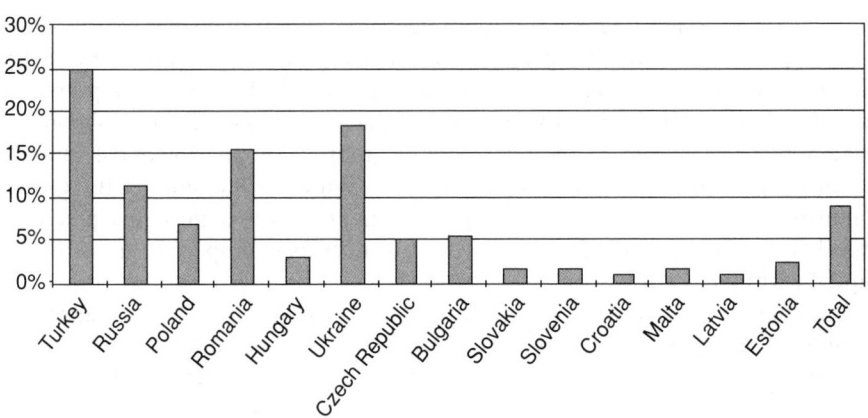

Figure 21.2 Total Exposure of Dutch Banks: Market Share in CEE Area (in percent)

Source: DNB and BIS.

Of course, the fragmented approach by which these groups are currently supervised in Europe follows from the national supervisory mandates in the respective European jurisdictions. Those mandates are based on the structures of the respective national

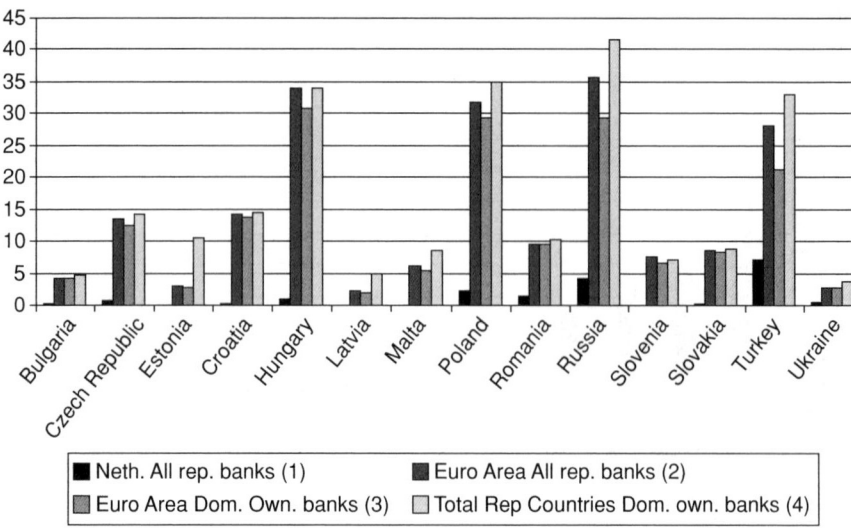

Figure 21.3 Foreign Bank Exposure in CEE Countries

Source: DNB and BIS.

(1) Local exposure Dutch banks (Dutch supervisory reports to BIS, both cross-border and domestic), as compared to (2) all reporting banks in the euro area (same as 1 for all euro area banks), and (3) domestically owned banks in the euro area (as 2, but foreign owned banks excluded), as compared to (4) total exposure reported by countries to the BIS. Differences exist in statistical definitions.

financial systems. But fragmentation implies a loss of grip that supervisors should not accept. When each EU supervisor has its own practices for subsidiaries in its jurisdiction, those subsidiaries are able to decide upon their own risk policy, as agreed with national supervisors. This might be acceptable within national borders, but among the ideas of international banking groups is the sharing of risks among the group and the incentive compatible allocation of capital among the group, following the rules of risk versus capital. Fragmentation in supervisory practices, especially in the solvency field, hampers this incentive compatible allocation of capital within a group.

This chapter is not about capitalization at the group level, for capitalization per jurisdiction remains important for most supervisors. The Dutch are known for their international focus and their consolidated supervision, placing DNB well in explaining the home supervisory perspective. DNB believes in the added value of consolidated supervision. At the same time, DNB hopes that it is also known for the pro-active way in which it involves and respects all hosts in the supervision of Dutch groups. Experience with DNB as a home should show that DNB truly cares about what happens in all the areas where Dutch groups operate—a comprehensive view, with risk-based details to focus on. DNB is the first to admit that hosts are needed for a better assessment of risks in foreign areas, stressing the emphasis on a coordinated way to supervise capital allocation within European groups.

A regulatory response to these economic dynamics is the new European capital requirements directive, which calls for cooperation between supervisors. The recitals in this directive mention the direction which supervision is taking: toward consolidated supervision of international groups. The EU supervisors do not have the choice between whether or not to stick to the current practice of fragmented supervision. For the other countries in CEE there is no such legal or political pressure, but the argument for cooperation remains the same.

II. Groups have internal capital markets

Lending activities by foreign banks in host countries will to some extent reflect decisions by the foreign head office.[5] Especially in rapidly expanding markets like the CEE countries, banks' credit supply may become constrained, because of limitations on the liability side of the balance sheet, while foreign bank subsidiaries may face fewer credit growth constraints, if they receive additional funding from their parent banks, either equity or debt. A subsidiary that has trouble raising new capital may receive funds from the parent in exchange for (new) shares. When the subsidiary requires additional liquidity rather than equity, the parent bank may provide it with funds in exchange for debt titles. Supervisors, aiming to ensure the soundness of the banks that are licensed, have an interest in understanding how the internal capital market in a group works—and to achieve this for international groups, they need each other. Thus, coordination and cooperation is a two-way process, which comes from interdependence.[6]

Research shows that local book capital (regulatory capital) is booked mainly because local regulation requires it. Banks check whether local book capital satisfies local capital adequacy rules and local large exposure rules. Fiscal incentives, which, if required, replenish capital levels, might be involved too. Economic capital, on the other hand, appears to serve different goals than what is locally booked as regulatory capital. Economic capital allocation is determined by the group's view on global portfolios on the one hand, and a hurdle rate on risk versus return on the other. The first implies a limit on local activities, the second is a filter for low-return exposures. What is important for supervisors is to understand how this risk-return driven allocation process works, what really serves as a driving force for the business activities of the local bank, and what serves as the capital buffer for unexpected losses.

For the home, it is important to know what buffers must be available for the globally distributed exposures, and whether total capital satisfies that global need. In order to assess whether economic capital for local exposures is sufficient, the home needs the host to check upon local estimates of risk, both on the individual level as well as on the portfolio level. What transpires is a consolidated picture.

For the host, it is important to know whether the group will always have sufficient capital available to protect the customers of the local bank, what buffers are available for the local exposures, and how certain the role of the bank is in the local banking system.

The CEBS home-host framework aims to give better answers than just a dialogue with the subsidiary itself, using essential information shared among the group, and the assessment of cross-border impacts in each step of the Risk Assessment System.

It is evident, therefore, that homes and hosts need each other when assessing the licensed banks (both parents and subsidiaries) in their respective jurisdictions. Since this relationship is not bilateral but multilateral, this implies a coordinating role for the home on information sharing with the network of supervisors involved in the supervision of a banking group. At the same time, this argument shows that bilateral MoUs fail to meet the need to get the full picture.

III. CEBS' home-host framework

The ideal European situation for the supervision of European financial groups would be one of low costs and effective supervision, of streamlined supervisory processes, and of converged standards. But before supervisors can achieve that situation, some very complex issues have to be solved: depositor protection, lender of last resort issues, failure management, crisis management, liquidity supervision, and integrity supervision. For now, CEBS cannot go further than stating its intention to make the supervision of international groups more efficient, to reduce the administrative burden on banks, and to start to focus on solvency. Effectiveness could only increase once the other issues have been solved.[7]

Key words in the home-host framework are "proportionality, significance, and risk-based supervision." "Proportionality" refers to efficiency and effectiveness, benefits exceeding costs, and actions serving a supervisory purpose. "Significance" refers to the importance in a jurisdiction, either quantitatively (market share) or qualitatively (e.g., a clearing role in a national system). Materiality (relative size of the entity within a financial group) is one of the factors that determine significance, but sometimes a non-material entity is still significant.[8] "Risk-based supervision," which is one of the spin-offs of the Basel II exercise, refers to the focus on where the risks actually are, instead of merely ticking a check box of risks.

Having a home-host framework appears to be a good thing in itself. In this framework, supervisors are talking about a common format and sharing and exchanging information in a common language, as opposed to the current situation, where every bank delivers different information packages to the respective supervisors. The intention to increase cooperation among CEBS members has already had the immediate effect of learning from each other, and building trust. The second immediate effect has been the sense of relief that capacity problems caused by the Basel II implementation can be covered by a wider range of possibilities: supervisors of groups determine in a coordinated way who is doing what—proportional and significance (or risk) based. This in turn reduces work duplication.

Although the capital adequacy directive gives the option to delegate the assessment of capital adequacy to the home supervisor of the group, most subsidiaries are also checked on a solo basis. Thus, the situation among EU supervisors is, in practice, not very different from the situation in other European countries, although within the EU, the delegation of supervisory powers to the home is a legal possibility. The main principle of the licensor supervising the licensees applies to both.

In order to achieve the prerequisites to actual cooperation, namely a common language and information sharing, CEBS came up with a list of essential information and an interpretation of relevant information. "Essential information" is information that all supervisors need for the assessment of the soundness of a bank, either the group, the parent, or the subsidiaries: governance structure, legal structure, main business units, responsible business units in host countries where the bank is significant, and so on.

The role of a host in the supervision of an international bank is made explicit with regard to the national mandates of the host and the explicit obligations of a licensor in supervising licensees. This is not for the objective of improving the cross-border framework, but to fulfill this prerequisite before a host can enter into an international cooperation arrangement. Also the proximity of hosts (geographically and culturally), together with the resulting knowledge of local risk estimates and local market circumstances, is acknowledged as valuable input into the building of a comprehensive picture.

IV. Proof of the pudding: Dutch implementation of home-host cooperation

Part of the preparation for the Basel II implementation in Dutch international banks is the structured information sharing with the hosts of the Dutch banks. DNB entered into Step 1 of the CEBS home-host framework, by inviting all hosts at the beginning of 2005, and talking to them about the significance of the Dutch banks in their countries. An in-depth questionnaire on the implementation plans and legal processes for Basel II showed that there are no legal impediments to cooperation and coordination.[9] In January 2005, Dutch banks presented their progress with regard to Basel II implementation to their European hosts, including the CEE countries. The meetings were followed by bilateral talks with hosts on significance. In Fall 2005, DNB sent out communication plans in order to be prepared for the arrival of the first Basel II applications. The communication plans include validation plans, models used, and requirements for local checks of local risk estimates. DNB observed a sense of relief among the supervisors present in this exercise, that the operational workload of the labor intensive Basel II kind of supervision could be shared. It appears to be possible to talk about a group and its entities and determine the interests of home and hosts in a risk-based manner.

Finally, the Basel II risk management systems are actually a blessing in disguise: not only has supervision forced banks to think about risks much better than anyone ever did, but supervisors have also forced themselves to determine which risks have a greater influence on the solidity of the banks and the financial systems and which have a lesser influence. The Basel II exercise and the home-host framework coming from Basel II give an opportunity for supervisors to get a better grip on internationally active groups, with a view to carrying out more effective supervision and ensuring a sound, European based banking system. This makes banking supervision today a challenge that has probably never been more interesting.

Notes

1. De Nederlandsche Bank (DNB).
2. European Central Bank (ECB) (2005), unweighted average.
3. De Haas and Van Lelyveld (2006), and De Haas and Naaborg (2005).
4. Zartl in this volume on CEBS' home-host cooperation framework elaborates upon the reasons behind the framework. Among those are the European Company statute, the evolving organizational structures of European banks, and the obligations laid down in the new Capital Requirements Directive (CRD).
5. De Haas and Naaborg (2005b) elaborates upon this argument.
6. For argument's sake, we stick to the solvency supervision argument, but we are aware that issues like deposit protection and liquidity supervision should be integrated into the argument.
7. See Zartl in this volume.
8. For example, Bank Slaski covers less than 1.5 percent of ING's balance sheet total, but 7 percent of the Polish deposit protection scheme. Thus Bank Slaski is not material, but it is significant.
9. As an exception, Russia made a formal reservation.

Bibliography

CEBS, 2005, Consultation on the Guidelines for Validation and Assessment of the Risk Management and Risk Measurement Systems Used by Credit Institutions and Investment Firms (CP10).
——, Consultation on the Guidelines for Supervision of Cross-border Banking and Investment Firms Groups (CP09).
——, Consultation on the Role and Tasks of CEBS (CP08).
——, Second Round of Consultation on Supervisory Review Process (CP03, second).
De Haas, Ralph and Ilko Naaborg, 2005a, "Does Foreign Bank Entry Reduce Small Firms' Access to Credit? Evidence from European Transition Economies," DNB Working Paper 50.
——, 2005b, "Internal Capital Markets in Multinational Banks: Implications for European Transition Countries," DNB Working Paper 51.
De Haas, Ralph and Iman van Lelyveld, 2006, "Foreign Banks and Credit Stability in Central and Eastern Europe, A Panel Data Analysis," *Journal of Banking and Finance*, June.
European Central Bank, 2005, "Banking Structures in the New EU Member States," report by the Working Group on Developments in Banking.
Zartl, K., 2005, "Cross-Border Supervisory Coordination," paper presented at the Conference on Rapid Growth of Banking Sector Credit to the Private Sector, Sinaia, Romania, October 7–8, 2005.

22
Home and Host Supervisors' Relations— A Host Supervisor's Perspective

Piotr Bednarski and Dariusz Starnowski[1]

As in other Central, Eastern, and South-eastern European (CEE) countries, almost all major domestic banks have been privatized and sold to foreign banks in Poland. As a result, foreign banks dominate the banking sector in Poland through their subsidiaries and branches. All the major banks are listed on the Warsaw Stock Exchange and have local minority shareholders. Overall, foreign banks control more than 67 percent of Polish banking assets (Figure 22.1). As in the Czech Republic, Hungary, and other CEE countries, almost all systemic banks are foreign-owned.

Furthermore, foreign banks individually hold very substantial market shares in host countries, which are often much higher than their share in their home country banking sector. In G-10 countries, it is almost an unknown that a single foreign

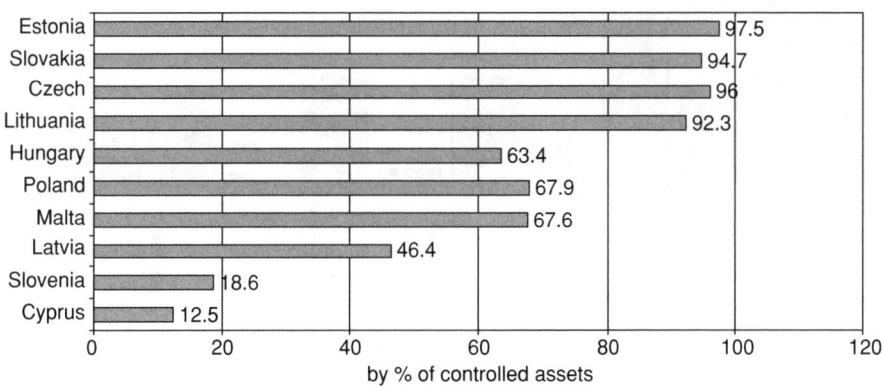

Figure 22.1 Predominant Presence of Foreign Investors in the Banking Sector Assets in the New Member States of the EU

Source: European Central Bank (ECB), as of end-2003.

bank controls a quarter (or over half) of the banking sector of the country, but this is not uncommon in CEE countries (Figure 22.2).

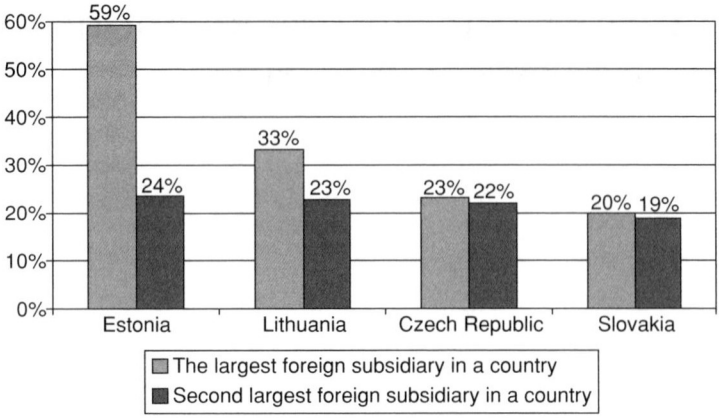

Figure 22.2 Share of Foreign Financial Groups in the Banking Sectors in CEE Countries via their Subsidiaries

Source: Central banks' reports and banks' financial reports available at their websites, as of end-2004.

Another important feature of CEE banking systems is asymmetry in the relative size of a foreign-owned bank in the bank's group and in the host country. The share of a major foreign subsidiary in a host country like Poland (and other CEE countries) is almost always much bigger than in its own banking group, where the foreign subsidiary is almost immaterial from the group perspective. Figure 22.3 illustrates this situation.

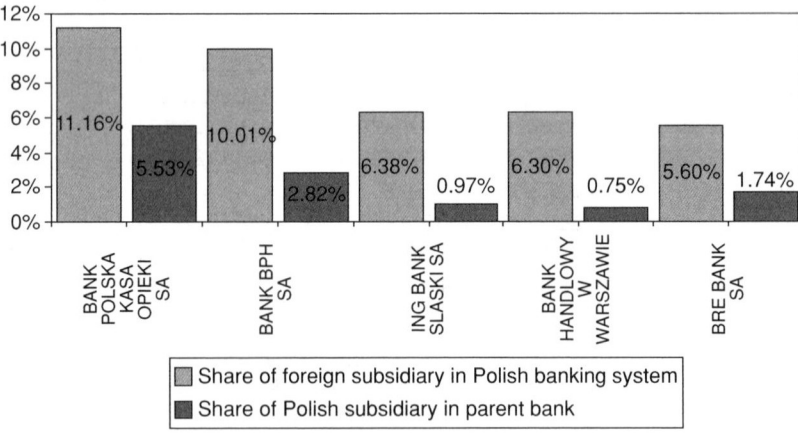

Figure 22.3 Share of Foreign Subsidiary in the Polish Banking Sector and Share in its Parent Bank

Source: NBP data and financial reports of the banks available at their websites, as of end-2004.

Finally, it should be added that the banking sectors of all EU new member states are relatively small; for example, total bank assets of all these countries are equivalent to around 63 percent of ING Bank assets.

To illustrate the relatively small size of CEE banking sectors, it is worth comparing them with international banks. Figure 22.4 provides a comparison of the size of the Polish banking sector with that of major foreign banks operating in the country.

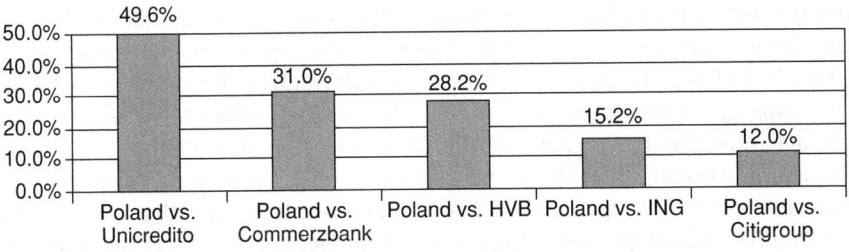

Figure 22.4 Share of Polish Banking Sector in Parent Institution Assets (in percent)

Source: NBP data and financial reports of the banks available at their websites, as of end-2004.

I. Impact of systemic foreign banks on the stability of the local financial sector

As noted above, CEE countries are predominantly the host countries of banking sectors that are mostly foreign controlled. Foreign control of local banking sectors has resulted in closer interdependence between local systemic banks and foreign parents, as well as between home and host supervisors. The emergence of foreign systemic banks in CEE countries necessitates oversight not only of the local bank but also, to some extent, the safety and soundness of the parent bank, since the latter may affect the condition of the local bank, as well as the stability of the financial system in the host country. A spillover of systemic risk across borders has become more likely.

As a consequence, host supervisors have started to emphasize a need to realign Basel and Brussels guidance and directives, respectively, to address the growing information needs of host supervisors towards home or consolidating supervisors. This is especially the case for local foreign subsidiaries that may influence negatively the stability of the whole financial system of the host country. A full picture of the risks posed by a bank in the host country may require knowledge of the parent bank's financial situation and global risks. This knowledge is partially included in published information, but what is crucial is the information received from and evaluated by the home supervisor.

Another aspect in the parent bank–foreign subsidiary discussions should be the source of funding for local subsidiaries. All in all, from the host country's point of view, it is not the shareholders' money that is predominantly at stake but depositors' money and/or local deposit insurance.

II. Cooperation between home and host supervisors

One of the key answers to the issues identified above is the "stand alone principle." We believe that in banking sectors dominated by foreign banks the "stand alone principle" makes sense. It does not exclude cooperation, exchange of information, and cross-border crisis management.

In parallel, however, especially in Europe and somewhat stimulated by Basel II and the lobbying of banks, a new concept has been promoted that would give more decision-making powers to the "consolidating supervisor." One purpose of this trend is to lower the burden for the industry through the introduction of "one-stop shopping," which implies a centralized supervisory authority—a single point of contact and decision, which would effectively limit the role of the host supervisor while retaining his responsibilities. There is a clear imbalance in this concept because the greater power being given to the home supervisor is not paralleled with more responsibility, including bearing the costs related, for instance, to crisis resolution.

At a global level, the relations of home and host supervisors are governed by Basel Committee guidance, including the Basel Concordat (1983) and the Core Principles of Effective Banking Supervision. Bilateral or multilateral relations are often formalized in the form of Memoranda of Understanding (MoU), and tested in practical daily collaboration. Within the European Union, the principles of home and host supervisor relations are established in Directive 2000/12 relating to the business of credit institutions (Codified Banking Directive), and the Capital Requirement Directive (CRD), which is still in draft.

Following the EU Directives, a consolidating supervisor (a home supervisor) shall coordinate the exchange of information as well as the supervisory activities, also in time of crisis, with a view to avoiding unnecessary communication and duplication of tasks for both supervisors and supervised institutions. This role has been substantially expanded and enhanced in the CRD draft.

In our opinion, both solo and consolidated supervision are important, as the former complements the latter. There should be no conflict of interests between them. In the last ten years, cooperation between supervisors has improved and now follows Basel standards. Interestingly enough, the Basel Committee standards recognize more and more the emergence of systemic foreign subsidiaries and the need for a more balanced exchange of information between home and host supervisors. On the other hand, the growing complexity of large groups, functionally integrated and linked by intra-group transactions, causes group-wide monitoring to be increasingly important from a financial stability perspective. At the same time, such monitoring is more difficult to perform without adequate information sharing by all the authorities involved. The need for effective cooperation is communicated by MoU and ongoing collaboration (various working groups at Basel and at the regional level).

III. Industry concerns

From the perspective of some participants in the industry, the current practice of cross-border supervision is not appropriate and probably too costly, as there are: too many regulators to deal with; excessive reporting burdens (risk of duplicative work); duplicative supervisory activities; multiple supervisory approvals; and differences in interpretation of the same laws, rules, regulations, and regulatory practices.

Some financial institutions are keen to see greater cooperation, coordination and convergence of supervisory practices in the EU (a more streamlined approach to cross-border financial supervision), mainly for reasons of efficiency. An initial step toward achieving that concept is the proposal of having a lead supervisory body designed to reduce the duplication of supervisory activities. This body would be in charge of supervision on a consolidated, as well as on the local level, responsible for prudential supervision not only of branches in other EU member states, but also of fully owned subsidiaries in other EU member states. It would be the single point of contact for all issues in the field of prudential supervision and would coordinate all reporting duties, on-site examinations, and licensing procedures. Also, it would be responsible for group-wide model validation, capital allocation at group level, and liquidity rules at group and branch level. It would approve the cross-border set-up of central functions. The host supervisor would carry out local examinations, based on delegation by the lead supervisor, while both home and host supervisors would form a college of supervisors for a specific group.

The idea of a lead supervisor is quite radical for a number of reasons:

- First, remaining legal differences between member states could impair the practical functioning of this approach (the lead supervisor may not always be adequately equipped to perform supervisory duties that extend to another country where the subsidiary is located, because he/she may lack the necessary supervisory powers, knowledge, and tools).
- Second, it may be difficult to gain sufficient political support for a transfer of supervisory responsibility to the lead supervisor.
- Third, the commitment of the lead supervisor to the host entities may not always be fully clear and certain, especially in those cases where there might be some divergent interests (for example, when a parent bank is not systemically relevant while its subsidiary is a systemic bank in the host country).
- Fourth, it may be hard to apply the principles in a crisis situation. Present arrangements for crisis management, emergency liquidity assistance, insolvency and winding-up procedures, and deposit insurance are all based on the existing, clear allocation of supervisory responsibilities and potential costs.

Therefore, the introduction of the concept of a lead supervisor, while retaining all other components of the supervisory system intact, would result in an unbalanced transfer of powers to lead supervisors without the transfer of legal and financial responsibility.

The European legislators, under huge pressure from the industry, have accepted some of these ideas. As a result, a softer version of the lead supervisor concept for the model validation in Basel II is proposed. According to the EU Commission's proposal, the scope of the home (consolidating) supervisor's powers would be broadened. The consolidating supervisor would plan and coordinate supervisory activities, coordinating the gathering and dissemination of information about the group, both on an ongoing basis and in emergency situations (the consolidated supervisor will also be required to alert central banks and finance ministries). The most important change concerns the right to lead the consultation process of the college of supervisory authorities with regard to the validation of group-wide advanced models, and to take the final decision as regards the handling of the bank if the various competent authorities are unable to come to an agreement within six months.

IV. Prospects for supervisory cooperation

Currently, we are facing two possibilities. The first one is to recognize that each country is an independent regulator, and has full rights to decide about requirements to be placed on foreign subsidiaries, such as the approval of the models used in the calculation of capital requirements. Such an approach should, however, be accompanied by progress toward the convergence of practices. In this way, industry concerns would be at least partially addressed, making the cross-border supervisory process comparable, easier, and cost-sensitive (Basel II could be a pilot test).

The second option is to further develop the idea of lead supervisor, where the host supervisor would be quite limited in its powers, and become a sort of secondary supervisor. There is also a more radical version being promoted by some European and other industry groups and supported by some academics that happen to come from home countries. It is the idea of a more radical overhaul of the existing system of supervision toward a sort of European supervisory framework but not covering the safety net and other elements. This approach seems to lack balance and completeness.

A more integrated supervisory system could be considered only if one can guarantee a global budget in case of crisis, global depositor protection, and home or global emergency liquidity assistance. But the stability of the financial system is still perceived to be for the common good of individual national markets. Thus, the centralization of supervisory functions without first solving the problem of crisis management will not eliminate a basic inconsistency: depositors and taxpayers from one country cover the loss from banks in another country.

Another aspect is cooperation of home and host supervisors. Host country supervisors' needs, especially in countries dominated by foreign banks, should be understood and recognized. These needs include the possibility of receiving evaluated information on the risk and financial strength of the overall group. This would not contradict the principle that the consolidating supervisor is responsible for the supervision of the group-wide functions and the overall solvency of the consolidated group. As a consequence thereof, supervisory powers remain in full with the authorities that have licensed individual institutions; consolidating supervisors will thus have to continue to rely on their host peers for effective intervention at subsidiary levels.

At a practical level, home and host supervisors should work towards greater convergence, comparability, and practical coordination in supervising cross-border banks. However, the sovereignty of particular countries' jurisdictions and the interests, both of home and host supervisors, and the "supervisory level playing field" should always be respected. Home and host supervisors have a common interest in ensuring, to the extent possible, that cross-border activities are subject to effective supervisory arrangements. The emergence of large and complex cross-border banking groups has highlighted the importance of effective information sharing and coordination between authorities.

More open and symmetrical information exchange—proportionate to the entity's systemic relevance and risk-focused—is the very starting point for developing sound relations between supervisors. Information exchange should be a two-way process also from home to host supervisor. In the exercise of supervision on a consolidated basis, the consolidating supervisor may need information from the host supervisor to make an appropriate assessment of a particular situation, paying due consideration to the local conditions. The host supervisor is the best placed to collect and assess information that could be of interest to the consolidating supervisors as regards the national banking landscape and assessment of the local risks faced by subsidiaries and branches. In addition, the host supervisor is the only one to have the necessary legal prerogatives and authority to adopt supervisory or precautionary measures in respect of the subsidiaries in the event of contingencies or crisis.

Enhanced cooperation should seek to reduce the implementation burden on the banks by avoiding requiring redundant or uncoordinated approval and validation work, and hence duplicative work on supervised institutions. Another goal is to use effectively, and conserve, scarce supervisory resources—especially in small countries. Cooperation arrangements for the supervision of subsidiaries of banking groups should be based on written agreements.

Note

1. National Bank of Poland (NBP).

Part Five
Concluding Remarks

23
Lessons from Country Experiences with Rapid Credit Growth, and Policy Implications

Charles Enoch and İnci Ötker-Robe[1]

The chapters in this volume set out a wide range of country experiences and of measures taken to cope with rapid credit growth. In this concluding chapter, we discuss some common themes that emerge from the experiences of the countries in Central, Eastern, and South-eastern Europe (CEE) as well as those of the three countries in the euro zone that have been also experiencing rapid credit growth in recent years—Greece, Portugal, and Spain (GPS). We draw some tentative policy conclusions.

I. Observations from country experiences

The nature of the credit growth

Bank credit to the private sector has expanded rapidly in many of the CEE countries covered by the case studies, on average about 20 percent per year during 2000–04. The credit expansion has been characterized by the following common features (Table 23.1):

- In most countries covered, credit expansion has been mainly driven by foreign banks, though domestic banks also accelerated credit. Foreign banks hold on average about 80 percent of total domestic banking system assets in these countries, ranging from 47 percent in Latvia to over 90 percent in Croatia, Estonia, Lithuania, and Slovakia (see also Mihaljek and Arcalean et al in this volume).
- The rapid credit growth was financed both by a steady growth of banks' deposit base (particularly as confidence in local banking systems was regained) and, especially more recently, by bank borrowing from abroad, including from

parent banks (Bulgaria, Croatia, Estonia, Latvia, Lithuania, and Romania, similar to what had been observed in GPS during their convergence to the euro zone).
- Lending to the corporate sector contributed significantly to rapid credit expansion in Croatia, Estonia, Poland, Ukraine, and at least initially, in Latvia, Lithuania, and Romania. In more recent years (especially from 2002–03), household loans have dominated the credit growth in almost all countries covered. Similar developments were observed in GPS. Among household loans, consumer loans have made a larger contribution in Bulgaria, Croatia, Poland, and Romania, while in the remaining countries (Estonia, Latvia, Lithuania, and Slovakia), housing loans (including mortgage loans) have been the main driving force (also see Mihaljek in this volume). Credit growth in Spain has been similarly driven by housing loans.
- In all the CEE countries covered, bank lending has had a very significant foreign exchange (FX) component in recent years, ranging from over 45 percent to 80 percent in the Baltic countries, Bulgaria, Croatia, and Romania.

What motivated rapid credit growth?

A combination of supply and demand factors has been underlying the rapid growth of bank credit in the CEE region (see Table 23.2, as well as Arcalean et al; Boissay, Calvo-Gonzalez, and Koźluk; Duenwald, Gueorguiev, and Schaechter; and Hilbers, Ötker-Robe, and Pazarbasioğlu in this volume). Similar factors have played a role in stimulating credit in GPS. These similarities underpin the regional aspects of the rapid credit growth.

- The **most common demand factors** included the easing of borrowing costs with declining interest rates in the region, combined with increased confidence in domestic economies, rising incomes, and optimistic expectations, particularly in the context of EU accession prospects; all these factors led to a shift in attitudes toward borrowing, and were important in stimulating demand for both corporate and household loans. Stable and predictable exchange rates, particularly with the prospect of adopting the euro in the future, stimulated foreign currency denominated borrowing, by reducing perceived exchange rate risks, and hence the cost, of such borrowing (Bulgaria, Estonia, and Lithuania with currency boards, and Croatia, Latvia, Romania, Slovakia, and Ukraine with pegged or tightly managed exchange rate regimes).
- **Additional factors that strengthened the demand** for bank loans included: imbalances in the housing market (with rising real estate prices), which encouraged the demand for housing loans including by raising expectations of future price increases (Latvia, Lithuania, Romania, and Slovakia), and various fiscal incentives associated with mortgage subsidies, guarantees, and tax deductibility of mortgage repayments, all of which helped reduce the effective cost of such borrowing (Estonia, Lithuania, and Slovakia at the initial stages).

Table 23.1 Nature of the Credit Growth

Nature of credit growth	Bulgaria (2001–)	Croatia (1995–98) (2000–)	Estonia (1996–98) (2002–)	Latvia (2000–)	Lithuania (2002–)	Poland (1996–97)	Romania (2001–)	Slovakia (2003–)	Ukraine (2000–)	Greece (1998–2005)	Portugal (1995–)	Spain (1995–)
Foreign bank driven	✓	✓ (2000–)	✓	✓	✓	✓	✓	✓	✓			✓ (from end-1990s)
Financing mainly from:												
Increased borrowing abroad (e.g., from parents; securitization)	✓	✓ (2000–)	✓	✓ (since 2003)	✓	✓	✓		✓		✓	
Increasing deposit base	✓	✓ (1995–98)	✓	✓	✓	✓	✓	✓[a]	✓			
FX-denominated credit significant	✓	✓	✓	✓	✓	✓	✓		✓			
Fastest growth in:												
Corporate sector	✓		✓	✓ (initially)	✓ (initially)		✓ (initially)	✓	✓[b]		✓	✓
Household sector for:	✓	✓[b]	✓	✓[b,c]	✓ (from 2003)	✓	✓ (from 2003)	✓	✓	✓[b]	✓[b]	✓
Consumer loans	✓[b]	✓[b]			✓		✓	✓	✓	✓		
Housing/real estate	✓	✓	✓	✓ (from 2003)	✓[b]	✓	✓[b]	✓[b]		✓		✓

Source: The country case studies, and Duenwald, Gueorguiev, and Schaechter in this volume.

[a] Only for corporate loans which is not a fast growing component of total loans and the corporations are in general naturally hedged with their strong export orientation. The share of FX loans in total household loans (the fastest growing component of total loans) is low.
[b] More dominant in the rate of growth.
[c] Since 2000, growth rates of credit to households have constantly been higher than for corporates. However, contribution to overall credit growth of credit to households picked up substantially only since 2002 due to initially low base. As of end-2005, contributions to overall credit growth by both sectors are approximately equal.

- **The most common supply factors** contributing to the growth of bank lending included: the privatization, deregulation, and reform of the domestic banking systems and the legal infrastructure; the arrival of foreign banks that offered new products, expertise, and improved risk management practices, while providing easy access to funding from parent banks; and increased competition in the banking sector that increased willingness to extend loans to gain/maintain market share. Improved economic fundamentals and income prospects also helped reduce risk premia of the borrowers in the private sector, and increased banks' willingness to extend loans. The opening of the capital accounts brought abundant inflows, helping ease banks' liquidity constraints in financing new loans. The lack of well-developed capital markets has also made banks the main funding source to satisfy the growing demand for loans; the share of bank assets in total assets of the financial system generally exceeds 75 percent in these countries. Finally, the need to cofinance projects supported from EU structural funds provided an additional stimulus to credit growth (e.g., Latvia and Lithuania).
- Many of these supply and demand factors reflect the process of catching-up from low levels of financial intermediation to the market economy levels that prevail elsewhere in Europe. As EU accession and European integration progresses and the degree of financial deepening converges to levels in western Europe, the pace of credit growth may be expected to slow down.

What are the main risks associated with the credit growth?

While the rapid credit growth in CEE countries may be part of a catching-up process, policymakers have been concerned about the potential implications of its pace for macroeconomic and financial stability, in particular where rapid credit growth has coincided with a weakening current account and vulnerabilities in the financial systems. These concerns call for a careful look, not least because there are some preliminary indications that the observed rates of credit growth may have been "excessive" in some of the countries in the region (see Boissay et al in this volume) or may soon lead to private sector credit-to-GDP levels that are higher than suggested by fundamentals (see Backé et al in this volume).

- On the **macroeconomic front**, the episodes of rapid credit growth have been associated with a deterioration in the current account balances (Bulgaria, Croatia, Estonia, Latvia, Poland, Romania), and in many of these countries with an increase in net foreign liabilities of the banks that increased external vulnerabilities (see Table 23.3). Banks have been borrowing funds from abroad (including from parent banks) and/or have been drawing down their foreign assets to fund the rapid pace of credit expansion (the Baltic countries, Bulgaria, Croatia, and Romania). Inflation has remained subdued in general despite the rapid credit growth, except in a few cases where the authorities were concerned about some upside risks (e.g., Latvia, Poland, Romania).
- On the **financial front**, many banks in CEE markets have comparatively new and untested credit risk systems. While most financial soundness indicators do

Table 23.2 Factors Stimulating Credit Growth

Factors stimulating credit growth	Bulgaria (2001–)	Croatia (1995–98, 2000–)	Estonia (1996–98, 2002–)	Latvia (2000–)	Lithuania (2002–)	Poland (1996–97)	Romania (2001–)	Slovakia (2003–)	Ukraine (2000–)	Greece (1998–2005)	Portugal (1995–)	Spain (1995–)
Demand factors												
Increased confidence in the economy, rising incomes, and associated rise in demand	✓	✓		✓	✓	✓	✓	✓	✓	✓	✓	✓
Catching up from low financial deepening	✓	✓	✓ (initially)	✓	✓	✓			✓	✓	✓	
EU convergence issues	✓		✓	✓	✓		✓	✓		✓	✓	✓
Lower interest rates, and easing of liquidity constraints	✓		✓	✓	✓		✓	✓		✓	✓	✓
Stable/predictable exchange rates	✓	✓	✓				✓		✓			
Imbalances in housing market (including rising real estate prices)				✓	✓		✓					✓
Shift in attitudes toward borrowing, with optimistic expectations				✓			✓	✓	✓	✓	✓	✓
Taxes/subsidy factors that lower effective loan rates (e.g., for housing, consumer loans,...)			✓		✓	✓		✓ (initially)				
Supply factors												
Absence of funding sources other than banks	✓			✓	✓		✓	✓	✓	✓	✓	
Competition in the banking sector	✓	✓	✓	✓	✓		✓	✓	✓	✓	✓	✓
Privatization/deregulation of banks	✓	✓	✓	✓	✓		✓	✓	✓	✓	✓	✓
Capital accounts liberalization and abundant inflows		✓	✓	✓	✓		✓					
Arrival of foreign banks and new products	✓		✓			✓	✓					
Availability of EU funds			✓	✓								

Source: The country case studies, and Duenwald, Gueorguiev, and Schaechter in this volume.

not seem to indicate a clear rise in financial risks in the banking system, they are usually viewed as lagged indicators of banking system problems. In fact, there have been some indications of rising financial sector risks in a number of countries in the group:

- Banks have significant exposure to indirect FX risks through their FX lending to corporate and household sectors, where information on customers' foreign currency exposures and the extent of their hedging remains limited. In some of these countries, the authorities view FX related risks as relatively low, given the importance of the euro in the current arrangements, the credibility of the prevailing pegs vis-à-vis the euro, and plans to adopt it as the national currency in the future (Bulgaria, the Baltic countries, Slovakia). In some countries, FX exposures are assessed to be reasonably hedged (Latvia, Lithuania, Slovakia), though not with respect to the euro; the latter may leave the banks potentially exposed to indirect FX risks through a rise in their borrowers' debt burden, in case of unexpected, though seemingly improbable, adverse exchange rate movements.
- There are potentially higher credit risks (Bulgaria, Croatia, Latvia, Lithuania, Romania, Slovakia, Ukraine), with increased sensitivity to interest rates or real estate prices (Slovakia), faster loan impairment (Bulgaria), sectoral concentration of risks on the household (especially housing and construction) sector (Estonia, Lithuania), and some indications of growing strains on bank supervisors' and banks' capacity to assess risks (Bulgaria, Croatia, Slovakia).
- Though still high, and generally still above the required minimum, capital adequacy ratios seem to be declining in a number of countries (Bulgaria, Croatia, Lithuania, Ukraine) in the last few years, and there is some pressure on bank profitability (Bulgaria, Romania, Ukraine).

How have the authorities responded?

Policymakers in many of these countries have been concerned at the emerging signs of macroeconomic and financial stability risks. As a result, a range of measures have been used in responding to the rapid credit growth (see the country case studies, Duenwald, Gueorguiev, and Schaechter, and Hilbers, Ötker-Robe, and Pazarbasioğlu in this volume; and see Table 23.4):

- **Monetary policy measures** in the form of: raising interest rates (Croatia, Latvia, Poland, Romania); changes in reserve requirement parameters (Bulgaria, Estonia, Latvia, Poland, Romania) or delays in their reduction (Estonia, Lithuania); and increases in liquidity requirements (Croatia, Estonia).
- **Greater exchange rate flexibility** in the form of adjustments in the parameters of the crawling band regime (Poland), and switching to a more flexible exchange rate regime (Romania).
- **Fiscal measures** in the form of fiscal tightening (Bulgaria, Croatia, Romania), and reductions in fiscal incentives—limiting mortgage interest rate

Table 23.3 Risks Associated with the Credit Growth

	Bulgaria (2001–)	Croatia (1995–98, 2000–)	Estonia (1996–98, 2002–)	Latvia (2000–)	Lithuania (2002–)	Poland (1996–97)	Romania (2001–)	Slovakia (2003–)	Ukraine (2000–)	Greece (1998–2005)	Portugal (1995–)	Spain (1995–)
Macroeconomic risks												
Inflation pressures	✓			✓	✓	✓	✓			✓		
Widening C/A deficit		✓	✓	✓	✓	✓	✓					
Dependence on foreign capital, increase in external debt		✓	✓									✓ (from end-1990s)
Financial sector risks												
FX exposure risk	✓*	✓	✓*	✓*	✓*		✓	✓*				
Market risk (e.g., interest rates, housing prices etc.)					✓		✓	✓	✓		✓	
Potential credit risks		✓		✓	✓	✓	✓	✓	✓		✓	✓
Some decline in capital adequacy	✓	✓			✓				✓			
Faster loan impairment	✓											
Pressure on profitability	✓						✓		✓	✓	✓	✓
Sectoral risk concentration (e.g., real estate, mortgages)			✓ (households, housing market)		✓ (real estate, construction, households)							
Deterioration in risk assessment/internal risk control systems	✓	✓			✓	(imperfect to begin with)		✓				

* Although FX denominated component of lending is high, FX related risks are viewed relatively low, given the importance of euro in current arrangements, credibility of the prevailing pegs vis-à-vis the euro, and in the context of adopting the euro as the national currency in the future. In some countries, the FX exposures are assessed to be reasonably hedged (Latvia, Lithuania, Slovakia), although the calculation of FX positions usually exclude the positions in euro.

Source: The country case studies, and Duenwald, Gueorguiev, and Schaechter in this volume.

deductibility and housing activities of a quasi-government loan guarantee agency (Estonia).
- **Prudential/supervisory measures** in the form of:
  – tightening existing supervision/prudential regulations, with adjustments in FX risk regulations, surveys of banks' FX exposures, adjustment of capital requirements for market risks and different categories of loans (e.g., consumer or housing loans), tightening the eligibility criteria for various loans, loan classification and provisioning requirements (Bulgaria, Croatia, Romania, Greece, Portugal, Ukraine), and dynamic provisioning to reduce the cyclical behavior of loan-loss provisions (Spain);
  – close monitoring and assessment of loan procedures, risk management systems, and asset quality of banks, and closer and more frequent inspections (Bulgaria, Croatia, Estonia, Latvia, Lithuania, Romania, Slovakia, Greece, Spain);
  – closer supervision of nonbank financial institutions (Bulgaria, Romania); and
  – increased cross-border supervisory coordination in the form of greater dialogue and exchange of information with home-country supervisors (Estonia, Latvia, Lithuania, Greece).
- **Market/institution development and information enhancing measures** in the form of establishing credit registries, credit bureaus, and broadening banks' information base (Bulgaria, Estonia, Lithuania, Romania, Greece).
- **Moral suasion and communication tools** (Bulgaria, Croatia, Estonia, Latvia, Lithuania, Poland, Slovakia, Portugal) in the form of issuing moral suasion letters to the banks and closer consultations to warn against the risks involved, as well as promoting better understanding and awareness of risks. This tool has also been used in Spain, where the central bank Governor gave speeches warning about the risks associated with rapid credit growth.
- **Administrative measures** in the form of controls on credit growth above certain levels of credit growth (Bulgaria, Croatia, Greece); marginal reserve requirements on foreign borrowing (Croatia); limits on banks' FX lending to unhedged borrowers (Romania); central bank collection of public/interbank deposits to absorb liquidity (Poland, Greece); and an obligation to finance mortgage loans through mortgage bonds (Slovakia).

II. Some common themes, lessons, and policy implications

The following common themes emerge from these country experiences:

1) Many countries have faced challenges (and indeed continue to do so) in finding the appropriate measures to deal with the ongoing credit booms, and hence have resorted to a combination of various instruments aimed, in general, both at reducing the pace of credit growth as well as at maintaining the quality of credit.

Table 23.4 Policy Responses to Credit Growth

	Policy responses to credit growth	Effect to date
CEE Countries		

Bulgaria (2001–)	Policy measures aimed at slowing down the pace of credit growth:
	• Information enhancing:
	  – abolition of the minimum loan amount threshold for reporting loans to the central credit registry (CCR), thereby incorporating all consumer credits into the CCR, reduction in the grace period for reporting, and in the fee banks had to pay for inquiry from CCR (2/2004);
	  – requirement on banks to disclose effective interest rates on their consumer loans (12/2005), on all household loans from (6/2006);
	  – moral suasion to convince banks' management of the risks of credit growth.
	• Prudential and regulatory:
	  – broadening of the coverage of reserve requirements to liabilities previously exempted (6/2004), increase in the ratio of reserve requirements applied to such liabilities (12/2004); and reduction in the share of cash in vault that could be used for reserve requirements (to 50 percent in 10/2004 and 0 percent in 12/2004);
	  – adjustments in the capital adequacy requirements (risk weight of mortgage lending increased and loan to-value ratio of 70 percent introduced (12/2004), later reduced to 50 percent (4/2006), current profits excluded from capital base (4/2005);
	  – tightening of loan classification/provisioning requirements (4/2004; 4 and 11/2005);
	  – tightening of household loan eligibility requirements, with inspectors reflecting the information in their reports with appropriate supervisory measures (2/2006).
	• Administrative:
	  – limits on excessive credit growth in the form of a nonremunerated reserve requirement on banks whose credit portfolio exceeds 6 percent per quarter (2/2005).
		• Moral suasion has not been an effective tool in constraining credit growth.
		• Tightening reserve requirements did not help slow down credit growth but served as a warning signal from the BNB on the degree of toleration of the ongoing credit growth.
		• Overall, the prudential/administrative measures of 2004–05 to slow down credit growth have been effective (some slowdown in credit growth; the decline in the capital adequacy ratios kept at a comfortable level appropriate for each bank's risk profile; some decline in the risk appetite of main market players; improvement in risk management systems).
		• But they also led to some creative attempts to circumvent them (e.g., banks establishing their own leasing companies to avoid the limits, funding some domestic customers through bonds and other debt instruments that are riskier than standard credit), thereby leading to adoption of further measures to limit scope for circumvention (extension of the measures, inclusion of instruments subject to the limits, strengthening of nonbank financial institutions' supervision, etc).

Table 23.4 continued

	Policy responses to credit growth	Effect to date
CEE Countries		
Croatia (1995–98, 2000–)	• Tighter monetary policy (mid-1997), but limited use, given weak transmission mechanism based on FX market and high level of euroization, possibility of higher interest rates triggering more capital inflows and having adverse implications for public finances; • Chilean-style capital controls (4/1998): nonremunerated 30 percent deposits on all financial credits from abroad with maturity less than one year, 5 percent on those up to three years; marginal reserve requirement on foreign borrowing (7/2004), increased several times (currently 55 percent); • Administrative measures: direct credit controls aimed at slowing growth, not at preventing asset quality problems per se: "16 percent rule"—banks must buy low-interest rate Croatian National Bank paper if growth of risk assets exceeds 4 percent in a given quarter (during 2003); liquidity requirements: "35 percent rule"—banks must hold liquid foreign exchange assets equal to at least 35 percent of their total foreign exchange liabilities (from 2003); lowered to 32 percent currently; • Prudential measures: maintaining minimum capital adequacy requirement at 10 percent (since 1999); adding market risk into capital adequacy calculations, increased provisioning for banks with rapidly growing portfolios, and higher weight for calculating risky assets for FX-denominated or indexed loans; requirement to form special reserves (0.10 percent of risk assets) for banks that grow faster than 20 percent similar to a temporary increase in capital requirements, with the exception of banks if they meet higher capital standards (during 2004); • Moral suasion: on a few occasions, the CNB indicated to commercial banks that it would relax or tighten some of its instruments depending on banks' foreign borrowing.	• Credit growth slowed down significantly in 1998–99, but the banking crisis in 1998 was mostly responsible for the slowdown. • Effect of 2003 measures: loan growth slowed down from 30.2 percent in 2002 to 14.6 percent in 2003 and 13.0 percent in 2004, but: banks have shifted their assets within categories, e.g., decreasing available but unused lines of credit, increasing write-offs, to show lower loan growth; rapid growth in leasing activity; greater direct foreign borrowing by corporates, which indicated a much smaller decrease in the total of bank loans, leasing activity and corporate foreign borrowing than the decrease in bank loans alone. Also, the rate of credit growth rose again in 2005 (to 20.3 percent). • Moral suasion did not have a material effect on banks' behavior.

	Policy responses to credit growth	Effect to date
Estonia (1996–98) (2002–)	First credit cycle, given limited monetary policy tools under the CBA: • Forming Stabilization Reserves from increasing fiscal surplus that were shifted out abroad from commercial banks • Increasing the capital adequacy ratio for banks • Strengthening compulsory reserve requirement framework and introducing an additional liquidity requirement. Second credit cycle: • Monetary measures: limited under the CBA, hence mainly in the form of: delaying the relaxation of the reserve requirement to the euro area levels; abolition of vault-cash deductibility; inclusion of foreign liabilities into the reserve base on gross basis; • Prudential measures: maintenance of the higher capital adequacy requirement, and an increase in risk weightings of mortgage loans from 50 percent to 100 percent (March 2006); • Promoting better understanding of risks: pointing out the risks of excessive credit growth, especially in the household mortgage loan market; • The "communication tool" and "moral suasion tool" with the BoE recommending that the government abolish certain tax relief and guarantee schemes in the mortgage market so as not to interfere in market developments on the relaxing side; "moral suasion" letters sent to the banks, their Scandinavian owners, as well as to the respective supervisory authorities in the region; • Capital or direct credit controls were ruled out, given the authorities' desire to avoid policy reversals and inconsistencies with the EU directives, as well as the recognition of their limited effectiveness in a system made up of large conglomerates and dominance of foreign banks.	• First credit cycle: Credit growth slowed down considerably in late 1997, though the period also coincided with the halt of capital inflows following the Asian and Russian crises that created speculative pressures in the Estonian money and FX markets and banks' liquidity position. Uncertainties in banks' exposure to the affected countries and a decline in credit demand led to a cease in credit growth in the late 1990s. • Second credit cycle: rapid credit growth in the current cycle has continued with a peak in the annual growth in real sector credit at more than 50 percent at the end of 2005. The measures in the last four years have not yet had any visible impact to slow down credit growth: – Government reluctance to make unpopular decisions to abolish relevant tax relief and state guarantee schemes in the housing loan market, especially in the context of local and parliamentary elections. – Moral suasion not helpful as foreign banks pay more attention to instructions from parents and strong competition prevents banks from slowing credit growth so as not to lose market share – Easy access to funds through parent banks. • Scope for extending cooperation between home/host supervisors beyond MoUs, regional cooperation agreements with shared resources and responsibilities in crisis management, coordinated efforts to curb unsustainable developments.

Table 23.4 continued

	Policy responses to credit growth	Effect to date
CEE Countries		
Latvia (2000–)	• Monetary policy tightening: increase in the main refinancing rate (3 and 11/2004, 6/2005), increase in the reserve requirement (7/2004, 6/2005) and a broadening in the reserve base to include banks' foreign liabilities with shorter maturities (11/2004); • Prudential and supervisory measures: increase in supervisory reporting requirements—tightening of onsite/offsite inspections, introduction of a rating system for banks, periodic stress testing activities, increased supervision of banking groups on a consolidated basis (2004); dialogue and exchange of information between home and host supervisors; • Moral suasion: periodic consultations with individual banks and bank association; communication of BoL's concerns about rapid credit growth to banks (through letters to and meetings with banks) and the media; efforts to raise public awareness (e.g., through conferences); • Administrative controls are seen as a step backward and as a last resort.	• Monetary measures were not sufficient to put sufficient downward pressure on lending growth—credit growth has remained very strong throughout (2002–05); though the term structure of banks' borrowing abroad improved (reasons for limited effectiveness of measures: lack of independent monetary policy under the fixed ER system and high dollarization; high foreign ownership and hence unlimited access to funding resources; high competition and profitability in the banking sector). • Effects of efforts to raise public awareness are hard to assess.
Lithuania (2002–)	• Monetary measures: with limited interest rate policy under the CBA, postponement of the planned reduction in reserve requirements to the euro zone levels; • Prudential/supervisory measures: keeping capital adequacy ratios high, especially on banks specialized in housing finance; continued bank monitoring measures with frequent inspections; greater cooperation with home supervisors of foreign banks; • Moral suasion/risk awareness/market development measures: broader bank disclosure/reporting requirements; collection of more comprehensive information in the credit registry for risk assessment and management; policies aimed at better understanding of risks; moral suasion letters to banks; public statements on risks related to housing boom; consultations with banks and internal ratings based risk assessment measures.	The authorities' policy response to rapid credit growth is not to reduce the growth rate per se but to reduce the risks involved, including by reducing the factors that may be stimulating the credit growth and taking excessive risks: • Credit growth has remained very strong throughout (2002–05).

	Policy responses to credit growth	Effect to date
Poland (1996–97)	With assessment that there was no serious threat to banking system stability, and with already a strict supervision of the banking system, policy response mainly took the form of monetary policy measures: • Exchange rate policy: NBP maintained its crawling band mechanism but refrained from further reductions in the rate of crawl, with the intention of reducing imports and stimulating exports; • Monetary measures: increase in reserve requirements; open market operations to sterilize the FX interventions that aimed at supporting the crawling band; raising the official and market interest rates to absorb liquidity; NBP collection of deposits directly from households at higher rates than those offered by commercial banks, so as to encourage banks to raise their lending and deposit rates (given the problems in the transmission mechanism).	• Difficult to assess the effect of the individual instruments used to reduce the pace of credit expansion. However, the package of measures seemed to prove effective. Banks started to pay more attention to deposit collection. The growth of lending slowed significantly. Corporate credits responded more rapidly to the interest rate impulse, whereas household credits reacted stronger only after the introduction of the NBP deposit measure. For the commercial banks, the acceptance of households' deposits at the NBP was a clear sign that the central bank would make determined efforts to rebalance the economic situation. The impact of the exchange rate policy measures on the current account imbalances was positive, though difficult to assess the impact on credit expansion. Interest rate measures had limited effectiveness, given the limited cost elasticity of demand for credit and the weaknesses in the monetary transmission mechanism in affecting the retail interest rates. Limited effectiveness of reserve requirements with banks passing their costs on to depositors through lower deposit rates.
Romania (2001–)	• Monetary policy measures: ceasing of the declines in the policy rate (6/2003); gradual increase in the policy rate (8/2003); increase in minimum reserve requirements on FX liabilities (8/2004, 1/2006, 3/2006) and expanding the reserve base to longer term liabilities; FX market intervention to introduce two-way FX risks (up to 10/2005); • Prudential measures (to slow down consumer and mortgage credit growth and FX denominated lending): loan-to-value limits, down payment and collateral requirements for consumer and mortgage credits (2/2004); tightening of eligibility criteria for individuals for consumer and real estate loans (8/2005); refinement of loan classification and provisioning requirements to incorporate borrowers' FX risks (9/2005); broadening supervision and regulation to nonbank financial intermediaries (2/2006); • Market development measures: establishment of a credit bureau to monitor consumer loans and business credit (end–2004) and expanding the database.	• Strong credit growth remained persistent throughout 2005. • Persistent expectations of exchange rate appreciation continue to feed demand for FX-denominated loans under an open capital account. The measures to slow FX-denominated loans have evidently been followed by banks raising capital rather than restructuring and reducing their FX-denominated loans, and by various window-dressing activities.

Table 23.4 continued

	Policy responses to credit growth	Effect to date
CEE Countries		
Slovakia (2003–)	• Supervisory measures: close monitoring of all relevant risk categories to identify potential vulnerabilities through: introduction of a new reporting system for banks, bank lending survey, stress testing by the NBS for various scenarios; • Moral suasion/market development measures: increased frequency of meetings with commercial banks, informing the general public about the risks the household sector is exposed to in various NBS publications; • Administrative measures: an obligation for banks to finance mortgage loans through mortgage bonds (to limit banks' excessive funding of long-term mortgage loans through short term foreign or domestic funds), and a limit on the loan-to-value (LTV) ratio for mortgage loans of 70 percent.	• The monitoring/supervisory measures help the NBS to identify potential vulnerabilities in advance. • The administrative measures cover only part of the housing loans/mortgage loans. The final impact of these measures is limited, since banks also provide other loans without a specified purpose that are mostly used for housing purposes.
Ukraine (2000–)	• Supervisory and regulatory measures: increase in CAR, strengthening of the definition of capital, tightening of loan classification rules, raising provisioning requirement for FX denominated loans, tightening of related party lending regulations, new risk assessment methodology for supervisors.	• Credit growth continues to be rapid. A temporary slowdown at end-2004 and early 2005 can be attributed mostly to political uncertainties.
Euro convergence countries		
Greece (1998–2005)	• Severe quantitative restrictions on the rate of bank loan growth to the private sector (early 1999-March 2000); • Monetary measures to limit the liquidity impact of convergence to euro area interest rates: the release of additional reserves resulting from the reduction in reserve requirement ratio from high levels to low euro levels in tranches (mid-2000), and the offering by BoG of very high interest rates to collect voluntary interbank deposits (1999-2000). At the end of convergence, banks had additional reserves to lend to the private sector; • Prudential, supervisory, information disclosure measures (1999-2005): stricter monitoring framework for credit institutions, in particular for capital adequacy (differentiating ratios for vulnerable banks), provisioning (a supervisory provisions matrix with differentiated provision coefficients by loan type and past due and dynamic adjustment of coefficients to market developments), transparency and disclosure; surveys of household debt; strengthened on-site, off-site inspections; stress testing of the banking system; monitoring of banks' risk management and procedures; close cooperation with European and international institutions for knowledge transfer and supervisory coordination (including MoUs with neighboring countries); minimum information requirements by product type (deposits, loans, cards) and distribution channel (branch, internet, etc) (2002); upgrading credit bureau services.	• The quantitative restrictions were quite effective, as indicated by a very low growth of credit at end-1999, and an immediate jump in credit growth in late 2000 following their elimination. But were used only temporarily since they were viewed as not compatible with the way monetary policy is carried out in the euro area. • Improved supervisory, prudential and monitoring system since 1999 has helped identify and manage financial sector risks.

	Policy responses to credit growth	Effect to date
Portugal (1995–)	• Supervisory/monitoring measures: Monitoring tools to analyze banks' liquidity position, with a new emphasis on supervisory guidance for banks' internal control, risk management, and contingency procedures. Fine-tuning of changes in general and specific provisioning (to differentiate consumer credit from other segments) and solvency and specific provisioning requirements (for loans with LTV above 75 percent) to ensure adequate buffers under EU-type overall supervisory infrastructure. Measures motivated by prudential and financial stability goals and not designed to curb or target aggregate credit growth per se; • Moral suasion: extensive use of interactive dialogue with banks.	• Measures have not been introduced for the purpose of reducing the growth of credit, but ensuring that there is an adequate supervisory infrastructure and banks had appropriate risk management skills.
Spain (1995–2004)	• Supervisory, monitoring measures: close monitoring of financial developments, projections of financial indicators, such as indebtedness or debt burden, conditional upon the expected macroeconomic scenario, stress testing to evaluate the potential impact of (unlikely) negative shocks on the Spanish economy; • The statistical or dynamic provisioning was used as a prudential tool to reduce the strong cyclical behavior of the loan loss provision ratio, and to better synchronize risk-taking and provisioning, and not to restrict credit growth; • Moral suasion: warning speeches by the Governor about the risks of rapid credit growth.	• While making credit growth significantly more costly (it absorbed close to 20 percent of banking institutions' pre-tax profits during 2002–04), dynamic provisioning has not prevented credit to the private sector from continuing to grow at very high rates in recent years.

Source: The country case studies, and Duenwald, Gueorguiev, and Schaechter in this volume.

2) Efforts to slow credit have in general been frustrated by:
   - the limited number of monetary instruments available to policymakers, especially as countries approach EU and then euro membership, as well as the limited effectiveness of monetary policy instruments, when available, in an environment with a high degree of euroization and capital account openness;
   - the significant foreign bank presence with easy access to funds to finance rapid credit growth, including through borrowing from their parent institutions; and
   - the circumvention by borrowers, for instance through direct borrowing from abroad or from less well-supervised nonbank financial institutions, and by banks, for instance through window-dressing activities.

3) There has been only limited resort to using capital controls or administrative measures to directly control credit growth, given the authorities' concerns about their circumvention and undesirable effects; such measures have also been generally seen as incompatible with the economic policies pursued from the beginning of the transition process and the EU directives.

4) Nevertheless, administrative measures have been used in a few countries where strong credit growth had been continuing unabated and with growing concerns about macroeconomic and financial stability risks. While the measures may have had some limited short-term impact, they evidently prompted creative attempts at circumvention, including through shifting lending to nonbank financial institutions, such as leasing and insurance companies, and various window-dressing activities, such as write-offs, and use of bank guarantees. Such attempts have prompted the respective authorities in some cases to broaden and extend the coverage of the regulations, and to better monitor, and strengthen the supervision of, nonbank financial institutions.

5) The use of moral suasion as a tool to warn banks against possible risks of credit growth also has not proven to be effective in limiting credit growth, especially in the presence of foreign banks, with foreign branches evidently paying less attention to local supervisors than to the home supervisors of their parent banks. Strong competition between banks to avoid losing market share has also limited the effectiveness of this tool.

6) The scope and channels for circumvention of prudential and administrative measures, and more generally the apparent divergence between the interests of host supervisors and the constraints on the operations of the nonbanks and the branches of foreign banks, highlight the importance of better coordination and cooperation on two fronts: (i) coordination between supervisors of bank and nonbank financial institutions, and (ii) cross-border coordination and the exchange of information between home and host supervisors. There have indeed been increasing efforts to increase such cooperation by many countries in the region (Bulgaria and Romania, for bank–nonbank supervisory coordination, and Estonia, Latvia, Lithuania, and Greece for cross-border supervisory cooperation). Mihaljek in this volume draws attention to one of

the most critical debates ongoing in this area—how to rein in the behavior of foreign banks in a liberalized open economy, in particular under circumstances where the bank is not of systemic importance from the viewpoint of the home country supervisor, but clearly is from the viewpoint of the host.
7) With the increased globalization and sophistication of the financial systems in these countries, and continued concerns about the pace of credit growth, intensification of efforts for close cooperation and coordination between home and host supervisors with shared tasks and resources in normal and crisis times are a critical element for effective management of rapid credit growth. The importance, as well as the complexity, of these issues is brought out clearly in the chapters by Bednarski and Starnowski, van Goor, and Zartl in this volume.
8) Coordination efforts should be complemented with host supervisors' continued endeavors to enhance understanding and awareness of risks associated with excessive credit growth, and to develop markets and instruments to manage such risks (see e.g., Hilbers, Ötker-Robe, and Pazarbasioğlu in this volume); it is also important to encourage the relevant authorities to pursue a sound macroeconomic policy mix that focuses on limiting the incentives for taking such risks (for instance, avoiding fiscal incentives through interest deductibility for interest payments for mortgages and large domestic interest rate differentials that are inconsistent with the prevailing exchange rate regime).
9) The host supervisors may wish to consider also measures to reduce the risks that may arise in a crisis. In some crises in other countries, some banks have declined to remain involved, preferring simply to write off their past investments in the country. To reduce the impact of any such action, host countries may wish to examine whether to require all foreign banks to capitalize themselves within the host country on a stand-alone basis, i.e., to treat them all, from a supervisory perspective, as subsidiaries rather than branches, even while the banks are planning global strategies, treating even subsidiaries as branches (as discussed by Mihaljek in this volume). However, this independent decision will not be possible when a country becomes a member of the EU, in which case it has to implement EU directives and adhere to home country control principles.

III. Looking ahead

The rapid credit growth of recent years has been pervasive and in many ways welcome. To some extent, this trend reflects a catch-up of the region, assisted by a favorable conjuncture, including rapid economic growth and low interest rates in the region. Nevertheless, studies of past crises show that these have nearly all been preceded by rapid credit growth, so at a minimum one needs to monitor the situation carefully to ensure that such a situation does not recur. Aggregate credit growth is to a large extent a story of the rapid growth of finance for housing and other personal loans, and so safeguarding the financial system must involve looking particularly closely at these two areas.

The present situation is complicated by the unprecedented constraints on policy options, both as regards the authorities' legal constraints in many cases, as they seek to converge to the requirements of EU or euro membership, and market constraints, given the porous nature of financial flows in systems that have been liberalized across countries and sectors. Monetary policies may therefore not be able to do much to slow credit growth, and administrative policies also have at most a temporary and limited impact, possibly offset by the distortionary impact of any controls. Clearly, insofar as countries are not operating prudential policies in line with best practice, achieving best practice should be a high priority (see papers by Hilbers, Ötker-Robe, and Pazarbasioğlu and Josefsson in this volume). Similarly, any fiscal distortions that stimulate credit artificially, such as interest deductibility for mortgage payments, should preferably be eschewed.

Beyond that, the countries of the region face an asymmetry, in that the foreign banks operating in their countries are likely to be of systemic significance to them, but may well not be for the authorities in the home countries. This understandably leads to proposals, for instance, that all foreign banks should be treated on a stand-alone basis, for instance in meeting their capital and prudential requirements. More generally, greater interaction between the central banks and regulators of the region, and those of the countries where the major foreign banks are located, to discuss the challenges and propose solutions, is likely to be important to ensure that effective and cooperative management of the ongoing credit growth can be taken forward. The conference hosted by the National Bank of Romania, which has led to the preparation of this book, would be one example of such interaction. The issues discussed here and the policies put forward will hopefully make a significant contribution to understanding and reducing the risks from the continuing rapid credit growth across the central, eastern and south-eastern European region.

Note

1. Both International Monetary Fund (IMF).

Index

Compiled by Sue Carlton

Abiad, A. 78
acquis communautaire 273
administrative measures (quantitative limits) 148, 151, 189, 225, 234, 259, 285, 356, 366
Albania 13, 36, 275
Arcalean, C. 271
Asian financial crisis (1997–98) 6, 138, 141, 175, 254
Association of Commercial Banks (ACB) 149
Autoregressive Distributed Lag (ARDL) 77

Backé, P. 77
Balassa–Samuelson effect 26
Bank of Estonia (BoE) 175, 177, 179
Bank of Greece (BoG) 285, 289–90, 291–4
Bank of Latvia (BoL) 187, 188
Bank of Lithuania (BL) 200–2
Bank of Portugal (BoP) 302, 303, 307
bank privatization 23, 47, 49, 60, 61, 92, 145, 276, 352
  see also foreign-owned banks; *under individual countries*
Bank of Spain (BoS) 315
bank supervision 23, 28–9, 40, 51, 96–9, 102–7, 119, 279–81
  administrative measures (quantitative limits) 148, 151, 189, 225, 234, 259, 285, 356, 366
  communication tool 179, 356
  cross-border cooperation 107, 321–30, 331–7, 341–5, 356, 366
  cooperation between home and host supervisors 342
  industry concerns 342–4
  lead supervisors 343
  information enhancing measures 148–9
  monitoring measures 122–4
  moral suasion measures 96, 149, 167, 169, 179–80, 188, 202, 259, 308, 356
  prospects for 344–5
  prudential measures 120–2, 137–40, 149–50, 152, 167, 169, 291–2
  role of supervisors 137–42
  see also Bulgarian National Bank (BNB); Croatian National Bank (CNB); *under individual countries*

banking sector
  bank failures 138–9, 141
  competition 36–7, 48, 49, 93, 149, 160, 183, 230, 231–2
  and deposit growth 100, 174, 181, 209–10, 212, 247, 307
  foreign ownership 7–8, 23–5, 39–40, 60–1, 92, 274–9, 339–42, 366
  reform 23, 29, 49
  shock-absorbing capacity 37–40, 86, 93, 138, 217, 257
  see also bank privatization; bank supervision
Basel Concordat (1983) 342
Basel I 145, 296, 304
Basel II 202, 293, 332, 336, 337, 342, 343
BCR bank (Romania) 215
Belarus
  nature of credit growth 111
  policy responses 92
Boissay, F. 75
Borio, C. 49, 96
Bosnia and Herzegovina 13, 22
  policy responses 98, 129
Bulgaria 145–52
  bank privatization 243, 245, 246, 247
  bank supervision 150, 244, 246, 259
  credit boom 236–60
  credit-to-GDP ratio 54, 55
  currency board arrangement 245, 247, 259
  equilibrium credit-to-GDP ratios 79, 81
  and excessive credit growth 56, 58, 60, 61–2, 75
  exchange rate regime 59
  factors underlying credit growth 145–8
  financial crisis (1997) 26, 47, 55
  and foreign currency lending 72, 244, 247
  foreign-owned banks 243, 257, 275
  household lending 246–7
  interest rates 146, 149, 245
  macroeconomic background 239
  nature of credit growth 111
  policy responses 129, 148–51, 245, 259
    effectiveness of 151–2

Bulgarian National Bank (BNB) 47, 148–52, 245
Bussière, M. 253

Calvo-Gonzalez, O. 75
Central Credit Register (CCR) 148–9
Committee of European Banking Supervisors (CEBS) 321, 322, 329, 331–2
  guidelines/home-host framework 321–4, 336–7
  Supervisory Review and Evaluation Process (SREP) 321, 324–9
    allocation of tasks and legal responsibilities 328–9
    information exchange 327–8, 337
    significance/systemic relevance 325–7
consolidating supervisor 323, 324, 325–9, 341, 342, 343–5
consumer lending 9, 148, 220, 279
  see also household debt
consumer protection 9, 149, 291, 292
Core Principles of Effective Banking Supervision 342
corporations/enterprises
  financial structure of 17–19
  loans to 25, 55, 69, 70, 74, 76, 87, 229, 270, 286, 306
Cottarelli, C. 50, 74
crawling band mechanism 205–6, 354
credit, importance as source of finance 15–21
credit booms 49–50, 154, 168
  and bank supervision 139–40, 150
  and banking crises 14, 33, 85–6, 254
  in transition countries 14, 30, 75–6, 236–60
    background 237–44
    causes 238, 244–6
    characteristics 238, 246–8
    Croatia 155–69
    macroeconomic risks 250–4
    opportunities 248–50
    policy options 257–60
    risks for financial stability 254–7
credit growth
  analysis of 84–9
  causes/factors 21–8, 40, 154, 231–2, 312–15, 353
    cyclical factors 26–8, 271
    demand-side factors 183–5, 286–8, 296, 305–6, 350
    policy-related factors 26
    supply-side factors 181–3, 289–91, 296, 306–7, 352
    transition-related factors 22–6, 47–8
  common trends in CEE countries 268–71
  and credit composition 61–3
  measuring 5
  monetary/prudential interface 6–7
    see also monetary policy; prudential regulations
  nature of 87–8, 111–14, 229–30, 349–50, 351
  popularity of 5
  problems of 8–9
  recent developments in CEE countries 89–93
  risks from 34–7, 103, 104–5, 254–7, 315–17, 352–4, 355
    see also macroeconomic stability/risks
    see also credit booms; excessive credit growth
credit-to-GDP ratios 13–14, 22, 30–1, 48–9, 54, 55–6, 68–70, 240–1
  equilibrium levels 50, 51–2, 56, 59, 67–8
    estimating 74–9, 81
      method and data issues 74–7
      and observed credit-to-GDP ratios 78–9, 80
      results 77–8
Croatia 154–69
  bank privatization 158–61
  banking crisis 155
  credit booms 155–699
    first (1995–98) 155–8
    second (2000–present) 158–68
  credit-to-GDP ratio 22, 54, 55
  current account deficit 156–8, 162
  equilibrium credit-to-GDP ratios 79, 81
  and excessive credit growth 56, 58, 60, 75
  exchange rate regime 59, 60–1
  features of banking system 157
  foreign currency lending 72, 162, 163, 168, 279
  and foreign-owned banks 60, 158–60, 161, 275
  and household debt 34, 156, 161, 165
  interest rates 156, 160, 162–3, 168–9
  nature of credit growth 112
  policy responses 98, 130, 162–8, 169
  rising foreign debt 162–8
Croatian National Bank (CNB) 61, 155, 162–8, 169
Croatian Postal Bank 160
currency board arrangements (CBAs) 101, 172, 173, 174, 178, 179, 245, 247, 259

current account deficits 30, 92–3, 147, 156–8, 162, 186, 197
Czech Republic
  and foreign currency lending 72, 74
  foreign-owned banks 7, 275, 339

De Nederlandsche Bank (DNB) 331, 332–5, 337
Dell'Ariccia, G. 74
deregulation 22–3, 26, 300, 314–15, 318, 352
direct inflation targeting (DIT) 212
dollarization 244
Duenwald, C. 253
dynamic provisioning tool 317, 356

EBRD (European Bank for Reconstruction and Development) 29
  index of banking sector reforms 23, 255–6
  Transition Reports 13, 240
ECB (European Central Bank) 14, 17, 294–5, 299, 310
Égert, B. 77
EMU (European Economic and Monetary Union) 8, 305–7, 308, 310, 314, 318
equity financing 17–19, 20–1
ERM (Exchange Rate Mechanism) 304
  ERM2 101, 183, 186
Estonia 172–80
  bank privatization 172
  bank supervision 178, 180
  credit growth cycles
    first (1990s) 172, 179
    second (2001–present) 176–9
  credit-to-GDP ratio 54, 55
  currency board arrangement (CBA) 172, 173, 174, 178, 179
  equilibrium credit-to-GDP ratios 79, 81
  and excessive credit growth 56, 60, 61–3
  exchange rate regime 59
  and foreign currency lending 72, 74, 176–7
  foreign investment 173–4
  foreign-owned banks 7, 60, 61, 176, 178, 179, 180, 275
  and household debt 34, 61–3, 177, 178
  interest rates 178
  nature of credit growth 112
  policy responses 92, 98, 131, 178–9
  Stabilization Reserves 174, 175
Euribor 56
euroization 100, 101, 176, 220, 222, 225, 364
European Company Statute 323–4

European Economic and Monetary Union (EMU) 8
European Monetary System (EMS) 304
European Union (EU)
  accession to 7, 55, 84, 93, 100, 154, 216, 350, 352
  Bulgaria and 246
  Croatia and 162
  Estonia and 176
  Latvia and 181–3
  Portugal and 300
  and property market 272, 273
  Romania and 223, 227, 239, 245, 246, 247
  and bank supervision 342, 343–4
  Capital Requirements Directive (CRD) 322, 323, 327, 328–9, 335, 342
  Codified Banking Directive (2000) 323, 329, 342
  Second Banking Directive (1993) 301, 304
  structural funds 197, 200, 352
'evergreening' 254
excessive credit growth 5–6, 47–64, 67, 257–8, 267, 352
  credit composition 61–3
  detecting 50–8
    data 54–5
    estimating credit elasticities 52–3
    test strategy 53–4
    test using benchmarks 55–6
    test using CEE country data 58
  empirical literature 49–50
  and exchange rate regimes 59–61
  see also credit-to-GDP ratios, equilibrium levels
exchange rate regimes 26, 30, 35, 59–61, 74, 92, 258, 271
  crawling band mechanism 35, 205–6
  and flexibility 30, 35, 59, 96, 101, 245, 271, 354

financial accelerator effect 194
financial accelerator mechanism 32, 33, 85
Financial and Capital Market Commission 188
Financial Sector Assessment Programs (FSAPs) 244, 294
financial soundness indicators (FSIs) 6, 88, 352
financial stability 33–40, 81, 84, 85–7, 147, 203, 279–80, 316–17, 352–4
  and banks' shock-absorbing capacity 37–40, 86, 93, 138
  risk factors 34–7, 254–7

financial structure, and economic growth 15, 16, 25, 28–9
fiscal policy 101, 115, 205, 251, 259, 354–6, 366
foreign currency lending 8, 26, 34–5, 59–60, 70–4, 88, 200, 268, 278–9, 350
  foreign sources of financing 18–19
  see also under individual countries
Foreign Direct Investment (FDI) 32, 35, 146, 176, 236, 239, 240
foreign-owned banks 7–8, 23–5, 39–40, 60–1, 92, 274–9, 339–40, 366
  and efficiency 276–7
  and financial stability 341–2
  and internal capital markets 335–6
  policy implications 279–81
Furfine, C. 96

Glogowski, A. 34
Goldstein, M. 85
Goodhart's Law 5, 11
Greece 284–95
  bank supervision 291–4
  causes of rapid credit growth 286–91
    demand side 286–9
    supply side 289–91
  evolution of private sector loans 284–6
  household debt 287, 288, 294
  interest rates 287, 287–9, 289, 290, 291
  policy responses 131, 291–4
    prudential measures 291–2
    recent developments 294
    supervisory framework 293–4

Hellenic Data Protection Authority 292
Hernando, I. 316
Hodrick-Prescott filter 49
Home-Host guidelines *see* Committee of European Banking Supervisors (CEBS), guidelines
household sector
  assets and liabilities structure 17, 18
  and excessive credit growth 61–3
  house prices 26, 37, 61, 273–4
  household lending 25, 26, 74, 75–6, 79, 87, 147, 149, 150
  see also under individual countries
  housing market 9–10, 61–2, 184–5, 196, 267, 271–4, 279, 305, 315, 318, 350
Hungary
  credit-to-GDP ratio 54, 55
  equilibrium credit-to-GDP ratios 79, 81
  and excessive credit growth 56, 58, 75
  foreign currency lending 279

  foreign-owned banks 7, 275, 339
  nature of credit growth 112
  policy responses 92
HVB 280

Iceland 131
inflation 10, 29–31, 78, 156, 162, 174, 186, 192, 200, 203, 250–1, 258
  disinflation 186, 205, 212, 215, 225, 239, 244, 245
  targeting 212, 221, 225, 245
information enhancing measures 148–9, 356
initial public offerings (IPOs) 17
interest rates 24, 25–6, 34, 56, 75, 78, 254, 270, 273, 286, 350
  foreign currency borrowing 8, 59, 61, 74, 88, 92, 101, 165, 276, 278
  international 154, 162, 165–6, 168, 279
  see also under individual countries
International Monetary Fund (IMF) 3–5, 6, 49–50, 217, 250, 294

Jankov, L. 155
Joshi, B. 253

Kaminsky, G. 85
Kiss, G. 75
Kozluk, T. 75
Kraft, E. 155
KredEx 63

Latvia 3, 181–9
  bank supervision 188
  credit-to-GDP ratio 54, 55, 181
  current account deficit 186
  equilibrium credit-to-GDP ratios 79, 81
  and equity financing 19
  and excessive credit growth 56, 58, 61, 63
  factors underlying credit growth 181–5
    demand factors 183
    supply factors 181–3
  foreign currency borrowing 72, 186–7
  foreign-owned banks 275
  household debt 181, 183, 185, 186, 188
  interest rates 183–4, 188
  nature of credit growth 113
  policy responses 98, 131, 187–9
    future options 188–9
  and risks of credit growth 185–7
Law on Banks and Savings Banks (1993) (Croatia) 155
liberalization 22–3, 26, 48, 51, 78, 154, 155–6, 168, 231

Lithuania 190–202
  assessing risks to banking sector 197–200
  bank privatization 193
  bank supervision 192, 201–2
  banking crisis (1995–96) 192
  catch-up processes 190–2
  credit-to-GDP ratio 54, 55
  current account deficit 197
  current phase of credit expansion 194–7
  equilibrium credit-to-GDP ratios 79, 81
  and equity financing 19
  and excessive credit growth 56, 60
  exchange rate regime 59
  foreign-owned banks 7, 192–3, 275
  household debt 191, 193, 196, 199
  interest rates 192–3, 194, 197, 200, 201
  lifting of credit constraints 192–3
  nature of credit growth 113
  policy responses
    dilemmas 200–1
    measures taken 201–2
Lizondo, S. 85
loan-to-value (LTV) ratio 291–2
loans
  eligibility requirements 150
  loan classification 150
  loan quality 38–9, 186, 254
  provisioning requirements 150
  see also foreign currency lending;
    household sector, household lending;
    mortgage; nonperforming loans
Lowe, P. 49, 96

Macedonia, foreign-owned banks 275
macroeconomic stability/risks 25, 29–33,
    84, 85–7, 147, 185–7, 203, 205, 250–4,
    315–16, 352
Maeso-Fernandez, F. 78
Marginal Reserve Requirement (MRR) 96,
    165–6, 167, 169
Martinez-Carrascal, C. 316
Mean Group Estimator (MGE) 77
Mehl, A. 29
Mexico, banking crisis (1994) 254
Mody, A. 78
Moldova
  nature of credit growth 113
  policy responses 98, 132
monetary policy 26, 101, 115, 258–9, 354,
    358–62, 364, 366
  Bulgaria 245
  and Croatian credit booms 156–8, 160–1,
    162–3, 168, 169

  and currency board arrangements (CBAs)
    172, 179, 245
  Greece 285, 295
  Latvia 187–8
  Poland 205–6, 212
  Romania 221, 222, 225–6, 245, 259
  Spain 316, 318
monetary transmission mechanism (MTM)
    207–8
moral suasion 96, 149, 167, 169, 179–80,
    188, 202, 259, 308, 356
mortgages 34, 61, 63, 70, 87, 184, 185, 223,
    234–5, 247, 259, 274, 307

Nagy, M. 75
National Bank of Poland (NBP) 205–12
National Bank of Romania (NBR) 214, 217,
    221–5, 239, 245, 259
National Bank of Slovakia (NBS) 233–4
National Bank of Ukraine (NBU) 259–60
nonperforming loans (NPLs) (bad loans)
    38–9, 49, 93, 139, 141–2, 186, 203,
    276–7, 299
  Bulgaria 150, 254, 255
  Croatia 161
  Greece 289
  Romania 215, 254, 255
  Slovakia 229
  Ukraine 254, 255
Nordic bank crisis (1990s) 138, 141

Osbat, C. 78

Pesaran, M.H. 77
Poland 203–13
  bank privatization 208, 339
  bank supervision 205
  equilibrium credit-to-GDP ratios 79, 81
  and equity financing 19
  foreign currency lending 34–5, 72, 279
  and foreign-owned banks 7, 339
  growing economic imbalances 204–5
  household debt 17, 203, 204
  and household deposits 209–10, 212
  interest rates 205, 206, 207–8, 212, 280
  policy responses 99, 101, 132
    assessment of adopted measures 207–12
    measures taken 205–6
policy responses 92–107, 115–36, 187–9,
    291–4, 354–66
  targets and instruments 10–11
  see also bank supervision; fiscal
    policy; monetary policy; prudential
    regulations; *under individual countries*

Pooled Mean Group Estimator 75
Portugal 296–310
   bank privatization 296, 302, 303
   banking liberalization 299–305, 310
   credit growth in run-up to EMU
     demand-side factors 305–6
     supply-side factors 306–7
   indebtedness 297–9, 309
   interest rates 299, 300, 303, 304, 305–6, 307, 309, 310
   monitoring build-up of risk 307–10
   new financial institutions 300–2, 303
   policy responses 133
   state-owned banking sector (1975–83) 299–300
privatization 22–3, 184–5, 239, 240, 272
   see also bank privatization
prudential measures/regulations 102–5, 137–40, 149–50, 188, 221, 225, 291–4, 356, 366

quantitative limits *see* administrative measures

Reinhart, C. 85
Romania 214–27
   bank privatization 215, 243, 245, 246, 247
   bank supervision 216–17, 220, 225, 244, 246
   characteristics of credit growth 217–20
   credit boom 236–60
   credit-to-GDP ratio 54, 55, 56, 257
   equilibrium credit-to-GDP ratios 79, 81
   excessive credit growth 58, 61, 75
   foreign currency lending 72, 226, 244, 247
   foreign-owned banks 215–16, 243, 257
   household lending 217–18, 223–4, 246–7, 259
   interest rates 217–18, 220, 224, 225, 259
   macroeconomic background 239
   nature of credit growth 114
   policy responses 99, 134, 220–6
     and currency mismatches 220–3
     measures taken by NBR 221
     monetary policy 225–6, 245
     options 259
     and sustainability 223–5
   underlying fundamentals of credit growth 215–17
Russian financial crisis (1998) 175–6, 192

Savings and Loans crisis (USA) (1980s) 138

Scandinavian banking crises (1990s) 254
Schadler, S. 50
Schnatz, B. 78
seasoned equity offerings (SEOs) 17
Serbia
   foreign-owned banks 275
   nature of credit growth 114
   policy responses 99, 135
Shin, Y. 77
Slovakia 229–35
   bank privatization 229, 231
   bank supervision 233–5
   determinants of credit growth 231–2
   excessive credit growth 61
   foreign currency lending 72, 230
   foreign-owned banks 7, 231, 275
   household lending 17, 70, 229–30, 231, 232–3, 234–5
   interest rates 230, 232, 233, 235
   nature of credit growth 229–30
   policy responses, measures taken by supervisory authority 233–5
   risks from credit growth 232–3
Slovenia
   credit-to-GDP ratio 54, 55
   equilibrium credit-to-GDP ratios 79, 81
   and equity financing 19
   excessive credit growth 56, 58, 61, 75
   exchange rate regime 59, 60
   and foreign currency lending 72
   foreign-owned banks 275
   household lending 17, 70
   nature of credit growth 114
Smith, R. 77
Šonje, V. 155
Spain 312–18
   credit growth
     consequences for financial stability 316–17, 318
     explanatory factors 312–15
     macroeconomic consequences 315–16, 318
   and EMU entry 314, 318
   financial liberalization 314–15, 318
   interest rates 314–15, 316
   and labour market reforms 314
   policy responses 135
surveillance 3–4
System of European Central Banks 294

Tobin's q 194, 196
trade balance 81, 250, 251–3
Turkey 22, 36, 275
   financial crisis (1997) 26

Ukraine 3
  bank privatization 243, 245, 246, 247
  bank supervision 244, 246, 259–60
  credit boom 236–51, 254–60
  credit-to-GDP ratio 257
  foreign currency lending 244, 247
  household lending 246–7
  macroeconomic background 239
  nature of credit growth 114
  policy responses 99, 136
    options 259–60

Unicredito 280

vestor error correction model (VECM) 50
VILSE 194
Vladkova-Hollar, I. 74
Vonnák, B. 75
Vujšić, B. 155

Zochowski, D. 34
Zumer, T. 77